To Use The Sea

2nd Edition

Readings in Seapower
And
Maritime Affairs

Naval Institute Press
Annapolis, Maryland

Library of Congress Card Catalog Number 77-78390
ISBN 0-87021-707-0

The following articles are reprinted from the United States Naval Institute
Proceedings:
Ruhe, W. J., Captain, USN, "Seapower in the Seventies." April © 1970 by
the United States Naval Institute.

Winnefeld, James A., Captain, USN, and Builder, Carl H.; "ASW—Now or
Never" September; Nichols, W. R., "Ships at Sea—Maritime Facts of Life"
April; copyright © 1971 by the United States Naval Institute.

Truax, R.C., Captain, USN (Ret.), "Surface Effect Ships in the Surface Navy".
December; Turner, Stansfield, Vice Admiral, USN, "The United States at a
Strategic Crossroads" October; Kidd, Isaac C., Admiral, USN, "The View
from the Bridge of the Sixth Fleet Flagship" February; copyright © 1972 by
the United States Naval Institute.

Knott, Richard C., Commander, USN, "Who Owns the Oceans?" March;
copyright © 1973 by the United States Naval Institute.

Charlier, R. M. and Vigneaux, M., "Towards a Rational Use of the Oceans"
April; De La Mater, Stephen, Captain, USN (Ret.), "Naval Aircraft in the Next
Decade", May; copyright © 1974 by the United States Naval Institute.

Gorshkov, S. C., Admiral of the Fleet of the USSR, "The Development of the
Art of Naval Warfare" June; Miller, F. C., Lieutenant (j.g.), USN, "Those
Storm-Beaten Ships . . ." December; Kehoe, James W., Captain,
USN, "Warship Design: Ours and Theirs," August; Garde, Hans, Com-
mander, RDN, "Where is the Western Navy? The World Wonders," April;
Hopker, Wolfgang, "Soviet Global Strategy: The Great Challenge to the West
at Sea," December; Copyright © 1975 by the United States Naval Institute.

O'Rourke, Gerald G., Captain, USN (Ret.), "Why V/STOL?", January; Steele,
George P., Vice Admiral, USN (Ret.), "The U.S. Seventh Fleet", January;
Ackley, Richard T., Commander, USN (Ret.), "The Soviet Merchant Fleet",
February; Zumwalt, Elmo R., Admiral, USN (Ret.), "High-Low", April; Chase,
John D., Rear Admiral, USN, "U.S. Merchant Marine—For Commerce and
Defense", May; Ruhe, W. J., Captain, USN (Ret.), "Cruise Missile: The Ship-
killer", June; Holloway, James L., USN, "The U.S. Navy: A Bicentennial Ap-

praisal", July; Reynolds, Clark B., "The Sea in the Making of America", July;
De La Mater, Stephen, Captain, USN (Ret.), "The Carrier", October; Parks,
W. Hayes, Major, USMC, "Foreign Policy and the Marine Corps", November;
Copyright © 1976 by the United States Naval Institute.

The following articles are reprinted with permission from the *Naval War
College Review*:
Reitzel, William, "Mahan on the Use of the Sea," May/June 1973
Barber, James, Commander, USN, "Mahan and Naval Strategy in the Nu-
clear Age," March 1972
Ambrose, Steven E., "Seapower in World Wars I and II," March 1970;
Booth, Ken, "Foreign Policies at Risk: Some Problems of Managing Naval
Power," Summer 1976.
Patterson, Andrew, "Mining; A Naval Strategy," May 1971;
Ackley, Richard T., Commander, USN (Ret.), "Soviet Navy's Role in Foreign
Policy," May 1972;
Smith, Clydé A., Commander, USN, "The Meaning and Significance of the
Gorshkov Articles," Mar./Apr. 1974, and "The Constraints of Naval Geogra-
phy on Soviet Naval Forces," Sep/Oct 1974.
Ra'anan, Uri, "Soviet View of Navies in Peacetime," Summer 1976; Hynes,
William R., Lieutenant Commander, USN, "The Role of the Kiev in Soviet
Naval Operations," Fall 1976; Ashmore, Edward, Amiral, RN, "The Possible
Effects on Maritime Operations of Any Future Convention of the Law of the
Sea," Fall 1976.

The following article is reprinted with permission from the Center for Continuing Education, Naval War College: "Major Ocean Areas," *Guide to Committee Discussions,* Naval War College Global Strategy Discussions, 1971.

The following articles are reprinted with permission from *Sea Power*, official
publication of the Navy League of the U. S.:

Ennis, John, "Deep, Cheap and Deadly," *Sea Power*, December, copyright
© 1974, by *Sea Power*.

Paone, R. M., "The Big Three and the Indian Ocean," August, copyright ©
1975 by *Sea Power*.

Canan, James, "Today's Marine Corps: Stepping Out Smartly," November
1976. Palmer, J., "NATO's Tender Watery Flanks," March 1976; Bissell,
Richard E., "The South Atlantic: A New Order Emerging," October 1976;
Griswold, Lawrence, "The Scrambled Geometry of the New Pacific," April
1976; MacBain, Merle, "Constitution or Chaos for the World's Oceans,"
March 1976. Copyright © 1976 by *Sea Power*.

Introduction

To gain an understanding of the world in which we live, the geopolitical factors that shape a nation's policy—especially its foreign policy—must be carefully studied and assimilated. The United States must import vast amounts of strategic materials necessary for its survival, yet few Americans are concerned about or even realize the extent to which this country depends upon the sea. Because of our geographic isolation, our unimpeded use of the sea is not optional—it is an absolute necessity. Any attempt to disrupt or inhibit free passage over the oceans must be regarded as a potential threat to our national interests and to the peace and stability of the world community.

In strategic policy, U.S. thinking has been dominated by the theories of Alfred Thayer Mahan for over half a century. The USSR on the other hand has based its doctrine on Clausewitzian concepts of a "continental" or land strategy. As indicated by the growing Soviet fleet, these traditional doctrinal concepts appear to be changing.

This publication is a compilation of articles and maps originally published in *United States Naval Institute Proceedings, Naval Review, the Naval War College Review* and *Sea Power*. It represents a cross-section of recent views on the subjects of sea-power and maritime affairs and is intended as a source book for a seminar-style analysis and study of these areas. We hope it will be of value to instructors and students alike.

Lieutenant Commander F. C. Rouse, USN, Editor

CONTENTS

Seapower

MAHAN ON THE USE OF THE SEA

An article

by

Mr. William Reitzel

Maritime power is a comprehensive and complex system that if judiciously developed will advance a nation's well-being. As a system it consists of two subsystems: seapower (commercial movement) and seaforce (navy), both of which must necessarily complement each other in the development of maritime power. Inasmuch as trade overseas has traditionally played a significant part in the U.S. economy, the size of its Navy is an accurate indicator of the economic and political status Americans feel their country must occupy.

It is not easy to recapture Mahan's idea of maritime power. Although statesmen were supposed to have slept with his books under their pillows, the evidence is that they merely made extracts, summaries, and highly selective formulations of his views, using these chiefly to justify the role of a navy in relation to such national interests and policies as they wished to develop.

Mahan, taken as a whole, was not a thinker whose generalizations were of universal validity. Actually, once the skeleton of his concept was constructed, his preference was to persuade his fellow countrymen to action, applying his generalizations to the analysis of issues and situations of current liveliness. The climate of American opinion was highly receptive, combining as it did a feeling that the United States had a role to play in the world with diverse uncertainties about what that role was or should or could be.

Mahan, along with the bulk of his contemporaries, was exhilarated by the idea of the United States flexing its economic and political muscles in the world arena. He and they saw the country's economic maturation as both necessary and desirable and accepted as natural the implication that this might well involve conflict with other muscle flexers. The basis for acting on this conviction was, according to Mahan, an understanding and proper use of seapower.

The elaborate historical analysis on which this rested was, for the most part, confined to narrow professional circles. For the greater number of his contemporaries, civil and military, his views were used in fragmented, particular snippets. In the hands of the military, especially those of naval advocates, these selections tended to become formulas, repeated to justify claims that were no longer unhesitatingly accepted by Americans generally. The change can be succinctly illustrated by an exasperated remark of Secretary Stimson: "The peculiar psychology of the Navy, which frequently seems to retire from the realm of logic into a dim religious world where Neptune is God, Mahan his prophet, and the U.S. Navy the only true church."

The piecemeal use of Mahan still goes on. Its use, however, after three-quarters of a century, naturally raises the question of the real applicability of Mahan's concept to the present-day international scene. In order to provide a reliable basis for examining this question—if necessary, a basis for rewriting Mahan—the original full-dress thesis must be recovered, recaptured, one might say, from the accumulation of cliché-ridden formulas in which it is now expressed.

Thus, the sole purpose of what follows is to get back to the original.

Mahan's methods make it difficult to do this with any assurance. Like many sweeping generalizations, his core idea was not reached after slow and painful research. It sprang from a sudden insight, which research was then brought in to confirm, organize, and expand. Mahan knew what he wanted to prove before he set about proving it.[1] Consequently, Mahan's history is deliberately selective.

A further difficulty is that he expands and develops his basic insight in a variety of contexts—seapower in peace, in diplomacy, in commercial competition, in imperial expansion, in armed conflict—and does not always make it clear in which context he is working at any particular moment. He applies his key generalization somewhat indiscriminately to specific international crises, to the role and policy of the United States, to the world in general. He moves from the present to the past, and back again, with a freedom of analogy that is indifferent to the critical changes that time may have brought about.

In spite of these hazards, a reconstruction is necessary. What follows is such a reconstruction. It is given either in Mahan's own words or in a close paraphrase. The structure has also been given a logical coherence. Except for these devices, the following is Mahan's concept of seapower.

The Concept. The concept of seapower derives, in the last analysis, from Mahan's assumptions about man and society. Two quotations are enough to set the tone.

Power and force is a faculty of national life; one of those talents committed to nations . . . no more than any other can it be abjured without incurring the responsibility of him who buries in the earth that which was entrusted to him.

National power is surely a legitimate factor in international settlements; for it is the outcome of national efficiency, and efficiency is entitled to assert its fair position and chance of exercise in world matters . . . the existence of might is no mere casual attribute, but the indication of qualities which should, as they assuredly will, make their way to the front and to the top in the relations of states.[2]

The sea is to be considered in the glare of this "actual world." It is a common over which men can pass in all directions. It is a great medium of communication established by nature. But it is important only to the extent that men use it.

Man's interest in the sea, and hence the interests of nations, is almost wholly interests of carriage, that is, trade. Maritime commerce, in all ages, has been most fruitful of wealth. Wealth is a concrete expression of a nation's energy of life, material and thinking. Given the relation between wealth and maritime commerce, the sea is inevitably the major arena of competition and conflict among nations aspiring to wealth and power.

The capacity to move freely on the sea oneself and to inhibit as need be a similar capacity in others is a critical consideration. For it is a fundamental truth that an ability to control movement on the sea is chief among the purely material elements determining the comparative power and prosperity of nations.

There are four basic requirements for desiring, achieving, and maintaining this freedom of movement. First, a nation must produce and exchange products. Second, shipping, the instrument of exchange, must be available. Third, colonies and bases—at any rate, nationally held points of safety—must be secured to enlarge and protect the operations of shipping. Fourth, armed force—a navy—must be available to guard and keep open communications between these points of safety and the home base.

Put another way, seapower is shipping, bases, and their supporting adjuncts. Seaforce is a navy.[3] When brought into being and kept in motion by national productivity, a system of maritime power exists. Recognition of these interdependent elements is the clue to understanding the policies and actions of nations that use the seas and for whom the use of the sea is vital to national life.

Any nation bordering on the sea can, in principle, aspire to develop a system of maritime power; but, on the evidence of history, only a few have achieved it in fact. Maritime states differ widely in respect to the characteristics that are definitive. These characteristics are geographical location, physical configuration, territorial expanse, size and nature of population, nature of the political system. The value of these characteristics is not absolute. They can and do change with time and circumstances. But, in a general sense,

● If a nation has easy access to the oceans of the world and is, as well, in a position to dominate major trade routes, it is in a position to develop maritime power; and,

● If its physical configuration provides harbors and puts a productive hinterland in easy touch with its sea frontiers, an impulse to develop maritime power naturally follows; and,

● If its territory is extensive or diversified, its population large and active, and its political structure encourages productive energy and gives it an outward thrust, an irresistible pressure to exploit the sea commercially and militarily demands and gets concrete expression in the form of seapower and seaforce.

In short, a true maritime state comes into being; and as long as time, circumstances, and faults of policy do not undermine its advantages, its maritime power increases and becomes its distinguishing feature. Maritime power, at this point, represents a tightly knit system of national activity critically meshed with the life and well-being of the nation.

Great Britain is the classical illustration. Throughout the 18th century it was the one nation that consistently earned its wealth in time of peace by seapower and in time of war ruled the sea by virtue of its seaforce. It spread its bases of maritime operation over the globe, bases that would have been valueless if seapower and seaforce had not combined to keep communications open. No one can fail to conclude that British maritime power was, by long odds, the dominating factor in this century of conflict.

The constant exercise of maritime

power, however, cannot be equated with peace. Commercial interests, the foundation underlying any maritime country's vitality and power, may tend to deter war from fear of the presumed losses that war might bring, but from its very nature commerce is competitive and engenders conflict by fostering ambitions that lead to armed collision. For when a nation sends its merchant ships abroad, it naturally looks for positions upon which those ships can rest for trading, for supplies, or for refuge. From this follows the need for control, primarily a matter of ensuring communications, which, in turn, multiplies the number of positions needed for the effective exercise of control. Since this progression does not take place in an empty world, the upshot is that a nation's seapower cannot be brought to its full value except by the addition of seaforce.

A navy follows from the existence and needs of peaceful shipping. The extent to which a navy subsequently takes on functions unrelated to the protection of trade, shipping, and commercial communications is a matter to be considered separately. But it can be said in anticipation that if these acquired functions displace or weaken a navy's capacity to fulfill its primary historical role, the maritime power of a nation is correspondingly reduced.

The efficient use and control of sea movement is but one link in the chain of exchange by which wealth accumulates, but it is the central link, for it puts other nations under obligation to the wielder of maritime power. The end result of the sustained exercise of maritime power is a nation geared to the production and exchange of goods, conducting its commerce freely and safely with all continents, possessing a network of colonies and bases, a visible presence of power and force on the high seas and in the world's ports.

When this stage has been reached in the life of a nation, maritime power has become the basis of a system for the creation and expansion of national wealth and greatness. It is now essential to the life of the nation, and its maintenance and advancement are the major considerations of national policy. But the system is now one of immense size and complexity, as well as being ex-

tremely sensitive to interruption. It is in connection with the various possibilities and modes of interruption that we come to the navy, that is, to the addition of seaforce to seapower.

The basic relation of seaforce to seapower is simple and direct. The navy springs from the needs of merchant shipping. Though it would be theoretically possible to argue that if maritime commerce ceased to be essential to the life of the nation the navy could disappear, this conclusion is no longer practically tenable. The present realities of international life forbid it.

As things now stand, and have stood historically, the operations of seapower create competition, and competition is always capable of taking an armed form. A navy, accordingly, operates in peacetime to check inevitable disagreements from recklessly growing into armed clashes. At the same time, the necessary readiness to shift from the day-to-day work of deterring conflict to the occasional role of fighting a war has the effect of giving a navy a specialized life of its own with specialized requirements. This can, and sometimes has, tended to obscure the navy's fundamental relationship to seapower.

One must be clear. Navies do not exist merely to fight one another—to gain the sterile glory of fighting battles to win them. They do fight battles, but the purpose of the battle is to maintain maritime power. Thus it follows that in war a navy must aim first and always at depriving an opponent of sea movement in its broadest sense. This is not a matter of casual commerce destruction. It is a matter of strategically dominating sea movement so that every form of movement is at the mercy of decisively superior maritime power.

A fully established maritime nation, if it is attentive to the conditions that dictate its policy, will aim at acquiring and maintaining that superiority in seaforce that enables it to project its seapower to the most distant quarters of the earth. In fact, it might well be argued that such a nation would be well advised to increase its navy above those arms more narrowly styled military.

Once a navy is developed, it begins to take on functions additional to the basic role for which it was created. It be-

comes an instrument of national policy in the broadest sense. When commerce expands a nation's contacts beyond its shores, a navy converts contacts into interests and consolidates interests as political influence. Statesmen, habituated to the concept and use of maritime power, find in a navy a means of forcible, yet beneficent, adjustment in international affairs, adjustments that would be impossible without the existence of seaforce.[4]

One should note in passing the case of a nation which, though not possessing seapower, nevertheless seeks to develop seaforce. Such a policy, in the absence of a significant seapower interest, inevitably produces the effect of planned aggression. The creation of such a force automatically makes its possessor an uncertain and threatening factor in international life. The policy cannot fail to stimulate vigorous defensive action in already developed maritime states, since it implies not commercial competition, but armed threat.

The essential structure of a system of maritime power can now be summed up. It rests upon a geographical location and a productive society. From this base springs seaborne trade and all its supporting agencies. This is seapower. The net of trade thus built up must then be protected. Seaforce becomes an integral part of the system. The navy, in turn, has its own requirements. These often include the acquisition of extracontinental territory. Such holdings frequently prove valuable as new markets or sources of raw materials, and then navy needs and seapower become reciprocal.

By this time the maritime system has become an intricate mesh of interlocked components, a system in which the parts must be kept in balance if the system is to function effectively and economically. If any one element gets out of balance—if seapower declines, if seaforce expands for reasons unconnected with seapower, if national productivity falters—the system either demands internal adjustment or it loses ground in the international arena. On the other hand, if the system as a whole acquires colonies and bases beyond what is required by the commercial activity of the nation, the expansion becomes a source of national weakness by entailing division of energy and resources in order to maintain communications that have become too complex.

Application of the Concept. The experience of Great Britain brought a new dimension into thinking about maritime policy. In support of Britain's maritime growth there was developed, first, a mobile navy; and, second, local posts along the great sea routes for use as naval bases. In the seas where there were no national possessions, the navy first depended upon friendly harbors, but the uncertainties of such dependence soon led to territorial acquisition. The results were so striking that, in our time, this pattern of expansion is being followed by all states with maritime aspirations.

It will be readily appreciated that the pattern has implicit in it the constant threat of conflict. Furthermore, commercial competition being now worldwide, the regions of potential conflict are now global. Communications on a global scale are inevitably maritime, and conflict over such communications can only mean sea war. This defines the essential task of the navy.

But, to perform this task, an opponent's navy must be dominated. This is the true object to be assailed on all occasions. While fixed positions are important, a fleet itself is the key position. A crushing defeat of a fleet means the ultimate dislocation of an entire system of maritime power, irrespective of the spot on the seas where the defeat is administered. With the elimination of opposing seaforce, the remaining elements of maritime power are wholly exposed to destruction. This is the foundation of control of the seas. From it follows the true objective—the sole end of naval war: to protect one's own commerce and to deprive an opponent of that great resource.

It is vital, in this connection, to disabuse American minds of their erroneous views of the function of a navy. These have historically been held to be: to defend American territory and to engage in commerce raiding. The defensive role was established as guarding coasts and harbors, and, by this measure, the demand was for many small ships, since tonnage put into large vessels could not be subdivided to cover all

the points to be defended. The offensive role, commerce raiding indulged in by individual ships, could not bring down an opponent that had and knew how to use maritime power. It could not be the taking of single ships, or even convoys, that would strike down the money power of such a nation; only overbearing seaforce, literally driving the enemy's flag from the sea, could achieve this end.

Such narrow views ignore a critical fact. Political status in the world, to which a productive nation must aspire, involves activities that imply conflict. The real question for Americans, in respect to a navy, is a clear judgment of the political status they wish their country to occupy, for this determines the character and size of their seaforce. If the United States were an aggressive nation and not simply a maritime state, the measure would be what it was desired to accomplish by aggression. But, as a productive society with potential maritime power, the true measure becomes what Americans are willing, or not willing, to concede to other states in a world of commercial competition and potential armed conflict.

It is impossible, as one reviews the part played by maritime power in the history of the prosperity of nations, not to consider the implications for the United States.

The great civilized nations of the world now feel a strenuous impulse to find and establish markets outside their borders. This is leading to manifold annexations and naval aggressions. The United States has, as yet, taken no part in this, though it constitutes a situation that adds immensely to American political and commercial anxieties. No one can ignore that seapower and seaforce play a leading part in these developments or that the United States, by its geographical position and by the expansive pressure of its industrial and commercial activity, must of necessity become a participant. Necessity, like a blind force of nature, is sure at last to overwhelm all that stands in the way of a movement of the nation toward acquiring a wider influence in the world.

When the United States is impelled to play its inevitable role in the world, it can no longer leave to one side the need for seapower and its essential adjunct, a

navy. The commercial interests at stake are so great and the political considerations so uncertain that the desire to secure advantages leads countries that possess force into a dangerous temptation to use it. Force, when remote localities are concerned, means seaforce.

The development of maritime power by a state should not in itself be considered a threat, since maritime power is not aggressive. In fact, the interests of such a state are generally peaceful, since it acquires too great an interest beyond its shores to wish to expand by force. But the superior influence of such a state is a condition that must be competed for.

The march of events not in the United States alone but all over the world—political events, events economic and commercial—has brought about a necessity for active seapower and larger navies. Furthermore, a world in which other states press competitively to all corners of the globe is one in which it is highly improbable that the seas will ever again be exclusively dominated by a single nation. Unless the United States is prepared to maintain its interests in this kind of world, its people may find themselves excluded. It must either participate or be shut out from the essentials of national growth. It follows that upon the seas must be developed the means to sustain the requisite external policy, and the means are seapower defended by seaforce.

As Mahan Saw the World. There were two basic assumptions by which Mahan viewed international life. The first was that it was a struggle for survival, with the best fitted coming out on top—what we would now call Social Darwinism. The second was that his historical evidence, drawn largely from the 17th and 18th centuries, provided a complete analogy with the situation of the late 19th and early 20th centuries. The two assumptions reenforced each other and furnished a picture of the world to which the concept of maritime power was totally applicable.

Consequently, Mahan's thinking cannot be fully recreated without adding—again in his own words or by paraphrasing—his view of the world around him.

There is no region so remote or forsaken as not to be possessed by some human group. Many of these groups lack the capacity to organize themselves to hold what they possess. Civilized man—that is, modern, organized, and productive societies—needs and seeks space that he can control and use on his own terms. The chief feature of the present world is the extent to which feeble groups are pressed upon by strong groups.

This pressure is a natural force and, like all natural forces, takes the line of least resistance. When it comes upon a region rich in possibilities but unfruitful through the incapacity or negligence of those who dwell there, the incompetent race goes down before the persistent impact of the superior. The feeble may have a vast preponderance of numbers but, being disorganized, are helpless in the face of organized power backed by material prosperity. To this historically recurring situation is now added steam which, applied to seapower and sea-force, has multiplied the points of contact between peoples and made proximity a significant characteristic of the times.

In these circumstances, enterprising commercial nations are not content to move patiently. Commercial activities are invariably followed by demands for settled government, for security of life and property. Productive nations proceed to control the centers of commerce they have opened, well aware that control is a powerful influence on the course and security of trade. And trade, as they envisage it, goes far beyond a question of bare existence. It is the source of national wealth and the measure of national importance.

It should be no cause for surprise that the competition for such great prizes results not only in growing armaments, but in the increase of a national spirit of which armaments are but an expression. Artificial institutions of adjustment may serve to soften somewhat the competition of organized and powerful states, but they are not applicable to the relations of strong advanced peoples and weak backward peoples. The present stage of evolution is one in which enterprising nations will productive societies—needs and seeks space that he can control and use on his own terms. The chief feature of the Their leading political interest is to

provide and maintain outlets for the productive energies of their people. They will seek solutions by methods that are inherently combative. But, not merely do they confront societies that are resistive, even if feeble, they compete with each other for exclusive positions. Since the underlying spirit is one of domination, the possibility of military action is always present. The world is clearly in a state of transition, and some new order must evolve out of the chaos. But the order that emerges will be desirable and lasting only to the extent that the natural forces involved act freely and find their own equilibrium.

The power to act effectively in these circumstances is no mere accidental attribute. It is the natural concomitant of the qualities that have set advanced nations to expanding and that keep them in active motion. However, the relative ease with which they now deal with weaker opponents is not a permanent condition. The lesson they teach is one that can be learned. Present collisions are bound to become more frequent and more intense.

Since these confrontations are widely scattered and remote from the territories of advanced nations, the capacity to bring, first, influence and then force to bear, is the prerogative of nations that possess maritime power. In fact, this is the means by which they can compensate in distant places for their inferiority in numbers, their disadvantages of position, and their difficulties of communication. In short, this is an age in which maritime power fully predominates. With the extension of overseas commerce, the control and safety of maritime routes and positions have become the first aim of national foreign policies. Consequently, all advanced nations vigorously compete to develop the elements of maritime power.[5]

Summary Restatement. In anticipation that someone may wish to analyze the applicability of Mahan to the contemporary scene, it will be useful to summarize the concept of maritime power in contemporary terms.

Maritime power is a comprehensive and complex system. In addition to certain attributes that belong to the

system as a whole, maritime power contains two subsystems: seapower and seaforce (navy). Each of these subsystems has its specialized attributes. The whole, in its operation, reflects a national maritime policy, that is, maintaining and using maritime power systematically to support and advance national well-being under conditions of international competition.

In detail:

● *Maritime Power*, given the requisite geographical advantages and national will, is generated initially by an economic activity that produces surpluses for exchange. These surpluses must be disposed of and seaborne trade results. The process, however, requires institutional machinery—financing, in-

BIOGRAPHIC SUMMARY

Mr. William Reitzel served in World War II as a commander in the U.S. Naval Reserve in the North Atlantic and Mediterranean theaters. He has served as professor of social science at Haverford College, occupied the Chester W. Nimitz Chair of National Security and Foreign Affairs at the Naval War College, been active with the Central Intelligence Agency and the Brookings Institution, and served as a Director, Division of Strategic Studies, Center for Naval Analysis at Cambridge, Mass. His publications include *The Mediterranean: Role in U.S. Foreign Policy, Major Problems U.S. Foreign Policy, U.S. Foreign Policy: 1945-1955, Background to Decision-Making*. Mr. Reitzel resides in Newport, R.I., where he is engaged in independent research and writing at his leisure.

surance, exporters, importers, brokers, et cetera—and specialized industry—shipbuilding, ship repair, cargo handling, and the like—for its operation. Without such machinery in place and working smoothly, domestic and foreign markets cannot be developed, cargoes cannot be found, ships cannot be moved, and whatever maritime potential a nation may have cannot become a reality.

● *Seapower*, given the initial impetus to develop maritime potential, is a specialized subsystem of sea movement. Its basic element is merchant ships (cargo carriers), but their effective use

8

depends upon the buildup of the supporting facilities mentioned above. With these facilities systematically related and employed, seapower can be presumed to compete successfully in world commerce and even to absorb increasing shares of world markets and to gain greater access to raw materials needed by the nation's economic activities. The thesis is that the interplay between the national productive base of the maritime system and the sea movement capacity of seapower systems steadily adds to national wealth and influence, and the end product is maritime dominance. But seapower is an exposed system. It is open to every variety of interference, from political and economic impediment to armed attack. It requires organized protection.

• *Seaforce (Navy)*, a highly specialized subsystem geared primarily to the support and defense of seapower. The components of this subsystem need no detailed description here. It should be noted, however, that, like seapower, it has its own specialized shore-based requirements and that these are only to a limited extent interchangeable with those of the seapower system. Furthermore, as the special uses that could be made of seaforce came to be more fully appreciated, policymakers tended to give a lower priority to the primary and original function of seaforce—namely, the support and defense of seapower. The result in time was increasingly to equate the navy with the military elements of national power rather than to see it as a specialized subsystem of national maritime power.

So far, Mahan. In his view, a maritime power system was an integrated whole, working to forward a nation's position in the world. It worked as a stimulus to a nation's total capacity to produce, to distribute, and to influence in its favor the trend of international life. It used its seapower component offensively in commercial competition. It used its seaforce component defensively in a world of incipient conflict. Mahan's consistent reminder was that he was talking of a tightly knit system of institutions, facilities, commercial carriers, and naval fleets and that no one of these elements of the system could be allowed to become inadequate without the system losing its effectiveness.

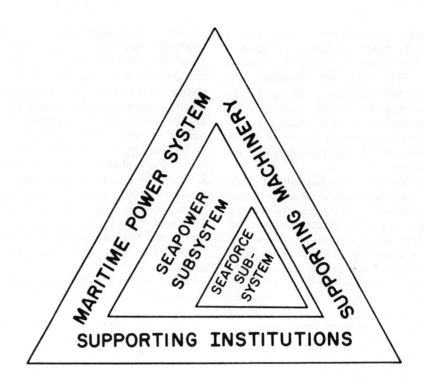

FOOTNOTES

1. In 1884, then 44 years old, Mahan sat in the library of the English Club in Lima. He was reading Theodor Mommsen's *History of Rome* (New York: Scribner's, 1887). Puzzling over Hannibal's dramatic failure as a conqueror, "... there dawned upon me one of those concrete perceptions..., that the control of the seas was an historical factor which has never been systematically appreciated and expounded. Once formulated consciously, this thought became the nucleus of my writing for twenty years to come."

2. The Chief of Mission at a Hague Conference reported on Mahan's contribution to discussion as follows: "... his views have effectually prevented any lapse into sentimentality. When he speaks, the millenium fades and this stern, severe actual world appears."

3. Seaforce is not Mahan's term. It is introduced in order to make more explicit Mahan's argument that maritime power is a system formed of distinct but interlocked elements.

4. Mahan cites the Monroe Doctrine as a case in point. Here a comprehensive position was taken whose only guarantee was naval.

5. To illustrate the fact that Mahan's view was not unique but shared by many of his generation, compare Brooks Adams in his *American Economic Supremacy* (New York: Macmillan, 1900).

Towards 1890, a new period of instability opened. Civilization then seemed to have entered upon a fresh period of unrest, and the inference is that no condition of permanent tranquility can be reached until a new equipoise shall have been obtained. ... conflict will be between the maritime and non-maritime races, or between the rival merits of land and sea transport.

The importance of understanding history when confronting today's problems frequently is not appreciated, particularly when present realities seem to differ sharply from the circumstances of the past. At first glance, the applicability of Mahan's theories on seapower may seem to be totally confined to the days of heavily armored battleships, but such an uncritical derogation of all his writings is unwarranted. While Mahan can never completely solve the problem of developing an appropriate strategy for the constantly evolving technological and political environment we find ourselves in, his writings are based on certain fundamentals of maritime strategy, many of which retain their validity today.

MAHAN AND NAVAL STRATEGY

IN THE NUCLEAR AGE

A lecture delivered at the Naval War College

by

Commander James A. Barber, U.S. Navy

My objective in this lecture is "to examine the validity and applicability of Mahan's principles and concepts of seapower to the role of naval forces in the modern environment." An easy manner in which to dispose of the subject would be to say that since Mahan was concerned with the naval strategy of a day in which the heavily gunned ship of the line dominated all other strategic considerations, in which aircraft and submarines were only experimental toys, and in which such facts of modern life as nuclear weapons and guided missiles were not even imaginary considerations, it is quite obvious that his answers can have no relevance to our present concerns.

Yet Mahan himself faced a similar problem. In a letter to his Naval Academy classmate Samuel Ashe, Mahan wrote that his difficulty lay in the fact that "all naval history hitherto had been made by ships and weapons . . . wholly different from those now in use," and that he was striving "to view the lessons of the past so he could mould them into lessons for the future."[1] Mahan told Ashe that his project was "to wrest something out of the old woodensides and twenty-four pounders that will throw some light on the combinations to be used with iron-clads, rifled guns and torpedoes."[2]

Mahan believed that it was possible to formulate general principles of strategy that would remain valid despite technological change. He asserted: "while many of the conditions of war vary from age to age with the progress of weapons, there are certain teachings in the school of history which remain constant, and being, therefore, of universal application, can be elevated to the rank of general principles."[3] Unfortunately for us, Mahan does not set down these general principles in any systematic way, but rather analyzes a series of historical employments of seapower as illustrative examples of general principles—often leaving his reader with the problem of determining which of the lessons to be drawn should be taken as unchanging general principles and which are of a lower order because they were based upon temporary factors.

One of the few systematic treatments that it is possible to find in Mahan's writings is his listing of the six factors which are the natural conditions for the growth of seapower.

- Geographical Position,
- Physical Conformation, including, as connected therewith, national productions and climate,
- Extent of Territory,
- Number of Population,
- Character of the People,
- Character of the Government, including therein the national institutions.

While there is little to argue with in the above factors, it is still necessary to summarize Mahan's main points about naval strategy which lie scattered through his major works before attempting to assess his applicability to the problems facing us today.

The most fundamental conclusion reached by Mahan through his study of history was that command of the sea brings victory in war and riches in peace. This conclusion permeates almost everything he ever wrote—and may also explain the Navy's fondness for Mahan as a strategic theorist. Because Mahan does not spell out the essentials of his theory of strategy in any systematic way, different interpreters offer different lists of the essentials of his seapower theories. My interpretation of his writings is that the four most important concepts in Mahan's strategic theory are:

- Command of the sea,
- Concentration,
- Strategic position,
- Communications.

I would like to discuss each of these basic concepts briefly before turning to their contemporary applicability.

Command of the Sea. Command of the sea is the basic concept in Mahan's strategic theory, and all other parts of that theory are directed to the problem of gaining command of the sea. For Mahan the sea is indivisible, and, as a consequence, command of the sea is also indivisible, with the dominant naval power able to dominate sea communications worldwide. This kind of command is to be gained through decisive defeat of the enemy by means of a superior fleet. Mahan emphasized and reemphasized the necessity for positive and offensive employment of the fleet to gain control of the sea. Once such control was gained, it permitted the superior seapower to operate along interior lines through the use of sea transport and provided the initiative in projecting power against an enemy.

This command of the sea, in Mahan's day, meant superiority in capital ships, with the primary objective of the battle fleet being the destruction of the enemy battle fleet. Mahan tended to dismiss commerce raiding as an appealing but ineffective strategy and emphasized the dominance to be gained by the offensive use of the concentrated battle fleet to destroy the opposing fleet or drive it from the sea. Although Mahan introduced a number of qualifications, it is hard to avoid the impression that he thought most of the time in terms of a single large setpiece battle, the outcome of which decides who commands the sea and who is driven from it.

Concentration. Closely related to this picture of the showdown battle between opposing battle fleets is Mahan's emphasis upon concentration. He repeatedly makes the point that the real essence of naval strategy, even the real essence of all military strategy, is to achieve concentration of power at the decisive point. Despite his oft-repeated admonition not to divide the fleet, Mahan was not simply talking about physical proximity. The more correct interpretation of this dictum is to think in terms of mobility and interior lines of communication, which permit a superior seapower to concentrate at decisive points more rapidly.

Mahan's emphasis upon concentration must be interpreted more broadly than just not dividing existing military forces. In *The Influence of Sea Power upon the French Revolution and Empire*, he wrote: "... concentration of effort will as a rule be a sounder policy than dissemination."[4] The Germans, who used Mahan as a textbook, really did not always properly understand what he had to say. In the First World War the German Navy violated Mahan's principle of concentration by dividing

its effort between the submarine war and the surface battle fleet and, as a result, lost the war. Quite possibly a purer concentration of effort would have resulted in a different outcome.

Strategic Position. Despite Mahan's insistence upon the indivisibility of command of the sea, he is well aware of the problems introduced in exercising such command at considerable distances from home. I think that perhaps his ideas were molded by his concentration upon European experience, where command of European waters was sufficient to dominate all of the world's important trade routes. As a result, he does not appear to see any inconsistency between insisting upon the indivisibility of command of the sea, in the sense of being able to control the use of the sea for transport, and his recognition of the need for local bases if seapower is to be effectively exercised at any distance from home.

The technology of Mahan's day dictated the need for coaling stations, and he urged the need for properly prepared advanced bases in any area in which military operations were anticipated. Such bases should be as self-sufficient as possible and should be capable of self-defense. By no means did he wish to see an indefinite proliferation of overseas bases, however, for he saw them as a source of potential vulnerability as well as a source of strength. Thus, overseas bases should be limited only to those necessary for essential support of anticipated fleet operations.

Communications. The fourth of Mahan's fundamental concepts which I want to discuss briefly is that of communications. Mahan uses the term "communications" in a broad sense, encompassing all of what we would now call logistics, as well as information flow and the ability to exploit the inherent mobility of seaborne forces in moving to or within a theater of action. Understanding of the concept of communications is crucial to an understanding of Mahan. He repeatedly emphasizes the point himself: "... communications, in the full meaning of the term, dominate war. As an element of strategy they devour all other elements."[5] Elsewhere he calls communications "the most vital

and determining element in strategy," and goes on to assert that "all military organizations, land or sea, are ultimately dependent upon open communications with the basis of national power."[6]

At the same time Mahan drives home the surpassing importance of communications to all military strategy, he also tells us how it is to be obtained: "Secure communications at sea means naval preponderance."[7] Which brings us full circle and back to command of the sea as the basic concept in Mahan's treatment of naval strategy.

This leads us to the question, Is Mahan still relevant? Mahan stated quite clearly that he was seeking to uncover fundamental principles of strategy that were applicable to all times and places. Unfortunately, like all of us, he was not entirely successful in escaping from some of the limitations imposed upon him by the realities of the time and place in which he was writing. It seems to me that there are at least four areas in which Mahan's strategic thinking is weak as a guide to action in the nuclear age:

• Reliance upon mercantilist economic theory,
• Assumption of direct link between naval power and ability to use the sea,
• Disregard of uses of the sea other than for communications,
• Dismissal of the *guerre de course*.

There are, of course, other lessons in Mahan which have clearly been overtaken by events, such as his emphasis upon the surface battleline as the most important element of any navy. But that kind of problem is sufficiently clear so that no one is likely to be misled. The four weaknesses I want to discuss are of a more subtle sort and, if not understood, might very well provide incorrect guides to action. Let us take each of these points in turn.

Reliance upon Mercantilist Economic Theory. A great deal of Mahan's belief in the virtues of seapower is founded upon mercantilist economic theory, which emphasized the value of colonial trade and a large national merchant marine as essential elements of national wealth. Mercantilist theory had been attacked as early as the end of the 18th century by Adam Smith, and much of the 19th century saw a movement away from mercantilism and toward national free trade policies, but two circumstances combined to make mercantilist theory important to Mahan's doctrines. First, mercantilist thought dominated the period from the mid-17th century until the early 19th century, and this period provided the great majority of Mahan's historical examples. Second, the end of the 19th century saw some revival of mercantilist thought as an intellectual underpinning for colonial expansion, and Mahan himself was a leading exponent of this expansionist movement.

Nevertheless, most economists now dismiss mercantilist theory as both obsolete and seriously defective. They cite such examples as Japan, who has achieved a buoyant economy and most of her "greater East Asia Co-Prosperity Sphere" objectives despite losing a major war and failing to gain any of her territorial objectives of World War II. Today the relationships between economic prosperity, large merchant fleets, the requirement for naval forces, and the value of overseas possessions are much more tenuous than they appear in Mahan's theories.

As a parenthetical observation, however, perhaps we should be a bit cautious in completely dismissing the relevance of mercantilist economic theory. We may consider it obsolete, but in many ways the policies being followed by the Soviet Union appear to parallel those of classic mercantilist theory. After all, much of the economic theory of Marx himself was derived from the mercantilist tradition. There really is not much difference between the Marxist view of colonialist exploitation and the mercantilist concept of colonies as a source of wealth for the motherland. In some ways Mahan and Marx were not really too far apart in the way they viewed the economy of the world—they just made different value judgments.

Freedom of Action. A second weakness of Mahan's strategic theory as a contemporary guide to action lies in his assumption that superior naval forces enjoy freedom of action. This may have been at least partially true in earlier days, but quite clearly no longer holds. For a number of reasons, including the always present threat of nuclear war, the growing influence of international

law and international organization, the development of rapid worldwide communications and a consequent increase in the impact of both domestic and international public opinion, and probably a number of other reasons as yet unidentified, powerful nations are under much tighter restraints on their ability to take military action than they once were. Two graphic examples are the inhibitions on the United States in responding to the *Pueblo* incident and the regular resupply of Haiphong by unescorted Russian merchantmen, despite our virtually uncontested "command of the sea" in the South China Sea. Whether we like it or not, there *are* serious inhibitions on our ability to employ military force which are not consonant with Mahan's theory of seapower. The strictures under which major powers must act in a nuclear world have led Herman Kahn to assert, only partly in jest, that there are only two real superpowers in the world— Israel and North Korea.

Mahan can be misleading in another related way. Because of his acute sensitivity to the vital role played by sea communications, he tended to fall into the error of making the use of the sea even in peacetime appear to depend upon military control. Yet even in his day, nations such as Greece and Norway had large and profitable merchant fleets combined with insignificant navies. Carl Amme has pointed out that there is an antipathy between the concepts of "freedom of the seas" and "command of the seas" and that in the modern world "freedom of the seas" has tended to gain the upper hand.[8] Even in Mahan's sense, command of the sea really does not exist except as an act of war, and today, in an era of cold war, limited war, and undeclared war, the simple and straightforward concept of indivisible command of the sea loses much of its validity.

The Emphasis upon Sea Communications. The third weakness I would submit has to do with Mahan's emphasis upon maritime communications as the *sole* overriding and dominating consideration of naval strategy. Mahan repeatedly states that "communications dominate war;" indeed, the concept of maritime communications dominates

not only war, but all of Mahan's strategic theory. The whole meaning of "command of the sea" to Mahan was insuring to oneself the ability to transport things at sea, while denying this ability to one's opponent. He went so far as to declare that the sea was an unfruitful possession " . . . except as a system of highways joining country to country."[9]

However, in recent times we have become more and more aware of the increasing importance of two other uses of the sea which were specifically dismissed by Mahan. These are (1) the sea as a power base from which to extend power against the land, and (2) the sea as a valuable resource in and of itself. I will discuss these two new uses of the sea in somewhat more detail later, but for now I would like to address only the importance given by Mahan to sea lines of communication. Our experience in two World Wars strongly confirms the validity of Mahan's emphasis upon sea communications in conventional general war. The problem is that conventional general war may not really be the issue we need to address in modern naval strategy. Our experience since World War II has been that the use of the sea as a highway has not been often contested in limited wars, and inhibitions against risking nuclear war probably make a repetition of the WW I and WW II Battles of the Atlantic improbable. As a result, military contest over sea communications may no longer occupy as central a position in naval strategy as it did in Mahan's day.

This point is also closely related to the restraints on military action already discussed. Possession of superior naval force no longer automatically confers the ability to control lines of communication in limited wars. The ability to act must be accompanied by the decision to act, and in a nuclear world that decision may be a difficult one to make. As a result, we may more frequently see situations in which both sides are able to use the seas as if in time of peace, even though a limited war is being fought.

Dismissal of the Guerre de Course. The final weakness of Mahan's strategic theory to be mentioned is a somewhat more obvious one than those we have been discussing. As you know, Mahan dismissed the concept of a war against commerce as a weak and losing strategy: not without value, but of minor importance compared to the main issue to be decided between the battle fleets.

Based upon his historical analysis, Mahan was perfectly correct, and faced with the lessons of World Wars I and II he would have undoubtedly revised his estimate of the value of the *guerre de course.* As a less obvious point, he would also have had to revise his notion of the indivisibility of control of the sea, since in both World Wars it became painfully obvious that the ability to control the surface of the ocean was by no means a guarantee of the ability to control the subsurface. Control of the surface meant that the Allies were able to prevent Germany from transporting goods at sea, but it took some time and many lives to decide the issue of whether they were going to be able to use the sea to transport their own goods in the face of submarine opposition.

x x x x x x

I would like to return now to Mahan's idea of the indivisibility of command of the sea to try and analyze it in terms of our present world. Every element of Mahan's strategy is directed to the importance of sea lines of communication. I have already suggested that although this is still an important concept, new developments have compelled us to add two other elements. Thus we have three important uses of the sea which must serve as the foundation of modern naval strategy. These are: (1) Mahan's classic concern, maritime lines of communication; (2) the use of the sea as a base for military power to be exercised against the land; and (3) the increasing importance of the sea as a resource.

The importance of sea lines of communication to traditional maritime strategy has always been, and is still, based upon the efficiency of sea transport. Until the development of long-range aircraft, the sealanes were often the *only* means of transport between many locations. Even now, though we hear a great deal about developments in air transport, most goods are moved by sea. This is a familiar concept, and I do not think it is necessary to develop it any further here.

Less well recognized, even by Mahan, is the second of the three uses of the sea—the use of the sea as a base for military power. Until World War II the ability of naval forces to exert power directly against the land was relatively limited. The restricted range of cannon meant that only targets directly along the coast could be attacked by naval gunfire. Mahan noted "A ship can no more stand up against a fort costing the same money than the fort could run a race with the ship."[10] Seaborne raids against the land were largely limited to brief forays, and large-scale amphibious operations against a defended coast were impractical.

Several developments of this century have completely changed the ability of seaborne forces to exert power directly against land targets. Chief among these developments are the fast carrier task force, the development and demonstration of the techniques and equipment necessary to successful amphibious warfare, the development of the underway replenishment techniques necessary for extended at-sea operations, and most recently, the development of long-range, sea-based missiles for use against land targets. In combination these developments add a dimension to maritime strategy which is barely hinted at in Mahan's writings.

Finally, the third use of the sea which is important from the viewpoint of maritime strategy is the use of the sea and the seabed as resources in themselves. Man has extracted goods from the sea—principally fish—from time immemorial, but there is now a new element in the equation. Until recently we have treated the sea as inexhaustible—as a free and unlimited resource—and we do not fight over goods which are in unlimited supply.

We can no longer treat the sea in this way. Three interrelated things are happening: (1) we are making progress in great leaps toward economic exploitation of the sea; (2) the demand for the products of the sea is steadily increasing; and (3) we are coming to realize that the resources of the sea, though vast, are not inexhaustible. In the baldest possible terms, this makes the sea itself worth fighting for. The

business of dividing up the resources of the rest of the world created a long series of wars between the European colonial powers. We are now on the verge of having to work out the similar problem of how to divide up the resources of the sea. This introduces an entirely new element into the considerations of maritime strategy.

The basic aim of maritime strategy in the support of national strategy is to insure these uses of the sea to yourself and your allies and to deny them to your enemies. There are, therefore, six tasks to be performed by naval forces: insuring to yourself the three uses of the sea and denying the same three to your enemy. What I am saying is that in the contemporary world "command of the sea" is not quite so simple and indivisible a concept as it was for Mahan. It is necessary to control the sea in different ways to accomplish different tasks, and it is entirely possible to be in complete control for some purposes, while being unable to control the same area for other purposes. Perhaps this idea will become clearer if we consider what is involved in several kinds of command of the sea.

The most conventional kind of command of the sea is that necessary to insure your own ability to use the sealanes at will for purposes of transport. This is the kind of command of the sea that was at issue in the Battles of the Atlantic in World Wars I and II. We solved the problem of gaining command principally through convoy escort and ASW, but it is important to note how close we came to not being able to solve it in time.

The reverse of this kind of command of the sea is the task of denying to your enemy the use of the sealanes. We did this quite effectively to Japan during World War II through submarine and mine warfare and to Germany through blockade. More recently we performed a similar task in the form of the Cuban "quarantine," which led the Soviet Union to withdraw its missiles from Cuba.

It is important to recognize that, contrary to Mahan's concept of the indivisibility of command of the sea, there is a difference between being able to use the sea yourself for transport and being able to deny the same capability to your enemy. There have been times when both sides were able to protect their own transport quite adequately, yet were unable to deny use of the same water to their opponent. An example of this is the Mediterranean in 1942 when the Axis vessels were able to make resupply runs to North Africa, and the British were able to keep at least tenuous sealanes open to Malta and Alexandria.

The opposite case, where both are able to deny an area, but neither is able to use it—a kind of nautical no man's land—can be illustrated by the situation in the English Channel and North Sea in 1942. This kind of a situation was also nearly reached in the Mediterranean in late 1942 and again in Japanese home waters in mid-1945. Improvements in offensive weapons systems since that time make such a nautical no man's land even more likely today.

The second major use of the sea, as a base for power to be exerted directly against the land, was largely dismissed by Mahan: quite correctly, for the technology of his time made it impossible. The ability of seaborne forces to strike deeply and forcefully against land targets was first demonstrated only about the time of World War II, a step-level change vividly demonstrated in Japan's attack on Pearl Harbor. With the development of nuclear weapons and long-range missiles, sea-based forces are now capable of striking devastating blows at almost any point on the earth's surface.

In less catastrophic kinds of conflict there has also been a dramatic change in the capabilities of seaborne forces. The combination of the attack carrier, our amphibious forces, and the logistic train of replenishment ships gives the Navy the capability of exerting military force in carefully controlled ways throughout the world.

The international character of the sea permits these forces to be deployed freely without the necessity of intricate negotiations with other nations and lets them be as visible or as inconspicuous as the situation requires. Parenthetically, it must be noted that any large-scale or long-term use of naval general purpose forces is very nearly as dependent upon the maintenance of sea lines of communication as were the fleets of Mahan's

day.

The reciprocal of insuring to ourselves the use of the sea as a power base is being able to deny such a use to our opponents. In many ways this is a much more difficult task than using the sea as a power base yourself. The task of finding a missile-carrying submarine is a formidable one. I am personally not very optimistic about our ability to deny to the Soviet Union the capability of using the sea as a basing point for Polaris-type missiles.

It is possible to be at least a little more optimistic about being able to deny the use of the sea as a power base in limited wars. The Soviet Union's amphibious forces have been growing but are still relatively limited in capability, and the lack of aircraft carriers limits their range of operation to areas permitting land-based air cover. A reasonable assessment would be that—at least for now—we could, if we wished to, prevent most kinds of Soviet use of military power based on naval forces so long as there was blue water between them and their objective.

It is necessary again, however, to remind ourselves that there is a vast difference between capability and intent. There is no doubt that we have the *capability* of denying seaborne support to North Vietnam, but because of our desire to limit the war, and a concomitant reluctance to take the risks involved in a direct confrontation with the Soviet Union, we have not exercised that capability.

The Vietnam war is a good illustration of the divisibility of military uses of the sea. In that war we have had clear command of the sea and have used it *both* as a means of communication and a base for power directed against the land. Despite our command of the sea, however, the Communists have used the sea effectively as a means of communication. They have, however, made no serious attempt to use the sea as a power base—and I do not believe that we would have permitted such a use, despite the inhibitions on action already discussed. My point, once again, however, is that in modern naval strategy command of the sea *is* divisible.

The third major use of the sea, and again one given almost no weight by Mahan, is as a natural resource. It seems

certain that it will become a more and more important resource in the future. We are already finding a tendency for countries to claim larger and larger portions of the sea for their own uses. This encroaches upon the traditional international character of the sea, and, in situations of less than total war, it can have a serious inhibiting effect upon the use of naval forces.

The other strategic consideration raised by the increasing importance of the sea as a resource is that it can easily become a source of friction and conflict as nations compete for the riches of the sea. Quite certainly many wars have been fought over resources less valuable than the potential of certain areas of the sea. It will be some time before all of the implications are worked out, but at a minimum it must be recognized that the concept of "command of the sea" must now be expanded to include some idea of control of the resources of the sea itself.

Mahan's fundamental concept of command of the sea retains its validity. His corollary of the indivisibility of command of the sea does not. If we are to be able to solve the problems of maritime strategy that face us today, it is necessary to deal with the several aspects of command of the sea in all their complexity.

While I have not even begun to sketch out the details of what a contemporary version of Mahan's strategy would look like, I would like to examine at least in part the role of naval forces in the modern environment by discussing a single aspect of contemporary naval strategy: the deterrent role of sea-based forces. In a thermonuclear world there are two fundamental requirements to be met by military strategy. One is to prevent the kind of large-scale conflagration which could destroy our civilization; the other is to be able to utilize military force to control lesser conflicts and to bring them to acceptable conclusions.[11] For the remainder of this discussion I would like to address the problem of avoiding the nuclear holocaust and the role of naval forces in accomplishing that task.

You may think that Mahan would have had nothing to say about deterrence, but he did: "The clear expression of the national purpose, accompanied

14

by evident and adequate means to carry it into effect, is the surest safeguard against war."[12] Mahan was not talking about nuclear weapons, but he states quite clearly the central notion of deterrence, though in modern strategic terms, when the word "deterrence" is used it generally refers only to threatened actions at the upper end of the spectrum of conflict. It is this kind of deterrence that I would like to discuss: keeping any potential opponent from considering a surprise attack against the United States by convincing him that he would inevitably suffer unacceptable damage in return.

During the coming decade it is difficult to imagine any viable alternative to maintaining a U.S. nuclear strike capability with sufficient survivability to insure the destruction of any opponent, even after a surprise attack. To use the strategic jargon, we must have an assured second-strike capability—that is, nuclear strike systems that can survive any kind of a surprise attack and still be able to strike back massively at the aggressor.

On the other hand, a capability on our part of disarming the Soviet Union by attacking first is neither feasible nor desirable. It is not feasible, because no matter how massive our attack is, the Soviet Union would almost certainly have sufficient deliverable weapons remaining to destroy the United States as a viable society. It is not desirable because the possession of a first-strike capability by the United States would have the inevitable effect of making the Soviet Union trigger happy in a crisis, for fear of being disarmed by such an attack.

To maintain the assured U.S. capability to strike back even after a surprise attack, we should place additional emphasis on sea-based strategic weapons systems. I think that there are persuasive arguments in favor of doing this.

First, the sea-basing of strategic systems directs any attack against these systems seaward, rather than against the U.S. landmass itself. Any attack against Minuteman sites would cause widespread collateral damage, whether such damage was intended or not. Attacks directed against sea-based missiles would not involve this kind of damage to nonmilitary targets.

Second, sea-based systems are, in most cases, more survivable than equivalent land-based systems. This is a particularly important point with respect to second-strike capability. A deterrent system which cannot survive a surprise attack is worse than useless. Sea-based systems, particularly submarine-based systems, have a high survival value. We are made particularly aware of this when we face the problem of trying to counter equivalent Soviet systems.

Third, basing deterrent missiles at sea complicates the defensive problem of any potential opponent. Because of their mobility, he cannot do much in the way of pretargeting. If he attempts to counter a seaborne missile threat after the missiles are launched, he has a greatly increased defense problem. From the Soviet point of view, ICBM's based in the continental United States simplify defense, since all the missiles have to come through a narrow corridor, significantly limiting the problem of missile defense. Sea-based missiles, on the other hand, present almost a 360-degree potential threat and greatly complicate the necessary defenses. Further, the shorter range of sea-based systems reduces the vulnerability time of the offensive missile, making defense even more difficult.

For these reasons I believe that we should move toward placing a large portion of our strategic deterrence forces at sea. We should, however, stop short of total dependence upon sea basing to avoid becoming vulnerable to technological breakthrough and to avoid giving potential enemies a single defense problem to solve. It is to our advantage to force them to consider defense against a variety of systems.

As I have indicated, I do not see a great deal of difficulty in insuring to ourselves the use of the sea as a base for strategic deterrent forces. Denying this same use to potential opponents is another matter. The Soviet Union has been greatly expanding its capability to use the sea for its own strategic purposes. Barring an unforeseen technological breakthrough, there is little more prospect of our being able to effectively deny the Soviets this use of the sea than there does of them being able to deny it to us. From this point in time and technology, there seems to be no work-

able alternative to mutual strategic deterrence. This makes for an uncomfortable world, but it can be a more stable one if we make proper use of a blue-water deterrent strategy.

There is much more than can be said about contemporary naval strategy, especially about the problems of usefully employing naval forces in that large portion of the spectrum of conflict which lies between peace and nuclear holocaust. Much of what Mahan wrote 70 years ago still has value today, but anyone tells you that "all we have to do is apply Mahan," you can be reasonably sure he is wrong. On the other hand, the dismissal of Mahan as irrelevant is also wrong. His lessons on command of the sea, concentration, mobility, and strategic position are, when correctly applied, as useful as ever. If we are to understand strategy we must understand Mahan—along with Clausewitz, Sun Tzu, Liddell Hart, and Mao Tse-tung—but none of them will ever completely solve for us the problems of evolving particular strategies to meet particular problems. To understand strategy we must study the masters, but we must face and solve our problems ourselves.

BIOGRAPHIC SUMMARY

Comdr. James A. Barber, Jr., U.S. Navy, did his undergraduate work in economics at the University of Southern California. He holds an M.A. in economics from Vanderbilt University and an M.A. in international relations and a Ph.D. in political science from Stanford University. His primary operational experience has been in destroyers, most recently as Executive Officer of the U.S.S. *Henry W. Tucker* (DD 875) and as Commanding Officer of the U.S.S. *Hissem* (DER 400). He recently served as Plans Officer on the staff of the Naval War College and is currently assigned as Commanding Officer of U.S.S. *Schofield* (DEG 3).

FOOTNOTES

1. William D. Puleston, *Mahan: the Life and Work of Captain Alfred Thayer Mahan, U.S.N.* (New Haven: Yale University Press, 1939), p. 77.

2. *Ibid.*

3. Alfred T. Mahan, *The Influence of Sea Power upon History, 1660-1783* (Boston: Little, Brown, 1894), p. 2.

4. Alfred T. Mahan, *The Influence of Sea Power upon the French Revolution and Empire, 1793-1812* (Boston: Little, Brown, 1892).

5. Alfred T. Mahan, *Naval Strategy* (Boston: Little, Brown, 1911), p. 255.

6. *Ibid.*, p. 167.

7. *Ibid.*

8. Carl H. Amme, "Seapower and the Superpowers," *United States Naval Institute Proceedings,* October 1968, p. 33-34.

9. Mahan, *Naval Strategy,* p. 139.

10. *Ibid.*, p. 144.

11. James A. Barber, "War: Limitations and National Priorities," *Naval War College Review,* January 1971, p. 4-16.

12. Alfred T. Mahan, *The Interest of America in Sea Power Present and Future* (Boston: Little, Brown, 1897), p. 124.

ψ

War cannot be made a rule of thumb; and any attempt to make it so will result in disaster, grave in proportion to the gravity with which the issues of war are ever clothed.

Alfred Thayer Mahan, Naval Administration and Warfare

SEAPOWER IN WORLD WARS I AND II

The concept of seapower has undergone considerable change during this century as a result of two world wars and a tremendous increase in technology. The experience obtained during these years indicates that many of the traditional concepts of seapower need to be reexamined. In this first of three papers, Professor Stephen E. Ambrose describes the major military events of the first half of the 20th century in the light of their effect on the concept of seapower. In two future articles, Professor Ambrose will deal with Grand Strategy and Applied Strategy in World War II.

A lecture delivered at the Naval War College

by

Professor Stephen E. Ambrose

Ernest J. King Chair of Maritime History

Seapower in World War I

He who controls the sea controls everything—or nothing. It all depends on where he is and what use he makes of his control. He controls some, but not all, of the world's great commercial routes; but, except for the fisheries, he controls almost none of the earth's currently usable resources. In order to get the coal and iron and oil that make a modern industrial state go, he must be able to extend his control to one of the world's great landmasses. Obviously, then, nonexpansive nations that already occupy a large landmass do not need to control the seas, or at least they do not need to do so as badly as island empires do, a fact not often recognized by British and American naval strategists.

To continue for a moment in this heretical vein, it is possible that the purpose of a continental navy is *not* to destroy the enemy's navy in order to gain control of the sea. Perhaps France and Germany have followed the correct

strategy in pursuing a *guerre de course.* Certainly for Napoleon, the Kaiser, and Hitler, one of the keys to victory was denying the British access to their world market and sources of supply, but it is not at all certain that this required the destruction of the British battle fleet. There are enough "ifs" in the submarine campaigns of this century to lead one to suspect that it is theoretically possible to deny to the enemy the use of the seas without yourself controlling the ocean and, in an immediate crisis the objective for continental powers is not so much to control the sea in order to use it as it is to deny its use to the British.

What I wish to suggest is that Mahan's concept that national greatness can come only through control of blue water is a limited one that must be examined with regard to a specific time and place. Surely the ancient Mongols, Napoleonic France, and modern Russia and China were, or are, great nations by any standard, yet none of them controlled the seas. German commerce

raiding in this century posed, potentially, a more dangerous threat to the Allies than Allied control of the water did to Germany. German submarines, by themselves, could have defeated England; English battleships, by themselves, could never have defeated Germany.

It is clear enough that had England lost control of the surface water at any time between 1914-18 or 1939-45, she would have lost everything. The same observation would apply to Japan, with even more force, for her relative paucity of resources at home, combined with the tremendous distances in the Pacific, made control of the seas vital to her if she wished to play the role of a great power. But it is not much more than a commonplace to say that island empires depend on control of the waters around them for their greatness.

What is necessary, it seems to me, is to realize the limitations inherent in any given situation; to be more specific, to recognize that it is well-nigh impossible for any one nation to control both the land and the sea. Only two nations in this century have really tried, Germany from 1900 to 1916 and Russia today. America does not challenge Russian control of the land in the Eurasian heartland nor China's domination in Asia. England has never by herself thought of challenging for control of the European landmass. For all the power of the combined British and American Fleets in World War II, without the Red army the Western Alliance could not have won the war.

Clearly, then, Mahan was wrong in intimating that control of Europe depended on control of the sea. In both World Wars the Germans were brought down only by massive engagements on the land, brought about through alliances. Allied control of the oceans denied certain things to the Germans, to be sure, and therefore contributed to the victory, but the Allied navies, in the nature of the game, could not be decisive. By the same token, in Vietnam today, where the United States has total control of the sea, the Navy has helped enormously in deploying and maintaining American power at a vast distance from the homeland, but it is able to give only limited help in achieving a tactical victory or, far more important, imposing a political settlement.

This rather long-winded introduction to seapower in World War I is meant only to suggest that German's naval policy ought not to be condemned out of hand. Insofar as Germany followed a *guerre de course* policy, I believe she had a correct strategy; insofar as she tried to challenge England on the high seas, she was mistaken. The geographical position of the two nations dictated certain rather obvious policies, of which by far the most important was that in allocating resources, Germany had to put her major effort into the army, Britian into the navy. The more resources Germany put into the *guerre de course*, with its promise of a high return for a low cost, the better off she was.

But this was not so clear to the Germans, of course, and in fact, they put their major naval effort from 1900 on into big ships. Great battleships brought great prestige, and the Kaiser wanted his share of them. Realizing that the British would never allow Germany to outbuild the English Fleet, Tirpitz

came up with a theory to justify the construction of the High Seas Fleet, the so-called "risk fleet theory." Tirpitz argued that Germany's overseas trade and colonies could be effectively protected only by constructing a fleet so strong that even "the strongest naval power" could not fight it without seriously weakening its own naval power and leaving it helpless against a coalition of other naval powers. In other words, the German Fleet did not have to be as strong as that of Britain, because England would never dare concentrate all its naval power against Germany. The cold calculation behind this doctrine was that England, rather than risk a clash with a powerful concentrated German Fleet, would prefer to make concessions to Germany in the colonial field. In short, the new fleet would be used as an instrument of coercion.

There were a number of assumptions in Tirpitz' risk fleet theory, none of which proved justified. Perhaps most important was the idea that big ships were the only way to challenge Britain on the high seas. Cruisers built for commerce raiding and, of course, submarines would have worked much better. Tirpitz also assumed that it was important to Germany to protect her colonies and overseas trade—yet, in practice, Germany carried on for 4 years of arduous war without them. Germany's colonies were by no means as important to her as England's were to Britain. Finally, the risk fleet theory was based on the concept that if war with England came, Germany would have allies in possession of fleets that would be capable of taking on a weakened British Fleet. This turned out to be not so, as German statesmen proved to be incapable of so arranging things as to bring about this desired political result. Germany's main ally, Austria-Hungary, was almost exclusively a landpower. The risk fleet theory proved to be a costly error.

Let me here just cover one highlight of German strategy, beginning with the observation that German naval strategy was governed in large part by the tools available at the beginning of the war. There was always a controversy over how to use these tools; to oversimplify, Tirpitz wanted the High Seas Fleet to accept risks, while the commanders of

the fleet itself were cautious. Tirpitz virtually accused the commanders of cowardice. He argued that the High Seas Fleet was more at liberty to take risks than the British since Germany's fate did not completely depend upon the High Seas Fleet, whereas the fate of not only Britain, but that of her allies, depended on the Grand Fleet. There was some truth in his observation—Germany could have lost the High Seas Fleet and still won the war—but the commanders of the High Seas Fleet would have none of it. They were always weaker in capital ships, and their only hope of victory in an all-out encounter was luck—luck with destroyers, U-boats, or mines.

So the High Seas Fleet, built at such cost, both financial and political, contributed little to the German cause. Until 1917 submarines did not do much better, partly because of political limitations, more because there were not enough of them and their tactics were deficient. Finally, in early 1917, after the underwater fleet had been built up and following long discussions in which General Ludendorff seems to have taken the lead, the decision to introduce unrestricted submarine warfare was taken. It changed the nature of the war at all levels. Ludendorff knew it would bring America in on the British side; he reasoned that America could not make a contribution, however, until it was too late, and, given the information available to him at the time, it is hard to see how he could have reasoned otherwise. The decision gave Germany the initiative at sea, putting its navy on the offensive and challenging Britain in a way that had not been done since the Spanish Armada. Significantly, Germany made no bid to wrest control of the sea from Britain; the U-boats did not waste their effort in trying to get at the Grand Fleet. Instead, the sea war became an all-out *guerre de course*, with not only the submarines, but also surface vessels, switched to the attack on commerce, concentrating on traffic in the English Channel and the Mediterranean and against the Scandinavian trade.

To inaugurate deliberately a policy that would surely bring the world's greatest industrial power into the war as an enemy was a great gamble. The

Germans realized this and regarded the decision as the most important of the war. Within weeks of taking it, they had reason to believe victory was in sight. Germany was on the verge of victory. Incapable of destroying her enemies on the ground on the Western Front, she had—in effect—successfully blockaded Russia and thereby contributed to the withdrawal of that nation from the war. Now she was blockading Britain, with startlingly effective results. One of every four ships that left England was sunk. Britain was replacing only one ship for each 10 sunk: No pit props were arriving from Norway, which threatened to destroy the coal industry. Wheat supplies were down to 6 weeks (although there were piles of grain in France, belonging to the British, which Haig insisted on hoarding to feed the horses, so that when the breakthrough occurred his cavalry would be in good shape for the dash to Berlin).

How did the Royal Navy respond to this, the greatest crisis in Britain's history? Jellicoe, now First Sea Lord, admitted his helplessness by saying, "There is absolutely no solution that we can see." When Vice Adm. William S. Sims, USN, arrived in London on 9 April 1917, he was astonished at what he learned. Jellicoe told him, "It is impossible to go on with the war if losses like these continue." Yet Jellicoe had no solution nor could he even think of new methods to try. Britain was failing—and it is only a slight exaggeration to say that the Royal Navy decided it could do nothing about it.

There were other shocks for Sims. America had begun a great naval building program in 1915 and had naturally followed the British lead and concentrated on dreadnoughts. Sims now learned that they were not needed, indeed, not even wanted. If they were brought over, they would just burn oil needed for destroyers. Destroyers were what was wanted, but America had only a few to offer, not nearly enough to save the day. It was quite a commentary on a whole generation of naval building, not to mention the way in which Germany, with a relatively small expenditure on submarines, had been able to change the entire nature of the war at sea.

The story of how Britain overcame

the crisis is one of the most dramatic of the war; naturally, with so much at stake, there are a number of versions, with various people taking credit for the solution. The Americans claim that Sims was chiefly responsible. Actually, many contributed, but the key figure seems to have been the Prime Minister, David Lloyd George, that shadowy figure who reveled in the hatred of the entire British establishment and who was, according to A.J.P. Taylor, the greatest Prime Minister of the century.

Lloyd George first asked Jellicoe to devise a solution. Jellicoe said nothing was possible. Lloyd George then turned to the publisher Northcliffe, who suggested consulting Hankey, Secretary of the War Cabinet and father of the Committee of Imperial Defense. Lloyd George discussed the situation with Hankey, who recommended the convoy system.

Lloyd George then returned to the Admiralty and demanded the initiation of the convoy system. He pointed out that the Grand Fleet never moved except in convoy. The Admiralty rejoined that merchant captains could not keep station, that the convoys would just offer larger targets to U-boats, that unloading facilities were inadequate to handle all the ships that would come into the ports at once. On 30 April 1917, nevertheless, on the only occasion in British history when a Prime Minister directed a great department of state in the teeth of the minister responsible, Lloyd George ordered the institution of the convoy. It was his greatest and most decisive achievement of the war. The first convoy left Gibraltar on 10 May. Others were organized from Canadian and American ports. Slowly but surely, the curve of sinkings went down. By 1918 over 80 percent of the shipping coming into Britain came in convoy. Less than 1 percent of ships in convoy were lost from all causes. By 1918 Britain was building more ships than she was losing. The convoy enabled England to survive and win the war.

Nothing illustrated quite so clearly how fully Germany had taken the initiative by launching unrestricted submarine warfare than the British decision to go to convoy. Because the destroyers' primary task now became escorting convoys (as well as search and destroy

missions through patrolling), the Grand Fleet was deprived of its screen and therefore, in effect, blockaded in its harbors. The effect was strikingly and tragically illustrated by Admiral Beatty's position as Commander in Chief of the Grand Fleet. At an Admiralty conference on 2 January 1918, Beatty said he no longer considered it wise to provoke a fleet action, even if an opportunity occurred. This from the dashing Beatty, the man who had writhed under Jellicoe's cautious leadership at Jutland. Beatty argued that trade came first, that ships detached to protect convoys must be written off the strength of the Grand Fleet; that the German battle cruiser fleet was now more formidable than his own; that he had detached too many destroyers for the Grand Fleet to safely issue forth to take on the High Seas Fleet. Nelson turned in his grave as Beatty spoke, but there was no gainsaying that Beatty was correct.

What, then, of the Grand Fleet, that magnificent collection of gigantic dreadnoughts and cruisers that were hardly smaller? It had been the number one priority of Great Britain, built at enormous expense, and was regarded as the first line of defense. What was the strategy governing the use of this weapon? How successful was it? In the end, what contribution did the Grand Fleet make to victory? Did it justify the allocation of resources necessary to create it in the first place?

There are no clear-cut answers. Certain it is that the Grand Fleet kept German surface raiders under control and helped to keep the submarine menace from becoming worse than it did. The British blockade of Germany would hardly have been possible without the Grand Fleet, and there are scholars who argue vehemently that in the last analysis it was the blockade that brought the Central Powers to their knees. This, however, is conjecture and to my mind not valid. The German spring offensive in 1918 (the Ludendorff offensive) was an extraordinarily powerful one and came close—very close—to total success. That Germany could mount such an offensive so late in the war indicates that, great as the contribution the blockade made to reducing German strength, it was not decisive.

As early as 1905 Admiral Wilson, the Channel Commander in Chief, considered the problem of what the British Navy could do to tip the balance in a war that would be primarily fought by mass armies on the Continent. He believed that "no action by the Navy alone can do France any good," and declared that the best and most valuable contribution the navy could make would be to capture the mouths of the Elbe and Weser Rivers through combined military and naval expeditions—amphibious assaults, in short, somewhat like First Sea Lord Fisher would propose as the Baltic alternative in the early stages of the war. Wilson recommended that when the serious possibility of war arose he be placed in communication with the commander in chief of the expeditionary force in order that they could prepare plans for combined operations "on the largest scale possible," with the objective of drawing German troops away from the French frontier and threatening Germany's rear. He argued that all available small craft, as well as overage battleships, could be used to bombard the shore and prepare the way for the landing.

As noted, Fisher would later propose a similar idea as a proper use of seapower, but, unfortunately, the reforms he introduced during his first term as First Sea Lord, beginning in 1905, led to the creation of a navy ill suited to combined operations. Fisher concentrated on dreadnoughts; his critics at the time argued, among other things, that in weeding out the smaller ships of no great power and taking them out of commission he was concentrating his attention too exclusively on the fleet as an engine of fighting at sea, thereby ignoring its enormous possibilities for influencing operations ashore, especially through amphibious assaults. Fisher stuck to the dreadnoughts, nevertheless, with results that are well known.

It is also true that the one great combined operation tried in the war was an unmitigated disaster. The reasons for the failure at the Dardanelles remain controversial; the list of mistakes is almost endless. Certainly, had the British used World War II amphibious methods the campaign would have been

a success, but one can wonder if they should have tried it at all since they knew nothing of World War II methods. Had the overage battleships pushed just a little harder, they could have forced the straits, but none of the commanders knew that at the time, and it is difficult to see how they could have known. Had the soldiers been more aggressive once they had landed, they could have carried the day, but it is much easier to be aggressive after the fact, when the enemy's strength and disposition are known, than it is when under fire.

I am not so foolhardy as to try to settle the Dardanelles argument, I would, however, like to make one observation on a broader aspect of the campaign. Almost everyone who writes about it seems to accept Churchill's basic justification for the attempt to force the straits—that opening a pipeline to Russia would have had immeasurable effect on the war. Dr. Lundenberg suggests that if a supply route to Russia had been opened, the Czar would have remained in control, the Russians would have fought on, and there would have been no Communist Revolution. Most Western writers seem to accept this idea, usually without thinking about it very hard.

It is time to call the idea into question. Great political upheavals do occur in a time and at a place, to be sure, so that they are influenced by immediate events. But it seems to me to be questionable to assume that the overthrow of the Czar, and later of Kerensky, could have been prevented by shipping some ammunition to Russia. Dramatic history and romantic historians to the contrary notwithstanding, world events do not turn on such small matters. More concretely, one must ask how many supplies the Western Powers could have shipped to Russia in 1917. Even had the straits and/or the Balkan route been open, did England and France, in fact, have the ships and, more important, the guns and shells to spare? I doubt that they had anywhere near enough to supply the Russian Army adequately, especially when one recalls that the Russian Army needed everything—food, clothes, shoes, shelter, as well as implements of war. Finally, everything I have read about conditions among the officer corps in the Russian

Army leads me to believe that whatever was sent would have been sold on a black market for individual gain. More and more supplies cannot overcome ingrained corruption. They just add to it.

The other great naval event of the war was a battle that, like Waterloo, has been analyzed *ad nauseum*. Jutland was the first great encounter between dreadnoughts and the last of the gigantic surface actions in that war. Tactically, it is intensely interesting, and the personalities of the commanders on both sides add to the fascination. As with the Dardanelles, I intend to settle nothing here, but again some suggestions may be in order.

First, much of the criticism of Jellicoe for not being more aggressive seems out of touch with the realities he faced. That he was overly afraid of torpedoes, mines, and submarines is obvious now, but who was so sure then? He had, in any case, always made his position clear enough. As Arthur Marder writes,

> Jellicoe's position never altered. He refused to be stampeded into any hazardous adventures: no risks must be run that would threaten the British command of the sea. Jellicoe believed that the fleet should always seek a decisive victory at sea, but he always qualified it with two powerful considerations: (1) a recognition of the practical obstacles: the submarine and the mine danger; and (2) the knowledge that, because a defeat would be catastrophic, they must ever be on their guard against being drawn into action under conditions favorable to the enemy and deliberately planned by him.

Jellicoe's fears were exaggerated, because everyone was always telling him how important he was. As usual, Churchill put it best by saying Jellicoe was the only man who could lose the war in an afternoon, which was true enough but which, because everyone was saying it, had an unhealthy effect on Jellicoe's mind. As Professor Donald Shurman has pointed out, "Jellicoe more and more saw himself as the focal point for the whole war," the Grand Fleet as the key to victory. Since Jellicoe also felt, as

Hankey put it, that at any minute a German was going to jump through the Admiralty window behind him and hit him a poke when he least expected it, he was quite naturally cautious.

But as Marder reminds us, one of the critics, Admiral Beatty, when he became First Sea Lord, changed nothing at all. For all his dash, Beatty would not dream of risking the Grand Fleet except under favorable circumstances, which meant north of the latitude of Horns Reef. Since the Germans would not fight except in waters comfortably close to their bases, the result was stalemate.

Now, everyone knows that neither of these two great fleets was willing to take risks, for reasons on both sides that were sound enough. Nevertheless, there is a feeling of frustration about Jutland. The two fleets that sailed through the misty night to their encounter at Jutland constituted "the culminating manifestation of naval force in the history of the world," and they were unable to reach any decision. This was frustrating, especially for the British, who loudly demanded, "Was this the spirit of Nelson?" Nelson, Jellicoe's defenders rejoined, did not have to face torpedoes and mines. It is generally accepted today that Jellicoe was correct, perhaps not tactically, but strategically, for the maintenance of British control of the sea was even more vital than the defeat of the German Fleet.

There is great force in this argument. I am compelled to ask, however, if it was the only factor in Jellicoe's, and later Beatty's, mind. The navies of World War I, on both sides, can with some justice be accused of sentimentally valuing things more than lives or even causes. The artilleryman's love of his guns and readiness to sacrifice his life to avert the disgrace of losing them is paralleled by the sailor's adoration of his ship. Liddell Hart suggests that this attitude may have its foundation in totemism, but it is accentuated by the military man's peacetime shortage of material and the penalties attached to any loss of it. The attitude hinders the soldier or sailor from adopting the commonsense view that a ship or a gun, like a shell, is merely a weapon to be expended profitably.

A very curious thing happened in Britain in World War I, and it happened twice. In early 1917 the Admiralty could think of no way in which the Grand Fleet, built at such an enormous national effort, could help overcome the submarine crisis. We have already covered the results. Then it happened again, in 1918. Ludendorff's spring offensive threatened the entire position in France. Another crisis was at hand. Again, the Grand Fleet could propose nothing.

I don't know of anyone who has studied this astonishing fact. I asked Arthur Marder, who by all odds is the expert to ask, about it last spring. He said that Beatty made a couple of halfhearted proposals to Jellicoe, which were turned down, and the fleet did nothing. It is astonishing to realize that while English soldiers were dying by the thousands, with their backs to the wall, and the fate of the Empire trembled in the balance, the Grand Fleet felt it could do nothing at all to help.

Younger officers in the fleet disagreed at the time and urged action of some sort. The crux of the matter, as Marder emphasizes, was Beatty's conviction that there must be no gambling with the navy; the whole Allied cause was based on the latent power of the Grand Fleet. I am suggesting that Beatty was wrong; that even had the Grand Fleet remained intact, even had it defeated the High Sea Fleet in action in 1918, Britain and France still could have lost the war to Ludendorff's troops. Beatty's view of war was too narrow.

There is another disturbing element to naval warfare, 1914-18. Liddell Hart has said that a fundamental difference between the higher naval and military leadership in the World War was that the admirals would not intentionally give battle unless reasonably sure of an initial advantage, whereas the generals were usually ready to take the offensive whatever the disadvantages. This is true, and one must wonder why. How did it come about that while Beatty was carefully preserving his ships, Haig was spending tens of thousands of lives in absolutely useless offensives? England paid practically no attention when a hundred men died in the trenches because of a stray shell; England went into national mourning when a dreadnought was lost. Why?

Let me make two highly tentative suggestions. First, the dreadnoughts had been tied in with the whole idea of national prestige. In Germany the schoolchildren collected pennies to build the ships. No one had ever thought to collect pennies in the schools to buy the soldier a rifle. In World War II there was relatively little of this mystical nonsense about ships—aircraft carriers were seen as tools of war; expendable tools to be used profitably. Some flattops were lost, but they were used to advantage. They were not regarded as entities unto themselves, to be spared and protected for their own sakes. They were implements of national purpose, nothing more—and nothing less. Ships like *Lexington* are remembered today precisely because they did fight—who now remembers any of the dreadnoughts?

The second tentative suggestion I should like to make as to why the dreadnoughts did not fight, even in moments of supreme crisis, is this: it was a machine-oriented age. Social historians stress this point all the time. The industrial system of the time was geared to machines, not to men. As one quick example, if a machine worked most effectively by going 24 hours a day, 7 days a week, then men had to adjust to it, and night shifts were invented. No one thought of adjusting the machine to the needs of men. So, too, with the armed services. Britain was willing to make any sacrifice in men's lives required to win the war, but she was unwilling to sacrifice her machines. Haig, Jellicoe, and Beatty all came from the same generation, all had comparable values, standards, and education. Yet Haig thought of nothing but attack, while the sailors thought of little but protecting their ships. There had to be a reason. Mine may not be the right one, but hopefully the question will at least provoke some discussion.

These criticisms of British naval strategy in World War I apply equally to the other powers, especially Germany. More important, I really don't see how Jellicoe, Beatty, and the others could have acted much, if any, differently. They were human beings, not computers, and they were the prisoners of their time and place. Their attitudes toward strategy were shared by nearly every important sailor. Their professional knowledge and experience were excellent for 1914-18. They all did their best, and one cannot ask humans to do more. It is the function of history, as I see it, to point to errors and make suggestions, based on hindsight, so that we can do better in the future, but who among us can say he could have done better at that time and in that place? Certainly I cannot.

Seapower In World War II

It has long been my contention that there was no major technological breakthrough in land warfare between the beginning of the First World War and the conclusion of the Second. The major weapons of the 1914-18 period were also the major weapons of the 1939-45 period. There were improvements on basic designs, to be sure, and the tacticians of the Second World War used the weapons better than they were used in the First World War (tanks are an obvious example), but in basic essentials, both wars were fought with the same weapons.

This was not the case at sea. World War I had inaugurated a new era, that of underseas warfare, which drastically changed the old strategies, especially that of the nature and extent of the *guerre de course*. Before the submarine, the ships that were capable of gaining command of the sea were also capable of destroying commerce raiders. After submarine development this was no longer true. Thus I would contend that the major breakthrough of World War I was the development and extension of underseas warfare. In World War II one sees refinement and improvement in submarine techniques, as well, of course, as in antisubmarine warfare, but no basic change. In essence, the *guerre de course* of World War II was similar to that of World War I. On the high seas, however, there were fundamental changes, which meant in practice that admirals in 1939 had to consider much more in the way of technological change than did the generals. The two most important changes were the revolution in amphibious warfare and the coming of age of the aircraft carrier.

There was also a change in attitude on the part of the British. In effect, the British armed services rejected the World War I experience totally. On the ground, the soldiers were determined to avoid the blood baths of 1914-18, and British strategy returned to the traditional practice of staying out of the mass warfare on the Continent, hitting at the enemy's periphery, and going onto the Continent only when the enemy was exhausted. At sea, British sailors were concerned with much more than just protecting the fleet in being, and British ships compiled an outstanding combat record, as they sought out the enemy at all possible opportunities. The British made especially great contributions in support of amphibious attacks, exposing the fleet in return for a measurable profit.

Throughout human history, navies have been used to transport soldiers to hostile shores, land them, and provide logistical support. In a sense, then, the United States and British Navies of World War II only did what had been done before, albeit on a far larger scale. But the scale was so enormous that the difference was not just quantitative, but qualitative. Just as the aircraft carrier allowed navies to increase dramatically the area over which they could influence events, so did improvements in amphibious techniques make navies far more valuable by making it possible for them to project their power up to and beyond the coastline.

It was not just that the ships carried the men to the shores, although obviously that was the *sine qua non* of amphibious warfare. In nearly every amphibious operation of World War II, it was naval gunfire that saved the day. At Sicily, in July 1943, a German counterattack against the beaches by the Herman Goering Panzer Division threatened to drive the Americans back into the Mediterranean. The troops had few antitank guns and practically no artillery ashore. The air forces were off flying strategic missions, for at that stage of the war they could not be bothered with close-in tactical support. The destroyers and cruisers, British and American, stepped into the breach. In one of the few actions in history that pitted tanks against ships, the ships demolished the tanks and thus secured the bridgehead.

At Salerno, in September of 1943,

and again at Anzio, in January of 1944, the same story unfolded. Once again the size and accuracy of naval bombardment—mostly British—made it possible for the troops to hang on in the bridgehead. At Normandy it was ship-to-shore bombardment, much more than air strikes, that softened up the beachhead for Eisenhower's troops. Surprisingly, this story is seldom told and little known. One reason, I suppose, is that the air forces have better publicity departments than the navies. Another is that the airplanes are more spectacular, especially to the soldiers on the ground. Thus, in his memoirs, Eisenhower related how touch-and-go things were at Salerno, until the air force began to fly tactical missions and forced the Germans back. He did not mention the naval support fire. Yet the navies fired 10 times more shells than the air force dropped, and I hardly need to remind this audience that the naval shells hit what they were aimed at while the free-falling bombs seldom did more than make large holes in the ground.

The navies' contribution to the revolution in amphibious warfare did not end with fire support. Indeed, the scale of amphibious warfare could hardly have been possible had it not been for the enormous strides made in landing craft in World War II. Here I am not so much concerned with getting the men ashore—its importance is too obvious to belabor—as I am with the ability to supply them once there. The development of vessels that made it possible to bring supplies in over open beaches along with the British development of artificial harbors and breakwaters were the chief innovations of World War II. I would go so far as to say that more than any other technological development of the war, the ability to supply troops over open beaches shaped the strategy in World War II.

Most of the great operations of the war, on both oceans, would hardly have been possible without this development. The Allies could not have invaded Sicily nor Italy nor Normandy, not to mention the Pacific islands, without it. Supply over beaches enabled the Allies to exert their power in areas previously denied to them and thus greatly extended the strategic scope of the war. Had it not been for the new landing craft and the artificial harbors and breakwaters, the Normandy invasion would have been a bloody failure. In fact, it would not have been tried, and since Hitler's defenses around the ports and harbors on the coast of France were so strong, it is doubtful if the Allies would have been able to return to the Continent at all.

Even after the capture of ports, most land campaigns would have failed had it not been for the navies' new-found abilities. In the French campaign, for example, the artificial ports (and Pluto) brought in by far the bulk of the supplies until the late autumn of 1944. The troops that overran France drew only a small percentage of their supplies from Cherbourg, the only working port available. It was not until Antwerp was opened and winter weather set in that the artificial harbors were overshadowed.

What the revolution in amphibious warfare meant was that no open coastline was safe from Allied power (the invasion of Casablanca in November 1942, may I remind you, was mounted in Norfolk, Va.). This forced the enemy to protect all coastlines or face defeat. It is only a slight exaggeration to say that the Allies could strike anywhere with terrible swiftness (MacArthur's landing at Inchon is a later example of the effectiveness of this technique). It was all dependent, of course, on control of the sea, which is another way of saying that in World War II the Anglo-Americans used their control of the sea for positive purposes, as they had not done in World War I. The Grand Fleet made practically no contribution to the land battles in France in 1914-18; the Anglo-American fleet of 1942-45 was the decisive weapon in the European war. This is using resources effectively.

The success of Allied amphibious warfare was dependent on the ability to produce the necessary landing craft (more about that later), but an essential ingredient to the mix was men. Combined planning and control of operations reached new levels in World War II. If landing craft were the decisive factor in the strategy pursued in Europe and if the aircraft carrier revolutionized naval strategy in the Pacific, it was combined planning that made the new tools usable. The achievement was espe-

cially impressive because, in Europe, it did not just involve getting the army and navy to work together—a difficult enough task by itself—but rather included the air forces plus officers of two distinct nationalities. In effect, men from six different backgrounds had to be brought together—British Army, Navy, and Air officers, as well as American officers from the three corresponding branches. The first time it was tried, in the early days of planning for the North African invasion, they "fought like cats and dogs."

Time and again, Eisenhower said that his success all came down to one word —the team. He always emphasized that he felt his greatest contribution was getting everyone to work together toward a common objective. He himself used the term triphibious warfare to describe his operations and he became a great advocate of unification after the war. He thought the National Security Act of 1947 did not go nearly far enough in unifying the three American services and even went to the length of advocating a uniformity of curriculum among the service academies and a single uniform for all officers in the armed services. He also felt that integration of the Anglo-American armed services was a desirable goal.

Eisenhower's success did not come easily, but he did have certain advantages that should not be ignored. There was, first of all, the common language and heritage, something hardly ever found in alliance warfare. Still, there was a certain amount of Anglophobia among the Americans which Eisenhower constantly fought. Another great advantage was the relative absence of political bickering. The British and Americans shared the same general goal—the total defeat of Nazi Germany, and because Eisenhower always insisted on making his decisions on purely military, as opposed to political, grounds, there was little bickering. There were, of course, differences, the most important of which was British insistence on fighting in the Mediterranean as opposed to the American desire to get into northwest France as soon as possible; but these differences were ones of approach and method, not goals.

Eisenhower, in fact, had as much trouble in integrating some American

officers into the team as he did with the British. I'm glad to relate to this audience that it was the Army Air Force, and not the U.S. Navy, that gave him trouble, although the reason was not necessarily that the naval officers had a broader vision. The Air Force, of course, had its own strategic doctrine and fervently believed that it could win the war on its own, if only the ground troops would stop bothering them with requests for support. Eisenhower fought some momentous battles with the flyers before he could get them to cooperate, especially with those Air Force officers who believed the invasion of France was unnecessary and who maintained that they could bring Germany to surrender through massive air raids alone.

The navy was a different story. The admirals, like the flyers, had a strategic doctrine of their own, command of the seas, which might have led them to drag their heels in combined planning and to withdraw their vessels from support of the troops had there been a challenge to their command of the sea. But there was no such challenge, and since the navies already had command of the sea, they could willingly pitch in and give their all to supporting the troops. MacArthur's experience in the Southwest Pacific indicates that had the Germans maintained a large surface fleet however, Eisenhower might not have enjoyed such full cooperation from the navies.

But the important point is that he did have it, most notably in the planning stages. British and American naval officers worked closely with soldiers and flyers, from the level of lieutenants up to admirals and generals, toward a common objective. In a way, however—to end the discussion on combined planning on a slightly sour note— the success may have been unfortunate for the future. It seems to me that the American and British armed services came out of World War II with a faith in the possibilities of combined planning in an alliance that was out of proportion to the reality. The only situation that I can envision in which an alliance could work so smoothly again would be to repeat World War II. That is, the alliance would have to be between Britain and America, the enemy a threat as obvious as Hitler was. This situation does not appear likely to be repeated. Even if something like it did come again, I doubt that the alliance could work as well because another essential factor has forever disappeared. I am referring to the relative equality of the contribution Britain and America made to the common cause. Throughout much of World War II the partners were more or less equally strong. After America became the senior partner, in late 1944, the British found that they were increasingly discriminated against in the strategic decisions—especially in the broad-front versus single-thrust controversy and the question of going into Berlin.

To return to the subject of cooperation between the U.S. Army and Navy in World War II, the story is not altogether one of easily achieved success. There were bitter fights, especially at the higher levels and on the JCS, over worldwide strategy. To oversimplify, the Army wanted to fight in Europe and take care of Japan after Hitler was finished, while the Navy's war was in the Pacific. Alan-Brooke, CIGS, used to complain that Admiral King slept through CCS meetings, awakening only when someone mentioned the Pacific. As I hope my account of the Navy's contribution in Europe has made clear, that was not true, but it was the tendency.

This basic difference in emphasis led to problems all along the line. On the fundamental question of industrial priority, King wanted to build fighting ships, while Army Chief of Staff Marshall wanted the shipbuilding program to concentrate on landing craft. In effect, King won, which meant that the chief limiting factor in all strategic decisions of World War II was the relative absence of landing craft. Churchill once growled that history would always wonder at how it happened that the fate of two great empires was tied up in some god-damned things called LST's. He was both right and wrong. Every amphibious operation of the war in Europe was delayed because of the shortage of landing craft, while in the Pacific some major operations had to be called off altogether for the same reason. There were never enough landing craft to go around. But Churchill was wrong in speculating that historians would not be able to explain this shortage, for the reasons are clear

enough.

First and foremost, King was faced with a challenge on the high seas in the Pacific. He reasoned, correctly, that the Europe-first decision, while basically sound, had to be modified in practice. The Allies could not concentrate everything in Europe and remain on the passive defensive in the Pacific, for that would allow the Japanese to build up their Empire to such an extent that it could never be cracked. In order to undertake limited offensives in the Pacific, King had to have surface ships. If he were going to get them, the shipyards had to build them. In addition, the surface fleet program was not entirely a Pacific program, for many of the destroyers the shipyards turned out were vital to the antisubmarine war on the Atlantic. All the landing craft in the world would not have mattered had it not been for the victory in the submarine war.

The real culprit, I think, was the Air Force. Priorities got mixed up, not in the shipyards, but on a national level. To put it bluntly, the Anglo-Americans built far too many bombers. All the men and money and material that went into the Lancasters and B-29's would have been better used on landing craft. This is not to deny that the bombers made a contribution to victory, for of course they did, but it seems to me clear that any honest cost-effectiveness analysis would indicate that landing craft were a better buy than bombers.

In any case, there were not enough landing craft. The issue then became one of where to use those that were available. In this area Admiral King was playing a delicate game. The Navy controlled the craft, and King wanted as many as possible for the Pacific war. He therefore kept the total number of craft a closely guarded secret. More to the point, he used his possession of the craft as a weapon to influence strategic decisions. In July of 1942, for example, when the Anglo-American struggle over whether to invade the Continent in 1943 or to go to North Africa in 1942 was being decided, King was willing to make sufficient craft available for a 1943 cross-Channel attack. When the British won, however, and North Africa was decided upon, King suddenly found that he did not have enough craft

available for the operation. The issue could not be settled by the CCS, and eventually President Roosevelt had to step in and order King to deliver the necessary landing craft.

Again, in 1944, worldwide planning on landing craft was impossible, since only Admiral King knew how many there were. He was willing to make more available to Europe if the British would promise to use them to invade the south of France, but he would not make them available if they were to be used for operations in Italy or against the Balkans. The British were furious, but nothing could be done about it. Once again Roosevelt had to step into the breach and order King to give up more craft when Eisenhower said they were necessary for the cross-Channel invasion. To my mind, by the way, King was correct in doing everything he could to prevent operations in the Mediterranean; his strategy, like Marshall's, with its emphasis on coming to grips with the Wehrmacht on the Continent as soon as possible, was the one with the greatest promise of a quicker victory.

The lesson in all this, I suppose, is the great events turn on comparatively little matters, or, to use Churchill's phrase again, the grand strategy of World War II turned on some god-damned things called LST's.

No one ever called the other great development of naval warfare, aircraft carriers, those god-damned things, although in the early years of the war they too were in short supply. Like the landing craft, the most important contribution of aircraft carriers was vastly to extend the areas over which the navy could influence events. Fleets could see farther and hit farther. They could sail closer to enemy-held shorelines for they could now provide their own protection in the air. Land-based fighter planes could not drive away a fleet that had sufficient aircraft carriers. In the Pacific this meant that landing craft could be used for the purposes for which they had been designed. It is doubtful that the amphibious operations in the Pacific could have been undertaken at all had it not been for the air cover provided by the aircraft carriers. It is notable in this regard that in Europe where, generally speaking, there were not enough Allied aircraft carriers, every invasion from

1943 onward was strictly limited to areas that could be covered by land-based fighter airplanes. In the Italian invasion, for example, Salerno was as far north as Eisenhower dared to go, even though the strategic rewards of going further up the coast were obvious, because Salerno was as far north as his Sicily-based fighters could provide cover.

In listing the virtues of the carrier and its impact on naval warfare, it need hardly be added that the carrier was absolutely essential to gaining command of the sea. Navies without aircraft carriers were like babies still in the womb; they were tied to the short and inelastic umbilical cord of land-based air cover. They were incapable of challenging for command of the sea and were limited to sending submarines into blue water. Submarines, of course, could only carry on a *guerre de course.*

Which brings us back to the point at which I began the lecture on World War I—the value of command of the seas. In World War II, control of the oceans was vital to England, the United States, Japan, and, to a much lesser degree, Russia so that she could receive lend-lease goods. Without the ability to move men and supplies across blue water, none of these nations could have carried on in the war, and, indeed, Japan was doomed when she lost that ability. For Germany the key was denial of the use of the seas to the enemy. In practice these distinctions in definition meant little except insofar as they applied to the manner in which the war at sea was waged. As in 1917-18, it was the war under the seas that counted, because no matter how great Allied superiority on the surface, no matter how many aircraft carriers and landing craft the Anglo-Americans had, they could only win the war by getting cargo vessels into the ports. (Incidentally, the Navy's work in clearing demolished ports and keeping them working afterwards has always impressed me as one of the significant, although least noticed, achievements of the war.)

I cannot comment on the techniques of antisubmarine warfare as it is outside my field, but I would like to say a word or two on what did not work. All prewar, and to some extent postwar, claims by the advocates of strategic air

forces to the contrary, it is clear that the submarine had to be met and defeated on the high seas. That is another way of saying that ASW had to be done the hard way—there were no shortcuts. The big bomber boys claimed they could knock out the submarines in their pens. The major effort came in the late summer of 1942 as the air forces concentrated on the pens in the Bay of Biscay. The campaign was an utter failure. Then the airmen said they would do the job by destroying the submarines in the manufacturing stage, at the factories. That effort, too, failed. The same was true, by the way, of the attempt to destroy the German fighter planes at their source; as with the submarine, the Allies discovered that the only way to do the job was the hard way—destroy the German fighters in the sky in combat. Airplanes were, of course, extraordinarily helpful in spotting submarines at sea, and fighters could do good work in attacking them, but the big bombers were practically helpless.

All of which points to the obvious conclusion, hardly original with me, that modern war is a team effort. No one service is capable of winning by itself. Victory in either world war would have been impossible without the navies, although both wars could have been lost by the Allies even though they retained command of the sea. Without the navies, the Allies could not have exerted their power on the Continent, but without the armies there would have been no power to exert. The chief responsibility of the strategist is to find a proper balance between the services in allocating resources. To reiterate my own assessment of the Anglo-American effort in World War II, I believe far too many resources were put into big bombers. The German error was not putting enough into submarines. But, of course, it is much easier to do better after the event than before it.

BIOGRAPHIC SUMMARY

Professor Stephen E. Ambrose received his bachelor's degree from the University of Wisconsin and his master's degree from Louisiana State University in 1958. He completed his doctorate at the University of Wisconsin in 1963. Professor Ambrose has taught at both Louisiana State University and Johns Hopkins University. He has written or edited six books, including *Eisenhower and Berlin, 1945* (Norton, 1967), numerous articles, and a variety of book reviews. He is presently occupying the Ernest J. King Chair of Maritime History at the Naval War College, as well as serving as the Associate Editor of the projected 15-volume edition of the Eisenhower papers.

Seapower in the Seventies

By Captain W. J. Ruhe, U. S. Navy (Ret.)

"Sea power in the broad sense, includes not only the military strength afloat that rules the sea or any part of it by force of arms, but also the peaceful commerce and shipping from which alone a military fleet naturally and healthfully springs, and on which it securely rests."

Captain Alfred Thayer Mahan, U. S. Navy

Seapower once involved, fundamentally, only the surface of the seas. In the past few decades, however, aircraft operating over the seas and submarines operating just below the surface of the seas have increased the dimensions for the applications of seapower. Today, not only are we experiencing the revolutionary effects of radical changes in the sea transportation industry, but we are apparently also on the threshold of an even more profound change in the nature of seapower.

Ahead of us lies a decade of development of the underseas—a breaching of a new frontier of the earth. The movement into the depths of the oceans to exploit the wealth of deep-seabed resources and to use the potentials of the vast bodies of water covering the earth, is accelerating. The years ahead, the 1970s, should demonstrate clearly the value of seapower in the traditional sense, but, in the immediate future, we should see also the creation of a new and additional extension of seapower—underseas power.

Freedom of the seas (even for electronic intelligence ships or nuclear ballistic missile submarines) has created a somewhat different ocean environment than that which Mahan observed; one where merchant marine power is vastly different from naval power and cannot be exercised in the same way.

Admiral John McCain, Jr., the most persuasive advocate of seapower today, is acutely aware of its changing nature. He notes in *The Expanding Scope of Sea Power,* NavPers 15223, that four major developments since World War II required a re-evaluation of the scope and importance of seapower.

The first major development is political in nature, involving the rapid increase in number of new nations since World War II. Africa offers a striking example. On V-J day, ten nations held control of that vast land area. Today there are 39 independent nations on this awakening continent. For the most part, these new nations are underdeveloped economically, socially, and politically and are good targets for aggressive nations—either through subversion or by direct intervention—and the seas are the main avenue of approach to these countries.

The second major development is also political in nature. The United States now has more commitments, in more places, with more nations, involving more people than any nation in history has ever had to meet. The United States is committed to the defense of some 60 nations, either by treaty or by other agreement. And the great majority of these nations border on the oceans of the world. The United States has moved irreversibly away from isolationism. Today and in the future, events halfway around the globe will profoundly affect our own national life. Most significant in this trend away from isolationism is the tremendous amount of U. S. big business involvement overseas and the rapid growth of U. S. sea-trade to over 400 million tons annually.

The third major development, technical in nature, represents one of the most profound changes in military strategy in the history of warfare. Seapower is no longer confined to the vast, trackless wastes of the oceans, but now represents an additional element of military power which can strike inland at land targets anywhere on the earth's surface. This fact means that all previous strategies dealing with seapower must be revised drastically to include this new inland-reach of naval striking power, in any consideration of land hostilities. This new naval strike-power is three-fold in nature consisting of long-range ballistic missiles, jet-powered aircraft, and helo-lifted marine forces.

The fourth major development is nuclear power. The destructive power of the nuclear warhead has added a new dimension to the power which can be exerted at and from the area of the sea. And with this added destructive power from sea-based naval units, the big wars are increasingly deterred by seapower. On the positive side, nuclear power also means a new dimension of endurance for naval ships, freeing them from the limitations of logistics. Politically, nuclear power changes the need for well-spaced refueling facilities worldwide, giving seapower a total oceanwide effectiveness. Additionally, the nuclear-powered submarine has demonstrated that strategists of naval warfare must now add the Arctic to their thinking and planning.

A fifth development, though in its infancy, should be added. This development, as illuminated by Albert Wohlstetter, in his January 1967 *Foreign Affairs* article, "Illusions of Distance," stems from the use of satellites for extremely long-range communications, the use of large, fast aircraft for the rapid movement of people, and the use of increasingly larger ships for the transporting of liquids and bulk materials, thus decreasing communication and transport costs significantly. With the use of satellites, distance becomes relatively unimportant in the sending of messages to far-off and isolated locations. Jet aircraft now move people across the oceans in a matter of hours. And the introduction of tremendous ships to ocean trade, (Japanese construction of 500,000-ton tankers is planned for the 1970s) provides such a drastic reduction in the long-haul costs of bulky, primary commodities as to cause new economic groupings of nations to emerge. A new type of "regionalism" or economic grouping of countries because of low-cost sea transportation is thus developing, and seapower is the dominant factor creating this regionalism.

Today, seapower represents: new dimensions of destructive power; increasingly cheaper long-haul transportation of bulk commodities; unfettered world trade across the seas; significant extensions of naval power from the seas into the land masses of continents; extensive worldwide commitments and alliances with maritime nations, as well as a control of the seas in specific areas where dominant force can actually be brought to bear at any given moment. This latter attribute of seapower stems from the great degree of power which the air forces and submarines of many of the nations of the world could apply to a limited locale of the oceans to gain temporary control of that sea area. (Even with the Seventh Fleet deployed in the Far East, Red Chinese air power, through concentration of forces, might hold temporary control of the Taiwan Straits.)

Despite the changing dimensions of seapower, its importance in the Mahan sense should not be lost sight of. Today, 40 of the 50 largest cities in the United States have thriving port activities located either close to or with easy water-access to the sea. These port cities have developed on waterways that were sufficiently deep to allow great tonnages of commodities to be delivered to the doorsteps of thriving industries. For the first half of this century, these 40 locales could have been called deep-water ports. But for the last part of this century, only a few can provide sufficient depths off their piers (even with extensive dredging) to handle the super bulk-carriers of raw materials—so necessary to the cost-competitive production of basic industries. The importance of this new need for very deep-water ports can be illustrated by the Japanese success in producing steel at lower cost than U. S. steel industries. With Japanese steel mills newly located adjacent to pier areas for the off-loading of ore ships (drawing up to 57 feet), the savings in transportation costs are sufficient to provide a major cost difference in offsetting the efficient U. S. steel-production operations. (The cost of loading ore into freight cars and the additional freight costs in trans-shipping by rail, although less than one cent per ton-mile, creates a significantly greater cost.)

In bringing the definition of seapower up to date, former Secretary of the Navy, Paul Ignatius, has said:

> To many, the term Sea Power defines the act of controlling the world's sea lanes through the employment of combatant ships. In reality, Sea Power has a broader definition. It encompasses the Merchant Marine, oceanography, ocean engineering, marine research and technology as well as naval power.

The Soviets appear to have recognized the new dimension of seapower inherent to an understanding and use of the underseas areas of the world. In "Report on the Soviets and the Seas," a report of a Congressional Delegation to Poland and the Soviet Union, 4 August 1966, the Congressmen who participated said:

> Since World War II the Russians have realized that knowledge of the oceans' secrets would be mandatory if the Red goal of world naval, economic and maritime superiority was to be achieved . . . Highly directed Soviet planning in oceanography is one of the reasons for their present progress. It was our impression that these are their major goals:
> Rapid and efficient conversion of the results of basic oceanographic research into economic development.
> World respect for Soviet scientific achievements.
> Gaining leverage with the international scientific community and making use of the accomplishments of foreign oceanography.
> International political leverage as a result of assisting nations to establish their own oceanographic programs.

The Congressmen noted that the Soviets have over 200 oceanographic and hydrographic vessels at work and about 9,000 oceanographers and technicians as compared to our 3,000. Their edge in fisheries is just as significant, a catch of 5.6 million tons of fish in 1965, to 2.3 million for U. S. fishermen. And the Soviets planned a 50 per cent expansion of their catch by 1970. But more than the differential in catch is the oceanographic use of much of this fleet. Additionally, the Soviets are building

a merchant marine with a target of 20 million deadweight tons by 1980, which is double the present declining U. S. tonnage.

To this listing of areas of Soviet emphasis to gain primacy as a seapower should be added their recognition of the growing value of underseas naval power. Their more than 350 operational submarines and a nuclear submarine building program which is considerably in excess of that of the United States indicates a belief that the "military strength" which is required of a great seapower is best exerted by underseas systems.

Whether the definition of seapower by a former Secretary of the Navy or by the Soviets (as interpreted by our Congressmen) suffices for a use of the term, applicable to the 1970s, should be examined in light of both the expected values of seapower in the world environment of the Seventies as well as the expected oceanographic and technological developments in the province of the oceans and particularly the underseas.

The values of seapower in the 1970s will, for the most part, be the same as those of today. Thus, in its all-inclusive aspects, seapower should:

▶ Provide a general reputation for power which would give a nation considerable leverage in international affairs.
▶ Comprise extensive worldwide sea trade, of great importance to the national economy.
▶ Provide a continuing bond between maritime nations which both ensures mutual protection of their sea trade and through military alliances guarantees a continuing free use of the oceans.
▶ Guarantee adequate logistics in time of war for support of the economy and military forces.
▶ Deter general nuclear war by assuring massive destruction from the oceans. (This value accrues to nuclear powers who use the sea for the deployment of deterrent weapons systems.)
▶ Provide a capability to muster sufficient sustained power in an area of the oceans remote from own land-based air power to pose effective control of that area.
▶ Represent technological leadership in the development of the potentials of the oceans, with its many benefits, commercially, politically and militarily.
▶ Comprise a technological base which permits build-up and reinforcement of sea forces, if necessary.
▶ Provide a capability to act independently at sea for political and economic national interest. (The capability for unilateral action not only increases military options but also increases the ease and credibility of political maneuvering.)
▶ Create prestige in the international scientific community by being authoritative on ocean matters.

In relating these values of seapower to U. S. self-interest and national well-being, it should be noted that an expanded, efficient U. S. flag merchant marine will be necessary to provide for support of military operations in order to retain the flexibility of unilateral action. (The success of the naval quarantine of Cuba as a unilateral application of military pressure must be recognized in contrast to the uncertain, slow, and tenuous processes in the past which have been involved in obtaining consensus for military action from our maritime allies.) Without a strong flag merchant marine a number of unilateral military options are lost. Additionally, being pre-eminent in technological knowledge for exploiting of the oceans should produce new areas for the worldwide expansion of U. S. business. This leadership in ocean exploration may prove of foremost value in the future development of U. S. seapower as related to our national economy. Similarly, pre-eminence in oceanographic matters will cause the United States to retain its image as a leader in the scientific world, as well as to reap the practical benefits from fall-outs which are only too often unpredictable ahead of time. The international image is important, not only to the foreign buyers of U. S. products, but to U. S. international relations, where alignments may to some degree depend upon a belief in the future strength of the United States.

Since the Soviets, with their emphasis on undersea power, offer the major challenge to U. S. seapower primacy in the 1970s, the possible uses of seapower to further their own interests should be recognized. In a speech, Admiral McCain identified a specific Russian interest in the oceans for providing a new means of solving the food problems of a growing and hungry world population. His words put focus on this one aspect of seapower:

> Russia is quick to realize what the Western world is equally quick to forget, namely, the increasing importance of the oceans to the entire human race.

L. W. Martin, in *The Sea in Modern Strategy*, focuses on the probable use of Soviet military strength at sea. His estimate of the Soviet's sea strategy differs from that being used by either U. S. or other NATO military planners, and appears more reasonable—particularly in view of Soviet development of a considerable overseas tender-based capability for their submarine forces. Martin sees a use of Soviet naval forces "for limited assaults on communications that might attempt to single out particular powers within a loosening framework of alliances." Such limited assault would be in the context of hostilities restricted to limited parts of the oceans, with naval forces enjoying sanctuary outside a defined combat area. Hence, the factor of present base limitation would weigh less. In this context, "provision for distant replenishment would be desirable and in many cases essential."

But the usefulness of Russian seapower, Martin feels, need not be limited to conflict:

> The value extracted from nonbelligerent deployments of naval and amphibious power by Western nations, gives rise to speculation as to whether Russian ventures of this kind may be anticipated . . . . Russian help in a new state's need for intervention could be attractive . . . . .
>
> In such affairs to be *first* is a great advantage . . . . Some form of peacekeeping action, so called, may well prove to be the way in which Soviet maritime power at last moves on to the political offensive. Well calculated, such a move would present the Western alliance with difficult and divisive problems.

What Martin describes, a strategy where the Soviets could separate the United States from its allies, is a somewhat different type of threat to U. S. seapower than is generally discussed.

It is not difficult to visualize the Soviets using their naval power to intervene in the revolution of an African state while the United States was attempting "to keep the peace." Military pressures against U. S. shipping only could be applied on a low key in areas of the oceans remote from U. S. bases. Such pressures would probably skyrocket insurance costs for U. S. shipping, as well as the cost of carrying U. S. goods in foreign ships. This type of military action would have, primarily, economic and political overtones and would be more in consonance with the Soviet's accelerated expansion of its own merchant fleets.

The military implications of this rival seapower of the 1970s are certainly different than in the past few decades.

The technological and oceanographic developments in the arena of the ocean which affect the nature of seapower in the 1970s appear to be predictable from the present trends in surface transportation technology, deep-ocean technology, and the ongoing research which is designed to increase knowledge of the oceans themselves.

The development of massive bulk-carrying ships, as noted earlier, will have a profound effect on the nature of seapower in the next decade. To the previous comments might be added: sea trade becomes more worldwide; business becomes increasingly international in scope; sea trade becomes more vulnerable to interdiction in time of war; and geographical bottlenecks in sea trade decrease in importance. Suez, for example, even before the closure of the canal, noted a decrease in the use of the canal by tankers owing to the increasing use of the supertankers in the movement of oil around the Cape of Good Hope.

The projection of man's capability to work as a free swimmer, down to depths of 1,500 to 2,000 feet, within the next decade will open up industries aimed at exploiting the seabed to at least these depths. With the technological developments which will be sparked by the promise of profitable industrial operations at such depths will come a host of capabilities for utilizing the sea-bed and water column to this limit. Dr. William A. Nierenberg of Scripps Institution of Oceanography notes that, with the proliferation of underseas installations, military posts on the bottom will follow, to be used as a source for intelligence on the movement of hostile submarines. He also notes that control of the depths of the oceans—a three-dimensional form of control—will have to be seriously considered as an extension of the limited aspect of control of the surface of the seas, as in the past. "The possibility of exploiting the ocean basins for material purposes have added possession of the oceans as an objective, even if in a limited sense of the word. The drive toward possession, and its accompanying technology, will return naval warfare to its earliest origin, which was that of economic domination by the country that had most succeeded."

Man's increasing capability to move about freely under water will have a great impact on amphibious operations—an important extension of naval power. A lock-out technology from submerged vehicles will be translated into an extensive capability for launching large numbers of assault troops from bottomed submarines. The *Grayback*, a fairly modern conventional submarine, still retaining the two bow tanks which housed Regulus missiles, can lock-out simultaneously several dozen troops, mounted on underwater sleds and equipped with infantry weapons. This is only the start of a new concept for powerful attack forces launched from underseas against defending forces in virtually any coastal area.

The movement of vehicles close to the bottom, or on the bottom itself, will translate into a capability for military vehicles to operate close to the bottom and thus enhance their security by minimizing the dangers of detection and destruction. (Aircraft in daily operations over Vietnam have minimized their detectability while approaching land targets by flying low and thus using the irregularities of the terrain to shield their movement from radar detecting devices). What this new capability to hug the bottom might mean, in view of the trend toward the use of new hull materials, such as glass or ceramics and the consequent rapid extension of submerged operations of vehicles to about 20,000-foot depths, is difficult to predict. And the new types of antisubmarine vehicles which must necessarily be developed are even more difficult to visualize. But the chief trend in military submarine technology should be

toward operation at very great depths, and the hunter-killer submarine may have to be prepared to go to any depths to meet her objective.

Floating platforms, which can provide offshore ports as well as airfields outside of territorial waters, are in the offing. With their appearance, in a world political environment which continues to recognize a freedom of the high seas, the nature of seapower becomes more autonomous—less dependent upon a worldwide network of land bases. The political influence of seapower is thereby strengthened and the flexibility in the use of seapower is heightened. This development alone may provide the most significant increase in the influence of seapower, to be seen in the 1970s.

New types of sea-based nuclear deterrent systems should emerge, as the requirement for security, second-strike capability, assured destruction of enemy targets and survivability of such systems are increasingly hazarded by technological developments.

In fact, what is most easily predictable is that a whole new family of military weapons systems will grow out of man's mastery of the deep oceans, and their natures are extremely difficult to even guess at. Looking back to the 1930s, only a handful of visionaries foresaw the aircraft systems used in World War II (only a decade later)—and even fewer could sense the revolutionary role to be played by the jet engine.

Just as sea trade on the surface of the oceans has for the past thousands of years been a prime factor in a nation's peacetime and wartime viability, the next decade should begin to demonstrate the importance accruing to the exploitation of the underseas and sea bottoms. The vehicles and industries developed, and the skills acquired in the process will create a new dimension of seapower in the Mahan sense.

Maritime powers have dominated the past. Those who will master and use the ocean environment through its entirety may similarly control their destiny.

A graduate of the U. S. Naval Academy with the Class of 1939, Captain Ruhe served in submarines during World War II and later commanded the submarine *Sturgeon* and *Seadevil*. Following a tour in the Bureau of Naval Personnel, he commanded the destroyer *Beale*. Destroyer Division 262, Submarine Division 22, and the USS *Topeka*, in Vietnamese waters during the initial escalation in 1964. From 1960 to 1962, he was Deputy Director of the Strategic Plans Division in the office of the Chief of Naval Operations, and during this period served on the first major systems analysis ASW study. Later, as a member of the Chairman, Joint Chiefs of Staff Special Study Group, he was project officer for the Navy's first General Purpose Forces Study. In 1965, he was project officer for the Navy's major ASW Study, Cyclops II, and finally served two years as Deputy Director Navy Program Planning prior to retiring in December 1967. He was military consultant to the President's Commission for Marine Science, Engineering and Resources, until September 1968, when he joined General Dynamics as Corporate Director of Engineering and Program Development.

The Sea in the Making of America

By Clark G. Reynolds

*A 19th century marine artist has split his canvas to suggest the dark
sense of sadness and foreboding of those left behind on the land and, through
the soft reflections of moonlight and lamplight on the sea, the
mood of hope the Pilgrims must have felt as they embarked in the Mayflower.
As deftly as Edward Moran leads our eye from moonlight to lamplight,
Professor Reynolds offers our mind's eye a loving look at the land; but in
this, his "bicentennial appreciation," he celebrates the sea—that vital
force in the making of America.*

The dependence of the American people upon the sea—to utilize it for political and economic power and even for cultural growth—has been so dramatically demonstrated throughout our history as to make the image of the republic incomprehensible without it. Without American activity upon the waters, alone and with allies, how different the course of American and world history would have been—from the crossing of the Pilgrim fathers on the *Mayflower* to the recovery of the Apollo astronauts. Without the central role of New England shippers within the British Empire, how could the colonies have achieved their economic importance and urge toward independence? Without the support of the French fleet at Yorktown, how could the Continental Army have ever culminated that movement to independence? Without British and American naval patrols, how could the Monroe Doctrine have been enforced and thus American continental expansion accomplished without European interference? Could the Union have been preserved without Lincoln's blockade? Would the nation have connected the oceans without Mahan's ideas and Teddy Roosevelt's Panama Canal and modern fleet? Indeed, would not the continent of Europe have become German and all East Asia Japanese without the intervention of the U. S. Navy and the sealifted American ground, air, and logistical forces in two World Wars?

On this auspicious occasion, the 200th anniversary of the birth of the republic, an accounting is in order of just how important has been the role of sea power in the history of the United States. So let us now recall the monumental importance of our citizenry upon the sea in those 200 years. With even a superficial appreciation of this historical force, we can then better understand the vital role of the United States in the progress of the human race.

THE *PAX*

O Sea! Thou Sea!
What nations thou hast framed,
What thoughts inspired,
What fires kindled high.

Americans have always prided themselves on being "peace"-loving people, preferring to compete in the economic, technological, diplomatic, and even athletic arenas rather than resorting to armed force. However, as every student of politics and international affairs knows all too well, each nation has unique interests and goals, and no two nations have ever coexisted in complete harmony. International tensions between national powers have been the norm since the beginning of recorded history. Simply put, when these tensions are in balance, we have peace, and when the balance of the powers is upset, we have war. Thus, this country has sought peace but has occasionally had to resort to war with the shifting power balance.

The United States has always been a virtual island nation in relation to the other great power centers of the world. The surrounding waters have been less a natural barrier than the medium upon which naval power has kept the nation isolated from the wars between those other powers, or have been used to project American power hence on the few occasions when the country felt forced to fight. Had the nation been threatened by the presence of large standing armies perpetually on its land borders, no doubt it would have relied on a similar large army of its own. But such a threat has never existed (save for the Civil War period), whereas America's enemies and potential enemies have always threatened from the sea, making the Navy the first line of defense.

The U.S. Navy, however, has not always possessed the capability to provide this defense unilaterally. Indeed, throughout most of American history, it was never strong enough to protect America's political interests alone. It thus had to act instead as a diplomatic tool in political situations dominated by other and larger navies. Consequently, from 1778 to 1781, isolated Continental Navy vessels and squadrons merely augmented the allied French fleet which then insured ultimate independence. In the 1798-1800 quasi-war, the new and small U.S. Navy supported the Royal Navy against the French, then reversed its support again from 1812 to 1815. During most of the *Pax Britannica*, Britain's Royal Navy deterred general war in Europe and policed the sea-lanes of the world; the latter function was shared by the U.S. Navy. And between 1898 and 1947, a general if sometimes shaky Anglo-American naval partnership existed in peace and war between the two powers until, finally, after 1947 general deterrence became chiefly an American responsibility, giving the period its strategic identity as the *Pax Americana*.

The great goal of American foreign policy throughout these two centuries has remained constant: the maintenance of international law and order throughout the world so that the American people might go about their business peaceably. Consequently, the nation has insisted on freedom of the seas for trade; on the suppression of illegal use of the sea by pirates, slave traders, and smugglers; and in the present century on the preservation of the global balance of power to insure political and economic stability. Throughout, sea power has been the primary means of enforcing this American interpretation of international maritime law.

The desire for economic independence by maritime New England most directly triggered the War for Independence (1775-1783) from the British Empire, the quasi-war with France (1798-1800), the Barbary Wars (1801-1815), and the unsuccessful attempt at neutrality during the Napoleonic Wars (1803-1814). Though the application of sea power in each of these affairs resulted in defeats as well as victories, the net effect was to convince Britain to drop her trade barriers and to accept free trade (completely by the 1850s) for which the United States and other nations had been fighting and bargaining.

Henceforth, the Anglo-American peoples shared a common interpretation of international law, although the United States refused any official tie and declined to endorse the general European Declaration of Paris (1856) on international law. The desire for free trade with Britain played a large part in America's decision to intervene in World War I following the German declaration of unrestricted submarine warfare on our shipping (1917). And freedom of the seas was a pillar of President Woodrow Wilson's Fourteen Points at the Versailles Conference (1919). In this case, the policy was aimed against the British. A strong Navy—able to deter or fight those nations which would deny us the free use of the sea—made such policies possible. Even when the British blocked our neutral trade with wartime Germany in the early years of both World Wars, we ultimately chose alliance with Britain against a common foe.

Illegal use of the oceans by violators of international law led to an active American role of naval policing, usually in concert with other Western nations. The Barbary pirates were only the first of many such maritime outlaws to feel the weight of American naval guns and cutlasses. The Navy was especially active between 1815 and 1860 in the Caribbean, Southeast Asian waters and the South Atlantic, where slave traders defied Western laws against the practice. Piracy still occurs, as shown in the *Mayaguez* incident (1975). Anti-smuggling work was the province of the Revenue Marine Service, later the U.S. Coast Guard. And adventurers who attempted to run the declared Union blockade in defiance of federal authority found themselves hunted and ultimately thwarted by four Union blockading squadrons (1861-1865). Warships of a growing Navy were the agents of enforcement of international law as interpreted by our government.

The desire of 20th century American governments to preserve the balance of power in Europe and Asia has led to several major unilateral American interpretations of international law. The interpretations have succeeded because of the Navy's ability to enforce them. Presidents Wilson and Franklin D. Roosevelt both regarded the possible collapse of Britain to the international outlaws of Germany as inimical to American interests—political, economic and moral—thus prompting our intervention in both World Wars. And all American Presidents from William McKinley (1897) to FDR (1945) regarded Japanese incursions into China with similar disdain, leading to the Open Door Policy (1900) and eventually to our unofficial participation in the Sino-Japanese War (1941), climaxed by Japan's treacherous and illegal attack on Pearl Harbor. In the thermonuclear Cold War, the United States interpreted the presence of Russian missiles in Cuba as a threat to the global balance of power and hence intervened with a naval blockade in 1962. In each such crisis, the U.S. Navy applied its sea power in concert with the sister services to affirm the American view of international law and order.

Indeed, since 1945, American sea power has grown beyond the confines of being a mere diplomatic tool in the shadow of the Royal Navy. It has become the prime deterrent global force as well as the most important police force in maintaining the worldwide *pax.* Before World War I, Theodore Roosevelt's battleship diplomacy helped deter the Germans in the Caribbean (Venezuela, 1903, and the "Big Stick") and Mediterranean (Morocco crisis, 1904-05 and 1913) and Japan in the Pacific (especially with the Great White Fleet, 1908), while American warships patrolled in such diverse places as the Yangtze River and the Virgin Islands. In the 1920s and 1930s, this policing was intensified, with the U.S. Fleet concentrated in the Pacific to deter Japan. When the United States allowed this deterrent and the patrol forces to deteriorate, Japan was encouraged to initiate the war against China in 1937.

World War II—won largely by superior Allied fleets, sealifted armies and air forces, and seaborne logistics—destroyed not only the German and Japanese Empires but proved equally fatal to those of Britain, France, and Holland. Into the resulting power vacuum stepped the United States, its fleets henceforth patrolling the oceans of the world and projecting American military power ashore in troubled coastal regions from Korea (1950) and Vietnam (1965) to Lebanon (1958) and the Dominican Republic (1965). This strategy, at first (1947) politically designed to "contain" global Communism, eventually matured into the Nixon Doctrine (1969) which formalized America's basic maritime strategy of controlling the sea and air of the Asian periphery while its allies provide the manpower. In so doing, American sea power acts as a deterrent to limited war in those regions and throughout the world.

The 20th century also witnessed the first attempts at international arms control, wherein quantitative measures were established to limit arms production and inventories. Significantly, such yardsticks were not in armies or land weapons or in aircraft but in capital ships and seaborne weapon systems. The first halting attempts, at the Hague conferences of 1899 and 1907, considered several issues but focused mainly on the laws of naval warfare and neutrality—partly because of the contributions of Alfred Thayer Mahan of the U.S. Navy. The subsequent rise of American naval strength enabled the United States to convene the Washington Conference on the limitation of naval armaments in 1921-22. In this conference arms controls were established through battleship and carrier tonnage quotas, gun restrictions, and the freezing of the general strategic-geographic balance in the Pacific. This successful arrangement—due largely to Anglo-American-Japanese cooperation—was renewed at the London Conference of 1930 but then collapsed in 1936 with the rise of the uncooperative dictatorships. This experiment in arms control, in which the world's navies remained the object, set important precedents for the future—namely, the limitation of missile-launching submarines and their warheads.

Throughout our history, the Navy has taken its major inspiration from the Royal Navy, although we have drawn on particular technical and tactical innovations of most of the other major navies. By the present century, when the Navy became a true oceangoing force, it shared with Britain a common concern over Germany and Japan, with both English-speaking navies developing doctrines, bases, and tactics with which to counter these two belligerent nations. Following the victory over them in World War II, the Anglo-American Navies looked upon Soviet Russia as the common foe, and since Russia's naval strength lay in its submarine armada, Allied naval doctrines shifted to antisubmarine warfare. With the advent of nuclear weapons, however, the U.S. Navy developed its own nu-

clear war capability, matching that of the new U.S. Air Force after severe interservice battles in the late 1940s. During the 1950s, the Navy deployed nuclear warheads on carrier-based A3D Skywarriors and developed the Polaris submarine/missile system for deployment during the 1960s. Such seaborne mobility and range gave the Navy the ability to attack continental targets in Russia just as it had struck Japan in the closing months of World War II. The arms race of the years 1945-1962 gave the Russo-American Cold War its character, based on the belief that a thermonuclear exchange in a World War III was a viable military alternative.

The Cuban Missile Crisis of 1962 showed the folly of this assumption, the aftermath being the tacit recognition by the United States and the Soviet Union that such a general war would be counterproductive to both nations and indeed to the survival of industrial civilization. Nuclear weapon systems—America's being matched by similar Soviet systems—have since been regarded as a separate political category outside the normal conduct of military and naval operations, although the advent of tactical nuclear weapons like the ship-to-ship cruise missile has weakened distinctions between general and conventional war forces. Nevertheless, the tense thermonuclear arms race, or Cold War, reached its climax during the Cuban crisis. Since then, the Americans and Russians have sought to control these weapons, culminating in the Strategic Arms Limitation Treaty (SALT I) in 1972 with revisions during the present year. The Polaris/Poseidon/Trident ICBM submarines and carrier-based, nuclear-armed attack planes have great mobility and range—unlike the Strategic Air Command's fixed, hardened missile silos and bomber bases—which add a unique dimension to Russia's strategic woes, since both require constant surveillance by the Russians. The sea-based nuclear deterrent therefore remains the key to the current arms balance as the ultimate form of military power projected from the sea. What third parties such as China, France, India, or Israel do in the nuclear arena only time will

tell, but for the moment these American and Russian weapons are the yardstick for offensive deterrence and arms control and thus act as the strategic umbrella over the current *pax*.

Just as Soviet Russia developed its own strategic missile subs to match ours, it has also greatly expanded its surface fleet and antiship submarine attack forces for a conventional naval presence. In addition, it has taken a commanding lead in seagoing fishing factories and oceanographic research vessels and has significantly enlarged its merchant marine. Also, the Russians have supplied naval vessels and weapons to their allies and third world countries, just as has the United States. The U.S. Navy thus has had to counter all these activities by maintaining a viable strategic deterrent against the Soviet (and Chinese) interior and coast, including naval bases and air fields, against Russian surface forces and attack subs, and against Russia's commerical fleets. At the same time, we must look to our tactical fleet defenses in order to maintain our ability to control the open seas. This Russian naval and maritime growth has caused great concern and debate within American naval and political circles. At the very least, we need new ships and weapons to meet this vast and complex challenge. If we have them, the Navy should be able to maintain a credible conventional naval deterrent stance. For Russia lacks the doctrines, balanced fleet, overseas bases, at-sea logistics, major amphibious forces, and—above all—the *experience* to wage a conventional war on the oceans. Strong at sea, the U.S. Navy can deter Russia from strategic adventurism in this or any environment.

Needless to say, whenever deterrence and maritime policing—and the *pax*—have failed, war has followed, and therein sea power has assumed its most violent manifestations. America's cruisers and gunboats of the sailing era, though few in number, gave distinguished accounts of the nation's military prowess from 1775 to the 1830s in otherwise defensive wars—defensive of the coast and of commerce. Blockade, amphibious, and riverine operations in the Mexican War, the Arrow War in China, and Civil War (1846-1865) initiated the Navy into a limited offensive stance. The Spanish-American War (1898) began the modern offensive American Navy, projecting sea power and armies into Cuba, Puerto Rico, and the Philippines, then throughout the Caribbean (1901-1914), to North Africa and France (1917-1918, 1942-1945), into Russia (1918-1919), the Black Sea and Eastern Mediterranean (1919-1923), the Pacific islands (1942-1945), Korea (1950-1953), and South Vietnam (1965-1973). American ''peacetime'' aid went by sea to Western Europe on three occasions (1914-1917, 1939-1941, and 1946-1949) to shore up the Western democracies. These temporary measures resulted in war for America in the first two cases and in the latter in the country's first peacetime defensive alliance, the North Atlantic Treaty Organization (1949). NATO's communications and flanks ever since have been protected by American-centered naval forces.

By 1976, American sea power has extended the nation's peacetime policy of freedom of the seas over the entire globe, enabling general intercourse between all seagoing nations to continue unabated, save for local disputes such as the Anglo-Icelandic ''cod war.'' If international agreements on laws to govern the sea finally emerge, or if new defensive treaties are enacted, it will still be American sea power which will enforce them. Even should new agreements not occur, or should they fail, the United States will unilaterally continue to use its sea power to enforce free exchange upon the sea. This is the legal right of any maritime nation—in our case the most powerful nation in history at that—much of whose livelihood is derived from the sea. Happily, most of the civilized world—which profits thereby—is grateful for it.

ECONOMIC GROWTH

And Sea! Our Sea!
From Cretan birth to Athens' main -
By star and wave
We learned to fly.

Sea power has been a vital ingredient of American economic growth in both overt and less obvious ways. Inasmuch as capitalism is based upon trade, the merchant and manufacturer have been interdependent foundation stones within the American economic framework and thus accountable for America's overall prosperity. Overseas trade has therefore been the basis of what has been somewhat inaccurately termed America's ''empire.'' In the 18th century, Britain's colonies provided both the markets and sources of raw materials as part of a closed mercantilistic system, leading Mahan at the turn of the present century to the false conclusion that colonies therefore must provide an inevitable link in American sea power. But unlike the British, Americans have never been overseas colonizers, relying more so on trade, internal resources and domestic as well as global markets, so that their brief imperial experience in 1898 was unusual. The Philippines were hardly comparable to India, nor Puerto Rico to Transvaal. No, Americans have preferred their economic competition straight—by private enterprise, with a minimum of governmental interference, regulation, and taxes and therefore in a peacetime environment rather than under wartime controls.

Since the bulk of American foreign trade has been by sea, carried in private hulls and protected by government warships, shipbuilding and the carrying trade have provided major stimuli to the American economy. Competition has been fostered by the American belief in free enterprise and free trade, though protected by government tariffs and treaties and assisted by government subsidies and warship/weapon system contracts. The presence of Navy yards in certain coastal areas has also helped to stimulate the local economies in those regions. As for actual oceanic commodities, the fisheries (including for many years pelagic sealing and whaling) have been important down to the present, and offshore petroleum drilling and seabed mining have been recently added. This intimate interrelationship between the sea and economic power is older than the republic itself.

The North American colonies of Massachusetts and Virginia were originally founded by enterprising joint-stock companies following the English peace with Spain in the early 17th century. Joined by subsequent colonies, they soon became an integral part of England's sea-linked empire. By the next century the colonial seaports were prospering by direct and indirect trade with Europe, Africa, and the West Indies. This was so to the extent that especially maritime New England resented crown controls and eventually led the movement toward independence. These Northeastern merchants exhibited similar truculent economic independence under the new government, notably through the ''Essex junto'' and then the Hartford Convention which protested the economically-adverse War of 1812. Allied with coastal New York and to a lesser extent with Philadelphia and Baltimore, all connected to the interior by rivers and canals, and championing the business-oriented politics of New York's Alexander Hamilton, maritime New England remained the undisputed center of American commerce for the first century of the republic.

American economic prosperity throughout the 19th century depended as much on the trade with Britain as America's strategic insularity rested on the good offices of the Royal Navy. In the 1790s, Anglo-American trade developed first in the Carribbean and spread outward from there, interrupted only by the American embargo of 1807-1809 and War of 1812. Both events were largely American economic protests against British policies. These temporary dislocations in fact stimulated internal American industrial development which then helped to magnify postwar trade. The Anglo-American seaborne exchange so prospered after 1815 that commercial reciprocity was accomplished by 1830, open free trade by the 1850s.

Economic surpluses that were thereby accumulated through overseas trade went into federal internal improvements—notably canals and turnpikes—which linked up the Great Lakes and the interior with the seaboard, especially as the river steamboat became available. In this way the Erie Canal alone from 1825 stimulated "seaport" development at Buffalo, Detroit, and Chicago, whence goods traveled via the canal to Albany and New York City. Jefferson's purchase of the vast Louisiana Territory in 1803 made New Orleans a seaport rivaled only by New York and Boston and turned the Mississippi River into a virtual second coastline along with the Atlantic Coast. The great river and its tributaries opened up the Midwestern interior to port developments as far northeastward as Cincinnati and Pittsburgh, southeastward to Nashville, westward to St. Louis, and northward to St. Paul, while Chicago was linked by canal to the Mississippi in 1848. By such river, coastal, and overseas traffic, culminating in the magnificent clipper ships, the volume of American merchant traffic nearly equalled Britain's by the 1850s, with an American near-monopoly over the key Liverpool-New York run.

Geographical expansion south and west during the 19th century—made possible partly by North America's physical isolation behind the Atlantic Ocean—had equally dramatic economic consequences. New Orleans was joined by Mobile, Pensacola, Galveston, and Houston in the Gulf maritime traffic as Spain's American empire waned. Diplomatic compromise with Britain resulted in the acquisition of port sites in the Pacific Northwest, and victory in the Mexican War added the tremendously important San Francisco Bay to the American economic complex. The gold rush—by "'49ers" on board swift clippers around Cape Horn to

California—and American commercial inroads into China, Japan, and other Far Eastern markets stimulated the rise of the United States as a Pacific and thus global maritime power. The use and eventual acquisition of Samoa and Hawaii provided commercial way stations across this great new highway, creating the economic basis for the United States making the Pacific a sphere of economic and thus political influence by the end of the century. All these trade routes also served as avenues of immigration to America, to which foreign peoples came largely in hope of economic gain.

American economic power at sea suffered drastically for a number of reasons from the middle of the 1850s. The new railroads provided a more convenient and profitable means of freight and passenger transportation throughout the expanding continental interior, so much so that it successfully outstripped shipping from the beginning of the railroad boom in the 1850s. The financial panic of 1857 had a disastrous impact on world shipping, not least that of America whose shipbuilders and shipowners failed to respond with vessels more utilitarian than the speedy but small capacity clippers. Furthermore, the steam revolution had gone to sea; the British Government subsidized private steamship development, while the United States did not. British steam thus rapidly bypassed American sail power. The American seagoing merchants instead shifted away from oceanic to coastal trade, thus surrendering commercial leadership at sea to the British. Confederate raiders hastened this shift, sinking many Yankee vessels and frightening even more to shift to neutral British registry because of lower wartime insurance rates and the protection of the Royal Navy. Finally, after the Civil War, an irate Congress refused to allow such errant merchantmen to return to the flag.

The American merchant marine never recovered from such reverses. The emergence of the modern dynamic American industrial state in the post-Civil War period did, however, lead foreign powers to eagerly seek trade with the United States, regardless of the registry of the carrier. And where the American merchant marine failed, high protective tariffs guaranteed enormous profits to entrepreneurs. Also, American business investments and close trade associations abroad provided powerful stimuli to American political and military interventions after 1898 in the Caribbean (Cuba and the Spanish-American War; Roosevelt Corollary to the Monroe Doctrine; Taft's Dollar Diplomacy), in China (Boxer Rebellion; Open Door Policy; Yangtze gunboat patrol), and in Europe (World War I).

Despite U.S. difficulties in oceanic trade, the nation's simultaneous territorial expansion reflected another key economic role of the sea. The acquisition of new coastal areas on the Gulf and Pacific Coasts broad-

ened the range of the coastal fisheries from the cod of New England to the tuna of the Pacific Northwest, with increasing varieties of fish in between. Also, American dietary habits changed as lobster, shrimp, and abalone were added to the established shellfish tastes for oysters and clams late in the 19th century, and whales for oil and seals for hides sent Yankee fishermen into the colder waters of both major oceans. The purchase of Alaska and the Aleutian Islands from Russia in 1867 greatly extended the range of American commercial activities in the Pacific. They became even more pronounced following the discovery of Alaskan gold in 1897. The next year Hawaii became an American territory, giving the country not only a major new seaport at Pearl Harbor but the pineapple industry.

These sudden developments, combined with the receipt of the Philippines and Guam as spoils of war from Spain and the annexation of Wake, all in 1898, made the matter of interocean commerce especially urgent for economic as well as military reasons. The narrow isthmus of Panama had for centuries served as a terminus for ships transferring goods between oceans, but the hopes for a canal intensified to the point where Teddy Roosevelt supported the successful Panamanian revolution against ruling Colombia there in 1903 and then leased the Canal Zone. Construction was completed in 1914, just in time for the United States to exert international control over this vital new waterway at the outbreak of World War I. That control has con-

tinued down to the present, and though the railroad and commercial trucking eventually became preferred transcontinental carriers, the Panama Canal remains a major link in international trade. The Canal Zone and the states of Alaska and Hawaii are linked to the mainland states by ships—coastal merchantmen, warships, and Coast Guard vessels. Small wonder, then, that these acquisitions helped the republic to become the commercial colossus of the Western Hemisphere.

The United States, like the major industrial powers of Europe, sought economic self-sufficiency, a chief cause of the neo-imperialism fervor and arms race of the pre-World War I era. One such area of vital strategic importance was warship construction, leading to the Domestic Materials Act of 1886 in which Congress ruled that henceforth all American naval vessels were to be manufactured entirely in this country (a rigidity that has since been slightly relaxed). The burgeoning new American steel industry thus obtained rich government contracts for the new steel Navy. Such a policy did not follow for merchant shipping because of general and ever-growing British friendliness. But as the United States drifted into World War I, such independent American hulls became badly needed. Consequently, through the concerted efforts of President Wilson, Congress created the United States Shipping Board in 1916 and the Emergency Fleet Corporation in 1917 to provide additional vessels. The former achieved enormous success. After the war, the government disposed of these merchantmen and by the Washington Conference agreements froze its capital warship inventory; both deeds severely hampered the shipbuilding industry. The Merchant Marine Acts of 1928 and 1936 and the Public Works Administration of the New Deal stimulated some merchant and warship construction respectively, but neither could reverse the disastrous economic effects of the great depression.

In the 1940s, the previous wartime and postwar pattern was repeated. The rapid construction of the great two-ocean Navy which relieved Britain and Russia, helped to defeat the German and Italian Navies, and to destroy the Japanese Navy in World War II. This was both a tribute to American industrial capacity and a powerful stimulus to the American maritime economy. Postwar demobilization hindered naval construction until the Korean War, during which the Navy began to be revitalized. In the merchant marine, the Maritime Commission, created in 1936, achieved the epitome of American mass production techniques by directing—largely through the efforts of industrialist Henry J. Kaiser—the rapid creation of the wartime emergency merchant fleet of Liberty and Victory ships. But again, after the war, these were disposed of outright by sale or gift to destitute foreign nations or were mothballed.

The Merchant Marine Act of 1970 resumed federal efforts to stimulate American merchant ship construction, although longshoremen and mariners alike demand such high wages and safety measures by international standards that foreign registry continues to be economically preferable. The modern Navy continues to be a vital force in the American economy, but the costs of contemporary weapon systems have tended to stifle competition in favor of super-rich corporate conglomerates.

Interrelationships between sea power and American economic growth remain strong as ever today. As the world's major industrial power, the United States—by example, trade, and foreign aid—has made the sea into a greater arena of international intercourse and "peacetime" rivalry than ever before. By example, the American maritime success has prompted Soviet Russia to compete in virtually every sphere of oceanic activity. Also, small countries with coastlines have learned to insist upon their fair share of the maritime economic pie—the basic cause of their insistence upon the 200-mile limit to protect their fisheries and ocean bed resources. Such nations which are oil rich have been major determinants in the current energy crisis, especially as they affect an oil-driven U.S. Navy and merchant marine and those of our allies.

By trade, the United States has come to depend upon the cheaper registries of minor states like Panama, Liberia, and Greece to carry American goods. Furthermore, American seaborne manufactures and foodstuffs led to the recovery of postwar Western Europe and Japan until each has become a major economic competitor. By the same token, any country that urgently desires American economic and technological aid—now virtually *every nation in the world*—knows that such goods must come by sea.

Hence, the age-old American policy of free enterprise upon the seas has been not only a bedrock of American prosperity but has evolved into a prerequisite for the future economic survival of the human race.

The sciences of the sea and seafaring have always had far-reaching implications for human knowledge and skills, giving the notion of "sea power" an even broader range. From the simple need to travel upon the waters have stemmed the fundamental challenges for naval architecture, navigation, meteorology, and hydrography. Drawing upon its experience within the British Empire, undisputed leading power in these matters during the 18th century, the young republic soon became an active participant and then partner with Britain over the two ensuing centuries. From such a practical maritime base, American science and technology expanded into other physical frontiers, exploring new waters and lands and studying in land, air, and space environments; into pure scientific research, especially in astronomy and oceanography; and into the applied areas of steam propulsion, modern ballistics, aeronautics, communications systems, medicine, and nuclear physics. All of these disciplines have merged with general American and world scientific developments, but one inescapable fact is that the sea and especially the U.S. Navy have been major catalysts.

To the naval architecture of sail, the United States contributed a great deal once it established an independent fishing fleet, Navy, and merchant marine. Pioneers in the fast fishing schooner from the early 18th century, the New England-centered Americans continued to excel in these two-masted workhorses throughout the 19th century. Such sleekness and speed also typified the early Navy's heavy 44-gun frigates, the revolutionary, record-setting 18.5-knot clipper ships of mid-century, and the racing yachts epitomized by the schooner yacht *America*'s victory in international competition in 1851. Even with the advent of steam, iron, and steel, the Americans continued to excel in sailing ship design, construction, and racing. The biggest wooden sailing ship ever built (reinforced with iron strips), was the four-masted, "jigger-rigged" ship and aptly-named *Great Republic* of 1853, built for trade with Australia. The big four-, five,- and six-masted schooners of the end of the century were topped off by the seven-masted *Thomas W. Lawson* of 1902, while the longest wooden sailing ship ever constructed, the 350-foot six-masted *Wyoming* of 1910, was built in this country. Finally, the America's Cup has been successfully defended down to the present, most dramatically by the fastest and biggest (Class J) yacht ever built, the 1937 *Ranger* designed by W. Starling Burgess and Olin J. Stephens.

SCIENCE AND TECHNOLOGY

The tides of time, the winds of change
By Venice to the Dutch—
Salt air for life;
Eternal vigor, power complete.

Whereas they could be viewed as latecomers in the age of sail, the Americans were present at the beginning of steam propulsion, iron ship construction, and the general industrial revolution. Pennsylvania inventor Robert Fulton from 1793 worked on steam, canal, and submarine navigation. His efforts were crowned by the world's first practical commercial steam vessel, the *Clermont,* in 1807 and seven years later by the first steam warship, the *Demologos.* The first sail-steam schooner to cross the Atlantic, the *Savannah* in 1819, was American, and it was the American Collins ocean liners of the 1850s whose superior hull lines produced the best speed and motion through the water. Immigrant engineer John Ericsson designed the screw-propelled warship *Princeton* in the 1840s, the prototype of all modern steam vessels, and in the 1860s the celebrated *Monitor,* model for the first generation of the world's all steam-iron warships. Connecticut-born David Bushnell pioneered the submarine in 1775, and with the first real submarine of John P. Holland in 1900, the United States became a leader in this revolutionary field of naval design and construction. The nation also led in modern steel battleships, their armor upgraded by the American "harvey" process, and of aircraft carriers and many smaller warships. The epitome of the Navy's contribution to nautical propulsion systems has been the nuclear-powered ships and submarines of Admiral Hyman G. Rickover since the 1950s.

Just as immediate and profound as the practical effects of such progress in naval architecture and propulsion on the growth of the republic were concurrent developments in navigation. Massachusetts master mariner Nathaniel Bowditch built upon British work in nautical tables to publish in 1802 *The New American*

Practical Navigator, which became the Navy's standard navigation text. To survey and chart America's long and expanding coastlines, five years later President Jefferson created the U.S. Coast Survey, which began (haltingly, to be sure) with the tides and currents, gradually worked inland to become the Coast and Geodetic Survey in 1887, and ultimately in the 1920s moved under and over the earth (seismology and air currents).

Without an established scientific community, the nation relied upon naval officers to promote this work during most of the 19th century. Consequently, Lieutenants Louis M. Goldsborough, Charles Wilkes, and James M. Gilliss developed the embryonic Naval Observatory with its navigational instruments and charts from its initial offices in 1830 and then official establishment in the 1840s, when Lieutenant Matthew Fontaine Maury became the first Superintendent and began his influential pioneer work in charting ocean and wind currents. In 1845 the Observatory initiated its first time signals to the American public, and 20 years later it first transmitted them nationwide via the new telegraph of Western Union. From the Observatory stemmed the Nautical Almanac Office (and its published annuals) under Lieutenant Charles Henry Davis in 1849 and the Hydrographic Office in 1866.

The crowning achievement of this practical use of the sea occurred in the fertile mind of Samuel F. B. Morse, the New York artist who in the 1830s invented the telegraph and conceived the idea of an underwater cable. In 1842 he laid such a line under New York Harbor, whereupon Congress funded his larger scheme the next year. Private capital enlarged his budget, leading to a temporary transatlantic telegraphic cable in 1858 and then, with important British help, a permanent cable in 1866. The impact of such mechanical communication under the sea on American—and world—progress can hardly be overstated.

To the science of ballistics and the general area of ordnance, the Navy has contributed importantly. From the "soda-bottle" muzzle-loading gun of Lieutenant John A. Dahlgren in the 1850s and 1860s to the powerful breech-loading 16-inch rifled guns of the last generation of battleships in the 1940s, the Naval Gun Factory and related agencies have supplied the armament for America's warships. When the range of naval firepower was extended with the invention of the airplane in America, the Navy lost no time in contributing to the growth of combat and civilian aviation and of ordnance. The same has been true of guided missilry and indeed of associated scientific and technological innovations such as radio, radar, loran, and computers, beginning with the Navy's IBM Naval Ordnance Research Computer in 1954. By the post-World War II era, the Navy's work in these fields had been absorbed

into the larger arena of the new American technocracy.

Practical innovations in navigation were naturally supported by the American shipping industry and the Navy which needed such vital navigational data, freeing the young republic from utter dependence on the tables and charts of the Royal Greenwich Observatory and the Royal Navy. One must concede, however, that such an overriding concern for the pragmatic uses of astronomical data tended to thwart government support for pure scientific work in the nation. But it did lay the foundations for future developments along such lines. Also, such work served to initiate the country in the field of overseas exploration, notably into the Pacific and Antarctic waters before the Civil War and into the Arctic after it.

The advance from practical technology to pure scientific research and development proceeded rapidly from the late 19th century, with the U.S. Navy playing a key role. The U.S. Naval Observatory and Nautical Almanac Office (finally rejoined administratively under the former in 1894) began the transition from nautical exploration to that of space. With the talented mathematician Admiral C. H. Davis as superintendent during the 1870s, the observatory installed the largest refracting telescope in the world with which the masses of the planets were calculated and the two tiny moons of Mars discovered. The observatory sponsored expeditions to observe solar eclipses and the transits of Venus, while Lieutenant A. A. Michelson first measured the speed of light at the U. S. Naval Academy. Admiral Davis' counterpart in the Almanac Office, the esteemed civilian astronomer Simon Newcomb, so improved the planetary tables for navigation over a 20-year period that in 1896 by international agreement they became the basis for the almanacs of every nation. And in 1904, the Naval Observatory adopted Guglielmo Marconi's wireless to initiate the worldwide transmission of its time signals via U.S. Navy radio stations, an important activity which has continued uninterrupted down to the present.

The final period of terrestrial exploration occurred with the union of the modern ship and the airplane, with Americans as leaders. Robert E. Peary began to explore the Arctic regions by sea and dog sled from the 1880s, pushing steadily northward until he reached the North Pole in 1909, after which he turned to aviation for the remainder of his life. The Navy wedded the flying machine to the boat hull to develop new seaplanes (''hydroaeroplanes'') before World War I and utilized the seaman's knowledge of wind and sails to study aerodynamics. In 1919, the Navy's NC-4 flying boat became the first aircraft to fly the Atlantic. The navigational information for that flight was the work of a Naval Academy graduate, Lieutenant Commander Richard E. Byrd. He later applied the airplane to exploration by being the first person to fly over the North and South Poles, in 1926 and 1928 respectively. During the ensuing two and a half decades Admiral Byrd continued to lead the major American research and discovery efforts in the Antarctic. Simultaneously, it was the U.S. Navy which first published an air navigational almanac (1933) and which superintended the nation's program in rigid airships, a system which, however, failed in competition with heavier-than-air craft.

The zenith of sea power's impact on American and thus world scientific and technological progress arrived with the space age. The traditional stimulus of the sea in exploration has been easily transferred to what President John F. Kennedy in 1962 aptly termed ''this new ocean.'' The means were also similar; the oceanic ship and the space ship are both closed eco-systems and administrative units with comparable logistical, medical, manning, and command situations. The same self-discipline and technical expertise for operating seaborne vessels pertains to space craft, so that the Navy immediately assumed a leading role alongside the Air Force and NASA in the American space program.

The celestial navigation techniques and tools pioneered by Captain P.V.H. Weems of the U.S. Navy were extended to the space environment, with navigational and communications satellites playing essential roles for ocean and terrestrial navigation and communications. The recovery area of American manned and unmanned space vehicles became the sea, with tracking ships linked to land stations and carrier forces retrieving reentered space craft. Finally, Navy-trained pilots provided a major element of the astronaut program. Lieutenant Commander Alan B. Shepherd, Jr., became the first American to fly in space. In 1961, he manned the Mercury Freedom 7 capsule in sub-orbital flight before being recovered, by the carrier *Lake Champlain* (CVS-39). And in 1969, the Apollo program achieved ultimate success when former Navy pilot Neil Armstrong became the first human being to walk on the moon. The Navy has therefore played its part to the full in the space effort in the tradition of oceanic exploration. Just as the *Mayflower* brought the American colonists to our new world in 1620, it is their descendents who have sent the unmanned Viking lander to the surface of the planet Mars in this very month of July 1976.

Without the presence of the sea, and the manifold challenges it has provided Americans, one simply cannot imagine how the republic and the race at large could ever have reached the level of scientific and technological brilliance that they have today. How this knowledge and sheer physical power will be ultimately utilized—for good or ill—of course depends upon human wisdom, and wisdom depends less on hard technology than on the human condition.

SOCIETY

At the helm, full sail,
Does mankind rush—
'Tis England, Olde and New—
The cargo hope—yea, promise.

The power of the sea has been a fundamental ingredient in the social life of the republic. More than any other single physical element, it has shaped the character of American society and has acted as a force of continuity throughout our history of change and uncertainty. It has broadened our horizons, intellectual and cultural, and has made us the envy and hope of the world. It has inspired our dreams and made us respect nature as no other force can. The sea has been our avenue to greatness, its intellectual power acting as the foundation of a folklore that will never die as long as the republic stands or is remembered.

From the first colonial settlements, America's cities have grown and prospered on the great watercourses of

the continent. These cities have been the economic focus of our national life, the physical centers of our population, the meeting places of our businessmen and artists, the crossroads of American civilization. The merchants of New England and New York thus set the tenor for a capitalistic, cosmopolitan, bourgeois society, largely middle class and generally devoid of the elite aristocratic upper classes or suffering, hopeless peasant classes more typical of non-maritime nations. Even as the Northeast (and the agrarian South) declined in political importance with westward expansion, Wall Street lost none of its economic power, and New York City blossomed into the cultural capital of the nation. The great seaports thus remained both the jumping-off bases for American activity abroad and the front door for incoming immigrants, goods, and ideas from foreign lands.

Inevitably, the original cultural heritage of America—like its political and economic foundations—lay in its colonial maritime roots and has been centered in the Northeast from the earliest days. No better examples can be found than in two great American families, Adams and Roosevelt. Both are inextricably linked to the sea, its art and history, to business and politics, and to the American dream, all of which their members have championed. The original Englishman Henry Adams came to Braintree, Massachusetts, in 1636 and ultimately fostered, among many luminaries, Presidents John Adams (1797-1801) and John Quincy Adams (1825-1829), statesman Charles Francis Adams, historians Charles Francis Adams, II, Henry Adams, and Brooks Adams, and banker-yachtsman Charles Francis Adams, III, who was also Secretary of the Navy (1929-1933). The Roosevelts can be traced to a Franco-Dutch settler of the Plymouth Colony in 1621 and a Dutchman of New Amsterdam (New York) about 1649. From that beginning ultimately emanated Presidents Theodore Roosevelt (1901-1909) and Franklin D. Roosevelt (1933-1945). Both were Assistant Secretaries of the Navy as well, (1897-1898 and 1913-1920 respectively), as were Theodore Roosevelt, Jr. (1921-1924) and Henry L. Roosevelt (1933-1936). Like the other Massachusetts and New York businessmen and leaders around them, the Adamses and Roosevelts reinvested their material profits into the arts and humanitarian purposes in general. They were patrons of the spiritual components to material prosperity.

The rich literary heritage of the New England community arose from the early 19th century authors and poets who wrote near and/or about the sea. America's first true philosophical movement of Transcendentalism centered here in the works of Ralph Waldo Emerson and Henry David Thoreau, while Herman Melville

in his *Moby Dick* tried to fathom the mysteries of the sea and men against it. Ordinary seaman Richard Henry Dana did likewise in *Two Years Before the Mast*, and Henry Wadsworth Longfellow used the ship as a metaphor of the republic when in 1849 he wrote, "Sail on, O Ship of State. . . ." The likes of novelists James Fenimore Cooper and Nathaniel Hawthorne and poets Walt Whitman and John Greenleaf Whittier helped give America its literary character, and young Oliver Wendell Holmes, Sr. helped save the USS *Constitution* from being broken up with his moving poem of 1830, "Old Ironsides."

These traditions have survived undiminished throughout the 20th century. In the 1920s, Melville's lost novel *Billy Budd* received critical acclaim. Harvard graduate Charles B. Nordhoff, whose grandfather had sailed in Yankee windjammers, moved to Tahiti with James Norman Hall where in the 1930s they produced the epic trilogy *Mutiny on the Bounty, Men Against the Sea,* and *Pitcairn's Island*. The most successful recent fictional works have been the penetrating novels *The Caine Mutiny* and *Winds of War* by Herman Wouk. And one must not forget the unsurpassed historical prose of Harvard historians Samuel Eliot Morison of Massachusetts and Robert Greenhalgh Albion of Maine. Their histories of Americans and Europeans at sea have flowed continuously from their pens over the past half-century.

As for painting, generations of artists, following the example of Winslow Homer, have captured the power and majesty of the sea from the vantage points of the Maine and Massachusetts coasts. One such individual, John Marin, in a reflective moment in 1938, perceived the unique advantages of the republic's proximity to the sea when he observed, "Isn't it funny that Dictators *never never never* live by the sea?" While a storm pounded the shore, he considered the fascist rulers abroad: "Don't lock the tyrants up—make them look at this great sea manifestation taking place." The awesomeness of the ocean environment—portrayed so vividly, for example, in the canvases of C. G. Evers—has been understood by such artists as a special force in the shaping of unique American social qualitites. So the quiet fishing village scene of downeast Maine tells as much of the people as does a mural showing a square-rigged ship under full sail in a gale. It captures the very quality of individualism that has been the basis of American democracy, of this Columbia, the Gem of the Ocean.

The severe demands on the merchant and warship sailor to survive have been common to all seafaring nations, but it has been the great liberal maritime democracies of Britain and the United States which have pioneered in humanitarian reforms ashore and afloat. The new republic has led in many respects, however, in keeping with its strong libertarian ideals. The unpopular British practice of impressing common seamen by force was abandoned largely at American insistence in 1815. The British habit of the grog ration outraged American temperance reformers and Congressmen who thus outlawed it in the U.S. Navy in 1862, while Secretary of the Navy Josephus Daniels abolished all alcohol on board ships in 1914. Needless to say, such a purification scheme was and still is regarded with much skepticism by thirsty swabs, but it was all a part of the very necessary effort to clean up the harsh conditions of shipboard life, to eliminate alcoholism, and thus to enhance performance of duty. Besides, enlisted men's and officer's clubs ashore, liberally rationed medicinal brandy, and privately-kept liquor under personal lock and key at sea (and ingenious concoctions of ''torpedo juice'' in World War II) have compensated for the official ''dry'' policy. The need for improved diet, medicine, and general health at sea, along with the social, educational, and religious requirements of the individual sailor, have kept the Navy in the important business of providing essential services to the average sailor, most recently in the area of drug control and rehabilitation.

Life at sea and along the urban waterfronts was still rough-and-ready even as late as the turn of the present century. This writer well remembers his late grandfather, Gilbert P. ''Curly'' Reynolds, fireman first class and coal passer in the armored cruiser *Maryland* (1912), tattooed eagle emblazoned across his chest, telling how he once flattened a junior officer one day after the latter had kicked him as he scrubbed the deck. Grandpa spent some time in the putrid brig until the truth became known and the officer replaced him there. He and his mates of that era worshiped a man like Admiral Robley D. ''Fighting Bob'' Evans, whose son Captain Franck Taylor Evans was a chip off the proverbial old block. One day about 1913, after a shore leave at the notorious ''Barbary Coast'' of San Francisco in which a number of his men had been beaten up and robbed by the proprietors, their bouncers, and ladies, this Evans led a shore party which tore up the place and henceforth gained his sailors the respect they deserved while ashore. My other grandpappy, Charles C. Clark, still vividly recalls an occasion in Seattle when bluejackets from the Great White Fleet rallied to their threatened comrades in the red light district in like manner.

A similar problem which appeared in 1917 had a profound impact on American music. The port was New Orleans, already infamous for its ''Storyville'' red light district, but under wartime conditions a menace to young seamen on liberty. The musical entertainment at the ''sporting houses'' was provided by black musicians playing the new type of jazz music which was in fact becoming America's only original contribution to the arts. The Navy Department closed down the district as a wartime measure, forcing the jazzmen to seek new employment up the Mississippi River, on the river boats, at Memphis, Kansas City and Chicago, thence to New York. Thus did jazz begin to sweep the nation and the world.

Eventually, the music matured into ''swing'' and found its way back to the Navy, as each major warship

during World War II formed her own swing band. In the tradition of U.S. Marine bandmaster of the 1880s John Philip Sousa and his stirring marches, these orchestras were terrific morale builders, as were ''name'' touring units like that of Navy bandmaster Artie Shaw which toured the South Pacific or Saxie Dowell's group as it played on board the bomb-stricken carrier *Franklin* (CV-13) off the Japanese coast. The crowning glory occurred in England in 1944 in a ''battle of the bands'' in which Sam Donahue's U.S. Navy band thoroughly outplayed Glenn Miller's Army Air Forces orchestra.

Progress in 20th century photography, still and motion, greatly enhanced the image of the sea in the public's mind, making legendary heroes at once even more larger than life and more personal, especially via television. From the novels noted above and the Broadway stage came Hollywood scripts, as well as original screenplays. In the 1930s, the sailing ship era received much attention through the swashbuckling performances of such characters as Errol Flynn, and the prewar Navy received a romantic image through dramas like ''Helldivers'' and even musicals like ''Follow the Fleet.''

But World War II marked the pinnacle of the naval film, between the documentary stills of Captain Edward Steichen, documentary movies like Commander John Ford's filming of part of the Battle of Midway, and Lieutenant Dwight Long's story of the new carrier *Yorktown* (CV-10), ''The Fighting Lady.'' Many fictional/semi-documentary movies starring such actors as John Wayne, Dana Andrews, and Tyrone Power captivated American audiences during and long after the war. So motion pictures from ''A Wing and a Prayer'' to ''Sands of Iwo Jima'' to ''In Harm's Way'' not only entertained but educated the public and even proved to be effective recruiting devices. Cinematized Pearl Harbor has kept Americans sensitive to sneak attack in dozens of films, culminating in the epic ''Tora! Tora! Tora!'' Ship types received their due from PT boats (''They Were Expendable'') to carriers (''Task Force'') and especially submarines, through the eyes of the attacker and the victim (''Destination Tokyo,'' ''Action in the North Atlantic,'' and ''The Enemy Below'').

And since the war, the Navy has provided an even broader stage for portraying on film the human drama as embodied in the republic's actions on the waters. The documentary television series ''Victory at Sea'' even utilized a brilliant musical score by Richard Rodgers. The Korean War found expression in ''The Bridges of Toko-ri,'' based on James Michener's book. He had earlier written the story behind the successful Broadway musical ''South Pacific,'' the score by Rodgers and Oscar Hammerstein. Potential nuclear war found naval settings in ''The Bedford Incident'' and

O Sea! Eternal Force!
Sing, Voyagers;
We're upward bound,
For God has smiled.

"On the Beach," Hollywood's version of Armageddon. And on a more optimistic note, "Mister Roberts" and "Kiss Them For Me" (based on Frederick Wakeman's novel *Shore Leave*) captured the great good humor and human pathos of the American sea fighter in war.

Between the old and young salt represented by John Paul Jones, Captain Ahab, Bull Halsey, and one Ensign Pulver emerges the composite of a naval character unique in the annals of history, a uniqueness which can best be understood by the term "American." Until the British naval bombardment of Falmouth (Portland), Maine in 1775, Americans had so revered their naval heritage that the Washington family of Virginia could name its plantation in honor of a British admiral, Edward Vernon. Post-Revolutionary naval heroes were similarly honored, but they were never given political authority or prestige, nor did they want it. The Secretary of the Navy held absolute control over the Navy down to World War II, while the rank of admiral—considered aristocratic and un-American—was not even created until the 1860s.

Indeed, the nation's sailors have stayed generally out of the political arena—as all navies do—preferring instead to practice their art far away, at sea. The only time a flag officer was even mentioned as possible Presidential material—George Dewey in 1900—was an aberration which lasted but a few weeks without serious impact. In fact, just as the United States at the turn of the century created a major standing battle fleet officered by products of the highly professional U.S. Naval Academy (from 1845) and Naval War College (from 1884) and who maintained their closest dialogues in their own private U.S. Naval Institute (from 1873),

the Navy began to foster non-professional sources of officer and enlisted manpower: the Naval Militia (1888-1918), the U.S. Naval Reserve (from 1915), the Naval ROTC (from the 1920s) and Naval Aviation Cadet programs (from the 1930s). With the coming of World War II, the Navy finally expanded into an institution representative of a true cross section of the republic—typified by the fact that the last four Presidents, John Kennedy of Massachusetts, Lyndon Johnson of Texas, Richard Nixon of California, and Gerald Ford of Michigan, were wartime Naval Reserve officers.

The U.S. Navy has become a major component of the contemporary American consciousness, but at the same time it has maintained its traditional political aloofness. Unlike Army and Air Force officers who deal with large administrative organizations and masses of personnel and who thus develop political savvy and clienteles which can project them into high political office, regular Navy personnel have stayed oriented to shipboard activities, out of touch with landlubbing politics. Retired admirals may utilize their logistical expertise in corporations, but few have had sufficient talents to achieve elective office. They are by nature and preference seamen first and foremost, for which the republic can be grateful.

By the same token, however, naval leaders often suffer in political battles with more politically-seasoned civilians and generals. Some of the more well-known examples are Admiral James O. Richardson's dismissal by FDR when the former tried to remove the U.S. Fleet from Pearl Harbor just prior to World War II, Admiral Ernest J. King's repeated failures to reorganize the Navy Deparment during the war, the "revolt of the admirals" against post-war unification, and Admiral George W. Anderson's relief over the TFX controversy. Notable and rare exceptions have been Admiral William A. Moffett's successful crusade for naval aviation in the halls of Congress during the 1920s and 1930s, Admiral William D. Leahy's role as chief of staff to the President during the 1940s, and Admiral Hyman

Rickover's dogged but successful campaign for nuclear-powered warships throughout the government and industry over the past 30 years. The Navy's success in Congress has depended almost exclusively instead on civilian leaders like Carl Vinson who have understood and appreciated the Navy's missions.

The subtlety of sea power has been the major stumbling block to the public's developing a full awareness of its importance. The vision of a naval battle is real enough, but Congressmen and Presidents have traditionally had precious little sympathy for the financial needs of the fleet and the merchant marine, vital as these are. Even when a major naval philosopher emerged in the person of Captain Alfred T. Mahan in the 1890s, his ideas were more oversimplified and uncritically cannonized than really understood—inside the Navy as well as outside. Naval historians in general have been read for their action narratives, not for their philosophical insights. And even in the wake of naval victories in all of the nation's major wars, immediate, rapid, and dangerous postwar naval demobilization has inevitably followed.

The republic appreciates the power of the sea only superficially, but that influence endures more importantly now than ever in the past. We underestimate or ignore it only at our peril.

The final measure of any nation's power upon the sea is its ultimate impact on the race at large. The original seafaring nation or thalassocracy was fifth century, B.C., Athens, whose democracy, empire, economy, and culture not only dazzled the ancient world but laid the foundations for all Western civilization. Though the state of Athens was eventually destroyed politically by jealous rivals and through internal decay, Athenian culture conquered Alexander the Great and his successors (fourth to second centuries, B.C.) and the Roman Republic and Empire (second century, B.C., to fourth century, A.D.) and provided the seeds of the Italian Renaissance (14th to 16th centuries). This latter event centered on maritime Venice and neighboring Florence and to a lesser extent on seafaring Genoa and Pisa—all republics which rescued Europe from the stultifying dark ages and from Oriental enemies, propelling Western civilization into the modern age. The torch of enlightenment passed by sea to the republican Netherlands and democratic England (17th and 18th centuries), the latter spreading this Western culture across the globe via its ships.

The United States—a democratic republic—has gradually replaced Great Britain as the defender of Western ideals and culture, the model of aspiring nations in political freedom and economic prosperity. On three occasions, World Wars I and II and the Cold War, the republic rescued Western Europe from the threat of authoritarian overthrow and cleared the Pacific

of similar dangers. But victory was only the beginning, for conquered Germany and Japan were transformed into giant models of the American colossus, with Soviet Russia and Communist China and every developing small nation unabashedly seeking American aid or imitating American techniques in the hope of achieving those material advantages which Americans hold dear. They thus take to the sea in search of wealth. If they succeed fully, however, they will prosper in many more ways than simple treasure. For the American Republic is also rich in the common human aspirations held sacred by all freedom-loving people since the beginning.

The republic is not a utopia. Though motivated by the noblest of human ideals—life, liberty and the pursuit of a happy life through material well-being—two centuries ago, Americans have shown themselves to be heir to the same frailties that plague the race at large. We have made mistakes, abused power, often fallen short of our ideals. Even when our intentions have been well-meant, we have often stumbled, out of ignorance or inexperience. And yet, painfully and persistently, we have striven to overcome our deficiencies, to correct our mistakes and even to learn anew. Perhaps this challenge is the source of the drive and the excitement that keep us active, growing and prosperous.

And yet, there is something more than mere challenge, something unique, subtle and unspoken, that continues to shape and propel us, something that must account for our success where others have failed. In the view of this historian, it has been the sea—its mere presence, its riches, its horizons, and its awesomeness. Other challenges and other factors have influenced our history, to be sure, and often they have eclipsed our awareness of the waters. And yet, we always return to the sea—that vital force in the making of America, its importance no less now than 200 years ago or at any time in our past.

Professor Reynolds, a graduate of the University of California at Santa Barbara (1961) with an M.A. and Ph.D. (1964) in history from Duke University, taught at the U. S. Naval Academy (1964-1968) before going to the University of Maine, where he is now professor of history. His first published work appeared in the December 1961 *Proceedings,* and his books include *Carrier Admiral* (with Admiral J.J. Clark, 1967), *The Fast Carriers: The Forging of an Air Navy* (1968), and *Command of the Sea: The History and Strategy of Maritime Empires* (1974). This *Proceedings* essay completes a bicentennial trilogy for Dr. Reynolds. The other articles are "American Strategic History and Doctrines: A Reconsideration," in the December 1975 *Military Affairs* and "The British Strategic Inheritance in American Naval Policy, 1775-1975," in the 1975 book *The Atlantic World of Robert G. Albion,* edited by B.W. Labaree.

All the paintings in this article are by Edward Moran (1829-1901) and are the property of the Naval Academy Museum

The United States At a Strategic Crossroads

By Vice Admiral Stansfield Turner, U. S. Navy

"With the emphasis on sea control and sea-based projection forces that a maritime option entails, we would automatically have a force structure that provided a credible deterrent and significant quick-response capability in a NATO flank war, a conflict-at-sea, a unilateral intervention or a sub-theater war."

There is a momentum to military and strategic concepts which on the one hand is reassurance against whimsical tampering, but on the other hand is the cause of the traditional accusation that the military are always planning for yesterday's war. Surely there have been enough jolts in recent months to accepted patterns of diplomacy and military operations to warrant a close review of whether our overall military strategy fits our best understanding of national interests and aspirations.

Three changes in our strategic environment are particularly pertinent: (1) the movement away from a bipolar world, (2) the waning domestic support for traditional policies, and (3) changing Soviet capabilities and strategy.

By the end of this decade, we can expect to be dealing with four other major power centers: the U.S.S.R., China, Japan, and a united Western Europe. China is already a factor politically and militarily, including nuclear capability. It needs only economic strength to become a full major power. Japan has more than enough economic leverage and needs only an increased military potential, including nuclear weapons, to move into the major league. United Western Europe has all the ingredients of a major power now, and needs only political cohesiveness.

The world's political structure is beginning to acknowledge this potential five-sided power relationship. The freedom of each of the major powers to maneuver is becoming affected by the positions of the other four. In the future, alignments are likely to vary from issue to issue. Each major power will seek to avoid being on the minority side of any issue, especially the one-out-of-five side. While these restrictions on maneuver are likely to act as a damper to rash destabilizing moves by the large powers, they have the disadvantage of tempting smaller nations into actions that could result in pitting the major powers against each other.

The American people appear to be desirous of reducing the world-wide roles we have been filling for the past 25 years. Whether or not this represents a long-term change of attitude, it supports current pressures to reduce defense spending. Those pressures will be difficult to reverse, even if there is a change in attitude toward our world responsibilities. The portion of our Federal budget that can be considered discretionary is largely in Defense. Thus, any sizable increase in Defense spending would require that Congress reverse various legislative actions which have created "non-discretionary" demands on the budget; e.g., social security rates. This would be difficult, in view of pressures for increases in welfare, education, ecology, etc. These sections of the budget are already growing at three to five times the rate of the GNP.

Thus, it is becoming increasingly difficult to pay for all the forces needed to support the strategy of containment of Communism that has remained largely unchanged over the past quarter-century. This strategy was carried out first by maintaining strong NATO forces, then by helping threatened nations around the world. The means until now have been large balanced Army, Navy, and Air Force forces keyed mainly to controlling a possible ground war in Europe. This strategy is beginning to change and the thrust of the changes have been defined in the Nixon Doctrine.

For instance, the reduction of our forces in Korea and the accelerating withdrawal from Vietnam, plus the Presidential statement that we expect our allies to carry a greater share of the burden for their defense indicate that the future will see less reliance on the use of U. S. military forces.

Because of the reductions in our forces and the changes in Soviet capabilities, we are now being forced to make hard choices, both between the Services, and within the Navy. If national objectives have changed, we must develop military capabilities that serve these new policies, or we may find that we have insufficient resources to meet the old strategy and have not developed the right kinds of forces to support a new one.

There are two facets to trends in the Soviet threat. The first is the unchanging nature of the buildup and improvement in Soviet general purpose force, as well as strategic capabilities. The second is the changing emphasis of the threat towards its maritime features.

One apparent reason for the accent on Soviet naval forces is that the Soviets are using their seapower to leapfrog the stalemate we both face on the central front in Europe. They, as we, recognize how destabilizing any attempt would be to change the territorial frontiers in Central Europe that have been frozen since 1948. Thus they are exerting strong pressures on the flank nations of NATO. They would like to create the impression that the eastern Mediterranean and the Norwegian Sea are areas which the U.S.S.R., not NATO, will control. Without firing a shot, they hope to pressure these flank NATO nations into "Finlandization." Additionally, the Soviets are increasingly concerned with the threat on their eastern front, even to the extent of redeploying sizeable forces to their Chinese borders. On top of this, they must contend with uncertain lines of communication across Eastern Europe. Overall, the probability of a Soviet military assault into Western Europe today is lower now than in many years.

This does not mean that we can disregard the Soviet threat to the land areas of NATO Europe. Any of a number of events could reverse the apparent movement toward détente and heighten tensions rapidly. It does seem mandatory, though, that we regard the Soviets' growing capabilities at sea as providing them with the option of expanding the traditional areas of confrontation and potential conflict beyond Europe to include other areas reachable by sea. In short, the contingencies which we may have to face have multiplied, while the resources and facilities available to us, owing to a combination of escalating costs and constrained budgets, are, in effect, declining.

The United States is facing a new challenge. We must review our strategies to determine whether the changes in the world situation that we have discussed call for substantial changes in our military posture.

NATO: Looking at NATO first, we see that our strategy is based on a joint conventional defense with our NATO allies. Of the three changes in the world environment, the one that most affects this strategy is the emergence of a united Western Europe as a major power. If that united Europe elects to cooperate more frequently with the Soviet Union than with ourselves, there will be little significance to our military alliance and strategy. Our military, diplomatic and economic actions in Europe, then, must be keyed to ensuring close relations with Western Europe. One way in which military strength can help is to offer assurance to the Europeans that we can and will assist them if they are attacked either frontally or in nibbles.

The cornerstone of such assurance is our ground forces in place in Europe. There can be no clearer earnest of our intent. Yet, those forces today are only a small part of the help we estimate that we would have to provide against a major Soviet attack. And the size of that contingent in Europe is under pressure from the Senate, the doves in general, and from mutual and balanced force reduction negotiations. It is obvious that, even without further reductions, our strategy in Europe is viable only if rapid sea resupply is feasible.

This brings us up full against the third change in the world environment, the increasing Soviet challenge at sea. The real challenge lies hidden below the seas and on Soviet air bases. The Soviets have, however, made pointed efforts to make their threat visible by means of an impressive surface fleet. The utility of Soviet surface forces after the first blow in a war with the United States is highly questionable. Their peacetime usefulness in making the Europeans aware of the threat lurking in the wings is highly effective.

A key issue in our review of our NATO strategy is what, if any, steps we might take to accommodate possible uncertainty in the European mind of our ability to reinforce them in an emergency. No change would be necessary if:

▶ We, and the Europeans, estimate that our combined naval forces can prevail rapidly enough to strengthen the central front on time; or

▶ We agree that the front can be stabilized by the forces in place and airlifted forces with their pre-positioned equipment and supplies; or

▶ We agree that the war will be over or go nuclear so rapidly that reinforcement could not take place.

If none of these assumptions is acceptable, we must consider trade-offs for improving our forces that can ensure the rapid reinforcement of Europe by sea. If we voluntarily or involuntarily reduce ground forces and land-based air forces in Europe, we could decommission those forces to pay for increased sea control capability. If we do not reduce forces in Europe, we could decommission ConUS ground or air forces and rely more heavily on mobilization of Reserve and National Guard forces. Either of these courses of action would increase the time for us to complete our reinforcement of Europe by the mobilization factor (though this might not really be the case if the seas were not safe for shipping in the early days of war). The choice of strategy should be made largely by answering the question as to whether the West Europeans would feel a greater assurance with our present posture (with possibly some force transfers to (ConUS) or with our having a greater capability to reinforce them by sea at the expense of some readiness in ConUS back-up forces.

There are two related considerations. One is whether the West Europeans could and would pick up the expense of improving our total sea control capabilities. This would play as naturally into the Secretary of Defense's Total Force Concept as would greater reliance on Reserve Army and Air Force forces for ConUS back-up. The problem is complicated by a divergence of views within NATO. The United States wants its allies to recognize sea control as a problem to be solved by all NATO nations. Most allies are allocating an increasing percentage of defense resources to land and air forces so that they may be in a better position if U. S. forces in Europe are reduced. Their navies receive, on the average, 17% or less of national defense budgets and the trend throughout NATO Europe is toward smaller, less expensive navies. In particular, the number of open ocean escorts is declining while coastal capabilities are increasing. On balance it appears unlikely that we will be able to divert our allies from emphasizing their land-based forces and coastal navies at the expense of open ocean sea control forces.

The second consideration is how a mix of forces that was richer in sea control than our present force would respond to possible non-NATO requirements. This leads us to a review of our other national strategies for military force.

Asia: Of the three changes in the world environment, again the emergence of the five-sided world is the primary consideration in our Asian policy. Three of the major powers are resident in Asia. We enter the scene as outsiders and are anxious not to end up on the short side of 3-against-1 alignments on particular issues. One way to achieve this would be to maintain our past close ties with Japan. If we also assume that only on unusual issues such as Vietnam are China and the Soviet Union likely to take the same side, we can expect to be on the high side of three-against-one if we stay close to Japan. Thus our military input to an Asian strategy should be keyed to promoting close ties with Japan.

The second change in our world environment, the reduced national will to become involved abroad, markedly limits our options for doing this. Clearly we are neither likely to station more forces in Asia, nor are we likely to become involved in new ground conflicts there. We are more likely to reduce our earnest forces in this theater. This may not be all bad. In terms of our relations with the Japanese, reduction of U.S. ground forces throughout Asia would lessen Japanese concern that its ties to the United States could draw it into a conflict against its will. Additionally, relative to the Chinese, withdrawal of our inevitably visible ground forces from the periphery of China and replacement with less obtrusive sea-based forces and Guam-based bombers would remove what must be a major irritant to our relations with China.

If, in partial compensation, we increased the naval component of our Asian force posture, there would be several advantages. Japan is totally dependent on sea communications. It clearly cannot have naval forces adequate to cover its extensive sea lanes for many years. To the extent that U.S. sea control forces in Asia appear to be capable and available, they could make it attractive for the Japanese to maintain their ties with us.

A maritime accent in Asia would also have its impact on our relations with China. As China re-enters the mainstream of world affairs, we wish to remove irritants from our relations with it and afford it the opportunity of working constructively with us. At the same time, we want to be in a position to apply appropriate pressures to China if it should move in an expansionist direction. Asia, after all, is an area of potential instability in the decade ahead. Naval air and amphibious forces are appropriate to signalling U.S. attitudes toward China according to whether they are paraded visibly and threateningly or held in remote reserve.

In summary, our primary interests in Asia lie with Japan, a maritime nation. A force posture with a maritime accent is appropriate. Such naval air and amphibious forces would not have the staying power to take on a major Chinese ground thrust, but we really do not have a practical option of planning a strategy around winning a ground war on mainland Asia. We would do well to have strong and "relevant" naval

power in this theater—relevant in the sense that a President might be able to deploy it for its deterrent impact or even engage it in lower order conflicts. This leads us to consideration of possible conflicts in Asia and elsewhere not involving the Soviet Union or China directly.

Conflicts in Asia, Africa, or the Indian Ocean Basin Not Involving the P.R.C. or U.S.S.R. (Sub-Theater Wars).

The objective of our military forces in all situations is deterrence. Our specific military posture may have greater deterrent impact on possible sub-theater conflicts than on major tensions in Europe or Asia simply because there are not so many other factors involved such as the restraint stemming from the magnitude of the stakes. The role of military posture in the sub-theater situation is also important because of the dangers of our precipitately relinquishing the responsibilities we have shouldered in these situations for the past quarter of a century. It is therefore important to examine the characteristics of different forces for such conflicts with a view toward determining which are best suited for deterrence.

Forces stationed overseas are the best deterrent. There are, however, four factors working against reliance on overseas basing. One is the domestic pressures to bring such forces home for both policy and financial reasons. The second is the pressures of negotiation for mutual reduction in forces. The third is the pressures from some of the host countries themselves. The fourth is that the diminishing size of our armed forces will make it increasingly difficult to provide adequate coverage in many areas of the world and still have any contingency reserve. Overall, then, we should not anticipate any increased reliance on stationing forces overseas in the near future.

Thus, what we want to consider is how we can substitute a capability to introduce ground and/or air power into a troubled sub-theater. Basically we are talking about rapid introduction of modest-size forces. Most wars of this type are likely to be small initially and the application of sufficient power in the early stages may be decisive. In light of the Nixon Doctrine that we will support our allies in Asia primarily through air, naval, and economic means, the emphasis is on air power. There are essentially three separate means by which we can introduce air power into such conflict.

Long-range, land-based bombers operating from distant bases such as Guam can be effective against well-identified large targets. Their shortcoming is their limited capability for accurate, quick-reaction, direct support of ground forces in changing tactical situations. This problem would be magnified if it were a question of direct support for foreign ground troops. Additionally, we must always be cautious in the employment of strategic forces anywhere near the U.S.S.R. or the P.R.C., e.g., Korea. The potential ambiguity between a long-range conventional strike and a surprise strategic nuclear attack could be most dangerous.

The second means of introducing airpower into a conflict would be through the tremendous air lift capabilities of the C-5A. This transport gives the Air Force a considerable capability to introduce tactical aircraft into sub-theater areas through the use of "bare base kits." This concept provides us maximum flexibility with minimum forces since a force based in ConUS can react equally quickly in either an easterly or westerly direction. The bare-base concept has three principal limitations. The first is dependence on en route over-flight and staging rights. The second is reliance on the availability of bases with prepared runways, adequate security and a capacity for rapid buildup of water supply, POL storage and ammunition storage. The third limitation is the fact that the trends of the time in terms of increased sophistication of aircraft, and hence maintenance and repair requirements, makes it more difficult to have confidence that all of the elements necessary for a true combat capability will be available in a timely manner.

The third means of introducing tactical air power into a sub-theater situation is the attack carrier. Non-deployed attack carriers cannot arrive on the scene as rapidly as long-range or air mobile land-based air if we are caught without adequate warning. If we do have some warning, sea-based tactical air can be in place well in advance of hostilities without committing us to intervention. Sea-based tactical air carries its own spare parts, personnel, maintenance equipment and hence is as much a going concern in peacetime as it is in wartime. It takes with it its own POL, ammunition, and water supplies. Additionally, carrier vulnerability is essentially nil in a sub-theater situation. It is clearly less than that of land-based air located in the area of combat.

A similar situation exists with regard to a comparison of the means of introducing ground forces. One means is to air-lift the initial elements of army forces in very rapidly. We are again dependent on both internal security at the arrival base and upon assurance that sea support will be forthcoming shortly for both logistics and reinforcement. Another means is to introduce ground forces from amphibious ship platforms. If security exists, they can be introduced administratively. They have the added advantage of being able to go in against opposition if required. Amphibious ground forces have the obvious disadvantage of lesser relevance to situations remote from the sea.

Going back to our basic purpose of maximizing

deterrence with a minimum commitment of forces, there are several other aspects of these alternatives which must be borne in mind.

First, long-range bombers, bare-base tactical air and air mobile ground forces are capabilities which are difficult to demonstrate to others in peacetime. They are thereby less useful in creating the impressions desired for deterrence, namely that they probably would be dispatched and that they likely would succeed if they were. Sea-based forces, on the other hand, can be paraded as much or as little as desired to create a deterrent impact, e.g., Jordan in 1970.

Secondly, we must also consider the fact that the use of sea-based forces, especially carriers, minimizes the likelihood of extended military involvement. At least as far as aviation is concerned, there is no commitment on the ground because there need be no introduction of forces in-country. If a decision should be made to introduce ground forces, but subsequently we elect to withdraw that commitment, amphibious forces have the advantage that they can be withdrawn by the same means as they arrived even in the face of opposition.

Finally, a distinct limitation on reliance on sea-based air and amphibious forces is that they constitute a limited war fighting capability in the event prolonged conflict ensues. It is thus essential that they be backed up by mobile Army and Air Force forces. Thus the unique contribution of naval forces is that they provide the most credible deterrent that we can offer short of stationing forces overseas, but they do so essentially by evidencing a commitment of the United States to rapidly introduce its full gamut of Army and Air forces if necessary.

Unilateral Involvement. Still another situation that requires review is what is described as unilateral involvement. This is simply a situation in which we become involved with the Soviet Union militarily without drawing in our respective allies. Support for two client states such as Egypt and Israel is the most frequently cited instance of this possibility. In the Middle East case, our assistance would almost certainly have to be primarily naval. To begin with, keeping the sea lanes open would be a prime requirement. Conducting amphibious assault operations might well be another.

For air superiority and air strike missions we would have options of sea-basing, basing on foreign allied bases, or of introducing forces directly onto Israeli bases. The latter course depends on staging and transit rights, would encounter base-loading limitations, and would be ultimately dependent on resupply and support by sea. The use of allied bases in Greece, Turkey, or Cyprus could bring land-based air within extreme range for such support. The issue here, and with the unilateral case in general, is whether we want to count both on handy allied bases within reach of possible involvement, and on our allies being willing to become involved along with us.

At the same time, we must recognize forthrightly that the threat at sea that the Soviets can pose in a region like the eastern Mediterranean would inevitably reduce our ability to mount offensive strikes. If, for example, the Soviets were willing to expand an Arab-Israeli war to an attack on the U. S. Sixth Fleet, a large portion of that Fleet's resources would first have to be devoted to neutralizing the threat from submarines, surface ships, and land-based aircraft. We must keep in mind that in a unilateral war, such as we are discussing here, there would be limitations or inhibitions on how extensive a force the Soviets would commit. Would they, for instance, use aircraft from Europe and from the Soviet Union, or only those few that can be based in Egypt? Still, there is no doubt that the emergence of a threat to us at sea for the first time since World War II limits the speed with which we can react offensively. This, in turn, places a premium on our being able to exert control rapidly over the sea and air environment, primarily by having adequate numbers of carriers immediately available.

Case for a Maritime Strategy. In summary, greater reliance on sea-based forces is not the answer to each of our prospective uses of military force. Under the new strategic considerations which we must take into account, however, sea-based forces have increased applicability across the spectrum of our requirements.

In NATO, those strategy options that do not call for an increase in sea control capability are optimistic about our ability to stabilize the front on the basis of limited prepositioning and air lift capability or be very hopeful about our ability to protect our sea lines of communication. There are risks in relying too heavily on these possibilities. Furthermore, when we consider the NATO flanks, it appears that devoting more of our resources to sea control and sea-based projection forces would be shifting our strength with the shifting threat.

In Asia, we will continue to have commitments and interests that require a means of coming to the aid of our allies rapidly, primarily with air power but maintaining the option for deeper commitment if necessary. Placing primary emphasis on sea-based forces for rapid response with the option of introducing ground-based air forces as the need develops provides a posture of capability without commitment. We probably cannot expect domestic attitudes to tolerate much more than this in the near future.

For sub-theater and presence situations the most visible deterrent forces we can maintain as our numbers of forces stationed overseas diminishes are naval air and amphibious forces. For the full credibility of this deterrence they must be backed by air mobile ground and land-based air forces.

Because unilateral involvement would generally preclude reliance on allied bases, we would be in a dangerous position if we were to count on being able to move forces, other than naval and long-range air forces, into position quickly enough to be effective.

What are the objections to greater reliance on the maritime elements of our strategy? One is the reputed high cost of naval forces. Another is the alleged vulnerability of sea-based forces, especially attack carriers.

Various analyses have demonstrated that naval forces may be shown to be more costly, less costly, or cost about the same as other forces of comparable capabilities. When naval forces are shown to be more costly, it is often because portions of the costs of competing systems, e.g., base defense and logistics, are neglected or understated and certain benefits of naval forces, such as mobility, are under-valued or given no value at all.

The real issue is the spotlight that can be pointed to the initial cost of a CVAN. As a percentage of the life cycle system cost, this is really very small. Moreover, the only significant difference in the cost of building a sea base and a land base is the mobility of the former. Thus the real cost differential lies in our estimate of how many land bases we would need to build overseas to match the mobile sea base.

Recent joint Navy-Air Force efforts to study actual historical costs of sea and land air-basing have shown such close comparability that opponents of carriers have significantly muted their tone on costs in recent months. Overall, the qualitative differences in the basing of land- and sea-based air are clearly the dominant factor in selecting the best mix.

To assess the vulnerability of sea-based forces, we should consider three levels of conflict: presence, sub-theater conflicts (including the P.R.C. but not Soviet involvement), and wars involving the U.S.S.R.

In a presence or peaceful deterrence situation, there is little threat to naval forces, while there is an appreciable one to land-based forces (e.g., abandonment of Wheelus Air Force Base, non-availability of NATO southern flank bases during the Jordanian crisis, etc.). In sub-theater situations, there may be a threat to carriers, but it is likely to be moderate in comparison with the threat to land-based forces. In the Vietnam war, for instance, many hundreds of aircraft were lost on the ground to guerrilla action, while no losses were reported for carrier-based aircraft from enemy attacks on carrier bases.

In a war with the U.S.S.R., there would certainly be a serious threat to our carriers. Most frequently, discussions of this issue focus on the question of a surprise from trailing ships and submarines. All military forces are quite vulnerable to a well-timed and organized surprise attack. However, the enemy would have problems of coordination, particularly if the attack amounted to more than a conflict-at-sea. In addition, because the Soviets on an average day have only one or two of our CVAs within firing range of their missile units, they would have to change their posture significantly in order to be ready to inflict major damage on our overall carrier force. Such a change in posture would almost certainly alert us and under these alerted conditions, our tactical commanders could assume progressively improved defensive postures. This could reduce our vulnerability, though damage could by no means be prevented entirely. Initial damage or losses need not be crippling if our force levels are adequate to regain and preserve control of the seas after a surprise attack.

Once hostilities with the Soviet Union have commenced, we have another ball game. As pointed out earlier, we can expect some inhibitions on their commitment of forces in a unilateral involvement situation. This should reduce our defensive problem significantly. In a total war situation, we would undoubtedly give ground, take losses, delay offensive operations and fight a difficult fight (as would ground and air forces also). If we are so pessimistic as to not rely on naval forces at all under these circumstances, we need to return to square one and rethink our entire military strategy. The issue under these circumstances would be whether we can conduct military operations outside ConUS. It is not a question of whether naval forces are more or less vulnerable than Army or Air Force tactical air forces based overseas, but whether the Army and Air Force can have the reinforcements and supplies upon which they are dependent and which only the Navy can assure their receiving.

What would a national military strategy with a more maritime orientation look like?

On the NATO Central Front it would reduce U.S. ground forces and some of their ConUS backup. It would encourage the West Europeans to replace the forces that we withdraw. Of the forces withdrawn, a substantial portion should be replaced by sea control forces and airlift capability. The balance should go into the ConUS reserve.

In Asia, it would acknowledge the improbability of our employing sizeable ground forces and rely on Navy forces for sea control and combined Navy and Air Force forces for projection of power ashore in order to prevent conflicts.

With the emphasis on sea control and sea-based projection forces that a maritime option entails, we would automatically have a force structure that pro-

vided a credible deterrent and a significant quick-response capability in a NATO flank war, a conflict-at-sea, a unilateral intervention or a sub-theater war. We would want to increase our rapid air lift capability and regularly exercise our air mobile forces to ensure that a maritime-oriented force structure also contained a credible capability for rapid augmentation by ground and land-based air forces. The threat of such augmentation is essential to deterrence. It is the key to any large-scale or prolonged military involvement, and in such event should replace our quick-response sea-based projection forces.

What would be the benefits of such a strategy?
▶ It would implement the Nixon Doctrine with forces that were less dependent on political constraints arising from overseas basing and the attendant risk of unwanted involvement.
▶ It would stretch limited military resources by being more flexible and more useful over a variety of contingencies.
▶ It would make it easy for the President to signal others by means of military forces even with domestic pressures against military involvement.
▶ By thus providing an improved capability to protect our sea lanes, it would guard our access to raw materials and commerce and impart to our allies a higher level of confidence in our ability to come to their aid.
▶ It would address directly the Soviet naval build-up, which could, if it continues, shift the balance of conventional war-fighting power in their favor.

For a variety of practical reasons, a shift from our current strategy to a maritime strategy would have to extend over several years. Our allies, for instance, would need time to understand the change in U.S. posture and to realize how NATO can be strengthened by it. Mutual and balanced force reductions negotiations would have to be taken into account. Attention would have to be paid to domestic political factors. And it would take time to rebuild the naval force structure that has been in such precipitate decline in the past few years. It is because of this inherent time constraint that an early, decisive start toward a new strategy is necessary.

A graduate of the U.S. Naval Academy with the Class of 1947, Admiral Turner served at sea for a year before being appointed a Rhodes Scholar. After acquiring a master's degree from Oxford University, he returned to sea in 1950, serving in destroyers in both the Atlantic and Pacific. His sea commands include the USS Conquest (MSO-488) from 1956 to 1958, the USS Rowan (DD-782) in 1962, and the USS Horne (DLG-30). After a two-year tour as Naval Aide to the Secretary of the Navy, he assumed command of a carrier task group with the Sixth Fleet in the Mediterranean. In April 1971, he was assigned as Director of the Systems Analysis Division in the Office of the CNO and, in June 1972, he became the President of the Naval War College.

The U.S. Navy: A Bicentennial Appraisal

By Admiral James L. Holloway III, U. S. Navy

The Naval Appraisal: The ritual of our bicentennial celebrations has been very properly characterized by a review of the history of our first 200 years as a nation, an appraisal of our position today in both domestic and international affairs, and a forecast of the future directions of our great republic.

It seems most suitable and timely that the U. S. Navy, which recently celebrated its 200th birthday, be included in our bicentennial appraisal.

I think there is no question that the United States needs a Navy; history has demonstrated its essentiality to our security and to the sustaining of our American way of life. The discussion, understandably, centers on the future course of the Navy—what should be its size, character, and composition—as we as a nation enter our third century as an independent democratic republic.

The Navy must be constituted in such a way to best serve the nation. That is its purpose. Naval requirements must be related to national needs. And that must be the objective of any appraisal of the U. S. Navy.

The mission of the Navy is established by law—Title X, U. S. Code—and, in its simplest terms, expresses this mission as a preparedness to conduct prompt and sustained combat operations at sea.

To carry out this mission, the Navy needs ships, aircraft, and the people to man them. But to best serve the national interest in the prosecution of this mission requires the most refined and considered judgment to determine the kinds and numbers of ships, aircraft, and people to constitute our operating fleets:

▶ We must have ships and aircraft individually capable of coping with the most advanced weapon system technology which can be expected during their tenure of service in the active forces.

▶ We must have a dedicated corps of competent professional manpower to maintain and operate the ships and aircraft to their maximum design potential.

▶ We must have enough of these capable ships, aircraft, and people to constitute a fleet which in the aggregate will provide us with the requisite level of

★★★

maritime superiority to support our most fundamental national interests, a fleet that can effectively conduct combat operations at sea across the spectrum of conflict, from crisis management to general nuclear war.

The determination of the proper force structure of the Navy depends upon three main factors: our national strategy, the principal military threats we must face in execution of that strategy, and the degree of risk we are willing to accept for the successful execution of our strategy against the projected threat.

Strategy: **The national strategy of the United States is a forward strategy, driven by the basic considerations of world geopolitics. There are two superpowers, the United States and Soviet Russia. The U.S.S.R. is entirely located within the Eurasian landmass. Her principal allies, the nations of the Warsaw Pact, are contiguous to her western border. The two most probable adversaries of the U.S.S.R. are the NATO forces in Western Europe and the People's Republic of China. Both are located on the Eurasian landmass —on the flanks of the U.S.S.R. The Soviets can defend themselves, support their allies, or strike their most threatening adversaries without ever having to cross a major body of water.**

In contrast, the United States is characterized by its insular position on the North American continent, where there are no potential enemies on our borders. Two of our states essentially lie overseas. All of our territories, and 41 of the 43 nations with whom we have treaties or security arrangements are also located overseas. It is clear that support of U. S. allies, as well as attacks against the United States, must be overseas operations. In essence, our forward strategy uses the oceans as barriers for our defense and avenues to extend our influence abroad.

The Navy carries out its mission within the broad framework of national strategy in joint coordination with the other services, and in combined planning with our allies.

Within this strategy the Navy has two primary responsibilities:
▶ To provide forward deployed forces overseas in support of our allies and our overseas national interests.
▶ To insure the security of the sea lines of communication between the United States and its overseas forces and allies.

Combat-ready forces, organized into numbered fleets with balanced capabilities across the spectrum of naval warfare, are strategically deployed to those areas of the world of critical importance to our security. These fleets:
▶ Provide visible reassurance to our allies
▶ Deter aggression on the part of potential enemies
▶ Protect the terminal ends of our essential sea lines of communication and our remote national interests
▶ Respond quickly to local crises
▶ Are positioned to initiate combat operations immediately against the U.S.S.R. and its allies in the case of general war.

Today, about 30% of the active operating forces of the U. S. Navy are maintained in a forward deployed posture. The balance of the combat-ready elements of the fleet are immediately available for overseas reinforcement in contingency situations, as well as for general war tasks. A major part of the total fleet ballistic missile submarine force is deployed to operating areas where the validity of the concept of an invulnerable strategic deterrent is being continually demonstrated.

From the mission of the Navy its two principal functions are derived:
▶ Sea control
▶ Power projection

By sea control we mean the capability to use those portions of the high seas essential to our national interests. This includes the capability to deny their use for purposes hostile to ourselves or our allies. Sea control is a prerequisite of all other naval tasks and most sustained overseas operations by the general purpose forces of the other services. An effective sea control capability provides secure areas for amphibious and carrier strike operations, enhances the survivability of the strategic deterrent, allows other deployed naval forces to operate as required, and protects commercial shipping.

Sea control is primarily accomplished by carriers, surface combatants, attack submarines, and patrol aircraft—normally operating together in integrated task forces for mutual support—with the common objective of destroying hostile air, surface, and submarine targets which constitute a threat to the survival or operations of our own forces or those of our allies.

The second function of the Navy, the projection of power from the sea—although dependent upon sea control for assuring secure areas for the operation of projection forces—represents a discrete and essential instrument of national power in terms of pure war-fighting capability and for projecting power in support of our national policy.

The first and perhaps the ultimate means of power projection is through the fleet ballistic missile (FBM) submarine force. This essentially invulnerable force—capable of assured retaliation—is the backbone of our nation's strategic deterrent capability. The flexibility of the FBM force fits well into the flexibility of our national defense planning for warfare appropriate to varying levels of hostilities. The FBM force characterizes our national will to deter nuclear aggression.

Our second means of projecting power from the sea is by tactical aircraft operating from aircraft carriers. Although the carrier's primary mission is to maintain our general superiority at sea in support of the sea control function, the principal employment of our carriers since World War II—projecting air power over land in support of national objectives—has convincingly demonstrated the effectiveness of this collateral function as a major element of national power.

The third means of power projection is the ability to put Marines ashore in an opposed operation by sea-borne assault: to seize, occupy, or control as necessary those land areas required by our strategic and tactical planning, and in support of our national interests.

Essential to amphibious operations is naval gunfire, another means of power projection. This capability today provides selective strike operations along coastal areas. However, new technology promises to extend the range and improve the accuracy and effectiveness of that capability substantially.

There are special advantages and broad options inherent in the employment of naval forces that make them uniquely valuable to the national command authorities. Naval forces have the organic capability to respond to contingencies or crisis situations worldwide with the precise type and magnitude of force necessary to achieve a given objective, from classic show of force,

through landing of troops, to strategic nuclear attack.

Freedom of the sea has long been a principle highly valued by seafaring nations, and one almost universally recognized and accepted. Because of the international character of the sea, several benefits accrue to naval forces:

▶ Naval forces may be positioned near potential trouble spots without political entanglement. Naval forces do not have to request overflight authorization or diplomatic clearances before taking a position in an area of potential crisis. By loitering in the proximity of a potential or real trouble spot, naval forces communicate a capability for action without entering the sovereign waters, air space, or territory of another country. Thus, naval forces provide decision-makers the capability of influencing events without committing forces to combat, and allow a flexibility with regard to commitment and withdrawal.

▶ Although bases on foreign soil may be desirable, they are not mandatory for most naval forces. Ships are integral units which carry their own support, and, through mobile logistics, can be maintained on forward station for long periods of time. Naval forces, therefore, are relatively insensitive to the political difficulties which can be generated by bases on foreign soil, and they do not involve the same pressures toward involvement that exist when U. S. forces are ashore in an area of crisis. If U. S. forces in an area are sea-based, they can provide military or logistics support, or protect or evacuate U. S. citizens, without becoming involved in a land war which may be contrary to both our intentions and our national interest. Additionally, sea-based forces cannot be subjected to host country employment limitations.

▶ The mobility of naval forces allows them to gain full benefit from the free use of the international seas and operate over vast areas of the ocean. In many cases, naval forces, particularly fast carrier task groups, can carry out assigned missions while remaining beyond the range of the enemy threat. Such mobility provides the naval force the initiative as to when or if land force should be engaged, thereby retaining the elements of surprise and concentration of force.

The second major advantage of naval forces is their ability to commence combat operations immediately on reaching a crisis location. They are ready on arrival. As the number of U. S. overseas bases dwindles, the ability of a military force to arrive in an area fully prepared to conduct sustained combat operations will take on added importance.

▶ Finally, naval forces are effective across the entire spectrum of warfare, from peacetime presence, through crisis management, contingency operations, limited war, major conventional war, limited nuclear war, to general nuclear conflict. Furthermore, naval forces are able to make the transition through these stages with minimum risk of escalation, due to the flexibility of forces in international waters. For example, the presence of naval forces can be carefully modulated to achieve the desired effect. If naval presence is designed to deter actions inimical to U. S. interests by projecting a stabilizing influence into a particular location in time of crisis, then by its clearly visible presence, deliberately made known, it can put a potential adversary on notice or assure an ally that the United States has both the ability and the will to influence events in the area. Under other circumstances where the presence of raw military power could be misinterpreted or serve to destabilize an ameliorating situation, naval forces can remain at the ready, but over the horizon, out of sight. At the other extreme, all major U. S. naval combatants are nuclear-capable, and should the national command authorities decide to exercise nuclear options, naval forces would play a major role. Should a nuclear war occur, sea-based nuclear systems present several advantages. They are highly mobile and carry their nuclear weapons with them with the same degree of security against seizure, and availability for use when directed by the national command authority, as those weapons on U. S. sovereign soil. They are capable of executing a wide variety of either pre-planned or *ad hoc* attack options and can conduct either limited or all-out nuclear strikes under all circumstances of war initiation. Moreover, retaliatory attacks against naval forces in open ocean areas would not result in large scale collateral damage on U. S. and allied soil.

Threat: **The principal maritime threat to the U. S. is that posed by the Soviet Union. To a lesser extent, other nations with air and naval forces possess the potential for maritime harassment. However, of all these threats, the Soviet Navy is clearly dominant. The Soviet Navy has considerable capability now and is growing both in sophistication and scope of operations.**

Only the Soviet Union possesses military forces whose quality and numerical strength can threaten the ability of the United States to carry out its national strategy worldwide. Other coastal nations with modern weapons can temporarily threaten U. S. forces acting in support of the national strategy, but they lack the numerical strength to sustain that threat when subjected to attacks of attrition by the United States.

It is difficult to make a universally acceptable comparison of the U. S. and Soviet fleets. What must be understood is that the general purpose forces of the two navies have been developed for different missions and functions, which are themselves evolving. U. S. Navy force structure emphasizes sea control and distant power projection capability in the form of aircraft carrier task forces, long-endurance surface combatants, nuclear-powered attack submarines, amphibious forces, maritime patrol aircraft, and support forces to keep the fleet supplied at sea. The Soviets' force structure is changing rapidly as the role of their navy moves from coastal defense to a worldwide instrument of Soviet power. The Soviet fleet of 20 years ago was largely built for relatively short-range coastal defense. It now includes large, long-range, offensively capable surface combatants, a developing amphibious capability, aviation-capable ships in the form of *Kiev*-class carriers, and a formidable force of long-range, nuclear-powered attack submarines.

In assessing the maritime balance, it is more important to focus on trends than raw statistics. Three points deserve emphasis. First, over the past decade, Soviet naval construction has progressed at a rate four times that of the United States. Second, the growing Soviet fleet increasingly has been making its presence felt in areas more distant from the Soviet Union. Third, the dependence of the United States and its allies on the sea lines of communication will continue to be more crucial than that of the Soviet Union and its allies. Our dependence upon these sea lines of communication is especially significant when one considers that a sea denial capability requires a much smaller investment than the sea control capability required to defend against it.

The recent Soviet *Okean* 75 exercise demonstrated advanced command, control, surveillance, anticarrier and antiballistic missile submarine operations on a worldwide basis. For the first time, we observed the Soviet Navy exercising interdiction of sea lines of communication—combined submarine, ship, and aircraft operations against convoys—and operational employment of the new and highly capable Backfire aircraft. The growing maturity of the Soviet naval threat and the confidence of the Soviet hierarchy in employing maritime power must give us pause. We face a serious threat to our free use of the seas for the first time in more than 30 years.

Risk: **We must weigh the capability of our naval force structure to carry out U. S. strategy in the face of an expanding maritime threat. Today, we retain a slim margin of superiority with respect to the Soviet threat in those scenarios involving our most vital national interests. The concern is for the future, because the trend line in U. S. Navy capability has been on a downward slope.**

Over the 30 years since 1946, we have fought in two major conflicts. On the one hand, this has resulted in a reservoir of combat experience which must be considered as a major element of the naval balance in our favor. On the other, it has meant protracted use of weapon systems and hardware which has left the material condition of the fleet at a low ebb. During the same period, the Soviet Union—not engaged in naval combat—has optimized the design of its fleet to counter our obvious strengths. The Soviets have dispersed standoff offensive weapons (air-delivered, submarine, and ship-launched missiles, primarily) over a great number of platforms. They continue to develop, improve, and deploy their attack submarines and provide them with effective antisubmarine and antiship capabilities. And they have put to sea an impressive surveillance and targeting system. The trend line of the Soviet Navy is constantly moving upward on a steady incline of total capability. At some point in time, unless those trends are altered, the lines are going to cross. Once they cross, the balance of maritime superiority will have tipped in their favor. Therefore, it is essential that we embark on a procurement program that will provide a Navy in the future which will, at least, maintain this slim margin of superiority that we have today over the Soviets.

Fleet Readiness: **The fundamental responsibility of the Chief of Naval Operations is to ensure that the Navy provides trained and ready forces to the operational commanders within the Unified Command Plan, to be employed as the National Command Authority shall direct. In meeting this responsibility, the CNO must provide not only for current fleet readiness but also must direct those programs necessary for the long-term Navy force structure.**

As the Chief of Naval Operations, I have established combat readiness of the fleet as the Navy's number one priority. The fleet must have the ability to successfully carry out the responsibilities with which it is charged in support of national security.

If the fleet is clearly ready and capable of carrying out its mission and functions in defending the United States and responding to crises in the areas of the world remote from our own national borders, then it will be perceived as such by potential adversaries, and their perceptions will serve to deter war and hostile acts which could lead to conflict. Our paramount national interest in promoting peace through a stabilizing influence will have been realized.

Fleet readiness is a product of several factors—personnel, material, operational—all of which tend to be interrelated:

▶ Personnel readiness depends upon having enough manpower with the necessary skills, training, and experience to properly operate and maintain the ships, aircraft, and weapon systems in the fleet.

▶ Material readiness refers to the designed capabilities, and the operating condition of the ship, aircraft, and weapon systems in the fleet. Personnel readiness contributes directly to material readiness in its influence on maintaining the material in good operating condition.

▶ Operational readiness describes the proficiency of fleet units in performing their warfare tasks in a realistic mission environment.

To meet the expanding threat, the U. S. Navy has continued to improve the capabilities of the current forces. Carrier aircraft, which constitute the primary offensive punch of the fleet, are being equipped with standoff air-to-surface weapons: Harpoon, Condor, and Walleye. These weapons will significantly enhance the kill probabilities and survivability of our aircraft against the expected threats.

At the same time our surface ships and submarines, now faced with a potential and expanding enemy surface fleet to fight, will have their long-range offensive capability improved by the installation of weapons such as Harpoon and the sea-launched cruise missile which has recently been named "Tomahawk."

Predicting the outcome of conflict between our two fleets involves enormous uncertainties on both sides. We examine and reexamine these variables and their importance in a number of scenarios in arriving at force structure capabilities. In the last analysis, it is the balance of capabilities we achieve and the innate flexibility of naval forces that weigh most heavily in any assessment.

In the broadest sense, for the immediate future, I believe that the U. S. Navy will be able to carry out its mission and functions within the national military strategy. Our Polaris and Poseidon forces will continue to provide a credible deterrent to nuclear war.

The Navy of the Future: **It is clear that the most powerful influence on the Navy's ability to carry out its mission against the threat is the size and composition of the fleet; yet we have no positive influence on today's force levels. The numbers and kinds of ships and aircraft in the fleet today were established by the Congress over the past three decades or more. In the same sense, the ships and aircraft which we would propose to acquire this year would contribute only to future capabilities. They would become operational in the fleet three to seven years hence and remain in the active inventory over the next 20–30 years.**

Required Characteristics: **We cannot limit ourselves to the acquisition of weapon systems designed to satisfy narrow requirements of a single theater or a current political pressure. Naval**

weapon systems—ships and aircraft—must have a worldwide effectiveness across the range of possible geographic, political, and technological applications envisioned in the next two or three decades.

Considerations of strategy, mission, and threat determine the required characteristics of our deployed naval forces. To operate globally, against the most advanced weapons technology, without logistic dependence upon a forward base system, the operating forces of the U. S. Navy must embody the following military characteristics:

▶ Offensively powerful enough to defeat any potential maritime force routinely deployed in the area of responsibility.

▶ Defensively strong enough to defend against attacks from aircraft and missiles.

▶ Capable of projecting power, or operating in support of other U. S. forces or those of our allies.

▶ Logistically able to operate worldwide on the high seas without absolute dependence on forward land bases, utilizing an underway replenishment capability in our combatant ships, and a military force of ships able to resupply combat consumables in a combat theater of operations.

▶ Capable of being controlled by a command organization and communication system which provides swift, accurate, and secure collection and transfer of information upon which commanders may make recommendations to the National Command Authority, coordinate with allies and other commanders, and make decisions to effectively direct their own forces.

Ship Construction Programs: In planning for the future, a stable long-term shipbuilding and aircraft procurement program is the key to achieving the necessary capabilities to maintain our margin of superiority. Most importantly, this plan must be affordable within the defense budget guidelines.

The Navy's five-year shipbuilding program provides a sound basis for planning, demonstrates to the Congress our intentions for building the Navy of the future, and sets targets for the shipbuilding industry. It is derived from a logical, analytical, and disciplined process of force structure development.

As pointed out initially, fleet force structure requirements are determined by three factors: the national military strategy, the potential threat, and the degree of risk.

It should be reemphasized that the Navy carries out its mission within the framework of the national strategy. U. S. naval force requirements cannot be regarded in isolation from our foreign policy, domestic

considerations, and the force requirements and capabilities of the U. S. Army and Air Force.

The methodology of applying these factors in the determination of force structure requirements involves the application of solid analytical procedures.

Today's forces are limited to what we have in the active fleet inventory and the ready reserve. There are no significant ships in mothballs which could be used to quickly increase our active fleet force levels.

The starting point for future fleets resides in today's assets. Our fleet, on the average, is only about 15 years old. These ships, in general, have a nominal useful life expectancy of about 20-30 years, depending primarily on the type of ship. We cannot retire capable units with useful life remaining, simply to replace them with more modern versions. Therefore, the planning starts with the current inventory.

This force structure is projected five to ten years into the future by dropping ships as they attain the limit of their useful life and adding those ships which have been authorized and funded by the Congress. Also added are those ships included in the approved five-year ship construction program.

Because it takes about five years after authorization, on the average, for a ship to enter operational service in the fleet, and because we are already working with a five-year shipbuilding program, it is therefore more convenient and most significant to base our planning on a force structure ten years from now.

In a similar manner, based upon agreed intelligence estimates, the main naval and maritime air forces of the Soviets are projected to a force structure ten years into the future. Then, the U. S. naval capabilities against the Soviet forces are analyzed in various scenarios generated by our strategy. A number of iterations of these analyses are conducted to include the participation of allied forces at different levels and to incorporate variables in possible enemy strategies as well.

From these analyses, we determine the deficiencies in our projected force structure. We then add components to our force structure to reduce or eliminate these deficiencies. These additions, accomplished incrementally, will establish a range of force structures which will, as they increase, represent increasing levels of assurance that we can defeat the enemy, taking into consideration the significant uncertainties inherent in our ability to forecast future Soviet force levels and predict their strategies and actions. It is these uncertainties in battle outcomes, due to the unknowns in future Soviet intentions and capabilities, which result in a range of future force requirements which are described as risk. These uncertainties, likewise, prevent us from determining a fixed number for our future force level which can be fully agreed upon by all responsible authorities. Working as we are, ten years into the future, faced with the uncertainties of world politics, emerging weapon technologies, and difficult-to-define Soviet capabilities and intentions, these future requirements cannot be exact nor inflexible, but must be continuously monitored and periodically updated as required.

In spite of the inexactitude of the analytical results, we can, through the application of sound judgment, determine force level goals for the future which will conform to national policy decisions on strategy and the affordability as well as the acceptability of various levels of risk.

From this force structure goal ten years hence, we then work backwards to develop a multi-year shipbuilding plan. This plan will provide us the new ships that will be requested by annual authorizations. These ships, when added to current forces, minus the ship retirements, will provide us with the desired force structure.

The foregoing approach will provide a range of force structures which will be related to varying degrees of risk.

The minimal force structure would be that of today's fleet which numbers 477 ships, a marked decrease from the 976 ships in the active inventory in 1968. Although numbers are not a complete proxy of naval capability—which is the product of numbers of ships and unit capability—the decline in force levels indicates that the trend in U. S. naval capability is downward. This downward trend is the result of several factors which include the retirement of large blocks of World War II ship construction as they reach the end of their useful service life, the application of resources to combat operations in lieu of modernizing by new construction during the Vietnam War, and a decision to retire older ships as they approach obsolescence in order to free funds for new construction.

The shipbuilding program presented to the Congress with the fiscal year 1977 budget is the product of such analyses, including the fiscal constraints. It is a shipbuilding program designed to arrest the downward trend in our naval capabilities.

The five-year totals are most significant. There will be an increase in the annual start of production of ships from 16 to 31 for a total of 111 over the five-year period 1977-1981. During the past ten years, we have averaged about 15 new ships per year. It is a balanced shipbuilding program, with balance among types of ships—carriers, surface combatants, submarines, amphibious ships, and support ships—and balance between those very capable multi-purpose but, relatively expensive ships (such as carriers and cruisers), and the useful single-purpose and less expensive ships which are affordable in greater numbers (such as the frigates).

However, the results of a shipbuilding program cannot be seen until five to ten years into the future. Simply to maintain the size of today's fleet of 477 ships, the long-range program must provide about 18 ships per year to replace those which will drop from the active inventory at the end of their normal service life.

Conclusion: In summary, an appraisal of this nation's maritime posture at the turn of the second century of our existence, must take into consideration our current naval forces and capabilities, our national interests and objectives, our military strategy, the contributions of the other services and our allies, the inherent advantages of naval forces, the military capabilities of the Soviet Union, and the competing priorities of other U. S. foreign and domestic programs for critical resources.

From this appraisal we can conclude that the trend of U. S. naval capability has been on the decline and in comparison, as well as in absolute terms, the Soviet naval capability has been characterized by steady and significant growth. The United States still retains a slim margin of maritime superiority, mainly in those areas of most vital national concern.

From these conclusions, we can infer that unless the decline in U. S. naval capability is arrested and indeed reversed, the balance of maritime power will tip in the Soviets' favor as their capabilities increase.

It is in the face of a clear challenge to our maritime supremacy that our country and its Navy enter the third century of their history.

All too frequently considerations of the use of naval power as an instrument of foreign policy dwell on its positive results without adequate consideration of its costs. A fundamental step in sound military planning is determination of acceptability—what is the objective worth to me and what is its projected cost in political, materiel, and personnel terms? Ken Booth discusses some of the political costs involved in the peacetime use of naval power. These costs and problems can be ignored only at our peril. His conclusions in regard to the Soviet Navy are rather startling.

FOREIGN POLICIES AT RISK:

SOME PROBLEMS OF MANAGING NAVAL POWER

by

Professor Ken Booth

To know the pain of power, we must go to those who have it; to know its pleasures, we must go to those who are seeking it; the pains of power are real, its pleasures imaginary.

Charles C. Colton
Lacon (1823)

The aim of this essay is to show that naval power can be an unfortunate influence on foreign policy as well as a useful instrument; that naval power can contribute to the distortion of foreign policy, as well as to its support; that it can be the vehicle for irrational as well as rational behavior; and that it can bite the hand that feeds it, as well as snarling at adversaries. The essay is an attempt to present the other side of the coin to the neo-Clausewitzian emphasis on clinical instrumentality, in which armed forces are conceived in terms of the clear-cut missions which they perform in the pursuit of political goals.

The picture to be presented is entirely and deliberately one-sided, but it is an approach which has several values: (1) By aggregating certain types of naval behavior, it might help to clarify some of the inherent problems of using navies as instruments of policy in distant regions. (2) In so doing it may contribute to the debate about the utility of navies. This debate often polarizes the relatively straightforward concepts of *naval missions* as against the *oppor-*

tunity *costs* of maintaining expensive warships. In this polarization, political costs, which are often indirect, uncertain, and fuzzy, tend to be ignored. (3) By articulating some of the major problems of managing naval power, it should help those involved to think in advance of how to avoid the possible pitfalls. Forewarned is forearmed.

This essay, therefore, is the ugly sister of that numerous and optimistic breed entitled "The missions of superpower navies." However, the conclusion which the reader should draw is not that warships are not and cannot be useful instruments of policy.[1] Rather, it is to remember that since "the pains of power are real," it is well that we are conscious of them.

The Developing International Context. Concern with the problems of managing naval power reflect the feelings of an age in which there is not as much optimism as even 20 years ago, but in which there is much more worldly wise experience. There has been an important change in some Western attitudes toward the use and maintenance of armed forces in the modern world. We are not just concerned with the benefits which power brings: we are equally concerned with the problems which the possession of that power entails. We are not just concerned with the advantages accruing from the attribution of prestige: we are equally concerned with the pitfalls of being thought prestigious. We are concerned not just with the impulse to win friends and

influence people: we are equally concerned with the obligations and problems which follow from such entanglements. We are not just concerned with the problems of weakness and failure: we are also concerned with the problems of power and success.

Such concerns are appropriate in the changing international context. However one chooses to describe the late 1970's and 1980's, the late 1930's is not an appropriate analogy. The Western World is not facing a massive military threat on the Hitlerian model, ready to strike out and conquer territory through deliberate military aggression. As long as Soviet leaders remain prudent, nuclear deterrence takes care of such a possibility. What causes most worry today is not another 1939, but another 1956 or 1965 or 1973. Suez, Vietnam, and the October war are our most relevant memories. The most immediate problem is not an imminent *blitzkrieg* across Europe, but concern about intervening against our interests, becoming sucked into local international and civil wars, or of being drawn into dangerous confrontations with the Soviet Union as a result of "competitive meddling."[2] These are all genuine concerns, for if one thing is certain as we contemplate the world for the foreseeable future, it is that there will be an abundance of economic, political, social, and military problems in the countries bordering the west Pacific, the Indian Ocean, the South Atlantic, and the Mediterranean. There will be a surfeit of opportunities for being drawn into disputes and for competitive meddling, especially now that both superpowers have significant amounts of naval power deployed in distant waters.

In a world of fierce nationalism, power diffusion, and frequent ungovernability, those interested in navies must ask themselves not only how might warships contribute to the success of foreign policy, but also how might they contribute to its failure. How might warships divert, spoil, undermine, or channel a government's policy in a particular region? What foreign policy risks are entailed by the very possession or use of warships in distant waters?

The Provoking of Third Parties. An immediate problem concerns the question of threat assessment from the perspective of third parties. It is an old and familiar problem. What country A does out of prudence or self-defense might provoke countries B, C et cetera, into hostility and suspicion. In this respect it must be remembered that many countries have a very much more traditional view of the usability of military force than is supposed by some Western commentators. If so-called "gunboat diplomacy" is not as likely as in the age of imperialism, some states still have to worry about the threat of force from the sea, perhaps used in support of hostile neighbors or internal opponents. In this respect one might cite the provocation felt by India at U.S. naval activity in the Indian Ocean in recent years. This activity caused a negative input into Indian (and other) thinking about the United States. This created problems for U.S. diplomats (at the end of 1974, for example) when they were attempting to build up their country's diplomatic capital with the Indian Government. It must be remembered that one naval power's so-called "blue water" is another country's maritime backyard. Superpowers must not be surprised if local countries are overly sensitive about what happens there. The yearnings (if not the capabilities) for local Monroe Doctrines are not the prerogatives of the militarily mighty.

A naval power might argue that third parties should not feel provoked if they are not actually targeted. This is not how it will look, however, from the perspective of worst-case forecasting by

the planners of the country concerned. This is true not only of their attitude to naval presences, but also of their attitude to so-called goodwill visits by naval units of powerful states.[3] Newly independent countries often have ambivalent attitudes toward such manifestations of naval reach. One man's goodwill visit may well be another man's gunboat diplomacy.

The Provoking of Adversaries. Unless a rising naval power manages its growing strength and/or expanding activities with great subtlety and tact, it may well provoke its adversaries into counteravailing efforts. This may produce unacceptable tensions or, in the long run, no net strategic advantage but greater costs. The loudly publicized entry of very limited Soviet naval forces into the Indian Ocean has had the effect of spurring U.S. naval efforts in that region.

The Costs of Meeting Challenges. Naval considerations can have foreign policy implications in various ways. If, for example, a country is faced with a naval challenge which it cannot counter with the forces presently at its disposal, it has a range of alternatives: it has either to engage in a naval arms race, seek allies, appease the putative enemy, or otherwise try to manipulate relations with it. Each of these alternatives entail political or other costs and risks. The problems faced by British foreign policy because of the overstretch of the country's naval commitments in the first 70 years of the 20th century are the most prolonged illustration of the painful adjustments necessary when a country's power and responsibilities are not in accord.

In addition to diverting foreign policy to meet naval challenges, naval considerations might direct foreign policy in certain directions because of what might be called the *strategic scarcity*[4] of certain geographical locations. The importance of Gibraltar, Iceland, Malta, the Turkish Straits, the passages through the Indonesian archipelago, the eastern horn of Africa, in addition to many others, are evident for certain maritime countries. Superpower naval requirements with respect to these areas will affect their foreign policies in various ways. At the minimum they will

generate the need for interest and attention and the desire for a degree of influence. There will inevitably be an attempt to keep these areas out of hostile control. Just as economic scarcity constrains and determines economic policy, so the strategic scarcity of some locations can constrain and determine foreign policy.

Some Political Costs of Naval Bases. The operational advantages which result from the use of overseas bases for navies which operate at a great distance from their homelands are self-evident. For present purposes, our concern is with possible political disadvantages. There are five main problems:

1. *Uncertainty.* If a country's naval operations in a particular area depend to an important extent upon the use of forward bases,[5] this means that the government concerned will have to rest at least its medium-term naval strategy in that region upon the goodwill or sufferance of the government of the country with the facilities. Sometimes, this will present few difficulties, because of mutual confidence. This is the case with the United States and Britain. But such a relationship is the exception rather than the rule. More typical are the problems faced by the United States over its military bases in Iceland and Turkey, countries with whom the United States has been an ally for a generation. The instabilities are considerable: in an era of sensitive nationalism and frequent domestic instability, the enjoyment of military advantages in foreign countries cannot be taken for granted. Bilateral relationships can change with great rapidity. In this respect it is interesting that despite its much smaller involvement in global politics, the Soviet Union has suffered relatively more repudiation than the United States. Over the last 15 years it has been repudiated by Guinea, Ghana, Indonesia, the Sudan, and Egypt—relatively small Third World countries on which it had lavished some hopes and attention. This uncertainty undermines confidence about the long-term enjoyment of facilities, and it goes without saying that governments prefer to avoid instabilities in their programs.

2. *Dependence.* Although confidence about bases has decreased, they

still exist. Once they exist, the naval power becomes dependent to some extent upon the good favors of the host government. This dependence will make the naval power vulnerable to some extent to the host government. The latter will be able to hedge the use of the base with restrictions, as with the Egyptian restrictions on the Soviet use of its ports. It will have the power to threaten its free use in crises, just when the base may be most needed. A degree of dependence opens up the naval power to the possibility of political manipulation by the host country.

3. *Provocation.* In a postimperialist, postcolonialist world, bases (or rumors of bases) are almost certain to be a provocation to local nationalists and local political opposition. They are always a boon to adversary propaganda.

4. *Inertia.* Naval bases have always tended to have a multiplier effect. Once immediate operational requirements have been met, there has been a tendency for needs to expand. Mohamed Heikal has described how Soviet naval requirements in Egypt grew after the June war, such that President Nasser lost his temper with President Podgorny, declaring: "This is just imperialism." Admiral Gorshkov fared no better when he visited Egypt in 1970.[6] The expansion of Soviet naval "needs" in Egypt resulted in important damage being done to Soviet-Egyptian political relations.

Once the use of a base becomes well-established, inertia tends to result in inflated attitudes concerning its importance, especially if there are no ready alternatives. The multiplier effect spawns ideas about "vital interests." This happened with the High Tory School of British naval thinking with regard to Simonstown, South Africa. Rightly or wrongly, their desire for good relations with a country which offered a secure naval base and other facilities was thought more important than the possible policy repercussions of closely associating with a country whose domestic policies were regarded as outrageous by most of the Commonwealth. With naval bases, as with many useful things in life, it is often difficult to imagine how one will manage without them: that is, until one has to, and does.

5. *Domestic political costs.* As the attitude of some people in Britain showed over the Simonstown issue, there are sometimes domestic political costs attached to the use of bases. This has also been the case in the United States over Diego Garcia. The Diego Garcia affair shows that even if those responsible try to remove possible opposition by quietly removing the resident population, one does not necessarily free oneself of political costs in a democracy, because of the political capital to be made by journalists and political opponents at home.

Despite the various costs which might accrue from foreign bases, naval powers will find them useful. This is still true for the U.S. Navy, despite its impressive afloat support capabilities. The need for shore support is even greater for the Soviet Navy, despite its long-established propaganda stance against such manifestations of "imperialism" and foreign domination. The Soviet Union has taken the political risks rather than provide alternatives: greater numbers of ships, more skilled manpower for self-maintenance, or sufficient quantities of afloat support. The need to make the Soviet domestic economy work to a minimally satisfactory level gives them little choice but to base naval planning on the risky expedient of the use of foreign ports.

The Costs for Third World Countries. Almost more than anything, Third World countries want independence. Freed from colonialism within living memory, they want to avoid falling under the domination of other external powers. For this reason the provision of naval bases involves costs for small countries as well as the naval power. There is the risk of falling into client status. There are various opportunity costs: perhaps "tilting" to one side will mean that economic or other advantages from different sources are foregone. There is the risk to prestige. If a Third World country offers base rights to a superpower navy (or even if they are only rumored) some neighbors will scream. In the middle of 1975 the Egyptians were provoked by rumors that Libya had offered base rights to the Soviet Union, and Saudi Arabia has objected strongly to Soviet naval activity in the Somali Republic and the Republic of Yemen. Third World sensitivity on this matter sets limits to the possible penetration of the naval power.

Who Manipulates Whom? Influence is almost always a two-way process. We often have a fixed mental image of one-way influence being exercised by the physically strong over the physically weak. This bears little relationship with the facts. Parents understand that with children there is no direct relationship between physical strength and real influence. Between a superpower and a smaller country it is hardly ever clear *who* is manipulating *whom*. This is all the more so in a world where the militarily strong do not feel free to deal with the militarily weak by carrying and wielding a big stick.

Naval bases may be the opportunity for the small to manipulate the mighty. Because a country with the use of a foreign base desires stable evaluations for planning purposes, it automatically has a stake in the preservation of a government which seems favorably disposed toward it. In a world where friends are in short supply, one must nourish those one has. It would be a particularly naive host government which did not recognize the potential leverage which this partial superpower dependence gave it. The maneuverings of Nasser's Egypt, Mintoff's Malta, and Hallgrimsson's Iceland are instructive in this respect. Often, the dependency will not be upon a particular government as much as upon a particular individual. Magnified by an ignorance of local politics and uncertainty about future changes, a naval power might come to feel that its privileges in a particular country depended almost entirely on a single local leader. At its simplest it is the old idea of "better the devil you know..." In the second half of the 1960's the Soviet leaders found themselves in this position with respect to President Nasser. Like almost everybody else, Soviet observers could not easily imagine Egypt without Nasser. By cultivating him, they then opened themselves up to his influence. While the Soviet position in Egypt seemed to depend upon Nasser, his position did not depend upon the Soviet Union. Indeed, too overt an identification between a local leader and an external power can provoke internal opposition. It is now well known that the Egyptian Armed Forces had no affinity with the "Ugly Russian." In Third World countries, leaders do not win laurels for being thought the puppet of any foreign power.

If the local country is successful in its manipulation, it may result in the naval power having to pay more in economic and political costs than it originally expected. History is full of examples of how small commitments can insidiously expand into large entanglements. Americans do not need reminding of this. Soviet leaders have been luckier, and perhaps more prudent, in limiting their commitments.

On the whole, the Soviet Union has done badly in her relationships with small countries far from its borderlands. The picture of one-way Soviet influence into the Third World is misleading. The Soviets have given help and encouragement (and the importance of this is not to be underestimated), but they have not been able to make Third World countries into puppets. There are many constraints on Soviet influence-building efforts, from nationalism in general to Arab distrust of a godless civilization. Outside the Warsaw Pact (itself not the monolith our cold war mind-sets still project) there are no Soviet "clients," whose foreign and domestic policies are pulled by strings from the Kremlin. The forward deployment of the Soviet Navy has certainly not helped to produce Soviet clients. However, by making Soviet foreign policy vulnerable to the manipulation of some small countries on which it depends for bases, it has opened up Soviet foreign policy to more influences and more complications than ever before.

Local Conflicts. When a naval power identifies its policy with a particular country, this can result in its becoming involved in local problems. If the country with which the naval power is identified is involved in squabbles with its neighbors, then the naval power's relations with these neighbors will be adversely affected, and so its regional influence-building efforts will be limited. The Soviet experience is instructive in this respect. The Soviet involvement in the Somali Republic,

largely because of naval factors, increased the distrust of Saudi Arabia, Kenya, and the Sudan. By supporting Iraq, the Soviet Union increased the suspicion of Iran. By its moves toward Libya, it increased Egyptian wariness. The more a naval power becomes involved in a local area, its problems and responsibilities grow. In the summer of 1973 Soviet warships transported Moroccan troops to Syria. This has rightly been put forward as one of the ways in which the Soviet Navy has been used to support foreign policy: in this case it was a means of giving concrete encouragement to Arab unity in its fight against "Zionism." Whatever diplomatic capital was gained by the Soviet Union with the Moroccans was surely shattered at the beginning of 1976 because of Soviet support of Algeria, a country with whom Morocco is in contention over the Spanish Sahara. When the Moroccan Navy apprehended a Soviet Merchant ship with an arms shipment for Algeria, the goodwill created by the Soviet naval instrument must have been erased.

Identification with a particular country can cause problems in other ways, as has been illustrated by British-South African relations. Not only did the maintenance of a military and naval relationship tend to exacerbate British relations with the black Commonwealth, but even the residual relationship of the mid-1970's gave the South African Government the opportunity to manipulate British naval visits as gestures of solidarity. A good example of this occurred in October 1974, much to the embarrassment of the British Labor Government.

Forward deployment might result in naval powers being dragged into local conflicts in a serious way. Before moving to forward deployment, it would be relatively easy for a naval power to avoid direct involvement in a local conflict. With no capability for intervention, no intervention is expected. Propaganda capital could be made at little cost: words are usually (though not always) cheap. The situation changes with impressive naval units over the horizon. The pressures for intervention will be greater: because of the temptations of gain, because the possession of an instrument tends to shape

the will to use it, because of the possible entreaties of local associates, because of the desire to protect established positions, and because of a conviction that prestige demands some concrete action. Once a degree of military access is possible, expectations change. In some circumstances the pressures might prove irresistible. Forward deployment increases the likelihood of involvement and the risks of escalation in local disputes.

How might a superpower be drawn into a local conflict, perhaps against its interests or wishes? This question can be answered in several ways. One approach is to draw up scenarios. A pro-Soviet regime facing internal threat might call upon immediate Soviet assistance; this could lead to increasing involvement in a civil war. Another possibility is suggested by the situation in southern Africa. One might envisage South Africa fighting for its life in the last laager against both a guerrilla and conventional attack from the north, heavily supported by Soviet equipment and delivered in Soviet ships. In hard-pressed circumstances, the South Africans might ignore the sanctuary accorded to shipping in several limited wars since 1945; they might try to destroy the Soviet military aid at sea rather than wait until it is in the hands of enemy troops a month or so later. Such sinkings might not only be more "efficient" militarily, but might also be calculated to be a catalytic action, to draw in Western Powers in direct support. A second way of speculating about future risks is to consider recent "might-have-beens." How would the U.S. Government have reacted if the June war had broken out just a few days earlier and had trapped the U.S. carrier sailing through the Suez Canal? How would Britain, the United States, or Israel have reacted had the *Queen Elizabeth II* been sunk with heavy loss of life as a result of President Ghadaffi's orders in April 1973? How would the Soviet Union have reacted had anti-MPLA forces sunk Soviet ships transporting supplies to Angola? A third approach is the least precise but most telling. This approach tells us not to be complacent and to remind ourselves that almost all crises in history have been surprises to those most centrally involved. That we do not know how something might come about does not mean that it will not happen. Anything can happen in international politics, and usually does. History is full of "unthinkables." It is worth recalling in this context that Lord Carrington, then British Minister of Defense, admitted in 1971 that an analysis of 45 engagements of British forces between 1945-1959 revealed that on no single occasion had the engagement been foreseen. There is little reason to suppose that the British are worse at prediction than anyone else. Military history was surely the inspiration for Murphy's Law: "If anything can go wrong, it will: and when you least want it to."

One particular catalyst to involvement in local troubles might be the initiative of local commanders, either one's own or those of a local power. There have been some suggestions that the *Pueblo* and *Mayaguez* captures were the result of the initiatives of relatively junior officers. A naval power cannot control how the locals behave. It should be able to control its own commanders, but this is not always the case, and this is a danger to consider. What if there had been a precipitate response by 6th Fleet commanders to the sinking of the *Liberty*? On this occasion Navy commanders had a better appreciation of the situation than the Pentagon, but the U.S. Navy has not always been an obedient instrument of a political will. In the Cuban missile crisis, which is passed down as a legendary example of crisis control, there were at least two examples of the U.S. Navy failing to act in concert with Presidential wishes.

The Problem of Local Expectations. Many of the problems for a naval power arise because of the changing expectations of local powers. If a naval power does not have the capability or will to live up to these expectations, then disappointment will be the least of the consequences. By visiting ports in west and east Africa at various times, including some sensitive times, Soviet warships have been used to try to increase Soviet influence with particular governments. It would not be surprising if the leaders of these countries had a rather higher expectation of Soviet sympathy and willingness to help than any Soviet leadership would allow. This

could cause strain if the local leader called for serious help.

Even if help is given it might not be appreciated, and it goes without saying that the local power will not necessarily offer any concrete rewards for help given. This was the case in Soviet-Egyptian relations in the late 1960's. Some Egyptian opinion did not appreciate the significance of Soviet gestures of support such as the deployment of warships in Egyptian ports vulnerable to attack.[7] From its point of view, the Soviet Union received little thanks for acting as Egypt's supporter and arsenal.

Changing Naval Balances and Changing Intentions. If a naval balance changes, either favorably or unfavorably, then this will result in changed naval evaluations and expectations. These might ultimately result in changed foreign policy intentions. If the changed balance is to one's advantage, the outcome might be an encouragement to a more ambitious or opportunistic foreign policy, the result of more confidence or the arrogance of power. On the other hand, a relative decline in naval power might result in decreased estimations of what might be achieved. There might be less self-confidence in using what one has. Over the last few years this has been the cause of a worry on the part of many of the allies of the United States: they fear that some in the United States have thought themselves and talked themselves into passivity as far as using their naval instrument is concerned, just because the Soviet Navy has broken the former U.S. position of comfortable monopoly. While it is clear that in most circumstances the Soviet Navy cannot stop the U.S. Navy from carrying out its missions without shooting at it, an attitude of self-denial has been generated. And if Americans say that they are inhibited by Soviet naval presences, third parties will listen and presumably adjust their behavior in respect to both parties. If Americans do not have confidence in their power, what right have third parties to disagree?

While friends of the United States worry about its post-Vietnam uncertainties, a longer term question concerns the Soviet Union. Will its changing naval capabilities affect its foreign policy in-

tentions? How will forward naval deployment affect Soviet foreign policy in the long term? Will they use their navy to take advantage of opportunities that arise around the world? The answer so far is affirmative, but so far the naval support of foreign policy has been very restricted in scope, limited in impact, and cautious in implementation.[8] Whether or not they use them, forward deployed warships give Soviet decision-makers new options. And even if the forward deployment was originally a response to U.S. naval activity, it cannot be taken for granted that Soviet decisionmakers will abjure their use for other purposes. Although there is little or nothing to suggest that the Soviet Union planned to create an overseas intervention force on traditional Anglo-American lines, they could cobble something together for a small intervention. When governments look back, they are almost always surprised at the way things turn out.

Perpetuating Old Habits. Warships can create new intentions, but they can also perpetuate old habits. It is sometimes said that the maintenance of Britain's role east of Suez in the 1960's was more useful for the future of the Royal Navy than was the role of the Royal Navy for the future of British policy east of Suez. British decision-makers were inclined to think that Britain had a military role to perform east of Suez because British ships were there. British ships were there because they had always been there. The existence of warships can adversely affect foreign policy by encouraging policy-makers to put the cart before the horse.

Have Gunship Will Travel. In all aspects of life, instruments can shape the will to use them. It is one of the reasons why British policemen are not armed. The idea that weapons shape the will to use them has long been one of the themes of the proponents of disarmament. It is the belief that policies will become unduly militarized if military capabilities are readily available.

Some Americans have always feared that the possession of particular instruments might shape their own will. This was the case with Woodrow Wilson before the First World War and was the case with the cancellation of the proposed Fast Deployment Logistic Ships over half a century later. The idea was classically expressed by Senator Richard Russell: "If Americans have the capability to go anywhere and do anything, we will always be going somewhere and doing something." A recent example of the possession of local naval power shaping the will to use it was the U.S. response to the seizure of the *Pueblo.* The task force which assembled in the Sea of Japan seemed an appropriate response to the seizure of a ship. But the show of force was not a credible threat. Furthermore, it distracted attention from subtler and possibly more efficacious approaches. Whether or not alternative approaches would have secured a more favorable result, at least it would have avoided the unfortunate image of the U.S. Navy as a "paper tiger," snorting around the Sea of Japan with an abundance of politically unusable naval power.

One bizarre example of the instrument shaping the will occurred in April 1973, when President Ghadaffi ordered an Egyptian submarine to sink the *QE II,* in the aftermath of the shooting down by Israel of a Libyan airliner, with heavy loss of life.[9] The episode is an important reminder of the role of personalities in politics; that the scope for "unreasonable behavior" is greater than political science "analysts" often give credit; and that mature naval officers and effective command-and-control arrangements (the Egyptian submarine commander reported to his own authorities before taking any action) are vital. The possession of even a small amount of naval power can shape some wills.[10] We wait to see whether and how far Soviet decisionmakers may have their wills shaped by their modern and rakish-looking warships.

Warships as Catalysts. In sensitive situations warships can be vehicles of risk as well as instruments of opportunity. They can provoke or attract trouble, and major incidents involving ships (and especially warships) are always dramatic. Attacks on ships (real or imaginary) have played a part in the outbreak of all but one of the major

wars in which the United States has been involved in the last 80 years. These incidents were occasions rather than basic causes of war, but they are not to be overlooked because of that.

In the present Soviet-United States naval confrontation, especially in relatively restricted areas such as the Mediterranean, some have feared the possibility that close interaction in a crisis might be the spark which will kindle serious conflict. In a tense crisis, might not one side misperceive the tactical behavior of the other? Might there be a temptation to take preemptive action rather than be sunk first? Close interaction puts a premium on speedy (perhaps hasty) decisions: sink or be sunk.

The Pitfalls of Prestige. Naval prestige, like sex appeal, is a great advantage for those wanting to operate in the world of affairs. But both can lead toward serious pitfalls. Both can be "corrupted."

Navies can be used to support a policy of bluff. The situation does not have to be as dramatic as the sinking of the *Prince of Wales* and the *Repulse* in 1941. One might expect Soviet naval prestige to fall in "anti-imperialist" circles if it never actually stops the United States or its allies from carrying out their "imperialist" business. The possession of naval prestige might be costly if it produces complacency. One manifestation of this might be a "negative policy of prestige," resulting in a lack of concern about what others think. The United States discovered the possible consequences of this at Pearl Harbor. The greatest naval power in the world was not sufficiently credible to deter attack by a smaller one. Credibility is not synonymous with strength. It is not enough to be strong: it is also necessary to let allies, third parties, and adversaries be aware of that strength. Oversensitivity about prestige, on the other hand, can result in a naval power being dragged into disputes against its interests. One might be tempted to escalate trouble because of a feeling that one's prestige is always on test, and that one must prove oneself. Feeling "chesty" might produce an arrogance which leads a power to have expectations beyond its capabilities. Demands might arise because of the stimulated

expectations of local associates. Problems will occur if the latter have expectations which the naval power has neither the capability nor will of fulfilling.

Prestige can lead to pitfalls if it is possessed: it can lead to pitfalls if it is not taken care of. While overemphasis on prestige can encourage the arrogance of power, a neglect of the prestige factor in naval policy might encourage the ambitions of adversaries and might contribute to a lack of self-confidence. One can become victim of one's own negative prestige: this might inhibit a naval power from effectively using its real capabilities. Some observers have criticized what they see as a mistaken policy of negative prestige on the part of the United States in recent years. One consequence of this has been that third-party perceptions of the naval "balance" give a picture which objectively is too flattering to the Soviet Navy. It also gives a picture of Soviet success and influence-potential which the strained decisionmakers in the Kremlin would find impossible to recognize.

Gorshkov Plus 30. This essay has shown some of the problems involved in managing naval power in distant regions. It has suggested that the Soviet Navy in forward deployment (unless accompanied by great good luck and used with much care) is a risky new feature on the international scene not only for Western and Third World countries, but also for the Soviet Union itself. The Soviet Navy creates options, but it also risks provoking the United States into naval expansion; it risks provoking the suspicions of local powers; it opens up the Soviet Union to manipulation by small powers and to propaganda attacks by adversaries about its "gunboat diplomacy"; it risks being dragged into local squabbles and thus alienating many countries; it risks being sucked into conflicts and having policy shaped in undesired ways; it risks the raising of expectations which cannot be fulfilled without the Soviet Union facing dangers and taking on obligations beyond its norm. These outcomes are all possible. It should not be assumed that the Soviet Navy in forward deployment will always be used cautiously and in very limited

66

ways and will always be attended with success. These risks facing Soviet policy give us ground for speculating about a future Soviet Navy which will be rather different from the one most frequently envisaged in the West.

In a generation's time the Soviet Navy might be like it is today, only slightly more so. Because of economic constraints (and nobody foresees these getting easier for the Soviet leaders), it is not likely to be greatly different in size. But there is an alternative future. This is the possibility that the Soviet Navy will have retreated (except for SSBN's and some residual patrols) to its more traditional continental orientation. This might come about as a result of a combination of developments: (1) The present Soviet Navy will have provoked the U.S. Navy into qualitative and quantitative supremacy in decisive areas. (2) Soviet naval diplomacy over a 20-year period will not have proved a cost-effective instrument of policy: it will have drawn the country into some scrapes with Third World countries, alienated others, and brought about dangerous confrontations with the West; it will have raised some local expectations which could not be fulfilled; it will have been exposed as a paper tiger in revolutionary circles, by looking impressive but not actually being used; and it will have contributed to the development of an "Ugly Russian" image in many parts, magnified by Western, Chinese, and local propaganda.

These developments might not much matter for the Soviet leaders but for one other possibility, namely that they will have decided to drop out of the anti-SSBN mission as a result of *Trident* and whatever comes after it. Despite their traditional emphasis on a damage limitation philosophy, the Soviet leaders are willing to recognize insuperable economic and technological constraints. They called it a day with the ABM, and the same is likely with the anti-SSBN mission unless a massive breakthrough occurs in the detection of nuclear submarines. Even if such a breakthrough occurs, there will still be enormous cost constraints. Thus, over the long term, the Soviet Union will disengage from the anti-SSBN role. Presumably this will not be until the ships presently being built have had their day: they have

them and therefore will use them. When the damage limitation mission fades, forward deployment will have to be justified in terms of the support of foreign policy rather than in terms of general war missions. If the warships have been used in support of foreign policy only on a small scale, then the benefits will have been small scale; this will mean that the continuance of this role cannot be justified in relation to its enormous costs. On the other hand, if the warships have been used more aggressively and opportunistically, then all the problems and risks of failure will have occurred, and, without a doubt, the problems of exercising naval power will surely be greater than ever in a world of power diffusion and in which increasing importance is attached to maritime sovereignty. The Soviet Navy's blue water will be somebody else's maritime backyard, and other countries will be highly sensitive about its behavior.

For all these reasons, when the second series of *Navies in Peace and War* comes to be published, it will have been written not by a navy commander in chief advocating a larger navy, but instead it will have been written by the political leadership and signed by a pliant CinC. The series will include a strong critique of the adventurism of the Gorshkov period and the accompanying cult of personality. The critique will be supported by numerous statements and eulogies by Western admirals in the 1960's and 1970's describing Gorshkov as a "Russian Mahan." What could be worse for him? "Mahanian" is a pejorative word in the vocabulary of Soviet naval doctrine. *Morskoi sbornik* for 1972-73 will disappear from shelves, and the Soviet Navy will be told to return to its traditions. Not for the first time, Russian warships, after a few decades of out-of-area operations, will be pulled back.

Conclusions. Whether or not the arguments of this essay are correct in detail, they do lead to a number of important conclusions which might be expected to command general support:

● Warships are vehicles of political risk and cost, as well as of military and foreign policy opportunity. Further-

more, the clinical image of a functional relationship between a policy and an instrument of policy is misleading. "Missions" are only part of the story, if its most important part. It is safer to keep in mind that in some circumstances the naval tail may wag the foreign policy dog.

● We should not be unimaginative in our thinking about naval developments. Irrationality, drift, the impact of personality and chance, loss of control, surprise—these are the stuff of politics. The history of strategy is full of cases of weapons and men being used for one purpose, when their initial rationale was very different. We have heard plenty of threats that leave something to chance: we should hear more about analysis and forecasting that leaves something to chance.

● The problems of naval power indicate the complexity of the debate about the utility of superpower navies. If the debate is to be an informed one, more public education is required on naval matters. This puts a responsibility on the service concerned to explain its role carefully to its interested public. Outworn slogans will not suffice.

● In an era of naval diplomacy rather than of war at sea, a premium is put on politically mature and sensitive naval officers steeped in the law and politics of the sea, governmental policy, and international relations.

● As far as policymaking is concerned, it is dangerous to think in terms of "vital interests" in relation to bases or dependence on particular foreign rulers. The term "vital interest" can easily be debased through overuse. His-

BIOGRAPHIC SUMMARY

Ken Booth received his B.A. in the Department of International Politics at the University College of Wales, Aberystwyth. He has taught there since 1967, specializing in strategic studies. His publications include *The Military Instrument in Soviet Foreign Policy, 1917-1972* (1974); Joint Editor of *Soviet Naval Policy: Objectives and Constraints* (1975); co-author of *Contemporary Strategy: Theories and Policies* (1975), and *Navies and Foreign Policy* (forthcoming, late 1976).

tory shows that yesterday's vital interest is very often today's bad memory.

● As far as the carrying out of policy is concerned, the variety of political costs underlines the importance of clear foreign policy goals and good intelligence. This essay is a reminder that the instrument can shape the will, and so a warning against decisions determined by reflex actions rather than due consideration. It is a reminder that influence is almost always two-way, and so a warning about always considering how *one might be* manipulated rather than simply concentrating on how *one will* manipulate. It is a reminder that naval diplomacy is a matter of diplomats on land as well as ships at sea and of the role the former can play to ensure that naval messages are not misperceived. It is a reminder of the importance of imagination in thinking about the ramifications of one's acts. In particular it is a reminder of the importance of imagination in trying to think how one's actions appear through the eyes of others. It is a reminder that a superpower's blue water is almost always somebody else's maritime backyard, and that whatever a superpower navy does there, the local power will always regard it more seriously and more emotionally.

NOTES

1. Lest anyone misunderstand my position on this point, I would refer them to my *Navies and Foreign Policy* (London: Croom Helm, to be published late 1976). Much of the material in this essay is based on episodes, developments, and instrumentalities discussed in detail in this book. For this reason footnotes have been kept to a minimum.

2. The phrase is L.W. Martin's. See his "The Utility of Force," *Adelphi Papers* (London: International Institute for Strategic Studies, 1973), No. 102, p. 19.

3. This was most clearly expressed by L.W. Martin, *The Sea in Modern Strategy* (London: Chatto and Windus for the ISS, 1967), p. 140.

4. This phrase was suggested in conversation by Michael K. MccGwire.

5. For the purposes of this essay it is not necessary to become entangled in the thorny problem of the meaning of "bases," "facilities," et cetera.

6. Mohamed Heikal, *The Road to Ramadan* (London: Collins, 1975), pp. 47-8, 163-4.

7. Edward Luttwak, *The Political Uses of Seapower* (Baltimore: Johns Hopkins University Press, 1975), p. 67.

8. For a list of such usages, see Robert G. Weinland, "Soviet Naval Operations: 10 Years of Change," chap. 20 in Michael MccGwire, Ken Booth, John McDonnell, *Soviet Naval Policy, Objectives and Constraints* (New York: Praeger, 1975).

9. Heikal, pp. 192-4.

10. The dynamics of weapons innovation increases this problem. Note the relevance of the comment made about hovercraft: "a solution looking for a problem."

The Development of the Art of Naval Warfare

By Admiral of the Fleet of the Soviet Union S. G. Gorshkov
Translated by Theodore A. Neely, Jr.

The century began badly for a Russian Navy whose powerful Far Eastern Squadron barely escaped entrapment (only temporarily, as it turned out) at Port Arthur by four antiquated, stone-laden Japanese merchantmen, foreground, in the opening days of the Russo-Japanese War. But the modern Soviet Navy, below, led by perhaps its ablest admiral since Makarov, is not likely to be either as outmaneuvered or frustrated ever again.

The revolution in military affairs, which has been expanding over the recent decades, has governed the increasingly rapid replacement of some weapon systems by others possessing improved operational and combat qualities. This circumstance has accelerated the rate of development of the supporting base for warfare and of methods of force employment. In this connection, the study of the prospects for the development of military affairs, including also the theory of the art of naval warfare, is becoming particularly significant.

Let us briefly analyze the individual component parts of the art of naval warfare, i.e., its categories. These categories are those elements of the art which are the most immediately and readily affected and sensitive to changes in naval hardware. Therefore, their transformation can be regarded as the primary, concrete, and objective consequence of the change in this hardware.

Certain component parts of the art of naval warfare are evident in all of its levels. Thus, one may speak of the mutual support and control of forces on the strategic, operational, or tactical plane.[1] This pertains to the same degree to such concepts as, for example, strike and concentration. Other categories—e.g., battle and attack—are limited to the area of tactics.

The Scope of the Conflict. The constantly growing capabilities of navies to carry out strategic missions are elevating the naval role in warfare. The significance of the blue-water theaters of military operations is also being elevated accordingly. As a result, an even further increase in the scope of naval warfare as one of the most important parts of warfare as a whole is foreordained.

Such characteristics of a modern navy as its versatility, mobility, and capability to concentrate its striking power, which can be utilized not only in combat with a naval adversary, but also within the zone of operations of other branches of the armed forces, will

Reprinted by permission from *Morskoy Sbornik*, No. 12, 1974, copyright 1974 *Morskoy Sbornik*
For footnotes, please turn to page 63.

affect the character and results of armed combat to an ever greater degree in the future.

In examining the scale of a conflict on the strategic plane, it is essential to note the ever-growing capability of the navies of the great sea powers to achieve increasingly more critical goals. This particularly pertains to operations of strategic offensive forces with regard to destroying major groupings of the enemy, and above all in crushing his military-economic potential, which can have a direct effect on the course and even the outcome of a nuclear war. It is natural to surmise that the further development of navies will allow them to wage war on an even greater scale.

The scope of individual operations conducted by navies is also sharply increasing. In particular, the increase in the capabilities of strategic missile-armed submarines to prosecute missions entailing the destruction of land targets makes it possible to expand the front and increase their depth of penetration in operations against the enemy. For instance, the range of the American Polaris-Poseidon strategic submarine nuclear system in the last ten years has more than doubled. The transition to the new Trident submarine nuclear-missile system, about which the Western press writes so much, will double this range again. And the front of operations will be expanded accordingly.

Thus, the sharp expansion of the spatial scope of operations against land objectives is not merely a general pattern, but is also the general future prospect for the development of the art of naval warfare by nuclear navies. Hence, the corresponding growth in the spatial dimensions of operations against naval strategic nuclear weapon systems is also quite clear. As a result, naval combat activity may embrace almost the entire expanse of the World Ocean and assume a global character.

The sharp increase in naval offensive and defensive capabilities is being achieved not only and not so much by an increase in the number of ships and other weapon platforms as by expanding the range of missions which each platform is able to prosecute through its more advanced weaponry. In other words, clearly it is not the quantity but the quality of the weapons platforms, i.e., the total power of the potential combat capabilities concentrated on them, which is becoming the ultimate criterion of the scope of operations.

For example, after the end of World War II, the U. S. Navy had 263 submarines. At the end of 1974, while possessing incomparably greater capabilities and while constituting a most important part of the country's strategic assets (which could not be said of the 263 submarines in 1945), U. S. submarine forces numbered only 114 submarines, of which 102 are nuclear-powered (41 missile-armed and 61 multi-purpose submarines) and 12 are diesels.

The increase in the scope of warfare in the oceanic theaters entails the participation in it of groupings of other branches of armed forces on an ever greater scale. And this foreordains the emergence of a strategy of warfare in the oceanic theaters within the framework of a single military strategy.

Strike. At a certain stage in its development, the growth in the power of naval weaponry imparted a totally new meaning to that category of the art of naval warfare known as the strike. Previously accompanied by such amplifiers as "artillery," "torpedo," "bomb," (and in ancient times, even "ramming,") such strikes were limited to the tactical realm. In certain instances the expression "strike from the sea," underscoring its operational correlation was justified. Today, however, this concept has also been extended to the strategic realm. In the future, clearly the strike will become the main method of using naval forces. In this connection, it will be the solitary method in the strategic field, since only the delivery of strikes from vast ranges and different directions will make it possible to achieve such a strategic goal as crushing the military-economic potential of the enemy.

The strike concept apparently will be retained and strengthened in the operational realm. The term "strike" will signify one of the basic methods of accomplishing combat missions. In this connection, a strike will be not only a combination of certain operations united by a single goal or mission, as it is now, but it will also become an independent operation and, in a number of instances, a single operation by one weapon platform or grouping or another.

For instance, a strike against a surface force can be delivered by a group of ships armed with cruise missiles which will fully accomplish the mission of knocking it out. This also pertains in equal measure to independent naval air operations.

On the tactical level, in contrast with the past when it was only one of the elements of a battle and was regarded as a combination of attacks united by a single tactical mission, the strike will assume a status equivalent to the battle itself. Thus, a combat mission may be accomplished by delivering a strike against a major target. For instance, a single submarine is capable of destroying a major surface ship with a salvo of cruise missiles. The development of this trend is being fostered by the increase in the range and power of weaponry which permits, in certain cases, the accomplishment of tactical missions not through a duel, but by a unilateral, and sometimes single operation against the enemy.

Thus, a strike makes it possible to achieve strategic, operational, and tactical goals. Moreover, sometimes a strike (e.g., delivered against land targets by a missile-

An F-class submarine and a Kashin-class destroyer in the Mediterranean.

A Soviet fleet oiler refuels a Kashin-class guided-missile armed destroyer.

armed submarine), delivered "according to tactical standards and rules" will permit strategic goals to be achieved by a single combat unit. In the future this may become a characteristic feature of the strike.

Battle. This form of operations, combining fire and maneuver, has always been and will remain the main method of accomplishing tactical missions. For a long time it was the solitary form of the combat employment of naval forces. Yet, it too, is undergoing evolution. One of its more characteristic features is the increase in the ranges of engagements (and consequently also the spatial scope), due to the increase in the range of naval weaponry, in maneuverability, endurance, and in the cruising (flight) range of weapons platforms, and also due to the participation in the battle of other types of naval forces and the employment of various means of influencing the outcome. When navies were young, no one spoke of range in battle, since the outcome was determined by the possibility of boarding or ramming an enemy. With the appearance of projectile weaponry, range in battle not only became a reality, but it has continued to increase. The warships of the opposing sides became capable of destroying the enemy at ever greater ranges.

During World War II, this distance equaled the visible range to the target, using not only visual, but

"It is natural to surmise that the further development of navies will allow them to wage war on an even greater scale . . . naval combat activity may embrace almost the entire expanse of the World Ocean and assume a global character."

also the technical means of detection existing at that time. Yet even that was not the limit: in that very war several battles took place without such contact. The first naval engagement marking the beginning of "contactless" ship combat operations is considered to be the battle of Midway Island in the Pacific Ocean on 4 June 1942 between the American and Japanese forces.

In today's context, these distances have already increased up to several hundred kilometers. In the future, the effective range of naval weaponry will increase even more. Therefore, it will be commonplace for a naval battle to range over vast areas, and the coverage of the situation in the region of the battle will become possible only with the aid of specialized (primarily airborne) means.

The three-dimensional character of naval battle is another special feature of its evolution. Initially, battle

72

"When navies were young, no one spoke of range ... With the appearance of projectile weaponry, range not only became a reality, but it has continued to increase. The warships of opposing sides became capable of destroying the enemy at ever greater ranges."

was waged only by surface forces, and, consequently, only on the sea surface, on the interface between the water and air media. Later, forces operating in the water (submarines) and air (aircraft) began to participate.

Another feature is the ever-growing importance of destroying (or diverting from a given trajectory) the enemy's means of destruction (torpedoes, missiles) before they reach their target. This is giving rise to a specific special feature of the modern naval battle and is engendering a totally new quality in it which will distinguish the battle of the future from that of the past, when every effort of the opposing sides was directed toward the destruction of the weapon platforms, and not the means of destruction which they employ.

The vast destructive effect of weaponry and the timely deployment of its platforms will reduce the time needed by forces to accomplish combat missions. Therefore, one of the important factors bringing about significant changes in the nature of a battle is the acceleration of the rate of development of events and the ever greater transient nature and dynamism of them.

A naval battle is almost always waged to destroy the enemy. In the future, this special feature will become indispensable in connection with the equipping of navies with powerful forms of weaponry.

Maneuver. For a long time, the main essence of naval tactics was practically covered by "fire and maneuver." Through maneuver, the weapon platform was able to put itself into such a position relative to the enemy, where its technical potential capabilities could be employed in a strike to the fullest degree. Moreover, in certain cases, maneuver assured the necessary concentration of forces.

Maneuver in battle, as executed on the tactical deployment level, is decreasing in direct relationship to the increase in the effective range of weapons. Thus, with the appearance of smoothbore guns, the need to close on enemy ships was removed, and maneuver became shorter. It was curtailed even further by the entry into service of long-range rifled guns. And with the creation of missiles having a great horizontal flight range and high accuracy in hitting targets, it has acquired an essentially new quality which has made it possible for maneuver by weapon trajectories to replace maneuver by the platform to a considerable degree.

Calculations show that as the effective range of a weapon increases by one order of magnitude, the area within whose limits a target can be hit increases by two orders of magnitude. Therefore, strategic weapon systems have the capability of hitting targets within vast areas. The naval Trident ballistic missile being developed in the United States, it is believed, will have a range of more than 10,000 kilometers and in principle possesses ample capabilities for trajectory maneuver to hit targets within vast areas.

However, it by no means follows from this that the role of maneuver in battle is diminishing and that its execution is becoming simpler. On the contrary, the maneuvering of forces situated outside the detection range of the enemy (who, in turn, is also taking measures to get into an advantageous position which is also located beyond detection range) raises special demands for supporting the maneuver with information obtained from reconnaissance and target data. The maneuver must be carried out on the basis of data obtained through various electronic means and in a context of the most intensive electronic warfare, the correct organization of which can theoretically completely paralyze the system for monitoring the situation and the gathering of essential information. This requires the skill of not only carrying out a maneuver, but also of employing various technical means of monitoring the situation and for target indication. In this connection, a critical need arises for efficient mutual support between the attack groups and not only the reconnaissance forces but also external means of target indication.

Inherent to the maneuver of ship forces is the attribute of swiftness, which is acquiring new significance owing to the widespread introduction in the many navies of surface effect ships which have a speed several times greater than conventional displacement ships. The American press has been openly writing of the possible development of a fundamentally new class of aircraft carriers which will be equipped with powerful engines and will be in the form of air-cushion surface ships developing speeds up to 180 knots (333 km/hr), i.e., some five times greater than present carriers.[2]

In examining maneuver's effect on the operational plan, it should be noted that its significance as a form of operations aimed at supporting the operational deployment of forces and the concentration of them in certain areas of the oceanic theaters is rapidly increasing.

The Massing of Forces. Since ancient times, massing of forces has been due to two basic and mutually dependent circumstances. First, the relatively modest effective range and destructive power of weaponry, the low hit probability, and also spatial limitations for placing weaponry on board ship. Second, the constantly improving armor plating and survivability of warships. The eternal struggle between the means of destruction and protection has also evoked a need for the massive employment of strike forces.

When the chief weapons of navies were guns, torpedoes, and bombs, massing in battle was practiced primarily with the employment of high-speed forces with no armor, such as torpedo boats, minesweepers, and aircraft. Only the participation of a significant number of these combat units resolutely closing on the enemy at high speed under his heavy fire to a range sufficient for the effective employment of their own weapons could (and frequently at the cost of high losses) make it possible for them to take up a launch position and carry out the assigned mission. Therefore, in naval battle, the massing of forces has always taken the form of a large number of weapon platforms participating in an attack, with their make-up being predetermined to allow for considerable losses. The more powerful the weapons the enemy had, the greater the massing of platforms needed to accomplish the assigned combat mission. The criteria for massing were either the damaging effects of one type of weapon or the concentration of these capabilities in conjunction with various other combat means.

Massing, as such, doubtless will retain its significance, but clearly will assume another form. Already under today's conditions even in the employment of so-called conventional weaponry, whose destructive effects are continually growing, the number of platforms needed to carry out missions similar to those of World War II has decreased sharply. Hence it is logical that the massing of forces, while previously representing the optimal concentration of weapons firepower needed to destroy an enemy, no longer necessarily has to be carried out in the form of the participation of a large number of ships or aircraft. Today we can employ a considerably smaller number of combat units having a power equivalent to earlier weapons.

In this change in the concept of massing, we clearly see one of the manifestations of the dialectics of the development of military affairs and, in particular, of naval affairs; thus, the very same content (the defeat of the enemy) can have various forms, beginning with the concentration of a large number of platforms, as in the earlier context, and ending with the con-

centration of an equal (or even greater) striking power on a fewer number of platforms under today's conditions.

However, the main content of massing continues to remain the same: the concentration of the firepower of one's own forces necessary to carry out a combat mission reliably and to disperse the enemy's defensive efforts over many sectors and targets.

Thus, massing in naval battle, by retaining its former meaning under existing conditions, still basically takes the form of a concentration on board a relatively modest number of platforms of highly effective weapons necessary to prosecute a combat mission advantageously through a single action against the enemy. In this instance, the platforms, as a rule, will be dispersed over considerable areas.

The massing of forces, as implemented on the tactical level, undoubtedly is also displayed on the operational level when the main efforts must be concentrated in the critical sectors of combat with the enemy fleet. Thus, the mass employment of aircraft in an operation appears not merely in a single powerful strike, which must be regarded as the basic form of operations, but also in the successive delivery of strikes to soften up and later also to fully annihilate groupings of enemy forces. As the maneuvering capabilities of aviation increase, this form of massing will be employed on an ever greater scale.

Mutual Support. One of the most important categories of warfare, including naval warfare, is mutual support by mixed forces. The optimal combination of the offensive and defensive capabilities of mixed groupings makes it possible to carry out missions considerably exceeding in scale those missions which forces of one type, by simply adding up their capabilities, could accomplish. However, these mixed forces must provide mutual support for one another in order to achieve this.

The organization of mutual support (especially tactical support) is becoming more and more complex and its importance is growing as the effective range, power, and diversity of the employed weaponry increases and also as the speed of the weapon platforms is improved. We may assume that in the future all of the above factors will influence mutual support in the fullest measure. Therefore, the increase in the role of tactical and operational mutual support of forces in accomplishing all missions levied on navies should be considered to be a basic pattern. In this connection, the tactical mutual support of mixed forces in the battle against strategic nuclear weapon platforms will be organized so as to take into consideration the urgent need to prosecute this mission in the shortest possible time.

On one hand, the further mutual penetration into the zone of combat operations of other branches of armed forces complicates the organization of mutual support between the Navy and these other branches on the operational and tactical levels, yet, on the other hand, it makes mutual support an essential condition for achieving victory in operations in the continental and oceanic theaters of military operations. This is explained by the fact that the capabilities of the other branches of the armed forces to operate in concert with the Navy within the Navy's mission sphere, as well as the Navy's capabilities to carry out missions on land and in the air, are continually increasing.

Thus, the complication of the organization of mutual support, the growth in the degree of its importance, as well as the increase in the diversity of the forms and methods of implementing it are the basic features characterizing the development of this category of the art of naval warfare.

Surprise. In the theory of naval warfare, surprise formerly meant taking advantage of the enemy's lack of preparedness to conduct combat operations in order to accomplish your own missions. Today, surprise presupposes active, strictly goal-oriented actions to create conditions hindering the enemy's capability to react operationally to the actions of the other side. This thesis stems from the development of military equipment and the pattern of military operations in nuclear warfare when surprise can put not only the advantage in the hands of whoever holds the initiative, as was previously true, but even victory in a battle or operation.

Therefore, the struggle to achieve surprise is becoming particularly critical. It comprises an important part of staff efforts to ensure the possibility of taking advantage of such an important factor to the fullest measure.

Intelligence, which to an ever greater degree is based on the employment of electronic means, has always been the enemy's opportunity to utilize the surprise factor. That is why electronic warfare is a most important trend in the achievement of surprise in a battle or operation. Also security in all of its forms, as before, is of great significance in achieving surprise.

From what we have said it follows that surprise is a multifaceted category having many direct and inverse relationships with other categories of the art of naval warfare. In examining it from the point of view of the ability to achieve the unexpected, one could conclude that it is especially important at all levels of the naval warfare, whereas if we approach it from the standpoint of ensuring the achievement of the final goals of military operations, then we see that surprise is immediately and more fully displayed primarily on the operational-tactical plane. Here the achievement of

surprise, in a context where reconnaissance means and automated systems for analyzing and predicting situations are being continually upgraded, to a great degree is the province of the skill of the flag officer, since only surprise, when both sides have practically equal material capabilities, can yield a definite operational-tactical advantage for one side over the other.

Swiftness.[3] A characteristic feature of all forms and varieties of combat operations at sea is the rapidly unfolding nature of events, the rapidity of the change in the situation. This trait is a consequence of the development of hardware due to which previous methods of waging naval battle, including continual maneuver of forces and repeated and prolonged operations against the enemy, have lost their significance and have been replaced by dynamic, decisive, and more fruitful combat engagements transpiring over ever shorter time intervals. And this is understandable, since scientific-technical progress is leading to the creation of more mobile platforms and high-speed, long-range weaponry. Therefore, swiftness is becoming a more and more important and indispensable feature of a strike, an operation, and a battle. Its manifestation on the operational plane is expressed in the further reduction in the duration of pressure on the enemy by increasing the power of this pressure. Hence, the increase in the effectiveness of combat operations. The swiftness of operations of various forces aimed at the main enemy targets is becoming a most important, main, and deciding factor in methods of attaining goals, since it ensures a fuller use of all combat capabilities of the weapons platforms and makes their strikes unstoppable.

Swiftness permits an all-round reduction in the time expended on achieving the assigned goals. Only quickly-developing operations combined with surprise make it possible to beat the enemy to the punch, to quickly achieve the advantage in maneuver, and to deliver a strike against the entire depth of the enemy forces' combat alignment. Swiftness has been and will be one of the most important methods of achieving surprise.

Thus, surprise and swiftness are closely related categories of the art of naval warfare.

The increase in scope of naval warfare and the further enrichment of it with combat operations accenting swiftness at every level is imparting a special dynamism and effectiveness to this warfare. The totality of the entire combat activity of the Navy is represented by the complex combination of instantaneous and successive quickly developing strikes and operations accomplished through the achievement of critical goals, and having, in certain instances, a direct effect on the course and outcome of the war as a whole.

Thus, swiftness is an indispensable factor in naval

Soviet Naval Infantry fire their rockets.

"The capabilities of the other branches of the armed forces to operate in concert with the Navy within the Navy's mission sphere, as well as the Navy's capabilities to carry out missions on land and in the air, are continually increasing."

warfare, whose role is constantly growing, and the ability to utilize it in one's own interests is one of the more important elements of the art of naval warfare.

Tempo. From the well known Marxian dialectical definition of time, we clearly see the importance of tempo as a category of the art of naval warfare, since all military events at sea develop not only in space, but also in time, i.e., at a certain tempo. In this connection, tempo always has been and will remain one of the indispensable conditions for the planning and conduct of all types and forms of naval combat operations.

As naval hardware developed and the speed of platforms and range and power of weaponry increased, the art of naval warfare was faced with the need to carry out an ever-growing volume of missions in an increasingly short period of time. Even in World War II, the destruction of a certain enemy grouping was not always limited to a definite time frame. In those days, for example, a mission was assigned of annihilating the enemy during a sea transit. Yet it could have been carried out anytime during his entire transit, lasting days or even weeks. And, in principle, it was not important whether it was at the beginning or the end of this period. What was important was to accomplish the mission while the enemy was at sea.

Today, such an approach is impermissible. In today's context, a hostile group of naval forces must be destroyed in a strictly defined and very short time frame—before it is able to employ its own weaponry in full measure. Thus, the time factor, i.e., the tempo of events, is an element of the success of combat operations.

The characteristic feature of the category of the art of naval warfare which we are now examining is that the time needed by a fleet to carry out strategic missions is becoming of the same order as that expended on prosecuting tactical missions. Thus, it is becoming more evident that today the possibility exists in certain cases of achieving strategic goals through tactical operations (as we mentioned above).

The constantly growing requirements for reducing mission execution times in naval warfare are finding expression in the need to maintain forces at a high readiness posture to immediately deliver attacks on the enemy and also in the widespread introduction into navies of various automated systems.

The categories of the art of naval warfare examined above are very closely related to the ability to employ one's own forces in the rigidly limited frames allocated for the accomplishment of a mission.

Control. A great deal of significance is attached to the art of control in today's context. The materials of the 24th Communist Party Congress stress that effectiveness of control can be achieved only through the ability to see the prospects, to correctly define priorities, to take advantage of the latest achievements of science and technology, and the latest experience, and to react quickly and efficiently to changing conditions. These theses must be the basis for solving the problems of the development of such categories of the art of naval warfare as control of forces.

Requirements for the control of forces have continuously grown with the development of naval forces and with changes in the conditions under which they operate. For example, control even in complex and multiphased combat operations, as a rule, formerly was implemented on the basis of direct visual observation of the situation. In this instance, decisions were made by the flag officer, to a considerable degree, on the basis of his own experience and intuition. Later, as a result of the sharp increase in the scale and rapid pace of combat operations due to improving performance characteristics of weaponry and combat equipment, control was transformed into a complex process requiring the employment of long-range and very-long-range technical equipment. Under today's conditions when opposing groupings of forces have nuclear weapons at their disposal which are essentially sufficient to completely destroy one another many times over, control of forces is related to the employment of various automated equipment to ensure surprise and swiftness of operations and to gain time over the enemy. In this case, control of forces is a guarantee of success. It has become especially critical in the realm of the employment of nuclear forces and of the forces whose mission it is to knock them out.

As was noted earlier, one trend in the development

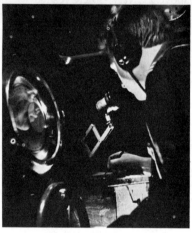

"Despite the appearance of powerful weaponry, highly efficient control systems, etc., the role of man in the development of all branches of the art of naval warfare is constantly increasing."

of naval warfare is the increase in its scope. Yet this increase in itself entails a further increase in and concentration of information traffic and in the intensity of its circulation through various circuits and spheres of control. In order to receive and process all incoming information and, on the basis of it, to prepare and make the optimal decision in a short time, there is a need for an increasingly broader introduction of scientific methods of control based on the use of the latest technical means (of communications, automation, and computerized equipment).

The postwar development of submarine forces having great strike and defensive capabilities in all of the navies of the sea powers has complicated the control of submarine forces located in distant regions of the World Ocean. Moreover, the transfer of the main efforts

of naval warfare to the subsurface medium has engendered a principally new quality of the art of naval leadership, based on the employment of modern control systems and complexes. Together, they must provide the flag officer with accurate information on the air, surface, and subsurface situations and aid in making the optimal decision on the employment of a large number of forces.

It must be noted that the problem of the control of forces is related not only to the comprehensive introduction of automated equipment, but also to the inclusion of groups of highly qualified officers and admirals in the control system.

Automated control systems, which are being used more and more widely, today call for highly intellectual human effort as an indispensable element, i.e., a combination of the objective and subjective principles of the control process in which man, to an ever greater degree, is supported by "machines" with the data to be used by him in optimal decision-making.

Organization. The employment of diverse organizational forms fully corresponding to actual capabilities and conditions for the employment of naval forces and means, has always comprised and comprises one of the important branches of the art of naval warfare.

Naval forces, which have had quite definite operational and combat capabilities and properties in every historical stage of their development, can be regarded as the object to which a concrete organizational form must always correspond. Therefore, over the entire history of naval development, organizational structures have continually been replaced, and as naval hardware has been upgraded, they have assumed one system or another of permanent force formations or battle alignments. For example, at a certain stage squadrons made their appearance as a permanent organization. At the same time, we observed a tactical reserve of high-speed, well-armed frigates in the combat organization of Admiral F. F. Ushakov's forces, and in Admiral D. I. Senyavin's forces, we saw tactical groups together with the traditional line alignment of forces with the dispatching of an independent formation of two ships to attack the enemy flagship.

In more recent times the organization of forces in a battle, and later also in an operation called for a considerable number of different groups and detachments. The totality of these groups in battle assumed an organizational structure which has come down in the art of naval warfare as the concept of "battle alignment" and in an operation as an "operational alignment of forces."

During the Great Patriotic War major organizational changes in the Navy were evoked by the emerging operational-strategic situation in the ground theaters of military operations, and in particular in the littoral sectors, and also by the need to carry out the missions assigned to it.[4] This was expressed in the creation of new, and restructuring of previously existing flotillas, naval bases, maritime defense regions, and forces of ships, aircraft, and rear logistic organs, etc. The taking of organizational measures in a timely and efficient manner comprised a definite part of managing the Navy in that era.

Questions of the organization of naval forces have always been decided in response to the requirements of the art of naval warfare in a certain period and, to the extent it was rational, they were a unique form corresponding to the content entailed in the form of the certain potential combat capabilities of the naval hardware. This affirms the well-known thesis of Marxist philosophy of the correspondence of form to content. Undoubtedly it will also be displayed in the future as the missions of the Navy develop further, and as its missions, the military-political situation, and the conditions for waging naval warfare change.

The revolution in military affairs is having an ever greater effect on organization. This is particularly expressed by the fact that computerized equipment and automated systems (which serve as the basis for the creation of new organizational structures) are being introduced into various areas of control. Therefore, there are increased demands on organization, since only a rational variant of it will permit the fullest realization of all the capabilities in the control of forces which an automated system offers.

As we have seen, the development of the art of naval warfare is related to the affirmation of all of its traditional categories using new quality criteria which are characterized by continually growing requirements, a rigidness of standards, a strengthening of efforts, a reduction in decision-making time, and increased re-

sponsibility for the flag officer. Despite the appearance of powerful weaponry, highly efficient control systems, etc., the role of man in the development of all branches of the art of naval warfare is constantly increasing.

One should consider the following to be the important trends in the development of the art of naval warfare: a steady extension of the concept of optimization to wider areas, and an increase in the role of the engineering and technical fields and in the emphasis on physical and mathematical sciences as the basis needed to resolve theoretical and practical questions.

This article touches on only a part of the questions comprising, in the aggregate, such a broad problem as the employment of a modern navy, whose solution is considered to be one of the tasks of the theory of the art of naval warfare. Clearly, review of all the questions constituting the art of naval warfare should be made on the basis of a strict consideration of the changing operational and combat capabilities of naval hardware which are the basis for the formation of all of its categories.

Sergei G. Gorshkov was born 26 February 1910 in the Ukraine. He graduated from the four-year Frunze Higher Naval School in 1931, and his first career assignment was the destroyer *Frunze*. He served in the Black Sea Fleet and later the Pacific Fleet. By 1938 he commanded a brigade of destroyers, and when war with Germany broke out in June 1941, Gorshkov commanded a cruiser brigade under the Commander-in-Chief of the Black Sea Fleet. In October 1941, having commanded a successful amphibious landing at Odessa the month before, Gorshkov was promoted to rear admiral at the age of 31. After the war, he commanded a squadron of ships in the Black Sea Fleet, became fleet chief of staff in 1948 and fleet commander in 1951. After a brief period as First Deputy Chief of the Soviet Navy, Admiral Gorshkov became its Commander-in-Chief in June 1956 and has held the post ever since. During that time he has been instrumental in transforming the Soviet Fleet from a coast defense force to a true blue-water power.

[1] Though the U. S. Navy generally distinguishes between only strategy and tactics, many European navies—parallel to land warfare—insert the concept of "operation" between the two. Moreover, the terms are used with slightly different connotations. Rear Admiral Edward Wegener, Federal German Navy (Retired), explained this point on page 198 of his essay in the 1972 *Naval Review*: "Strategy is the 'grand design' for the totality of military activities. It is brought into reality by operations. To clarify how these terms are applied, we might take the example of the *Bismarck*'s cruise in May 1941: The decision to use major fighting ships in raider warfare was a strategic decision; the decision to employ specifically the *Bismarck* at that time of the year and under the circumstances of that spring was an operational decision; and the decision of the admiral on board the *Bismarck* to engage in combat with the British capital ships, *Hood* and *Prince of Wales*, was a tactical decision.

[2] *The New York Times,* 21 October 1970.

[3] Translator's Note: The term "swiftness" here does not do justice to the original Russian word *stremitel'nost'*, which also includes the meaning of "dash," "impetuosity," and "rapidity," yet "swiftness" seems the most appropriate translation in the context of this category.

[4] The term "Great Patriotic War" refers to the part of World War II in which the U.S.S.R. participated.

View From the Bridge
of the Sixth Fleet Flagship

By Admiral Isaac C. Kidd, Jr., U. S. Navy

On occasion, Admiral Kidd's Sixth Fleet shared a Mediterranean anchorage with sleek Soviet warships.

A new chapter in the textbook on naval tactics is being written in the Mediterranean today. Departure from traditional doctrines of naval employment occurs daily. The Mediterranean has seen the first signs of new naval tactics in the missile age. The Jordanian crisis in September 1970 proved that no longer may naval task forces expect to group in classical manner, search out the enemy, and engage. On that occasion, Sixth Fleet and Soviet Mediterranean Fleet units were interspersed at times.

It has become routine practice for Soviet men-of-war to shadow our attack aircraft carriers. We, in turn, trail their "high-value" units. Soviet surface ships and land-based aircraft monitor Sixth Fleet and NATO exercises. New Soviet ships of all types now train and exercise routinely in the central and eastern Mediterranean.

The growing Soviet naval strength in this area has caused many to question the capability of the U. S. Sixth Fleet to perform its stated mission of helping to maintain peace and stability on NATO's southern front. The fact is that under existing pressures, we are walking a tightrope of adequacy; at some points, the rope is beginning to fray. Our still formidable fleet is being forced to accommodate to a new environment far different from the one which it dominated for almost a quarter century. The change has come about chiefly through design but also somewhat as a result of neglect. The designing influence is the Soviet Navy and its Mediterranean Fleet, which gives ever more convincing evidence of its growing capability and professionalism.

Generally, it is a "have" fleet. It has new ships, modern weapons systems, well-trained and highly

motivated personnel, and a "back yard" logistics base with prepositioned stocks of ammunition and fuel plus a reinforcement capability which is the envy of every naval commander. This force has very few apparent weaknesses. It lacks only two very important assets: sea-based aircraft, and the experience the men of the Sixth Fleet have acquired on frequent deployments to the Mediterranean and in recent years to Southeast Asia where combat operations have molded them into top professionals with a confidence and skill equal to any challenge. It is the American Bluejacket's proven performance which somewhat quiets a growing anxiety for the future. We have been asking virtually wartime-type sacrifices and devotion to duty from him for almost 25 years. Pride alone will not sustain him indefinitely. He must continue to have the best available ships in which to fight.

The U. S. Sixth Fleet. The attack carrier striking force is the heart of our Sixth Fleet. It comprises two attack carriers and their assigned destroyers. It is a mobile, self-sustaining force independent of base support except for major repairs. The Sixth Fleet spends about 50% of the time at sea training and exercising in the western, central, and eastern Mediterranean. Each area is covered through a series of continuing unilateral, bilateral, and multilateral (or NATO) training exercises conducted with the various friendly nations bordering on the Mediterranean.

The Sixth Fleet's concurrent role as a NATO striking force requires that it be ready to provide assistance and support to Italy, Greece, and Turkey. The Fleet's presence has long been recognized as being of prime importance in maintaining Greek and Turkish ties to NATO, since almost the only external support, immediate or over the longer term, that either nation may rely on in the event of conflict must come by sea. The most capable aircraft available in the southern region of NATO are those of the Sixth Fleet. Within the balanced force operating concept is a combined Navy-Marine Corps amphibious team of some 1,500 Marines embarked in four or five amphibious ships. Theirs is the traditional Marine mission: land and stabilize the situation, as they did in Lebanon in 1958.

A Fleet Without Bases. The Sixth Fleet operates independently of fixed bases. The Fleet does, however, receive significant support from U. S. and Allied shore bases in the northern Mediterranean littoral. Through Naples and Sigonella in Italy; Athens, Greece; and Rota, Spain, are staged considerable logistics. The commercial airfield at Soudha Bay, on the Greek island of Crete, provides back-up support. The Soviets have a logistical advantage, since their lines of logistics communication are so much shorter. The Soviet capability is most impressive in the eastern basin of the Mediterranean where Egypt and access to the Black Sea provide essential resupply and reinforcements. Conversely, the Soviets are painfully aware of the need for air support. In recognition of these factors, they generally operate close to their supply base and under their shore-based air umbrella.

The Importance of Logistics. The question of a logistics base is critical to any military operation. In this respect, problems confronting the Sixth Fleet and the Soviets are vastly different. To support the normally 40-ship Sixth Fleet, seven or eight auxiliaries—one repair ship, three oilers, two ammunition ships, and one or two refrigerator ships—are generally on call. For the day-to-day consumables not immediately available overseas, support from the United States is conducted on periodic replenishment cycles. Some supplies are prepositioned in limited quantities, e.g., petroleum, oil, and lubricants (POL) and ammunition in NATO stock farms and depots throughout the Mediterranean. Such Service Force ships as the USS *Seattle,* a new combat support ship, carry the burden of sustaining the Fleet over one million square miles of ocean. She and her sister ships, which performed superbly during the Jordanian crisis in September and October of 1970, can be likened to a one-stop country store with a gas station out front.

To support their 50-plus ship Soviet Mediterranean Fleet, the Soviets usually have about 15 support ships prepositioned within the Mediterranean. They have the additional option of using their merchant shipping or deploying additional ships on short notice from their Black Sea Fleet. It is common knowledge that the Soviets use their commercial vessels both for military and political purposes. Their central and western Mediterranean units are normally replenished underway or at anchor, but the bulk of their force gets its provisions from shore-based facilities in the Black Sea or from selected Arab ports, such as Alexandria. The close proximity of the "locker room" to the "playing field" gives the Soviets the decided advantage in this critical resupply-reinforcement aspect and they are aware of this advantage. They normally have the oilers available and on station in sufficient number to accommodate a much larger combatant force. When a contingency situation arises, their combatants are deployed from the Black Sea to where their logistic support awaits. Probably in the hope of expanding their logistics base, and no doubt for other reasons, the Soviets are now providing military and financial assistance to Mediterranean nations who will accept it. The Arab Republic of Egypt provides support facilities to Soviet naval forces. Recently Soviet merchantmen have quadrupled their calls to Libya.

The geographic advantage, already described, which enables this large, modern, and growing Soviet Fleet

to move quickly to and from the Mediterranean is important. In this respect, the Soviets have a choke-point factor—the Montreux Convention controlling the Turkish Straits. It is somewhat restrictive on surface ship movement, specifying total tonnage allowed in the Straits and requiring advance notice for transits.

Sea Control. The problem of protecting long sea lines of logistic communications is directly proportional to their length and to the ability of the opposition to challenge. The heavy concentration of Soviet surface, subsurface, and air forces in the Mediterranean—some

A Soviet Yurka-class fleet minesweeper studies Sixth Fleet underway refueling techniques. Although still badly base-limited, it is only a matter of time before the Soviet Navy acquires the expertise necessary to perfect their rudimentary techniques of underway replenishment.

sea-based, some land-based—combined with the great transiting distances from the continental United States to Gibraltar and then across 2,000 miles of the choke-point-studded Mediterranean is a sobering prospect.

The situation is reminiscent of the early days of World War II when the Allies were trying to supply Malta and the Germans and Italians operated from air fields along the North African coast and Italy. The Italian Fleet was the largest in the Mediterranean. German and Italian submarines were taking an awesome toll of allied shipping. Heavy losses among Allied oilers, stores, ammunition and combatant ships forced us to

sail through Gibraltar three times the tonnage necessary to sustain Malta. Two-thirds of our shipping and supplies were lost to enemy action during the most critical months. Considering that Malta is only halfway across the Mediterranean, the problem confronting us today is doubly serious. NATO has been concentrating on a solution. Only through the combined efforts of our NATO allies is the problem solvable.

Commander Naval Forces Southern Europe (ComNavSouth) is responsible for protecting the logistics line across the Mediterranean in the event of hostilities involving NATO. Toward this end, ComNavSouth

A Soviet Sverdlov-*class cruiser refuels a Riga-class destroyer escort by means of the alongside method. Having studied the U. S. Navy's underway refueling techniques, the Soviet Navy has adopted this method, which is faster and far more efficient than the old method of trailing a hose astern.*

will use ships of the United Kingdom, Italian, Greek, and Turkish Navies with Sixth Fleet support. The carrier strike forces of the Fleet can be used to provide air protection, and would attack those sea forces and bases which threaten the mission.

Soviet Land-based Air Support. The port facilities now available to the Soviet Navy and the possibility that the Soviets will obtain the use of more such facilities have led some observers to conclude that the maritime age in the Mediterranean may be a thing of the past. The implication that the assumed decisiveness of Soviet control of important airfields in turn guarantees, ipso facto, the control of strategic bodies of water, i.e., the Bosporus and Dardanelles, is dangerously overstated. Critics of seapower further contend that the Soviets can "control" the Mediterranean Sea, even though denied free passage of their ships through the Bosporus and the Dardanelles, purely by the establishment of a series of airfields along the North African coast. The inference that airpower in the Mediterranean, as represented by Soviet land-based aircraft, together with their political machinations which have gained them access to strategically located airfields, is a decisive factor neutralizing the presence of Allied naval forces is open to challenge.

While hostile aircraft based along the southern edge of the Mediterranean certainly could take a heavy toll of shipping in that sea—until the aircraft and their bases can be destroyed—they can in no way "control" the Mediterranean in the sense of denying its use to properly defended mercantile and naval ships.

In addition to being counterbalanced by Western control of the land on the opposite side of this inland sea, the Soviet African bases must withstand the sea-based airpower present in NATO's Southern Striking Force.

For the massive logistic support which would be required for sustained Soviet air operations, the Soviets would be dependent upon resupply from the sea. This would be denied them by (1) control of the straits of ingress, and (2) by the Western naval forces in the Mediterranean, which could be resupplied and continually augmented by sea.

Moreover, although Soviet airpower based in North Africa is indeed a capability to be considered seriously and one that might initially cause great problems at sea in the Mediterranean, Soviet airpower could, in time, be reduced to manageable proportions, leaving NATO and the Western nations in control of the sea lanes. The important consideration is to prevent any Soviet capability from gaining a military edge which could not be overcome.

The Soviet Mediterranean Fleet: Capabilities and Limitations. Although it possesses a powerful offensive capability, the Soviet Mediterranean Fleet, like its sister fleets (the Northern, Baltic, and Pacific Fleets), is still very much defense-oriented. Necessity dictated this approach because the Soviet Navy is designed for one objective—to counter the efforts of the U. S. Navy to establish control of sea lines of communication and to project seapower ashore. Its concurrent missions are oriented to destruction of our carriers, the defense of a burgeoning merchant marine, and to "show the hammer and sickle." The growing Red Fleet in the Mediterranean was and is base-limited; although it is only a matter of time before the Soviets acquire the expertise

necessary to perfect their rudimentary techniques of underway replenishment. They have the necessary support ships. Their use of commercial shipping has already been mentioned, but they labor under certain handicaps. Lacking sea-based air cover, their surface units are vulnerable as is their logistics train.

The Soviet Mediterranean Fleet is heavily dependent upon surveillance provided by surface combat units, submarines, and intelligence collection ships (AGIs) using visual means and a few reconnaissance aircraft. It is vulnerable to air attack. It is analogous that the more numerous the Soviet Fleet, the more attractive aircraft carriers are in quickly reducing the overall effectiveness of this force. Given Soviet superiority in naval guns, an advantage which can be achieved quickly by deployment of additional ships from the Black Sea, and long-range strike capability provided by surface-to-surface missile (SSM) equipped ships and submarines, only aircraft carriers among all existing Allied navy ship types provide even the opportunity of quickly overcoming this threat. Given ample nuclear submarines and ample time, a submarine fleet might attrite the Soviet Fleet forces, but it would take too long.

The Missile Threat. The Soviet SSM weapons system threat is well suited to surprise attack. For use at ranges beyond its own radar horizon, it is heavily dependent upon accurate target locational information from a "forward observer." Because of the size of the SSM, and the limited number which can be carried on board any ship, proper target identification is a primary requirement. Ships are maneuverable. Their relative motion both to the firing ship and to friendly ships in company complicate both location and identification problems for the SSM. The missile is also highly dependent upon a favorable electronic environment. Since Soviet Fleet units in the western Mediterranean are virtually without air cover, they are dependent upon surface-to-air missiles (SAMs) and conventional AA guns for defense from air attacks—defensive systems that are themselves vulnerable to jamming, electronic deception and to low-level aircraft attack. Their SAMs cannot be hidden, as they were in North Vietnam. When one considers the range of uncertainties involved in the Soviet SSM system on the one hand, versus the relatively straight-forward (and predictable) problems that we face using carrier aircraft and relying on human judgments for problem-solving on the other, the great advantages enjoyed by aircraft carriers become apparent.

If we postulate "open ocean" situations after an outbreak of hostilities, aircraft carriers are vastly superior to SSM ships by every measure. Why, then, were SSM ships built? The Soviets know their limitations better than we do. In attempting to offset or neutralize the power of the U. S. Navy, they developed the SSM and

To support their Mediterranean Fleet of 50-odd ships, the Soviets usually have about 15 prepositioned support ships, such as the Soviet oiler Koida, *seen refueling the guided missile helicopter ship* Moskva, *while a Kashin-class destroyer in the background awaits her turn.*

built a number of ships with that system as its main battery. They built SAMs to defend their SSM ships from air attack, and developed a family of air-to-surface missiles (ASMs) for their aircraft. The Soviet Union had already developed a substantial and increasingly proficient submarine force. When one considers the Soviet problem in shifting from a defensive naval posture, heavily oriented towards the use of submarines, to a more expansive navy capable of exercising control of the seas, and of effecting that transition in the face of the awesome power of the U. S. Navy (not to mention British and other navies), the attractiveness of SSMs becomes very great. It provided the earliest possible achievement of a credible threat against more numerous U. S. and Allied surface ships.

The SSM ship can be used in surprise attack against aircraft carriers at an outset of hostilities. However, at over-the-horizon ranges, it always remains dependent upon surveillance, which must be provided by others.

No Longer a Permissive Environment. The presence and capability of this Red Fleet has forced a new approach to Sixth Fleet planned operations in the Mediterranean. The fact is that there is no longer a permissive environment where once the Sixth Fleet moved at will. Formerly, there was no opposition force powerful enough to contest the availability of the sea lines of communications in support of NATO in the event of a confrontation.

In recent speeches, the Chief of Naval Operations has identified the modern roles and missions of the Navy. He has dwelled heavily on the sea control mission and capability. In the absence of any potential opposition, there is no problem with sea control. What is available by way of naval competence can be used exclusively for the projection role. In Vietnam, we enjoyed a permissive sea environment. In the Mediterranean, there is an opposition Navy; forces at sea able to say, "Look fellows, you'd jolly well better be aware that we're here and think about us before you start committing everything to this projection mission. Because, if you don't take care of that threat at sea, then you're not going to have anything to project with." And, if the projection force were launched, there might well be nothing to come back to. This "threat elephant" must be eaten one bite at a time. The immediate threat—the air, the missile, the ship—must be accommodated, and after that is resolved in a kind of ink blot manner, the capability can be expanded into the project mission.

First, one must plan on protecting the sea lines of communication—protecting the oilers, the food ships, the ammunition ships that would be needed, together with the reinforcement ships with the soldiers and Marines who might be required to reinforce the NATO flank. Recall the previous reference to World War II when the Allies had this very salutary experience in the resupply of Malta requiring sea control. The decisive factor then, as it is today, was the availability of sea-based air. Until carrier air support was forthcoming, the Allies got a bloody nose. This force must control the seas. If total control cannot be exercised, then there must be concentration on sea protection in the hemisphere immediately above and below this logistic force or this Marine force or Army force, or whatever reinforcing force, as it moves.

The Sea Control Mission. How ready is the Sixth Fleet to accomplish the task of sea control? Aging ships and budgetary restraints have been affecting readiness. Secretary of Defense Melvin Laird has said that he anticipates readiness will suffer in the face of the severe budgetary cuts the military has experienced. The ships are there. To begin with, the average age of U. S. combatant ships assigned to the Sixth Fleet is about 19 years. The average age of the Soviet force in the Mediterranean is about seven years. The disheartening thing is that the Soviets have already begun to phase out certain types of ships which they apparently consider obsolete, replacing them with new and more capable construction. These "obsolete" ships are about 10 years old.

There is no way of correlating dollars directly to readiness. In fairness one must admit that, despite a drastic ship deactivation program in the U. S. Navy, there are still only slightly less than the same number of ships deploying, on roughly the same deployment cycles, to the Mediterranean. In certain cases, capability is improving owing to the availability of newer weapons systems, such as more advanced high-performance attack aircraft for our carriers and improved ASW aircraft. In the present Mediterranean environment, the Fleet Commander must settle for many old ships in numbers sufficient to permit partial surveillance and escorting of high-value ships (CVAs, AOs, Amphibs). Given the choice (and all else being equal), the preference is for high-performance new ships in fewer total numbers. Budget restrictions on fuel money, limiting operating days, and flight hours, have hurt. Something as important as training cannot be curtailed without it hurting. The controlling factor is the continuing growth of Soviet naval forces in the Mediterranean. If the Soviet build-up continues, there must be a commensurate increase in the Sixth Fleet, either in numbers or quality (preferably both) and certainly an increase in operating funds. The disadvantages, should war be thrust upon us, are obvious. The degree of reinforcement required is difficult to establish; but, depending on the extent of this growth, the need for additional assets is an inevitable conclusion.

At what level will they be required? In September and October 1970, the Soviets had 52 ships in place as tension in Jordan grew. In very short order the number rose to 72. At that point there was a requirement for the USS *John F. Kennedy.* The *Kennedy* arrived as did additional support ships—missile ships, most of them—and it was just like the sun coming up in the middle of the night. It was not a question of numbers. Numbers alone are incomplete indicators. It is the capability of the ship that counts. From the American point of view, the arrival of the *Kennedy* was the hoary

The U. S. and U.S.S.R. Fleets (Submarines not shown) during the peak period of September and October 1970.

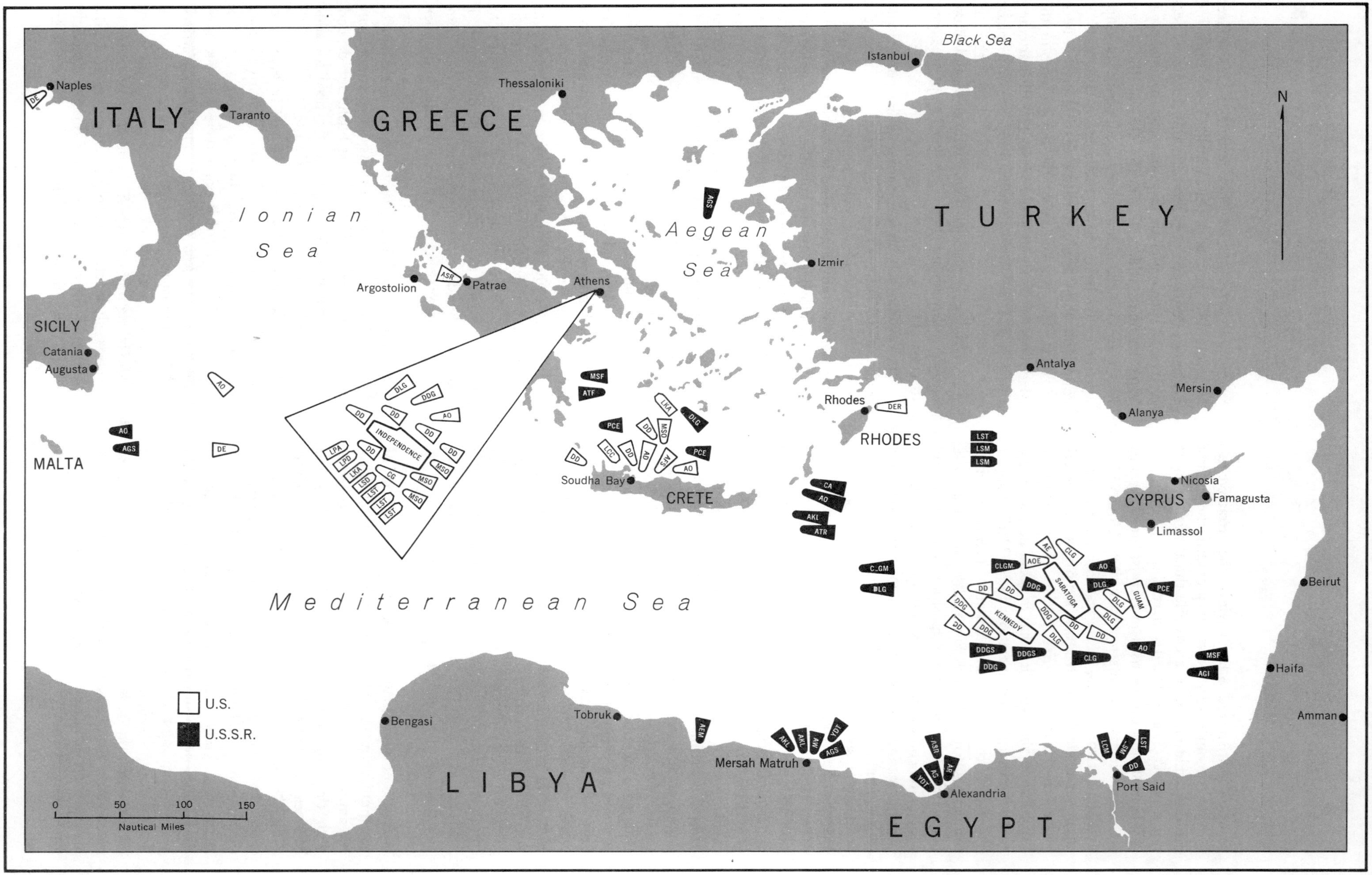

N

Black Sea

ITALY

Naples

Taranto

SICILY

Catania

Augusta

MALTA

GREECE

Thessaloniki

Istanbul

Izmir

TURKEY

Mersin

Alanya

Antalya

Patrae

Argostolion

Athens

Ionian Sea

Aegean Sea

RHODES

Rhodes

CRETE

Soudha Bay

Mediterranean Sea

CYPRUS

Nicosia

Famagusta

Limassol

Beirut

Haifa

Amman

Port Said

Alexandria

Mersah Matruh

Tobruk

Bengasi

LIBYA

EGYPT

U.S.

U.S.S.R.

Nautical Miles

0   50   100   150

Texas Ranger riot story all over again, wherein the Ranger, asked why he was the only man who had been sent to quell the disturbance, replied, "You only got one riot, aincha?"

The presence of that third carrier contributed substantially to my peace of mind and, so much more importantly, to the peace of the world.

The Jordanian Crisis. A brief look at the Jordanian crisis situation as it developed last fall will provide some insight into Soviet capabilities. As the Sixth Fleet, on orders from the Joint Chiefs of Staff, deployed eastward toward Jordan to take up a position and be prepared to assist U. S. citizens in that country, it numbered 45 ships. As stated above, the Soviets had approximately 52, the majority of which were already in the eastern Mediterranean. The Sixth Fleet was augmented by an additional carrier task group and escorts. The USS *Guam* and other amphibious ships already earmarked for NATO exercise "Deep Express" sailed from the east coast a day early. When the two fleets were joined in the area of Jordan, there were some 40 ships standing-to in what resembled an international boat show. The Soviets had approximately 20 ships and submarines in the immediate area. Within less than one day's steaming time of U. S. forces, the Soviets maintained approximately 50 additional ships and submarines, 26 of which were combatants, including seven SSM firers and eight ships carrying surface-to-air missiles. Parenthetically, additional reinforcement for the Sixth Fleet was ten days to two weeks away. Soviet ships followed all major Sixth Fleet ships as they cycled in and out of the area of operations from Greek and Turkish ports. As the Sixth Fleet watched and waited for orders at "Camel Crossroads," the Soviets also watched and waited. The two fleets gave no evidence of undue stress. Both sides operated in a normal and restrained manner. There was none of the nonsense of their ships running in and around our men-of-war at close range. It was evident the Soviets were under the direction of a seasoned seaman who not only knew well the capabilities and limitations of his equipment, but also was sensitive to the potential seriousness of the situation.

The Eastern Mediterranean. Before and since that crisis, the Sixth Fleet has been accused of abandoning the eastern Mediterranean to the Soviets. If there has been a reduction in numbers there, it has been by design rather than default. U. S. units continue to operate in the eastern Mediterranean and sometimes into the "deep eastern" basin when necessary. If additional presence is required there, the Fleet will go. The proposition that we should stay and train in the deep eastern basin in strength is unrealistic and wasteful. In order to be useful we must be well honed all the time. That means intensive training all the time. For example, the young

gentlemen who fly our high-performance aircraft must do it day in and day out. The eastern basin has a low ceiling of interlaced commercial airline routes. During the Jordanian crisis, some 75% of the aircraft that were intercepted and escorted were commercial airliners. Under the circumstances, adequate exercising and training cannot be conducted in that area. This doesn't mean we intend to ignore it. We can and do monitor activity in the eastern Mediterranean. Furthermore, it isn't necessary to be alongside or in the immediate vicinity of targets to conduct contingency air operations. Our carrier-based attack aircraft have very long ranges.

As important as it is to keep track of Soviet high value ships, there simply are not sufficient assets to put one on the tail of each of their units. To do so would interfere with training. And obviously spreading out ships very seriously affects the ability to capitalize on the capabilities of the numbers available and to deploy them in positions of tactical advantage.

The Three-Dimensional Threat. The size and capability of this Soviet Fleet presents a three-dimensional threat. Working from the overhead down, first is the air threat which at the present time is constrained by their reliance on shore bases and by problems associated with over-flight rights. A relatively small air contingent of Soviet-made TU-16 Badgers, BE-12 Mail Amphibians, and AN-12 Cubs conduct reconnaissance of U. S. and other nations' naval forces in the Mediterranean. They provide, among other things, locational information and identification of specific units, and they facilitate submarine and surface-to-surface missile employment. The TU-16 Badgers are not suitable for direct bombing attack on maneuvering ships because they are highly vulnerable to our surface-to-air missiles as well as to our defending fighters. However, their use of long range air-to-surface missiles is a serious consideration.

Next are the previously mentioned SSM weapons and their surface ship launching platforms. Missiles from ships have altered traditional naval tactics and formations. Because of them, the practice of placing a circular screen around a high-value ship has changed. If there were more missile ships, the days of the circular screen might be entirely over. The fact that sonar detection ranges are so radically reduced in the Mediterranean complicates the defense. To take full advantage of a missile ship's missile radius envelope, ships are positioned with a little overlap. But these ships have an ASW mission as well. If their sonar ranges do not match their missile range, they must be positioned closer together to ensure that a submarine doesn't get between them. This diminishes their AA posture. The solution lies in adequate numbers of ships to do the job. With our present number, we rarely achieve a satisfactory defensive posture. We are always forced to compromise.

Finally there is the Soviet missile-firing submarine. This submarine with its missiles is potentially the most serious, for, first, we must find it. Failing that, we have to contend with the missile once launched.

The primary weapons system which counters this triple threat is the CVA. The aircraft carrier has considerably longer strike ranges than have SSM ships, many more attack vehicles, its own inherent and vast surveillance capabilities (electronic and visual), several thousand tons of offensive ordnance and an intelligent identification and guidance system that can accommodate to uncertainties—a pilot. It has a formidable defense capability. It is capable of sustained action in a wide variety of roles. Assuming that we don't lose our shirts in a surprise attack, the Sixth Fleet aircraft carriers can concentrate an awesome air power strike against Soviet combat ships and maintain this power in sustained combat, since aircraft are in a sense re-usable missiles. The ability to concentrate air strike forces against targets of our choosing, simultaneously, in widely separated areas, is a fundamental advantage that the Sixth Fleet enjoys. Our intensive surveillance efforts are partly for reducing the prospects of a successful surprise attack and partly to prevent technological surprise.

The Gatekeepers. The Soviet force has established several patterns of operations. They make great use of their intelligence collectors, the AGIs. One is always maintained off Rota to observe Polaris submarine movements and to watch the Straits of Gibraltar.

They usually keep an AGI and an hydrographic survey ship in the Strait of Sicily's choke point. They also maintain another off the coast of Israel. In addition, they use their combatant ships for surveillance. There is usually a missile or rocket ship in the area between Sardinia, Tunisia, and Sicily, and there are usually combatants either east and/or west of Crete. They trail our high-value ships with combatants. Normally, when our important units—the amphibious ready group with Marines and the aircraft carriers—are at sea, their forces will closely intermingle with ours. When not working in a surveillance role or exercising, they are normally in Port Alexandria or Port Said, A.R.E., or at anchorages. These anchorages are located throughout the Mediterranean, in international waters, where the depth is usually less than 100 fathoms. No nation's permission is required for their use. The most frequently used anchorages are Mellila Anchorage just north of Morocco; Alboran Island, east of the Strait of Gibraltar; the Gulf of Hammamet, northeast coast of Tunisia facing the Strait of Sicily; Hurd Bank, just east of Malta; Kithira Island, south of the Greek Peloponnesus; east of Crete; in the Gulf of Sollum, at the northwestern corner of Egypt; and east of Cyprus. Constant surveillance of geographic choke points or "turnstiles" is a

well established Soviet practice. This tactic is clearly a part of their battle plans. Their interest in controlling the choke points is apparent in their exercises in the Mediterranean and worldwide. For example, exercises in the Mediterranean have included as objectives amphibious landings along the shores of the eastern Mediterranean. To protect the landing they use a defensive force of submarines, surface ships, and aircraft as a buffer against any attempt at intervention from outside sub-surface, surface, or air forces.

While the exercise is proceeding in a particular area, locally defended by the defensive forces just mentioned, they also put combatant forces into the strategic choke points. Thus, they accomplish their objective. They protect the area of assault and on a Mediterranean-wide strategic basis, they exercise at preventing any intervention by any country of the objective area by choking off access routes. This strategy could also serve to interdict the sea lines to the southern flank of NATO as previously described.

The NATO Surveillance Effort. Our own CTF-67, (ComASWForSixthFlt) has a concurrent NATO hat as the Maritime Air Command Mediterranean (MarAirMed), a NATO command located in Naples, Italy. He coordinates the collection and continuous dissemination of air surveillance information to the navies of participating NATO member nations. Through MarAirMed, the Sixth Fleet actively shares its aircraft assets and information to help provide effective surveillance of the Mediterranean Sea without duplication of effort. No aircraft are assigned to MarAirMed in peacetime; they remain under national control. Of the highest priority is the further strengthening of surveillance efforts of all types.

ASW in the Mediterranean. The problem of greatest magnitude in the Mediterranean is antisubmarine warfare. The "ground rules" of the ASW game—something like having all three outfielders on a baseball team wearing blindfolds—would be intolerable were it not for the fact that these handicaps apply alike to both teams. Speaking of ground rules, the aforementioned Montreux Convention, signed in 1936, restricts the passage of Soviet submarines through the Turkish straits. Thus, most of the Soviet submarines in the Mediterranean come the long way down from the Northern Fleet, which is the largest of the Soviet submarine fleets.

Once they reach the Mediterranean, Soviet submarines may operate almost without limitation. However, the Mediterranean is no goldfish bowl. There are high ambient noise levels in the water owing to the high density of shipping (2,000 ships are estimated underway in the Mediterranean every day) and "layering" in summer months make sonar conditions extremely difficult. As indicated, these same water conditions appreciably increase the difficulties facing an attacking submarine.

The reduction in the number of ASW carriers seems to be a paradox in view of the Soviets' heavy emphasis on submarine warfare and the unique problem ASW presents in this part of the world. Only periodically since World War II have we had ASW carriers in the Mediterranean. We have never been able to afford a steady-state deployment.

This leads to another important subject: carrier use and air group composition. For example, during her Mediterranean deployment last fall, the USS *Independence* had an ASW helicopter squadron embarked. This is the second time this has been done. Of course, there have been the traditional differences among the proponents of strike aviation on the one hand, the proponents of ASW aviation on the other; and the supporters of the Hunter Killer group (HUK) concept versus the land-based patrol aircraft believer. Then there are the submariners who feel that the best way to find a sub is with another sub. Our best results have accrued from the complementary capabilities of all hands applied to the problem. In this, we are showing a healthy departure from the traditional by experimenting with a mix of planes on our carriers to meet specific missions. There is considerable promise from putting a composite capability on certain of our floating airfields, but at a cost in reducing our strike potential.

Conclusion. The United States can no longer with impunity allow its oilers and other support ships to steam unescorted. Sea protection and sea control is critical to such ships. Sea control must be earned. In this small sea, it is no longer available by assumption. That logistic umbilical must be inviolate; otherwise, operations come to a grinding halt very quickly. The plain numbers limitation in the Sixth Fleet is becoming aggravated for several reasons. One, the age and material reliability of the older ships work increasingly against us. We are having a difficult time with these older ships. They are breaking down, and repair parts are not always available. Additionally, the problem is aggravated by inadequate numbers of first-line types of ships, such as those with a missile capability and long-range sonar. The third factor of aggravation keys to a requirement to keep ships of high interest and potential under surveillance to preclude surprise, which tends further to fragment our limited forces.

Aircraft can indeed help with surveillance. Surveillance around the clock, 24 hours a day, could become a necessity because reaction times are becoming shorter and shorter.

In 1967, there were 25 Soviet ships in Mediterranean waters. That number more than doubled in two years

from 35 in 1968 to as many as 72 in 1970. At this writing, there are 64, while our force numbers have declined. Now, in view of the magnitude and capability of this Soviet presence, the combined support of the NATO navies becomes increasingly important. NATO works in the Mediterranean. It is working daily in the valuable exchange of information and the perfecting of operating techniques at sea on bilateral and multilateral exercises. We must and do depend more and more upon our friends for help. The net result is most gratifying. It is an absolute necessity that the quality of performance continues to improve. This can only occur through the acquisition of additional numbers of new aircraft, ships, and missiles with high-performance capabilities for all Free World nations, not just the United States.

Lately we are hearing encouraging statements from authoritative spokesmen regarding the so-called renaissance of the U.S. Navy. Congressman F. Edward Hebert, the new chairman of the House Armed Services Committee, has promised more funds to rebuild the Fleet. He has predicted that reconstruction of the Navy will go forward until we have, in his words, "a more modern Navy, a Navy that will challenge your wildest imagination." These are heartening words indeed.

In the interim, the Sixth Fleet will continue to do its job. In this regard I have charged my shipmates in this Fleet to direct their energies to becoming so proficient in the fundamentals of naval matters that the unexpected can be taken in stride. This is our operational goal. But, while readying ourselves for the unexpected, we must not overlook the obvious.

Whatever the cost, we must prevent the Soviet Union from gaining a military edge which could not be overcome.

Admiral Kidd has just been relieved as Commander Sixth Fleet to assume the position of Chief of Naval Material. He has served as Commanding Officer of the USS *Ellyson* (DD-454) and the USS *Barry* (DD-933); Commander Destroyer Squadron THIRTY-TWO and Destroyer Squadron EIGHTEEN (the Navy's first all-missile ship squadron); Executive Assistant and Senior Aide to the Chief of Naval Operations; Chief of Logistics, Allied Forces Southern Europe; Commander Cruiser Destroyer Flotilla TWELVE, and as Commander First Fleet.

Those Storm-beaten Ships, Upon Which the Arab Armies Never Looked

By Lieutenant (junior grade) F. C. Miller, U. S. Navy

In The Influence of Sea Power . . . , *Mahan wrote movingly of the far-distant, storm-beaten Royal Navy ships, upon which France's Grand Army never looked, yet which stood between Napoleon and dominion of the world. So, too, did the ships of the U. S. Sixth Fleet influence the outcome of the fourth Arab-Israeli War in 1973.*

The shooting had not yet died along the banks of the Suez Canal and on the rocky wastes of the Golan Heights before analysts began to dissect and discuss the results of this, the fourth Arab-Israeli war. The October 1973 struggle called forth several questions about previously accepted military doctrine, and the so-called "lessons learned" were duly noted and published. Two of these revolved around the role of the modern foot-soldier. The accuracy and effectiveness of the portable Soviet-built Snapper and Sagger antitank missiles had restored something of a measure of equality to the infantry; thus, the prominent battlefield position which armor had occupied since the Wehrmacht devastated France in 1940 suddenly appeared much less unassailable. Similarly, the introduction of the highly mobile truck-mounted SA-6's and hand-held SA-7's demonstrated that air power can indeed be countered from the ground; ground forces now possess the capability not only to defend themselves against air attack but to greatly inhibit an enemy's employment of close-in tactical air support as well. On the other hand, proponents of air power could draw considerable comfort from the strong evidence confirming that a massive airlift capability remains a crucial weapon in a Great Power's national arsenal. The rapid resupply effort undertaken by the United States and the Soviet Union which made it possible for the belligerents to continue fighting in the face of extremely heavy losses could not have been accomplished so quickly without aircraft. A final lesson (or, more correctly, a reassertion of a lesson from the past) was drawn from the apparent ease with which the Egyptian Army shattered the highly vaunted Bar-Lev line: static lines of defense remain extremely vulnerable.

The publicity and attention devoted to the above developments have created a tendency to sum up the entire October 1973 war solely in terms of them; from the strictly tactical/immediate theater of operations standpoint, it would not be totally incorrect to do so. If one considers the broader scope of the crisis, however, it becomes apparent that one major and extremely vital lesson has been overlooked in the headlong rush to discover the more novel and spectacular aspects of the conflict. The eventual outcome of the war, and the avoidance of direct Great Power participation in it, was brought about in part by the decisive and intelligent exercise of American sea power. Such action has been so natural in the past, so familiar and so commonplace, that no attention has been devoted to it at all. In a sense, this is entirely in keeping with historical tradition, for American disregard for sea power is not new: we have as a nation generally ignored the fact that the world's oceans serve as platforms for national policy. For this reason, three-quarters of a century ago Mahan undertook to educate this country to the very real, yet unperceived, exercise of power by naval forces; today's crises continue to provide further case studies which bear close scrutiny. In this regard, the October war may be seen as yet another chapter of an already bulging textbook.

To understand this latest chapter, the role played by the Sixth Fleet from mid-October 1973 to mid-December 1973 should be divided into three distinct phases. The first, best described as the "replenishment phase," began on 15 October and continued until 25 October. Phase II, the actual crisis, was initiated by the change in LertCon status early that day, and lasted roughly until 15 November. The final, post-crisis period extended for an additional month after that, concluding about the second week of December.

At the time of the outbreak of hostilities, the Sixth Fleet's striking force consisted of two carrier groups: the Athens-based Task Group 60.1, centered about the USS *Independence* (CVA-62), and Task Group 60.2, in the western Mediterranean, built around the USS *Franklin D. Roosevelt* (CVA-42). The first days of the war, during which the United States adopted a "wait and see" posture, saw both Arab and Israeli forces make initial advances which neither side was able to fully exploit; both sides were suffering extremely heavy materiel casualties in the fighting, especially in aircraft and armored vehicles. As the week progressed, however, and the Soviet Union undertook to replace the Arab losses with new equipment, it became apparent that without similar aid Israel would soon be fighting a tenuous campaign against steadily mounting numerical odds. Soviet four-engined turboprop transports were flying south in a constant stream, pausing only to refuel at Budapest or Prague before proceeding onward to Syria and Egypt. That weekend, the decision was made in Washington to provide Israel with the tools of war she needed to adequately defend herself. Speed was of the essence: if the American equipment was to have any effect on the outcome of the war, it was absolutely imperative that it be introduced immediately into the theater of operations. Thus U. S. Air Force C-5As and C-141s would carry armor, ordnance, and repair parts directly from bases in the continental United States to Tel Aviv. To aid a beleaguered and hard-pressed Israeli Air Force, A-4s and F-4s were to be taken out of United States stock and flown to the war zone.

This solution immediately presented two problems, one general in nature, and one quite particular. The former was that of command and control: the size and complexity of the contemplated operation (formidable in and of itself) was aggravated by the fact that the aerial supply pipeline running over the Mediterranean was parallel to several thousand miles of hostile Arab airspace, and thus subject to possible attack. This called for constant monitoring and precise command and control, extending to the highest national levels, of all aircraft transiting from the Straits of Gibraltar to Israel and back. The latter problem related specifically to the logistics of ferrying the fighter aircraft. Unlike the larger C-5s and C-141s which carried sufficient fuel to fly the distance with only one intermediate stop, the Skyhawks and Phantoms needed to refuel at least three times between the United States and their ultimate destination. The logical solution, using American bases in Europe, could not be employed to support the mission. As in the 1970 Jordanian crisis, some of our NATO allies, fearing Arab reprisal in the form of oil embargoes, did not make their airfields available for the United States to land aircraft which were destined for Israel. The presence of the Sixth Fleet, however, gave U. S. policymakers an option they would not have otherwise had: the answer to both problems was resting at anchor in the ports of Europe. Thus, the replenishment phase was inaugurated.

By the evening of 15 October, the Sixth Fleet was at sea. A floating and mobile chain of communications and support had been created which extended from the guided missile frigate *Harry E. Yarnell* (DLG-17), near the Straits of Gibraltar, to an area 100 miles southeast of Sicily, where the *Roosevelt,* accompanied by the escorts *Trippe* (DE-1075) and *Joseph Hewes* (DE-1078), had taken up station. Intermediary PIRAZ (positive identification and radar advisory zone) stations between the *Yarnell* and the *Roosevelt* were occupied by the escort

With anxious Israeli pilots awaiting them, Skyhawks, en route from the United States to Tel Aviv, had to refuel both in the air (while avoiding hostile Arab airspace) and also on one of three carriers, including the Independence, below.

The Sixth Fleet signalman sending his semaphore message from the flagship Little Rock to the destroyer Manley is reminiscent of the way Horatio Nelson's "storm-beaten ships" communicated at sea.

Edward McDonnell (DE-1043) and the guided missile ship Claude V. Ricketts (DDG-5). East of the Roosevelt, the USS Dewey (DLG-14), occupying another PIRAZ station, linked the above-listed ships of TG 60.2 with the Independence task group, which was maintaining a station south of Crete. Thus, in less than 24 hours, the command and control problem had all but disappeared. Extensive and secure communications facilities were available to pass and receive information to and from the transport aircraft. The possibility of surprise attack on the transports similarly had been eliminated, for, through the naval tactical data systems' (NTDS) Link 11 and Link 14 data links, the PIRAZ ships kept constant track of all aircraft in their vicinity, including any potentially hostile air contacts. And, should the need have arisen, the forces to defend the transports were always at hand, in the missile batteries and air intercept controllers of the ships. Thus, as the C-5s and C-141s approached Gibraltar they were picked up by the Yarnell, who handed them down the long line, each ship assuming responsibility in turn until they were safely on the ground at Ben-Gurion Airport in Tel Aviv. The logistical support problem for the Phantoms and Skyhawks had also been solved. The attack carriers, American airfields in the sea, were eminently well suited to act as supply platforms for the ferrying fighters. Initially, some of the A-4s were refueled on board the USS Kennedy (CVA-67) and the rest at the Azores. The

F-4s were refueled in flight over the Azores (where the C-5s and C-141s had set down for their one refueling). After refueling, some of the A-4s continued to the Roosevelt, and Independence from which, after "touching down and gassing up," they flew on to Tel Aviv. The stated mission of the Fleet, to act in support of U. S. policy and interests in the Mediterranean area, was therefore successfully accomplished.

It is important to note that the Sixth Fleet did more in furtherance of national policy during this period than merely monitor the replenishment operation. Indeed, through its very existence and presence, it made the policy of supplying aid to Israel possible: by virtue of its forward deployed status it provided Washington with a means of attaining a desired goal which, under other circumstances, might have had to be abandoned. Had a standing American naval force of sufficient size and strength not existed in the area, the policy options (and consequent results) would have been much more

94

severely limited. Secondly, again due to its "on-station" nature, the Fleet allowed the policy option, once decided on, to be put into effect with an absolute minimum of delay. No weeks of staging and preparation, no time-consuming negotiations for overflight rights and other privileges had to occur: the orders were given, and, within a day, had been carried out. This, too, was crucial, for, given the circumstances, the alternative to prompt action was no action at all.

By the middle of the week of 21 October the momentum on the battlefields had gradually shifted in Israel's favor. Finally at full mobilization strength, and bolstered by the influx of American materiel, Israeli forces were advancing on both fronts. In the north, the Syrians and their Iraqi allies were being pushed back along the road to Damascus; simultaneously, Israeli troops had crossed the Suez Canal, encircling and isolating the Egyptian Third Army. A short truce failed to materialize into a cessation of hostilities. With her clients' position deteriorating, the Soviet Union belatedly took interest in a ceasefire. In response to an Egyptian initiative, the Russians proposed the creation of a buffer zone between the belligerents: the Israeli side was to be patrolled by American troops, and the Egyptian side, by the Soviets. Moscow's plan was not a viable one. History records that regional conflicts are not settled by an imposed truce forced on the warring parties by more powerful external states. More important, the proposal was fraught with the peril of direct Great Power involvement in the hostilities: should the truce break down, the possibility existed that American and Soviet units might be drawn inexorably into combat, with the implicit threat of escalation of a global nature. Finally, there was considerable doubt, and much negative speculation, as to the integrity of the Soviet Union's motives for seeking to introduce Russian combat forces into the war zone. The entire idea was therefore emphatically rejected by Washington. The fighting thus continued unabated, and along the canal the Third Army was facing the very real prospect of complete annihilation within days. By 24 October, Moscow began to signal its intention to implement its half of the ceasefire proposal unilaterally, i.e., land Russian troops in Egypt for the ostensible purpose of creating a demilitarized strip and bringing the fighting to a halt. According to *Time* magazine of 1 July 1974, at 2125 (Washington time), the Soviet ambassador in Washington, Anatoli Dobrynin, passed a message to Secretary of State Kissinger from Chairman Brezhnev; in it, the Soviet party leader is said to have warned that if the United States would not cooperate in bringing the fighting to an immediate halt, the Soviet Union "should be faced with the necessity urgently to consider the question of taking appropriate steps unilaterally."

The Russian statement reportedly was emphasized by Soviet amphibious ships which, carrying Russian troops, began to move south from the Dardenelles towards Egypt. Additionally, seven Soviet airborne divisions in eastern Europe apparently were placed in an alert status.

Washington necessarily regarded this Soviet action in an extremely grave light. The introduction of Soviet combat forces would completely disrupt the delicate balance of power that the Super Powers had theretofore maintained in the Middle East. There was no guarantee that, rather than acting as peacemakers, the Russian forces would not add their considerable weight to their client's cause. (On the contrary, strong indications existed that the Soviets would do exactly that.) If and when Soviet forces were actually committed to battle against the Israelis, the United States would face the agonizing decision of either abandoning Israel to whatever fate the Russians intended for her or facing a major war with the Soviet Union. The need existed, therefore, to prevent the situation from deteriorating that far by thwarting the introduction of those Soviet forces into the war zone.

Early on the morning of 25 October (Alfa time zone), the Sixth Fleet received word that Washington had placed the American Defense Establishment in DEFCON III. In the continental United States, first-line units were taking steps to insure maximum readiness, instituting recall bills, and loading and packing equipment. Much closer to the scene of action that was not necessary. The Fleet was already in peak condition; as soon as their orders were received, American naval forces in the Mediterranean were reacting to the crisis. The ships of TG 60.2 turned east at flank speed, heading for rendezvous with TG 60.1 off Crete. The Sixth Fleet flagship *Little Rock* (CLG-4), with Vice Admiral Daniel J. Murphy, ComSixthFleet, on board, was already in the eastern Mediterranean. A task group that had four weeks earlier been relieved as TG 60.2 was conducting an exercise in northern European waters prior to returning to the United States. Immediately redesignated as Task Group 60.3, this force, consisting of the carrier *John F. Kennedy* and her escorts the *Dale* (DLG-19), *Connyngham* (DDG-32), *Byrd* (DDG-23), *Elmer Montgomery* (DE-1082), *Glennon* (DD-840), and *Sarsfield* (DD-837) also turned east and passed through the Straits of Gibraltar en route to rendezvous with the other carrier groups. Having departed her East Coast home port several days earlier when the crisis began building, the helicopter carrier *Iwo Jima* (LPH-2), with her Marine Amphibious Unit embarked, entered the Mediterranean hard on the heels of the *Kennedy* group. Task Force 61, the Sixth Fleet's amphibious arm, consisting of the command ship *Mount Whitney* (LCC-20),

Guadalcanal (LPH-7), *Austin* (LPD-4), *Nashville* (LPD-1), *Fort Snelling* (LSD-30), *Pensacola* (LSD-38), *Manitowoc* (LST-1180), *Sumter* (LST-1181), and *Harlan County* (LST-1196), sortied from Greek and Cretan harbors to form up with the rest of the Sixth Fleet, their Marine detachments on board. Thirty-six hours later and in Sea State 9 (so rough that Soviet tattletale units had to drop their pursuit of TG 60.2), the Sixth Fleet was maintaining a combat ready station south of Crete, prepared to carry out any assigned mission and, by its location, in position to interpose itself between the Soviet amphibs and the combat theater.

It would do well at this point to examine the composition and capabilities of this force so rapidly gathered off of Crete. With the bare minimum of staging time that is the hallmark of deployed naval forces, the U. S. Navy had assembled the single most potent and powerful force in the immediate area of the war zone. Its primary strike element lay in the air wings of the *Independence, Roosevelt,* and *Kennedy,* with their balanced mix of fighter and attack aircraft. Closely linked to this air superiority was the unmatched capability to intervene inland to fulfill a wide range of functions ranging from the evacuation of American citizens to whatever direct participation might be required. The ships of Task Force 61 held about 6,000 combat-ready Marines with their supporting equipment; they had the option of being placed ashore either by direct assault, via the landing craft carried in the well-decks of the LPDs, LSDs, and LSTs, or by the tactic of vertical envelopment, using the Marine CH-46 and CH-53 helicopters on board the *Iwo Jima* and *Guadalcanal.* Escort ships, all qualified in naval gunfire support procedures, were present to provide backup firepower should the need to project power ashore become necessary.

Soviet warships, cargo vessels, and tankers are visible in this photograph of the Kythira anchorage during the height of the fourth Arab-Israeli War. But there is no carrier. And it was the absence of Soviet carriers that so severely limited, as it continues to limit, the Kremlin's options.

Primary force antiair and antiship missile defense was furnished by Combat Air Patrol (CAP) from the carriers; secondary protection was afforded by the Talos missile-equipped *Little Rock,* and by the medium-range Terriers of the DLGs. Localized defense capability lay in the Tartar-firing DDGs, and in the Standards and close-in Sea Sparrows of 1052-class DEs. Protection against the subsurface threat was particularly strong. All of the destroyers carried ASROC and ASW homing torpedoes; the majority of the escorts were specifically designed as antisubmarine warfare platforms, and possessed the long-range SQS-26 sonar. This capability was greatly enhanced by the SH-2 LAMPS detachments on board the *McDonnell* and the *W. S. Sims* (DE-1059), which were invaluable in over-the-horizon classification and prosecution. Additional support was furnished by Navy P-3 Orion patrol aircraft. The surface warfare aspect was more than adequately covered by the surface CAP of the carriers, the six-inch guns and Talos of the cruiser, and the Terriers, ISSMs, and five-inch guns of the missile frigates and destroyers. The essential ability to remain on station continuously was achieved through the dedicated efforts of the Sixth Fleet's Service Force, Task Force 63. Twenty-year-old oilers worked around the clock in the time-honored routine of the underway replenishment, flanked by spanking new fast stores ships which were demonstrating their immense versatility by using their helicopters to vertically replenish food stores and supply items. In short, this was a well-balanced, multipurpose, self-sufficient force capable of fulfilling a wide range of missions, and it thus gave the U. S. government the latitude of choosing any action from a simple showing of the flag to graduated intervention.

One of the inherent beauties of naval power however, so well illustrated throughout modern history (especially by the U. S. Navy in the Cold War era) is that, unlike any other form of military power, it can remain at a distance, unengaged, and nevertheless have a profound effect on the development of an international crisis. Essentially, this is possible due to what may be termed its "representative" role or function. A naval task force is a highly mobile symbol, an indication of the resolve and determination of a nation in its foreign policy and a clear and present expression of its willingness to exercise power to support that policy should the need arise. Following from this, it can be seen that in October 1973 the Sixth Fleet was exerting influence in two separate but inter-related planes. On the global level, the Fleet was the on-scene representative of the entire American defense establishment, the visible element of the power which, at every American installation throughout the world, was at that moment being readied to act. As such, the force off Crete was a symbol of the awesome potential of the world's most powerful nation. On a secondary scale, the ships and men of Task Forces 60, 61, 62, 63, and 67 were symbolic of their own power and of their own position as the single most powerful military factor in the Mediterranean area. It should be noted here that the Sixth Fleet was by no means the only naval force present: some 50 to 60 units of the Soviet Navy were similarly on station in the eastern Mediterranean basin. The effectiveness of the Russian ships was, however, severely limited by the very nature of their role: the primary and overriding *raison d'etre* of the Soviet Navy is to deny control of the seas to the Western maritime powers, specifically, the United States. It is, by virtue of its lack of aircraft carriers and their attendant tactical air support, necessarily a first-strike force, whose mission is to launch a surprise attack on an unsuspecting and unready Sixth Fleet with the intention of sinking the American CVAs; this would enable the Russians to destroy the superior strike capability of the U. S. forces before the latter are able to react. Soviet ships are good platforms for carrying out this role, but they are ill-equipped to perform the many other functions traditionally ascribed to naval forces. And, with the ships and aircraft of the Sixth Fleet operating in Condition III readiness, the possibility of a successful surprise attack and quick victory had been so substantially re-

duced (if not virtually eliminated) as to effectively blunt the presence of the Soviet ships.

This, then, was the situation confronting Kremlin policymakers in the wake of the American alert. It was as impossible for the Soviet leaders to disregard the seaborne signal of American resolve as it was unthinkable for their generals to further contemplate inserting forces in Egypt with the Sixth Fleet sitting firmly astride the sea and air lanes running from the eastern European staging areas to the theater of operations. The stakes had suddenly risen enormously, far exceeding those risks deemed justifiable in light of the limited gains Moscow could hope to make. Thus, the insistence on a ceasefire involving the active participation of Soviet forces was dropped, the amphibious ships halted their southerly passage, the airborne divisions remained in eastern Europe, and the door was opened for the creation of a United Nations peacekeeping force which excluded the two super powers.

The lowering of the level of Soviet-American tensions and the uneasy but effective ceasefire between the Arab states and Israel which followed several days later did not signal an end to the Sixth Fleet's role in the Middle East crisis. Because the truce was an uneasy one which, given the all-too-volatile political climate of the Holy Land, could on short notice degenerate into renewed hostilities, the Sixth Fleet remained on station in the area, fulfilling the same basic mission which caused its sortie from European ports two weeks earlier: providing the U. S. government with the means, and therefore the ability, to implement a wide range of graduated policy options. Thus, while other American units had resumed a normal DEFCON IV status by the end of October, the Sixth Fleet continued to steam and operate at Condition III in the eastern Mediterranean.

By mid-November, with the ceasefire remaining intact and in effect, the situation in the Middle East presented all the appearances of becoming stabilized. Accordingly, Condition IV watchstanding was resumed, and the presence of TG 60.3 was no longer deemed necessary; it was dissolved, and its ships, accompanied by those elements of TF 61 due for rotation, departed the Mediterranean en route to their East Coast home ports. With the return to two on-station carriers and peacetime steaming, the crisis phase concluded. Stabilization, however, by no means insured that a real defusing process had begun and, as before, the requirement existed to have a continuous on-scene force-in-being to cope with contingencies. This need was satisfied by maintaining one carrier task group in the vicinity of Crete at all times; a rotational cycle was set up so that while one task group was at sea, the other would be in port for a much needed rest. This arrangement endured until the second week of December, at which time Washington determined that the cease-fire was proving viable enough to permit the Sixth Fleet to return to its *status quo ante bellum.* The *Roosevelt* and her escorts thus returned to the western Mediterranean, a move which marked the end of the post-crisis phase of the Sixth Fleet's involvement.

In recapitulating, it should be stressed, first and foremost, that the success of American policy was neither accidental nor fortuitous. It was rather the result of the intelligent exercise of naval power in precisely the manner in which naval forces should be employed. As such, it was the product of the combination of the high degree of professionalism of the U. S. Navy (itself the reward of intensive training and an easy, long-standing familiarity with the task at hand) and the keen appreciation on the part of America's leadership of the many and varied roles which the Navy is capable of playing. In passing, it is worth noting that this last-mentioned factor is far too often taken for granted: national leaders, even in maritime states, are not always cognizant of the proper employment of naval power in the furtherance of foreign policy.

A second important lesson of the crisis is the re-affirmation of the tremendous value of maintaining regularly deployed naval forces. As was brought out time and time again during the crisis, the forward-deployed nature and on station presence of the Sixth Fleet first created, and then preserved, a full range of policy options for Washington and, in the case of the replenishment phase, actually made a policy choice viable. Had there not been a Sixth Fleet present, the outcome might have been quite different, and far less favorable for America. It is nothing short of imperative, therefore, if the United States is going to preserve this freedom of action, this ability to be flexible in choosing among a wide range of potential courses, that a strong and consistent American naval presence be maintained in the Mediterranean and in other areas of possible international crisis.

An adjunct to the above, somewhat tangential, centers about the continued role of the aircraft carrier. The past several years have seen much controversy generated on this subject, with a fair amount having been written on the "obsolescence" of those ships. The October 1973 experience, however, starkly underscored the very real and tangible need for the carriers. It cannot be forgotten or overlooked that so-called friendly airfields in allied countries are not always available, that twice in the past four years some airfields have been unavailable precisely when they were needed most—in a crisis situation. The United States must retain the ability to be self-reliant in the Mediterranean theater in situations short of general war, and this calls for the continued

presence of aircraft carriers in the Sixth Fleet to provide both landing platforms and air support. Secondly, it was the aircraft carrier which, more than any other single factor, tipped the naval balance of power in the eastern Mediterranean in the Sixth Fleet's favor. Their unmatched ability to establish local air superiority, conduct long-range strikes, and project power ashore was the actual vital difference between the American and Soviet fleets. Had no U. S. carriers been present, the results, again, would have been vastly different.

The above discussion of the relative strengths of the U. S. and Soviet Navies points to the final lesson of the conflict, one which is perhaps best stated as a *caveat*. American control of the seas can no longer be taken for granted in international affairs. The ability of the United States to act in a manner similar to last October's may be seriously diminished in the future as Soviet naval capability continues to grow. This is especially true in light of the launching of the first Soviet aircraft carrier—which must be seen as their primary step in the development of a full-fledged Fleet Air Wing. As was noted at the outset, the modern American citizen has, by and large, remained blissfully ignorant of the importance of sea power. It was extremely fortunate for him in that ignorance that the world's oceans were dominated first by the friendly forces of the Royal Navy, and, more recently, by our own. Except for tanker torpedoings off the East Coast and momentary invasion scares in the Pacific states in 1942, the United States has never felt the effects of a denial of the use of the seas. But the *Pax Americana* which reigned over the oceans beginning in 1945 is over—and a serious contender with interests antithetical to our own is mounting a powerful challenge to our ability to "go anywhere, anytime." The American citizen and his elected representatives need to develop an increased sense of awareness on the crucial importance of this subject. If we are to continue to exercise the freedom of action of the type demonstrated 16 months ago, we must maintain a naval establishment which is literally "second to none." Should we fail to do so, the day will inevitably come when the United States will be unable to respond adequately to a crisis, and will be forced to suffer the consequences.

Lieutenant (junior grade) Miller is a 1972 Phi Beta Kappa graduate of Williams College, where he received honors in History and highest honors in Political Science. Designated a Distinguished Naval Graduate at Officer Candidate School, he reported upon commissioning to the USS *Joseph Hewes* (DE-1078), and served as Communications Officer for 15 months before assuming his present duties as Antisubmarine Warfare Officer of the *Hewes.*

Ready Power for Peace—
The U. S. Seventh Fleet

By Vice Admiral George P. Steele, II, U. S. Navy (Retired)

On guard in about 30 million square miles of the Western Pacific and the Indian Ocean is the largest of the deployed fleets of the U. S. Navy, the Seventh Fleet. This enormous ocean area borders nations containing about half of the world's population. The Seventh Fleet was born in early 1943, and in the years since World War II, it has been the only American fleet to fight.

The presence and strength of the Seventh Fleet made possible the successful defense of the Republic of Korea during the Korean War more than two decades ago. In those days, there was no threat from any other sea power; the U. S. Navy was unchallenged and supreme at sea. The assignment of the fleet to the Taiwan patrol at that time guaranteed the survival of the Republic of China government and the security of Taiwan against Communist attack from the mainland of China. Taiwan could have been protected in no other way.

The American effort in the Vietnam War was made possible only through control of the sea. The Seventh Fleet secured the sea-lanes, projected strong air power against the enemy ashore, conducted amphibious landings, provided naval gunfire support to Allied troops, and made an indispensable contribution by air and mine warfare to the negotiated end of the U. S. military involvement. The fleet could have done far more—far more quickly—to help bring about an end to that tragic war. The wisdom of the political decisions that restrained the Seventh Fleet and other U. S. forces for so long will be the subject of long debate by scholars, but the naval capability there cannot be questioned.

Toward the end of the Vietnam War a new reality emerged: the Seventh Fleet no longer enjoyed unchallenged supremacy in the Western Pacific. The Soviet Pacific Fleet today faces the Seventh Fleet with a powerful force of nuclear and conventionally powered submarines, armed to the teeth with missiles and torpedoes. It has a number of modern, missile-equipped surface ships and is backed by numerous, effective long-range maritime aircraft carrying air-to-surface missiles. So the attitude and policy of the Soviet Union in a crisis are factors to be considered, as never before, if the employment of the Seventh Fleet is contemplated.

Several other rival navies in the Seventh Fleet area of responsibility are growing in modern capability and strength. Although the tactics of the Seventh Fleet have been modified as necessary to confront the modern arms possessed by some of these navies, they pose no serious threat to the Seventh Fleet today. Further development of the People's Republic of China Navy at the present pace would be cause for concern, but the modernization of the U. S. Navy should keep the Seventh Fleet in a commanding position.

The mission of the Seventh Fleet is to conduct operations necessary to support our national objectives. That simple mission statement keeps the fleet hopping. A heavy training and exercise schedule is required to keep up the fitness to fight across the whole spectrum of naval warfare. A visible presence must be maintained in the area, and visits to friendly countries are both a pleasure and a duty. In many cases, exercises to strengthen mutual defense are conducted with the military of these nations; recently combined exercises have been held with the armed forces of the Republic of Korea, the Republic of China, the Republic of the

U. S. NAVY

U. S. striking power in the Western Pacific is exemplified by these aircraft carriers steaming in the South China Sea: left to right, the USS Enterprise *(CVN-65), USS* America *(CV-66), USS* Ranger *(CV-61), and USS* Oriskany *(CV-34).*

Philippines, Thailand, United Kingdom, Australia, New Zealand, Pakistan, Iran, and Canada. The fleet keeps watch on the forces of potential adversaries and is always on the lookout to help mariners in distress at sea or to render humanitarian assistance ashore in case of natural disasters. In 1975, for example, the Seventh Fleet provided major assistance to the small Indian Ocean island nation of Mauritius, which had been hard hit by a tropical cyclone. Flood relief in the Philippines is a periodic task.

There are those in the United States who believe that

the Seventh Fleet has no business being in the Far East and Indian Ocean. This belief is shared by few governments in that area. Indeed, there have been repeated statements on the vital importance of the presence of the Seventh Fleet by the leaders of friendly governments. Despite a substantial opposition, Japanese leadership has emphatically supported and provided bases for the Seventh Fleet. Premier Chou En Lai of the People's Republic of China has been reported as favoring the presence of the Seventh Fleet.

Throughout the Seventh Fleet area there are ancient tensions and fears. Because of the presence of the American fleet, the Japanese need not fear the U.S.S.R. or the mainland Chinese. Taiwan is safe, the Republic of Korea can expect effective support, and the Philippines are immune from invasion, so long as the Seventh Fleet is deployed and used to enforce the peace.

The composition and organization of the Seventh Fleet provide remarkable flexibility for quick response to any routine task or emergency. It is currently a strong fleet, including a full Marine division and Marine air wing, 55–60 ships, and 55,000–60,000 sailors and Marines. The fleet has more than 500 Navy and Marine aircraft of all types and is normally composed of the following:

Carriers	3
Cruisers	4–5
Destroyers or frigates	18–19
Amphibious ships	8
Submarines	5
Tow, salvage, and rescue ships	5–6
Repair ship or tender	1
Mobile logistic support force ships	9–11

Charged with search, reconnaissance, and surveillance through daily air patrols in the Seventh Fleet ocean area, about 30 P-3 Orion antisubmarine patrol planes and one reconnaissance squadron of specially-equipped aircraft of Task Force 72 operate from Japan, the Philippines, and Guam. Flights in international air space are conducted from the far Arabian Sea to the Sea of Okhotsk. Task Force 72 has primary responsibilities in ASW and as the eyes and ears of the fleet.

The principal punch of the Seventh Fleet is delivered by the carrier striking force. Task Force 77 draws on other task force commanders for the supporting ships and aircraft to form carrier task groups. Roving through the area with Task Force 72 aircraft and mobile logistic support ships, these carriers and their associated cruisers, destroyers, and submarines can be found from time to time as far west as the Persian Gulf, down under off Australia, in the Sea of Japan, and in the South China or Philippine Seas. When necessary, a special concentration can be achieved rapidly, as

happened during the evacuation of South Vietnam.

The cruisers and destroyers of the Seventh Fleet carry a heavy load. Escorting the carriers, participating in exercises throughout the Seventh Fleet area, and racing to the rescue at sea when called, the ships of Task Force 75 lead a busy life. The May 1975 rescue of the containership *Mayaguez* and her crew, assisted by the USS *Harold E. Holt* (DE-1074) and the USS *Henry B. Wilson* (DDG-7) shows the readiness and flexibility of these ships. After two days of high-speed steaming, the former received a Marine boarding party, an explosive ordnance demolition team, and a Military Sealift Command volunteer group from hovering helos, went alongside the *Mayaguez,* boarded her, and towed her to sea. Later, the *Henry B. Wilson* delivered naval gunfire on hostile positions ashore on the Tang Island to assist Marines landed there. She even armed her gig and used it successfully to suppress and divert fire, aiding extraction of the Marines from the island. With very little time for planning, all this was done with cool professionalism, in the best tradition of destroyermen.

The amphibious force, Task Force 76, and the Fleet Marine Force, Task Force 79, are virtually inseparable partners in carrying out their jobs. The 31st Marine Amphibious Unit, composed of a battalion of marines and assigned helos for vertical assault, embarks in Amphibious Ready Group Alfa. Amphibious Ready Group Bravo carries a battalion landing team. These ready groups are capable of amphibious assault providing tailored landing teams with tanks, artillery, and helicopter gunships. An amphibious command ship carries the Navy and Marine Corps commanders and their staffs to run the show.

The submarines of the Seventh Fleet are few in number, and thus Task Force 74 has to make every minute count. As a submarine proceeds from one area to another, she will be simultaneously providing tracking services to aircraft and surface ships. The role of the nuclear attack submarine in the defense of a carrier task group is now widely acknowledged. A feature of fleet exercises, therefore, is submarine protection and support for other naval forces.

While the fleet depends upon bases for refit and upkeep, as well as stores and supplies of all kinds, its range would be narrow indeed, except for the mobile logistic support force of Task Force 73. Normally, Seventh Fleet ships reserve periods at sea for taking on fuel, food, ammunition, and stores to exercise at underway replenishment. The oilers, ammunition ships, stores ships, and ships that combine two or more of these capabilities are a vital part of the Seventh Fleet. The fast combat support ships are especially valuable with their great capacity for fuel, ammunition, food, and general cargo; they can carry more fuel than the

Considering what it took to get it and what it takes to hold it, the "high ground" of South Korea ranks among the most expensive real estate in the world. Yesterday, U. S. Marines helped take it; today the U. S. Army (above) supports the ROK Army in holding it; and, for the foreseeable tomorrows, the Seventh Fleet stands ready to guarantee the freedom of its people.

largest fleet oiler and more ammunition than the largest ammunition ship. The combat stores ship is a welcome sight to ships long at sea with her general provisions, refrigerated food stocks, and aviation supplies.

Most of the ships and aircraft of the Seventh Fleet deploy for a period of six months, but one attack carrier, two cruisers, a destroyer squadron, and two combat stores ships are homeported in Japan; a submarine and the tactical support squadron are based in the Philippines; and the reconnaissance squadron is based in Guam. The Marine division and Marine air wing are based in Japan and furnish forces for operations at sea; their personnel are on unaccompanied, one-year tours.

When there is an emergency, the Seventh Fleet is augmented as required by the situation from the rest of the Pacific Fleet. Ships about to depart the Seventh Fleet may be held on if necessary. When it became obvious that evacuation of South Vietnam was imminent, the Seventh Fleet was temporarily boosted by a full carrier task group and an amphibious squadron. Almost all of the Seventh Fleet ships were concentrated off Saigon, ready for any eventuality.

The magnificent base at Subic Bay, Republic of the Philippines, provides needed repairs, supplies, and recreation to the Seventh Fleet. Yokosuka and Guam follow in that order of importance as bases for the Seventh Fleet. Some support is also available at Singapore and Sasebo. Aircraft of the fleet are supported or based in the Philippines at Cubi Point (part of the Subic Bay complex), Kadena on Okinawa, and at Atsugi and Misawa on the island of Honshu, Japan. These bases are not subordinate to the Commander, Seventh Fleet but are charged with fleet support.

Scheduling operations of the Seventh Fleet are quite complicated. Much of the planning work is done at quarterly scheduling conferences attended by representatives from all task forces, as well as representatives from the United Kingdom, Australian, and New Zealand Navies. These conferences review the forces assigned to the Seventh Fleet, including Allied ships and aircraft that will exercise with it, and piece together a schedule of exercises, refit periods, port visits, and various special operations. Some of the guidelines that must be observed include: port loading must be within the capability of the particular port to absorb the liberty party; ship repair facilities must not be overtaxed; economical speed must be used when exercise realism does not require fast movement; exercises with Allies are a priority commitment. But after about three days of hard work, the schedulers come up with a compromise plan to submit to the Seventh Fleet Commander and higher authority for approval.

The story, of course, does not end there. The Seventh

Fleet operating schedule is under practically constant revision for one reason or another. Important world developments, such as a war in the Middle East or the fall of a friendly government mean that the whole schedule has to be taken apart and put back together again. Minor events, such as a material casualty, can cause the substitution of one ship for another in an exercise, with a cascade effect. Unusual activity by the Soviet Navy calls for a surveillance effort which dislocates the Seventh Fleet employment schedule. Change is the normal mode of Seventh Fleet operations and becomes an accepted way of life.

The USS *Oklahoma City* is the fleet flagship. Styled these days as the "command ship," the guided-missile cruiser carries the fleet commander on a series of protocol visits. He needs to know the chiefs of friendly navies in the area, as well as other senior foreign officers and officials in order to be ready to cooperate in mutual defense and exercises to improve combat readiness. It is important, also, for the fleet commander to know as many as possible of the U. S. ambassadors in the area in order to provide the best support.

Wherever the *Oklahoma City* (CG-5) is, her specially-configured communications suit serves the flag and staff in the direction of fleet operations. A continual stream of reports, instructions, plans, and discussions flows between the Commander, Seventh Fleet, his subordinate commanders, and his boss, the Commander-in-Chief, U. S. Pacific Fleet. A quiet Sunday afternoon in port may suddenly become hectic when a disaster at sea requires quick reaction by the staff duty officer to get a plane or ship on scene as quickly as possible. At sea, the *Oklahoma City,* may join an amphibious task group, with her 6-inch guns and Talos missile battery, or she may help protect a carrier. She is a well-preserved old lady, first commissioned in 1944. Her smartness sets the fleet standard.

The fleet is not without problems. The rush of international events has called our ships out of port repeatedly when they should be undergoing needed upkeep and materiel improvement. There remains a great deal of work left over from these intensive efforts required in the national interest. Money to buy spare parts, make repairs, and provide consumable stores has been short. Many gaps appear in the rosters of skilled personnel and, in some cases, ships have been unable to steam at full power due to lack of men to stand watch; under these circumstances, even routine maintenance suffers, and the overall quality of material readiness goes down. Instead of being able to conduct all of the advanced exercises needed, too much time has to be spent doing leftover maintenance work and in kindergarten or first grade exercises at sea due to lack of experienced personnel. Yet, progress is made, and the fleet is at a much higher standard of combat effectiveness for blue water operations in 1976 than it was at the end of the Vietnam War, which so narrowed the operational focus.

Because of the great distances in the Seventh Fleet operating area, logistic support would be greatly simplified if more nuclear-powered surface ships were available. The distance from Norfolk to Alexandria, Egypt for example, approximates that from San Diego to Guam—but then on to the Arabian Sea is another 6,000 miles. Nuclear power is especially suited for the Pacific Fleet.

Another problem within the Seventh Fleet has been a lack of knowledge by one community of another. Patrol planes working with surface ships have not fully understood the surface ships' capabilities and limitations and vice versa, causing operations to falter. A program of cross-fertilization has provided insight into the other man's game. For example, pilots look at and go to sea in submarines, and submariners do the same with aircraft carriers. A thorough understanding of the capabilities and limitations of other types of ships and units is necessary in order to strengthen team play and mutual support. Progress has been made, but much more effort is necessary to make everyone appreciate that it is the *fleet* that wins the battles and not just the destroyers alone, or attack aviation independently, or submarines on distant patrol.

If deterrence, toward which the Seventh Fleet plays a part, should break down, and there should be a war with the Soviet Union, there is concern about the control of the sea-lanes by the United States and her

U. S. NAVY

The Seventh Fleet flagship—USS Oklahoma City *(CG-5)*

Allies. Much discussion goes into setting up convoy routes, surveillance of the ocean, and protection of naval bases. It must not be forgotten that until and unless the U. S. Navy maintains control of the sea in this vast area, none of the Indian and Pacific Ocean sea-lanes would be safe. The target in such a war would be the combat forces of the enemy. And that is what the training program of the Seventh Fleet aims at. The readiness to meet and defeat any potential enemy is the paramount objective.

On a given day in the Seventh Fleet, one might find several ships well east of Japan entering or leaving the Seventh Fleet area of responsibility. An antisubmarine warfare exercise is in progress off Tokyo Bay. An aircraft carrier with her cruiser-destroyer screen and a submarine are exercising in the Okinawa operating area, while another carrier task group is in port at Subic for maintenance. A third carrier task group is visiting Mombasa, Kenya. An amphibious exercise involving ships and Marines of Amphibious Ready Group Bravo is in progress on the coast of Korea. Marines of Task Force 79 are exercising on Okinawa, and at Iwakuni, Japan, and Camp Fuji at the base of the famous mountain. Individual ships are exercising in operating areas off Subic and Guam. Ship visits are in progress in Hong Kong; Beppu, Japan; Kaohsiung, Taiwan; Manila; Sattahip, Thailand; Singapore; and Penang, Malaysia. A salvage ship is towing a barge from Sasebo to Subic. Various types of ships are undergoing upkeep at Yokosuka, Sasebo, and Guam, as well as Subic. Oilers, ammunition ships, and stores ships are underway to replenish the at-sea forces of the Seventh Fleet. Patrol planes of Task Force 72 are conducting ocean surveillance in the Indian Ocean in support of the carrier task group there and range along the Asian mainland at a respectful distance on the lookout for unusual happenings. Soviet intelligence collection ships are watching and being watched off Guam, Subic, and the southern coast of Korea. British and Australian destroyers are engaged in an antisubmarine warfare exercise with U. S. destroyers and a submarine in the Subic operating area. Several cruisers and destroyers are making preparations for a missile shoot on the Poro Point Range nearby.

The fleet commander leads an exceptionally active life. His first attention is focused on improving the ability of the fleet to fight in war. This means constant work to perfect and improve war plans. Exercises must be carefully tailored to test the plans and train the units of the Seventh Fleet to carry them out. The Seventh Fleet must also be ready to conduct a number of contingency operations, and the planning effort to keep contingency plans current never ends.

It is important for the fleet commander to see his principal subordinate commanders frequently. When the flagship is in port, it is often necessary for him to be flying off for a visit or an inspection. He cannot afford to be tied to the location of his command ship. The fleet commander tries hard to visit all of his ships, squadrons, and units ashore frequently enough to keep personal touch with their efficiency and morale. He may give drills so that he can personally check readiness. Informal discussions with officers and men of the fleet provide instructive insight into the feelings and attitudes and also provide an opportunity for junior personnel to hear his views.

A good part of the effectiveness of the Commander, Seventh Fleet, stems from his social contact with senior officers and officials of other countries. It is a great deal easier to settle difficult problems with people after you get to know them well at a pleasant dinner or athletic afternoon. Foreign dignitaries may not be able to judge the efficiency and effectiveness of the fleet except by the quality of service and food. So, no detail is spared.

Ceremony plays a considerable part in the life of the flagship. Honors to a visiting chief of state must go off with precision. The parade of lesser officials and officers whose rank warrants some ceremony is interesting and varied. Study of the customs and courtesies expected in each country is most important, because attention to protocol is a hallmark of the fleet commander.

Duty as Commander, Seventh Fleet is probably the best the U. S. Navy has to offer because of the size of the fleet, the enormous area in which it operates, and the scope allowed in exercising command. The opportunity to deal directly with the officers and men of the fleet, to work with ships and aircraft underway on exercises, representing the most powerful naval force in the area during visits to exotic foreign ports, and the chance to make so many overseas friends combine to make it a splendid experience. He lives a great six years in a two-year tour.

Vice Admiral Steele graduated from the Naval Academy in 1944 and entered the submarine service. He commanded the diesel submarine *Hardhead* (SS-365), and then as first commanding officer of the nuclear-powered attack submarine *Seadragon* (SSN-584) he took her on the first transit of the Northwest Passage by any vessel via the classic Parry Channel, went under icebergs for the first time, and visited the North Pole. He was the first commanding officer of the USS *Daniel Boone* (SBN-629), making the first Polaris patrols in the Pacific Ocean. As a flag officer he was successively Commander, U. S. Naval Forces Korea; Commander, Antisubmarine Warfare Group Four; on the staff of the Supreme Allied Commander, Europe; and was for nearly two years Commander, Seventh Fleet. He is the author of two books, *Seadragon: Northwest under the Ice* and *Vengeance in the Depths,* and the coauthor of a third, *Nuclear Submarine Skippers and What They Do.* He has also written a number of articles published in the *Proceedings* and other journals. Vice Admiral Steele retired from active duty on 1 September 1975.

Tactics and Tools

MINING: A Naval Strategy

A lecture delivered at the Naval War College

by

Professor Andrew Patterson, Jr.

The potential significance and utility of the mine in naval warfare has seldom been appreciated since its invention at the time of the American Revolution. The following historic narrative and analysis offer the reader not only a valuable review of past successes and failures of mine campaigns, but also a series of unique insights into possible roles for the mine in contemporary warfare.

The constraints of time require that my talk deal with the major considerations of mining as a naval strategy. I shall therefore limit my observations to an outline of the history of mine warfare and mention certain specific engagements of great naval significance, then comment on the mine and strategic materials, and conclude by summarizing some generalizations which become evident to one who has had the opportunity to study mining extensively. These generalizations will tell us a good deal about how the mine has been employed and how it might better be employed in the future. Although this approach is not exhaustively academic, I think it will provide a summary look at the subject.

If we define a mine as an instrument of warfare which is placed on or near a ship under the waterline to cause damage by the effect of its explosion alone, then we can clearly place the origin of mine warfare with one of my fellow Yale men, David Bushnell of Connecticut, class of 1775. Bushnell demonstrated to his fellow students and his professors that gunpowder could be exploded under water and then postulated and demonstrated experimentally that the bottom or side of a ship is more vulnerable to explosions under water than are sections above the waterline. He spent a considerable portion of his undergraduate years, even as Yale students do today, on something other than his studies, for by 1775 he had built and tested an operational one-man submarine and an explosive magazine or mine to be emplaced by it. His inventions were used in the War of Independence by the United States, but they had no notable success.

Robert Fulton, whom Americans credit with the invention of the steamboat, made the next major advances in the technology of mining. A man of innumerable mechanical schemes and unbelievable energy, he first designed mines and then persuaded Napoleon to use them against the British. However, after losing the confidence of the French, he went to England and convinced the British to use his mines against the French. After leaving Britain, he tried to sell his idea for the defense of New York harbor to the American Government but failed, despite his strikingly modern McNamara-style cost analysis entitled "Torpedo War."[*][1] He calculated that a third-rate ship of the line (one of 80 guns and 600 men) would cost $400,000 to build and equip, while the same 600 men placed 12 at a time in torpedo boats, would cost, for the craft plus outfitting with torpedoes, only $24,300, resulting in a saving of $375,700. He also assessed the relative safety in a major battle of those in a defending ship of the line *vs.* those in

---

[*]Bushnell who first used the term, chose to call his weapon a torpedo, after the electric torpedo fish found off European coasts; the root Latin verb, torpere, means to stun. This name was used for the weapon we now call the mine through most of the 19th century when the advent of the self-propelled torpedo caused the named stationary device to be called the mine.

the torpedo craft and concluded the latter would be better off. Fulton's ideas, while definitely sound, were ahead of the technological level of his weapons.

Samuel Colt, also of Connecticut and famous for his invention of the revolver pistol, began to experiment with mines at the age of 15. In 1842 he adapted an electrical firing device to his mine designs, developed and built a successful sheathed underwater cable, and conducted numerous spectacular and successful demonstrations of his system, some of which were against moving craft at considerable distances from the firing point. Again, the U.S. Navy could not be sold on the idea of mines, in spite of the public and political popularity of Colt's devices and system.

Further developments took place then on the Continent, leading to the planting of electrically detonated wine-cask mines at Kiel during the Schleswig-Holstein War of 1848-1850. Mines were planted by the Russians in the Crimean War of 1854-1856 at Sevastopol, Svea-borg, and Kronstadt. These utilized the Jacobi fuse, a kind of chemical horn firing device. In the French-Austrian War of 1859, the harbor of Venice was protected by mines containing up to 450 pounds of guncotton rigged to be fired electrically. Finally, these European developments were also recognized in Asia where the Chinese used mines in their war of 1857-1858 with the English.

None of these installations entailed any actual battle experience, however. It was not until our Civil War that mines were seriously and effectively employed. Matthew Fontaine Maury, the noted American oceanographer, concluded early in the war that the vast shoreline and river systems of the South could not be protected by a new nation which had no navy to speak of, except by the use of mines. If we define tactical to mean operations within an engagement limited in space and in time and strategic to mean the deployment of forces and materiel on a large scale—often in advance or over a protracted period—the South was unable to develop any overall strategic concept for the use of mines. It had no time for advance preparation and was lacking in both resources of men and

material and, therefore, could do little other than meet immediate threats. Nevertheless, the events of the obviously successful Southern mine and spar torpedo campaign speak for themselves. By the end of the war, 29 Federal vessels were sunk and 14 damaged in major degree. Certainly, considerable planning went into the installation of several electrically controlled minefields in strategic rivers, but the majority of the efforts were in the form of improvised but ingenious tactical maneuvers in the face of a vastly better equipped and numerous enemy. These efforts created stalemates in nearly all the major rivers, notably the James, prolonging the war not just for months, but for years.

I should like now to pass rather rapidly through the years 1865 until the present, picking out some engagements involving mines which were decisive in establishing the strategic and tactical uses to which mines could be put.

In the Russo-Turkish War of 1877-1878, the Russians wished to keep the elements of the Turkish Fleet separated and immobilized. They did so by planting mines at strategic spots in the Danube, spots so well chosen that the British planted aerial-laid mines at the exact same places in WW II. Although only one sinking is credited, the Turkish battleship *Suna*, the combined Russian effort with spar torpedoes and mines reduced the effective strength of the Turks to zero and transferred the initiative into Russian hands.

You will recall that this was the period during which the iron navies were developing and replacing sailing ships. It is curious to us today that developments in ships and armament, particularly including mines, were widely publicized and discussed. The Austrians, for example, displayed their mining system at the Paris exhibition of 1867, and Maury would give instruction in mining systems to the representatives of any government which could pay his substantial fee. This openness continued to the turn of the century.

Then the Russo-Japanese War of 1904 and a new climate of international mistrust changed things. The Russo-Japanese War constituted the first major confrontation between world powers

using modern mines, a confrontation which warfare theorists had been calling for if mines were to be tested in the heat of battle as a system of weaponry. The Japanese mined offensively, placing fields across Russian harbors with considerable daring and then enticing the Russian Fleet out with a show of inferior forces. The Russians mined defensively, managing thus to extend their shorelines effectively to seaward, making it impossible for the Japanese Fleet to bombard the shore defenses. Six Russian ships were sunk by Japanese mines, one by a Russian mine. Eleven Japanese ships were sunk by Russian mines. Many ships and small craft of several nations fell victim to floating mines after the war was over, giving rise to the Hague Convention on mines of 1907.

Perhaps the most classic and history-making strategic action employing mines was by the Turks, possibly with aid from the Germans, in the Dardanelles in 1914. Using a mixed bag of mines and nets of uncertain origin and quality, the Turks mined the straits, employing an inspired combination of shore and naval weaponry, and undoubtedly changed the course of history. The minefields, at first rudimentary but later expanded, were guarded by shore batteries and searchlight installations, making it impossible for the British to sweep the fields. Attempts to do so were abandoned after the British lost four dreadnoughts to mines and shore fire. As a result of the blockade, Russian wheat did not leave the Ukraine, Turkey was not surrounded from the north, Turkey and Bulgaria were not separated by the naval wedge that Britain hoped to drive between them; but, most of all, the British suffered a major psychological defeat as well as a significant loss of ships and men.

The campaign by Russian Adm. Nikolai von Essen against the Germans in the Baltic was well planned in advance and brilliantly executed. Unfortunately, it was terminated by the admiral's death in 1915. A concerted effort went into training elements of the Baltic Fleet in minelaying, and many destroyer hulls were converted to or developed as minelayers. Owing to the long 6-week period between the precipitating assassination and the declaration of hostilities, there was plenty of time to lay mines during the period of mobilization. While the Russians laid mines mostly for defensive protection of their own harbors and shore areas, they also mined offensively to interdict traffic on the Scandinavian-German iron ore routes. After the Germans laid minefields, von Essen expanded them and converted them into his own, creating havoc in the German Fleet. He then made fast runs into German harbors with minelaying destroyers, virtually cutting off the flow of iron ore, and preventing the German Fleet from giving fire support to shore-based forces. On one occasion alone, the Germans lost seven of 11 ships in the 10th Destroyer Flotilla.

A mine barrage of major proportions had been planned by the British Admiralty in WW I against the German concentrations at Heligoland, but its cost caused Churchill to turn it down as impossible. Furthermore, in 1914-1915, the British did not have a reliable mine to use, much less the numbers necessary to mount such a barrage. It was not until the United States entered the war and made its technological and production facilities available that it was possible to mount this offensive. By this time the British had developed the successful H2 mine, which was embodied into the Mk 6 mine, with float, antenna, et cetera. These made the mine barrage possible since they were able to watch over a much greater volume of ocean. Thus the decision was made to close off the entrance for German subs into the North Sea; by the end of the war, 70,117 mines had been laid. Not many sinkings can be attributed to the barrage—Roscoe in his British report claims five, and Admiral Scheer says none. However, the barrage did force the Germans to traverse a greater distance to open water, with consequent delay, and the morale effect for the beleaguered British and the anxious Americans probably was significant. The cost of the barrage has been reckoned as equal to the cost of running the war for 1 day. Hence, if it shortened the war by 1 day, which it may well have done through its morale (if not ship sinking) effects, it was a good investment.

During WW II the United States conducted two major mining operations in the Pacific. The initial campaign was in the southern and outer reaches, and this was followed by a close-in operation around the Japanese home islands in what has come to be known as Operation Starvation. These campaigns were singularly successful in spite of the fact that

There was at no time in the past war an over-all plan for a mining campaign against the Japanese, and as a consequence offensive mining was not included in the major strategy of the war.... Mines perhaps more than any other weapon of equal accomplishment, were orphans during the war. Even though approval and encouragement were received from the high commands, much of the initiation and promotion of the mine laying campaign can be traced to the relatively small group of enthusiasts engaged in the work.[2]

During the last 5 months of the war, more than 1,250,000 tons of Japanese shipping were sunk or damaged by mines, and a virtual blockade of the Shimonoseki Straits and of the inland sea was affected. The aerial mining campaign is credited by Prince Konoye (and other knowledgeable Japanese officers) with having an overall economic effect comparable to all the other bombing and incendiary raids conducted. Thus an effort in mining requiring 5.7 percent of the XXI Bomber Command's flying time was comparable to all of the remaining 94.3 percent given to strategic bombing. Mines sank and damaged more shipping than any other agent, whether it was submarines, Army or Navy air forces. Despite this phenomenal success, the attack was very nearly too little and too late, as had decidedly been the case with the North Sea barrage. The bulk of the mining was of a strategic nature, although a number of tactical mining campaigns were mounted in support of amphibious operations when it was desired to interfere temporarily with movements of enemy ships; examples of tactical employment of mines would be in the Solomons, Rangoon, the Marshall Islands, Palau Atoll, Truk, Woleai, and the Shimonoseki Straits.

I cannot end this brief historical recital without mentioning the incident at Wonsan, Korea. There was plenty of evidence that mines were being used by the North Koreans, for there had been sightings of drifting mines and of minefields on both coasts. Accordingly, plans were made to sweep for 10 days before the planned landing at Wonsan. What was not perhaps fully anticipated was that the Russians had given the North Koreans mines, torpedoes, and depth charges as well as technical training and direct supervision in planning and laying the fields at Wonsan. In the first 3 days of sweeping, American forces lost two large steel minesweepers and were so demoralized that the following message was sent to the Pentagon: "The U.S. Navy has lost command of the sea in Korean waters...." Sweeping was abandoned and searching for mines instituted for 2 days. Then as the sweepers had cleared a channel and neared the shore, influence mines were encountered. Seven more days were required to complete the sweep, and the commanding officer of the landing force wisely concluded that, because of ROK advances on land, the landing was not required until the sweep could be completed. Of the estimated 3,000 mines laid, only 225 were swept and destroyed. The remainder lay outside swept channels.

In retrospect, the major result of the Wonsan encounter was a revitalization of U.S. Navy mine countermeasure activity. One cannot view the Wonsan incident as anything but a major victory for the Russians. In exchange for 3,000 obsolete mines, many of WW I vintage, a majority of pre-WW II style, the United States, aside from losses of ships and men, was committed to a continuing program of mine countermeasure expenditures extending into the multimillion dollar range. While this was good for the United States, it was a cheap trade-off for the Russians to force us to spend that kind of money.

Turning to some selected historical observations carefully picked from the panorama outlined above, significant conclusions can be reached. It is a surprising fact that *all* ship sinkings in the European theater in WW II were in

110

depths of less than 600 feet, while in WW I the bulk of ships were sunk in similar inshore waters. During the 3 winter months of 1917-1918, 200 ships were sunk within 10 miles of shore (63 percent) while within 50 miles of shore an additional 35 percent were sunk, for a total of 98 percent ships sunk, all in waters not more than 50 miles from shore. From February 1917 to October 1918, 2,000 ships were sunk; 43 percent 10 miles from shore, 29 percent within 50 miles, for a total of 72 percent sunk within 50 miles of shore. In a similar way, during WW II every British battleship, fleet carrier, and cruiser sunk or damaged; every British submarine sunk in enemy action; every German warship, cruiser sized or greater; every German warship torpedoed by Soviet submarines; every Italian surface ship or warship damaged by submarine action; every Soviet warship sunk by submarines; *all of these* were sunk in waters of less than 600-foot depth.

The reason why these sinkings, a significant number of which must have resulted from mines, took place in comparatively shallow waters near shore is quite evident. Transiting upon the ocean's surface takes place between a comparatively limited number of ports, whose location is determined by favorable conditions both ashore and offshore, as well as by historical accident. These ports are quite commonly approached through waterways which are restricted in one way or another by local or distant geography. The economic health and survival of these ports hinges on access to and need for various commodities and strategic materials. Minefields have characteristically been placed at points where ship traffic is expected, and attack submarines or surface ships would hunt their prey in similar waters.

An obvious implication of these data is that very little mining has been done in deep waters and that, hence, there is an unfulfilled need for a good deep-water mining capability. Except for those areas where the Continental Shelf extends far to sea, as it does on the east coast of the United States, there are uses for deep-water moorable mines near shore. In addition, the paths of much ocean traffic in deep water are still fairly narrowly defined by the desire to sail the minimum possible distance between established ports, modified only by intervening geographical features or by wind or weather.

Three charts emphasize what I mean. First is a depiction of the narrow waters of the world. Places marked 1 are 25 fathoms or less; 2, 25 to 200 fathoms; and 3, greater than 200 fathoms. Much traffic seems to go through narrow waters. Next is shown the major ports of the world. If this were overlaid with the preceding chart, most of these would be within narrow, shallow waters. Finally there is a track chart of the world showing selected tracks between these major ports. It is here where most of the world's trade is funneled,

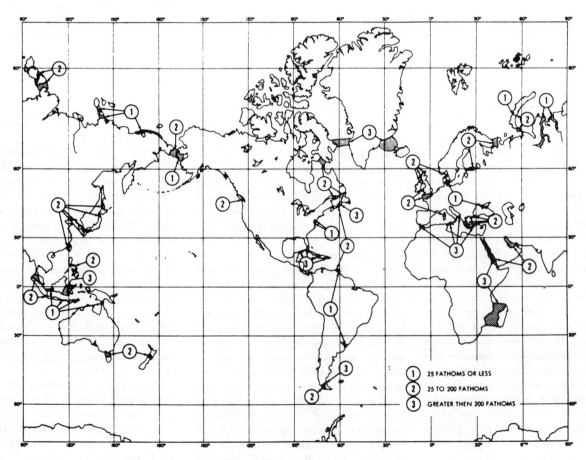

Fig. 1—Depths of Narrow Waters

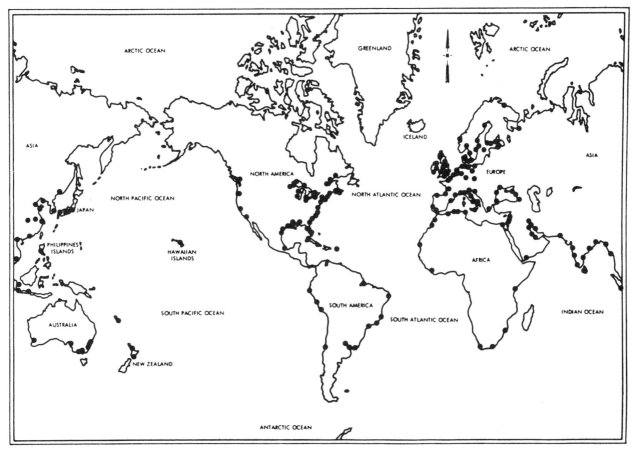

Fig. 2—Major Ports of the World

eventually through the narrow, shallow waters previously depicted.

I leap to a conclusion from these figures, and the history of mining seems to convey this point in general, that it is the ships and men themselves, more than the cargoes, which are the prime strategic materials. I leap also from strategy to strategic waterways. This was certainly Fulton's idea when he wrote *Torpedo War* in 1810. It was likewise the motivation for the use of torpedoes (that is, mines) during the Civil War, since the South could not blockade the North's sources of strategic materials. Only in WW I and WW II did the attack on cargo ships begin in a concerted way, and then, again, it was the ships and their generalized contents that were the targets, rather than attempts to control any particular materials. In both of these wars the attempts to establish the North Sea barrage or the Scotland-Iceland barrier were for general strategic and political objectives rather than for the control of

specific strategic materials. Not the least of the objectives of mining is to cause the adversary to expend relatively large amounts of his substance on mine-sweeping and countermeasures; large amounts of this substance consist of ships and men, to which a few strategic materials, like copper, are added. There are clearly notable exceptions to mining in this generalized strategic sense: the classic examples are the Russian and British use of mines in both World Wars to deny high-quality Scandinavian iron ore to Germany, both of which were singularly successful. These exceptions do not alter the conclusion, however, that in a large majority the targets of mining have not been specific strategic materials, but more generalized objectives. When these have not been men and ships, they have been political. Although in WW I the Allied Powers were anxious to get arms to Russia in exchange for her wheat, the Central Powers and Turkey undertook the mining of the Dardanelles not because

of these materials, however strategic they might have been, but for political reasons. The targets sunk by those 20 mines at Erenköi were British battleships, British seamen, and British national prestige and pride. Brittania no longer ruled the waves!

To rephrase the historical lesson another way, few mining episodes or campaigns have been undertaken with specific raw materials as their goals. The goals have been larger: political and strategic and directed against ships and men themselves. These I deem to be the prime strategic materials.

Why this should be so is puzzling. It would seem to indicate lack of foresight on the part of strategic planners. It is certainly true that the strategic materials we depend upon—food, fuel, and certain minerals—often come from a few limited places. Nickel is a good example. Until WW II nearly all came from Canada. Cuba is now a significant producer, ironically from mines developed by the United States during WW II.

Fig. 3—Track Chart of the World (Showing selected tracks, within distances from place to place in nautical miles)

There are numerous other strategic materials which come from only a few places, Persian Gulf oil being a particularly significant example.

I would go so far as to venture that, except in extended wars of the WW I and WW II types, it is not permissible to speak of the strategic uses of mining. The uses which have been made of mining lie elsewhere—in the political and psychological realms—a topic I shall defer to a subsequent part of this talk.

A second item which stands out in the historical record is the degree in which proponents and opponents of mining have been "true believers" in the Eric Hoffer sense of the term. From the times of Bushnell, Fulton, and Colt, mine developers have pressed and fought enthusiastically for the adoption of their ideas against others even more passionately opposed. Thus, when Fulton proposed mines first to the French, Admiral le Pelley, who was of the old school, refused to be interested because he had "conscientious scruples against such a terrible invention."[3] Fulton's

encounter with Commodore Rodgers was not very much different, the commodore finding Fulton's torpedoes to be "comparatively of no importance at all; consequently they ought not to be relied on as a means of national defense."[4] While the proponents of mining have evidently believed in the efficacy of their weapons, their opponents have been motivated by a variety of very human emotions. The Earl St. Vincent, First Lord of the Admiralty, feared he would soon be out of a job when he said to Fulton, "Pitt" [who had supported Fulton's experiments in England] was the greatest fool that ever existed, to encourage a mode of war which they who commanded the seas did not want, and which, if successful, would deprive them of it."[5] This polarization of true believers is no doubt connected with the quote given above from the Strategic Bombing Survey which found that at no time was mining a part of the grand strategy of WW II. I raise the issue to indicate that among the arguments which are neces-

sary if mining is to be used effectively as a weapon of war are those against prejudices of a number of different types.

A third feature of mines, which is of paramount importance in their tactical and strategic use, is their characteristically high degree of cost effectiveness. A string of 20 very ordinary mines off Erenköi in the Dardanelles probably altered the course of history in the Middle East. But of the mining expeditions which have been conceived on a large scale and postmortemed in detail, none is a better example than Operation Starvation around Japan at the end of WW II. Sherwood Frey has taken data from the 1946 survey [referred to above] and converted them into a modern cost-effective format, using contemporaneous dollar figures. Among the conclusions are: Mines laid by aircraft and submarines produced from 2 to 10 times the merchant ship sinkings yielded by submarine torpedoes per unit of cost. Air-laid mines, producing about eight sinkings per million dollars of cost, were about 50 percent more effective per unit of cost than were submarines laying mines. However, there were *no* casualties to submarines on minelaying missions. It thus appears that submarines achieved a greater cost effectiveness using mines than they did using torpedoes. The effectiveness-cost ratio for submarines using mines is 4.7 casualties per million dollars of cost, while for submarines using torpedoes it is only 1.1 to as low as 0.36 sinkings per million dollars of cost, depending on how the initial investment in the submarines is handled. A reverse datum which would be instructive is the expenditure the United States has made on mine countermeasure activity divided by the cost to the Russians and Koreans of the mining at Wonsan. The figure, indeterminate for the present, is undoubtedly very large; it would affirm again and with vigor the statement that mining is cost effective not only in targets sunk, but also in expenditures made by the reacting opponent.

One can, of course, quote less favorable data. The North Sea barrage was singularly ineffective in terms of the sinkings it achieved for the costs it entailed. This may suggest, as do other experiences, that we should devise more comprehensive methods of measuring costs to the opponent other than simply the number of ships sunk. We need to quantify how much a delay or a longer route costs him. How much is it worth to demoralize his seamen or strike fright in the heart of his populace? On these scores we know mines have been singularly effective also.

I would like to emphasize the obvious point that mines should not be utilized as a sole element in a strategy, as the figures quoted above may seem to indicate they have been. They should be used as a part of an integrated or coordinated strategic or tactical plan. In the Pacific,

on 30 and 31 March 1944, prior to the planned US landings at Hollandia in North New Guinea, carrier aircraft attacked Palau (Atoll) with mines and bombs in order to reduce its effectiveness as a base from which the Japanese could launch a possible counterattack. The attack consisted essen-

tially first of mining all exit passages to prevent the escape of enemy ships, then a direct bombing attack in which all the trapped ships were either sunk or beached, and finally the mining of the anchorage and the bombing of installations to prevent the further use of the Atoll by enemy vessels. The operation was completely successful, and Palau was abandoned as a forward enemy base shortly afterward.[6]

Thirty two ships were bottled up in the harbor; three were damaged by mines, and the rest would not risk trying the mined channels. All the ships were destroyed by bombing. A more successful combined tactical strike is hard to imagine.

But of all the factors which stand out when one contemplates the history of mine warfare, none is as noteworthy as the profound psychological and political impact of their use. Almost invariably the danger of mines is subjectively judged to be vastly greater than the actual or real threat the mines may present. Acknowledging that the "effect of mines" and "actual threat" are not easily quantifiable—or indeed as a very consequence of this unquantifiability—this general statement will stand unchallenged.

The simple mention of the word *mine* by governments has closed seaways and precipitated wars. It is interesting that the Egyptians seem especially prone to the use of verbal minefields: at least three historic instances bear recalling. In the Israeli 6-day war of 1967, Egypt announced a blockade of the Gulf of Aqaba, stating mines had been laid. In the Suez incident of 1956, Egypt stated the approaches to Alexandria had been mined and that the Gulf of Suez was dangerous to navigation. In both cases these statements were major factors in precipitating the crises into armed conflict. A much earlier incident throws illuminating commentary on the latter two. During the Arab-Pasha uprising of 1882, hundreds of steamers were tied up outside the Suez Canal because of the reported planting of mines. As an Italian warship steamed up, its captain, the future Vice Admiral Morin, inquired the cause of the congestion and was told of the mines. He

reportedly replied that the Egyptians had hardly the skill to lay mines properly, and if they had been laid as long as claimed they were probably ineffective, and steamed through the canal. His calculated risk broke the verbal blockade.

To repeat, the use of mines, or on occasion just the statement that mines had been planted, has most often resulted in extreme political reaction or overexaggerated psychological and emotional reaction. As Lott puts it, speaking of Farragut's fleet during the Civil War, "Sailors hardened to the smoke, noise, and pandemonium of close-range cannonading were stunned and demoralized by the sudden and unexpected mine blasts."[7] The fact that the mine threat usually remains hidden, unknown, uncalculated, and unassessed leads to the necessity to make decisions on what are emotional rather than rational grounds. I am indebted to Vice Adm. E.P. Aurand for a perceptive interpretation of this point. As he puts it, the important thing is not your calculation of the minefield's effectiveness or threat, but the enemy's *guess* of its threat. Historically, though with the usual exceptions (Damn the torpedoes, full speed ahead!), the tendency has been to overestimate the threat. The very great payoff rate of mines (a $350 mine can sink a $1 million ship) surely adds to this effect, since the risk is emotionally felt to be very great.

It is not going too far to say that the potential of mines excites a different sort of fear than ordinary weapons. Vice Adm. Friedrich Ruge puts his finger on this source of fear when he comments,

The mine is the only weapon of naval warfare that is to some extent capable of altering geographical circumstances by making certain areas unpassable to ships. Thus an area which has been declared dangerous because of the use of mines is usually treated with great respect and is avoided as though it were land.[8]

It is also true that mines have *not* been used on numerous occasions because of the political and emotional impact their use would entail. The rules of the game in Vietnam are so strange it is not easy to say much about it, but it is probably fair to say that political considerations have strongly guided military actions, including the use and nonuse of mines.

Mines possess a number of unique qualities as weapons which are significant in any consideration of how they might be used strategically.

Mines are versatile; they can do direct damage to military logistic units, but they can also attack broad facets of the enemy's economy. Because ships typically carry a large bulk of goods, they are much more vulnerable to attack than other modes of transport, especially on land. Mines can destroy and disrupt the enemy's merchant marine. They can increase the damage inflicted by other weapon systems by channeling traffic into positions favorable for attack. They can saturate ports, disrupt storage and loading as well as shore-based transport, and force diversion of traffic to decrease or even stop cargo flow. They have deterrent effects which weigh heavily in the political and psychological realms.

Mines are waiting weapons. The target must come to the mine. While this might at first be thought a disadvantage, it actually has a number of positive attributes. The mine maintains vigilance, possibly over a long period, without continued commitment of forces. The initiative or aggression must come from the enemy. A direct face-to-face confrontation can be avoided.

Mines usually are invisible weapons. If mines are laid surreptitiously, they can inflict maximum damage because of surprise. If they are announced, the psychological impact is maximized because of the ignorance of the size and nature of the threat.

Mines are selective weapons. Few other weapons can be made to select a very specific size or class of target or be selective in depth or range—clearly mines are vastly more selective than bombs.

Mines are flexible in duration and times of activeness.

Mines are ideally suited to providing graduated response in intensity, area, and time of attack. The minimum response required to attain a military goal can be chosen.

Mines change the geography of the battlefield.

Conclusions. Mining strategy and its

planning must be started in advance—it is not adequate to wait until later to decide that mining might be useful. The amount of logistic preparation is too great. This mistake was made by the United States in WW I and WW II and again—with respect to countermeasures—in the Korean war.

Offensive mining should be considered a complementary effort, not a competitor, to other forms of attack systems—submarine torpedoing, aircraft bombing, or whatever modern technique may be employed. Mining should be assessed on a cost-effectiveness basis, as with any other system, but in doing so it is necessary to be both honest and realistic about the assumptions put into the calculation. When mining is used, planners should endeavor to coordinate their mining effort with other modes of attack to gain maximum effectiveness.

Mine warfare has always been considered a contest between the mine designers on the one hand and the countermeasures experts on the other. Experience indicates, however, that mines can be made so difficult to sweep or hunt that practical countermeasures may take some time to develop, thereby assuring that the opponent will have suffered time-consuming delay and attrition of his valuable resources.

Since a mine campaign is closely related to the entire war strategy, the first task at hand is to convince strategists and tacticians that mines have any role at all to play in a modern conflict. Mine technology, to a greater degree than that of any other weapons system, exponentially decays after a conflict has been finished. Consequently, the planners of the current generation:
- assume mines are available and ready to use if they should want them, when in fact they are not,
- know nothing about how to use them and assume they can be employed only in long, drawn-out major strategic standoffs, when exactly the opposite should be true,
- fail to realize that mines are specialized weapons with requirements which demand training and preparation to use them advantageously.

Minelaying, as a general rule, should commence with a large initial attack—hence the need for advance preparation— and be continued by frequent

moderate-sized attacks rather than occasional large-scale attacks. Minelaying should be so dispersed as to put the maximum burden on the enemy's mine clearance forces.

Much of the value of a new weapon—e.g., a new firing mechanism—lies in its unexpected introduction and large-scale use before the enemy can develop countermeasures or adopt alternative courses of action.

One must also realize that there are values other than sinking ships that the miner desires and with which he is concerned because they redound to the benefit of the minelaying side:
- sinking ships is fine, but damaging a ship may be better—forcing the enemy to expend men and materiel on repairing damaged ships is advantageous;
- forcing the enemy to engage in mine countermeasures uses up men and resources at little cost to the miner;
- delay of shipping and disruptions of cargo handling at ports on both ends of a supply line are valuable byproducts of mining even if no ship is sunk;
- demoralization of both ship and shore crews is also a valuable byproduct; if the crew can be prodded to jump ship, so much the better.

Simplification of mine preparation in the field would make the mine a much more useful weapon as would relaxing some of the earlier strictures which I have noted above.

Every effort should be made to accumulate intelligence information on how and where best to use mines before and during hostilities. An equal and perhaps even greater effort should be made to determine the effects of mines on the enemy's war effort while they are being used as well as after the end of hostilities. One needs to receive feedback on the effects of mine weapon systems as quickly as possible if the minelayer is to get credit for what he has accomplished in his effort and if mines are to be credited with what they have done; otherwise, cost effectiveness will not be assessed correctly, thus reducing the chances of their intelligent and effective use.

The possible future use of mines in affecting and possibly settling international disputes should not be overlooked. Mines can be dropped so as to produce a blockade without actually resulting in direct harm or bloodshed to the local populace. The economic effects of such blockade might well assist the settlement of disputes without actual combat. It should be noted, however, that one must maintain a cadre of trained officers and men if one desires to have the option of a mine campaign open at any time to deal with international disputes.

In using mines we have erred in thinking of them as only long-term attrition weapons instead of using them as tactical weapons. We have failed to use them for their psychological and political effects by insisting that only a ship sunk is a valid test of whether the mine has accomplished its mission.

We have not devised a sufficiently evangelical approach to the conversion of true nonbelievers in that we have not convincingly shown that mines are important parts of overall oceanic and riverine naval strategy. We have not recognized or, more properly, minefield planners have not properly recognized the strategic character of ships and men themselves, but rather have preferred to consider such products as petroleum or platinum as the ultimate targets of mine warfare.

Many persons in the position to make decisions of military importance do not understand the characteristics of mine warfare or its underlying principles, so the potential of the minefield as a military weapon system is not well appreciated. Why does this situation exist?

● Military people are vehicle oriented, not weapon oriented. It is the Polaris submarine that claims the allegiance, not the Polaris rocket. Mines have the disadvantage of being even less dependent on a particular vehicular delivery sytem than are most other weapons.

● Mines lack bang appeal. The layer seldom gets to see one go off, and, as a consequence, his battle ribbons record few or no sinkings compared to the usual aviator, say, who gets to drop a bomb.

● Mines have commonly been the chosen weapon of inferior nations because of their cost effectiveness. This leaves the stigma that somehow it is beneath the dignity of the great nation to use such a weapon. There is the

feeling, expressed ever since the time of Bushnell and Fulton, that the mine is somehow an ungentlemanly weapon.

● Mine service is often thought not to contribute to professional advancement.

● The mine is a basic and ancient weapon, one for which it is not easy to devise novel innovations or arrive at a breakthrough.

In conclusion, it can be fairly said that the military has failed historically to appreciate the significant role the mine is capable of playing in naval warfare and continues to do so for a variety of reasons. It is only by dispassionate critical analysis of past successes and failures that we can hope to overcome the traditional prejudices against this useful weapon.

BIOGRAPHIC SUMMARY

Professor Andrew Patterson, Jr., did both his undergraduate and graduate work at the University of Texas, gaining his Ph.D. there in 1942. He has been actively associated with the Harvard Underwater Sound Laboratory (1943-1945), the U.S. Navy Underwater Sound Laboratory as a physicist and research consultant (1945-1951), and served as the Director of the Office of Naval Research at the Edwards St. Laboratory, Yale University (1951-1956). Professor Patterson was the Chairman of the Mine Advisory Committee, National Academy of Sciences of the National Research Council for 1958-1962. Since 1962 he has served as a consultant to the Mine Advisory Committee and presently is Professor of Chemistry, Yale University.

FOOTNOTES

1. Robert Fulton, *Torpedo War and Submarine Explosions* (New York: Elliot, 1810). (Fulton had the book privately published.)
2. U.S. Naval Material Command, *The Offensive Mine Laying Campaign Against Japan*, NAVMAT P-9810 (Washington: 1969), p. 25.
3. Paul D. Bunker, "The Mine Defense of Harbors: Its History, Principles, Relation to Other Elements of Defense, and Tactical Employment," *Journal of U.S. Artillery* (Fort Monroe, Va.: Coast Artillery School Press, 1914), v. 41, p. 129-170.
4. *Ibid.*, p. 136.
5. Fulton.
6. U.S. Naval Material Command, p. 19.
7. Arnold S. Lott, *Most Dangerous Sea* (Annapolis, Md.: U.S. Naval Institute, 1959), p. 11.
8. Friedrich Ruge, *Sea Warfare 1939-1945: a German Viewpoint*, trans. M.G. Saunders (London: Cassell, 1957), p. 13.

By JOHN ENNIS

John Ennis is a freelance writer and a former member of the Navy's mine force.

INFLATION is the number one peacetime enemy of the U.S. Navy. That, no one doubts. Yet, while costs of new weapons continue to soar and their need is questioned by disgruntled taxpayers, the Navy has scuttled one of its most economical and effective weapons: Mine Warfare.

The U.S. Surface Mine Force today consists of only five active duty ships. The average age of the vessels is 18 years. Breakdowns at sea are a way of life for the crews—one sweeper broke apart in a Pacific storm at the end of Vietnam's Operation End Sweep.

The Soviet Navy, on the other hand, has an active-duty fleet of 350 minesweepers, and is building more. The USSR's ships are faster and more sophisticated than U.S. mine force vessels. When a Soviet minesweeper becomes obsolete, it is placed in the reserve force or given to another Communist-bloc Navy. The Soviet Navy is now the world leader in mine warfare. The U.S. Navy ranks tenth. Moreover, the Soviet Navy has never thrown away a mine and has more than one-half million stockpiled.

Each year, the Soviet Navy awards diplomas to 100 graduates of its two-year postgraduate mine warfare course. The U.S. Navy has fewer than 70 officers who have attended even a six-month course—and fifty percent of that number graduated more than ten years ago. Only ten percent have served more than one hitch in the mine force.

That such a disparity could exist today is somewhat puzzling, considering that mines have played an extremely important role in every U.S. war to date, and were particularly important in World War II, when 25,000 mines were laid against the Japanese and more than two and a quarter million tons of enemy shipping was sunk or seriously damaged by mines.

Ships Sink, Lessons Don't

Combat vessels placed out of commission by Allied mines in World War II included two battleships, two escort carriers, eight cruisers, 38 destroyers, five submarines, and 54 smaller vessels. The closing days of the war found Japan's ports polluted with mines.

But the lessons of success sink in slowly: 27 years after the end of that war, a lonely man cast a final glance at a speech he had re-written numerous times. Precisely at 9:00 p.m. Washington time, Richard Nixon stepped before White House television cameras and announced that U.S. Navy planes were again mining the ports of Asia, this time the harbors of North Vietnam.

It had not been an easy decision. But the former Chief Executive was faced with the reality that a South Vietnam which for years had been under continuous attack might soon collapse. Fewer than 60,000 American troops remained in South Vietnam, and only a limited number were combat-trained. In deciding upon a course of limited response, the then-President chose one of the oldest, most successful—and most neglected—weapons in the U.S. military arsenal.

The U.S. sea mine was invented by David Bushnell,

Deep, Cheap & Deadly

Mine Warfare: The Most Economical Weapon, and the Most Neglected

who in 1775 filled empty beer kegs with explosives and floated them down the Delaware River toward British ships. The mines missed their targets but created tremendous confusion among the English crews; Bushnell's feeble attempt to sink the fleet failed, but nevertheless established the mine as a psychological weapon that would itself later pay a major role in sea warfare.

It was not until the War between the States that sea mines were used on a large scale. The Confederacy, which had practically no navy at all, found it much easier and cheaper to fight the Union's superior forces with underwater weapons. Confederate mines were crude devices filled with unpredictable black powder and ignited by home-made fuses. Many failed to explode on time and, worse yet, some exploded too early, making southern minemen their own unintended victims.

Mobile Bay and the Final Count

Despite such problems, Confederate mines were greatly feared by Union sailors, and it took strong leaders to overcome that fear. One such leader was Admiral David Farragut, who, sailing into a Mobile Bay cluttered with more than 80 mines, uttered his immortal "Damn the torpedoes; full speed ahead."

The count taken when the last Civil War shot had been fired showed that Confederate naval officers had sent 35 Union ships to the bottom with mines. Artillery fire and shore bombardment had sunk only nine.

Despite the success of the Civil War mine, Navy

officials again ignored the weapon until the United States entered World War I. For the second time in history, England convinced the United States of the efficacy of mine warfare. Royal Naval Intelligence, worried about German U-boats in the North Sea, prevailed upon the United States to supply England with mines. To combat the submarine threat, the allies cut off the only access route from the North Sea to the Atlantic by laying hundreds of mines beneath the surface of the choppy waters. The tactic succeeded in keeping the enemy fleet bottled up and had a great psychological effect on German sailors. One German U-boat commander who had been ordered to make the passage through the minefield had to cancel his mission because of widespread panic and mutiny. His submarine sailors were willing to fight but refused to transit waters filled with underwater explosives. The North Sea barrage was one of the most successful offensive tactics of the war.

The WWI mine battle was not one-sided. The German Navy itself laid many mines in the Atlantic from submarines and prompted the English to develop a primitive mine-countermeasures system. Many of the early basic MCM techniques developed then are today used by the U.S. Navy and by the fleets of other maritime powers.

During the early days of World War II, German submarines laid 338 mines along the east coast of the United States and sank 11 ships. The situation was so serious that the U.S. Navy refused to confirm the sinkings even though several had been observed by U.S. civilians from nearby coastal areas. Newspapers and radio stations were prohibited from mentioning the losses. The German mines kept U.S. ports closed for 32 days and forced the Navy to commit 125 minesweepers to the "clean-up operation."

The United States conducted extensive mining operations in the Pacific. More than 25,000 mines were, as previously noted, laid in Japanese home waters and 670 Japanese ships, including 109 men-of-war, were sunk or damaged by U.S. mines. At the end, because her ports were closed, Japan could not import food and her people nearly starved.

World War II also gave birth to aerial minesweeping. England again took the lead by outfitting a small squadron of Wellington bombers with large electrical coils energized by gas generators. The equipment, designed to explode magnetic mines, was extremely noisy, and useless in deep water, but the Wellingtons represented another milestone in mine warfare.

Lost: Five Ships, One Face

Several years later, North Korean mines caused the U.S. Navy to lose face at Wonsan Harbor when Soviet technicians helped their allies lay 3,000 mines before the path of invading forces. The mines held the U.S. Navy at bay for days and eventually sank three minesweepers and damaged two destroyers.

Tactical frustration and a rising casualty rate forced the Navy to assign nine minesweepers to clear the waters while an invasion force of 250 ships and several thousand troops waited offshore. By the time the dangerous operation was completed, South Korean Marines had taken Wonsan and the North Koreans had retreated. It was not the U.S. Navy's finest hour. Commenting on the painful lessons learned, Rear Admiral Brian McCauley, commander in the early 1970s of the U.S. Navy's mine-warfare force, said "It is almost unthinkable that a nation with no navy to speak of could delay, stop and frustrate the most powerful navy in the world by laying a mine-field with a fleet of decrepit fishing junks and sampans."

From Haiphong to Suez

It was McCauley, incidentally, who directed the removal of mines from the Suez Canal. He had trained for that mission by conducting End Sweep, the code name given to the operation which had been designed to deactivate the mines in North Vietnam's harbors and rivers.

Operation End Sweep was one of the most dangerous, complex and challenging missions the United States ever undertook to end a war. To understand why, a basic knowledge of mines and their capabilities is required.

The popular, artist's-concept idea of what a mine looks like is a big metal ball with spikes that bobs up and down in the ocean or is moored just under the surface. In World War II such weapons, contact mines, did exist. Simple in concept, they exploded when hit by a ship. Today's highly sophisticated mines are "can-shaped" and do not have spikes. They are called "influence mines" and can be detonated in many ways:

• A magnetic mine contains a magnetized needle similar to that in a compass. When a steel ship passes overhead, the vessel's own magnetic field deflects the needle and thereby detonates the explosive charge.
• A pressure mine is activated by a change in water pressure. When a ship steams through shallow water, the pressure of the water under its hull is lessened and a sensitive diaphragm in the mine triggers the charge.
• An acoustic mine, outfitted with sophisticated sonar equipment, is triggered by the noise "signature" of a ship's propeller or engine.

Numbers and Dates

All of which sounds simple. But the clincher in mine warfare today is that each type of mine can be equipped with more than one kind of detonating device, and all three classes can be set in the same minefield. Mines can also be set with counting devices so as not to explode when the first ships (usually minesweepers) pass overhead. Later ships, of course, passing through the "cleared" field, are exposed to the full fury of the mines.

Another new twist: modern mines can turn themselves on and off at certain times and will even self-destruct on a pre-set date. The twofold purpose of the self-destruct device is to keep the mines from falling into enemy hands and/or from exploding after hostilities have ended.

In Vietnam, while the mining of Haiphong Harbor

Navy Sea Stallion helicopter takes off, above, with Mark 105 minesweeping sled in tow for Suez Canal clearance operations, below. Had the operation been in deep water the Navy would have been in deep trouble.

received the most publicity (26 merchant ships were stranded in that port), Navy A-6 and A-7 jets also sowed mines at the doorsteps of 13 other coastal cities, including Cam Pha and Hon Gai, as well as the offshore shallows and inland waters. Prior to mining North Vietnam's intricate system of rivers and canals, U.S. intelligence estimated that 1.5 million tons of cargo per day were moved along the water routes. After the mines were dropped, the supply lines slowed to a trickle.

McCauley's mission was to deactivate all mines previously set. He received his orders two months after assuming command of the Navy's small and antiquated mine force, then and now headquartered in Charleston, S.C.—the Navy's top decisionmakers for many years had viewed the mine force as a financial drain and it was a much emasculated fleet that McCauley commanded.

McCauley selected eight of his best ocean mine-sweepers, or MSOs. The wooden-hulled ships, 173-feet long and with a shallow draft of 12 feet, had all been built more than 16 years ago. They were designed, in theory, to operate with impunity in the presence of magnetic mines. MSOs carry two types of minesweeping equipment—mechanical and influence. Mechanical gear, trailed far behind the sweeper, severs moored mines from their anchors. When they pop to the surface another sweeper destroys them with gunfire. Influence equipment generates magnetic and acoustic signals similar to those made by ships. The signals are amplified and directed in such a way that the mines explode at a safe distance from the minesweeping ship.

Marine Assistance Required

To augment his MSO flotilla, McCauley gave the Navy's only helicopter minesweeping squadron a chance to prove itself. Helicopter Mine Countermeasures Squadron 12 (HM-12) was then less than 18 months old and had spent most of its time flying CH-53 helicopters borrowed from the U.S. Marine Corps. McCauley had his men train Marine pilots to sweep mines. The U.S. Navy, in other words, no longer had the capability to perform a large sweep operation by itself.

The reason the Navy was again caught short can be gleaned from numerous public documents. The aerial mine countermeasures program dates in concept back to the year the service lost face at Wonsan Harbor, but it was not until 13 years later that the Navy in fact began limited aerial sweeping tests. And it was not until 19 years after Wonsan that the Navy's first and only helicopter minesweeping squadron was commissioned.

A Navy press release issued in conjunction with End Sweep leaves the impression that delays in implementing the aerial minesweeping phase resulted, almost incidentally, from the fact that it was a relatively low-keyed element of the overall operation.

But some mine force officers claim the Navy dragged its feet for years by refusing to allocate enough money to development of the system. The fact remained that 21 years after Wonsan the Navy still got caught short and had to seek assistance from the Marines.

In operation, minesweeping helicopters tow a 6,000 pound MK-105 hydrofoil sled, which trails two buoyant magnetic conductor cables. The helicopter pilot sends electronic impulses through the cables to explode magnetic mines. A three-foot MK-105 acoustical tube can be attached to the sled to explode sound-sensitive mines, and a series of cables and cutters can be added to snag moored mines. Aerial sweeping equipment is effective only in relatively shallow water. Deepwater mines have to be swept by ships with more powerful gear.

Captor: The Deep Threat

In the past, the use of mines has been restricted to some extent by water depth. But Soviet technology recently has been advancing so rapidly that communist navies may soon be able to mine any section of the ocean. The Navy would normally counter such a threat by building ships capable of destroying deepwater mines, but McCauley notes that "There is no new ship construction planned or anticipated." Fiscal constraints,

Soviet F-class submarine, a probable target for the "Captor" torpedo mine which is one of the few bright spots in the U.S. Navy's mine warfare inventory.

120

he claims, "have all but denuded the Mine Force of its most effective minesweeping vehicles."

There is a bright side to the otherwise bleak picture. The Navy is developing a torpedo mine capable of seeking out and destroying enemy submarines. The new mine is called "Captor"—the name is a contraction of "enCAPsulated TORpedo." Moored to the ocean floor, it will ignore surface ships, but when it picks up the acoustic signal of a submarine it will release a torpedo to home in on the sub's signature. The Navy will not say when the system will become operational.

Captor comes at the right time, because the major threat to allied shipping today is not the Soviet surface fleet, but the 170 submarines based at Murmansk. Naval officers say it would take as long as 90 days to neutralize the Murmansk fleet, during which period many U.S. and allied ships would be sunk.

Future plans, according to news reports not officially confirmed, call for placement of Captor mines: (1) along the Denmark Straits; (2) between Greenland and Iceland; and (3) between Iceland and the British Isles. But that plan will be implemented only in event of war—if for no other reason than the fact that the U.S. Navy does not have the equipment to sweep such deepwater mines once they are sown.

Words of Joy

The U.S. Navy recently swept the Suez Canal from Port Said to Suez City. It was a difficult operation. The canal had been closed for seven years and no one had any idea how many mines were planted in the waterway, nor was there an accurate record of what types of mines were in the canal.

But if it had been a deepwater sweeping operation, where powerful deep-probing equipment was required, the Navy would have had no way of carrying out its assigned mission. Such missions require ships that the U.S. Navy does not now have. The United States has, so to speak, put all of its nautical eggs into a shallow-water basket.

Rear Admiral Brian McCauley, right, who as commander of the Navy's Mine Warfare Force directed U.S. minesweeping operations both in Vietnam and in the Suez Canal, receives a check flight briefing from Lieutenant David I. Dries of Helicopter Mine Countermeasures Squadron 12.

The few minesweepers the Navy has today are slow. Their best speed is 12 knots. But by shifting to hydrofoils or hovercraft much higher speeds can be achieved. Minesweeping is a difficult, tedious, miserable job—completely devoid of any glamour. But it is a talent at which the Navy must excel.

It has been more than twenty years since Admiral C. Turner Joy told his fellow officers at Panmunjon, Korea, that "Today, not unlike days past when this great nation of ours was busy with the business of ending its involvement in a war, we are facing severe reductions in ships, hardware and manpower. It is indeed a period of fiscal austerity for the military. However, it is important that the United States not be reduced to having to bargain with other world powers from a position of weakness.

"We cannot afford to sacrifice the essential strength of our military to a pseudo-economy. It is in this light that mine warfare plays such a vital role in our national economy." ∎

Explosive Ordnance Disposal unit prepares to explode a WWII mine found on the beach at Cape Hatteras. German mine warfare strategy locked up U.S. ports in the early days of World War II and sank a number of ships within clear sight of U.S. coastal areas.

ASW – Now Or Never

By Captain James A. Winnefeld, U. S. Navy
and Carl H. Builder

The U. S. Navy must rethink the ordering
of its ASW mission priorities for, with the
emergence of a significant Soviet sea-launched
ballistic missile capability, the survival
of essential elements of all our nuclear forces
is now, more surely than ever, measured
in minutes.

Prize Essay 1971

FIRST HONORABLE MENTION

Item from page 2 of the London Times, *Wednesday, 25
September 1974: "It is only now, some three months after
the terrible events of 17 June, that some of the extraordinary details of the surprise attack on the United States
are becoming available through the deductions of Western
European military experts. While it was almost immediately apparent that the attack was intended to neutralise
the United States in a single, stunning blow, most of the
world found the outcome to be either incredible or inex-
plicable. Now, however, it is even more astonishing to
learn that the attack was far from an all-out effort.
Early accounts assumed that the crippling of U. S. strategic nuclear forces resulted from a massive attack by intercontinental ballistic missiles. But experts sorting through
the available evidence have concluded that not a single
ICBM was fired by either side. Perhaps the most revealing
statistic of the attack has come from an Admiralty report recently submitted to the Defence Minister showing
that the entire attack, from the closing of the first switch
to the last nuclear blast, probably took no more than ten
minutes.*

*"The Admiralty report summarises a priority study
demanded by the DM immediately after the Havana Conference in July. It provides, for the first time, an official
explanation of how U. S. nuclear forces were either destroyed or paralysed in a matter of minutes and why the
Soviets were able to take over most of West Germany in
the ensuing strategic standoff. Up to now, there has been
much speculation on why the U. S. strategic forces, despite
elaborate precautions to insure their survival, were unable
to respond during the world's first nuclear war. The explanation offered in portions of the Admiralty report released yesterday. . . ."*

*Excerpt from Admiralty Report No. NAV-ANAL/
PLAN-0014, dated 7 September 1974: "From the foregoing considerations, we believe that the following conclusions may be reasonably drawn:*

*"1. The attack, while carefully planned and executed,
was both daring and risky. The opportunities for failure*

The views herein are those of the authors and are not to be considered
as implying an official endorsement of factual accuracy, opinion, conclusions, or recommendations by the Department of Defense.

were numerous, and the remarkable success of the attack must be attributed to the bold acceptance of the enormous risks. There was no certainty of the U. S. response even if the attack was a technical success; but this risk, too, was apparently accepted by the Soviets because of the gravity of the German situation. Reference 14 shows that the German political crises of May were far more alarming to Moscow than to London or Washington.

"2. The attack on North America appears to have been carried out entirely by means of missile submarines in a carefully coordinated strike from close upon the Atlantic, Pacific, Caribbean, and Hudson Bay coastlines. Two types of submarine-launched ballistic missiles were employed, one type having multiple warheads. Most of the missile trajectories were purposefully lowered to shorten flight times and delay detection. It is estimated that the total number of submarines involved need not have exceeded a dozen, but the actual number may have been higher. In any event, there is no evidence that the Soviets augmented their normal on-station submarine forces for the attack.

"3. The most demanding aspect was precise timing as to launches and impacts. It is certain that the authorities and equipment exercising control over U. S. nuclear forces were the priority targets in time. The patterns of nearly 100 detonations, most of them on the U. S. mainland, correspond to our understanding of their nuclear control and communications structure. While some elements of that structure did survive the attack, the losses were so sudden and extensive—for example, only two secondary transmitters for communicating with the U. S. Poseidon submarines are known to have survived—it required nearly 15 minutes to clarify the vestment of authority. By that time, the attack was over, a substantial portion of the U. S. nuclear forces had been destroyed, and the Soviet ultimatum was being transmitted on all frequencies and the one surviving hot-line. It is estimated that most of the command and communications targets were struck within about six minutes of the first launch. It is doubtful that any of these targets enjoyed more than four minutes of general warning or more than two minutes of certain prior awareness that the country was under attack.

"4. The second-priority targets were the strategic bomber bases. The detonation patterns here suggest that airborne aircraft were also the object of attack at many inland bases. All of the bomber and tanker bases were probably struck within nine minutes of the first launch. Even so, a rather substantial fraction of the alert aircraft may have become airborne. The only reasonable explanation for the small numbers of bombers surviving (we estimate about a dozen) is the extensive targeting of aircraft flight areas near the inland bases that could have received the greatest warning. We doubt that any bomber base had more than six or seven minutes of warning.

"5. The third priority was apparently given over to the new antimissile installations protecting U. S. ICBMs in the northwestern states. The attack scheme here is readily apparent: only the radars and fire control centers were hit. Since the U. S. ABM system was designed specifically for self-protection and survival against an ICBM threat, the sensors were misoriented for a submarine missile attack. For example, the BMEWS radars here and in North America were not attacked and provided no indications that an attack had been launched, further adding to the initial confusion of U. S. authorities. It is estimated that all of the critical ABM sites were struck within about ten minutes of the first launch.

"6. The lowest priorities in time seem to have been the overseas communications installations and submarine bases for U. S. strategic forces. We have fairly reliable data on the one weapon that destroyed U. S. submarine forces at Holy Loch; it was delivered from a surfaced diesel-electric submarine. (We have intermittent radar and acoustic records on the transit of that submarine.) Radio message traffic intercepted here indicates that the few attacks outside the U. S. mainland (only 14 weapons in all) were withheld until it was certain that the attack upon the U. S. mainland was successfully launched. They could have been executed with older, less-sophisticated submarines launching ballistic or cruise missiles from the surface at relatively short ranges from their targets. These attacks, also, were completed within 10 minutes of the first launch off the U. S. mainland. The weapon at Holy Loch destroyed four Poseidon submarines and we presume that about 12 more U. S. missile-firing submarines were destroyed at their bases.

"7. We believe that the U. S. ICBMs would have been included in the attack except for the limited numbers and accuracy of the multiple warheaded missile carried by some Soviet submarines. Because of these limitations and the daring Soviet decision to withhold the use of ICBMs in the initial attack, the U. S. bombers and submarines in port offered the most lucrative targets for achieving a decisive shift in the balance of strategic forces.

"8. Any U. S. response to the attack appeared to be highly disadvantageous. Private discussions with General Tyer at the Havana Conference have shed some light upon the dilemma that the U. S. authorities faced immediately after the attack. By the time General Tyer was certain of his responsibilities, the following aspects of the attack were clear:

(a) The first phase of the attack was obviously over, for no new detonations had been reported for seven minutes and BMEWS stations continued to report no incomings.

(b) The attack was directed primarily at U. S. authorities, command and control, but not against the popu-

lation (as noted earlier, only three large metropolitan areas received substantial damage).

(c) No Soviet ICBMs had been employed in the attack, and they could be presumed temporarily withheld in a high degree of readiness.

(d) No U. S. weapon had yet been released and enemy defenses were undegraded. (The few bombers that had escaped destruction were recalled when it became clear that U. S. ICBMs were not under attack.)

(e) While it was apparent that the U. S. ICBMs had survived and could be fired upon any warning of further Soviet attacks, the same was true of an even larger Soviet ICBM force. The situation for the Polaris and Poseidon submarines at sea could only be presumed over the next several hours and days. But it was also obvious that the only rational option was to withhold these forces in the hope of not being forced into what would now be a lopsided exchange of either military targets or cities.

(f) A full text of the ultimatum was available. General Tyer said that the terms were such that there was little alternative but to acquiesce to the Soviet fait accompli in West Germany. . . ."

Excerpt from cover letter from the Defence Minister to the Prime Minister. ". . . so there isn't too much here that I haven't passed on to you at cabinet. It would seem to me that the key in this wretched mess was time. If the Americans had had even three or four more minutes, I believe that much of the apparatus that didn't work would have had a good chance. With a few more minutes I believe the President would have been safe, the bombers would have made it off, and we would have had an entirely different match to be played out. More important, I think it likely that if the attack had required more time for execution, the greater risks would have discouraged the entire enterprise and we would have had a chance to work things out at the conference table.

"Geoffrey tells me that the subs could have been kept far enough off to prevent anything as sudden as that from happening—something about conventional antisubmarine forces being used to control certain water areas. I keep telling him that I rather suspect he has an ax to grind, but if there is a way to buy a margin of time, we should probably look into it. . . ."

Fiction is a convenient technique for avoiding many complicated questions that must be faced and answered in order to make a scenario credible, and it would be imposing to argue for the credibility of this fictional autumn in 1974. The purpose was to dramatize the special capabilities and characteristics of a threat that is now present and growing in our coastal seas.

As a nation, we certainly are not in need of any

new strategic threats to further justify the many valid concerns for our strategic posture. There are hobgoblins enough in the SS-9 and Fractional Orbital Bombardment System without our searching for new possibilities to scare ourselves. However, the first-strike threat posed by Soviet submarine-launched ballistic missiles (SLBMs) has three ugly aspects that set it quite apart:

1. The required hardware types are already developed and operationally deployed. The principal future uncertainty is not the projected competency of the hardware, but the locations and concentrations of this hardware off our coasts, and Soviet intentions for its use. There are no technological developments that "bear watching," although the observation of Soviet SLBM flight tests could verify estimates of how far the trajectories might be depressed.

2. Not just one, but all of our strategic forces (or their supporting systems) fall under the shadow of this threat. Our strategic bombers have, for several years now, had their survival measured against the quarter-hour clock of an SLBM following a conventional, maximum-range trajectory. But if these flight times can be cut in half and if the numbers of missiles continue to increase, the SAC Wing Commanders will soon be joined by other worriers. Many important things that can reasonably be accomplished by human beings in 15 minutes become extraordinarily difficult and questionable when the time is cut to seven or eight minutes, or even less.

3. U. S. perceptions of strategic stability and arms control would appear to encourage the expansion of the SLBM threat. During the past year, the open literature in the United States has extolled the arms control virtues of SLBM forces, largely because of their relative invulnerability at sea. Many U. S. experts would apparently welcome a Strategic Arms Limitations Talks agreement favoring greater reliance by both sides upon SLBM forces. Thus, we can expect to see a growing Soviet SLBM threat, with or without a SALT agreement.

While the daring of the attack described in the opening scenario may seem incredible, the technical capabilities assumed for the attacking SLBMs should not. There are no points within the United States that are more than 900 nautical miles from open seas. An SLBM having a maximum range of 1,500 nautical miles and a normal flight time of 15 minutes theoretically could, by means of a depressed-trajectory, reach any Continental U. S. target in less than seven minutes. If it were assumed that the longest-range shots were fired first, and that the firing rates of the SSBNs were about four missiles per minute, then perhaps the time allowance of the opening scenario was too generous: it could all be over in seven minutes instead of ten. Even assuming reliable warning within one minute after the launching of the first missiles in such an attack, we could be left with less than six minutes to remove from harm's way the critically important people and equipment that do not lend themselves to protection through constant mobility or hardening.

It would be unfair to imply that compressing the time for an SLBM strike is a cost-free option to the attacker. Resorting to extreme depression of trajectories to shorten the time of flight, cuts into the range of the missile. As already indicated, however, SLBM range is not a very severe requirement for U. S. targets. (This is one situation where the U. S. maritime geography is unfavorable as compared to that of the U.S.S.R. For example, about half of the CONUS urban-industrial targets lie within 500 nautical miles of many potential SLBM launch points in the Atlantic Ocean.) However, reductions in SLBM range and time of flight will force the SSBNs to move in closer to shore, increasing the risks of exposure. The shallow reentry angles associated with depressed-trajectories can degrade the accuracy of the missile (because of greater sensitivity to atmospheric uncertainties), but high accuracy is not required for many of the soft targets, such as antennas and buildings, associated with our strategic command and control structure.

What are our options for coping with the first-strike threat posed by the growing number of Soviet SSBNs that could concentrate close to our shores? Even though the sharp edge of this threat is keenly felt by the Air Force in its concern for the pre-launch survivability of the SAC bomber force, it would be short-sighted to accept the threat as another example of the superiority of sea-basing strategic forces. Land-based bombers and missiles are key elements of our nuclear deterrent and will probably remain so for the foreseeable future. Additionally, most command and control facilities, including national command authorities, must by their nature be land-based. People, institutions and equipment of vital importance to our strategic capabilities will always be ashore. As the SLBM threat grows, so will the national interest in counter-options.

We might want to limit the consequences of a sudden SLBM attack. Without discussing all of the alternatives and problems that lie in these directions and without denigrating their importance, it is fair to note that limiting the *consequences* of an attack is a different form of deterrence from limiting the *means* of attack.

International agreements offer some possibilities. It is not the SLBM forces per se that we would want to restrict, since the relative invulnerability of SSBNs on patrol to a sudden nuclear attack is a quality we prize for deterrent forces. But, to preclude the use of SLBM forces for the kind of attack described in the opening scenario, we would have to forbid SSBN patrol areas close to shores. Would we be willing to give up some of our own SSBN patrol areas close to the U.S.S.R.? Could we confidently and unilaterally inspect for compliance?

A more direct counter to the first-strike threat posed by a minimum range/time SLBM attack might be based upon conventional ASW forces deployed to provide relatively dense ASW coverage of those ocean areas from which such SLBM attacks are feasible. While not denying peacetime passage to enemy submarines in our coastal seas, we might bring sufficient ASW attack capability to bear upon "excessive" enemy submarines to convince the enemy that provocative concentrations in our vital ocean areas will only degrade his nuclear delivery posture. The intent of this defensive option would be the intimidation of those SLBM forces that concentrate in areas where minimum range/time attacks are feasible. By exercising a very deliberate and finite amount of control over selected ocean areas, ASW forces could demonstrate to a potential enemy that his interests are best served by standing well off our coasts and that concentrations in ASW-controlled waters are almost certain to be counter-productive.

The enforcement of this control over the SLBM threat within certain vital ocean areas should not be destabilizing since it does not threaten the accepted retaliatory role of SLBM forces. The continuous targeting and timely response against retaliatory targets, using conventional near-maximum-range SLBM trajectories, should not be threatened because of practical limits on the size of the ASW-controlled areas. (As a first approximation, potential SSBN deployment areas increase with the cube of the range to target.) Development of longer-range SLBMs, such as Underwater Long-range Missile Systems, would be made more attractive, and the experience gained in the operation of ASW forces in the counter SLBM role would be the best possible insurance of timely recognition of developing ASW threats against our own SSBNs on patrol.

Two basic functional capabilities are needed in order to exercise this kind of preventive defense against minimum range/time SLBM attacks: (1) the ability to maintain a reliable head-count on submarines within the controlled-sea areas; and (2) the ability to position obviously competent attack forces in the vicinity of "excess" SSBNs and, if necessary, to escalate force levels at a reasonable cost exchange until the alerting of other strategic forces is clearly warranted.

The ASW force levels and compositions required to provide these capabilities appear to be fairly quantifiable and, hence, profitable opportunities for analytical study. A major issue in the economic feasibility of this continental defense concept is the amount of ocean area and the perimeters that would have to be controlled. Fortunately, geography is a little kinder to us in this problem. If the Hudson Bay is controlled (requiring a relatively small control perimeter), some key SAC bases in ConUS would be 200 more miles and about two more minutes away from an SLBM attack. Controlling the Caribbean also would greatly enlarge these time-sanctuary areas, and SAC could probably start to breathe a little easier. Controlling the North Atlantic, out as far as the arc from Newfoundland to Bermuda to the Bahamas would add 500 miles of range and more than four minutes of additional time for many potential targets of an SLBM attack. This would require controlling a perimeter of about 1,800 nautical miles. Control of the coastal areas of the Pacific would appear to be more difficult because of the long perimeters and lack of island bases.

Is ASW technology sufficiently advanced to provide the necessary hardware capabilities? Under satisfactory water and weather conditions, and with the correct mixture and quantity of both forces and surveillance sensors, nuclear submarines can be detected and tracked for extended periods with the products of existing technology. Much remains to be done, however, to improve the assurance that detection and tracking can be accomplished under less optimum conditions and with smaller forces. Improved sensors must continue to receive first priority in this effort. Our previous neglect to improve some of our sensor platforms will continue to plague us for years to come, but that problem is beginning to receive the attention it deserves. In sum, we face significant and continuing efforts if we are to have adequate tools to close the margin now enjoyed by nuclear submarines. But the evidence available indicates that the technical problems are not insuperable, particularly if sensor and weapon development receives the funding which the gravity of the developing strategic threat justifies.

Are the ASW forces required for continental defense reasonably attainable? The answer to this question requires an assessment of the importance of the threat in relation to others, the cost of the forces necessary, and our willingness to pay that cost. If one accepts the importance of the threat as drama-

tized in the opening scenario, the question becomes one of finding the most cost-effective way of doing the job. The design of the most effective force is beyond the scope of this essay. Further on, some force design considerations will be suggested based on a comparative analysis of ASW missions. But at this point, reference may be limited to the obvious: we require an initial detection capability, a tracking capability, and a kill capability against enemy SSBNs on-station off our coasts. For selected targets we have these capabilities now. However, the evidence indicates that current forces will be inadequate to cope with a Y-class SSBN force which could be comparable in size to our present Polaris/Poseidon force by 1974.

Although an ASW force to counter such a threat will be expensive, it probably would not be any more expensive, relatively, than our investment in continental air defense undertaken in the 1950s and 1960s. Rather, there is good reason to believe it would be considerably less, since ASW forces are required for missions other than continental defense. Other required ASW forces could be made available to augment continental defense ASW forces if they were in danger of being saturated. Because SSBN forces cannot be deployed from bases to firing stations overnight—with the obvious exception of Cuban basing possibilities—some strategic warning is available for reasonable augmentations of any dedicated continental defense ASW force. Hence, the alert (or nucleus) continental defense ASW force need only be adequate to meet the routine on-station threat (plus some safety margin). Such capabilities should be within our means if we establish the necessary resource allocations and mission priorities.

The question of priorities hinges on the relationship of the ASW missions to one another and to the total threat. Three principal ASW missions can be identified: continental defense, Fleet defense, and sea-lane defense. The force requirements in both quantity and mix are likely to be different for each of these missions. The evidence suggests we have optimized our forces for Fleet and sea-lane defense. Such emphasis in the past is understandable in view of the Navy's traditional sea control mission. However, the emergence of the Soviet SLBM threat should force us to reevaluate the old priorities.

As the opening scenario demonstrated, the survival and effectiveness of all our nuclear deterrent forces could be threatened by enemy SLBMs. The key position of our nuclear deterrent capabilities in the strategic balance logically leads to the conclusion that no Navy forces are more important than those that either comprise or defend our nuclear deterrent capabilities. It follows that those portions of the Fleet which provide for continental defense against missile attack and which protect our own SSBNs from enemy countermeasures deserve top priority, second only to our SSBNs, in the resource allocation process. Further, since Fleet defense is essential to sea lane defense, we can postulate the following order of ASW priorities: first, continental defense; second, Fleet defense; and third, sea-lane defense.

If this ordering of ASW priorities is accepted, our first order of business should be to design and deploy a nucleus continental defense ASW force and identify the augmentation forces required to keep pace with surges in the strength of enemy SSBNs on-station. That part of our Fleet defense forces (both ASW and strike) associated with protection of both our continental defense ASW forces and our own SSBNs should also be in the first priority category. Our second ASW priority should be Fleet defense of our carrier and amphibious forces. Finally, we must be capable of protecting our sea-lanes in such extended conflicts as the enemy may undertake.

The foregoing discussion suggests the following bare minimum ASW force for national survival:
▶ Nucleus continental defense ASW forces.
▶ Covering ASW forces to defend the continental defense force and our own SSBN forces from submarine attack.

The covering force is of marginal utility in some situations, such as the opening scenario, where the enemy would not risk losing surprise by a prior attack on either the continental defense or the covering forces. However, covering forces are necessary to discourage or counter non-nuclear attacks intended to reduce naval forces comprising or protecting our strategic deterrent.

These bare minimum forces, by definition, would not be adequate to cope with a surge increase in numbers of SSBNs on-station. Neither would they be adequate to provide the necessary ASW protection for our seapower projection forces. In order to meet these minimum requirements, we need two additional ASW force increments:
▶ A continental defense augmentation ASW force to counter surge increases in numbers of enemy SSBNs on-station (up to the numbers justifying a wider alert of strategic forces).
▶ A Fleet defense ASW force adequate to provide minimum cover for our seapower projection forces.

These forces in the aggregate must form the basis for our minimum acceptable ASW force if we are to retain the ability to project our power overseas and meet our mutual security commitments. However, these forces do not provide a capability to protect our sea lanes from enemy submarine attack, if the enemy simultaneously escalates his SLBM threat and engages our seapower projection forces with his attack submarines. The risk of the enemy's undertaking a "war at sea" is one of the key imponderables of naval force planning. Prudence dictates that we should develop and maintain some forces for this mission. This requirement generates a fifth ASW force increment:
▶ A sea-lane defense force adequate to meet essential requirements until mobilization generates the additional forces required.

Two world conflicts have demonstrated that we have paid a high price in war for economizing in this area during times of peace. Given the temper of the American people, it is probably unreasonable to expect them to maintain in peacetime the forces required to provide an adequate counter to a war at sea. Nevertheless, we need to define more clearly the risks we run in this area. If, in fact, our fiscal constraints leave little or nothing left over for this mission, we gain little in configuring any of our remaining ASW forces specifically for sea-lane defense. Previous ASW force level decisions indicate that we have tended toward spreading the risk among all ASW mission/force increments rather than concentrating it on the lowest priority missions and forces. Our large investment in DE/DEGs is an instance of such a practice, even though other factors were influential in their procurement.

The foregoing assessment of priorities in ASW force design has not addressed the optimum mix of forces. In view of the different missions of each of the five force increments, it is apparent that a high premium must be placed on employment flexibility. This flexibility must be such that forces are optimized for the higher priority missions, which in turn leads to emphasis on quality rather than numbers. Additionally, emphasis should be placed on forces in being rather than on mobilization capability. Thus, our NRT escorts and hardware air reserve ASW units should be dedicated to the sea lane defense mission where a modicum of time is available to generate forces in response to an enemy threat. Some fast reaction reserve forces may be suitable as augmentation forces for our continental defense posture.

The place of Allied ASW forces in meeting the five ASW mission requirements is almost entirely dependent on political assumptions. Because the first three ASW force increments are clearly related to protection of U. S. nuclear deterrent forces where rapidity of decision and response is of the essence, only limited reliance can be placed on Allied ASW forces for these functions, with the exception of Canadian forces similarly committed to defense of the North American continent. Allied ASW forces can and do make a significant contribution by their surveillance of the routes that Soviet submarines are constrained to use. However, these early warning functions supplement rather than substitute for the surveillance capability we require in our coastal sea areas.

This essay has examined a threat that the growing Soviet SSBN force poses to the survival of essential elements for all of our nuclear deterrent forces. In evaluating the nature of this threat, the critical dimension appears to be time: minutes that we can no longer afford to give away against a large-scale attack. With the emergence of a significant Soviet SLBM capability, we may find that conventional ASW forces are the most practical approach for denying the enemy an otherwise attractive option for a surprise first strike on time-urgent targets. Such ASW forces may not be cheap, but they should be attainable if we establish mission priorities in accordance with the risks we face.

In evaluating the various ASW missions, the critical dimension appears to be our requirements for continental defense ASW forces. If so, the Navy must rethink the ordering of ASW mission priorities, and then design and deploy forces to meet the highest

priority missions with a reasonable balancing of the risks. Our traditional view of the pre-eminence of Fleet and sea-lane defense is confronted with the new realities of the strategic nuclear power equation. We are up against a potential enemy who has learned that the sea presents him with new opportunities as well as the old perils. Our task is to deny him those opportunities whenever they tempt misuse.

A graduate of the U. S. Naval Academy with the Class of 1951, Captain Winnefeld served in the USS *Halsey Powell* (DD-686) from 1951 to 1952, and, following flight training, was assigned to Air Antisubmarine Squadron 23 from 1953 to 1957. He attended Stanford University from 1958 to 1960 and was awarded an M.A. in foreign affairs. He then served on the staff of the Commander Fleet Air Mediterranean (1960 to 1962), in Air Antisubmarine Squadron 26 (1963 to 1965), in the Strategic Plans Division, OpNav (1965 to 1967), in Air Antisubmarine Squadron 21 (1967 to 1969), and in the Bureau of Personnel (1969 to 1971). He is now assigned to the Staff of Commander Carrier Division Six.

Mr. Builder enlisted in the Navy in 1948 and served in the USS *Amphion* (AR-13). He was a Midshipman at the U. S. Naval Academy with the Class of 1954. He received both his B.S. and Master of Engineering degrees from the University of California at Los Angeles. His 18-year career in aerospace engineering has been devoted to advanced systems planning and analysis for a broad spectrum of military and civil systems. His industrial associations have been with the Marquardt and United Aircraft Corporations, directing analytical planning studies for weapon and transportation systems. Mr. Builder has also been associated with the non-profit Aerospace and RAND Corporations in the areas of space and strategic system analysis.

Cruise Missile:
The Ship Killer

By Captain William J. Ruhe, U.S. Navy (Retired)

The scene depicted below reflects the imagination of an artist, but it should also capture the imagination and consideration of a good many naval officers. For it is likely, if not certain, that naval wars of the future will involve exchanges of surface-to-surface cruise missiles. Soviet strategy is geared to the quick kill at sea. Will we be ready?

The antiship cruise missile now offers a form of long-range offensive striking power to those navies which have not been able to afford the luxury of sea-based, manned tactical aircraft. Although the carrier-based attack aircraft has supplanted the battleship's heavy gun as the dominant weapon on the oceans of the world, Admiral S. G. Gorshkow, the head of the Soviet Navy, writing in *Morskoy Sbornik* in 1967 suggested that the cruise missile had become the primary form of offensive power at sea: "Combat capabilities of aircraft carriers, even the atomic powered ones, cannot stand comparisons with the strike capabilities of (missile-armed) submarine-air forces."

But the introduction of the antiship missile involves far more than just a possible increase in the offensive power which can be exerted at sea. There are significant changes in naval strategy, tactics, and ship design also indicated. Such changes stem not only from the character of this new weapon but also from advanced technologies which help to optimize its usage. A new kind of naval warfare, different from carrier warfare, seems to be evolving. Hence, some rough guesses as to the impact of the cruise missile on sea warfare should be useful for a navy which, with its preponderant strength in manned aircraft, will less acutely feel the effects of this weapon, but will nevertheless have to adjust to it.

Cruise missiles comprise a family of long-range, antiship missiles which can be launched by aircraft, surface ships, and submarines. Virtually all of the very long-range missiles (over 100 miles) are jet-powered, but a sizable number of shorter-range missiles are solid-fuel, rocket-propelled. They range in speed from just under subsonic (about 600 knots) to several times the speed of sound (1,500 knots or greater). The cruise missile exists in a wide variety of sizes, airframe configurations, warhead sizes, and internal electronics. Although all are costly, the cruise missile generally does not require complex shipboard installations. It requires little on board maintenance and is easily launched after relatively simple tactical maneuvering and fire control direction to start it on course. The in-flight trajectory is normally correctable by broadcast directions, and it can terminally seek a target over a wide expanse of the ocean. It is hence readily proliferated to a variety of platforms and into the navies of even the less technologically developed maritime nations.

Actual wartime usage of the cruise missile has occurred only in recent years and between lesser sea powers in coastal waters. Such experience, while demonstrating the potential of this weapon, may not, however, be particularly pertinent to the use of the cruise missile between leading maritime nations whose battles are most likely to be fought far at sea. A review of cruise missile warfare is helpful in order to show some of the basic changes which the missiles seem to create in sea warfare and the implications of their—as yet unproved —tactical usage by major sea powers.

In the Arab-Israeli War of October 1973, the cruise missile engagements involved small, high-speed, missile-carrying patrol craft in inshore battles. The Israelis, although using the Gabriel missile with about half the range of the Arabs' Styx (a Soviet-exported missile of about 25-mile range), were able to sink a considerable number of Arab patrol boats and merchant ships without, reportedly, the loss of a single Israeli missile boat.[1] The Israelis' high-speed surface craft tactics, coordinated with the use of electronic countermeasures for diverting the Arab missiles (reported as 55 Styxes in one battle) from their trajectories, resulted in only a few of the missiles having to be destroyed by close-in Israeli ship defenses.

It is apparent that the Israelis were made aware of the location of the Arab patrol craft and of their missile launchings in sufficient time to optimize the use of electronic warfare to prevent getting hit by the longer range and earlier-fired Arab missiles. This would emphasize the great need for the element of surprise in missile attack.

In the earlier Indo-Pakistani War of 1971, three Indian patrol craft fired nine Styx missiles at Pakistani ships. They sank one destroyer and put a second one completely out of action.[2] The attack was outside of destroyer gun range and demonstrated the great over-the-horizon hitting accuracy of the cruise missile and its lethality against warships of far greater size than the missile-firing Indian Osa boats. This confirmed the startling results of the initial wartime use of this weapon in 1967. Then, two Egyptian Styx missiles fired from harbor-concealed Egyptian missile craft sank the Israeli destroyer *Eilat* 12 miles away.

The cruise missiles in the hands of lesser sea powers have, for the most part, been bought on the open world market to fit their inshore needs. Hence they have little identifiable general character. Their cruising trajectories tend to be low or sea skimming, but their warhead sizes vary greatly, as does the character of their terminal homing technology.

On the other hand, there may be a definable character for high-seas cruise missile weaponry—stemming from the tactical and technological limitations of this type of weapon. The Soviets, who place primary reliance on this weapon, and who are in the forefront of cruise missile developments, have evolved a sea war strategy for the best use of the missile. And from this strategy they have developed a philosophy for the character of cruise missiles.

It is questionable whether a navy with a different strategy would develop the Soviets' kinds of missiles.

But they apparently feel that their strategy magnifies the cruise missile's strengths and minimizes its weaknesses. And perhaps theirs is the optimum way to use an unmanned aircraft with built-in electronic intelligence. The Soviets' sea strategy is based on the use of cruise missiles of great warhead power in a brief, massive, coordinated, surprise strike against hostile forces.[3] It calls for very good intelligence on enemy movements, and this can be provided by an ocean-wide network of collecting units, including satellites. With quickly developing operations, a substantial number of missile-carrying naval units are moved swiftly and for the most part unobserved to diverse areas of the ocean without any semblance of tactical formation or grouping. Then, with a high element of surprise, missile launch would follow rapidly on orders from a command center in Soviet territory. This would ensure a near-simultaneous attack of large numbers of missiles, from diverse directions and with many varying trajectories, on the entire alignment of the enemy's forces. The missile strike would be carried out by those air, surface, and submarine forces which were geographically available at a tactically favorable instant in time.

The theory behind this strategy seems to be that many highly destructive cruise missiles—when attacking in a quick, massive strike—will produce a new dimension of confusion. Enemy defenses will be overwhelmed, with consequent destruction of the high-value ships of a force. Such high weapon effect, it is felt by Soviet writers, should cause a rapid disintegration of the organization of an enemy's defenses, resulting in the last arriving missiles getting a free ride into their targets and producing devastating effects.

This is a somewhat different strategy than the traditional sequential strike attacks used by sea-based

tactical air forces. In the Soviet strategy, a sea battle has to be decisive in the opening moments with a single strike, because all the power which can be mustered is thrown into this single concentrated effort. No follow-up attack is contemplated. Mop-up operations to fully annihilate the enemy are expected to be carried out by missile units in individual strikes of massed weapon power. Thus, a Soviet submarine with eight cruise missiles could produce an eight-missile strike against a crippled warship.

Consistent with Marxist-Leninist dogma, this Soviet strike strategy is designed to gain the initiative in the first salvo—a use of maximum employable force—and then to maintain the advantage gained through the initial strike. The Soviets feel that cruise missiles, in near simultaneous attack, allow them to produce a far higher level of weapon effect than even the attacks generated by sea-based tactical aircraft. They also consider their surface ships to be expendable early in a war. To maintain the advantage gained by an initial strike, nuclear submarines and land-based, long-range aircraft, working together, will do the follow-on job.[4]

Extending this strategy globally, the Soviet's missile-strike strategy calls for a beating of the enemy to the punch with all the weapon power which could be massed in either initiation of war or in its earliest moments. Global coordination of attacks against enemy forces in several oceans of the world was strikingly illustrated in the *Okean* exercises of 1970 and 1975. These exercises demonstrated the Soviet goal to launch their missiles from ships and aircraft in all oceans almost simultaneously against the deployed major enemy forces which were within the Soviet range of operations. In effect, this range was determined by the land bases for their aircraft and their range of effective operations. A 90-second response was announced as their goal for coordinated strike timing. It was an undeniable attempt to impress the world with the Soviets' high level of communications, command, and control of their worldwide forces—and to show that their strike strategy provides a viable threat to the major navies of the world. Comprehensive broad ocean surveillance, computerized data flow, computerized decision-making at high levels of command, and centralized coordination played a major role in showing how a strategy—which is highly dependent upon quickly developing operations and a high degree of surprise—can be made to work.

This strategy makes sense when the nature of Soviet cruise missiles is recognized. It can be estimated from the missiles they've produced to date that fundamentally they are all-weather in operation, are readily and rapidly launched, require only simple fire control inputs, and are capable of terminally homing on their targets with high accuracy. The Soviet cruise missiles have varying trajectories in flight and various angles of attack on their targets, seem relatively simple in their internal electronics (ensuring high reliability in flight), have large, powerful warheads of 1,100 or 2,200 pounds using high explosives, and are designed to overwhelm the enemy by numbers and diversity of attack rather than by sophistication of built-in countermeasures. Thus, the missile is kept as simple as possible to hold down the cost and allow for a stockpiling of large numbers.[5] Their technological simplicity is thus offset by the great numbers of missiles which can be employed in a coordinated attack. Even if a single Soviet missile is considered only a low-threat weapon, their numbers raise the threat level to one of great concern.

Since all Soviet cruise missiles have very large warheads with large radar cross sections, it can be assumed that their main purpose is to destroy the enemy's big ships by brute force. The primary intent of Soviet design appears to be the achievement of absolute certainty of destruction when the opportunity is presented to attack U.S. carriers.

Soviet missiles have a regular development pattern which tends to fill gaps and deficiencies. The Soviets improve their missile capability and hold costs down by frequent and modest updates of a few basic types of missiles. Successive missile developments show a pattern of steadily increasing speed—increasing and compounding the problems of defense against such missiles. These continuing changes provide their missiles with a capability to stay ahead of future responses or counters to their effectiveness.

The Soviets, then, have indicated a character and usage for the cruise missile on the high seas which is somewhat different than that which is applicable to inshore waters—as evidenced by wartime experiences to date. Hence, the impact of the cruise missile on coastal warfare is first examined so that generalizations which appear applicable to this type of warfare are readily recognized as not necessarily being valid for the kind of naval war which the United States will tend to fight with her high seas fleet.

The earlier cited wartime actions involving the use of cruise missiles show that missile-carrying craft—with their small radar cross sections—enjoy a high degree of visual and radar concealment. They are thus difficult to distinguish in the coastal clutter of small boats, small islands, navigational buoys, etc. Consequently, such craft can produce a high degree of surprise in their missile attacks.

The inshore tactical environment also favors the small missile-armed warship. The short ranges of coastal missile engagements, the short reaction times involved for defense against missile attack, and the predominant use of low-flying missiles to minimize detection range of the incoming missile, call for an expendable missile platform which emphasizes offense rather than defense. Additionally, the feasibility of electronic jamming of the reasonably close launching ships' fire control radars places a premium on highly maneuverable, small warships which can suffer considerable force losses and still launch enough missiles of high weapon power to produce decisive effects in battle. Redundancy in firing units thus appears desirable for inshore warfare.

Israeli success in countering Arab missiles by means of electronic warfare measures can be attributed only partially to the high maneuverability and speed of their missile craft. The Israelis also appear to have had ample warning of the time and direction of Arab missile attack. But, had the Arab missile boats received surveillance and fire control support from shore installations, they could have operated passively as a type of coastal artillery in offset, surprise fire—greatly reducing warning time of missile attack. In this mode of operations, surprise attacks of great weapon power are likely to be overwhelming to even a large warship which might move into a coastal area. The added threat of mobile shore batteries of long-range cruise missiles tends to force any threatening warship, regardless of size, far out to sea.

Even the peacetime "presence" of the large warship becomes highly hazardous in inshore waters if there exists the threat of small, unfriendly missile-armed patrol boats in significant numbers. Lesser sea powers can now mount a coastal area threat out of all proportion to their investment in ships. Thus, whereas the small missile-armed warship appears to assume a dominant role in inshore waters when used in considerable numbers, her combat successes are not necessarily translatable to warfare far at sea. It should be recognized that missile-armed craft have only a small range of operations, are markedly reduced in their effectiveness by bad weather, and are highly vulnerable when away from the inshore environment.

The infeasibility of adequately arming small warships with near-absolute defense systems, due mainly to cost and weight limitations and the very short time of flight of missiles for the likely engagement ranges, seems to make destruction of the missile firing platform before it can fire of first importance in battle in inshore waters. Admiral Sir Edward Ashmore, Royal Navy, summarizes this thought:

"Advantage is likely to lie with the offensive and not the defensive (in the antiship missile environment). This is because, with highly destructive weapons, nothing but a hundred percent defense is going to

132

prevent heavy loss, and a hundred percent defense is highly unlikely.''[6]

This again emphasizes the need for redundancy of missile platforms to ensure that some portion of attacking warships get their missiles headed for the enemy.

The impact of the cruise missile on amphibious assault concepts appears to be more profound than for any other type of naval operation. The extremely long range of cruise missiles in mobile shore batteries (as much as hundreds of miles), the substantial increase in effectiveness of broad ocean surveillance, and the missile power inherent in even the small coastal warship, place in particular jeopardy the large amphibious ships which would have to close the coast for offloading of their cargoes. Thus, the concept of using sea-based helicopters for a vertical assault might be ruled out by the excessive operating ranges which can be imposed by the missile threat. Troop landings using small amphibious craft may also suffer markedly from the long travel required through unfavorable seas and the long exposure to accurate, long-range shore defenses.

Shore bombardment by guns is suffering much the same fate. It becomes the height of folly to commit costly ships close to a hostile, missile-protected coastline

in order to use their 5-inch guns effectively. Experience in the Yom Kippur War similarly shows the high missile hazard to tactical aircraft which provide close ground support and short-range tactical air strikes. The alternative to gun bombardment and close support aircraft appears to be the use of the terminally guided, stand-off cruise missile, even though it seems exorbitantly costly for this function. But the precise hitting accuracy of this high-power weapon may make it a cost-effective replacement for the traditional, less accurate bombardment weapons.[7]

These new relationships in inshore waters would seem to indicate that the advantage in missile warfare is likely to lie with the defense. Ships offshore are readily targeted, whereas coastal defense units and other high-value targets enjoy a good deal of concealment. On the high seas, however, ships which need to be protected are difficult to conceal from the increasingly effective broad ocean surveillance inherent in new technologies such as the satellite. Their defenses are confronted with short warning times and great detection difficulties against attacking weapons—particularly if the weapons are launched by submarines or stand-off aircraft. The advantage thus tends to shift to the offense—with surprise a key factor in offensive effectiveness. (The Soviets have indicated their belief that this is true in modern naval warfare and have stressed the arming of their naval units with offensive systems to the detriment of their defenses.)[8] This seems apparent for a missile environment where nuclear warheads are used and perhaps for the 2,200-pound high-explosive warheads credited to the Soviet Navy. Moreover, navies which don't have a major job of protecting merchant shipping or specific high-value warships like the carrier may find it practical to emphasize the offensive. But for any navy, the practicality of placing major emphasis on offensive systems seems related to the effectiveness achievable by the use of considerable numbers of long-range expendable weapons in attacks of short duration.

The emergence in many of the navies of a potential for concentrating great missile power against a high-value ship seems to affect the concepts of naval warfare for even a navy which holds superior and unmatched assets of sea-based tactical air power. Tactical air war at sea thus becomes quite different because of the injection of expendable unmanned aircraft (cruise missiles) into the relationships of offensive sea warfare. On the one hand, the manned aircraft must be husbanded in battle, and sequential attacks are traditional in their employment. On the other, the expenditure of unmanned aircraft in a single coordinated and concentrated effort becomes an effective use of cruise missiles.

Since attack by cruise missiles can be initiated by many different types of platforms, including submarines and aircraft, and since a coordinated missile attack can be generated by several platforms from diverse sectors of the ocean, the concept of a threat-axis for orienting defenses becomes quite meaningless. Even attacking missile-armed aircraft are likely to make their stand-off attacks from several different sectors, in the missile strikes described by the Soviets.

Concentration of forces to maximize weapon effect in a battle, a principle of war, gives way in missile warfare to a concept of wide dispersion of forces with missile firers coordinating their attacks so as to provide a concentration of weapon force on the target. Thus, there is virtual elimination of tactical formations for the utilization of missile-firing ships both in deployments and in battle.

Maneuvering in battle by platforms, it can be observed, becomes of little importance in missile warfare, whereas maneuvering of weapons in their trajectories is of great tactical importance. The traditional naval battles between task forces or fleets (which have been dominated in the past decades by sea-based tactical air forces) have involved a concentration of force on only a few well-defined and relatively bunched targets—the carriers or other important major warships of the enemy. In cruise-missile warfare, however, every missile

platform with its potential of high weapon power must be a target for rapid destruction. This, then, creates a great dispersion in attack effort which will require different concepts of command and control of forces. Since the ranges involved between antagonists may be great and in widely diverse areas of the oceans, the possibility of destroying missile platforms before weapon firing is seriously reduced.

For a navy with great assets of sea-based tactical air power, this suggests that coordinated attack with manned aircraft and ship-launched antiship missiles becomes a means for near-simultaneous mass weapon attack on many enemy missile platforms spread out all over the ocean. In any case, the diverting of missiles in their trajectories or the destruction of the missile itself may be of growing importance in battle as compared to the past, "when every effort of the opposing sides was directed toward the destruction of the weapon platforms."[9] (In this context, the carrier-based manned aircraft which can destroy missiles in flight far out from their targets, such as the F-14 Phoenix system, might be considered an offensive weapon system). Thus, measures to destroy or to divert the unmanned missile aircraft away from its target by causing it to head for wrong targets or to make it lose its homing logic, are important.

Concealment on the oceans from long-range identification takes on a new meaning in today's antiship missile environment. Absolutely first-class intelligence on the enemy's location is required before coordinated massive missile strikes are employed, both because of the high cost of the weapons and their relatively limited numbers. Admiral Ashmore observes:

"The key to success is obtaining constant, accurate and up-to-date target information. The requirement is therefore for very high-class surveillance of enemy units. This entails a large deployment of reconnaissance aircraft and foolproof communications between aircraft and the missile ship."[10]

With broad ocean surveillance increasingly more efficient and with missile strikes heavily dependent upon the factor of surprise, there is a more critical emphasis on measures to provide covertness in operations, partially through increase in the level of concealment of forces. Additionally, successful missile strikes will depend heavily upon misleading the enemy through deception and preventing him from guessing one's intentions. But of primary importance is the capability to deny the enemy his intelligence-gathering activities (mainly through electronic warfare) while prosecuting quickly developing operations to minimize enemy reactions.

Carrier task forces are at a disadvantage in this environment because they are the prime targets for missile firers and are most easily located and identified on the oceans. Yet the oceans are still so vast for surveillance coverage, mainly by electronic means, and the environmental anomalies at the surface of the oceans are so frequent that with proper use of concealment and electronic warfare measures, an antiship missile-armed enemy is likely to find the opportunity to put together the ingredients for effective missile strikes. But somewhat different concepts for the operations of forces, which rely mainly on sea-based air, seem indicated.

Electronic warfare assumes a key role with cruise missiles, more so than manned tactical air systems where the human intelligence can be carried close to the target for last-minute identification and fire control. The fundamental need for intelligence gained by electronic means, both for long-range targeting and to deny the enemy's use of surprise in attack, and the similar employment of electronics to achieve surprise in missile attack, receive particular emphasis in Soviet concepts for missile warfare. Admiral Gorshkov notes that electronic warfare is "a most important trend in the achievement of surprise in a battle or operation."[11]

Another factor in missile warfare which assumes a new level of importance is speed. This could mean speed in positioning missile platforms for coordinated strikes, or rapidity of developing operations, or even speed in the missile itself in order to confound enemy missile defenses. The high speeds of ships and aircraft, combined with new technologies for rapid communications and split-second computerized decision-making, make quickly developing operations possible. These thoughts are particularly emphasized by Admiral Gorshkov for his Navy:

" . . . swiftness is becoming a more and more important and indispensable feature of a strike, an operation and a battle. . . . Only quickly-developing operations combined with surprise make it possible to beat the enemy to the punch."[12]

Platform speed and reliability for getting into strike position are essential. Thus, on the high seas the small heavily armed missile craft is likely not to be able to use her speed in heavy weather, and hence little dependence can be laid on her to meet suddenly developing opportunities. Large numbers of small, low-cost missile-armed vessels are not likely to be effective missile-strike systems. But the attractiveness of the 100-knot, good-seakeeping surface effect ship as a missile platform has been noted by strategists who are developing concepts for the sea wars of the future.

The adaptability of the antiship missile to unsophisticated platforms, the relatively modest demands on shipboard personnel who maintain and use such a

weapon at sea, and the feasibility of carrying such a weapon covertly, may cause a rebirth of the armed merchantman in sea warfare. Observations on the present use of the Styx missile by navies of lesser sea powers would lead to this conclusion. The armed, and clandestine-type merchant raider, like the Confederate *Alabama* in the Civil War, may thus be a viable and effective component in future wars at sea. It's a form of guerrilla war at sea which seems to have become feasible with the widespread use of the antiship missile.

Conventional missile-armed submarines, despite their shortcomings of lack of mobility, low submerged endurance, and poor surveillance capability have a new usefulness in areas of low antisubmarine effort and relatively close to their own bases. Thus, coastal defense and advanced-base defense appear to be their logical missions.

The nuclear submarine has assumed, in the Soviet view, a first importance in naval warfare. With long-range missiles, she can destroy or neutralize the most dangerous antisubmarine warships, well beyond their active detection ranges. This allows the submarine to reserve her torpedoes for easier targets and greatly increases her efficiency in war. But the submarine's best asset is her low susceptibility to electronic warfare.

Other thoughts on strategies, tactics, and ships which are changed by the advent of missile warfare can be generated with more reflection. The broadly ranging guesses which have been made are quite obviously only the tip of an iceberg which needs more consideration and definition.

But one thought predominates which seems to have a disturbing urgency. Cruise missiles provide the wherewithal in weapon power and flexibility to cause a lot of Pearl Harbor-type attacks worldwide if this potential for warfare is underrated and not adjusted to. The high level of power of naval weapons, not only in the hands of major sea powers with sea-based tactical air assets but also in the hands of the smallest of navies, indicates the need for a far higher state of readiness for naval units, at all times. And shooting first or immediate counteraction seems absolutely necessary to stay in contention:

"Delay in the employment of weapons in a naval battle or operation inevitably will be fraught with the most serious and even fatal consequences, regardless of where the fleet is located, at sea or in port."— Admiral S. G. Gorshkov[13]

Captain Ruhe, a graduate of the U. S. Naval Academy, Class of 1939, served in submarines throughout World War II and until 1952. Next, he had a mix of sea duties involving several destroyer commands, a submarine division, and finally, a cruiser command, the USS *Topeka* (CLG-8) in 1964. Later shore assignments involved major ASW studies, and his last Navy assignment was as Deputy Director of Program Planning in the Office of the CNO. After a year on the staff of the President's Commission for Marine Science, Engineering, and Resources, Captain Ruhe joined General Dynamics as Director of Marine Program Development. In this capacity, he has been assessing the impact of developing naval technology on new naval programs and the effect of our energy shortage on new commercial energy opportunities.

[1] Charles Mohr, "Israel Claiming Heights," *The New York Times,* 11 October 1973, pp. 1, 19. In the article from Tel Aviv, Mohr reported naval missile engagements of 10 October between the Syrians and the Israelis at the port of Latakia. Two Syrian missile boats were reported sunk. Robert Alden, "Israel is Accused in U.N. Of Sinking a Soviet Ship," *The New York Times,* 13 October 1973, pp. 1, 14. This article cited reports from Damascus, Syria, which credited the Israelis with sinking Soviet, Greek, and Japanese merchant ships in missile boat attacks on the ports of Latakia and Tartus.

[2] Lieutenant Commander Ravi Kaul, Indian Navy, "The Indo-Pakistani War and the Changing Balance of Power in the Indian Ocean," *U. S. Naval Institute Proceedings,* May 1973 (Naval Review Issue), pp. 190, 192.

[3] Admiral S. G. Gorshkov, Soviet Navy, "The Development of the Art of Naval Warfare," *U. S. Naval Institute Proceedings,* June 1975, p. 56.

[4] Admiral S. G. Gorshkov, "Navies in War and in Peace," *U. S. Naval Institute Proceedings,* November 1974, p. 62.

[5] F. K. Neupokoev, *Firing Anti-Air Rockets,* (Moscow: Military Publishers of the U.S.S.R. Ministry of Defense, 1970), p. 39.
"Guidance technology should be as simple as possible, have the least number of measuring devices, and not require an unduly complex computer component. These requirements, however, are always subordinate to tactical mission requirements."

[6] Admiral Sir Edward Ashmore, RN, "Guided Missiles, Fiction and Reality," *NATO's Fifteen Nations,* February-March 1972, p. 60.

[7] Brigadier General Edwin H. Simmons, USMC, "The Marines Now and in the Future," *U. S. Naval Institute Proceedings,* May 1975 (Naval Review Issue), p. 111.
"There has been some rudimentary examination of the use of ship-to-surface missiles in gunfire support roles, but the trade-off of expensive and scarce missiles for cheap and plentiful gun ammunition does not seem promising." Despite what the general says, the trade-offs must also include the high risk of loss of the gunfire support ship in an antiship missile environment in coastal waters.

[8] N. I. Belavin, "Rocket Bearing Ships," (Moscow: Military Publishers of the U.S.S.R. Ministry of Defense, 1967).
"An age old struggle between kill-weapons and passive defense appears to have been resolved in favor of the offense. It is natural, therefore, that (designers) are forced to search for new ways of assuring survivability of naval ships."

[9] Admiral Gorshkov, "The Development of the Art of Naval Warfare," p. 58.

[10] Admiral Ashmore, *op. cit.,* pp. 59-60.

[11] Admiral Gorshkov, "The Development of the Art of Naval Warfare," p. 60.

[12] *Ibid.*

[13] Admiral Gorshkov, "Navies in War and in Peace," November 1974, p. 64.

Surface Effect Ships in the Surface Navy

By Captain R. C. Truax, U. S. Navy (Retired)

Barring some completely unexpected difficulties, ships riding on a cushion of air will be joining the Fleet within the next decade. After more than 50 years of only trivial increases in the speed of ships, a tripling or even quadrupling of the maximum speed is within the U. S. Navy's grasp.

Two precursors of this new "100-knot navy" are in the later stages of their trials programs. The SES-100A, built by the Aerojet General Corporation, and the SES-100B, by the Bell Aerospace Company, are testcraft designed as "proof of principle" articles for the U. S. Navy. Resistance measurements at speeds up to 70 knots have thus far confirmed the design predictions.

The two testcraft are of about 100 tons gross weight each and, although comparatively small as ships go, are expected to be capable of speeds in excess of 80 knots. There appears to be no fundamental limit to the size of ships using the air cushion or surface effect principle and, in general, performance increases with size. Speeds up to 200 knots may one day be realized with surface effect ships (SES) larger than perhaps 20,000 tons.

The type of surface effect ship currently receiving the lion's share of attention is the "hard-sidewall" or "captured air bubble" configuration. Air is forced into the cushion by powerful fans. This air cushion is retained by flexible seals fore and aft and by rigid catamaran hulls along the sides. This air layer separates the hull plating from the water, effecting an enormous reduction in frictional resistance. The air cushion vehicle rides high enough to allow most waves to pass unimpeded beneath her. Only her side hulls pierce the surface. The end seals either ride clear on a thin film of escaping air or plane on the surface complying with the waves as they pass beneath. Leakage is replaced by the fans. In waves, the cushion also attenuates the effects of what otherwise would prove to be a very bumpy ride.

Although an SES can go very fast, her lift-to-drag ratio is inferior to that of a displacement ship at speeds below perhaps 50 knots. Weight, therefore, is important, and many design practices approach those used in aircraft.

SES will probably be highly automated with most machinery automatically or remotely controlled. High speed tends to minimize mission durations. This fact, coupled with automation, tends to make the crew small, with a minimum of "hotel" facilities. The crew quarters of the 100-ton testcraft resemble those of airplanes rather than displacement ships. The Bell craft has no below-deck accommodations. Her controls closely resemble those of a large multi-engined airplane. Crew members have only airline-type reclining seats. The Aerojet testcraft has somewhat more elaborate quarters with four bunks, a galley, and mess spaces below.

The hulls of the two 100-ton testcraft are made largely of marine aluminum, and the future may see materials of higher strength ratio extensively employed.

Propulsion and lift engines, for the foreseeable future, will be marine versions of aircraft gas turbines which alone adequately combine high power with light weight. The Bell testcraft uses Pratt & Whitney FT12 engines; the Aerojet uses AVCO-TF35s.

There are three candidate propulsors: waterjets, supercavitating propellers, and ducted fans. The SES-100A uses waterjets; the SES-100B uses semi-submerged, supercavitating propellers.

The propellers of the Bell craft are not like those found on displacement vessels. Normally, a propeller produces thrust by an increase in pressure on the face of the blade, and a decrease in pressure on the back. This latter pressure becomes lower and lower as relative speed is increased until at some point (usually near the leading edge on the back face) the pressure is reduced to the vapor pressure of water. At this point the water boils. No further decrease in pressure is possible, and the contribution to the thrust made by the backside of the propeller ceases to increase. Worse, when the vapor bubbles reach a region of higher pressure, they implode with great violence. If they are in close proximity to any solid surface, very high stresses are induced, and the surface may disintegrate.

Cavitation, as the phenomenon is called, normally places a limit on propeller speed, since impingement of the collapsing bubbles on blades or structure is difficult to avoid under all operating conditions. Some special blade shapes (super-cavitating propellers) encourage the formation of a vapor cavity in a controlled fashion. It is then possible, at the design point at least, to avoid bubble implosion near any solid surface. Further alleviation of the problem can be obtained by ensuring that low pressure areas are filled with air before vapor pressure is reached. With such ventilation, violent collapse of the bubbles is avoided. Appropriate design is required to ensure that all cavities created are properly ventilated.

Another problem with propellers is the drag created by the hub and by supporting struts. The solution to this problem adopted for the SES-100B is semi-submerged propellers, only the blades of which contact the water.

Waterjets, produced by a diffuser-pump nozzle combination, are another solution to the problem of high-speed ship propulsion. Cavitation is avoided by slowing the water down from ship speed, converting some of the dynamic head (velocity) into static pressure before it meets the energy-imparting blades. It is possible to keep the pressure well above that of water vapor, especially at high speed. Of course, the relative velocity of diffuser and the water is equal to the ship speed and, thus, care is required to avoid excessive lowering of the pressure before adequate slowing down takes place.

Stability and control offer special problems. Surface-effect ships tend to have a high center of gravity. Because the wetted surface must be minimized, buoyancy forces cannot provide any great measure of stability. Hydrodynamic, aerostatic, or jet reaction forces must be used instead. Appropriate shaping of the sidehulls or special foils can give adequate stability, but drag considerations militate against indiscriminate use of such surfaces. Only the area required at any given moment should be exposed to the water. The rough nature of the ocean surface makes such controlled immersion difficult.

Hydrodynamic surfaces or jet reaction must also be used for directional stability and control. Design of such surfaces is further complicated by the cavitation problem. Not only does cavitation lead to material damage, but also it gives rise to unsteady and rather unpredictable changes in the forces produced by the control and stabilization surfaces.

In spite of severe structural problems in regard to space and weight, despite the difficulty of maintaining an air bubble with acceptable leakage while traversing a rough surface, and notwithstanding the destructive effects of cavitation, acceptable design solutions appear possible. How well the first generation of SES has solved these problems will be known shortly.

The two testcraft have many similarities and many differences besides the difference in propulsors previously mentioned. The rakish SES-100A shows more attention to aerodynamic drag. The forward position of her cabin gives better visibility and, being partially submerged in the hull, she looks more like an airplane.

The SES-100B on the other hand has her crew quarters aft and entirely above the maindeck. The aft position reduces the accelerations resulting from pitching motion and may offer a more comfortable ride. The symmetrical outline was selected to minimize the tooling required.

Steering concepts for the two ships differ sharply. The Bell craft uses a more conventional system, with rudders providing the turning moment. The centrifugal force of the turn is balanced by yawing the sidehulls to generate "lift." The sidehulls are supplemented by ventral fins to provide enough wetted area.

Since the waterjet inlets on the Aerojet craft cannot tolerate appreciable angles of sideslip without cavitating, the SES-100A uses center of gravity steering.

To make a turn, hydrofoils are extended out the side by hydraulic rams, producing a side force which goes very nearly through the center of gravity.

The forward seals of the two craft are quite different. Bell uses a combination of bow bag and individual fingers. The fingers accommodate to small waves locally without causing the entire seal to deflect.

The Aerojet's forward seal is essentially a fabric membrane stiffened with fishpole-like fiberglass rods. Hinges and air springs provide adjustable compliance. The rear seal is similar to the forward seal but a hold-down bag is added to counterbalance the cushion pressure. The Bell stern seal also has a hold-down bag but does not have stiffeners.

Both ships are heavily instrumented. Several hundred measurements are taken and recorded. Many are monitored on a real-time basis.

The Aerojet craft, the SES-100A, is being tested in the convenient variety of sea states available in Puget Sound. The Bell boat (SES-100B) is being tested first on Lake Ponchartrain in the New Orleans area, and later in the Gulf of Mexico just off Panama City, using the Naval Coastal Systems Laboratory as a base.

The two craft have been tested by their builders for about a year. During this time, the performance of the ships was measured in a wide variety of conditions and these measurements compared with the theoretical predictions. If necessary, the design technique for future ships will be modified to conform with actual results.

The test programs include determination of speed, range, maneuverability, seakeeping characteristics, and ride characteristics or "habitability." Any special problems of maintenance and operation peculiar to this type of vessel will also be noted.

After the builders' tests have been completed, the Navy will take delivery of the craft for an extended period of engineering and simulated operational evaluation. For this period, a special facility has been constructed at Patuxent River, Maryland, adjacent to the West Seaplane Basin, originally built to accommodate large seaplanes. Here Navy crews and government engineers will put both craft through their paces and in general apply naval experience to the understanding and exploitation of this new capability.

Unless some major surprises are encountered, we may expect to see a progressive conversion of the surface Navy to an all-SES Fleet, for there is no major class of naval vessel that cannot profit greatly from the unique advantages of these air cushion ships. Except for garbage scows and a few auxiliaries, all naval ships should be fast. Speed not only allows getting there "fustest with the mostest" but once at the scene of the action, gives tremendous tactical advantages.

SESs, because of their high speed and shallow draft, are virtually invulnerable to torpedoes, and they present a much more difficult target for aircraft and missiles.

Except for hydrofoil ships, SESs are the only surface vessels that cannot be outrun by a modern submarine. So great is an SES's speed that she can stop dead in the water, listen, and still maintain a rate of advance greater than any surface or subsurface ship.

The SES, while not as fast as airplanes or helicopters, have a loiter capability comparable with conventional displacement ships.

Speed increases use. Many SES trips can be made in the time required for one by a conventional ship. Speed allows one task force to cover simultaneous potential threats in widely dispersed areas, and minimizes the requirement for America to maintain advanced bases all over the world.

SES have two additional characteristics that should allow them to be superb aircraft carriers. First, their speed allows wind-over-the-deck to approach aircraft takeoff and landing speeds. Deck size requirements, and the need for catapults and arresting gear should be greatly reduced. Landing techniques could be similar to those used on the airships *Akron* and *Macon,* where the plane is caught by a trapeze-like device and pulled inside the hull. Numbers of such devices might be installed, allowing simultaneous takeoff and landing of several aircraft. Second, the broad beam, which is characteristic of SES, lends itself well to formation landings and launchings.

The impact of surface effect ships on the Navy will be extensive. It will involve both pain and pleasure. On one hand, their new capabilities will provide an intellectual and professional challenge that will infuse a new enthusiasm into younger officers. At present, our Navy is only beginning to understand how best to exploit SES characteristics. New strategies, new tactics, new maintenance, and new operating philosophies will be needed.

SES-100B *built by Bell Aerospace.*

SES-100A *built by Aerojet General.*

On the other hand, new habits must displace old, cherished totems. With smaller crews, even big ships will not represent the "command" they used to. A captain's energy and effort will be concentrated more on machinery than on people. There will be fewer seagoing billets and thus, the shore establishment will grow. Navy yards will change radically, evolving into something of a cross between what they are now and an aircraft overhaul and repair (O&R) establishment. Drydocking facilities must change. And although the crews will spend more time on the beach than at sea, seagoing time will be more confining and more physically exhausting. This means there will be even fewer sea duty billets for older, more senior officers. All these pains must be borne, however, for the new level of effectiveness the SES will give to the Navy is a power that, for the good of both the Navy and our country, is inarguable.

There will be a transition period. The SES will not replace the conventional ship overnight. Neither iron hulls nor steam power elbowed their predecessors aside immediately despite a superiority that is now obvious. Technological problems alone will force us to climb the growth ladder a rung at a time. We need bigger engines. Those engines must be developed especially for SES. The airplane industry has, for the moment at least, reached a size plateau, and larger spinoff engines are not likely, for some time, to be available for SES. Big gas turbines cost money—as do other technological developments required for full exploitation of the potential inherent in SES. We will need SES-oriented weaponry, if not initially, then ultimately, for full effectiveness. We will have to reorient our thinking about research and development (R&D) costs for ships. We accept R&D costs for airplanes that are orders of magnitude greater than the cost of a single plane, yet R&D for a ship class usually runs to only a fraction of the cost of one ship. For displacement vessels, this ratio was probably justified. Such ships represent a mature technology, where the payoff from R&D is small regardless of the sums spent.

With the advent of the air cushion principle, however, whole new horizons are presented. We shall not realize the bright promises if the problems are approached timidly. Boldness of both an administrative and financial nature is required. Some naval officers will have to stick their necks out, perhaps even lay their careers on the line, if both the engineering and operational problems are to be solved, and solved with a speed that will allow the U.S. Navy to take maximum advantage of the higher effectiveness the air cushion principle allows.

Most of us realize that there is no ultimate weapon. A new discovery, properly exploited, gives a few days, months, or years of advantage to the nation that first recognizes and uses it. Every weapon, sooner or later, is either countered or encountered in all the major powers' arsenals. Thus time is of the essence, in peace as well as in war. What we gain from all our military R&D expenditures is but a transitory advantage over our enemies or potential enemies. Still, such technical advantages can often spell the difference between victory and defeat. Moreover, in time of peace, they can mean the difference between peace and war. A Scarlett O'Hara—"I'll think about it tomorrow"—attitude with any new development of potential military significance simply fritters away all or part of the weapon's benefit.

Finally, in time of peace, the absolute secrecy necessary to achieving technological surprise is next to impossible in our open society. It is primarily by taking financial risks that this country can maintain the technological superiority of its weapons. Financial risk, followed by both administrative efficiency and basic technical know-how in converting dollars to weaponry, is the *sine qua non* of the weapons game. The surface effect ship is not the kind of doomsday weapon the nuclear bomb was and is. It might be possible to win a war without SES or lose one with them, but these ships represent a new and important capability that must be taken advantage of—and quickly. Without ships we do not have a Navy. If the choice had to be made between a somewhat improved airplane and the beginning of a revolution in our surface ships, we ought to give priority to the latter. Sometime soon this choice may have to be made, because the SES revolution will not be brought to a successful conclusion with half-hearted measures.

Captain Truax is a graduate of the U.S. Naval Academy, Class of 1939. He was designated a naval aviator in 1943 and AEDO the same year. Most of his naval career was spent in Navy R&D, in rocket propulsion and guided missiles. In 1955, he was loaned to the U.S. Air Force ballistic missile program, where he initiated the Thor and Reconnaissance Satellite programs. After retirement in 1959, he worked for private industry for nine years, returning to the government as a civilian in 1968. He is presently Assistant Project Manager for Development, Surface Effect Ship Project Office (PM-17).

The Carrier

by Captain Stephen T. DeLaMater, U. S. Navy (Retired)

A great part of the Navy's difficulty in formulating its shipbuilding program to its tasks is that so much of the country's total military mission falls within the Navy's province. It is sometimes hard for a nation that pioneered world aviation and space technology to fully realize the role sea power still plays. We have fought all of our modern wars overseas, and it is certainly our goal to keep armed combat far from our shores. It is, therefore, obvious that a great part of our defense establishment must be devoted to those forces which keep potential intruders at arm's length. This means transportation and defense of lines of communication, and it means air and amphibious support of our own or allied troops overseas.

Theoretically, there are two ways to accomplish this—by air or sea. Air is certainly faster, but air forces suffer three very definite disadvantages: limited payload, short range, and high vulnerability at critical times. Again, theoretically, these disadvantages can be overcome by vastly increasing numbers of aircraft, enhanced inflight refueling, and by access to strategically located overseas bases. In reality, these bases are no longer available, and this concept, if carried to its ultimate and somewhat ridiculous end—supporting combat aircraft from domestic bases—would be vastly more expensive, or less cost-effective than the sea-based alternative. Unfortunately, sea power is also expensive, and therein lies the problem. To satisfy the requirements of the sea-based alternative within constraints of a reasonable budget would require a restructuring of the total armed forces away from traditional concepts. There have been some serious attempts to do just that. U. S. Senator Robert Taft, for example, has prepared an excellent white paper on defense, *A Modern Military Strategy for the United States,* which would support the added forces needed for an adequate sea power strategy by phasing out a large portion of our nonmechanized ground forces. Regardless of how improbable it may be that such a massive shift in our national defense philosophy will be accepted by Congress and the administration, we must keep working toward some such reorder-

ing of defense priorities, and our planning and our building programs should be fashioned with this in mind.

The carrier force level has declined severely in recent years. Although currently at 13, it faces the threat of being reduced to 12. The Navy is, in effect, at that level now since only 12 air wings are provided. This is compensated somewhat by the existence of reserves. But this is a controversial issue itself, and there is logic to support the proposition that reserves should not be relied on to man active ships. Reservists suffer attrition in making the transition to active duty because of job priorities and personal hardship exemptions even under full mobilization. In the initial phases of combat, aircraft losses can be expected to be significantly higher than ship casualties, and reserves are required as replacements.

It wasn't too long ago—less than ten years—that we operated 24 carriers. When reducing force levels, there is some point of no return in carrier numbers beyond which, as the British discovered, the potential results aren't worth the effort. But where this occurs is debatable. Some critics have put the total number needed at from six to nine. These figures are based on the traditional concept of having four or five ships forward based for deterrence and quick response. There would also be a small number in backup for maintenance and

"The argument for the small nuclear carrier just doesn't stand up as an alternative to continuing the classic carrier philosophy exemplified in the Nimitz class. . . . Once you have bought the expensive components of a ship—power plant, electronics, the housekeeping facilities, etc.—the steel for added hull, work areas, aviation fuel, and ammunition is cheap."

small contingencies. One problem with this scheme, of course, is that it assumes that the carrier will not challenge the Soviets directly in a major combat scenario. In a very real sense, it opts to foreclose any chance we might have to maintain a conventional war deterrent against the Soviets. Such a course of action would be tantamount to a decision that we not try to sustain a position of world leadership—something no one has ever been able to do with a second-rate military establishment.

The carrier is indeed a key element in our ability to contain a Soviet threat, and the number needed must be related to this requirement. An analytic determination of this sort is very difficult, particularly since it is not feasible simply to compare numbers as used to be done with battleships or ships-of-the-line whose primary purpose was ship-versus-ship combat. The carrier is not for fighting other carriers. The factors that determine the size of a carrier force are many indeed. The Navy knows that whatever the number of ships is at any given time, it never seems to be enough. The active carrier force has always been overworked. The most convenient rationale for an attack carrier force existed several years ago when we had two carriers in the Mediterranean committed to NATO and needed three in the Western Pacific to support the SIOP (Single Integrated Operation Plan). Since it takes three carriers rotating for each one continuously deployed, this automatically dictated a force of 15 attack carriers. Most people were reasonably satisfied with this for a good number of years, particularly since we also had nine antisubmarine carriers (CVSs) operational. The advent of ballistic missile submarines removed the need for carrier SIOP forces but not for an on-station conventional deterrent. In fact, the Guam Doctrine reemphasized the need for this reassurance of support since we were thereby sensibly backing away from troop commitments. But the wave of inflation and austerity hit the Navy hard, and one casualty was the CVS. The CVS and CVA (attack carrier) capabilities were integrated into the single large CVA hulls and the ships were redesignated CVs. While this conversion—and it entailed a rather extensive ship modification—was primarily motivated by a force reduction, the resultant ships have lost some of the specialized capabilities they had as CVAs. They did, of course, pick up much added CVS capability. The net effect has been ships of greatly enhanced ability as complete weapon systems. At the same time, they are flexible enough that—given some warning—they can be optimized for either a sea control or a projection ashore mission.

One of the weaknesses of the 15-carrier force level argument was that some critics took advantage of the fact that it looked on the surface as though the five deployed ships constituted the total carrier requirement,

and that the rest constituted a rather expensive logistic chain. The Navy even worked out some rather complicated overseas home-porting schemes that would permit deployment of five carriers with a force level of 11 or 12, but these have never been fully implemented. Also never completely understood in this argument was the fact that the five deployed with ten back for training, upkeep, and home port time, represented the best way to utilize in peacetime the force we maintain for war. The carrier is so useful in peacetime as a visible deterrent—displayable without diplomatic clearance—that we tend to forget that its wartime use obviously should determine force size.

In the two combat situations we have been involved in since World War II, the number of attack carriers was always less than could have been profitably used—11 to 22 in Korea and an average of 16 in Vietnam. But these situations were limited war involvements which can hardly be considered as truly indicative of the needs of a large conventional (or limited nuclear) confrontation between the United States and Soviets. In Vietnam and Korea, the requirement was simply to provide numbers of aircraft for air superiority, close air support, and interdiction of enemy lines of supply and communication. There was never any need to dedicate separate forces or parts of carrier deckloads to antisubmarine and antisurface ship warfare. Some aircraft were, of course, dedicated to force antiair defense as combat air patrol, but these numbers were minimal compared to what they would be in an actual hostile environment. Succinctly stated, the carriers were fully occupied as forward air bases without ever being used in their prime role of sea control. Future scenarios may not require the simultaneous use of CVs in both sea control and projection ashore roles, but it is realistic to think that one could follow the other very closely. In any event, planning for future wars should make some allowance for attrition. All in all, considering the worldwide, two-ocean Navy aspects of the U. S. commitment, a force level of 25 carriers seems justified. The trouble with calling for that many is that it looks almost impossible to get there from here. With competition from the B-1 bomber, the cruise missile, a new Army tank, and other expensive defense hardware, dollars for expansion of the carrier force—without a drastic reshaping of the entire defense posture—seem more a planner's dream than a realistic possibility. In any case, we must redouble efforts to resist further cutbacks. A force level of 12 carriers is probably about the minimum active force which retains any credibility as a deterrent.

What should a force of 25 aircraft carriers look like? Obviously, we don't mean 25 nuclear-powered *Nimitz*-class giants with full CV capabilities and aircraft complements. There is no way that a *Nimitz* could be authorized more often than every two or three years. This schedule should be continued at least through the period necessary to replace the *Forrestal* (CV-59) through *Constellation* (CV-64) as they reach respectable retirement ages of between 30 and 36 years. The *Carl Vinson* (CVN-70), the last of the original three *Nimitz*-class ships, had her keel laying in October 1975 and will join the fleet in 1981. With 12 ships, she replaces the *Coral Sea* which would be 34 years old. If CVN-71, for which long-lead items were authorized by Congress this year, comes into the force in 1985 replacing the *Forrestal* and then one more each two or three years, the *Constellation,* the newest of her class, would be 36 years old when retired. Extension of the service life of these ships much beyond this period is impractical. It can be done, but there are marginal returns for the money when compared to new construction. This building program would sustain a minimum force of 12 frontline CVs as smaller supplemental carriers (discussed later in the article) come into being. It will be expensive, but not prohibitively so within the present framework and

"It wasn't too long ago—less than ten years—that we operated 24 carriers. When reducing force levels, there is some point of no return in carrier numbers beyond which, as the British discovered, the potential results aren't worth the effort."

JAMES F. FALK

concept of our shipbuilding budget. These ships—follow-on *Nimitz*es—would be less expensive than a new class of smaller nuclear ships, and they would retain the full range of compatibility with our current inventory of aircraft. Since the aircraft that embark in a carrier are nearly as expensive as the carrier itself, it behooves us to make full use of these assets and not create cross decking and other problems just to satisfy an unreasoned desire to cut down carrier size. The argument for the

small nuclear carrier just doesn't stand up as an alternative to continuing the classic carrier philosophy exemplified in the *Nimitz* class. The argument for large size is persuasive. Once you have bought the expensive components of a ship—power plant, electronics, the housekeeping facilities, etc.—the steel for added hull, work areas, aviation fuel, and ammunition is cheap.

More than that, the large ship goes faster, carries more firepower, handles more sophisticated aircraft, is safer to operate from, will absorb more punishment, can sustain herself longer, and in fact, does just about everything better—except manage to be in two places at the same time. In carrier design, the economies of scale are devastating. Not only can't you get one-half as much aircraft handling space on board the carrier that costs half as much, but you can't even get the same kinds of aircraft. This means that no matter how many of the smaller ships you have, some capabilities will undoubtedly be diminished—reconnaissance range, fighter speed, ship speed, safety, survivability, and staying power.

An OpNav study completed earlier this year clearly shows this and says, among other things supporting continued construction of this size ship, "Carriers significantly smaller than the NIMITZ Class cannot support the practical minimum number and types of aircraft required to perform missions alone in the presence of an air threat. NIMITZ size carriers provide more than twice the combat capability of the smallest practical nuclear powered alternative. . . . Practically all design-to-cost, reliability, maintainability, and operability options for a new design carrier can be incorporated in a modified design NIMITZ Class carrier."[1] We see, for example, that on the smallest nuclear design considered by the CNO study, the theoretical number of aircraft carried would be only 53 as compared to 94. Moreover, on a buy of three ships, they would be more expensive than *Nimitz* hulls because of lead ship costs. Figure 1, from the study, illustrates other comparisons.

There is, of course, the related question, "Would it be better to build a ship larger than the *Nimitz?*" There are compelling reasons not to, ranging from psychological and diminishing return factors to port handling problems, but again the most persuasive are lead ship costs. Going up from the *Nimitz* would not be just a bit more expensive. It would be a lot more expensive. There are no serious advocates of a larger carrier.

It is a combination of these factors which should guide the decision to a follow-on *Nimitz* rather than a somewhat smaller and more expensive new design nuclear ship as our frontline carrier.

[1] Office of the Chief of Naval Operations, *CVNX Characteristics Study Group Report* (Washington, D.C.: Department of the Navy, 1976), p. IV-2.

144

Figure 1 Ship Characteristics Comparison

	A	B	D	CVN-68
Dimensions (Feet)				
Length on waterline	860	940	970	1,040
Beam at waterline	121	130	135	134
Depth, Keel to Flight Deck	94	94	94	100.5
Displacements (Long Tons)				
Light Ship	51,900	59,700	68,200	72,700
Standard	55,900	65,300	73,700	81,600
Full Load	64,600	74,800	84,800	93,400
Propulsion				
Plant	Mod. D2G (D2W Core)	Mod. D2G (D2W Core)	A4W	A4W
No. of Shafts	2	2	4	4
Aviation Features				
No. of Notional Aircraft	53	65	65	94
No. of Avn. Elevators	2	3	3	4
No. of C13-1 Catapults	2	3	3	4
Arresting Gear (No./Type)	3 + B/MK 14	3 + B/MK 14	3 + B/MK 14	4 + B/MK 7
JP-5 (Tons)*	0.74	0.82	0.92	1.00
Manning				
Air Wing	1,296	1,580	1,580	2,227
Ship	2,004	2,209	2,200	2,981
Total	3,300	3,789	3,780	5,208

* Relative to CVN-68

The considerations addressed thus far apply only to an alternative to the CV. They are related to a ship that would be built instead of the *Nimitz* follow-on. That, however, takes care of only half of the proposed 25-carrier force, and here is where the Navy needs to do some serious soul-searching to come up with innovative ideas and leadership. A new class of carriers or aviation sea control ships (or whatever we may want to call them) is long overdue. These would be ships 13 through 25 in the force level. We need a conventionally powered class designed from the keel up for a primary mission of sea control. The ship would be capable against submarines, surface ships, aircraft, and missiles but would have little left for projection ashore. The concept of such a ship is, of course, nothing new. This is the ship Admiral Elmo Zumwalt tried so hard to bring to fruition when he was Chief of Naval Operations. The many problems that face such a design include:

▶ A fear among planners that this proposed class (CVSC) would compete with the CV for budget priority.
▶ The opposition of Admiral Hyman Rickover to building any major warships without nuclear power.
▶ The lack of successful guidelines to follow. This is the

same factor that has inhibited the Soviets from getting into carriers faster. This ship would not be an evolution; it would be an almost completely new carrier concept.
▶ The uncertainty of the technology. V/STOL (vertical/short takeoff and landing) is an idea whose time has been a long time coming. First flown in the early 1950s, only the Marines have put them into operational squadrons, and they are still regarded as freaks.

This is unfortunate, and it is also a little hard to understand. We built small escort carriers in World War II, and they served well. They were cheap and expendable, but they performed better than we might have anticipated, and we actually "expended" only six of the 71 in U. S. Navy service. That same ship won't suffice now, and in the years that have intervened we have lost the capability to build and operate the small carrier. Basically, of course, the problem has been technological in that up to now high-performance aircraft have required more deck space, landing and takeoff areas, and maintenance facilities than could possibly be accommodated in a jeep carrier-size hull. Obviously, the Harrier is evidence that technology is here now to put a V/STOL on a modest size hull. The strange thing is that it has been here for sometime, but we haven't utilized it. Why? Probably there are several answers, but the prime one is lack of in-depth Navy support. Until OP-05 (Deputy Chief of Naval Operations [Air Warfare]) enthusiastically supports this ship, she will never get built. Indeed, OP-05 (and others, but this office is key) have got to do more than just enthusiastically support. They must get out and actively crusade as they always have for the large carriers.

How big should this "small" ship be? What will she carry and cost? It really seems strange that these questions are still being asked after all the study and analysis that went into development of a sea control ship concept. Proposals over the past five or six years for sea control ships—small carriers—have ranged everywhere from the 1,000-ton surface effect ship, with two or three aircraft embarked, on up through incremental steps to 50,000 tons. When the proposals get to that upper limit, they have reached the CV stage.

There must, therefore, be real incentive and leadership dedicated not just to holding the displacement down but insisting that the technology match the task. It is a herculean one. We have long complained that we never get a good airplane when we have to match a new airframe to a new engine. In this case, we may be asking more than that—matching a new airplane, new engine, and new deck. This author's view is that we should start thinking of a sea control ship (CVSC) at about 25,000 tons. At this displacement, we should be able to design a ship that would hold 20 to 25, maybe even 30 aircraft. These are not the F-14s, A-6s, and RA-5Cs that take up so much real estate on board present CVs. This will require development of a sensible, workable, high-performance V/STOL. The thing that has stopped V/STOL development in this country is the fact that neither the Air Force nor the Navy has had any clear concept of what to do with it. On the other hand, the Marines with their aviation leadership clearly behind the V/STOL have put it to useful application, have three Harrier-equipped operating squadrons, and are enthusiastically looking toward follow-on Harrier development. In spite of this, and the fact that prototype operations of the AV-8A on board the amphibious assault ship *Guam* (LPH-9) in 1973 were highly successful, this writer doesn't believe that the Harrier, which is basically a 29-year-old design, is the answer for the CVSC. The point is, however, that dedicated and persistent leadership can produce a family of aircraft that can operate off a 25,000-ton ship either STOL or V/STOL. These must be aircraft that will reasonably do the jobs now accomplished by the antisubmarine aircraft, helicopter, and the small fighter.

Basically, the CVSC would be designed as a sea control ship and would not have the flexibility of a CV to

operate interchangeably in a projection ashore role. She could carry out minor projection tasks, for instance, provide combat air patrol and hold-down operations to cover logistic, troop insertion, or evacuation operations into or out of a land base in an unfriendly area. Her primary limitation in this role would be lack of aviation ammunition carrying capacity and limited numbers of aircraft embarked with an attack capability. Although this could be overcome by tailoring an air wing, it would probably not be practical to do so because of the ammunition limitation and hopefully the availability of suitable ships—the CVs.

The CVSC should not be nuclear powered. This writer's answer to the nuclear power question is an ironic one. When the Navy was pressing hard for authorization for a nuclear-powered carrier to follow the *Enterprise* (CVN-65), an oil crisis such as we have undergone would have swung the balance. Now that the battle is

". . . the Harrier is evidence that technology is here now to put a V/STOL on a modest size hull. The strange thing is that it has been here for some time, but we haven't used it. Why? Probably there are several answers, but the prime one is lack of in-depth Navy support."

HAWKER SIDDELEY

won, the wisdom of building the large CVs with nuclear power is almost unassailable, and certainly we should plan to continue doing so. But for the CVSC carrier, nuclear power would not be suitable. It would be ridiculous to call this ship expendable, but she should be inexpensive enough and small enough that being damaged or taken out of action will not be catastrophic. She also will be needed in numbers that would be almost impossible to justify at the cost of nuclear propulsion. Further, her mission will require her to operate with other conventional ships. And though she may often have to come off the line to replenish, generally she will be operating in an environment where this is possible. So while it seems in a sense to be a backward step, these ships, at least the first few, should be oil-fired. Any breakthrough in nuclear costs would change this, but such a breakthrough seems unlikely to occur.

The sea control carrier, while not having the attack role of the larger CV, would, however, still be a full-fledged combat ship, capable of sustained operations in a combat environment. Her conventional power plant—perhaps augmented with gas turbines for a dash capability—should be able to sustain 27 knots. Hull design, point defense weapons, and her own embarked aircraft would give the ship excellent survivability characteristics. The CVSC would not generate additional escort requirements. In fact, in most circumstances such a ship would augment or replace conventional escorts. Properly designed with built-in automation and redundancy, the crew and air wing personnel requirements should total less than 1,500 per ship.

Costs are another matter. A lot of the research and development on the elements that would make up this combination has already been done, but much more is needed. On the other hand, once research and development and lead ship problems are out of the way, these ships would be significantly less costly than the big CVs. They might cost a fourth as much. Once the building program is well on its way, we should produce at least two ships per year, so that actually, allowing some time to evaluate the first one or two prototypes, the full CVSC force of 13 ships could be completed in a 10 to 12 year period after the "go" decision is made.

Integrating these costs into the present budget will be difficult indeed. At this level of added shipbuilding requirement, it will probably be necessary to effect some major program shifting. What these would be is hard to say as there are no longer any soft spots in the defense budget. Maybe as these ships come into being and their use is evaluated, they will replace some non-aviation surface ships in a shipbuilding program. However, since the total requirement right now is for additional ships, and the 13 CVSCs would not be replacements, then to the extent that CVSCs replace new construction escorts, on a ratio of two or three to one for example, it would be necessary to further increase carrier force levels, and savings would thus not be achieved.

At some point in the near future, the United States may decide—by treaty commitment or otherwise—to limit our expenditures on strategic weapons. This theo-retically could make funding available for conventional forces, including the CVSC. And lastly, it could well be that the armed services' growing personnel costs would compel us to consider—as Senator Taft, among others, has suggested—seriously reducing our standing Army and putting this money into more capital intensive weapon systems—such as the sea control carrier.

In any event, this clearly is a step the Navy must decide to take. Until we make a definitive, strong effort toward deploying a small carrier, we won't convince key decision-makers that we are not proceeding blindly down the big carrier route without giving any serious thought to a force that has real balance for tasks over the full spectrum of warfare.

A two-type carrier force such as described here would need to be employed and deployed in different ways than we do now. For example, it might be an excellent idea to replace the large CVs in the Mediterranean with CVSCs as a general deployment plan. This doesn't mean that the large CVs need to be kept at mid-ocean in a dispersed pattern at all times, but it does mean that as intelligence gathering capabilities continue to improve, it should be increasingly possible to position forces strategically in a very flexible rotation and not have them tied to rigid schedules. It means then that as a crisis approaches, since our response almost always is going to be reactive rather than preemptive, we might want to put the CVs to sea to hide for awhile. The carrier's only high vulnerability comes in the initial phase of hostilities when she must risk a surprise attack from ships in close proximity and against which there is no real defense since she has sacrificed the big advantage of standoff attack range.

Even though the Midway (CV-41) is now home ported in Japan with no major problems, in the future it may not be a good idea to home port either CVs or CVSCs overseas, particularly from the standpoint of air wing training and support. This is a costly process and is worthwhile only if forward basing is a most important consideration. As carrier force levels come back up and the visibility needed to support the Guam Doctrine is achievable through rotation, overseas home porting will not be so important as it is today.

With a reasonably sized force of CVs and CVSCs under coordinated command and control, a flexible, random deployment pattern with fully ready ships could carry out the fleet's deterrent, quick-reaction role. Obviously, this depends on good intelligence such as we have not always enjoyed in the past. If, however, while utilizing a random deployment, we hold to a policy of having one-third to one-half of all carriers either deployed, in transit, or ready in U. S. waters, then our response capability should at least be no worse than it is now with set, regular visit and revisit habits.

The carrier issue, while obviously a highly technical and complex one, lends itself to simplification on the basis of what is possible and the limited set of available alternatives. The United States, like it or not, has an overseas strategy and in order to carry this out will need many aircraft landing platforms and/or advanced bases. Since the concept of using foreign bases is almost totally eroded, and since land-based aviation is in no position to support operations over the oceans far from domestic bases or in most areas of potential conflict, carriers become the only feasible answer. How many? The growing size of the Soviet Navy indicates that we need as many as we can possibly afford or can physically build within our existing economic structure without emergency mobilization.

These constraints would limit CV construction to about one every two or three years at most, and this is sufficient to sustain a force of at least 12 large carriers indefinitely. Although not discussed in detail in this overview, it would also be feasible to augment this force for backup reserves and training with the *Midway* and the *Coral Sea* (CV-43) and with the older *Forrestals* as they phase out of the active force. Though it is not practical to keep these ships in a combat-ready configuration, they could continue for years in non-combat roles.

Since the ultimate objective of our naval forces is to deter a full-scale war against the Soviets—particularly a conventional war—then it becomes reasonably obvious that 12 CVs would not be an adequate number of aviation platforms both to perform the widespread tasks of sea control and to provide support for land operations where no other bases were feasibly available. These missions require dispersal of forces over thousands of miles of ocean area in a taxing variety of roles. More than 12 ships are needed to do it. Whether the number needed above the 12 CV platforms is five, ten, 20, or 50 is somewhat academic. The actual number almost defies

analysis and in the end requires a subjective judgment. But the simplest of scenarios—keeping the North Atlantic sea-lanes open against an aggressive Soviet submarine campaign while simultaneously protecting trade routes to allies in the Far East—will generate requirements that exceed the 25 ships we have picked as a target number.

The ships that will augment the CVs to make up this total have been the subject of controversy for many years. Intuitively, most naval planners and operators believe that a small, compact carrier can be built to fill this need. The problem has been to clearly define it, to push the aircraft technology, and to get on with the job of building prototype ships.

There will be problems over and above the basic ship/aircraft design and marriage difficulties discussed. Probably the most critical of these is personnel. The upgrading of service pay that has occurred in recent years and which is changing the services from being people intensive to a hardware orientation, should provide the incentive to continue a buildup of highly qualified technical expertise. We should be able to keep up with the influx of new ships, considering the two-to-four year lead times necessary to build them.

Another problem not addressed here in detail is weaponry for ship self-defense. Of course, basically, the CVs or CVSCs, by simply carrying out primary missions, contribute significantly to their own defense, and once they survive the potential for surprise attack at the

"The growing size of the Soviet Navy indicates that we need as many [carriers] as we can possibly afford or can physically build within our existing economic structure. . . ."

148

transition to combat, are formidable adversaries. The CVSC will be large enough at 25,000 tons to carry point defense weapons that can themselves be upgraded as more advanced and sophisticated systems become available. There is no valid reason that our defensive weapon technology should not be able to continue meeting the challenge—particularly since the vastly superior offensive aircraft system of the carriers gives them a leg up to begin with.

We see, therefore, that the problems are many, but they also are surmountable. What is needed is to make the hard decision and proceed. The course seen as needed and most practical from the standpoint of what can reasonably be done is this:

▶ Establish a nucleus force of 12 large, nuclear-powered carriers, capable of the most demanding tasks.
▶ Accept the *Nimitz* design and size as the optimal ship for this role and start one every two or three years.
▶ Commence a priority program to develop a small conventional carrier and compatible family of sea control mission aircraft to go with it.
▶ Plan to build two or three of these ships each year and work toward diverting funds from other major programs to do so—with nonmechanized combat forces as a candidate because of their costly personnel emphasis.

There are pitfalls which potentially stand in the way of completing or even making a good start on this program. CVN-71, for example, although long-lead-time items have been authorized, could be scrapped. If the future of the large CV new construction program is placed in jeopardy, it is necessary to look at alternatives. The most feasible of these would probably be a mid-sized conventional CV at around 50,000 tons. This design would produce a substantial advantage on the displacement-versus-embarked aircraft curve and could hold 50 aircraft, two C-13 catapults, and most significantly, arresting gear so that non-V/STOL aircraft could be operated from it. Once the lead ship is out of the way, the cost, since it would not be nuclear, could be considerably less than a *Nimitz,* albeit its capability would also. This ship would be compatible with most present aircraft though probably not the F-14 and RA-5C. Hopefully, also it would provide even greater incentive to supplement with CVSCs. Unfortunately, though, what is more likely to occur is that as the basic CV design gets smaller, it begins to look like the sea control carrier and would be built instead of both CV and CVSC. Probably it would be authorized at a rate greater than the one every two or three years planned for CVNs, but it would undoubtedly not be approved on the schedule proposed for the CVSCs. In fact, it is unlikely that more than one per year would get through Congress. Therein lies the critical problem. The nuclear

Nimitz-size CVN plus CVSCs is the preferred program. An alternative which substituted a mid-size 50,000-ton conventional CV plus the CVSC would be a considerably less than optimum alternative. A program that excluded either the large CV or the small CVSC would not meet the threat and would place us at a distinct disadvantage vis-à-vis the soviets.

But the number one priority for our shipbuilding program of the future would seem to be development of the small carrier V/STOL capability in order to maximize the number of aviation platforms. This would entail a change of overall carrier philosophy and is a decision which, hopefully, will not have to be made.

Whichever way the decision goes, the key to its success or failure will be a firm determination and commitment that the program be carried to fruition with the drive and enthusiasm that have always characterized our large carrier efforts. The Navy has plans for a ship that sounds somewhat like the CVSC except that it calls for an aircraft complement made up of today's aircraft, e.g., four Harriers, 16 antisubmarine helicopters, and six LAMPS helos. That is not the wing or squadron this writer's CVSC concept visualizes. The first new aircraft capability that is needed is a high-performance V/STOL fighter—perhaps like the XFV-12A. Next and maybe hardest to obtain since little has been done so far toward developing it, is a V/STOL with the S-3's antisubmarine capabilities. The wing would be filled out with helicopters of as advanced design as possible.

It is the area of aircraft design and technology that requires more push and determined, persistent leadership than any other. The task is formidable, and the naval aviation community must get solidly behind it. There will be new carriers in the Navy's future as long as we continue to find the right combinations of ship design, aircraft capability, and dedicated leadership.

Captain DeLaMater is director for government relations of the American Gas Association. His last two assignments, prior to his retirement in 1973, were as special assistant to the Chief of Naval Operations for organization liaison and director, naval air weapons analysis staff, office of the Deputy Chief of Naval Operations (Air Warfare). Captain De La Mater graduated from the U.S. Naval Academy in 1943 and, after service in the battleship *Colorado* (BB-45), entered flight training, which he completed in 1945. He has served in five fighter squadrons, including, in 1959, command of one, VF-92. He served as air operations officer in the *Coral Sea* (CVA-43); as head of the aviation ship readiness section, Office of the Chief of Naval Operations; and as special assistant to the Director, Navy Program Planning. Captain De La Mater commanded two ships, the USS *Francis Marion* (APA-249) and USS *Guam* (LPH-9). In 1963, he was coauthor of a study on nuclear propulsion for surface ships, and that same year won first honorable mention in the Naval Institute's prize essay contest for "The Navy Image." He has been a guest lecturer at the Air War College and the Royal Canadian Air Force War College and has written several articles for the *Proceedings* and Naval Review.

Why V/STOL?

By Captain Gerald G. O'Rourke,
U. S. Navy (Retired)

*For years, the vertical or short take-off
and landing aircraft has been a weapon
in search of a mission. It has been successfully tested on board the USS Guam
(LPH-9), and the Royal Navy is con-
templating a "Harrier carrier" of its own.
At a time when there appears to be a diminishing requirement for the Navy's
amphibious assault ships, perhaps they
could be better employed for sea control.
If so, the V/STOL will have found its
mission.*

U. S. NAVY

VOSPER THORNYCROFT

For well over a decade, the advocacy of high-performance jet V/STOL (vertical or short take-off and landing) aircraft has been loudly voiced in the Pentagon, in various government-supported think tanks, in the Congress, and in the pages of numerous professional journals and mass media magazines. Throughout this period, the U. S. Navy has sought a reasonable and sane V/STOL development program. Almost every effort, aside from the Marine Corps' venture into the AV-8A Harrier program, has proven either fruitless or disappointing, leading only to more "studies," more words, later estimates of introduction dates, and a general headache for Navy long-range planners.

Advocates of V/STOL aircraft have attributed this "lack of foresight of naval planners" to hidebound conservatism. Foresighted naval planners (who really *do* exist) have attributed "the impracticability of V/STOL schemes" to the lack of pragmatism in the thinking of the V/STOL proponents. The truth is both and neither. Funding for the basic research and component development for V/STOL has been a hit-or-miss budget item for years, reflecting the fears of many senior aviators that the program will somehow steal moneys that rightfully belong in conventional carrier aircraft programs. On the other hand, no combat requirement for V/STOL has yet been presented which could not be accomplished as well or better by existing types of carrier-based aircraft. To compound matters, neither the Army nor the Air Force has paid much attention to V/STOL since the early 1950s. This frustrates the visionaries no end.

The most devout V/STOL enthusiasts invariably wind up muttering things like "It could only *not* happen in America" or "Why wasn't I born in Switzerland?" While the United States possesses the full range of aerodynamic expertise, world mastery of jet engine propulsion, and an incredibly large research and development establishment which could readily produce any number of V/STOL aircraft, not a single one has actually been made. The reasons are many, complex, and could easily lead to lengthy finger-pointing discourse. The truth of the matter, after all is said and done, seems to be that America hasn't needed V/STOL. The Army has lots of helicopters and no particular desire to move forces or weapons any faster than the 100–150 knots available through those proven, cheap aircraft. The Air Force has plenty of long runways and airplanes to use those runways. Why compromise airborne performance for the ability to jump into the air from the parking ramp? The Navy has its aircraft carriers, complete with high-energy catapults, arresting gear, all-weather landing aids, and the intensely cooperative complex system of ships, airplanes, and people which enable the carriers to work. The Marines, for all their talk about close air support with Harriers, are hard pressed to convince anyone that they will be ordered to invade Europe in the foreseeable future. So, why V/STOL?

If there is a good answer, it pretty much has to arise from a naval requirement. In recent years, as the total number of aircraft carriers declined (despite their full-scale use in Vietnam), as the cost of new carriers and their aircraft soared, as aerodynamic and propulsion technologies offered confident estimates for the feasibility of high-performance V/STOL, as the Soviet Navy surged seaward on a global basis, as the fragility of the sea-lanes of commerce was brought to public attention by the oil crisis, and as the Marine Corps has proven that Harriers can operate from ships at sea, a new sense of realism, even of urgency, is appearing in naval requirements for V/STOL.

Former Secretary of Defense James Schlesinger, in his February 1975 posture statement to Congress, emphasized the need for increased strategic mobility within the non-nuclear general purpose forces, citing V/STOL as one of the key elements for improving the effectiveness of sea control forces. The V/STOL's design compatibility has been a long-standing issue in the Navy fighter program. Almost every new surface ship design includes some degree of air capability. A few Marine-piloted Harriers were used in the evaluation of the sea control ship concept. Some were deployed on board a ship of the Sixth Fleet, and a squadron is now being introduced to overseas Fleet Marine Forces in the Pacific. As a result, the U. S. Marine Corps has a good and growing understanding of V/STOL, as well as a long-range plan for its use in amphibious operations and close air support of ground troops. The Navy, however, still lacks a good overall V/STOL policy and has quite naturally not been realistic about funding allocations and priorities to support a long-range program. In the jargon of the Pentagon, this process is called "concept formulation." Stripping away the bureaucratic language, this involves describing the needs, listing the best solutions, and laying out a detailed plan for spending money to achieve one of those solutions within a reasonable period.

In order to understand the present V/STOL problems in this regard, a brief review of past efforts is helpful. A wide variety of uses has been postulated over years of spasmodic development. The Royal Air Force pioneered land-based applications. That concept, now in early operational implementation, entails the "hiding" of small Harrier detachments under foliage and camouflage, supporting them from a conventional rear area air base complex, and deploying sorties on short notice for close air support, strike and interdiction missions along the forward edge of the battlefield area. The U. S. Marine Corps concept is similar, substituting flat-

U. S. MARINE CORPS

An AV-8A Harrier is launched from the USS Guam *during interim sea control ship tests in 1972.*

topped amphibious ships for the rear area complex and focusing upon close air support of ground troops. Both the RAF and USMC concepts are often attacked by professional critics for their vulnerabilities in modern warfare. According to this argument, nothing can be "hidden" from sophisticated sensors near a battlefield, least of all a group of fragile aircraft with their fuel, ordnance, and supporting ground crews.

A growing number of navies throughout the world see V/STOL opportunities in a different light. Thus far, the naval planners seriously interested or committed to some degree include British, French, Spanish, Italian, Indian, Brazilian, Australian, and—most notably —Russian. To all of these maritime nations, V/STOL offers an alternative to the traditional aircraft carrier. Most have a past history of carrier experience and understand the tremendous advantages accruing from air-capable warships at sea. The British and French have been forced away from the large aircraft carrier for economic reasons, yet both have invested heavily in smaller, air-capable, cruiser-carrier combination designs. Spain has an extensive coastline and a highly strategic location astride Gibraltar, for which naval forces, including a former U. S. light aircraft carrier (ex-USS *Cabot* [CVL-28]), are considered essential. The Italian Navy, although small, is a highly professional force with innovative leadership. A major Italian concern lies in open sea-lanes of commerce along and across the Mediterranean. India and Brazil both consider themselves big naval "frogs" within very large, peaceful ponds. The Australians have always considered aircraft carriers as essential to their Navy, but they are now faced with the high cost of replacing the *Melbourne,* which was launched more than 30 years ago. The Russian motivation toward V/STOL shows evidence of serious and forceful direction. The Soviet naval goal is a two-ocean fleet with enough combat credibility to offset the global navy of the United States. This rival American fleet is built around large aircraft carriers, whose technological prowess is decades ahead of the

Soviets. Any Russian attempt to duplicate this force implies a lifetime of effort, dedication, and priorities. The largest Soviet warship ever built is the brand new *Kiev,* of about 45,000 tons, while the United States has been commissioning carriers of 75,000-plus tons for the past 20 years.

The Soviets have never designed or built a high-performance, carrier-based aircraft, while the United States has produced, among others, the world's finest fighter of its era, the F-4 Phantom, and the world's only combat-proven, all-weather tactical attack airplane, the A-6 Intruder. Dismayed by the prospect of this sort of competition, the Soviet naval planners have chosen instead to leapfrog a technological age through V/STOL. Two other factors are probably equally imperative. One involves the Soviets' lack of easy access to the deep ocean areas where big carriers reign supreme. V/STOL promises compatibility with smaller ships. The other is the need for antisubmarine weaponry to offset the relatively invulnerable Polaris/Poseidon nuclear strategic threat which rings their continental fortress. V/STOL and the *Kiev* class promise a long-range, wide-area ASW weapon system for use on the high seas where these submarines lie on station.

In the U. S. Navy, no similar requirements for V/STOL exist. The carrier fleet is already in being. The heaviest investment costs have been paid many years ago. A vast cadre of professional expertise in supporting and operating aircraft carriers and their sophisticated airplanes is fully occupied in exactly those tasks. An annual stipend of something between $6–12 billion (depending on how the costs are allocated) supports the concept. Fourteen carriers are now operational throughout the world's oceans, from the Persian Gulf to the North Sea. Included in that number—which will soon be reduced to 13 when the *Oriskany* (CV-34) begins inactivation—is the USS *Nimitz* (CVN-68). She joined the fleet last year. Two sisters—the *Dwight D. Eisenhower* (CVN-69) and *Carl Vinson* (CVN-70)—are now under construction.

U. S. Naval engineers, architects, and aircraft designers lead the world in producing good, reliable, effective combat weapons. The F-14 Tomcat is the ultimate in sophisticated air-to-air fighters, the A-6 Intruder in air-to-ground attack, and the S-3 Viking in antisubmarine warfare. The Navy A-7 Corsair II and A-4 Skyhawk designs represent the best in the world for inexpensive attack and close air support duties. Both the E-2C Hawkeye early warning aircraft and the EA-6B Prowler electronic jammer are superbly capable designs. The Phoenix, Sparrow, and Sidewinder missiles are all U. S. Navy-developed products, as are the low-drag conventional bombs, the Walleye series of super-accurate, electro-optical, air-to-ground munitions, and a host of long-range stand-off and antiradiation weapons. All of these aircraft and air weapons were originally built for carrier-based operation. Most were later used with great success by other services and other nations. As one result, long-range U.S. Navy planners are understandably cool to emotional proposals to scuttle the carrier fleet and climb aboard a V/STOL ship.

Sea control has many interpretations and examples. Licensing passage through a canal, restraining fishing fleets to a 12-mile limit, placing ocean blockades across commercial sea-lanes, and depth bombing a suspected submarine are all potential sea control missions. In the traditional U.S. Navy meaning, sea control translates most easily as "full use of an ocean area for U.S. purposes with denial of use to an enemy". The ocean area is generally considered to include the submarine strata, the surface, and the overhead airspace. In actual practice, outside of inland seas and territorial waters, the degree to which sea control is established and maintained is always less than absolute. In the past, and for at least the near future, sea control can be interpreted best as freedom of safe passage for merchant ships, warships, and aircraft.

The exercise of sea control requires either force or the threat of force, since international law governs only those who agree to be governed or can be compelled to. Sea control is also both transitory and dynamic in its application. The classic World War II Atlantic convoy is typical. Battles for control of the seas are traditionally fought in early stages of a conflict, with relative attrition the chief measure of victory. World War II battles for sea control pitted submarines against surface ships. The weaponry of future wars at sea will not be so conveniently categorized. Shore and sea-based long-range missilery and aircraft add to the threat. Satellite surveillance is available. High-capacity airlift is a present reality. High-speed surface ships are not far off.

Despite the new weaponry, the exercise of sea control in future warfare will require even more ships, aircraft, and submarines than it did in the past. The growth of the Soviet naval threat shows no signs of abatement. More and more potentially hostile submarines, armed with more and more sophisticated and deadly weapons, are showing up along America's sea borders and the Free World's vital sea-lanes. The natural foils of these submarines are airplanes and other submarines. Matching submarine to submarine is expensive, cumbersome, slow, and a very imperfect scheme fraught with all sorts of weird and unknown contingencies. Airplanes are really the major weapon and critical to successful control of the sea.

Bringing these air assets into play in the battle scene far at sea poses a difficult challenge. Long-range, land-based ASW aircraft are good for patrol and search duties, but just cannot mass, stay, and attack in the far reaches of the oceans. Sea-based air power is much more proficient at this game, and, up until now, sea-based air power has been synonymous with large aircraft carriers. Only helicopter types can now be accommodated on board the numerous small oceangoing warships. Helicopters are limited in speed, altitude, operating range, and sensor and weapon payloads. These limitations tend to restrict their operational employment to combat radii of 50 miles or less, well below the ranges of some of the offensive weaponry which can be anticipated. Employment of a large aircraft carrier in the sea escort role readily provides the range, area surveillance coverage, and the striking forces required. However, the availability of large aircraft carriers for such escort roles cannot be prudently presumed. The carrier inventory has been rapidly depleted in the past ten years as the numerous World War II-built hulls passed into the jaws of the scrap iron mongers. Large, nuclear-powered giants are always in high demand, since these ships have the awesome ability to apply devastating force on short notice almost anywhere in the world. However, their numbers are too limited to cover the many contingencies facing the United States in this turbulent and unsteadily peaceful world. Replacement large aircraft carriers are hard to come by, since their costs have spiraled enormously. It is preposterous to presume that new ones will be built in the numbers that are really required in coming years for the exercise of sea control. Navy planners must search for a cheaper alternative.

They don't have to look very far for the beginnings of the answer. This gap in the sea control force structure calls for ships smaller than present aircraft carriers and aircraft more capable than helicopters. Already on the rolls of naval combatants are scores of capable, fairly modern warships, all built with some sort of a helicopter platform or a full flight deck. Many were designed for—and are fully employed in—the mission of amphibious assault, a role of questionable priority for large American military forces today. The migration of these ships from this use to that of oceangoing antisubmarine forces for sea control missions seems not only logical but almost essential to the maintenance of naval combat credibility both at home and abroad. The ships are there, the low-speed helicopters are there, and personnel expertise in ASW and sea control is widespread throughout the Navy. The single missing link is the high-performance V/STOL aircraft to provide both the modicum of air defense needed and the long-range, wide-area search, surveillance, and ASW sensor coverage which are integral to the overall mission.

Naval forces of the future will move rapidly and

quietly across vast distances of open ocean. For the task force commander unlucky enough to have no large aircraft carrier at his disposal, surveillance requirements will be all-important and highly time-sensitive. V/STOL aircraft equipped with some of the new sensors, data links and navigational equipment now available could provide that surveillance. V/STOL aircraft, admittedly inferior to their conventional carrier-based brethren in range and payload, still have enough punch to knock off a surface ship, a submarine, or a few heavy long-range reconnaissance aircraft.

In antisubmarine roles, V/STOL aircraft can fill the large performance void between the short-range helicopter and the long-range patrol plane. Quick-response, wide-area, moderate-range coverage using several of the family of new sensors, is a natural role for V/STOL. Because they greatly extend both the eyes and the firepower of a surface warships, V/STOL aircraft can be extremely useful in a variety of over-the-horizon missions such as, mid-ocean blockade embargo, or stop-and-search operations against special interest shipping. V/STOL aircraft could provide a low, but meaningful degree of force application against terrorist or piratical units preying upon merchant shipping in constricted sea passages.

V/STOL aircraft can be used to vastly extend the range and accuracy of ship-launched, surface-to-surface missiles. They could provide vital radio and tactical data links among widely dispersed naval dispositions, and they could be extremely valuable when used as a "zero fuel flow" (compared to airborne combat air patrol) standby interceptor on the deck of a small, distantly stationed surface ship. The large aircraft carrier and her overpowering air wing need not be engaged or hazarded in many possible combat scenarios. In a low threat level police action, at sea or on some remote but critical shore, V/STOL aircraft could be used to quench the brushfire quickly.

Further in the future, V/STOL aircraft could be combined with ultra-high-speed surface effect ships to provide fast-reacting attack, surveillance, ASW, or reconnaissance units. However, the advocacy of V/STOL has all too often been closely tied to far-out schemes, and has fallen flat on its fuselage when the scheme was overtaken by reality. U. S. Navy V/STOL policy should studiously avoid such close and deadly associations. Like the helicopter, dozens of new roles and missions will appear as the V/STOL technology advances into practical operational use. Probably the most interesting, yet pragmatic concept concerns the V/STOL basing possibilities inherent in more than 100 U. S. flat-topped container cargo ships.

An amazing variety of V/STOL designs has been proposed, debated, analyzed, discussed, and dissected over the past two decades. Without exception, none of the schemes has fulfilled its initial advertised potential, and only one, the deflected thrust design, has progressed to an operational airplane. They can be generally classified into four groups to provide a basic appreciation for how they work and to identify their advantages and drawbacks.

The deflected thrust uses a high by-pass-ratio turbofan exhausting through four rotatable nozzles to provide either vertical thrust for lift-off or horizontal thrust for wingborne flight.[1] Its major advantage is relative simplicity, a single engine useful throughout the entire flight regime, the availability of deflected thrust in flight for maneuvering, and, most of all, proof that it actually works in operational hardware form. Its drawbacks are also numerous and include an overpowered engine, inefficient for any combat airplane except a fighter, too much by-pass-ratio in the engine for an efficient fighter, limited range and endurance because of weight considerations, and an overall lack of affinity for supersonic flight.

The lift-plus-lift/cruise concept, apparently in vogue in the Soviet design, involves the use of additional high-output, lightweight jet engines mounted vertically in an airframe. These are used in conjunction with a rotating exhaust nozzle on the regular cruise engine to provide a "three poster" effect for vertical flight and transition. In normal wing-borne operations, the lift

[1] By-pass ratio describes the relative portions of air which pass through the fan only and air which passes through the core combustion process. Thus, the BPR for a pure turbojet would approximate zero, while an airliner fanjet might have a BPR of 5 or more. Most military fanjets have BPRs in the range of 0.7–2.0.

The Navy's plan for a dedicated sea control ship was killed by Congress, but other, now-existing ships could do the job.

XFV-12A V/STOL fighter/attack aircraft

engines are shut down, the cruise engine nozzle is rotated to the horizontal, and the airplane flies in a conventional manner. Advantages include compatibility with supersonic flight and a relatively free choice of the cruise engine design to optimize the conventional flight mode. Disadvantages are complexity, reliance upon several engines for takeoff and landing, the inherent performance penalty to be paid for carrying unused lift engines in normal flight, and a nasty characteristic of blowing very hot, high-velocity exhaust gas onto the ground directly beneath the aircraft—leading to the "vertical blowtorch" nickname for these designs. Several have been built, and many more have been put together on drafting boards. These experiences tend to support a high degree of confidence that such an airplane can readily be built if anyone will pay the price for the necessary engineering development. Thus far, only the Soviets have proven willing to sponsor the concept beyond the prototype stage. Aviation enthusiasts of the world are eagerly awaiting its unveiling, probably this year, on board the *Kiev*.

Both the deflected thrust and lift-plus-lift/cruise schemes are basically "brute force" solutions to the problem, in that they generate the needed lift directly by blowing engine exhausts downward. There are many other ideas which rely instead upon some sort of thrust augmentation or "aerodynamic gear-shifting" to develop vertical lift. At present, the most interesting one

of these is the Navy-Rockwell thrust augmented wing technology prototype, the XFV-12A. This hybrid fighter design, put together from parts of old conventional airplanes, uses a single high-output turbofan engine exhausting through very large, spanwise, venturi-like nozzles in each of the four horizontal wingforms to generate vertical and transitional lifting forces. In normal flight, the nozzles fold into the delta-canard wingforms and a conventional rear exhaust, with afterburner, is used. The potential advantages are tremendous: a single engine, a wide dispersion of relatively cool vertical exhaust, and sparkling performance in short rolling takeoffs as a result of self-generated airflow over the wings from the venturi effect. Disadvantages are few but major. Most notable is the dismaying fact that large area nozzles in wingforms are a technological world in themselves, and all previous laboratory estimates of their characteristics are suspect when transferred to flying hardware. Beyond this, less damning troubles arise in trying to find areas under the wings free from exhaust flows for carrying bombs, missiles and the other accoutrements of combat airplanes. Nevertheless, the promise of a supersonic design free from the blowtorch syndrome is appealing enough for the Navy to continue at least a modest attempt to see the design through to a flying model. Some cynics still maintain that the "aug wing" will never fly. They could be right. Even so, the aug wing concept holds good potential for use in some transport or utility designs required for short, but not vertical, takeoffs and landings. Several of these are being developed by NASA.

Other augmentation, or gear-changing schemes are also under serious study both here and abroad. Most of these use large-diameter fans, housed either in horizontal form in the wings or in a vertical, ducted arrangement alongside the fuselage. Regular jet engines are used in banks as suppliers of high-velocity air which impinges upon tip buckets in the fans, and the fan output is then used for either lift or forward propulsion, or both. Large diameter fans are anathema to supersonic flight, so few of these designs hold much potential for high performance fighter type missions. A recent variation using horizontally mounted, small diameter, long-span, squirrel-cage fans in lieu of the larger ones, could well provide the answer to the fighter requirements, but this scheme is only in its infancy.

The final technological category of V/STOL designs is that of the "tail-sitter" or "wire-hanger." As the names imply, these designs involve aircraft which actually rotate through a 90° arc from conventional flight and land by either settling onto their own tails or hooking onto a suspended wire. The absence of conventional retractable landing gear gives these schemes a big performance advantage, but the intrinsic operational problems of highly specialized ground handling equipment have served to relegate the tail-sitters and wire-hangers to the science fiction category.

Which is best? No one really knows today. The answer won't be evident for at least several years, possibly not until the Soviets find it and decide to let us in on their secrets. Our speed in determining our own answer depends almost entirely on the rate of our progress in research and development of each of the ideas mentioned above, plus variations which may turn up along the way. A lot of money is involved. An annual Navy research and development program of $200–300 million is probably a pretty good guess, and that kind of spending has to come from budgets already strapped by peacetime defense constraints and inflation. Luckily, there is a reasonably sensible policy which might be successfully followed. In essence, this involves a "biting of the V/STOL bullet" by both the Navy and Congress—a reliance upon Harriers to provide the interim design for training and tactical evaluations, the diversion of amphibious assault ships (LPHs and LHAs) to sea control duties, and a carefully paced building program to provide a wholly new, inexpensive V/STOL support ship which would eventually fill the sea control gap between the large carrier and the small ASW surface ship. Despite its performance shortcomings, the AV-8A

Harrier is both available and proven and could fill the bill quite nicely as an interim aircraft design. It would be used until several of the more esoteric augmented wing, fan, or lift plus lift/cruise schemes can be wrung out through sensible design, test, and evaluation.

The practical obstacles standing in the way of a sensible and realistic V/STOL policy are many. Neither interservice role and mission assignments nor technological feasibilities can be ignored, since either or both can become formidable barriers to progress. Marine Corps leaders are not yet ready to fall back on their amphibious lift requirements, both from sincere professional reasons and from the undeniable implications for a much smaller number of U. S. Marines in uniform in the future.

A host of other potential impediments can also be identified. The blackshoe Navy, twice bitten by the ill-fated DASH (drone antisubmarine helicopter) and the sugarplum visions of the now-defunct sea control ship, are taking great pains to dissociate V/STOL from their operational requirements for the proposed strike cruiser, lest she follow her air-capable predecessors down the non-funded drain in Congress. Developmental funding in the Navy has traditionally been split along air, surface, and subsurface lines. Is the heavy funding required for V/STOL to come from the naval aviation share, to the detriment of the large carriers and sophisticated aircraft? Or is the cost to be borne by the surface Navy, to the detriment of the new cruiser, the long-range missiles, the hydrofoils, or the surface effect ships? Or should the money come from sources external to the Navy—the Army or Air Force—in reflection of the changing roles of the military in the modern world and to the detriment of the B-1 bomber, AWACS surveillance plane, or the main battle tank? Time and ever-changing requirements will provide the answers.

Captain O'Rourke is a U. S. Naval Academy graduate, Class of 1945, who served principally in carrier-based, all-weather fighter squadrons throughout his early career. He was officer-in-charge of a detachment of F3D jet night fighters in the Korean War, was a test pilot at Naval Air Test Center, Patuxent River, Maryland, and later led three F-4 Phantom squadrons, VF-101 Det A, VF-102, and VF-121, during the early years of that program. Captain O'Rourke served as aide to Commander, Sixth Fleet in 1958–59 and returned as Deputy Chief of Staff for Operations and Plans, 1968–70. He commanded the USS *Wrangell* (AE-12), 1967–68, and the USS *Independence* (CVA-62) in 1970–71. He served as OP-05W and Director, Navy Fighter Study Group prior to his retirement in 1974. He holds an M.A. degree in education from Stanford University and was a 1967 graduate of the National War College. He has written extensively on aviation topics, is a frequent contributor to the *Proceedings,* and was formerly a member of the Institute's Board of Control. He is presently an associate of Farnsworth Cannon, Inc., McLean, Virginia.

Naval Aircraft in the Next Decade

By Captain Stephen T. De La Mater, U. S. Navy (Retired)

Preceding pages: An F-14 on the tail of an F-4 during simulated combat early in 1973. The F-4, "generally acknowledged as the finest tactical fighter in the free world," is now getting along in years. The F-14, which came into existence as a result of the failure of the F-111, "exceeded expectations and turns out to be a superior dog fight airplane as well as an interceptor." It appears that the only important failing of the F-14 is that it is expensive.

We like to believe that each new aircraft brought into fleet use by the Navy is technology's best possible response to a well identified operational requirement. Sometimes, as with the AJ-1 Savage and the A4D Skyhawk, it is. These two aircraft were intended to carry nuclear weapons. In the case of the AJ, all the manufacturer, North American Aviation, had to go on were the dimensions and weight of a "box" the airplane had to hold. The Douglas A4D was to be a lightweight "day only" tactical nuclear bomber and the prime considerations in her case were to be able to straddle the weapon and clear the runway with it. Both aircraft performed admirably in their designed mission and then went on to do other things equally well or better.

But unfortunately, this is not always the case and more often than would seem reasonable, the airplanes we fly are the result of technology looking for an application. Probably the most recent example of this is the Harrier which has been under development by the British for many years (the first flight was in 1966) as an intriguing concept; but not until much later, when the Marines saw Harrier as the answer to some of their close-air-support-from-a-forward-base problems, was an application found that could get this aircraft into full economical production.[1]

Harrier is not the only example of the tail wagging the dog method of aircraft development, although it certainly is one of the more successful ones. One of the less successful examples of this procurement pattern

was the F-111B, an airplane which was such a mismatch of technology to requirement that the Navy bought only seven, eventually cancelling the contract as soon as possible in favor of the F-14, of which the Navy wants hundreds.

Still another route through which aircraft come into use is one followed by those developed to meet one requirement, which then are either adapted to other uses, or their mission changes and they must be used in new roles. Probably the most important recent example of this pattern is the F4H (F-4) which was conceived as an attack aircraft, built as an interceptor, and used in combat both as an air superiority fighter and as a "fighter/bomber," but not as an interceptor. Not only has the F-4 been used in those several different roles, but it has been so successful that it is generally acknowledged as the finest tactical fighter (including the attack mission) in the free world and is used as such by seven countries.

Many other aircraft fit into this development category including the A-7 attack aircraft, which is an off-shoot of the basic F8U (F-8) fighter design, and the RA-5C which, as the A3J, started out to be a replacement for the AJ nuclear bomber and ended up as a pure reconnaissance plane. An earlier example might be the F2H which, while it never completely relinquished its fighter role, was better known and was potentially more effective as a tactical nuclear bomber. As a night fighter, it was unsuccessful since its airborne intercept radar almost never worked and its auto pilot was unreliable.

The F2H, incidentally, while it was in operational service for over ten years, a period encompassing the Korean conflict, saw very little combat—possibly less than any other Navy fighter of comparable useful life span.

Probably the only valid conclusion we can derive from this cursory review of aircraft development is that it makes little difference which comes first, the requirement or the technology. We have been pragmatic enough in the past to make the best of this situation, and while there have been a few unqualified "lemons" in naval aviation's long and enviable history, most of these were for reasons which would hardly indict the procurement process.

For instance, the F3H Demon, though much maligned, was the first fighter with any kind of real all-weather, stand-off missile capability. It suffered its bad reputation partly because when it was introduced into the Fleet it had a tendency to flame out when it flew through rain—embarrassing for an "all-weather" fighter. Moreover, it came in an era of technological transition and was underpowered because the engine originally planned to power the aircraft failed. Also, it was difficult to peak up the Demon's airborne inter-

[1] The RAF also uses about sixty Harriers for dispersed base operation in the defense of NATO.

158

cept radar and fire control systems, and its basic maintenance manhour requirements[2] were excessive. But it
did fill a gap until the F-4 came along, and undoubtedly
it could have been greatly improved if the F-4 had not
immediately been so successful.

The F7U, the SB2C, the P6M, and the AM are examples
of failure that the Navy has suffered, but each failed
mainly because of technological shortcomings rather
than any mismatch between airframes and mission.

It would appear that except where a whole idea has
been discarded, such as that of seaplanes in ASW, there
are few examples of a good airplane that could not
be matched to some mission and be used effectively,
although it might be argued that because we found
no mission for them we didn't try very hard with the
VSTOL prototypes in the 50s. This suggests that perhaps
we pay too high a premium for designing to operational requirements and should do more to encourage
the development of new technology.

That, of course, is the underlying premise of the
prototype system now being espoused by the Defense
Department. Under this plan, rather than insist that
the airplane manufacturer meet performance specifications (as distinguished from reliability and maintenance
specifications which must be rigidly enforced), that may
not be reasonably obtainable, or which at least usually
add greatly to the cost, the manufacturer is permitted
to design to broad mission parameters. He is thus
placed in a better competitive position and tends to
be more innovative than before. This procedure gives
us a better chance to produce aircraft which, if not
exactly what the Service had in mind, may be more
useful than if they were.

With this as background we can begin to look at
the overall development cycle and speculate on some
ways that we may be going in the next ten or twelve
years. We shall look at the operation requirements and
at the technological forecast and then we shall predict
what the marriage of the two will likely produce.

We must recognize, however, that aircraft procurement in the past dozen years (and in fact all weapon
systems procurement) has suffered from the application
of a system of cost effectiveness analysis which, however
well intentioned, has not contributed toward putting
the best aircraft in the skies. It is true, however, that
the rising costs of aircraft and their electronics and
weaponry have made an evaluation system necessary and
while that which has been used recently has not been
overly successful, the need is still, or increasingly, there,
and we must consider cost-effectiveness analysis by the

[2]Because of such things as the fact that spotting was a problem aboard
ship and you had to pull its monstrous engine out the back for maintenance,
planes tended to get buried on the hangar deck where you couldn't get
to them.

Department of Defense as a factor in the procurement
cycle.

Intuitively, we realize that this is wrong, that cost-
effectiveness analysis is not a factor to be considered
as an element of procurement but is a tool which we
use to evaluate the other factors in reaching a decision.
However, since in truth the purpose of analysis is to
drive us toward the cheapest possible effective system,
we will obviously be driven to some different choices
than if the procuring service determined requirements
and ordered priorities according to its own judgment.
At the very least, this system layers an additional level
of review on the selection process and will inevitably
alter the end product simply because it permits more
"decision makers" to get into the act.

We have seen three factors governing the nature of
naval aircraft. In brief, they are (1) the operational
requirement—what do we need? (2) technology—what
can we build? (3) options developed by planning and
weapon systems analysts—how much will it cost? There
are other factors, of which the most important (especially to the Navy, which must fly off and onto ships)
is compatability to the platform—will it work?

Naval Aviation Operational Requirements

Naval aviation has never experienced a more turbulent period than that which started two or three years
ago as a result of several almost simultaneous, inter-
acting events: the high cost of Vietnam and the consequent slash in force levels, a recognition of the
changing nature of the Soviet threat, a quantum improvement in ASW sensors and systems, and the matur-
ing of VSTOL technology.

Coming into this period the Navy had, in addition to those forces in supporting roles, three distinct
aviation communities, each generating aircraft requirements: (1) the Attack Carrier Wings (CVW), each of
which was a composite element of fighter, attack, surveillance, reconnaissance, and support aircraft similar in
size to Air Force Wing, whose main mission was the
projection of air power ashore, primarily in support of
amphibious operations; (2) the sea-based ASW Groups
(CVSG), made up of fixed and rotary winged aircraft
which specialized in providing concentrated ASW protection to localized forces such as those in the objective
area of an amphibious operation; and (3) the shore-
based patrol squadrons, consisting of long-range aircraft
for open ocean ASW.

Until recently, the Navy has been able to keep separate its carrier-based attack and ASW air systems; and
without the impact of a tight budget might have
continued to do so indefinitely. Now, the CVS, or

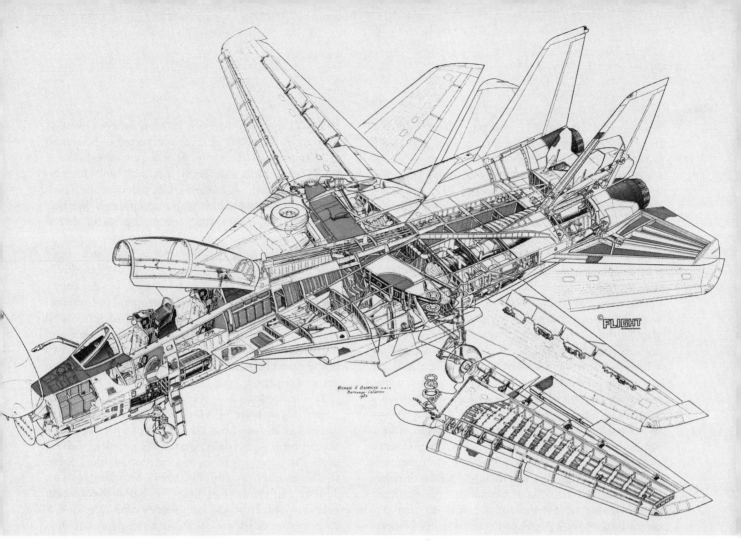

The F-14 in cutaway, drawn by Michael Badrocke of Flight International, *London. The wings are shown at both low-speed and high-speed angles. The engines are widely separated in order to provide good flow characteristics and to reduce the likelihood of a single hit damaging both. Notice the six-barrel M-61 Vulcan cannon right above the nose wheels, with a 1,000-round ammunition tank immediately behind the folding ladder. The airplane's top speed is reported to be slightly over Mach 2.2.*

antisubmarine carrier, has been eliminated from our active ship inventory. Hence, as rapidly as possible, we are integrating our ASW squadrons into our attack carrier air wings, thus changing attack carriers (CVAs) to plain carriers (CVs).

This would not have been feasible had it not been for the recent developments of both a truly modern ASW airplane, the S-3[3], and a sensor system for helicopters that makes them effective in today's submarine environment, an environment in which the submarine can not only go fast but it can do so without ever having to surface.

[3] The S-3 was originally justified on the basis that it would revitalize the CVS. This is another example of changing operational requirements and having a good airplane that could meet the new need. More on this aspect later.

Perhaps the evolution from CVA and CVS to CV was inevitable. The large number of Soviet submarines and their increasing quality made it obvious that in high threat areas, carrier task forces were going to need the heavy and extensive ASW protection that can come only from airborne systems. For reasons which shortly will be discussed, to all but the most stubborn opponents of ship-based-air it is clear that this protection could not effectively be provided by even very large shore-based aircraft. It also became clear that we were no longer going to be able to have a CVS to accompany each CVA force.

The obvious answer to this problem was to combine the attack and ASW capabilities in a single hull. But it was not quite so obvious that this would be efficient or even feasible. For example, suddenly we were going to have to operate a mixed bag of aircraft, all requiring different ship and staff expertises, more spares and ground equipment, more people, and different operating schedules (24 hours a day for the CVS people and aircraft, 12 hours for the CVA people and aircraft). It presented a lot of problems that would require strong will to overcome. In fact, the only "obvious" thing about it was that whether it was to be regarded as feasible, would depend on the attitude of the leadership running the evaluation. The concept was tested in the

Saratoga in 1970 and 1971, and was proved workable. Before long, when all the *Essex* class are gone, each carrier will have the option of operating as a CVA, as a CVS, or more usually, as a CV, with varying degrees of each capability embarked as needed. (The *Essex* class are too small to carry everything, considering the size of modern aircraft and their supporting component and supplies—not to forget the men who handle all that.)

It has been said by some that the feasibility test of the CV concept in the *Saratoga* was just a formality, that the Navy had already made up its mind to go the CV route and did so. Certainly there were pressures to make it work and within the parameters of the test plan, it did; but the test in the *Saratoga* was really only an attempt to find out if one ship could operate a fixed number of dissimilar aircraft where half the group was used to going like mad for 12 hours and recouping for 12, while the other half was used to a leisurely pace over the whole 24 hours, for several days at a stretch. There was no test of the ASW defense capability because the S-2 has little. Final testing must await the coming of the S-3 Viking and the other new or improved aircraft that will make up the CV air wings in the mid and late 70s. Since none of these aircraft were available at the time of the test, all that was determined really was the physical feasibility of operating a mixed wing of very different aircraft.

Though little publicized and still not operational, the S-3 has already had a profound impact on naval aviation. Planned originally to operate from the CVSs, it came along too late and the CVS, with the obsolete S-2 as its primary weapon, was doomed by the economy squeeze. The S-2, lacking speed and modern ASW and communications equipment, had little capability against the submerged nuclear submarine. As it turned out, we couldn't wait for the S-3. From a high of nine CVSs in 1965, we fell to only three in 1972, and they were in the fleet only to keep from losing the expertise built up over years of experience in conducting ASW operations from carriers. The next year saw the demise of even this limited capability and the CVS became a system of the past.

Concurrently the position of attack carriers became stronger. Though they are now called CVs they are, of course, the same ships that served so well as CVAs. They have survived severe analytical attack on their credibility because, with the S-3, F-14, and other highly capable aircraft embarked they have become a weapon system that can operate in high threat areas of any sort.

The S-3 has a good chance of becoming a classic Navy airplane. Although it arrived on the scene too late to save the CVS, it does make the CV concept practical. While not a glamorous, high performance airplane, it is potentially solid enough that its deriva-

tives will find useful service in many areas of aviation support. As a basic airplane, it is expected to be around at least through the 1980s. It will be a workhorse of the Navy, a right airplane at the right time. Its R&D costs are already amortized and, consequently, it is cheaper than comparable competing airplanes. We may soon see COD, tanker AEW, and perhaps other derivatives of the S-3.

The carrier itself is, of course, a basic and classic system. The heart of naval aviation, it has been threatened from time to time, not so much by the enemy as by its critics in the Defense Department, in Congress, in the press, and in the "think tanks." In spite of all the attacks, the carrier has justified itself over and over—Korea and the Jordanian Crisis being just two prime examples—and now seems in no immediate danger of extinction.

It is interesting to observe though that while the carrier is the heart of naval aviation, survival of the carrier has in turn been critically dependent upon the development of the right aircraft. We mentioned above how the advent of the S-3 permitted the carrier to sail through a credibility crisis with the analysts. That is neither the first time this has happened nor, probably, will it be the last. Shortly after World War II it was necessary for the Navy to develop rapidly a carrier-based airplane able to carry a nuclear weapon if the Service were to stay in competition with the newly independent Air Force. The AJ was the solution to this crisis. But the occasion was just one of many when the future need for a sea-based tactical air system was not readily apparent to our senior decision makers.

About the same time the Navy had to solve the new problem of ship and aircraft compatibility caused by the advent of the jet. This resulted in a two-part solution. We engineered excellent slow flight characteristics into the Navy jets so they could get aboard ship at safe speeds, and simultaneously we started a larger class of carriers—the *Forrestals*. There were other reasons for going to the *Forrestal* size, which was substantially larger than the existing carriers, but the overriding one was the requirement to operate jet aircraft from ships. We did this with much smaller carriers, of course, and still do, but not as well as with the big ones.

The S-3 is not the only aircraft that lends current credence to the CV concept. The carrier needs the promised air-to-air missile capability of the F-14/Phoenix system to counter enemy air and ship-launched anti-ship missiles.

So far as Navy systems go, the aircraft and platform are interdependent—each simultaneously enhances and limits the other. It is a tribute to our technology that for a long time Navy aircraft have not had to pay large

penalties for their compatability with the carrier. This is obvious in the fact that the Air Force has adopted several of our basic aircraft for their own use—the F4, the A-7, and even the old A-1, to cite recent examples (though one could go back as far as the pre-World War II Boeing F4B-4 for another example). But compatability has to be worked for. That recent example of non-compatability, the F-111, was an aircraft not designed by the Navy, and its basic failure to be carrier suitable has had major repercussions in both the Navy and Air Force with respect to the procurement of a follow-on fighter to the F-4.

The carrier, then, establishes the first and primary operational requirement for naval aircraft. But there are two other basic naval aviation systems, both of which will have a tremendous impact on future naval aircraft procurement. These are: the shore-based ASW patrol plane and the non-carrier, ship-based aircraft. The latter category is both the newest and the least understood member of naval aviation. It includes such members as the Sea Control Ship and the LAMPS destroyer, and we will have much to say about it later.

Platform Definition

First, however, we must recognize that the decision to accept the CV concept hardly solves all the problems associated with the future of the aircraft carrier. Just as we conceded that the jet was the prime factor in forcing us to the large *Forrestals,* the new VSTOL and related high performance technology improvements that are shaping up are causing us to relook at the question of carrier size. The last carrier authorized, CVN-70, carries a one billion dollar price tag, and many wonder if there isn't a cheaper way to put tactical aircraft to sea. While the main justification for the CVN-70s size is no longer aircraft compatability, but

more realistically to amortize the cost of nuclear power, the advantages derived from size are so attractive that the arguments to continue the class are quite compelling.

But so is the case for a smaller carrier.[4] Previously the small carrier brief has rested almost exclusively on economy; today, two new reasons may be evolving that make the moderate sized CV an attractive option.

One is that we need as many carriers as possible to cover the whole spectrum of possible warfare. To take care of the high end of the threat we have or will have, four large nuclear carriers plus eight *Forrestals.* At least half of the latter should be useful well into the 80s.

The other is that technology in the form of swing wings and higher thrust to weight ratio engines is making it possible to operate high performance jets from smaller decks. Although we may decide that we wouldn't want to, there is no restricting reason why we can't operate the F-14 off a forty or fifty thousand ton ship. Certainly all other candidate aircraft forseeable into the 1980s will be compatible with the decks of a new *Midway* size CV.

The foregoing should not be interpreted to say that carrier size is independent of aircraft design or vice versa. They are both still critically interdependent, but for somewhat different reasons than before. Forty to fifty thousand tons is probably still the smallest size that will permit us to operate fully capable, fully loaded aircraft. This does not apply to sea control ships or to such types as destroyers, amphibious ships, and underway replenishment ships whose interest in aviation is confined totally or mainly to helicopters.

It is necessary to make this point because many think

[4] See Captain Stephen T. De La Mater, U. S Navy (Ret.), "The Role of the Carrier in the Control of the Seas," U. S. Naval Institute *Proceedings* (*Naval Review* issue), May 1972.

that with the advent of VSTOL all we need do is provide any sort of unobstructed deck on a ship and we have a mini-carrier. It has been very difficult to keep the sea control ship from being called a carrier. It will have a flight deck and will be about the size of the jeep carriers of World War II. It will also have approximately the same mission. But there the resemblance ends for, unlike the CVE, the SCS will have none of the CV's air strike capability. It is not intended to be a system for projection ashore and it will have no basic offensive mission—though it could be used in offensive ASW and in a limited way for search and attack against enemy surface ships. Why the caveat and the limitation? First, VSTOL aircraft still sacrifice some performance in the STOL mode and a lot in the VTOL mode.[5] Secondly, at 20,000 tons or less, the aviation ship carries insufficient fuel, ammunition, and other consumables to be effective in anything more extensive than a small hit and run operation.

Air Support for Navy Missions

What we see evolving in naval aviation is a system that extends our capability over the spectrum of warfare and covers all sea and ocean environments. Without going far into the new liturgy for the uses of naval power, we see that from its beginnings aviation has learned, step by step, to assist in the performance of

The struggle for control of the central oceans probably will involve, on the one side many submarines supported by a few aircraft and, perhaps, surface ships; and on the other side, among other forces, a good many surface ships of modest performance in order to support an even larger number of modestly performing aircraft. The photograph above shows a model of the proposed sea control ship, with SH-3 antisubmarine helicopters and AV-8A VSTOL light attack aircraft on deck. The view at left shows both aircraft during tests aboard the USS Guam (LPH 9) during tests in 1972.

the basic missions by extending our eyes and ears over the horizon and doing the same for the range of our weapons.

The Navy has perhaps had a harder job than anyone in applying aviation to its tasks because of the difficulties involved in making the ship suitable as a base for airplanes. The maturation of the helicopter and more recently the VSTOL aircraft (and of course the helo is a form of VSTOL) has reduced these difficulties, and it is now possible to extend aviation support to a much broader scope of naval activity than before.

The Navy maintains forces to provide a nuclear deterrent, to project power ashore, to control the sea in areas of interest, and to influence political thinking peaceably. In support of these broad missions there are ten basic types of aircraft. Their use and application will depend on the scope and intensity of the battle or crisis, and on our ability to bring the aircraft to bear. The last brings up the problem of platform availability.

[5] And any modern aircraft operating off a ship of less than about 40,000 tons still has to be VSTOL or STOL aircraft, if not a helicopter.

If we could afford to provide a full fledged carrier (CV) in support of each evolution, we would greatly simplify the problem, but we can't. To spread the supportive arm of aviation as far as possible, we are developing lesser capabilities in the sea control ship and other non-carriers that increasingly are learning to operate airplanes.

In the remainder of this essay we shall look at the ways the Navy plans to combine aircraft and ships to ensure the best use of these costly assets. This means that there will be compromises. For example, the decision as to what aircraft eventually will go on the Sea Control Ship is tied to the Marine requirement for a follow-on to the H-46 for the lift of amphibious troops and equipment. One airframe may well serve these purposes, but whether it be a helicopter or a tilt wing bird remains to be seen.

This introduces a new element into the discussion: The relationship between Navy and Marine tactical aviation. Long a controversial subject, the cost of aviation hardware is bringing it increasingly into sharp focus. It is being said by some that we can no longer afford two separate air forces in the Navy Department. To a large degree the criticism has been unfair because the two forces have never been redundant. There has always been more than enough work for both, and any serious attempt to eliminate either will have far reaching consequences. In this discussion, we will consider Marine requirements in detail only to explain how a Marine need will influence a Navy decision with respect to aircraft procurement, as in the case of the use of Harrier for the SCS.

Specific Air Tasks

In the accompanying table we see a matrix of tasks, of aircraft that can perform these tasks, and platforms (mainly ships) for these aircraft. We see in some cases that we can double up on tasks with the same airframe, usually using a different model or variant, but in other cases we need more than one separate and distinct

Aircraft Used for Naval Air Tasks
(including Marines where there is joint use or where Marines fly from ships)

	F-4	F-14	F-X	FVX	A-7E	A-6¹	AV-8	AX	AVX	S-3²	SH-3H	SH-2	RA-5	E-2³	CX	H-53	H-46	HX	Tilt Wing	P-3C
Fighters	1,4	1,4	1,4	1,2,4,5			2,4,5													
Attack⁴	1,4	1,4	1,4	1,2,4,5	1	1,4	2,4,5	1,4	1,2,4,5	1,4	2									
Antisubmarine										1,4	1,2	2			2,5		1,2,3,4,5			1,2,3,5
Reconnaissance	1	1	1	1			2		2				1							
Surveillance										1	2			1	2					
Electronic countermeasures	1	1		1		1					2									
Mine countermeasures															2,5					
Tanker						1				1										
Troop Lift										1,4				1		4,5	4,5	4,5	4,5	
Logistic Support										1,4				1,4	1,2,4,5	1,2,3,4,5				1,2,3,4,5

PLATFORM KEY
1. CV
2. SCS
3. LAMPS
4. Land based (VP or Marine)
5. LPH/LHA

NOTES
1. Includes A-6E, KA-6, EA-6B.
2. Includes E-2C, C-2.
3. S-3, & C-2 are candidates. as well as new air frame.
4. Only the Marines now use the A-4. It is unlikely that this aircraft will often fly from ships again. This is not listed in the table.

aircraft. It is stimulating to the ingenuity of the designer to see what innovative uses he can make of a basic airframe. It is also a challenge to the cost effectiveness analyst to see if he can't force us into one airplane. One has a hard time finding pilots who are satisfied with the rationale of the cost effectiveness analyst. Ever since aircraft started being so expensive that it was necessary to consider cost (since about 1950), we have pursued commonality, but with little success. The essential problem faced by the Navy is that, as usual, it has more jobs to do than it has resources to do them with, and its requirements for equipment are staggering.

Fighters

The glamous aircraft is the fighter. It must be the dream of nearly everyone who enters aviation someday to be a fighter ace. The fighter is where the absolute maximum in performance must be extracted from both the man and the machine. For this reason there always seems to be a hot controversy with respect to fighter procurement. Moreover, the scope of the fighter mission means that a premium is put on maximizing different aspects of aircraft performance and it is almost impossible to find one airplane that will be competitive in all aspects of the mission—certainly not and be economically available in the numbers needed. This seems to contradict the argument presented earlier that it would be most cost effective to build from one basic air frame. There are cases where peerless capability in two or more areas could be built into one plane but at such a cost that it would be cheaper to design two

A UH-46 hovers over the flight deck of the escort ship Julius A. Furer (DEG 6) *during a missile replenishment operation in the Caribbean early in 1973. The combination of the helicopter and the conventional surface ship has long been with us. It has taken a long time to move the helicopter from merely the logistic support role of such ships, as seen here, into that of direct naval combat operations from those ships. But now with LAMPS it has happened.*

different ones. It is this fact that has kept the F-14 buy down. For instance, we need a fighter to provide the air defense of the surface task force. Such a force is so significant a danger to the enemy that he must be prepared to mount an expensive, sophisticated, concentrated, and coordinated mass air and missile attack upon it. This is the attack that the F-14 was designed to overcome.

We also need a carrier-based air superioity fighter to handle the other missions, such as gaining and holding air superiority, suppressing flak, providing combat air patrol in the amphibious objective area, and escorting our own attack aircraft. These are the prime roles of the F-4 now. There are many candidates now to supplant the F-4, and the right choice is both important and difficult. The F-14 can do all these things well, but the question is always, whether there is a cheaper way to handle some of those roles which are a little less demanding than that of providing distant air defense to the task force or convoy.

The concept and development of a family of fighters is fairly new. In World War II we simply had day fighters and night fighters and the difference was generally more in pilot training and experience than in aircraft and weapon. For instance, both the F6F and F4U came in day and night versions that were hard to tell apart. Slowly we changed to day and night "clear air mass" fighters (F-8) and "all-weather" fighters (F-4).

Much more than the Navy, the Air Force makes a distinction between fighters that are optimized as interceptors (F-106) and those optimized as air superiority fighters (F-15).[6] Certainly all first line fighters of the future will be good at day, night, and all-weather combat and will differ primarily in whether they are optimized for long range attack (interceptors) or for close, eyeball to eyeball hassle (air superiority). Depending on its mission and the weapons it carries, one airplane might be either an interceptor or an air superiority fighter. Where there are differences in the aircraft themselves, an interceptor is likely to have more speed but poorer turn and maneurverability characteristics than an air superiority fighter. In a fight between one of each, which would win? It is difficult to say. If he detects the opponent first, the modern interceptor, with his long-range missile, would probably be the victor. But if he doesn't and the air superiority fighter closes the range, the latter probably would win.

There are other differences in fighter types, and because they are confusing, the semantics of fighter nomenclature deserve a little more discussion. The term fighter-bomber, for instance, is a straightforward description of a fighter plane that could be used in a bombing role. The Navy used to have fighter-bomber squadrons, primarily using the F4U, the gull-winged Corsair. It was a great fighter and a pretty good dive bomber but used the "seaman's eye" approach to level bombing and was about as successful as you'd expect from "one potato, two potato, three pickle" bombing. The Navy does not emphasize the fighter bomber concept any more and now calls its bombers attack aircraft. The Air Force, on the other hand, uses most of its fighters as bombers today but refers to them as fighters rather than fighter-bombers. Most fighters have a respectable ground attack capability and quite often an airplane's use is simply a matter of meeting the most urgent need. The F-4s have been used by several different air forces, some primarily as a fighter and some primarily as an attack or bombing plane. The Israelis, for example, were impressed with the air-to-ground accuracy of the F-4 and saved them for strikes, leaving the air-to-air combat to the Mirage which, though not a better fighter than the F-4, has little air-to-ground ability.

Now we see cost introducing other distinctions between fighters, related mainly to their size and sophistication. We get into the lightweight fighter and the VSTOL. Certainly cost is not the total reason for development of either type, but it is a major factor. With VSTOL the savings are not so much in the aircraft as they are in the platform or basing system. Probably more than elsewhere, size in airplanes is directly related to cost and consequently there is a broad range of gross weights in the international fighter community. This extends from the British-designed, Indian-made Gnat of 6,650 pounds gross weight, through the Northrop F-5E (the latest version of the Freedom Fighter which, at 16,000 pounds gross, is still so small and unsophisticated that for the United States it is an export model only), and the most sophisticated free world fighter, the 57,000-pound F-14, to the Soviet Foxbat (MG-23) which grosses out at about 64,000 pounds. So we see that fighters differ from each other in size by as much as a factor of ten, and in dollars by as much or more. Operationally, the differences translate into speed, range, survivability, payload, all-weather capability, weapon flexibility, multi-purpose uses, stand-off capability, and endurance (the last named of which often is considerably different from range, with more time in the air being sought rather than more miles flown).

Where does the Navy, already heavily committed to the F-14, stand in the fighter picture? With 12 carriers (and this looks like the best bet as the number that we can expect to enter the 1980s with) the Navy would like to have two twelve-plane F-14 squadrons on each deck. We may have to settle for half of that, though if the carrier force got smaller we probably couldn't afford to be less than first class all the way across our reduced span of force.

A quick review of how we got where we are in the F-14 saga will help in understanding some of the problems and some of the pressures being felt. One thing that is confusing is that we keep designing an interceptor and finding out that we need a dog fighter (synonymous in this context with air superiority fighter). The F-4 is a classic case, but because of the belief that the next war is going to be characterized by air-to-air missile exchanges between fighters and bombers that will never see each other (a bet we still always must hedge against), the intended follow-on to the F-4, the F-111, was also planned as an interceptor.

Because it could hardly get off or back to the carrier, the Navy was convinced at inception that it wouldn't use the F-111 for any fighter task and plunged right on to the F-14. The Air Force, acting in an uncharacteristically pragmatic manner in this situation, after seeing that the F-111 was no interceptor was able to make a credible bomber out of it, both with the

---

[6] Probably the main reason for this was the Air Force division of responsibilities into major command elements: Tactical Air Command (with air superiority fighters) and Air Defense Command (with interceptors).

Tactical Air Command and, stretched out as the FB-111, as a mainstay of the Strategic Air Command. This satisfied their primary requirement for a while. They had a reasonably good interceptor in the F-106, and in Air Force circles the interceptor was losing its priority for replacement. The Navy faced a different situation and shifted from the F-111B to the F-14A, building on the promise of the Phoenix missile system and a still urgent fleet defense need for an interceptor. It came as a bit of serendipity though that, just as did the F-4, the F-14 exceeded expectations and turns out to be a superior dog fight airplane as well as an interceptor.

In developing the fighter to replace the F-4, because of the different experience with the F-111, the Air Force was about 18 months behind the Navy in bringing along the F-15. By the time the Air Force faced the reality that another new fighter, not the F-111, was going to be needed, three things had happened:

▶ We saw in Southeast Asia that the eyeball to eyeball dog fight days were not over.
▶ As mentioned above, the Air Force's incentive for an anti-bomber interceptor aircraft had diminished.
▶ The Navy had an interceptor underway. The last thing the Air Force wanted at that time was to be pushed into another Navy air frame. The Air Force fighter had to have significantly different specifications than the F-14.

Thus the F-15 emerged, identified as an air superiority fighter. Compared to the twin-engine, two-place, swing-wing, stand-off missile carrying F-14, the F-15, in concept, looked like a Light Weight Fighter because it was to have a one-man crew, one engine, and the short-range Sparrow missile as its main battery. Moreover, it lacked the swing wing. It was hoped the planes would not be competitive since they were different in concept in order to carry out different tasks. However, it wasn't long before the F-14 was in trouble with cost growth and because it was a key ingredient in the battle for the CVN-70's authorization. Any anti-carrier critic automatically took on the F-14 as well, since fleet defense was a large part of its cost justification. It was natural then that sooner or later it would be suggested, as part of the irrational argument that we can't defend against the Soviet threat anyway, that the F-14 was over-engineered and perhaps the Navy should look at an F-15N. What wasn't readily apparent was that the F-15 is not a Light Weight Fighter. At 40,000 pounds it is only slightly smaller than the F-14. The F-15's costs have also grown, mainly because of engine problems—there are now two engines in the F-15—so even if an effectiveness analysis could show any reason to switch, the cost to "Navy-ize" the design would make it even more expensive than the F-14 in the numbers being considered. Further, the fact that it lacks a swing

wing means that there is almost no way that it could be reengineered to match the F-14's carrier compatibility and, consequently, the cost analysis would have to reflect a higher and much more costly carrier accident rate for the F-15. On balance, it appears unlikely that anything could drive the Navy to accept the F-15, either in place of the F-14, or to make up the other squadron on each deck.

Nevertheless, the Navy needs a second fighter and must find a less costly alternative to the full system F-14. There are two immediately obvious choices, a slatted F-47,[7] or a stripped down F-14 with an AWG-10 Sparrow rather than the long range but expensive Phoenix weapon and fire control system. The Sparrow-armed F-14 would still be considerably more expensive than a slat-winged F-4; but it also would have much better overall performance, easily outfighting the slatted F-4 in mock combat; would reduce the price of all F-14s by increasing the size of the buy; would avoid an expensive maintenance problem by continuing the phase over to VAST compatable[8] aircraft on the CVs; and would minimize the requirement for different kinds of maintenance and ground handling equipment.

The best solution to the "other fighter" problem lies in the results of R&D programs now well under way. Hopefully that "other fighter" is the same airplane, a VSTOL, that will go aboard the sea control ship to replace the Harrier.

Everyone is expectantly looking for the breakthrough that will permit VSTOL operations in an airframe that doesn't have to pay a penalty for them and therefore can operate competitively from carriers using normal catapult assist methods to extend the range and payload. A small Mach two fighter that is equally at home on either a CV or a SCS will be necessary in the '80s. The number of airplanes needed for either the sea control ships' VSTOL or the "other fighter" for the carrier is not large enough to support two R&D and production tool-up programs.

There is a third piece in the fighter puzzle that has to be made to fit. The Marines need a new fighter also, and right now, in a sense, they are in the driver's seat. They have and control the Harrier. It may not be the ultimate in VSTOL but it is here today, it is flying operationally, and it is doing much better than many professionals would have dared to predict three or four years ago. The sea control ship's VSTOL has almost got to be the same type the Marines will use, which proba-

[7] A wing modification that enhances the maneuverability of the F-4 over a portion of the dog fight envelope but pays for this advantage with an energy loss.

[8] VAST (Versatile Avionics Support Shop Test) is a computerized avionics trouble shooting system being installed in all carriers. Not all older aircraft have systems that are compatible with it.

Two winners and a loser: the F-4 and A-7 (above) and the F-111B (right). Designed for the Navy, both the F-4 and A-7 have found favor in the Air Force as well, and in addition the F-4 serves in many foreign air forces. The F-111, designed to Defense Department specifications primarily for the Air Force, turned out to be useless for the Navy. The Air Force, having found it more of a bomber than a fighter, uses it accordingly.

bly means some advanced version of Harrier unless the Navy can come up with a fighter for the CV that will get on and off the sea control ship and has VSTOL and close air support capabilities acceptable to the Marines.

The most promising candidate in the R&D cycle is North American's augmented wing XFV-12A, which will duct hot gases through wing flap vents to achieve vertical lift. Much interest centers on this aircraft because, if it fails, the VSTOL-dependent community will be forced either to use the cruise-plus-lift engine concept with its inherent penalty of having to carry extra engines that mostly just ride, or to go back to the drawing board and take a new look at tail sitters and innovative vectored thrust concepts. In this connection, there is incentive to overcome the speed problems generally associated with the vectored thrust candidates, because vectored thrust has great potential for increasing combat maneuverability. This has been dramatically

demonstrated in flight tests of Harrier versus the F-4. The augmented wing airplane, in theory, sacrifices almost nothing in terms of high speed and unproductive weight to achieve VSTOL and, therefore, would be acceptable as a conventional carrier aircraft, probably using podded payloads to extend its range and weapon versatility. Such an airplane would of course also be welcomed by the Marines who would appreciate its Mach two speed. Of course, no such airplane has ever been flown. But it is certainly theoretically possible, and if it comes to pass, a lot of problems will be solved.

Attack

While perhaps not as glamorous as fighters, strike, or attack, airplanes are the bread and butter aircraft of "tactical" aviation. We need aircraft for a variety of attack missions, most of which come under the heading of close air support and interdiction.[9] It is acceptable that some of these aircraft be usable only when the pilot can see the target. But others must be able to attack no matter what the weather or visibility. The evolution of the attack aircraft since World War II has been even more complex in some ways than that of the fighter. Originally, carrier-based attack aircraft were classed either as dive bombers or torpedo planes. This distinction gradually disappeared as we came to use the aerial torpedo less and less, using the torpedo plane instead as a bomber. After World War II, as the TBM

[9]Close air support, in general, might be described as that air-to-ground attack which is under positive control and must be integrated into the efforts of the ground forces. Again, in general, interdiction is any other kind of air-to-ground attack except for that which is called "strategic."

(a torpedo plane) and SB2C (a dive bomber) were phased out, they were replaced on carrier decks by the AD. Tactical bombing was a daytime, clear air occupation. The only night bombing effort that took place, under the eerie light of parachute flares, was more for harassment than for accuracy.

About the same time we introduced the much larger AJ. This airplane had an almost exclusive atomic weapon mission, although later it pioneered our efforts in the field of ship-based tanking.

With the slow post-Korea conversion to an all-jet attack force (not ended until 1966), the classifications light, medium, and heavy attack came into use. These referred generally to differences in the airplanes' gross take-off weight; but, of course, they also reflected great differences in weapon sizes, missions, radius of action, and sophistication of bombing and navigation systems. Typical of these three classifications and obviously quite different in their application are the A-4, A-6, and A-3.[10] The A-3 was primarily a nuclear weapon delivery vehicle, the A-6 was, and is, a general purpose all-weather interdiction airplane; and the little A-4, which was conceived as a small tactical-nuclear daylight only bomber, found its most productive service as a close air support plane for the Marines.

During this period an all-weather capability was acquired. It appeared first as a radar bomb sight in the AJ. Gradually, as cockpit instrumentation, navigation aids, radar carrier landing approach, and air intercept radars came along, the concepts of all-weather flight and weapon delivery were accepted. But it was a slow process.

In fact, the transition to jets saw the development of a pure day attack plane, the A-4, whose only "all-weather" or night capability existed in dropping on signal while flying wing on a radar equipped A-3 or visually under a flare. The A-3, which replaced the AJ, had a night, or all-weather capability but primarily it was a nuclear bomber. The first real all-weather tactical attack plane was the Grumman A-6, a phenomenal

[10]Translational terms: In 1962 the AD became the A-1, the AJ the A-2, the A3D the A-3, the A4D the A-4, the A3J the A5, and the A2F the A-6.

aircraft which today, more than twelve years after its introduction into the fleet, is still not obsolete.

The A-6, although certainly representing a quantum leap ahead in all-weather capability, was prohibitively expensive for general tactical use and therefore did not replace the much cheaper A-4. Instead, it replaced only the elderly AD which was too slow to survive in a hostile environment. The A-4 was relieved by another airplane, the relatively inexpensive A-7. Compared to the A-4, this airplane had more speed, range, stability, payload, and survivability. Originally the A-7 was restricted to the day or clear-air mass delivery role. But updating of the A-7's weapons system (at a high price) has given it a very respectable "all-weather" weapon delivery capability and, in view of our experience in Vietnam, it is probably true that we will not again add to a carrier's complement an attack, or any other kind of, aircraft that does not have a reasonable all-weather capability. In the interdiction campaign against Vietnam the frequent heavy cloud cover meant that the "clear-air mass" attack plane couldn't bomb from high altitudes. If they went low, they were likely to have trouble finding their targets, getting enough altitude for release, and avoiding destruction by ground fire. They were not very effective over Vietnam—but weather was only part of the problem.

The evolution of the attack aircraft family provides another example of an air frame being diverted to a task not originally considered to be its prime one when it was being designed. Under the designation A3J, the RA5C was intended to be the next heavy attack nuclear bomber, to take the place of the aging and relatively slow A-3. It was designed around the innovative concept of expelling a bomb backwards out of an internal tubular bomb bay. The plan was to neutralize the bomb's forward speed to permit low level weapon delivery. But before the A3J ever became operational, a reconnaissance version was conceived and shortly thereafter an economy move, combined with the success of Polaris, led to the scrapping of the original bomber version. As a consequence, the A-3 represented the last of the heavy attack bombers, and today we find only medium and light attack planes on deck; with generally twice as many A-7s as A-6s in an air wing.

Both of these aircraft will probably be used for a long time. The A-6 is now entering the fleet in the A-6E configuration with a new radar, a new computer, and generally more reliable equipment all around for improved maintenance readiness. The A-7, in the D and E models, is one of the mainstay aircraft of both the Air Force and the Navy. It, too, has a radar, computer, and baro-assisted bombing and navigation system, and can do almost anything the A-6 can except pick out moving targets on the ground. However, it is a single place, single engine aircraft and cannot claim the sophistication, survivability, or total effectiveness of the larger, two-place, twin-jet A-6, which relies heavily on the very valuable Naval Flight Officer (NFO) in the second seat. As the weather gets worse, the NFO's value goes up. Both the A-6 and A-7 should be effective against enemy ships, no matter what the visibility. What they need is a good anti-ship missile, such as Condor or the forthcoming Harpoon. The ordinary bomb still has a place in battle against ships. First one can attack with an anti-radiation missile to destroy the enemy's ability to fight back and then come in with heavy bombs to sink the ship.

Eventually a new attack airplane (or airplanes) is going to be needed in the fleet. In spite of periodic interest in such an airframe over the past few years, concern with the F-14 and the S-3 has been far too intense to get involved with another major R&D effort. Of course there have been more systems than just the F-14 and S-3 competing for the R&D dollars, such as the much needed development of the helicopter and the light weight fighter.

But the thing that really has frustrated any serious effort to bring out a new attack airplane has been the acknowledged success of the A-6 and the A-7. The A-6 was almost an instant success as a weapon system but had trouble with reliability. The Echo version replaces second with third generation electronics and should represent a quantum improvement in readiness. The early A-7 (A and B) was built on the F-8's reputation and had little trouble acquiring fleet acceptance, but the attempt to upgrade the weapon delivery system's accuracy resulted in an Echo version that cost a lot more but flew less. Pushed into the fleet before its logistic backup was ready, it had a terrible spare parts problem. This has now been caught up with and both the A-6E and the A-7E are good for another ten years.

The argument continues, however, in the back rooms as to what after that. There are many theories as to what will be needed. As a prime example, there is still little agreement as to what the impact of "smart" bombs will be on attack plane design. Do the laser-guided and other modern delivery concepts that depend upon the bomb to solve the hardest part of the accuracy problem give us options for using significantly cheaper airplanes in larger numbers than nowadays?

If that is so, how much can be taken out of the airplane? Do we want to go to the Eagle/Missileer concept[11] for attack planes even though we never quite sold it for fighters?

Undoubtedly we wouldn't want to go that far, but there is some logic for cutting aircraft sophistication in favor of the weapon. For one thing there is the argument that we have to fly the aircraft in peacetime when we worry about costs, while in war, when we don't mind spending money, we can crank out costly missiles much faster than we can airplanes.

On the other hand, few are ready to give up our "iron bomb" capability totally, and depend exclusively on smart weapons. Certainly we learned in Vietnam that at least for that type of war, in which targets are hard to find, it would not be the answer. So it is questionable how much we can cut expenses even if we do plan on a primary missile capability. After all, we still need good speed to reduce the airplane's vulnerability during the penetration to target phase—the absence of enough speed was the trouble with the AD in Vietnam. The experience of the Middle East War in 1973 suggests that simple airplanes, even when fairly fast, such as the A-4, may be ineffective in a highly intense SAM environment. We need an ECM package to get into hard targets, and we certainly need a sophisticated communications and navigation package. With all that in the plane to start with, it doesn't cost much more to include radar ranging, an angle offset bombing system, and other refinements to enhance accuracy up to the bomb release.[12]

And that's what very often comprises cost overruns. Probably we will continue to compromise and use two or three types of aircraft in the attack role. Any new fighter, including the F-14, will undoubtedly have an active attack mission—much more so than the Navy's F-4 even though, as noted, it had an excellent air-to-ground capability. As force levels drop and as individual plane costs rise, they can expect to be more diversely employed.[13] The VSTOL Light Weight Fighter, for example, will have a limited attack role for employment from the sea control ship.

So for a best estimate of the attack aircraft of the '80s we can speculate on a cheaper counterpart to the A-7. But this is still a low priority project and unquestionably will see much change before an actual aircraft comes to function. The Marines, of course, have an attack helo, or gunship, capability in the AH-1. Though

---

[11] A concept of the late 1950s which argued that it was more practical to put a lot of smart air-to-air missiles on a large, relatively slow fighter than to pay the price for long range supersonic performance in each fighter aircraft.

[12] No aircraft bombing system can compensate for misjudging the wind that will affect the trajectory after release. This is why it is necessary to have a guided missile (five and ten foot CEPs) for pinpoint accuracy.

[13] This might also necessitate the development of a new concept of squadron organization and pilot training and utilization. If the pilot is required to be able to do more things with his airplane, to understand and master more warfare techniques, to compensate, he would have to be relieved of many of his administrative duties and additional ground officers would be needed. While this helps make the pilot a more professional airman it also, because of the cost of people in the modern Navy, raises the cost per airplane of doing the job.

this aircraft is in naval aviation, its mission is so closely related to the battle ashore that here we cannot go into it in detail. It is nearing the end of its useful life. Conceivably its replacement could be the same small helo that would replace the H-2. If so, the size of the buy would rise and the unit price would decline.

Antisubmarine Warfare

Antisubmarine aircraft come in three forms:

▶ Shore-based patrol (VP), which have essentially an offensive, broad-area search and destroy mission.
▶ Ship-based search and attack (VS), which are used for both close and deep defense of a task force or "sanitizing" an operating area or convoy route.
▶ Helicopter search and attack (HS), which are used for close in defense of a task force or an independently operating unit.

For two of these, shore-based patrol and ship-based search, the aircraft requirement is clearly defined well into the future. The P-3C Orion is the evolutionary product of a family of aircraft which has handled the long range search mission with at least moderate success since the end of World War II. However, measuring success in ASW is a very tricky business. For instance, it is probably not well understood that, until the advent of the P-3C, fixed wing ASW aircraft, particularly long range search and patrol aircraft, did not have a real capability against the submerged submarine. They could search the surface by eye and by radar; similarly they could pick up a periscope or snorkel trail; they could localize from a "flaming datum" or other contact using sonebuoys and MAD gear, but they could not sweep a large area to pick up submerged submarines. Before a large proportion of the submarines were nuclear, this fact did not keep them from being effective sub hunters. Conventional submarines spend quite a bit of time on the surface or submerged but with their snorkel and periscope raised. The nuclear boats have changed all that and have greatly reduced the fixed wing aircraft's ASW effectiveness.

In response, the Navy has come up with the P-3C and the S-3A, both of which, compared to earlier airplanes, have a greatly improved capability against the submerged submarine. They employ better sonobuoys, greatly enhanced on-board readout and analysis, computer-assisted localization and attack systems, data link equipment, radar, and all the other elements now considered necessary to a good ASW suite. The VP still works best with a SOSUS or other datum, but can effectively "sanitize" over a reasonable sized search area, and also can, as we will discuss in the following paragraphs, within reasonable constraints and within reasonable range of its base, help provide protection to transiting units or convoys.

As for the nature and tasks of seabased antisubmarine aircraft, we have said much already about the S-3 Viking which will fill this role for many years. There is no serious consideration of any alternative airplane for this job, although a proposed substitute is discussed below. It has been suggested by a segment of the analytic community that we might be able to accomplish the job by using shore based P-3s exclusively. Fairly well accepted studies have shown the latter to be of questionable feasibility. The P-3 is competitive in terms of time on station only when within 300 to 500 miles of its base.[14] This would occur too seldom to be practicable in "projection ashore" scenarios and would be completely out of the question for most sea control and escort missions. This basic question has been up and down through the Defense Systems Acquisition Review Council several times and if it is not yet a dead issue seems one that the Navy is fairly certain to win. In fact, a much better case can be made for using the S-3 ashore to supplement the P-3 when the former is not needed aboard the CV. And that of course is at the heart of the CV concept—to be able to move types of aircraft on and off the ship as needed to match the wing to the task to be accomplished. The S-3 contains the same sort of advanced ASW weaponry as the P-3C. It, too, is able to conduct an integrated search, independent of electronic assistance from either ship or land bases, and like the P-3C it can attack at ranges where enemy subs usually are unalerted or, in any event, are outside of their effective missile launch range. Fitted with a Harpoon missile, the S-3 would even have some value against a surface ship, though its lack of clear superiority in a duel with a ship's SAM missiles makes it unlikely that it would be much used for this in an offensive role. The CV, of course, carries attack aircraft much better suited to deal with this threat.

At least one admiral has suggested that the long range antisubmarine defense of a task force can be performed adequately by the A-6 or other high endurance carrier-based aircraft, using podded ASW components. Such aircraft would concentrate on search and the carrier on avoidance, neither giving much thought to making an attack. The thought here is that the CV does not want to risk damage by seeking out submarines but only desires to stay out of their way while it carries out its task. The trouble with this theory is that in the sea control role, the CV does indeed want

---

[14] In addition to the fact that the P-3 is not cost effective as a task force escort because of the distance it must fly from its base, there is the "time late" factor. Moreover, when a concentration of ASW capability is needed and the P-3 has to come a thousand miles, from a maintenance standpoint, it takes a nine plane squadron to support one aircraft on station at that range. The Boeing 707 and other large aircraft have been suggested for the VP role, primarily to increase range and on-station time, although additional weapon and sensor payloads could also be handled.

Seven of the new S-3 Viking antisubmarine aircraft are seen on the Lockheed flight line in November 1973 in the top photograph. The shore-based running mate of the S-3 is the P-3 Orion. The airplane shown in the middle photo is a P-3A. The most recent version, the P-3C, though externally almost identical, is a vast improvement on the P-3A. The RA-5C, seen in the lowest photo in Air Force style camouflage and small markings is an excellent reconnaissance plane with but a short future and no successor in sight. The photo was taken aboard the Kitty Hawk *in 1966. Notice the AD Skyraiders in the background.*

to seek out and destroy as many submarines as it can. Anyway, it seems obvious that the CV, as capital ship of the fleet, must have as good an ASW capability as can be provided and should not have to depend upon the secondary capability of other aircraft, the quality of whose ASW effectiveness would be marginal at best. Too much is at stake.

On the other hand, just as we see an increase in the use of fighters in an attack role, there is no reason not to provide a podded sonobuoy drop and monitor relay capability in other carrier aircraft to supplement the S-3, particularly in the high threat areas. This would then not be an alternative but simply a new way to make up for the slack in force levels and to get the maximum readiness out of our airplane dollars. Such pods have been under casual development for some time but without much push or priority. With the high tempo of the Vietnam fighting we were reluctant to saddle CV pilots with another mission until organizational and training arrangements could be made for it.

In any event, while obviously someday there will have to be follow ons for the P-3 and the S-3, both will be with us for some time. They are almost ideal for their job and they complement each other exceptionally well.

The ASW helicopter situation is something else again. While there is a wide variety of urgent helicopter requirements, there seems to be no ideal matchup between a new helo and any requirement. The following are the three most pressing helicopter tasks:

▶ Close in protection of the carrier task force with carrier-based helos.

▶ Convoy protection, a sea control mission with the helo being called upon to provide essentially all of the airborne ASW defense—as far out as 50 to 70 miles from the convoy. This is a sea control ship helo.

▶ The LAMPS helo, for contact prosecution from surface ships, to extend their weapon range, and to supplement the sea control ship and carrier helo effort.

No single design would be satisfactory for all three of these tasks. The mission from the sea control ship is more demanding than that from the carrier and because LAMPS lacks a search responsibility, both are more demanding than that. The sea control ship's task, therefore, would dominate as far as determining characteristics is concerned. Since the Navy also procures aircraft for the Marines, the airframe for any of these missions must be selected in coordination with them. In fact the Marines can be expected to have a particularly persuasive say in this selection since their helicopter force levels are generally larger than the Navy's.

If a helicopter alone were under consideration, one basic airframe could perform the sea control ship and carrier role and also meet the Marine requirement, though it would probably be too large for LAMPS. However, both the Navy for the SCS and the Marines for their lift tasks are also looking at a tilt wing airplane. While it is probably unlikely that such an airplane will be ready in the time desired, a tilt wing would not be satisfactory for the CV role, mainly because a tilt wing does not hover effectively and therefore could not serve as a plane guard. In the event a tilt wing was picked, it is probable that the CV would use the basic LAMPS helo or perhaps continue to use the still satisfactory SH-3 in order to have a sonar in the force.

This joint Navy-Marine development of a basic airframe is a relatively new venture. Though the Marines have always used naval fixed wing airplanes, the Navy and Marines have usually developed and used separate helos. Specifically, the Navy has gone to the SH-3 series for its ASW groups and to the H-2 for its utility missions, while the Marines have concentrated on the H-46 and H-53 for medium and heavy troop and equipment lift requirements. The H-46 and SH-3 are of about the same size but both were developed in an era when costs were lower; helo technology was expanding, and it was desirable to develop more, not fewer, different types; and both Navy and Marine force levels were much higher than now and could support separate R&D efforts.

In many ways the helo situation is one of the most confusing and complex facing our decision makers today. The sea control ship group sees the problem as a choice between either getting a major upgrading of the SH-3 airframe and deferring development of a completely new helo until the mid or late '80s or buying a number of new SH-3s with only minor mod-

ernization features and pushing the R&D on a new aircraft. There is also a proposed new version of the H-53 with double the original H-53's payload, and that has some attraction as a SCS candidate. The new H-53 will probably be pushed to fruition by the Marines as a heavy lift helo and it also has great potential as a medium range COD, but most Navy operators consider the H-53 to be too heavy for the SCS.

As far as the CV is concerned, the SH-3 is generally considered adequate. It serves very well as an ASW platform, plane guard, and air sea rescue vehicle, and therefore, regardless of which way the Marines and the SCS go, the CV will probably use new or reconditioned SH-3s for many years to come. The updated SH-3H will have an excellent ASW suite, with new MAD and radar, improved dunking sonar, the ability to take advantage of the latest sonobuoys, and other equipment which, together, will be an independent, integral system with a degree of sophistication approaching that of the S-3. As far as CV operations are concerned, we can place it in the category of aircraft, along with the A-6, S-3, and P-3C, which fortunately we won't have to worry about for some time.

The LAMPS helo problem is yet another matter. Using H-2s, we can fill out our quota of one LAMPS per escort ship for the next few years, but these aircraft are few in number and they won't last forever. As the thirty DD-963 class and the fifty PFs, each of which will take two LAMPS helos, begin to come into the inventory, we are just not going to have enough aircraft for them. As of this writing, a replacement has not been identified. Although the airplane probably will be, it doesn't necessarily have to be a helo. It could be a small tilt wing[15] or it could be a small, light VTOL. This is one of the murkiest areas when we look into the future.

Mine Countermeasures

The helicopter development picture is further complicated by the fact that naval aviation has recently taken on another new mission, mine countermeasures. The potential for helicopters in this role has only been explored in the last two or three years and is still not a fully developed concept. It is, however, evident that the helo is potentially a vastly superior vehicle for mine sweeping than the surface ship. On the other hand, all of the trade offs have not been clearly defined, and the full range of future requirement for this capability is still a matter for conjecture. One plan was to use the helicopter carrier (LPH) *Guam* to evaluate the H-53 in the mine countermeasures role after she finished the SCS evaluation. These have been pressures, however,

---

[15] But not the same one that would perform the SCS mission.

An E-2A surveillance plane banks sharply to the right while an earlier aircraft, the E-1B plods straight on. The most recent version of the E-2, the E-2C, is a very useful airplane.

from the Marine Corps to return the *Guam* to her normal amphibious service, and the SCS evaluation has stretched out well beyond the originally planned period.

The main point of interest in mine countermeasures is that it calls for a large helicopter. This fact supports those who are interested in development of a heavy helo and would like to see a careful evaluation of the H-53 as a multi-mission aircraft on the SCS. While the H-53 is more expensive than the SH-3H, and takes up considerably more deck space, its load and endurance potential make it an attractive, or at least competitive, alternative for the SCS role. In addition it is supposed to enjoy greatly improved maintainability over the H-3.

So while the helo's, and indeed naval aviation's, entry into the mine warfare mission is new and, even with our experience off Haiphong, only partly tested, it does add a new element of significant import to the helicopter community and the Navy.

Surveillance Aircraft

Often there is confusion over the terms surveillance and reconnaissance. In the Navy, at least, they have very distinct meanings, and their missions require different airframes. The surveillance aircraft is a defensive instrument. Usually it operates close to the force, keeping track of approaching air and surface targets. The concept of aerial surveillance of the force's environment is a relatively new one and awaited the development of adequate radar before it could be tackled. Before radar, the force relied upon the eyes of lookouts placed high on the masts of the ships and sometimes used scouting planes to search out the enemy (although the old scouting plane was probably closer to being the forerunner of the reconnaissance aircraft than of the surveillance plane). Radar gave us the ability to conduct close-in surface surveillance and long range air surveillance, but because both were ship-mounted, they were limited by the ship's horizon.

It was not until the 1950s that we were able to mount a reasonably satisfactory 360-degree search radar in a shipboard airplane—the WF or E-1A. This gave us the ability to search the surface to a range of about 150 miles from the aircraft, and it gave us a high altitude air search capability which could be used to extend the ship's radar range by stationing the aircraft out on the threat axis a couple of hundred miles. But it still did not provide the low altitude surveillance needed to warn of the low flyer; nor did it provide much air intercept control capability. In these respects, and in the fact that it was blacked out over land, its performance was primitive. The E-1A was followed by the E-2A and E-2B. But it was not until the E-2C entered the fleet a couple of years ago that we could really do what we had been suggesting we could do for sometime—cover the surface with confidence out to about 250 miles with one aircraft over the force, simultaneously keep track of the air picture out well beyond that, including the low flyers, and also be able to control over 20 intercepts almost automatically. This is particularly important in coastal waters. These aircraft are really sea-based warning and control aircraft. Though they are slow, they are dependable. They do an outstanding job, and they will be the right aircraft for that job for sometime. The replacement of the E-2C is not one of our airplane problems. At some point we may wish we had bought a lot more of them, but that will probably be true of almost any aircraft we own.

Reconnaissance Aircraft

Where surveillance is defensive, reconnaissance is offensive. Surveillance warns us when the enemy is coming to attack. Reconnaissance may spot the same enemy but generally in order that we may attack him. The difference is a significant one in terms of the type of aircraft that would be used in each case. The surveillance aircraft operates close to home and usually in a friendly environment. The reconnaissance aircraft must range far from the task force and seek out the enemy in his own territory. Hence, the reconnaissance aircraft must be fast and have long range. Reconnaissance uses electronic and photographic methods of gathering information—the sort of thing we do with the U-2 and satellites, except that neither of these has proven to be tactically responsive enough for the Navy's needs. Besides, the U-2 system wasn't accurate enough. It had a hard time correlating what it saw with its best guess as to where it was.

Tactical reconnaissance for the Navy used to mean photo planes and the mission was performed by a fighter, such as the F9F, F2H, and F6F, that had its nose stretched to accommodate camera installations (and then became F9F-5P, F2H-2P, and F6F-4P. Film was delivered right back to the ship, where it was developed and analysed, and the information used on tactical flights right away.

The Navy entered electronic reconnaissance with the shorebased RC-121, but this was really a national strategic mission and had little to do with fleet operations except as it helped in nuclear strike planning. The first carrier-based aircraft with both a photographic and electronic recce capability was the RA-3 version of the heavy attack Skywarrior.[16] But the only aircraft to go aboard ship with recce as its only mission was the RA-5C. The RA-5C, as we have mentioned earlier, started out to be the bomber replacement for the A-3; however, its inception coincided with deployment of the Polaris, and the need for a sophisticated reconnaissance capability was seen as a matter of higher priority. For its time, the RA-5C was a very advanced recce airplane. It embodied all the latest photographic and electronic (including radar) recce techniques and equipments, and it required a special, large, dedicated space aboard ship for processing, briefing, and debriefing.

The RA-5C was built for a war that fortunately we haven't had to fight. Because of its great accuracy with an inertial navigation system and other advanced features, it has been used strategically in many instances.

But the originally planned buy was cut back as money for airframes became critical. The scarce RA-5C will leave the fleet in a few years as attrition takes its toll (with economics killing the survivors), and there is much concern as to what will replace it. There are experts who insist that we need a dedicated recce aircraft to take its place. Most of these would settle for the F-14 airframe but contend that a complete recce package should go into it and therefore it could no longer double as a fighter. But the money-handling decision makers don't see any way that this could be afforded. Tactical reconnaissance for the fleet seems destined to take a step backwards, becoming again primarily a matter of photography, with the next recce package probably being in the form of a pod that can

be slung beneath whatever fighter is available. The airplane will still be a fighter, giving up only one or two missile stations in order to carry cameras.

But there is also much interest in an unmanned vehicle for the recce mission. The history of pilotless aircraft has never been one of the more exciting or successful chapters in naval aviation, simply, it is assumed, because they don't have the glamour of man in flight. Out limited excursions into this realm of flight have been marked by slow and inefficient progress. Much of this is probably because the concepts were never high in the interest scope of our leadership. Drones have a poor record of performance as can be attested to by the frustration of many a fleet pilot or gunnery officer who has tried to get a satisfactory drone for a scheduled missile shoot or gunnery exercise.

But the mission of tactical recce seems such a natural one for the drone that there is much new interest in the concept. It seems senseless to risk pilots just to get pictures. The mission doesn't require the accuracy and aggressiveness of weapon delivery, and it should be possible either to coordinate the transmission of satellite reconnaissance for tactical use or build a fast little drone that can penetrate a few hundred miles, fly low through enemy defenses, get its pictures, and get out. We tried this experimentally in Vietnam with some very limited success. The success was measured in terms of proving the concept, but never sufficiently to be tactically significant. We certainly have the technology, and all that is needed now is for our leadership to give the priorities necessary for development. It is a strange fact that the study effort aimed at developing the rationale to support this requirement has been remarkably unpersuasive. Still, this writer feels that pilotless aircraft are going to be the answer to many of our recce problems.

Electronic Countermeasures Aircraft

We noted that the future of reconnaissance is back full cycle to photography alone. While this is true so far as the task for the airplane goes, it doesn't mean that we no longer have a need for other intelligence. It means simply that we must get it from other sources—either from satellites or, for our real time, tactical electronic information; we must rely on the airplane that goes in with the strike force to neutralize the enemy's electronics. That airplane is the electronic countermeasures aircraft. Fulfilling a relatively new requirement for tactical naval aviation, that airplane makes it possible for today's strike aircraft to survive in a hostile missile and intercept radar environment. It jams the radars and sends false signals to the missile. These techniques were brought to a very high level in Vietnam. Success with these techniques and the fast

---

[16]The Skywarrior was to become one of the most versatile aircraft ever developed by the Navy and, by the time it is finally retired, it will have been used as both a "strategic" and "tactical" bomber, conventional and nuclear, as a recce plane, as a tanker, as a jet COD, and ashore as a VIP transport.

rate at which the key ECM units were introduced either into dedicated ECM airplanes or into the fighter and attack planes themselves shows what can be done when there is incentive—and there is nothing like high loss rates to create incentive.

The innovativeness of our technicians and the courage of our decision makers combined to give the fleet pilot this electronic assistance. They made it possible to develop a combination of tactics and electronics, each enhancing the effectiveness of the other, which reduced the enemy's expected missile kill probability from an estimated possible .8 or .9 to an actual .08 at the worst stage of the conflict, and finally down to something around .01! It was a remarkable achievement.

The aircraft that performs this mission today is the EA-6B, an aircraft of formidable complexity and cost but also one of remarkable accuracy, reliability, and capacity. The EA-6B marks the arrival of a new kind of warfare vehicle. There were predecessors—the EA-6A, the EA-3K, and one or two others—but their capability was so limited that their real worth lay mostly in pointing out the crying need for the development of an effective and reliable system. There is no obvious successor to the EA-6B, for it is a new airplane with many years of effective service to look forward to; however, EW is still in its infancy and it is difficult to predict where breakthroughs in this field could lead. This is also an area where breakthroughs might be most expected. The answer to electronic warfare may be silence. What would that do to our planning for aircraft in the future?

Troop Lift

The troop and amphibious lift requirements of the Marine Corps are, of course, an integral part of naval aviation, particularly with respect to those lift aircraft that operate from or are based aboard amphibious ships. Heretofore these requirements have been essentially independent of similar Navy systems; but as we have mentioned briefly in reference to other missions, the future procurement of amphibious lift aircraft will undoubtedly be part of a larger buy of a family of VSTOL airlift that will fill several roles.

The Marine Corps' dependence on the helicopter for the fulfillment of their basic mission[17] has been a rapid and relatively recent development. The helicopter has led to a whole new concept of amphibious operations based on vertical envelopment and, although the Marines use the helo to complement the other elements of a major landing, which is usually still largely boat oriented, amphibious operations today without the helo

are unthinkable.

The pioneer of the helo assisted landing was the H-34 Seahorse, which could lift a dozen combat troops (a squad), or could carry a jeep slung underneath. It revolutionized amphibious warfare, just as the World War II landing craft had only a short time before. The entry of the helicopter into the jet age brought the H-46 and H-53 into service as the backbone of the Corps' lift capability. With those aircrafts' increased speed, range, and payload, many amphibious commanders have begun to think in terms of small, totally air supported landings. This concept becomes more and more attractive as we contemplate a new generation of helos. We have already discussed the potential in this area of the new H-53 with a third gas turbine engine. Such an airplane almost qualifies for the term "heavy lift" and will be able to put just about any piece of Marine equipment on the beach.

On the other hand, the H-53 cannot fill all the Marines' lift requirements and a second new lift aircraft is urgently needed. The H-46, now more than ten years old, has never been a truly adequate or well accepted airplane, and soon it will have to be replaced. As pointed out in the ASW section, the selection of a replacement will ultimately have to be worked out in a compromise with other Navy requirements and the airplane choice may not even be a helo. A tilt wing would not displease the Corps because as a STOL aircraft it would have an enhanced capability, particularly when operating ashore.

Tilt wing and tilt rotor aircraft have been under development for a long time and, just as with any other VSTOL aircraft, have had a hard time convincing the leadership that they are worth the development costs and that they are safe enough. The issue might be closer to resolution in terms of their evident attractiveness for the sea control ship's mission if the decision could be made that we no longer need dipping sonar. Tilt wing and tilt rotor aircraft are uneconomical hoverers and would not be satisfactory if dipping sonar were a requirement. But this is a wide open area for innovative R&D and some far reaching decisions soon will need to be made. It is the writer's feeling that it would be foolish not to develop both a tilt wing or tilt rotor aircraft and a high performance, new technology helo using the hot blade exhaust principle: the former because such aircraft do not suffer the speed limitations that affect helicopters, the latter because the hot blade exhaust offers an enormous improvement in power for a given engine weight.

Tanker Aircraft

A product of the jet age is the airborne tanker. Two incentives led to the development of a tanking capabil-

---

[17]Today, probably not any more so than the Army and their operations which, since Vietnam, tend to look much like Marine amphibious landings in character.

ity, and although they are directly related, they are at the same time distinct. First we needed tankers to extend the range of our nuclear attack aircraft; secondly (and this is peculiarly a Navy problem not faced by Air Force pilots always operating ashore), we wanted the ability to refuel in the air as a safety feature for carrier operations. It soon became obvious that for all the speed and other performance advantages that we derived from the jet, we sometimes had to pay for it in loss of reaction time in around-the-carrier emergencies. Where before, a delay in landing aircraft caused by a deck accident was an inconvenience and schedule wrecker, now it could spell disaster. The high fuel consumption rates of jet planes compressed the time delays permissible by factors of ten, and "dog" times of five or ten minutes became an agony of suspense that too often had an unhappy ending.

But whereas the Navy has profited greatly in aircraft saved by having a tanker available to top off low-state aircraft arriving in the carrier's vicinity, the real push toward tanker development came from the need to extend the range of our nuclear attack aircraft. This was at a time when the carrier was a significant part of our strategic deterrent force. The carrier nuclear strike force was seen by the Soviets as such a formidable threat that their reaction to the carrier has been almost paranoid. Extending attack aircraft range has two advantageous effects. It permits us either to strike a much greater number of targets deeper into the heart of the

enemy than we would otherwise be able or it allows us to strike from farther out to sea beyond reach of many of the defensive aircraft that would wish to attack the carrier.

The first carrier-based tanker quite appropriately was the AJ Savage. It was fitted with a fuel tank package that went in the bomb bay, and the system worked compatibly with the F2H nuclear fighter-bomber. The next innovation in the development of a carrier tanking capability was the "buddy tanker." This system used a pod that could be slung beneath an attack aircraft to provide a drogue and hose for transfer of the tanker's fuel to the bomber, generally a like type attack plane. The scheme was for the two to take off together, fly toward the target as far as the tanker's point of no return, transfer the tanker's load to the bomber, with the tanker thereafter returning alone to the carrier. It

One well-designed airplane, an A-6 Intruder, refuels another, an F-4 Phantom. Both types have been with the Fleet in successively improved versions for many years. The F-4 is supersonic, the A-6 is not. But the latter proved itself in Vietnam to be the United States' best—if not only real—"all-weather" attack plane.

has been a very useful device, and A-1s, A-4s, A-6s, and A-7s have all been so employed. The buddy tanker has also been used to augment the dedicated tanker in providing life guard service around the ship for returning flights.

Eventually the AJ was replaced as the primary fleet tanker by the A-3 which served for many years, and only now is nearing the end of its employment.

Today the dedicated tanker is the A-6. It does a good job and is highly valued, but there just aren't enough of them, and it is a misuse of a very high priced airframe. We need a new tanker and probably an S-3 variant is the best prospect. We are a long way from seeing it in the fleet, but that eventually it will materialize is almost inevitable. With the cost of aircraft increasing and the corresponding emphasis on safety, the tanking mission is such an integral part of carrier operations today that we can hardly afford not to provide an adequate, sophisticated tanking capability. On the horizon right now there is no other airframe that seems as suited to this task as the S-3.

Logistic Support

Our discussion of logistic support aircraft will be limited to the COD (Carrier Onboard Delivery) family of planes. This, of course, largely ignores a very useful segment of naval aviation, the land-based transports whose pilots over the years have served the Navy valiantly and with little reward.[18] For a variety of reasons, the Navy and Marine Corps have always found it necessary to operate their own small and independent airlines in order to keep logistic delays at a minimum. Big brother MAC (Military Airlift Command—the old MATS) does a good job on a worldwide basis, but even years ago when the Navy participated, with several squadrons assigned to MAC control, they were not always responsive to the calls from small and out of the way units and ships in scattered ports that needed the priority service of a dedicated airline. It is the tag end of that line, the COD, that we will look at here. This is the uniquely naval application, the logistics planes that land aboard ship; getting the replacement electronics technician back to his squadron, bringing in a vitally needed spare part for a down aircraft, or taking a boatswain's mate from a destroyer in the South China Sea back home to his sick wife. Before, between, during, and after normal flight operations, a carrier deck resembles a commercial airport, with CODs and helos distributing everything from chaplains to cigars throughout the force and from ship to shore.

The COD concept as a sole purpose airplane is fairly new. Although we have always used operational aircraft as movers of parts and people from ship to shore and between carriers, it was usually on a haphazard, space available basis. Long after it had outlived its operational usefulness as a torpedo bomber, the TBM was still serving as an interim COD. Eventually it was replaced by a COD version of the AD-5N, a plane that, holding four or five passengers, several boxes of parts, and lots of mail, ably augmented the normal supply chain.

But the first aircraft built as a COD from the stringers up was the TF-1, or C-1. Although each C-1 was built as a COD, it was a variant of the Grumman S2F-1 (S-2) ASW plane. A real workhorse, the C-1 has been a consistent and reliable contributor to the fleet's efficiency since it was introduced about twenty years ago. It has a range of over a thousand miles and carried the ship to shore (and shore to ship) phase of the air resupply burden of the Vietnam War even though it was supposed to have some help from its planned replacement, the C-2.

Like the AJ and the A-4, the C-1 owes its start to the sense of urgency that was placed on developing a viable and effective nuclear weapon delivery capability. The C-1 came as the answer to the problem of weapon resupply at sea. It could hold the old Mk 5 atomic bomb which was the primary weapon of the AJ system. It was used for its primary purpose only in tests, but it very quickly became an indispensable part of daily operations at sea. It is the heart of one of those systems that moved quickly from the category of luxury to that of necessity, and we wonder how we ever lived without it.

If weapons were the driving force behind the C-1, engines were the incentive for the follow-on C-2. At the time of its inception, jet engines were the one high usage item that couldn't be airlifted to the carrier at sea. Deployment of the C-2 was expected to produce a large return in increased availability of aircraft. Unfortunately, the C-2 has not worked out, though Grumman is still trying and has, indeed, proposed a complete redesign for a next generation COD. Never a very comfortable plane (noisy and severe vibration in the passenger and cargo compartment), the C-2 suffered a devastating loss of pilot (and passenger) confidence through several tragic accidents.

The situation with the C-2 is unique. In spite of everything that the Navy and Grumman have done to get it into safe, productive operation, it still is not back in fleet service. The plane is grounded[19] and the burden

---

[18] In terms of recognition and promotion above the rank of lieutenant commander.

[19] As of this writing. But the E-2C, built around the same airframe and engine as the C-2, is still flying and has not yet evidenced the kind of troubles that have stopped the C-2. There is some fear, however, that this may be because the E-2C hasn't been used as hard as the C-2 and that fatigue may set in eventually with the same results.

Aircraft Type & Model	1981 Carrier Air Wings (National)		Basic Air Wing CV	For Sea Control—CVS	
	For Projection Ashore—CVA				
	Number	(± from CV)		Number	(± from CV)
F-14	12		12	12	
FX/FVX	12		12	12	
A-6E	12		12	0	(−12)
A-7E	24	(+12)	12	12	
S-3A	0	(−10)	10	20	(+10)
SH-3H	3	(−5)	8	16	(+8)
RF-14	6	(+3)	3	0	(−3)
E-2C	4		4	4	
EA-6B	4		4	0	(−4)

A carrier normally would embark the basic CV air wing but could change, emphasizing projection ashore or sea control as appropriate to meet the threat.

Possible deviations from the notional wing, by aircraft type, model, and number are too many to be reasonably footnoted but are discussed in the text. The chart represents one possible Air Wing for the early '80s.

of all COD work is back on the very old C-1s. Naturally, all of this adds to the requirement for a new aircraft for this mission. Unfortunately, at budget time, COD always seems to be a low priority item and gets cut out year after year. At some point we will have to face up to the need and put some money into a new COD. The most promising prospect at this time seems to be the S-3. A derivative of the Viking would be expensive, but there does not seem to be a cheap alternative, and certainly a derivative would be less costly and involve less development risk than a completely new airframe dedicated solely to that mission.

Such a wing is shown in the accompanying table. The numbers are presented as at least being typical of the mixes that are being considered for the CV of the '80s.

The strength of the Navy has always been its ability to recognize the need for change at a pace which ensures stability but at the same time permits innovativeness on the part of its leaders. Hopefully, this is the way naval aviation will continue to evolve.

Summary

This discussion of the aircraft of the Navy for the future has centered on the ship-based aspects of naval aviation and has purposely avoided high risk, long term conceptual designs. Hopefully it will provoke as many questions as it has answered. Probably there are readers who will contest the specific trails of aircraft evolution that the writer has suggested. We hope that they will share their theories with the Naval Institute.

One thing that has been touched on only lightly is an analysis of overall carrier air wing balance. That would be a separate task. We should however at least present a notional air wing for the CV, with possible aircraft allocations reflecting the threat, missions, and aircraft models that have been covered in the text, just to illustrate the type of combinations that are feasible.

Foreign Policy and the Marine Corps

By Major W. Hays Parks, U. S. Marine Corps

At 1020 on 23 February 1945, members of the 2d Battalion, 28th Marines, placed a small U. S. flag atop Mount Suribachi on the island of Iwo Jima. A short time thereafter, Joe Rosenthal took one of the most famous photographs of World War II as the first flag was replaced by a larger one obtained by Marines from their Navy comrades on board *LST-779*. That event, recreated in the Marine Memorial near Washington, has come to represent the mission with which the Marine Corps has been charged since the 18th century—projection of power ashore in furtherance of U. S. interests.

The Marine Memorial serves as a tribute to the forward thinking of the post-World War I Marine Corps planners who disregarded the pessimistic views of tacticians sounding the death knell for amphibious warfare. Pointing to the British-French failure at Gallipoli in 1915, the pessimists argued that the World War I development of the tank, airplane, and machine gun foreclosed the possibility of a successful assault from the sea against hostile, defended shores. Ignoring their critics, Major General John A. Lejeune, Brigadier General John H. Russell, Major Earl H. Ellis, and other Marines resolutely went about the business of adjusting to tactical and technological change, revolutionizing amphibious tactics and weaponry in the process. The wisdom of their efforts was manifested in the amphibious successes of World War II.

With the successful conclusion of World War II, the Marine Corps went through the transformation from its wartime posture as the "first to fight" to a ubiquitous *force in readiness*. Again, technological changes raised challenges to the Marine Corps and its amphibious mission. Amid arguments that the atomic age had revolutionized warfare, Marines assumed occupation duties in Japan, occupation and peacekeeping duties in China, and their portion of the presence mission performed by the U. S. Naval Forces Mediterranean (later the Sixth Fleet) in those perennially troubled waters.

It rapidly became evident that the defeat of the Axis powers had not brought international political stability and peace to the world. Neither the newly-founded United Nations nor our monopoly of nuclear weapons was a panacea for the challenges to the free world. Recognizing the necessity to respond to these challenges, Congress enacted the National Security Act of 1947. Reflecting upon the myriad missions assigned the Marine Corps over the years, Congress provided that the Marine Corps would be:

> ". . . organized, trained, and equipped to provide fleet marine forces . . . for service with the fleet in the seizure or defense of advanced naval bases and for the conduct of such land operations as may be essential to the prosecution of a naval campaign. In addition, the Marine Corps shall . . . perform such other duties as the President may direct."[1]

Again the Marine Corps rejected cries of obsolescence of its amphibious mission, seeking instead refinement of that mission in light of experience and technological advances. Changes were developed to respond to challenge. The concept of vertical envelopment—assault by helicopter—evolved to respond to the challenges of the nuclear age. Concepts developed at Quantico in the postwar years were refined in the years immediately following, soon to be put to use.

On 25 June 1950, overly relying upon the 12 January 1950 statement by Secretary of State Dean Acheson which excluded Korea from the security interests of the United States, the North Korean People's Army invaded the Republic of Korea. In a classic example of the consequences suffered by the occurrence of a vacuum between antagonists, North Korea rushed to fill the void, quickly forcing United Nations forces into a defensive toehold at Pusan. Relief came when the hastily-organized First Marine Division landed by amphibious assault at Inchon on 15 September, reversing the tide of the war. The lessons of the first three months of the Korean War remain valid a quarter century later:

▶ A lack of resolve to protect the interests of the United States and its Free World allies will always be met by Soviet challenge. Our experience in Angola reaffirmed this.

▶ Those challenges seldom occur according to any scenario or prediction envisioned by Free World planners, whether public or private. Although many have prepared for a major power confrontation in Central Europe, that arena has experienced 30 years of peace and prosperity. Rather than restrict themselves to a single scenario, our principal antagonists have sought a global challenge—usually by proxy—while avoiding direct confrontation.

▶ Any response to a challenge must be made with forces in being (including reserves). Our fast-paced world no longer permits the luxury of time enjoyed at the outset of World Wars I and II.

▶ To the enemy's chagrin, amphibious operations seek out his weak points rather than striking at his strong points. The Inchon landing of 1950, for example, served to deter the Democratic Republic of Vietnam from denuding itself of ground forces during U.S. involvement in Vietnam. Uncertain as to if, when, or where an amphibious assault would be made, major units remained tied down in anticipation of landings until the concluding months of the war in 1975.

▶ Challenges to the amphibious mission of the Marine Corps as obsolete neglect the propensity of the Marine Corps to anticipate and respond to technological and tactical change. Leadership in development of surface effect vehicles and V/STOL (vertical/short takeoff and landing) aircraft today carries on the forward thinking traditions which led to the development of the LVT (landing vehicle, tracked) in the 1930s and of modern-day helicopter tactics in the post-World War II era.

The quarter century which has elapsed since the Korean War has seen the Marines put to many tests, most within the naval missions of *naval presence* and *projection of power ashore*. The myriad missions assigned since U.S. withdrawal from Vietnam in 1973 are illustrative of the manner in which the Marine Corps is called upon to support our foreign policy objectives.

The ink was barely dry on the 1973 Paris peace agreements when amphibious forces carrying Navy helicopter squadron HM-12, Marine helicopter squadron HMH-463, and elements of HMM-165 were dispatched into North Vietnamese waters to conduct a minesweeping operation of Haiphong Harbor. Operation End Sweep commenced on 27 February 1973 and was concluded on 5 July, having been delayed at one point for two months by diplomatic discussions between North Vietnam and the United States.[2]

A few months later, 34th MAU, the Sixth Fleet Landing Force, was dispatched to the Eastern Mediterranean as the Arab-Israeli War commenced on 6 October 1973.[3] Other Marines of the Second Marine Division were immediately deployed from Camp Lejeune, bolstering the force to MAB level. Initially assigned to stand by for possible evacuation, their naval presence mission assumed greater importance on 25 October when—in response to threats of Soviet intervention—U.S. forces were placed on DefCon III status.[4] The 4,400 Marines of 4th MAB remained on station until mid-December.

Three months later, a contingent of Marine forces joined their Navy comrades to participate in Nimbus Star, the Suez Canal minesweeping operation. That operation barely was concluded when 34th MAU, engaged in a NATO exercise on the Peloponnesian peninsula of Greece, was dispatched to the waters surrounding the embattled island of Cyprus. The Marine force evacuated 752 persons (including 498 citizens of the United States) representing 22 nations to the amphibious ship *Coronado* (LPD-11). Predeployment planning for the ever-present possibility of evacuation had been so complete that the embarked stores of the amphibious force were able to supply diapers for the infant children of the evacuees.

Halfway around the globe, floods once again ravaged the Central Luzon basin area of the Philippines in August 1974. Marine helicopters on board the USS *Tripoli* (LPH-10) were summoned to assist Philippine government relief efforts. The mission was a familiar one to the *Tripoli*'s sailors and Marines. They had provided flood relief to the Philippines two years before.[5] During the six-day operation, Marine helicopters flew nearly one-half of the 249 individual sorties flown, providing food for an estimated 300,000 people.

As the Marine Corps entered 1975, it looked forward to the first year in more than a decade in which Marines were not being shot at somewhere in the world. That hope quickly diminished as the governments in Cambodia and the Republic of Vietnam began to collapse under the onslaught of Communist forces. Acting in Operation Eagle Pull in the former and Frequent Wind in the latter, 9th MAB evacuated more than 7,000 U.S. and foreign nationals from the two beleaguered nations.[6] Other Marines served as security forces on board the numerous Navy and merchant ships carrying out the seaborne portions of the Vietnam evacuation.

Less than two weeks after the conclusion of the Saigon evacuation, the American cargo ship *Mayaguez* was seized on the high seas on 12 May by naval forces of the revolutionary government of Cambodia. Marine forces were quickly dispatched from Okinawa to board the ship while her crew was being recovered, thus ending a tumultuous month.

The assassination of the U. S. ambassador to Lebanon and his economic advisor in Beirut on 16 June 1976 brought to the fore evacuation plans which had been executed in part the previous October. When partial evacuations were carried out on 20 June and 27 July, they were *seaborne* evacuations accomplished by amphibious craft from the Sixth Fleet Amphibious Force. A last-minute attempt by the Palestine Liberation Organization to exploit the 20 June evacuation for diplomatic and tactical gain (thereby jeopardizing the lives of the evacuees) was thwarted when President Gerald Ford announced his intention to land the MAU if necessary to safeguard the evacuees and the mission's success. Prior to each evacuation, the Navy-Marine Corps amphibious force had been in neighboring waters in anticipation of evacuation orders, discreetly out of sight, prepared to task organize its forces to suit mission requirements and diplomatic necessities.

The actions of the past three years illustrate the missions of the Marine Corps in its support of the foreign policy of the United States. With amphibious units simultaneously and continuously deployed in a naval presence role in the Mediterranean, Caribbean, and Western Pacific, they stand ready for any mission, ranging from those of the humanitarian nature of disaster relief and evacuation to confrontation with malevolent opportunists. By being sea-based, they remain a conspicuous and mobile example of the U. S. concept of forward basing, providing, in the words of Secretary of Defense Donald Rumsfeld, "the visible capability that serves to deter many acts of aggression."

The recent, well-publicized private study by the

Brookings Institution suggests that these needs are no longer feasible inasmuch as there now exists within the United States a "growing disenchantment with military ventures overseas."[7] The *Wall Street Journal*, responding to that study, suggested instead:

> "Americans have never been enchanted with overseas military ventures. But they have often backed such ventures when the reasons for them were clearly understood. Having a force in readiness is one way to discourage adventurism by other powers."[8]

The United States as a Sea Power: The substantial contribution of the Marine Corps to the foreign policy objectives of the United States is not accidental. It exists because of the necessary reliance of the United States upon the seas for communication and survival. Separated from 90% of the world by water, the sea is the economic lifeline of the United States. Foreign trade, of which 70% arrived by sea, was in excess of $142 billion in 1974. Vast amounts of strategic raw materials were imported from overseas: 100% of our cobalt, mercury, and natural rubber, 98% of our manganese, 91% of our chrome, 90% of our aluminum, 72% of our nickel, and 37% of our oil. Our demand for imported natural resources increases annually, as do our overseas investments, currently worth more than $130 billion. Indeed, the economy—and therefore the survival—of the United States is dependent on seaborne trade. While we value the fact that our political and military opponents are overseas rather than overland, we have become increasingly vulnerable in many respects due to our insular status. Our commitments to allies, economically or militarily, are fulfilled primarily by sea trade. Hence there exists a dependence on other states and their resources, on the oceans to deliver those resources, and on the oceans to preserve those resources. We utilize the seas to protect and maintain our national interests, to maintain the global balance of power, and, when necessary, for the support of diplomacy by force.

U. S. Foreign Policy: Like the foreign policies of all nations, that of the United States is concerned with questions of survival, security, and fulfillment. Our interdependent world precludes our seeking unilateral answers to these questions. The essentially bipolar

U. S. MARINE CORPS

Nobody won the Korean War, but America was very close to losing it before Marines stormed the sea wall at Inchon to turn the tide. Forgotten now by most Americans, Inchon must have been remembered by the North Vietnamese who tied up major units waiting for the amphibious assault that never came.

world in which we exist politically requires the establishment and maintenance of commitments with our allies.

Foreign policy must respond to change if it is to be effective. The foreign policy of the United States has been subjected to a number of influences in the last decade. International factors have had a significant effect. A new policy toward the People's Republic of China, relations with the Soviet Union based on negotiation rather than confrontation, and the emergence of a loosely unified but vocal third world, have forced rethinking of our foreign policy and the use of military force in support thereof. Domestic influences have had their impact. The foreign policy assertions of Congress have been influenced not only by the crisis of Watergate but by the demands of our democratic society to avoid what many honestly perceive to be unwarranted commitments. Resort to an all-volunteer military, concomitant personnel strength reductions, and demands for quality over quantity, both in personnel and equipment, reflect our capital intensive society in which emphasis is given to our technological and industrial capacity to minimize the risk of American lives. Our foreign policy and the military role in support thereof, like that of every other nation, are dictated by our history, geography, economy, politics, the foreign policies of other nations, and events within those nations.

The conclusion of the Vietnam War has had a demonstrable effect upon our foreign policy. Domestically we have faced not only the previously-mentioned personnel demands but the inevitable postwar reaction of isolationism to "bring the boys home." Both domestically and abroad, cries have been heard for the withdrawal of United States forces from overseas bases, although our allies are anxious that we maintain our defense commitments. With the reversion of Okinawa to Japan, for example, the Japanese have increased their pressure on the United States to withdraw our armed forces from Okinawa and Japan while insisting that the United States maintain the commitments of the Mutual Security Treaty of 1960 to defend Japan. Domestic political pressures exist for reductions in this nation's contributions to NATO forces even without resolution of the mutual and balanced force reduction discussions. Like reductions have been suggested for U. S. forces in Korea, while the Nixon-Ford Doctrine emphasizes the decreased role U. S. ground forces will play in the peacetime or low-intensity war environment.

Withdrawal of forces does not mean abandonment of allies and friends, however. Our lack of self-sufficiency and our desire to discourage aggression require that we continue to project our forces overseas. Obligations remain. Crises will continue to occur. The withdrawal of forces, rather than diminishing U. S. respon-

sibilities, has increased the need for our nation and its leaders to rely upon its sea power to provide the necessary response. Our experience during the Arab-Israeli War of 1973 showed that any attempt to deploy our forces by air would be fraught with difficulty in seeking landing, staging, and overflight rights, and it would be inadequate from a logistic standpoint.[9] Furthermore, crises often demand forces in being, on site. As suggested by the *Mayaguez* incident and the most recent evacuations from Lebanon, time frequently is of the essence. Rapid as air travel may be, the lengthy reaction time for deployment by air of any Army reaction force based in the continental United States impedes serious consideration of its use.[10] These factors suggest a greater reliance on Navy and Marine forces as the principal military tools for implementation of this nation's foreign policy.

The missions of the Navy are four: strategic nuclear deterrence, sea control, projection of power ashore, and naval presence.[11] We—and apparently the Soviets—have come to realize that the mutual capacity to destroy completely requires that force used in the pursuit of political objectives be amenable to selective and explicitly limited application. Thus, the success of the first mission has resulted in increased emphasis on the last three, which may be described as the historical and traditional roles of the Navy and the Marine Corps. The worldwide tendency of the last decade for states and factions within states to resort to violence as a first rather than a last resort has increased the importance of these missions, whether in discouraging expansionism or in protecting the lives of Americans and other foreign nationals unwittingly endangered by local violence. The role of the Marine Corps in each of these missions is significant.

Naval presence—historically known as "showing the flag"—is defined as "the use of naval forces, short of war, to achieve political objectives."[12] Although a mission with lengthy historical precedent, naval presence today is viewed more as a declaration of intent to honor our commitments to our friends and allies than in the 19th century context of "gunboat diplomacy." In an era in which emphasis has shifted from confrontation to negotiation, it has assumed increased significance—to the extent that Admiral Elmo Zumwalt, former Chief of Naval Operations, has predicted a "95% probability that the most likely future use of naval forces will be in the Presence role."[13]

The value of naval presence lies in its unused but highly visible potential rather than realized capabilities. It is a tactic of conflict avoidance executed through preventive deployments, such as the routine deployments made by amphibious forces to the Western Pacific, Mediterranean, and Caribbean, or through reactive

deployment, as was accomplished through the reinforcement of the Sixth Fleet Landing Force during the Arab-Israeli War of 1973. Deployment of Marine amphibious forces to Peru on a mission of earthquake relief in 1970 and to the Philippines in 1972 and 1974 emphasizes the use of these forces to "show the flag" on humanitarian missions while demonstrating the rapid deployment capabilities of our amphibious forces.

The greatest role of the naval presence mission, however, is that of deterrence of intervention. This was illustrated in the confrontation between the Soviet Union and the United States during the Arab-Israeli War of 1973 when the Soviet Union moved to achieve its long-held ambition of intervention in the Suez.[14] Notwithstanding the value of nuclear deterrence and *détente,* the principal stumbling block to Soviet ambitions was the Navy-Marine force of the Sixth Fleet, which lay astride the Soviet path to the Suez.

U. S. withdrawal from many overseas bases has increased the *naval* significance of the presence mission and, paradoxically, has occurred as U. S. interests overseas have increased. The myriad destabilizing factors and conditions which exist today suggest there will be no shortage of crises in the future. Experience has shown that few crises are immediately resolved. Military force, while ready, must rightfully defer to diplomatic efforts at peaceful settlement. The crisis in Jordan in 1970, the Arab-Israeli War of 1973, and the most recent

Because U. S. investments overseas and tourism—to say nothing of diplomatic and strategic U. S. interests—are likely to grow, not diminish, there will always be Americans who ignore State Department warnings and have to be evacuated from strife-torn countries, as was the case in mid-June 1976 at Beirut, Lebanon.

and prolonged crisis in Lebanon, for example, required the presence of Navy and Marine forces for extended periods of time. As in Jordan, they may serve principally as a passive deterrent to outside intervention. In the two more recent incidents, on the other hand, once needed, the need was immediate. The apparent requirement in each varied from day to day, suggesting the indispensability of a Navy-Marine Corps presence: a visible and highly mobile force, capable of remaining present in international waters for an indeterminate period, capable of projecting ashore on short notice a force task organized to provide the necessary response to any challenge to the interests of the United States.

The foregoing statement suggests that the missions of *naval presence* and *projection of power ashore* are inseparable except, perhaps, in academic definition. The practice of the past few years would seem to confirm this. Neither of the humanitarian missions of disaster relief or evacuation meet the technical definitions of *projection of power ashore* or *amphibious operation,* the latter being

184

one of three means by which the former is accomplished.[15] Perhaps what is absent in applying the latter definition to recent history is a clear-cut identification of shores hostile to the landing force, except in the cases of Pnom Penh, Saigon, and the *Mayaguez* incident. Herein lies the merging effect brought about by the on-site task organizing capability of the Marine Corps: that of responding to mission requirements, however unusual, including making a forcible entry if necessary.

The Marine Corps' capability is enhanced by its reputation both domestically and in the international arena as an elite, disciplined force capable of executing missions, when necessary, of *limited duration*. This reputation is essential. On the one hand, it deters the use of force by nations or factions within nations to oppose humanitarian missions, while on the other it assures those states of the ability of U. S. forces to execute a limited duration mission without threatening the territorial integrity or political independence of that state. It suggests the resolve to execute a limited duration mission while remaining neutral toward warring factions, as occurred on Cyprus in 1974. The international reputation of the Marine Corps as a professional military force permits it to accomplish its mission with a minimum of force in a minimum of time, displaying sufficient capability while reserving unused potential.

As a limited mission, limited duration force, the Marine Corps offers certain assurances domestically. Deployment of U. S. Army forces historically has been perceived as a commitment to a *sustained* land campaign. As Army Chief of Staff, General Frederick C. Weyand, stated before the Senate Armed Services Committee on 2 February 1976: ". . . in greater degree perhaps than the other services, if and when the Army is committed, the United States is committed." Secretary of War Patrick J. Hurley offered similar comments on 9 November 1931: "The Army is a little different from the Navy and the Marine Corps. The Marine Corps can land on foreign territory without its being considered an act of war, but when the Army moves on foreign territory, that is an act of war. That is one of the reasons for the Marine Corps." On the lower scale of the conflict spectrum, then, the projection of Marine forces ashore—whether in humanitarian intervention or in response to hostile actions, such as in the *Mayaguez* incident—suggests both internationally and domestically the limited nature of the mission while serving as a continuum of the naval presence mission. It is a reassurance to our friends of our capability and determination to honor our commitments while serving as a deterrent to the inimical intentions of adventurist groups or nations.

If there is a blurring or merging of images on the lower end of the spectrum of Marine Corps missions, the same occurs in Marine Corps support of the Navy's mission of *sea control*. Looking at the dual functions of the sea control mission of "*denying* an enemy the right to use some seas at some times, [while] *asserting* our own right to use some seas at some times," Marine Corps capabilities are supportive of each.[16] Projecting amphibious forces ashore, the Marine Corps can seize and defend advanced naval bases from which Navy and Marine forces can control essential geographic bottlenecks or "chokepoints," denying enemy naval forces egress from or ingress to an area of operations.[17] In the passive roles of deception and intimidation, that is, threatening an amphibious assault at any place at any time, we succeed not only in forcing the commitment of enemy naval forces but ground forces as well. The potential of the Marine Corps has not been lost on the Soviets, who in recent years have organized special amphibious defense units in recognition of the threat.[18]

Conclusion: International conditions suggest the unlikelihood of a world devoid of crises. The upward spiral of interstate and intrastate violence and counterviolence indicates that the mission of evacuating U. S. and foreign nationals will continue. Long-standing or emerging states can become battlefields overnight as factions wage bitter fights in the name of self-determination. American overseas investments and tourism, as well as diplomatic and strategic interests, suggest Americans will always be exposed to these crises as they occur. Experience lamentably shows there always will be Americans who, for business or personal reasons, fail to heed Department of State recommendations for timely departure from strife-torn countries, necessitating their subsequent evacuation by military forces. Requests for disaster relief will also continue to occur.

The action by Isreali forces at Entebbe, Uganda, on 4 July 1976, showed the feasibility of using a highly trained military force to combat international terrorism. The unlikelihood of an international antiterrorist force and the likelihood that Americans will be among the victims of terrorist actions paralleling the Entebbe episode suggest a mission for which the Marine Corps is suited, equipped, trained, and readily deployable.[19]

The events of the last 30 years indicate that major power confrontation will not be at the nuclear level, and that our principal antagonist will continue to test our resolve at every opportunity. Rapid development and worldwide deployment of a quality blue-water navy show Soviet appreciation of the dual roles of the Navy as demonstrable political power and a challenge to U. S. sea power. The appearance of Soviet amphibious forces off Angola one year ago reflects Soviet recognition of the importance of the naval presence mission and, in support thereof, the capability to project forces ashore.

Challenges to the survival and security of a nation dictate its foreign policy. The resoluteness of responses dictates the foreign policy of its challengers. The history of our nation is reflected in its use of the Marine Corps, the nation's *force in readiness,* as one of its principal tools of response. Our increased dependence upon sea power for security and survival suggests that use of the Marine Corps will not diminish but increase.

 Major Parks entered the Marine Corps by way of the Platoon Leaders' Class (Law) program in 1961. Although he always has been designated a Judge Advocate, he has served as a reconnaissance platoon leader, infantry company commander, and shore party company commander. He reported to his present assignment in the Office of Legislative Affairs, Secretary of the Navy, in August. In his previous assignment as the Marine Corps Liaison Office to The Judge Advocate General's School, U. S. Army, Major Parks taught international law at that school, the Army War College, the U. S. Naval Academy, and the Marine Corps' Amphibious Warfare School and Command and Staff College. Named one of the Outstanding Educators of America in 1975, Major Parks previously coauthored "If I Become a Prisoner of War . . . ," which appeared in the August *Proceedings.* A graduate of Baylor University and Baylor University School of Law, Major Parks is now completing the requirements for a master's degree in foreign affairs at the University of Virginia.

[1] National Security Act of 1947, as amended, §206(c) or 10 U. S. Code §5013(a).

[2] Lieutenant Colonel John Van Nortwick, USMC, "Endsweep," *Marine Corps Gazette,* May 1974, pp. 29–36. Rear Admiral Brian McCauley, USN, "Operation End Sweep, *U. S. Naval Institute Proceedings,* March 1974, pp. 18–25.

[3] A Marine Amphibious Unit (MAU) ordinarily is composed of a battalion landing team (a task-organized infantry battalion with armored, artillery, amphibious tractor, engineer, and other reinforcing units), a medium helicopter squadron, and a logistic support unit. A Marine Amphibious Brigade (MAB) usually consists of a regimental landing team, a helicopter group, and a combat service support unit group. A MAU normally comprises 1,800–4,000 men and a MAB, 8,000–12,000.

[4] Lieutenant (junior grade) F. C. Miller, USN, "Those Storm-Beaten Ships Upon Which the Arab Armies Never Looked," *Proceedings,* March 1975, pp. 18–25.

[5] Colonel Richard C. Kriegel, USMCR, "Operation Saklolo: The Battle of the Nutribun," *Marine Corps Gazette,* April 1973, p. 29.

[6] Colonel Sydney H. Batchelder, USMC, and Major D. A. Quinlan, USMC, "Operation Eagle Pull," *Marine Corps Gazette,* May 1976, pp. 47–60. Major General Richard E. Carey, USMC, and Major D. A. Quinlan, USMC, "Frequent Wind," *Marine Corps Gazette,* February (pp. 16–24), March (pp. 35–45), and April 1976 (pp. 35–45).

[7] Martin Binkin and Jeffrey Record, *Where Does the Marine Corps Go From Here?* (Washington, D.C.: The Brookings Institution, 1976), p. 35.

[8] "A Few Good Men," *The Wall Street Journal,* 11 February 1976, p. 12.

[9] Between 13 October and 14 November 1973, utilizing 24% of our active airlift capability, the military airlift to Israel transported 22,487 tons of cargo. Three times that amount went by sea. Of the heavy equipment required by a mechanized force, a Government Accounting Office study reported that "The [air] quantities delivered were not significant enough to have effected [sic] the war's outcome," further noting that "most of this [air] cargo did not arrive until after the ceasefire or until after the first shipload arrived." C-5A aircraft, capable of carrying 107 tons of cargo, averaged 73 tons per flight. Had refueling not been permitted in the Azores, those loads would have been cut to 33 tons. The extreme range would have prohibited the use of the C-141 without refueling in the Azores. *Report to the Congress, Airlift Operations of the Military Airlift Command During the 1973 Middle East War,* Washington, Comptroller General of the United States (GAO), 16 April 1975, pp. 10–15, 57–58. *See also* Colonel A. P. Sights, USAF, "The Projection of Power by Air," *Proceedings,* May 1975 (Naval Review Issue), pp. 86–101. See also Senator Robert A. Taft, Jr., "White Paper on Defense: A Modern Military Strategy for the United States," March 1976.

[10] Administratively moving combat essential elements of the 82d Airborne Division to the Middle East, for example, with a basic load of ammunition and a five-day supply of rations and fuel would require more than 700 C-141 sorties. Such a move would require ten to 15 days from a standing start, seven if alert times were sufficient to permit prior preparation. An airborne assault of the same force would require 1,200 sorties, including aircraft for a heavy drop. Estimates for other Army divisions are longer. *Oil Fields as Military Objectives,* Washington, Library of Congress, 21 August 1975, pp. 60, 64; and *United States/Soviet Military Balance,* Washington, Library of Congress, 22 January 1976, p. 30. Furthermore, heavily damaged airfields precluded the use of air transport delivered ground forces during the evacuations from Cyprus in 1974 and Lebanon in 1976.

[11] Vice Admiral Stansfield Turner, USN, "Missions of the U. S. Navy," *Naval War College Review,* March-April 1974, pp. 2–17.

[12] *Ibid,* p. 14.

[13] Commander James F. McNulty, USN, "Naval Presence—The Misunderstood Mission," *Naval War College Review,* September-October 1974, pp. 21, 22. Ironically, in order to strengthen its single scenario approach of a Marine Corps confrontation with the Warsaw Pact nations, The Brookings Institution study of the Marine Corps erroneously declared the Navy had ranked the presence mission lowest in order of priorities. Binkin and Record, *op. cit.* p. 33.

[14] Shlomo Slonim, "Suez and the Soviets," *Proceedings,* April 1975, pp. 36–41.

[15] Projection of power ashore "is concerned with the impact of naval on land forces, and can be divided into three categories: amphibious assault, naval bombardment, and tactical air." Turner, *op. cit.,* p. 10. The joint service *Doctrine for Amphibious Operations* definition of amphibious operations is an "attack launched from the sea by naval and landing forces, embarked in ships or craft involving a landing on a hostile shore." For further discussion see Brigadier General Edwin H. Simmons, USMC, "The Marines: Now and in the Future," *Proceedings,* May 1975 (Naval Review Issue), pp. 102, 108.

[16] Turner, *op. cit.,* p. 7.

[17] Colonel Marc Moore, USMC, "Strategy for a Triangular World," *Marine Corps Gazette,* August 1973, p. 31, which mentions 26 "chokepoints" around the world "where the land lies in close proximity to critical sea routes . . ." Deployment of a MAU to seize and defend a naval base for a squadron of the new *Pegasus*-class hydrofoil gunboats (PHM) in the Straits of Malacca, for example, would be supportive of Navy sea control measures.

[18] G. H. Turbiville, "Soviet amphibious landing defenses," *Marine Corps Gazette,* September 1975, p. 20.

[19] Recognizing the international law principles of *sovereignty* and the protection of human rights, the author limits his suggestion to the concept of self-help in cases like Entebbe, where the local government faltered in its upholding of the latter of the two principles. For a discussion of these principles, see Richard B. Lillich, "Forcible Self-Help By States to Protect Human Rights," *Iowa Law Review,* Volume 53, 1967, pp. 325–351.

'The Coasts of the World will be our Borders'

TODAY'S MARINE CORPS

By JAMES W. CANAN

James Canan is military correspondent for the Washington Bureau of the McGraw-Hill World News Service, and author of the book The Superwarriors.

THE U.S. Marine Corps is recapturing the individuality that makes it indispensable. In Korea and Vietnam, with only a few exceptions, the Corps engaged the enemy in inland campaigns which were virtually indistinguishable from those of the Army. Now, however, the Pentagon is dusting off the distinctive image of the Marines as soldiers uniquely capable of moving on, and striking from, the sea.

The Corps' *raison d'être*, the amphibious assault, is a military tactic whose time has come again. It is of a piece with the Navy's urgent preparations to assure U.S. control of the oceans, a mission of topmost Pentagon priority. That is perhaps why Defense Secretary Donald H. Rumsfeld praised the Corps in his posture statement this year, calling it "one of our most flexible assets."

The Chief of Naval Operations, Admiral James L. Holloway III, also is speaking out these days on the importance of the Navy-Marine team in protecting U.S. shipping and the country's economic and military interests abroad. In speeches and in testimony before Congress, Holloway has expressed regret that amphibious warfare "seems to be neglected when we discuss sea control" and

that it is mistakenly regarded as an element limited to land campaigns, as in Korea and Vietnam. The CNO makes the point that the Marines stormed Pacific islands in World War II not only to capture real estate but also to gain control of the sea approaches to the Philippines and Japan.

"Amphibious seizure of key bases and strait areas is going to be essential to sea control in the future," Holloway asserts.

Drawing the Fangs

A few months ago the CNO was asked at the National Defense University whether the Navy now considers sea control and power projection to be synonomous, not separate, missions. He replied, in effect, that, taken together, they are the same. Then he postulated an illustrative combat situation.

"Let's look," Holloway said, "at projection of power as it contributes to sea control. Our concept for the battle of the Atlantic goes something like this: We would attempt to shut off the access to ocean areas by the Soviet fleets coming out of their bases, blocking them coming out of the Kola inlet area, out of the Black Sea, out of the Sea of Japan, doing what we could with Petropavlovsk. Then we would try to attrite those forces which were at sea when the war began—their submarines and their surface ships.

"Some of this attrition would take place when one of their submarines shoots all his missiles and gets rid of his torpedoes. His fangs have been drawn. He's got to get back

Stepping Out Smartly

Members of the 4th Marine Amphibious Brigade from Camp Lejeune, N.C., in action during NATO Exercise Team Work 76, which began in late September in central Norway. (USMC photos.) Although used principally in the Pacific during most recent U.S. conflicts, the Corps emphasizes through such exercises that its commitments—and its capabilities—are truly "worldwide" in scope.

to the Black Sea, the Baltic, the Kola Gulf, or the Sea of Berbera.

"Now, how do you neutralize those bases? One way is to bombard them with gunfire. If you have to keep doing that all the time, it's rather expensive. Air strikes, that's merely suppressing them.

"The real way to take care of those bases is to go in there with the Marines and seize the territory, and then you own it, you've got it, and it's no problem."

Base Rights and Forcible Entry

The Marines relish the rejuvenation of their mission as seaborne troubleshooter and are, stepping out smartly. Late last summer the Commandant of the Marine Corps, General Louis H. Wilson, issued a point paper to commanders— "Subject: Role of Fleet Marine Forces in Sea Control." It directs that planning of strategic and tactical operations should take into account "the potential contributions of amphibious forces" in seizing or raiding enemy naval bases and airfields, islands, and littorals "from which operations could be conducted to dominate key straits or choke points and other vital sea areas."

Wilson already had delivered to Capitol Hill his message that the Marines are landing. His posture statement this year noted that the United States cannot maintain pre-positioned ground forces in every potential crisis area, cannot count on having base rights and overflight privileges, and cannot expect its troops to land anywhere unopposed.

"This," said Wilson, "is why the United States has a continuing need for its Fleet Marine Forces—to provide the nation's only major capability for forcible entry."

Ancient Roots; Classical Execution

The Marines have not really combat-tested that capability since World War II. They proved in Korea and Vietnam that they can fight prolonged campaigns ashore effectively and even, as at Khe Sanh, spectacularly. Their two most notable landings—at Inchon in 1950 and at Danang in 1966—were classically executed and resulted in stunning (but inland) defeats of the enemy. The landings themselves met little or no opposition.

Acknowledging the long time lack of battle testing on beaches, the Corps accentuates amphibious training in its tactical exercises. In the fiscal year which ended on 1 October, units of the Corps' one reserve and three active divisions conducted approximately 40 amphibious exercises, often in concert with troops of allied nations, and in climes and on coasts ranging from Scandinavia to Australia.

"We do not ignore training for extended operations ashore," says Brigadier General Calhoun J. Killeen, director of the operations division, plans and operations department, HQMC. "But we are *not* a second land army. We are structured as an amphibious assault force."

That structuring has its roots in ancient history. Amphibious operations have been around ever since the first company of spear-brandishing Phoenician foot soldiers jumped off their galleys and waded onto a hostile Middle East beach. But it took the U.S. Marines to develop amphibious warfare as a doctrine.

Shortly after the turn of the twentieth century, the Navy decided it might need to seize and hold overseas bases for harbors and refueling in the event of local or general combat. The Navy-Marine Advanced Base Force was created to prepare to carry out that mission, and the force's first battalion of Marines joined the fleet in 1903 for exercises off Culebra Island, near Puerto Rico. The Marines instituted formal amphibious warfare training at a new school in Philadelphia in 1910. Ten years later, all such training was consolidated at the big Marine base in Quantico, Va.

Throwback Orthodoxy: Questions and Answers

Following World War II, Marine General A. A. Vandegrift declared that the Corps actually had contributed much more to the Allied victory than its own smashing successes in the Pacific. Said he: "The basic amphibious doctrines which carried Allied troops over every beachhead had been largely shaped—often in the face of uninterested or doubting orthodoxy—by the United States Marines."

That same throwback orthodoxy seemed to have taken hold again in recent years. Former Defense Secretary James R. Schlesinger took note in his 1976 Posture Statement of "questions that have been raised about the need for an amphibious assault force which has not seen anything more demanding than essentially unopposed landings for over 20 years, and which would have grave difficulty in accomplishing its mission of over-the-beach and flanking operations in a high-threat environment." Then Schlesinger set the questions to rest, saying: "Despite these doubts, I believe that modernized amphibious forces will be well worth their cost. The entire globe is not defended by sophisticated surface-to-air missiles and high-performance fighters. Nor has the United States lost all interest in beachheads and flanking operations. Moreover, there is certain salutary value in having reinforced Marine battalions aboard their assault ships in various sensitive parts of the world."

The Sealift Shortage

Clearly, the Corps will stay the route. But just as clearly, as even its champions acknowledge, it needs some help—not in manpower, which has stabilized at a "lean and hard" level of about 192,000 (with a highly efficient 60-40 combat-to-support ratio), but in mobility and firepower, both at sea and ashore.

The U.S. Navy's trimmed down amphibious fleet of 65 ships now can transport simultaneously the assault elements of only slightly more than one Marine Amphibious Force (MAF), a division-air wing team. What's more, the ships are about equally divided between the Atlantic and the Pacific, and would have to join up in order to lift a full MAF in either ocean.

Overall, the Navy's amphibious lift capacity can handle, at the optimum, less than half of the total Marine fighting force. As presently constituted and arrayed, the amphibious fleet is barely sufficient to sustain the forward deployment of only two complete, battalion-size Marine Amphibious

Units (MAUs) with all the organic attack and transport helicopters they require for vertical envelopment of the enemy. The most glaring deficiency in the amphibious fleet is its lack of deck and stowage space for choppers. That deficiency could necessitate a lot of tactically unwieldy cross-decking of the choppers among the various types of ships, and tends to diffuse the combat units themselves.

The deficiency will be eliminated for a time, at least, by the addition to the fleet of five mammoth LHAs, general purpose assault ships second in size only to modern aircraft carriers and a dimensional matchup to the smaller carrier of World War II. Capable of exceeding 22 knots, the LHA is a landing force commander's every wish come true—the first amphibious ship ever designed from the keel up with the tactical needs of both the Navy and the Marines in mind.

The first of the LHAs, USS TARAWA, joined the fleet this year. The second, USS SAIPAN, is scheduled for delivery next May. All five will have been delivered by the end of 1981, providing that a long-running and acrimonious contract dispute between the Navy and Litton Industries, the builder of the ships, can be settled. Litton's Ingalls shipyard in Pascagoula, Miss., is now building the ships under court order, pending a final settlement of the cost disputes plaguing the billion-dollar-plus program.

Artist's concept of the LVA (landing vehicle, assault), being designed for the Marine Corps by Bell Aerospace Textron.

Marine Commandant General Louis H. Wilson meets with Marines at Camp Smedley D. Butler during one of his frequent visits to the field. (USMC photo.) Wilson often points out in such meetings that the Corps' air-ground/-amphibious team is today the only viable U.S. alternative to the economically and politically impossible strategy of pre-positioning troops and equipment in every potential crisis area of the world.

Flight deck and well deck views of LHA-1, USS TARAWA, first of five general purpose amphibious assault ships planned for Navy/USMC use. (Marine Corps photos by L. Connelly.) Even when all five are operational, however, the Navy and Marine Corps will still be faced with a severe shortage of amphibious lift capability.

Once the fifth LHA is operational, the Navy will have increased its large-force amphibious lift capacity to one and one-third MAFs—in either the Atlantic or the Pacific, but still not in both. A more significant point, however, is that the five LHAs will permit the Marines to forward-deploy two of their basic assault units, the MAUs, in each ocean with full complements of organic choppers and varying mixes of reinforcing armor, according to the particular mission or missions involved. "We can't forward-deploy four MAUs now simply because we lack the helicopter platforms," points out General Killeen.

The LHA combines the payload and the performance characteristics of four different types of amphibious ships

now in the fleet. Its versatility will vastly enhance the Marines' tactical integrity, which depends squarely on delivering, to the same point of attack and at the same time, assault units which balance and support one another.

The LHA does not mark the end of improvements planned for the amphibious fleet. Now in research and development is an air-cushion craft—the LCAC (or landing craft, air-cushion—also known as the AALC, or amphibious assault landing craft)—designed for carrying troops, armor, and artillery, and of surpassing speed and maneuverability, even across the surf line. "Technologically," says General Wilson, "it shows promise of being the greatest advance in amphibious capabilities since the advent of the helicopter." Also coming along, to replace the LVT (landing vehicle, tracked), is the LVA (landing vehicle, assault), which in one version utilizes a planing hull rather than the air bubble concept. Another amphibious vessel in R&D would feature a rotary diesel engine designed to provide high speed and enormous range at a minimal cost in fuel.

A Chop to the Capability

Those ships are several or more years away from deployment, however, and the Corps is not counting on them yet. Nor is it all that confident about acquiring all the LHAs it needs. Originally, it had planned on buying nine LHAs, but soaring costs forced the cancellation of four in 1972. Another cutback of LHA procurement would be a hard karate chop to the Corps, for, as Killeen puts it: "The five LHAs will give us the minimum acceptable lift capability." Moreover, as General Wilson emphasizes, even with the LHAs the amphibious fleet faces "a critical shortage of lift" in the 1980s upon the programmed retirement of the LSD-28 class of ships—unless the Navy moves swiftly with plans to replace them.

The Navy shares the Marines' concern about the plenitude and pace of amphibious ship procurement. But the Navy needs many other kinds of ships. Holloway provides this perspective: "It would not be wise to let amphibious shipping get out of balance with other naval capabilities. The Marines have to fight their way ashore. We need ships to provide them gunfire support and carriers to first gain air superiority and then provide them close air support."

Right now, the Navy is weak in gunfire support. Large numbers of World War II gun-equipped ships have been retired. The Navy's newer ships, far fewer in number, fire missiles. So the Navy has begun putting the eight-inch lightweight gun on its new SPRUANCE-class destroyers and will follow suit with other ship types as well.

Holding the Shore—Without Sea Transport

Getting to the beach is one thing; taking it and holding it, quite another.

Many critics of the Corps who nevertheless wish it well contend that it lacks the mechanized mobility and antitank firepower to fight effectively amid the ferocity of modern land warfare, as exemplified by the Middle East war of 1973. Among the more constructive critics is Senator Robert Taft, Jr. (R-Ohio), a member of the Senate Armed Services Committee whose recent "White Paper on Defense: A Modern Military Strategy for the United States" may be the most thought-provoking non-Pentagon document on

190

military affairs in recent years.

Taft argues generally that the Navy needs to be built up very quickly and that all Army and Marine infantry units need to be mechanized. He contends that the only U.S. forces capable of "forcible insertion" overseas—the Marines and the Army's 82d Airborne Division—are anachronistic because they are essentially light infantry.

"The airborne's key disadvantage compared to the Marine Corps," declares the White Paper, "is that its support transportation mode—aircraft—prevents it from ever becoming anything but an infantry force. A sea-transported force can be mechanized; an air-transported force cannot, without sea transport of its equipment."

Taft calculates the cost of completely mechanizing the Marines' three divisions at about $600 million. He advocates the movement of all infantry in vehicles that, unlike those presently in service, would serve as firepower as well as personnel carriers. Such mechanization would be cost effective, the Taft paper claims, because "the Marine Corps' current structure as infantry renders it increasingly incapable of defeating its opponents."

Taft selects the Middle East as a potential crisis area the Marines may well be called upon to invade, and draws some sobering comparisons: "Most of the area powers are mechanizing their land forces. Egypt today has 2,000 tanks, Iran 2,000, Syria 1,670, Iraq 1,400, and Saudi Arabia 500, including those on order. These tanks are integrated with other modern equipment into mechanized and armored formations. In contrast, the Marine Corps has a mere 477 tanks. To the extent that the Marines, as infantry, must fight a major mechanized or armored combined force, their chances of victory are not good."

Mobility and Firepower Programs

Those chances are, however, getting better all the time. The Corps has undertaken a number of mobility and firepower modernization programs which, as Wilson puts it, "selectively increase our capabilities to operate effectively in potential high-threat environments."

The Corps has begun buying, for example, the same chopper-fired, wire-guided TOW antitank missiles the Israelis used to smash an abundance of Arab armor in the 1973 war, and is procuring shoulder-fired Dragon antitank missiles as replacements for its recoilless rifles.

The first TOW units already have been formed up in the 2d Marine Division at Camp Lejeune, N.C., and more will follow as the missiles keep coming off production lines into the 1980s. The Corps' aircraft procurement in the current fiscal year provides for the first 15 of 24 AH-1T attack choppers configured with the TOW system. It also provides for the first six CH-53E "Sea Stallion" heavy-lift helicopters (which can carry 93 percent of all equipment items, including artillery pieces, organic to Marine divisions). Choppers are not a problem. "We appear to be in a good position on our helicopters," says General Killeen.

Armor and artillery are in the ascendancy as well. The Corps already has procured 406 of the latest-model M60A1 main battle tanks and will field 576 of them by 1981. Meanwhile, it is also benefiting from the Army's artillery modernization program. Within another year, moreover, the Marines will have finished extending the range of their eight-inch howitzers by fitting them with new cannon assemblies.

The Corps is obviously already on the move. But it also is scouting the terrain ahead. Led by Major General Fred Haynes, deputy chief of staff for R & D, a top-level panel of officers charged with studying future force requirements weighed in last year with several recommendations for increasing firepower and mobility. Last month (October), General Wilson was asked, during an interview on Armed Forces Radio and Television, what has happened to the "Haynes Report."

"We're working on it at headquarters," he replied. "They [the Haynes team] recommended one or two or three mobile assault regiments or mechanized regiments. I think perhaps we'll move in that direction, but it will have to be gradual. We have no place now where we could train such an organization. We are building up a very sophisticated training center at Twenty-Nine Palms, California, in the high desert, [but] we are short of billeting out there. The 3d Tank Battalion has just been formed there, and we will be sending infantry battalions from Camp Pendleton there to practice what will be a mobile assault regiment concept. But actually to form one of these—and it may be done out there—would take several years."

Needed: A More Revolutionary Pace?

It need not and should not take that long, however, according to William S. Lind, staff aide to Senator Taft for military affairs and Taft's right arm of authorship on the "White Paper." A military historian who describes himself as "pro-Marine but not uncritically so," Lind is among those who believe that the Corps moves but gradually toward complete mechanization at its own and the nation's peril. Says Lind: "The leadership of the Corps tends always to think in terms of evolution. It doesn't have the luxury. It must think in terms of revolution. Pace is crucial."

Characteristically, the Marines believe they can handle their mission. What matters most to them is that the mission, amphibious warfare, is philosophically secure in the Pentagon's strategic planning. The mood at HQMC seems peppery, and General Wilson declares that his troops are "looking good."

Nearly 15 years ago an earlier panel of Marine Corps planners assembled at Quantico to look ahead to the role of the Corps in its third century, which it has now well begun. That panel's report was right on the button.

"The strategic posture which we forecast," it said in part, "argues for substantial forward deployment of forces afloat and suggests that the Navy-Marine amphibious team will continue to constitute one of the most vital and useful elements of our military strategy. The close partnership of the Navy and the Marine Corps will become even more necessary in order to retain the naval supremacy the United States now enjoys. . . .

"Our defense will be essentially perimeter defense of key overseas coastal areas. The coasts of the world will be our borders. From those coasts our offense will be launched, and on those coasts our defense lines will be drawn. In this peripheral, littoral strategy, our amphibious capability will be a crucial element. . . . Many landings will control crises before they erupt."

And so it is, and likely will be.

A Course for Destroyers

What lies beyond the horizon for the destroyer? An experienced tincan skipper envisions the global environment of the next two decades and gives his candid opinion of the role of the destroyer on tomorrow's uncharted waters.

by Elmo R. Zumwalt, Captain, U. S. Navy

Proceedings *author in 1962; Naval Institute President in 1972*

"I first advanced this high-low concept in a November 1962 Proceedings *article entitled 'A Course for Destroyers,' in which I had used the terms 'the complex mainstream' for certain kinds of destroyers (including frigates) and 'the simplified mainstream' for others. Obviously 'high' and 'low' expressed the idea more clearly. 'High' was short for high-performance ships and weapon systems that also were so high-cost that the country could afford to build only a few of them at a time; there are some missions the Navy cannot perform without the great flexibility and versatility of such ships. 'Low' was short for moderate-cost, moderate-performance ships and systems that could be turned out in relatively large numbers; they would ensure that the Navy could be in enough places at the same time to get its job done."*

High-Low

By Admiral Elmo R. Zumwalt, Jr., U. S. Navy (Retired)

From the book entitled On Watch: A Memoir *by Elmo R. Zumwalt, Jr.*
Copyright © *1976 by Elmo R. Zumwalt, Jr.*
To be published by Quadrangle/The New York Times Book Co.
Reprinted by permission of the publisher.

The accelerating obsolescence of the U. S. Navy since the end of World War II as opposed to the impressive growth and modernization of the Soviet Navy during the same period was a contrast I emphasized and dwelt upon in the long interview I had with Secretary of the Navy John Chafee in 1970 when he was searching for a new CNO. Since he chose me I assume he agreed with what I said then on that subject, and I shall summarize it here. I said that, given the Nixon administration's determination to reduce military budgets, the only way I could see for the Navy to free funds for developing up-to-date ships and weapon systems that could cope with the new Russian armaments was to retire immediately large numbers of old ships and aircraft. That meant that the price the nation would have to pay for sufficient and appropriate naval capability in the 1980s would be a seriously reduced naval capability during at least the early Seventies, while the new systems were being designed, built, and deployed.

I said that this was true of both general-purpose (conventional) forces and strategic (nuclear-missile) forces. In the former case, some of our carriers and their escorts had seen service in World War II; in the latter case, the oldest Polaris-Poseidon submarines would, by 1980, reach the end of the 20-year life for which they had been built. I said that three sets of delicate decisions would have to be made. One was how far to reduce current capability so as to get the most money possible for modernization without becoming so weak as to tempt the Soviets into rash action. A second was how to bring the Navy into balance by supplementing the high-performance ships it was building in small numbers, because they were so expensive that small numbers were all it could afford, with new types of ships that had adequate capability for many missions and at the same time were inexpensive enough to build in the larger number required for an American naval presence in many parts of the oceans. The third was how to allocate resources between general-purpose and strategic forces so that the enormously important and enormously expensive strategic forces would neither starve nor consume so much as to reduce conventional capability to a point at which a major conventional threat could be countered only by a threat to escalate to nuclear war.

My colleagues and I made our decisions in those three areas against a background of asymmetrical U. S. and Soviet maritime development, which in turn had resulted from the great dissimilarity of the maritime situations of the two nations. To begin at the beginning, the Soviet Union is a land power in both an economic and a political-military sense, while the United States is, as I like to put it, a "world island" whose every activity is bound up with use of the seas. If it had to, the Soviet Union could feed itself and keep its industry going without ever sending a ship beyond its coastal waters. In addition, all the Soviet Union's most important political relationships, except the one with the United States, are with nations that also are situated on the Eurasian land mass. Russia can protect all her client states or attack all but one of her most likely enemies without going to sea. By contrast, the industry and trade of the United States depend on ocean traffic in both directions and most of her important allies are on the far side of broad oceans as well. The economy of the United States requires that she have a large maritime capability. The political interests and commitments of the United States require that she be capable of having a large military influence overseas. Both of those exigencies, in turn, make a powerful U. S. Navy imperative. Even more to the point, they define the double mission of the U. S. Navy: to keep the seas open for commercial and military traffic of all kinds, which we call "sea control," and to make it possible to apply military power overseas, which we call "projection." In World War II the U. S. Navy was called upon to perform both missions and at the end of that war it was the best balanced, most powerful Navy the world has ever seen. The Soviets on the other hand had virtually no Navy at all; they never had had much of one, and most of it had been destroyed or captured during the fighting.

In the late Forties and early Fifties, when the Cold War and their aspirations to become a world power led the Soviets to begin a naval buildup, they found that having to start from scratch was in one way a great advantage, for it allowed them to "optimize," that is build a Navy to precisely the specifications that would make it most capable of showing strongly against its only likely opponent, the United States. That meant a Navy that could challenge U. S. sea control—for it is obvious that without sea control the projection mission is impossible to carry out. In choosing this as their top priority mission, the Soviets gave themselves a second advantage. Denying sea control to an enemy is a far easier task than maintaining sea control oneself. Denying sea control means cutting lines of communication, which requires fewer ships, less sophisticated equipment and smaller risks than maintaining lines of communication, since a line of communication has to be maintained throughout its length, but can be cut anywhere.

In the war in Southeast Asia, as in the Korean War, the enemy could not dispute U. S. control of the seas and so the Navy's main business became projection: amphibious landings, air strikes, and occasional episodes of naval shore bombardment. Not only did the Navy's share of the budget shrink during those wars because the Army and the Air Force underwent greater attrition of equipment, but under the circumstances the Navy had to put a disproportionate share of the money it did receive into maintaining its capability for projection—its carriers and attack planes, its amphibious vessels, its ships with the weapons for bombardment. Sea-control forces—antisubmarine planes and their carriers and ships suitable for patrol and escort duty—were allowed to obsolesce and, finally, retire without replacement. More damaging yet, work on future sea-control requirements—new types of ships from which planes or helicopters could operate, new techniques for combating submarines, new vessels to escort convoys, new kinds of weapons with which to fight on the surface was postponed for many years. The one exception was nuclear-powered attack submarines, which through Admiral Hyman Rickover's special influence on Capitol Hill got built in ample numbers.

Internal forces in the Navy had contributed to unbalancing it in the 1960s. I no more intend to suggest that George Anderson, David McDonald, or Tom Moorer, the three aviators who preceded me as CNO, deliberately allowed the surface Navy to deteriorate than I would welcome a suggestion by them that I deliberately neglected air during my watch. The point is that for the last quarter-century or more there have been three powerful "unions" in the Navy—the aviators, the submariners, and the surface sailors—and their rivalry has played a large part in the way the Navy has been directed. (The submariners have not had a CNO in recent times, but they have had the aforesaid Admiral

Rickover, who most of the time is more than a match for most CNOs.)

The intense competition for resources and recognition among the three unions—for there is never enough of either to satisfy everybody, or even satisfy anybody—has had both constructive and destructive consequences. It tends to lead the Navy's civilian masters, who presumably are not parochial, to examine alternatives far more rigorously than they would if there were no push-and-shove. It develops a pride in service that is invaluable not only in combat situations, but as an antidote for the routine hardships of peacetime naval duty. It stimulates professional expertise. On the other hand it almost inevitably breeds a set of mind that tends to skew the work of even the fairest, broadest-gauged commander if he is given enough time. Whichever union such a commander comes from, it is hard for him not to favor fellow members, the men he has worked with most closely, when he constructs a staff or passes out choice assignments. It is hard for him not to think first of the needs of his branch, the needs he feels most deeply, when he works up a budget. It is hard for him not to stress the capability of his arm, for he has tested it himself, when he plans an action. I am not the person to evaluate the extent of my own bias, but I think it fair to point out that following three air CNOs in a row, as I did, I was bound to have some redressing to do. Regular rotation of the top jobs among delegates from the respective unions seems to me to be a prerequisite for institutional stability.

The union system has one other curious side effect. Certain crucial activities are outside the jurisdiction of all the unions and therefore tend not to concern them very deeply. No union has a vested interest in mines, which have no bridges for captains to pace. No union has a vested interest in the increasingly great variety of electronic surveillance instruments that operate independently of ships or planes. All the unions should have a vested interest in secure, high-speed communications, but somehow they too have been in no-man's-land. Such adjuncts to fighting, important as they are, receive no automatic institutional protection. Thus, the Navy was far behind the U.S.S.R. and our own Air Force and NASA with regard to use of satellites, computers, and modern communication management techniques. I resolved to do my best to protect the non-union shops from the indifference of the unions.

A final malady that afflicted—and continues to afflict—the whole Navy, though the surface Navy was and is the greatest sufferer, can be described in one word, a word I have used already: Rickover. By virtue of the force of his personality, his apparent permanence in office, his intimate relations with key members of Congress and his statutory independence of the Navy as

Director, Division of Naval Reactors, Energy Research and Development Administration (formerly the Atomic Energy Commission), Admiral Rickover for years had been able to tilt the Navy toward relying exclusively on nuclear propulsion. If nuclear power is not the earthly paradise that "Rick" makes it out to be, it is surely an excellent way to propel warships, chiefly because a nuclear-powered ship can steam at high speed without refueling for ten or 12 years. Thus nuclear power is particularly appropriate in strategic submarines, and advantageous in attack submarines and a limited number of big carriers and their escorts.

"For the last quarter-century or more there have been three powerful 'unions' in the Navy—the aviators, the submariners, and the surface sailors—and their rivalry . . . has had both constructive and destructive consequences."

However, it has a vice that outweighs its virtues in many kinds of vessels. Nuclear-propulsion systems are so big and heavy that making some types of ships nuclear means making them much bigger and hence much more expensive than conventionally powered ships that fight almost as well, as much as five times as expensive in the case of certain types. The sea-control mission, as I have just explained, requires a large number of platforms from which weapons can be fired and planes launched, a large number of ships. In most cases seven or five or even three ships of moderate capability would contribute far more to the success of this mission than one supership, as a series of analyses ordered by Robert McNamara, when he was Secretary of Defense, decisively demonstrated. For 20 years Rickover has been working successfully toward a supership Navy, and so it is partly his doing that for 20 years the Navy has been getting smaller except of course in the item of nuclear-propelled submarines. Occasionally, someone outside the Navy has made the obvious case for numbers of lower cost ships. One of them during my watch was U. Alexis Johnson, an entirely professional foreign service officer, who at the time was Under Secretary of State for Political Affairs. Twenty-seven days after I became CNO Alex wrote a letter to Deputy Secretary of Defense David Packard expressing his concern that the Navy was not adequately addressing the cost-numbers trade-off in going for fewer large expensive systems rather than large numbers of lower cost systems.

I was no stranger to problems of the kind I had to solve in order to "reoptimize" the U. S. Navy to meet the Soviet threat. As soon as President Nixon announced my appointment, in mid-April 1970, a month before I was relieved as Commander, U. S. Naval Forces, Vietnam, I began to create machinery to produce a long-term plan that I hoped would reconcile the dilemmas I had discussed with Secretary Chafee. The first thing I did was to persuade the commander of the Seventh Fleet to lend me Rear Admiral Worth Bagley, then commanding Cruiser-Destroyer Flotilla Seven, to serve as my principal assistant in this project.

I picked Worth for his brains, but it was no accident that I picked a brainy destroyerman rather than a brainy aviator or a brainy submariner. The first imperative as far as I was concerned was for the program to be conceptually ready in the shortest possible time. I had been around Washington long enough to have a clear idea of what was involved in bringing a program from concept to reality through the competitive officeholders in the Department of Defense, through the cheeseparers in the White House budget apparatus, through the political parochialists on four congressional committees and the political opportunists in two houses of Congress—and I had only four years. I named what Worth and I were starting to do "Project 60," to signify my determination to have something to put before John Chafee and Secretary of Defense Mel Laird by the time I had been in office no more than 60 days. Actually there was a lot more to Project 60 than the modernization program that this article deals with. Project 60 was nothing less than a comprehensive plan for my four years as CNO, and included a variety of programs for meeting the two other principal issues the Navy confronted in 1970: how to maintain a high-quality all-volunteer force when the draft expired, which it clearly was about to, and how to maintain sufficient capability during the modernization process for the Navy to continue to perform its assigned missions.

Worth was Project 60's full-time man. From the middle of April to the middle of May, I still had my wartime command responsibilities in Vietnam. Then I took a long trip home, visiting many Navy commands in various parts of the world. The trip made an important contribution to Project 60 because it gave me an opportunity to exchange ideas about it with most of the Navy's top commanders. Worth could not join me in Washington immediately; he was unable to leave his flotilla until August. However another destroyer officer of high intellect was available during the interim period, Captain Stansfield Turner, Secretary Chafee's executive assistant. Stan, a Rhodes Scholar, had just been selected for flag rank, but his new command would not be ready for him until Worth was ready for me, and the Secretary graciously relinquished him to me for six weeks or so. Stan, incidentally, got his fourth star not long ago as Commander-in-Chief of NATO's Southern Forces—CinCSouth. First Stan, then Worth, drew into the work on Project 60 on an ad hoc basis whichever other staff members they needed. I estimate I spent an average of two hours a day on it myself. At the time I also was spending about two hours a day on my new personnel program, about two hours a day on Joint Chiefs' work, and about two hours a day making myself known on Capitol Hill. That left the other eight hours of my working day for running the Navy.

There is an inherent difficulty or reluctance of a democracy, absent a crisis, to keep its attention on military possibilities and contingencies. Another of its effects is to preclude the kind of comprehensive planning and optimal use of assets that occur routinely in the Soviet Union. To speak only of the Soviet Navy, its chief, Admiral Sergei G. Gorshkov, has control of land-based long-range aircraft that can attack our naval platforms with bombs and cruise missiles; in lay terms, he has a piece of the Air Force. Every Soviet merchant ship serves as a surveillance and intelligence collection platform for the Soviet Navy. Many Russian merchant ships are configured so as to be readily useful as naval auxiliaries in the event of war. Even in crises short of war, these ships can be promptly diverted from commercial to military activity. Every Soviet fishing vessel, every space support ship, every oceanographic and survey ship contributes to the Soviet naval mission. From time to time over the years the U. S. Navy has tried to persuade the government to acquire similar assets in order to enhance the total power it might bring to bear in a crisis. However, under our system, with the co-equal Congress and its associated lobbies working outside the Defense Department, and with each agency of the executive branch applying parochial pressure on Congress, it has not been possible to achieve the total maritime strength of which this country is capable. But, this field of effort is potentially so fruitful that I decided during our Project 60 evaluation to see what I could do to make available the resources of outside agencies.

We examined the use of Army helicopters on merchant ships and on escorts on the theory that unless the Navy could control the seas, the Army could not be deployed anyway. This effort did not emerge from the bureaucratic jungle. We asked the Air Force to broaden its contingency plans to include the use of its strategic bombers for mining important waters. That was approved in 1971. We asked the Air Force to install our new Harpoon cruise missiles in its bombers so that it could give the Navy long range support of sea lines, similar to the assistance Admiral Gorshkov was getting. This initiative got nowhere.

I personally believed that the Defense Department was making a great mistake by not requiring some, if not all, of the Air Force's tactical air wings to be carrier capable so that the United States could have optimal air power to use in a typical crisis. In three of the four crises during my watch—Jordan, September 1970;

Indo-Pakistan, December 1971; Yom Kippur War, October 1973—the U. S. Air Force was totally incapable of playing a role due to lack of access to airfields, and only carrier aviation could be brought to bear. I brought this up personally with General Jack Ryan, Chief of Staff of the Air Force. After studying the problem, he declined to take it on. I gave the Secretary of the Navy a copy of a proposed directive for the Secretary of Defense to forward to the Secretary of the Air Force and the Secretary of the Navy on the subject of "employment of Air Force aircraft on carriers," that "died on the field of honor." I then went to Melvin Laird and his deputy David Packard and urged that they get it done. Both of them thought it was a good idea, yet both declined to touch it. Their reason was probably a good one, that the Congress and its lobbies would not permit it, and a jurisdictional wrangle would hurt the Defense budget. On the other hand, General Leonard Chapman, Commandant of the Marine Corps, readily agreed to use Marine aircraft to help augment carrier wings as necessary, recognizing that the Marines must be able "to get there" and had better help the Navy to do so, given our dramatic reduction in power.

We tried using merchant ships for refueling at sea and found they could do it. But we never could get the leverage within the executive branch to get the merchant ships being built in this country properly configured during construction so that they would be most efficient in that role. We examined the feasibility of using commercial container ships for replenishment of ammunition and other logistics in conjunction with a heavy lift helicopter. This proved practicable but no program was approved. We examined the feasibility of giving super tankers the capability to handle vertical-short takeoff or landing (V/STOL) aircraft and anti-submarine helicopters during wartime, together with the necessary shipboard equipment so that they could provide their own fighter, antimissile, and anti-submarine capability. The answer was that it was technically but not politically feasible to bridge the jurisdictional differences between DoD and the Maritime Administration.

As I have said, the underlying theory of that segment of the project dealing with modernization was to accelerate the retirement of obsolete ships in order to free as much money as possible for new development and construction. We then worked out a concept we called "high-low." I first advanced this concept in a November 1962 *Proceedings* article entitled "A Course for Destroyers," in which I had used the terms "the complex mainstream" for certain kinds of destroyers (including frigates) and "the simplified mainstream" for others. Obviously "high" and "low" expressed the idea more clearly. "High" was short for high-performance ships and weapon systems that also were so high-cost that the country could afford to build only a few of them at a time; there are some missions the Navy cannot perform without the great flexibility and versatility of such ships. "Low" was short for moderate-cost, moderate-performance ships and systems that could be turned out in relatively large numbers; they would ensure that the Navy could be in enough places at the same time to get its job done. In sum, an all-high Navy would be so expensive that it would not have enough ships to control the seas. An all-low Navy would not have the capability to meet certain kinds of threats or perform certain kinds of missions. In order to have both enough ships and good enough ships there had to be a mix of high and low.

The innovative part of this program was the low. In contrast with the Soviet Navy, which always has operated on the principle that "better is the enemy of good enough," the U. S. Navy has traditionally insisted on traveling first class. There was more than enough high, more than enough too high, already under construction or under contract when I began Project 60, and almost no low at all. This was true especially in the case of ships. A new group of too sophisticated, too expensive attack submarines, the USS *Los Angeles* (SSN-688) class, was being built at what would soon approach $300 million a copy. I knew something about that submarine because the concept for it had been sprung upon me as a fait accompli when I was director of the Division of Systems Analysis in the late sixties. That was the office where all concepts for new weapon systems were supposed to be worked up first. Somehow Admiral Rickover had gotten the work done elsewhere and without my knowledge. I protested, but my immediate boss, a submariner himself, approved the concept anyway.

Similarly, the Marines were in the process of getting something they had long wanted, a big modern amphibious ship, the LHA, which also was too expensive at $133 million a copy in 1973 dollars, but at least had the virtue that each one could carry as many troops as the several smaller landing vessels it replaced. (We used 1973 dollars in all Project 60's low calculations because the fiscal year 1973 budget would be the first in which low projects were funded.)

The day before I took command, but with my assent, the Navy signed a contract for 30 8,000-ton $100 million 30-knot destroyers of the new *Spruance* (DD-963) class to replace the almost obsolete 2,100- and 2,200-ton World War II destroyers that were still serving as escort vessels for carriers and convoys. At that time the Navy had in operation or under construction only 150 of the 250 escorts its studies showed were needed for the future. The *Spruance*s would raise that figure to 180.

The genesis of DD-963 is a story of some interest because it typified the Navy's institutional resistance to modest programs. When Paul Nitze was Secretary of the Navy in the mid-1960s he pushed vigorously for the development of a new class of inexpensive escorts to succeed the *Knox* (DE-1052), an escort that would begin to join the fleet in the late Sixties. The DE-1052 had been a breakthrough for advocates of low. It was a modestly equipped single-screw vessel that many sailors of the old school predicted would be unable to keep up with fast carriers, and in any case would forever be under tow because one propeller, one engine, and one boiler were obviously not enough for a warship. These forecasts proved to be almost entirely wrong. DE-1052 was no star, but she performed adequately and since her cost was low, the Navy could afford probably twice as many of her as of a more brilliant performer. It was a ship of this character, with somewhat improved performance, that Nitze wanted as the next class of escorts. However, the admiral he put in charge of the project, together with the engineering duty officers on the development staff, found a host of technical reasons to recommend a larger, more expensive ship. Paul fired that admiral and got a new one to manage the project. The new admiral came up with the same findings. My guess is that both of them thought they were speaking for the CNO. Anyway, three project managers later, when the new escort finally got designed, it was the far too expensive DD-963.

There were two other very high programs under way. One involved nuclear-powered aircraft carriers (CVANs), the most expensive ships there are. The *Nimitz* (CVAN-68) was under construction. The *Dwight D. Eisenhower* (CVAN-69) was being developed; that is, work was going forward on her long-lead-time components, the reactors particularly. The *Carl Vinson* (CVAN-70), was on the drawing board, but no money had yet been authorized. The second program involved DLGNs, nuclear-powered guided missile frigates, used to escort the nuclear carriers. A class of five was being planned by Admiral Rickover.

Most of those high ships, SSN-688, LHA, DD-963, CVANs, DLGNs were given. Congress had authorized them and appropriated funds for them and the Navy had signed contracts for them. Moreover there was no question about their quality. The trouble with them was that they were too good in the sense that the Navy had given up too much to get them. They came within the purview of Project 60 only to the limited extent that we could increase or decrease the construction tempo, or the total number of each ship delivered. And that narrow option was narrowed further by the absence from even a drawing board of any low types. We would have to start on low from scratch. That meant that for at least two years, while preliminary design work was proceeding, practically all the Navy's construction money, that which had been provided by my predecessor and that which we hoped to add by early retirement, would of necessity go into the high. Another of Project 60's theoretical underpinnings, to correct as rapidly as possible the tilt toward projection and away from sea control that the Korean and Vietnam wars had produced, dictated how the high money should be spent. We cut back the LHA program (projection) from nine ships to five, as the contract allowed us to, a decision made easier by the cost overruns and construction delays that were occurring at the Litton shipyard in Pascagoula, Mississippi, where the *Spruance* class also was to be built. Since we wanted to get an inexpensive escort into the fleet as part of our low, we resolved not to expedite DD-963. However, escort vessels are a critical component of sea-control forces, so we resolved not to slow down DD-963 either but simply to proceed with the program as it had been planned. We put DLGN in the same category. We decided we would try to expedite work on the fourth nuclear carrier since for reasons of both obsolescence and operating costs the carrier forces were dwindling fast. As for the SSN-688, like everything in which Rickover has a hand, it had complications leading to ramifications resulting in shenanigans.

Project 60 visualized starting work on four new classes of ships, all of them designed primarily for sea-control duty. Three of them were inexpensive and well within the means of existing technology, and one was a long-range research and development project. The simplest and cheapest was a high-speed 170-ton hydrofoil patrol boat, PHM, armed with a new weapon I shall describe later in this chapter, the Harpoon cruise missile. Its purpose is mainly as a strike vessel against enemy surface craft. It will patrol narrow or coastal waters like the Gulf of Tonkin or the Mediterranean or the Red Sea, or serve as a low-value trailer of high-value Soviet ships in such waters. We found this concept so attractive in Project 60 that we made a decision immediately to deploy two gunboats (PGs) with 3-inch guns to act as interim trailers in the Mediterranean. PHM's advantage to the Navy is that in those places where it can operate, it will replace on a one-to-one basis much larger ships, with much larger fuel consumption and big payrolls, thus freeing those ships for essential deepwater duties, and more important, making it possible for the larger and more valuable ships to be outside the range of surprise Soviet cruise missile attack.

Second there was the patrol frigate, PF (now FFG-7), another attempt to get that modest escort vessel that Paul Nitze had seen miraculously metamorphosed into DD-963. Like the *Knox* class, the FFG-7 is a single screw

ship of about 28 knots and, at 3,400 tons, about half the tonnage of DD-963, with a somewhat smaller crew, and about half as costly to build. We insisted on a top limit of 50 million 1973 dollars. Yet it is almost as heavily armed as DD-963, since Harpoon is the basic weapon in each and each carries two helicopters. The FFG-7 may have some limitations as an escort for carriers, particularly nuclear carriers. Part of its low cost comes from foregoing some speed and range and part from using certain less sophisticated kinds of sensing and communications equipment. However, it is quite adequate as a patrol vessel or as an escort for convoys of merchantmen or naval auxiliaries and, like the *Knox,* can serve as an escort for carriers in a pinch. The surface union was at first no more enamored of the PF than it had been of the DE-1052. That the program is on track and has turned out so well is a tribute to Vice Admiral Frank Price, the deputy charged with preventing a repetition of the DD-963 growth problem.

The third "low" component, and the one nearest my heart, was an extremely austere carrier we first called the "air capable ship," then the "sea control ship." She was to be a 17,000-ton 25-knot ship with endurance of 7,500 nautical miles at 20 knots. She was to be capable of carrying 14 helicopters and three Harrier V/STOL planes. She could handle only such aircraft because she would have no launching catapults or arresting gear for landings. Her price was to be 100 million 1973 dollars, about one-eighth the cost of a nuclear carrier. Her principal peacetime purpose was to show the flag in dangerous waters, especially the Mediterranean and the Western Pacific where the Sixth and Seventh Fleets operate, so that the big carriers that are the Navy's most important ships could withdraw from the front lines and deploy out of reach of an enemy first strike, thus putting themselves in a favorable position

"A final malady that afflicted—and continues to afflict—the whole Navy, though the surface Navy was and is the greatest sufferer, can be described in one word: Rickover."

to respond to such a strike—and therefore to deter it. To use the undoubted vulnerability of carriers to Soviet missiles as an argument for getting rid of carriers, as some Defense critics do, seems to me a classic example of throwing out baby with the bathwater. The solution to the problem is to deploy big carriers out of reach of cruise missiles and replace them with low-value ships that at the same time have some defensive capability, to wit sea control ships.

In a wartime situation the positions of the two kinds of carriers would be reversed: the big, powerful ones would fight their way into the most dangerous waters, destroying opposition beyond cruise missile range with their planes, and the sea control ships would serve in mid-ocean. The Navy's 12 or at best 15 big carriers would be needed in wartime for the large, complicated tasks of conducting air strikes against enemy vessels or shore installations, searching out and destroying submarines over long distances and at high speeds, providing air support for the land battle, interdicting land- or sea-based enemy air and cruise-missile attack against ships and ports. They had far too much offensive capability to waste on convoy duty. Yet in any real war situation there might be at sea as many as 20 convoys of merchantmen, troop transports, and naval auxiliaries in need of air protection from the time they left the reach of land-based air until they entered areas where the deployed carriers were operating. Providing this protection would be the chief wartime mission of the sea control ships. Eight vessels capable of that mid-ocean job could be built for the price of one full-fledged carrier, which in any case, if it was assigned to convoy duty, could protect only one convoy instead of eight. Moreover the SCS would be fast and easy to build because all of her systems—propulsion, weapons, sensing, communications—had already been proved out in other vessels and needed minimal modifications. Clearly SCS was a good investment. Unfortunately it was seen as a good investment when it was first proposed by no union but my own. Both the nuclear folk and the aviators saw it as infringing on their turf. Later the aviators got behind it.

Finally, for the future, there was the "surface-effect ship." This would be a 4,000–5,000-ton vessel that could skim just above the surface of the ocean at 80 to 100 knots. Such a ship, which could cross the Atlantic, say, in not much more than a day, virtually immune from underwater or surface attack, could revolutionize naval warfare. At that speed, it need not be equipped with a launching catapult and arresting gear; it could carry four or five carrier planes, even the big F-14s, and turn them virtually into V/STOLs. Thirty-five such ships, a member of my staff once calculated, could carry two divisions of troops to Europe in three days. The ramifications of such capability in antisubmarine, antiaircraft, and other kinds of warfare are endless. We put the development of this ship—for which the basic propulsion technology already was in existence—in a ten-to-15-year time frame. As of this writing two promising 100-ton prototypes have been built. I have ridden on one. It's quite a thrill.

In addition to these measures for increasing sea-control capability in the future, we hit upon one expedient for increasing it overnight, as it were. This idea, suggested by then Rear Admiral James L. Holloway, III, was to make all carriers, which customarily had been designated either as attack carriers (CVAs) or antisubmarine carriers (CVSs) into dual-purpose vessels. This increased sea-control capability because CVAs outnumbered CVSs by almost two to one. All that this involved was modifying the deck loadings so that each ship carried both attack and antisubmarine planes instead of one or the other, adding some minor command-and-control apparatus and, of course, installing the spare parts and the maintenance equipment that such change in deck loading necessitated. The cost of thus changing a carrier over was $975,000, a sum so miniscule by comparison with what almost anything else in Defense costs nowadays that even Senator William Proxmire might not bother to pick it up if he saw it lying in a Pentagon corridor, but just leave it for the sweepers. Of course, modifying carriers in such a way dissatisfied some people. They pointed out (correctly) that making a carrier capable of two dissimilar missions made it less capable than it had been of either one. They also pointed out (again correctly) that on the record of recent wars and crises a carrier was more likely to be called on for projection than for sea control. However, a 12-carrier Navy with as much water to cover as the U. S. Navy has would simply be incapable of keeping the sea lines of communication open in a major war if those carriers had no sea-control capability, and I thought that was too big a risk to run. Fortunately, the majority of my colleagues, including the most important sachems in the aviators' union, agreed with me.

As might be expected in a Navy that aviators had presided over for a decade, we were in good shape as far as types of planes were concerned. During the latter years of the Southeast Asia war, CVAs had carried two types of modern attack plane, the workhorse A-7, a light, relatively inexpensive machine that performed most strike and ground support missions, and the heavier, costlier A-6, which had similar armament but was built and equipped to operate effectively in bad weather and at night. Both were recent additions to the fleet. Both planes had proved their value in Vietnam. Both, with technical modifications, would be serviceable for another decade at least. The aviation admirals were content with them. There was no reason for me not to be.

On the sea-control side a new antisubmarine plane, the S-3, was about to go into production at Lockheed. It contained up-to-the-minute equipment that enabled it to drop sonar buoys over large areas, monitor the signals of those buoys and fire Mark 46 torpedoes at whatever enemy submarines the buoys—or other localizing sensing devices—find. There was every reason to believe that this plane would be serviceable for many years. The problem it presented was that at $13 million a copy it was not inexpensive, to use a cautious double negative, and Congress was showing some reluctance to buy as many as the Navy needed. The S-3 came into Project 60, therefore, as an action item for the Navy's legislative liaison people.

Somewhat further from production than the S-3, though already contracted out to Grumman, was the plane most of us thought of as the new star of the Navy's air arm, a fighter, the F-14. It was to replace the F-4, which had been designed in 1954 and had proved itself a superb one-on-one machine in fighting MiGs over Vietnam. However, with the massive deployment of cruise missiles by the Soviets, the day of the one-on-one fighter was ending; it was not capable of defending ships against a massive cruise missile attack. The F-14 was. In addition to excellent flight characteristics, it had a new missile system, the Phoenix, able to intercept Russian Foxbat aircraft at altitudes above 80,000 feet. And it had an extraordinary fire-control system that could track 24 targets simultaneously, automatically choose the six most threatening and fire at them simultaneously. Such equipment comes high. The F-14 is a very expensive plane, to use a well-justified double positive, even when you consider that the multiplied capability it gives a carrier makes operating with a reduced number of carriers feasible. The precise price of a single plane is harder to state than that of a ship, since planes are bought by the hundreds rather than by the fives or tens, and the unit price goes down sharply as the size of the buy goes up. However, it is pretty hard to find a way of stating F-14's price that makes it less than $14 million in 1973 dollars, and pretty easy to find a way of stating it that makes it a lot more.

I had become convinced that the F-14 was the world's best fighter plane long before becoming CNO. In 1966, when I came back to Washington from San Diego (after a year as a new rear admiral in command of Cruiser-Destroyer Flotilla Seven) to set up the Navy's Systems Analysis Division, my first assignment from Secretary of the Navy Paul Nitze was to study the cost effectiveness of the F-111B plane in comparison with all competition. The reader may recall that there had been quite a controversy in the Pentagon several years earlier when Robert McNamara had ordered that there be as much commonality as possible between the new land-based fighter plane the Air Force needed and the new carrier-based fighter plane the Navy needed. Thus was born the swing-wing plane that first was called the TFX, then the F-111, the Air Force's version being F-111A and the Navy's F-111B. Despite heroic efforts by the Secretary of Defense and Secretary of the Navy to make F-111B successful, the compromises that had to be made to develop an airframe capable of performing two different missions led over time to greater and greater weight, and it presently became a close question as to whether the plane could land on and take off from a carrier.

It was while this weight question was still in doubt that Secretary McNamara asked the Navy to examine again the cost effectiveness of the plane, assuming for the purpose of the study that it *could* land on and take off from a carrier. I soon learned that an earlier generation of analysts had done their work well. The fire control and missile system had been brilliantly designed to deal with the Navy's special problem—to crowd into a small airfield at sea a few fighter planes with the capability to search the air surrounding a carrier task force for hundreds of miles and provide a very long range capability to kill many airplanes and cruise missiles coming from several directions simultaneously. The study concluded that if the F-111B could use a carrier, it was by all odds the most cost effective aircraft for fleet air defense and other fighter roles.

However, by the following year it had become almost certain that the F-111B would not be able to use a carrier. Meanwhile, four companies had sent in bids to produce a fighter that put the F-111B's engine, fire control system, and missile in a new airframe. I did another study that showed that this new airplane, subsequently known as F-14A, was probably the way to go. The Navy decided to go that way. By March of 1973, to get ahead of myself, I was able to report to Congress that our calculations showed that when we compare a 13-carrier force carrying 301 F-14s with a 16-carrier force carrying 903 of the old F-4s, we found the smaller force to be militarily more effective; $2.5 billion cheaper in procurement costs; $500 million a year cheaper in operating costs; and requiring 17,000 fewer sailors.

Helicopters are coming into increasing use in naval warfare. They have been used for many years as rescue craft on board carriers, and for some time troop-carrying helicopters have been an important element in the amphibious forces. Project 60 demonstrated that we could achieve high payoff if escort vessels carried one or two helos on their decks to use as aids in detecting incoming aircraft, cruise missiles, and submarines. We had available in inventory over 100 SH-2s, a sort of all-purpose helo that was not highly satisfactory for the new mission, being too light to load with all the equipment the mission calls for, but it was adequate and inexpensive and available, so we decided to adapt the SH-2 for the near term and at the same time begin R&D on a more advanced machine. We called the new helo, together with its embarked detection and kill equipment, LAMPS, for light airborne multi-purpose system, a combination of sensors to find submarines and equipment to fire Mark 46 torpedoes at them. Expediting LAMPS, which was already in the design stage, was one of the high priority items in Project 60. The SH-3, the carrier rescue helo, which is bigger than the SH-2, is the one we planned to put on the sea control ship. The third important component in Project 60 that involved helicopters was to economize on and modernize minesweeping techniques by retiring almost all our surface minesweeping vessels and adapting the big CH-53 helicopters the Marines were using for amphibious operations for minesweeping. In the mid-Sixties, helicopters had successfully demonstrated a modest capability to sweep moored mines and a study had recommended they be used for this task. By 1970, helos had doubled their rates of sweeping mechanical mines

"In sum, an all-high Navy would be so expensive that it would not have enough ships to control the seas. An all-low Navy would not have the capability to meet certain kinds of threats or perform certain kinds of missions. In order to have both enough ships and good enough ships there had to be a mix of high and low."

and had demonstrated a significant potential to sweep magnetic mines. Our cost analyses showed that shifting the emphasis to helos for minesweeping could achieve significant savings on both operation and maintenance costs. In addition helicopters had the operational advantage over ships of being able to deploy rapidly to any location in the world. Developing the equipment and techniques took time and money, and meant going almost entirely without minesweeping capability for more than two years, which was a pretty big risk. Fortunately we got away with it. The new system was in operation by 1973, when the Navy was called upon to sweep the mines out of Haiphong harbor as part of the Vietnam cease-fire agreement, and the force that did that job proceeded almost immediately thereafter to repeat its performance in the Suez Canal. In these operations the ability of the helicopters to sweep areas much faster than surface ships and with less manpower demonstrated that this concept was a winner.

When it came to weapons, all of us who worked up Project 60 felt strongly that the most urgent task by far was to develop and deploy a proper cruise missile as rapidly as possible, in surface vessels, particularly escorts, first, then as soon thereafter as possible in planes and submarines. To my mind the Navy's dropping in the 1950s of a promising program for a cruise missile called "Regulus" was the single worst decision about weapons it made during my years of service. That decision was based on the theory that our carriers were so effective that we did not need cruise missiles, though I always have suspected that the reluctance of the aviators' union to give up any portion of its jurisdiction played a large part in the decision. In any case, without cruise missiles practically all our long-range offensive capability was crowded onto the decks of a few carriers.

Even those pets of Rickover's, the enormously expensive nuclear-propelled guided-missile frigates (DLGNs) remained almost purely defensive ships without cruise missiles. It was another case of numbers being more to the point than quality.

Fortunately, while I was heading the Division of Systems Analysis, the Secretary of the Navy had in effect rescinded the Regulus decision by directing my office to do a study that would lead to a program for a new cruise missile, Harpoon. The most significant string attached to this order was the verbal message relayed to me through the aide system that the missile was to have a range of no more than 50 miles if it was to be acceptable to the CNO, Admiral Moorer. Evidently the aviators' union was still nervous about its prerogatives. We did the study, it was accepted, and a development program got under way, in the course of which Harpoon's range increased a few miles. However, the program was not proceeding at a rapid enough pace to suit the needs of a Navy that was in the process of divesting itself of much of its other offensive capability. Expediting Harpoon to the maximum extent possible was one of Project 60's most urgent proposals. And to fill the gap until Harpoon became operational, we directed interim programs adapting various surface-to-air missiles into a short range surface role temporarily.

One other weapon whose development we proposed to accelerate was Captor, a rather spooky mine that, when it detects an approaching submarine, releases a Mark 46 torpedo to make a run against it. This was one of the cases of a program proceeding slowly for no other reason than that no union was pushing it; it clearly was a weapon that could be of great importance in fulfilling the mission of denying straits to the Soviets.

Finally, to round out only the most important of Project 60's 52 separate points, there were several kinds of "non-union" electronic systems that badly needed strengthening. These had been heavily on my mind since 1965–66, when I commanded a cruiser-destroyer flotilla in the First Fleet, and took part in four fleet exercises designed to test, among other things, communications, detection, and deception systems. Those exercises showed serious deficiencies in at least four areas where the Soviets were known to be extremely effective. The most important was in battle-condition communications within the fleet. In order to fight a modern battle successfully it is necessary to transmit and receive rapidly and securely—in other words without deciphering or jamming by the enemy—a staggeringly large volume of data about the rapidly changing speeds, courses and ranges of hundreds of ships, planes, and missiles, and about changes in the intentions of our own forces and in the estimated intentions of the enemy. Otherwise ships will not perform the correct maneuvers, planes will not go where they're supposed to, missiles will not hit their targets. Technological development in electronics has been so rapid that it is almost impossible to keep up with. When the World War II battleship *New Jersey* (BB-62) was recommissioned for shore bombardment duty during the Southeast Asia war, it turned out that her communications systems, the finest that could be produced when she was built, were so far out of date that she was virtually out of communication with the fleet. The communications systems in a modern front-line ship are probably a hundred times more effective and complicated—and expensive—than the *New Jersey*'s, yet they still have a hard time handling the amount of work they are given to do, reliant as they still are on high frequency transmission with manual transmission methodology. We proposed to increase our investment in this critical field by almost three-quarters. It is a large sum if you do not compare it with the cost, say, of one SSN-688-class submarine.

Besides this general problem in communications, a special, particularly difficult one was communicating reliably with submerged submarines. Historically submarines in naval engagements have operated almost entirely on their own because there was no way to control their activities, minute by minute, and fit them into a battle plan. But of course their effectiveness would be greatly enhanced if such coordination were possible. We wanted to work harder on this problem. A similar, and perhaps even more critical, problem is maintaining communications with strategic submarines without, of course, giving away their positions. The most persuasive criticism made of the effectiveness of the Polaris-Poseidon system is that sometimes it is difficult to stay in touch with the boats and that in a nuclear exchange situation a breakdown in communications would have major consequences indeed. This was an aspect of communications in which there was intense union interest; the reason progress was slow was the inherent difficulty of the problem.

In sensing and detection, acoustic and electronics, our equipment was quite good, but this is a field in which there always is need for improvement, especially in the electronics field where the Soviets were clearly ahead of us. We needed higher probabilities of detection in order to reduce the losses we would take in wartime from the undetected platforms which would get through. Much of the newest sensing and detection equipment operates out of buoys or satellites or other kinds of devices that no union cares much about, so it always is necessary for top management to take special care that work in this area is not neglected. The same can be said about the deception devices designed to frustrate the enemy sensing and detection system, with

the addition that this is one of the several places where the Russians are well ahead of us. One of Project 60's most potentially worthwhile innovations was to call for a central office with the responsibility for overseeing and coördinating all electronic warfare and command-and-control projects, instead of leaving them to the mercy of individual project managers as in the past. High energy laser development was accelerated as a result of Project 60.

I hope it is clear from this perhaps too discursive account of the main features of Project 60 that it had a central theme: to reoptimize the Navy so that it was equipped to meet the specific threats that the Soviet Navy posed. While we had been engaged in Vietnam, the Soviets, driven by the lesson of the Cuban Missile Crisis, had built a force that came close to being able to challenge our control of the seas. They had two-and-a-half times as many attack submarines as we. They had cruise missiles in many of these submarines and in many ships in their rapidly growing surface fleet and in their land-based naval aircraft. They had superior electronics. Meanwhile Korea and Vietnam had tilted the U. S. Navy dangerously away from sea control. Project 60 was an effort to begin to redress the balance. It was completed almost on schedule. I briefed the Secretary of Defense on it on 10 September, 72 days after I had been sworn in. The Secretary of the Navy had approved it earlier. Laird appeared to be pleased with it. My own attitude probably is reflected best in some comments I made to the very first meeting of my CNO's Executive Panel on 24 October 1970.

"I haven't really met my original objective. I had hoped that we could get going very quickly with Project 60 as a pilot effort toward changing direction, and by the end of that period we would have this group [the CEP] up to speed so that we could pass the baton without any significant missteps. As is so often the case we were just not able to get it set up that quickly. The Project 60 effort has been completed, and it expresses some changes of direction, but not as many as I would have liked. However, it represents the best we could do with a reasonable degree of consensus. This was also all we could manage in time to have much impact on this year's budget."

"I find myself with a great sense of impatience in that I have been in the job for four months (and that represents 8 percent of my time) and as yet I have only gotten the rudder over about 10 degrees. I am really looking forward to the fruit of this effort. I advised all flag officers in distributing the presentation to them on 16 September 1970 [that] I considered that [it] set forth 'the direction in which we direct the Navy to move in the next few years.'"

Warship Design: Ours and Theirs

By Captain James W. Kehoe, Jr., U. S. Navy

The design of current Soviet warships seems to give top priority to the same characteristics—firepower and mobility—that the United States did in World War II. Modern U. S. warship designs, however, stress electronics and habitability and give the lowest priority to those characteristics the Soviets rate highest: weapons and propulsion. We and they may both be right. A strategist/statesman of Admiral Gorshkov's stature ought to know what he wants of his ships—just as we ought to know what we want of ours.

Increasingly, over the past decade, American naval officers have been asking why Soviet surface combatants appear to be smaller, faster, and yet more heavily armed than those of the U. S. Navy. And, why do they appear to have better seakeeping ability? Have the Soviets learned something about designing ships that we don't know about? Why can't we build ships like the Soviets?

In an effort to answer these questions in a reasonable and quantitative manner, the Naval Ship Engineering Center, Hyattsville, Maryland, conducted an engineering analysis of selected U. S. and Soviet frigates, destroyers, and cruisers, with the objective of identifying and quantifying the differences in U. S. and Soviet design practices in the major ship subsystem areas of hull, propulsion, endurance, habitability, electronics, and weapons.

U. S. Navy ships are designed to satisfy specifically stated mission requirements in terms of payload carried and platform performance attained. *Payload* identifies the equipment carried by a ship to fulfill her military mission, i.e., weapons, ammunition, aircraft, detection, control, and communications equipment. While the term "load" denotes "weight," the ship designer is equally concerned about the other physical characteristics of this equipment, such as internal volume and support requirements. *Platform performance* is defined as maximum and sustained speed, cruising range and associated cruising speed, stores endurance, and the quality of the environment provided for the payload and the

USS Fox (*CG-33*)

"Kresta II"

personnel on board. The latter characteristic includes such diverse considerations as safety, comfort, availability of repair parts, ease of access, vulnerability, noise, and electromagnetic interference problems.

Mission requirements are derived from task and mission statements which in turn are related to potential enemy threats. The magnitude and priority of these requirements have a great influence on the size and cost of a ship's design. Also, for a given fixed value of size or cost, it is possible to realize a variation in performance by trading off capability among and between the elements of payload and platform performance.

Therefore, early in the conceptual phase of ship design, a series of trade-off studies are conducted to determine the combination of characteristics which can best fulfill operational requirements, optimize effectiveness, and keep the cost and size of a ship within limits dictated by both budgetary and performance considerations. Within such limits various combinations of endurance, armament, and other features are possible. For example, if the space provided for one function is increased, the space for another function must be reduced, or the ship's size and cost will be increased.

Because ship size and cost are so dependent on requirements, any valid comparison between U. S. and Soviet warship designs must be made on the basis of all the requirements. This is not always easy to do, particularly for Soviet ships, because the existence of some requirements is not nearly so evident as others. For example, habitability features, shock resistance, and fuel tankage are not outwardly obvious as is a gun mount, missile director, or electronic countermeasures (ECM) antenna. Yet, their implications on ship size and cost are just as real, and their influence on military effectiveness may be just as important.

It is also difficult to make valid comparisons between ships of the U. S. Navy and those of the Soviet Navy because the missions assigned to U. S. ships are not the same as those assigned to Soviet ships. For example, U. S. surface combatants must meet the demands of escorting fast carrier task forces worldwide, whereas Soviet ships do not have to meet this requirement. Soviet ships, on the other hand, require a much larger offensive capability against other surface ships which corresponding U. S. surface combatants operating with the support of aircraft carriers have not previously required, i.e., surface-to-surface missile systems. The U. S. Navy, however, is currently planning to enhance the offensive missile capability of its surface combatants to reduce their dependence on carrier air support.

Furthermore, the military effectiveness of a naval ship is determined both by the capability of her payload to detect and destroy the enemy, and by the platform's capability to transport this payload and the personnel who man it to the scene of action, and to support it there. In this article, consideration is given only to the effectiveness of the platform, and no attempt has been made to assess the effectiveness of the payload carried.

Much of the information on Soviet destroyers included in this report was obtained from *Jane's Fighting Ships: 1974–75, Weyer's Warships of the World: 1973,* Siegfried Breyer's *Guide to the Soviet Navy* (Annapolis, Md.: Naval Institute Press, 1970), and various other unclassified sources. Additional information on the Soviet ships was estimated by a process that is an adaptation of the one used by the U. S. Navy to do its own design studies.

Hull: A comparison of the trend in the hull size of the U. S. and Soviet surface combatants built since World War II is shown in Figure 1 in terms of the full-load displacements of U. S. ships and those which were estimated for Soviet ships. It is readily apparent that U. S. Navy Fleet operators are correct in their assessment that Soviet ships are generally smaller than their U. S. counterparts.

U. S. Navy frigates (FF), destroyers (DD), and cruisers (CG) have more than doubled in size since World War II.[1] The exception to this growth trend is the recently designed 3,400-ton guided-missile frigate (FFG-7), formerly called the patrol frigate (PF-109 class). Soviet frigates and destroyers, which appear to have been designed for a coastal defense and sea denial mission, have remained rather modest in size.

However, from the 5,600-ton "Kynda" in 1962, the

[1]As reported on pages 106 and 107 of the March 1975 issue of the *Proceedings,* as of 1 July 1975, U. S. Navy ships are now classified to conform to terms used by other navies of the world. Generally, and for this study, the changes are as follows: Ships formerly referred to as escort ships (DE) are now called frigates (FF); ships formerly referred to as frigates (DLG) are now called cruisers (CG); destroyers (DD) remain unchanged.

Figure 1 *Size Trend*

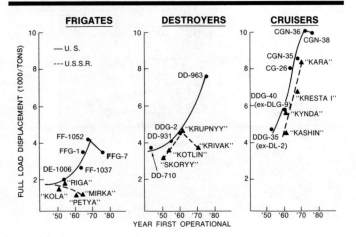

size of Soviet cruisers had grown significantly by 1972, with the introduction of the 8,500-ton "Kara." This growth in Soviet cruisers is in consonance with the introduction of the *Moskva*-class helicopter-cruiser in 1967 and the reported construction of two 35–40,000 ton *Kiev*-class ASW cruisers with a V/STOL aircraft and helicopter capability. Such growth in major ships may be indicative of a recent expansion in the Soviet Navy's defensive mission of sea denial to an expanded one of sea control and, perhaps, to one of being able to project military capability ashore.

To provide for the future modification of U. S. Navy ships, it is general policy to include a provision for a certain weight addition of a specified amount and vertical location. The stability, structural and, usually, speed calculations which are performed on the ship include this margin. Certain systems, notably electrical, are sized on the assumption of a future growth, and these margins are reflected in the ship as designed. In addition to provision for general growth, there have been occasions when design allowances were made for future weapons or sensor systems as replacements for interim systems with which the ship was initially out-fitted.

The compact design and smaller auxiliary systems estimated for Soviet ships appear to make them less amenable to easy modification than U. S. Navy ships. On the other hand, the Soviets appear willing to regularly update weapons, electronics, propulsion, and other shipboard systems through major modification during long overhaul periods.

In early 1973, the Naval Ship Engineering Center, with support from the Naval Ship Research and Development Center, Carderock, Maryland, completed a detailed comparative study of the slamming, deck wetness, and roll stabilization characteristics of U. S. and Soviet surface combatants. The results were published in the November 1973 issue of the *Proceedings*.[2] These results indicated that Soviet warships have better sea-keeping ability than their U. S. counterparts.

The results of slamming comparisons indicated that the average maximum rough water speed of U. S. ships with a relatively fine hull form and an extremely large bow sonar dome, is slightly less than Soviet ships of similar length with a relatively full hull form and without such a large bow dome.

The results of deck wetness comparisons demonstrate that the Soviets have built more hulls to designs which have good deck wetness characteristics than has the United States. The comparatively poor position of the U. S. in the deck wetness study was caused by the

[2]See J. W. Kehoe, Jr., "Destroyer Seakeeping: Ours and Theirs," U. S. Naval Institute *Proceedings*, November 1973, pp. 26–37.

performance of the DD-710, FF-1040, and FF-1052 designs, to which over one-third of all U. S. destroyer type hulls have been built.

The fact that Soviet surface combatants have been fitted with anti-roll fin stabilizers as a standard design practice since the early 1950s was an extremely interesting finding in the 1973 seakeeping study. This accounts for the majority of these Soviet ships having better rolling characteristics than comparable U. S. ships, since only the FF-1037, the FF-1040, and FF-1052 classes are fitted with fin stabilizers.

Propulsion: A comparison of the trend in the speed of U. S. and Soviet surface combatants is shown in Figure 2. The speeds of both U. S. and Soviet DDs and CGs show a decrease of about two to three knots since World War II, with the Soviet ships maintaining a two to three knot speed advantage over their U. S. counterparts. On the other hand, there has been an increase of about four to five knots in the speed of both U. S. and Soviet frigates with the Soviet ships maintaining a three to four knot speed advantage. The greater speed of Soviet ships is attributed to a mission requirement for this speed and to their willingness to invest in propulsion plants of substantially greater size and power than are provided for comparable U. S. ships.

A comparison of the estimated specific machinery volume of U. S. and Soviet warships, in terms of cubic feet of main machinery space per horsepower, indicated that Soviet ships require 25–40% less space than U. S. ships. This estimate accounted for the large amount of auxiliary machinery located in the main machinery spaces of U. S. ships but may not properly account for the auxiliary machinery located outside the main machinery spaces of Soviet ships. It is estimated that the volume and weight of Soviet auxiliary machinery is considerably less than that found on board U. S. ships for electrical power, fresh water distillation, and ship-

Figure 2 *Speed Trend*

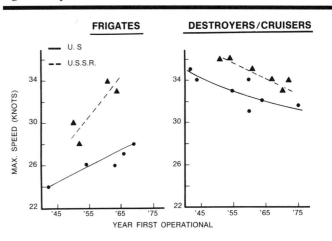

wide air conditioning. It is the tremendous increase in auxiliary machinery requirements which accounts for the major portion of the growth in the specific machinery volume of U. S. ships and a large portion of the overall increase in the size of U. S. ships since World War II.

In addition to the Soviet practice of designing propulsion plants with less specific machinery volume and more power than their U. S. counterparts, there are several other differences in Soviet propulsion plant design practice worthy of note.

First, unlike the present U. S. commitment to gas turbine propulsion for FFs and DDs with controllable pitch propellers and nuclear propulsion plants for CGs, the Soviets apparently have not committed themselves to any one type of fossil fuel propulsion plant scheme. Though emphasizing the use of gas turbine plants, the Soviets appear to be continuing the development of both pressure-fired steam plants and diesel plants, including combination gas turbine and diesel plants. However, there is no indication of any Soviet utilization of nuclear power in a surface warship.

Second, the Soviets appear unwilling to commit even small frigates to a single propulsion shaft. They apparently consider that the savings in volume, weight, and costs associated with a single-shaft ship design are outweighed by the increased maneuverability and availability associated with a multi-shaft ship design.

Third, the Soviets are reported to practice considerable standardization in the types of machinery and electrical equipment used in their auxiliary and propulsion plants. They also are believed to use more off-the-shelf mechanical and electrical equipment in new ship designs, as they also appear to do with their electronic and weapon systems. If in fact true, these practices, whether by design intent or as a by-product of their economic system, contribute to the design of ships with very little space and weight margin required for the uncertainties associated with concurrent development and competitive procurement of equipment for new ship designs.

Endurance: The trend in the cruising endurance range of U. S. fossil-fueled surface combatants compared to that estimated for comparable Soviet ships indicates an increase in the endurance of U. S. and Soviet ships that is proportionate to their growth in size. While the range of Soviet frigates and destroyers is only 55–60% of the U. S. range, the range of Soviet cruisers has grown impressively—at a rate similar to that of conventionally-powered U. S. CGs. Not considered in this comparison are U. S. nuclear-powered cruisers with their extended operational range.

In addition, the U. S. Navy has emphasized for a long time the underway alongside replenishment of a vessel's fuel, stores, and ammunition. Clear weather deck areas are reserved both fore and aft for vertical replenishment by helicopter. Wide accesses and passages are provided, both topside and below, for strike-down. The Soviet Navy has only recently appeared to be developing a limited capability in this area.

The added weight and volume requirements associated with this emphasis on endurance account for a large part of the overall growth in U. S. combatants built since World War II.

Habitability: A comparison of the trend in U. S. ship habitability design practice, and that estimated for Soviet ships is shown in Figure 3, in terms of cubic feet per man. The shipboard spaces associated with personnel are considered to include those designated for berthing, medical purposes, sanitation, food preparation, messing, stores, administration, services, and recreation.

The trend in habitability in U. S. surface combatants has been dramatic since World War II, increasing from 210 cubic feet per man in the DD-692 to 695 cubic feet per man in the new FFG-7 (guided-missile frigate). This more than three-fold increase was not matched by the Soviets, but on the other hand, their two-fold increase from 225 cubic feet per man on the "Skoryy" to 435 cubic feet per man estimated for the new "Kara"-class cruiser is probably a lot greater than most observers might have expected. In both cases, habitability standards seem to have kept pace with national living standards.

It is estimated that the space and facilities allocated to the berthing and medical care of Soviet crews are comparable to U. S. practice, while those allocated to sanitation, messing, food preparation, and stores are less. Space allocated to administration, recreation, and personnel services, such as the ship store, laundry, dry cleaning plant, barber shop, post office, and exercise room appears to be minimal in Soviet ships.

Summing up, the large amount of volume and

Figure 3 *Habitability Trend*

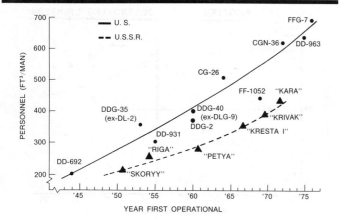

Figure 4 *Specific Payload Volume Trend*

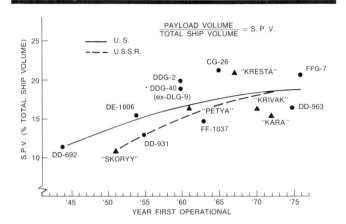

weight associated with meeting habitability requirements has had a significant impact on the overall growth of U. S. ships since World War II.

Payload: In this comparative study, the term "payload" has been used to identify the equipment carried in a ship to fulfill her military mission; that is, the weapons, ammunition, aircraft, detection, control, and communications equipment. When a comparison was made of the trend in the payload volume as a percentage of total volume of U. S. and Soviet surface combatants as shown in Figure 4, the results were extremely interesting. They indicate an increasing trend for both countries and that, while the Soviets put more weapons on their ships than does the U. S., both countries allocate about 15 to 20% of a ship's total volume to weapons and electronics.

This increasing trend in specific payload volume is attributable to the evolutionary change in weapons and electronic systems. Heavy and dense guns and ammunition and a small quantity of electronic equipment have given way to relatively light and volume demanding missile and launching systems and a larger quantity of electronic equipment.

It appears to be U. S. and Soviet design practice to allocate about the same relative percentage of total ship volume to payload. How is it, then, that the Soviets seem to arm their ships more heavily with weapons than the U. S. and with a comparable electronics suit without their ships having grown more in size than they have?

Electronics: The major design characteristic of Soviet electronic equipment that is thought to differ from U. S. practice is that, in general, Soviet radar and sonar systems do not possess the power-demanding performance of similar U. S. equipment. Hence, Soviet electronic equipment should demand less internal ship volume and require less electrical power and other support services than comparable U. S. equipment. The

one exception is in electronic warfare, where the Soviets have long employed an extensive variety of equipment. Their latest cruisers, the "Kresta II" and the "Kara," have been fitted with the new, relatively high performance three-dimensional Top Sail early warning air search radar. This new system may indicate a Soviet trend toward higher performance electronics which will require more space and electrical power in the future.

Weapons: The trend in the relative armament density on board U. S. and Soviet destroyers since World War II, in terms of weapon launchers per 1,000 tons of displacement, is shown in Figure 5. Counted were gun mounts, missile launchers, ASW rocket launchers, torpedo tubes, and helicopters, no matter how many barrels, tubes or launcher arms they had.

Figure 5 highlights the fact that as U. S. warships have grown in size, it has not been because a greater number of weapon systems were provided. The Soviet practice of providing frigates with six weapon launchers per 1,000 tons, compared to two on U. S. frigates is very impressive. Soviet frigates, however, have relatively low endurance and habitability and are not designed for extended open ocean operations.

The decreasing trend in armament on board Soviet destroyers and cruisers and its subsequent reversal in ships completed around 1963 is very apparent. These ships were in the planning stage about the time Admiral Sergei G. Gorshkov became Commander-in-Chief of the Soviet Navy. The present trend to increase the armament on board Soviet ships appears to be a reflection of his philosophy. In any case, their two-to-one armament ratio certainly justifies U. S. Fleet operators' observations concerning the well-armed appearance of Soviet warships. This observation is pictorially displayed in Figure 6, which shows a plan view of the 560-foot, 10,000-ton CGN-38 and the 538-foot, 8,500-ton "Kara"-class CG.

Figure 5 *Armament Trend*

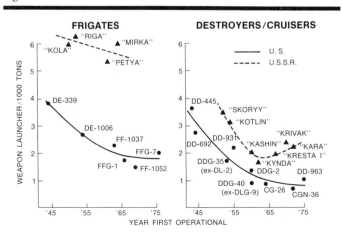

208

Figure 6 *Weapons Comparison*

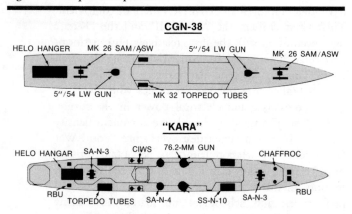

CGN-38

HELO HANGER   MK 26 SAM/ASW   5"/54 LW GUN   MK 26 SAM/ASW

5"/54 LW GUN   MK 32 TORPEDO TUBES

"KARA"

HELO HANGAR   SA-N-3   CIWS   76.2-MM GUN   CHAFFROC

RBU   TORPEDO TUBES   SA-N-4   SS-N-10   SA-N-3   RBU

The answer to the question of how the Soviets have managed to arm their ships more heavily than has the United States without enlarging their ships more than they have, appears attributable to several major differences in weapon design practice. To begin with, the Soviets seem to prefer the redundancy and firepower provided by more than one weapon system of a given type, even though:

▶ The combined ammunition magazine load of two Soviet surface-to-air missile (SAM) systems may be little more than that provided for a single U. S. multipurpose SAM system.
▶ The weapon systems may have to be located so that the arcs of fire covered by two systems are no greater than that which could have been provided by a single system more optimally located.
▶ The location of these multiple weapon systems along both sides of the main deck precludes a clear fore-and-aft topside access needed to facilitate the expeditious strike-down of underway replenishment stores and ammunition.

Another point is that, for weapon systems which are difficult to reload, such as surface-to-surface missile launchers and torpedo tubes, the Soviets seem to prefer multi-tubed launchers topside with no provision for carrying reloads on board ship in magazines below the main deck for protection.

A third facet is that, for other relatively small weapon systems, such as the close-in-weapon system (CIWS) and the surface-to-air missile launcher (SA-N-4), on board the "Kara"-class cruiser, the Soviets locate these systems on the weather deck with their ammunition magazines incorporated in and limited to the capacity of the deckhouse or the canister of the missile launcher.

In addition to carrying at least twice as many weapon systems on a ship as is typical of the U. S.

Navy, they are estimated to carry one-third more total weight of ammunition in their smaller ships and one-fifth more in their larger ships. The Soviets are estimated to carry fewer reloads of medium range surface-to-air missiles than comparable U. S. ships but more gun and ASW ammunition.

Finally, the Soviets appear more willing to accept the increased vulnerability associated with storing large amounts of ammunition in weapon launchers and magazines topside than is acceptable under U. S. design practice.

As a result of these overall differences in weapon design practice, the Soviets devote more topside deck area to weapons and associated magazines and relatively little more internal volume to weapon systems than is typical of U. S. practice. As a consequence, Soviet ships appear to have a main deck area and weight limitation as a design constraint as compared to the internal volume limitation of U. S. ships. Therefore, the installation of one weapon system using Soviet design practice has less influence on ship size than it would following U. S. design practice.

Two additional observations are worthy of note about Soviet weapon design compared to U. S. practice:

▶ First, the Soviets emphasize higher firepower in their warships, with either no reload or only a modest reload capability for their major missile and torpedo systems. This design philosophy suggests that these ships are being configured for a preemptive first strike in a short, intense conflict.
▶ Secondly, a mission of both the U. S. and Soviet warships is to provide peacetime presence, that is, "show the flag" in support of the nation's foreign policy. This mission has never influenced the visible design characteristics of U. S. warships. However, the number of visible weapon systems on Soviet ships makes them appear ominous, irrespective of their actual combat effectiveness.

Design Priorities: The ship design data that have been previously discussed were reviewed by several senior naval architects who have had extensive experience in the ship system preliminary design process. They were asked to use their experience and judgment to evaluate these data and rank them by major design characteristics—that is, propulsion, endurance, electronics, weapons, and habitability—into an apparent priority order.

The relative priority of ship subsystems was judged in terms of their comparative volume, weight, and capability impact on U. S. surface combatant designs during World War II and, then, on present-day designs. In other words, which of these design characteristics appeared to "get the biggest piece of the cake" in the ship design process? In conducting this evaluation, these naval architects looked only at the ships as they were finally designed and built, not at the original mission requirements that gave them birth. The results of this effort are shown in column one of Figure 7.

It was their opinion that, during World War II, U. S. frigates and destroyers were designed around a specified weapon suit and propulsion plant. Their size was determined primarily by the buoyancy required to adequately support the weight of this weapon suit and propulsion plant and their associated load of ammunition and fuel. The remaining volume in the fore and aft ends of the ship, and in the superstructure, was then allocated to electronics, habitability, and other features. Essentially, the philosophy was to design ships with good firepower and mobility, but of modest size, so that we could afford to build large numbers of relatively inexpensive ships for our wartime Navy. The naval architects used these same criteria in evaluating the design data applicable to recent U. S. designs, namely, the FFG-7, FF-1052, DD-963, and CGN-38. The results are shown in column two of Figure 7.

A review of the estimated design data for recent Soviet surface combatant designs, namely the "Krivak," "Kresta I," and "Kara," resulted in the priority order shown in column three of Figure 7. It seems that the priority with which the Soviets are designing their present warships is reminiscent of U. S. design priorities of World War II. That is, the Soviets are emphasizing firepower and mobility in ships of relatively modest size. They then appear to restrict electronics, endurance, and habitability characteristics to those which are barely adequate.

Thus, it appears reasonable to conclude that the Soviet philosophy is to design warships of modest size, with good firepower and mobility, so that they can afford to build a number of relatively inexpensive assets for the ever-growing Soviet Navy. This may explain why they have not yet used nuclear power in their larger cruisers.

Effect of Mission Requirements: At this point, a reader might logically ask to be shown by example the impact

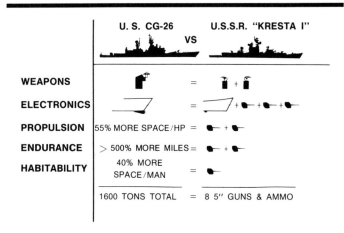

Figure 8 *Effect of Mission Requirements*

of present U. S. mission requirements in a specific U. S. ship design in contrast to a similar sized Soviet ship. By way of example, the impact of present U. S. mission requirements is shown in Figure 8, for the 7,900-ton CG-26 with seven weapon systems compared to the 6,700-ton "Kresta I" with 13 weapon systems.

Immediately obvious was that, in lieu of the multipurpose Mk 10 Terrier/ASROC launcher, a ship designer could have alternatively fitted the CG-26 with two missile launchers similar in size to the SA-N-1 launchers on the "Kresta." If he had done this, and the total missile load were reduced by 20%, it would not have required any increase in ship size.

Another obvious item was the SQS-26 sonar. A ship designer could have fitted the CG-26 with a sonar roughly equivalent in size to the sonar estimated on the "Kresta I." With the resultant saving in volume and weight, he could have alternatively fitted the ship with three 5-inch lightweight guns and 600 rounds of ammunition each. The 5-inch lightweight gun was used as a medium of exchange in this example because it is a highly visible item, the addition of which tends to make a U. S. ship look more like a Soviet ship from the standpoint of visible firepower.

An examination was made of the propulsion, endurance, and habitability requirements for the CG-26 compared to those estimated for the "Kresta I." Had these U. S. requirements been reduced to the equivalent level of Soviet requirements, the ship designer would have been able to alternatively fit the CG-26 with five more 5-inch lightweight guns and 600 rounds of ammunition each. With this previous example in mind, what would the 4,100-ton FF-1052 look like if she had been designed to estimated Soviet mission requirements and design practices? A possible answer is shown in Figure 9. A Sovietized version of the FF-1052 was designed as follows:

Figure 7 *Apparent Design Priorities*

U. S. WORLD WAR II	U. S. 1974	SOVIETS 1974
WEAPONS	ELECTRONICS	WEAPONS
PROPULSION	HABITABILITY	PROPULSION
ELECTRONICS	ENDURANCE	ELECTRONICS
ENDURANCE	WEAPONS	ENDURANCE
HABITABILITY	PROPULSION	HABITABILITY

▶ The maximum speed was increased to 33 knots by replacing two conventional boilers driving one screw, with four pressure-fired boilers driving two screws. This caused an increase in the overall size of the machinery spaces. However, by arranging the four boilers in one fireroom, rather than a less vulnerable two-fireroom arrangement, and reducing the auxiliary machinery, the specific machinery volume was reduced 35% to Soviet standards.

▶ The increased size of the machinery spaces was further compensated for by reducing the ship's endurance by 1,000 miles and reducing the habitability space by 40%.

The radar and sonar suits were replaced with other less volume- and weight-demanding U. S. equipment that reflect lower Soviet performance and support requirements. However, missile defense was upgraded by the addition of an antiship missile defense (ASMD) electronic warfare package.

▶ The weapon suit was doubled from six to 12 by the substitution and addition of "low ship impact" weapons topside. These weapons were placed without providing magazines below deck for reloads or concern for their arc-of-fire, vulnerability, or their hindrance of a clear fore-and-aft topside passageway for replenishment strike-down. Moreover, existing belowdeck magazine capacities were reduced to reflect Soviet practice.

The Sovietized FF-1052 is a feasible ship. She would cost an estimated 20% more than the original ship, primarily for the additional weapon systems. But, if U. S. Navy mission requirements called for more firepower and speed on ships of modest size—and engineering design practices were modified to meet minimum requirements—it is feasible for U. S. ship designers to provide them. However, it would obviously be necessary to compromise other features of these ships if they were not to grow in size and cost.

Summary: The Soviets have not made any breakthroughs in extending the state of the art in ship design. Rather, as competent ship designers and shipbuilders, they are building large numbers of relatively small, fast warships with impressive firepower to satisfy mission requirements and design priorities different from those of the United States. Other ship systems of lesser priority seem to be "fitted in" whatever space is available without allowing additional ship growth to accommodate them. This indicates a Soviet design practice to select subsystems which, if barely adequate, are accepted in preference to the ship growth that might be associated with additional improvements to optimize the subsystem design.

Soviet mission requirements account for the character of Soviet warship designs. Their sea denial mission is intended to deny other nations certain uses of the sea. The recent growth in size of Soviet cruisers, however, along with the building of 35–40,000 ton air-capable ASW cruisers, appears to indicate an extension of their ability to limit the use of world's oceans, or it could mean the emergence of a sea control capability. Their sea denial mission requires a design emphasis on a heavy firepower, first strike capability against a multiple air, sea and submarine threat, rather than an inherent shipboard self-sufficiency for extended deployments with limited dependency on shore based maintenance and resupply and the combat support of aircraft carriers. Finally, their sea denial mission requires emphasis on high speed and good seakeeping ability in all weather, rather than on endurance.

The principal design practices which also appear to account for the character of Soviet warships are: (1) topside "low ship impact" weapons, with either relatively modest sized magazines or no reloads at all, (2) high-power propulsion plants for high speed, designed with a relatively low specific machinery volume, (3) radar and sonar equipment of modest size, performance capability, and impact on auxiliary plant support requirements, (4) relatively low endurance, (5) habitability standards which reflect the modest standard of living in the Soviet Union, and (6) minimum provision for future payload modifications and equipment maintenance.

In addition, Soviet design philosophy does not appear to emphasize the concurrent development and multiple source procurement of weapon, electronic, propulsion, and aircraft systems to the degree that it is practiced by the United States. While the use of off-the-shelf systems often results in built-in obsolescence, it, along with equipment standardization, significantly reduces the design margins which must be allowed for the uncertainties associated with developmental or competitively procured systems. On the other

Figure 9 *U. S.-Soviet Design Practices*

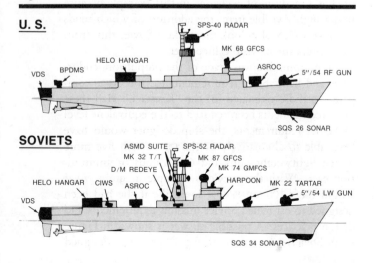

hand, the Soviets do appear willing to regularly update weapon, electronic propulsion, and other shipboard systems through major modification during extensive overhaul periods.

While Soviet ships are now generally smaller than their U. S. counterparts, there is a very definite growth trend in their size, endurance, habitability, and electronics, particularly in their cruisers. This growth is expected to continue as the Soviets experience the problems associated with extended operational deployments.

Finally, a review of Soviet warships built in the past 15 years seems to indicate that they are the product of a relatively consistent and strong design control process. One can almost visualize, by studying the naval architectural features of Soviet ships, the stamp of approval of a single design agent who has put his signature on each new destroyer design we have seen since about 1960. This suggests a stability in the Soviet ship procurement process that appears to be directly related to the 20-year incumbency of the Commander-in-Chief of the Soviet Navy, Admiral Sergei G. Gorshkov. It is from him that Soviet ship designers receive direction regarding mission requirements for warship designs. And, it has been variously reported that his attitude toward the ship design process is summed up in a few words on a sign, prominently displayed in his office, which reads, "Comrade, 'better' is the enemy of 'good enough'!"

Two classes of warships demonstrate the visible difference in the number of topside weapons. Top is the Knox-*class frigate* Lockwood *(FF-1064); below is a Soviet "Krivak"-class guided-missile destroyer.*

The opinions or assertions in this article are the personal ones of the author and are not to be construed as official. They do not necessarily reflect the view of the Department of Defense.

Commissioned through the ROC program in 1952 after receiving a B.S. in mathematics from Stonehill College, Massachusetts, Captain Kehoe holds an M.A. in education from San Diego State College. He has served in three aircraft carriers, most recently as engineering officer of the USS *Wasp* (CVS-18), and on board three destroyers, most recently commanding the USS *John R. Pierce* (DD-753). Ashore, he has had duty in nuclear weapons, the Polaris missile program, and instructing in project management. He is currently serving at the Naval Ship Engineering Center, Hyattsville, Maryland.

The author gratefully acknowledges the assistance of Dr. R. S. Johnson, H. A. Meier, J. D. Raber, J. L. Mills, Jr., V. W. Puleo, and N. T. Yannarell of the Naval Ship Engineering Center, Hyattsville, Maryland; K. Brower of J. J. McMullen, Inc., New York; and Lieutenant Commander C. Graham of M.I.T., Cambridge, Massachusetts, in conducting this study.

Shipping

Shipping

Ships at Sea
Maritime Facts of Life

By W. R. Nichols, Jr.

The sea and ships at sea have certain fundamental characteristics. The facts are few and simple. Their meaning is profound. Although the facts may appear evident to all, their meaning and application are understood by few. As a result of a national lack of understanding of ships at sea, the United States faces a fundamental crisis at sea. Data processing capability to handle complicated information about complicated problems sweeps simple concepts aside. Complexity seems almost a prerequisite for credibility.

Yet, simplicity does not detract from truth. The sea, for example, is one continuous highway that covers most of the Earth, about 70% of the surface. It is possible to travel from any point in the sea system to any other point in the sea system without requiring the vehicle ever to leave the system.

Conversely, less than one-third of the Earth's surface is land area. All land masses are isolated islands in that they are separated and surrounded by water. It is not possible to travel from any major land mass to any other land mass except by crossing the sea. In addition to the wide separation of the major land areas by major sea areas, there are also deep penetrations into the land masses by arms of the open seas.

To be usable for seagoing vehicles, some depth of water is needed. The sea is deep. Less than 10% of the ocean area is inside the traditional 100-fathom curve. Here and there are hazards and shoal water certainly capable of causing grief to the navigator. However, as a portion of the total surface, the unnavigable water area is exceedingly small. Essentially 100% of the ocean area is usable.

The sea is liquid, and like all liquids, the sea tends to seek its own level. The habitable areas on land vary in elevation by many thousands of feet. By contrast, the entire sea system presents a nearly uniform surface. The widest tidal range in the world is about 50 feet.

Because the sea is liquid, it is capable of supporting the vehicles of the sea by the phenomenon of displacement. The ship floats in the sea, and the sea is a worldwide, uniform or sea-level surface.

In any other vehicle, power is required to lift the vehicle and payload either uphill on the surface or bodily in the air above the surface. In ships, the lift is supplied by displacement of the operating medium without expenditure of power by the vehicle.

The ship operates on a worldwide interconnected highway; a gift of creation that requires neither construction nor maintenance. The existence of the highway and the minimum power requirements are the primary factors that make sea surface transport the most economical mode of transportation.

As a vehicle, the ship carries not only payload, but also carries within herself a largely self-sustained community.

The lack of penalty for weight has enabled man to build ships to carry crew, provisions, supplies, tools, and equipment to an unusually effective degree.

Although, in some conditions, it may be economically desirable to provide terminal facilities, the ship does not necessarily need such facilities to accomplish her task; the necessary equipment may be carried in the ship.

As a corollary, the operation of ships is not restricted to point-to-point operation between terminals. Operation is not restricted to location. The ship's task may be carried out anywhere on the surface of the seas: in harbors and ports, along the periphery or coastlines, and in the open ocean areas. The ship can go where she needs to go and be able to do what she is intended to do anywhere in the sea system.

These ship attributes are not the result of any 20th century technological development. Since man first put to sea in ships, his range has become global. Trans-ocean voyages are not a recent product of industrial progress; circumnavigation of Africa by the Phoenicians is reported in the times of classical Greece, and Pacific and Atlantic crossings are a thousand years old.

The factors that make the relationship of the ship at sea what it is are fundamental and timeless. Man did not invent them. Man learned of them.

All modes of transport have capabilities and limitations, and for a valid comparison to be made, some reference point in time is needed—today is convenient.

The ship does not require a prepared path for transit; the number of courses and routes between any two points is infinite. On land, even a footpath requires some preparation and maintenance; wagons need roads and bridges. The more effective the vehicle, the greater the need for the prepared path and, consequently, the greater the restriction to the path. The classic result of this development is the railway, which is absolutely confined to its specialized, prepared path.

On land, the path of transit is limited by natural barriers of terrain and water.

Where the prepared pathway is required, the heavier and more sophisticated the vehicle, the greater are the demands on the path. The weight of the payload is carried in the vehicle, the weight of both are in turn carried by the path—the road and all necessary structures, such as bridges, buildings, ramps, and the like.

Movement on land surfaces requires vertical movement, uphill and down. Power is required to lift uphill. Power is dissipated in braking systems going downhill. Contrast the ship, afloat in the worldwide sea-level system.

But, what of air transport? The characteristics of air transport are great speed and unlimited range—the operating medium is above both land and water—100% of the earth's surface.

The price paid for speed in the air is the requirement for power. The entire aircraft and contents, including payload, must be bodily lifted and carried in the air. Compared with other modes of transport this feat requires enormous power. Power takes fuel. Fuel is more weight, aggravating the problem.

Air travel is fast and expensive. Speed provides capability for high priority transport. The additional cost buys time—not additional transport.

Aircraft share with the ships the infinite choice of paths between points, but aircraft can also transit intervening land areas. While the paths are unlimited, the terminal points tend to be very definite. Aircraft operate from terminal facilities that tend generally to be fixed. Excepting for very specialized vehicles, the tendency parallels the need for paths by land vehicles. That is, as heavier and more sophisticated air vehicles are developed, the greater the requirement for terminal facilities from which to operate.

There are notable exceptions to fixed terminal facilities, particularly when air transport borrows from the sea. The seaplane can land nearly anywhere on water; facilities at the site are something else again. In special circumstances, the aircraft may take advantage of the ship's capabilities and use the ship as the terminal facility—the aircraft carrier.

With this briefest background of the attributes of modes of transport, alternatives may be examined. The relationship between various modes and the vast array of different vehicles involves an extremely large number of variables. At the risk of oversimplification, a graphic display or spectrum may be constructed to demonstrate the relationship of a few, primary variables.

Let the left side tend toward the displacement vessel. The further left, the greater the gross vessel in proportion to her relative power requirement. Approaching the extreme limits would be the raft. Airborne vehicles appear at the right, with increased speed further to the right. At the extreme right is missile or projectile delivery.

There are gaps and overlaps, but this crude array is useful. It helps demonstrate that selection of a mode of transportation, or a vehicle within a mode, involves compromises among the variables of capacity, speed, and economy. The claims by the supporters of any one vehicle that it is the answer to all problems simply will not stand up. No vehicle covers the entire spectrum.

New and revolutionary things continue to appear—surface effect vehicles, hydrofoils, and helicopters are examples. New devices fill needs, and they fill gaps in the spectrum. But, while a new device may add a new capability, it does not obviate or displace an existing capability. The aircraft will do jobs that the ship is simply incapable of doing. It is equally true, that ships are capable of doing jobs that aircraft cannot do. In reality, the area of overlap wherein there is a reasonable choice of alternatives between air and sea transport is quite limited. Controversy regarding these alternatives frequently has been a great waste of time and effort because arguments considered only the matter of capabilities, and evaluation of capabilities without concurrent evaluation of limitations is meaningless.

Economy of operation. In any instance where ocean transport is a reasonable alternative, it is the least expensive. This is readily evident in the comparative cost of moving a few thousand tons from one place to another—using other means of transportation.

Sustained Delivery. This has two aspects; rate and capacity. Rate is defined as cargo movement—ton-miles, per-unit time. To develop this concept, it is useful to construct an example:

Assume two vehicles—

Ship	Payload	12,000 tons
	Speed	25 miles per hour
Aircraft	Payload	100 tons
	Speed	1,000 miles per hour

In one hour of elapsed time the aircraft moves 100,000 ton-miles of cargo. In the same hour the ship moves 300,000 ton-miles of cargo. The ship delivery rate is three times the aircraft delivery rate in ton-miles.

The immediate counterpoint involves the number of units and the cycle time, or number of round trips per unit. The aircraft will get there first. No contest. The aircraft is capable of more round trips per unit. However, this is not a race between units. The topic is sustained delivery.

Take a North Atlantic trade route. Assume a conservative five days of transit and five days in port at each end of the run. Four ships in operation will maintain a continuous cycle; a new ship with 12,000 tons every fifth day, 2,400 tons per day. Comparable air delivery would require a 100-ton payload arrival every hour.

Increase the number of ships and the commensurate numbers of aircraft. Operate like any major port in the world; there are simply not that many aircraft—nor the capability to handle that many aircraft, if there were.

High-speed deliveries of individual units of high priority cargo can best use air transport capabilities. A particular shipment may be accomplished best by air where minimum transit time for that shipment is the controlling factor. This cannot be extrapolated indefinitely beyond the point where capacity becomes the limiting, and therefore, the controlling factor.

In transport of significant quantity, where sea transport is an alternative, sea transport enables the highest sustained rate of delivery. The reason is capacity, not the transit speed of the individual vehicle.

Capacity is the ability to move quantity. For those who do not deal in like quantities, the order of magnitude of quantity in seaborne transport is difficult to comprehend. Assume a mid-1969 world merchant fleet of 19,415 ships of 189,480,000 gross tons. This number includes only the larger ships, 1,000 gross tons and larger. These ships move vast quantities of cargo.

In one recent year, U. S. ports moved 471 million tons of foreign commerce and 208 million tons of coastwise domestic shipping. A total of 679 million tons through the ports does not include another 655 million tons moved in Great Lakes and inland waterways.

The quantities involved—hundreds of millions of tons—challenge the imagination. It is helpful to compare with other yardsticks. Compared to this 471 million tons is the airborne foreign trade of 503.4 million *pounds* for the same period, or slightly more than ¼ million tons. Today, there are individual ships at sea capable of moving, in one trip, tonnage equivalent to the entire national annual airborne foreign trade.

Truly, this international trade is a vital part of national life. Four hundred seventy-one million tons is more than two tons of foreign trade per person for every man, woman, and child, in the United States.

For bulk delivery between land masses, then, sea

transport is the *only* capability that has the capacity to carry the traffic. With the advent of large amounts of power in small packages, machinery was used as new forms of motive power on both land and sea, revolutionizing all existing forms of transportation. Rules of power use remain the same.

Further development of machinery enabled packaging of quantities of power required to generate the lift that made aircraft possible, and there was introduced a new mode of transport, with a new family of vehicles. Some attributes of that family have been examined.

The fact remains, however, that, in the history of the development and application of power to move mass in transit, whatever the form of power used, sea transport remains the most economical use of that power.

Every basic form of power that has ever been developed—muscle, wind, fossil fuel steam, internal combustion piston, gas turbine, nuclear fuel steam—has been successfully applied to ships at sea, and all are in use at sea today.

Historically, too, ships have been built of the widest range of materials, with every conceivable method of fabrication and fastening. On the one hand, ships are built out of whatever new materials and processes become available, and on the other hand, ships have been built, from necessity, with whatever materials were at hand.

Inherent limitations in operation of land and air vehicles have presented obstacles to the application of some materials and power plants. Not all have been used successfully on land or in the air. Ships, their construction and powering, are more adaptive to innovation.

What of the future? The major propulsion development being employed today, which will bear on transport in the near future, is nuclear power. Nuclear power has not yet been applied practically to land or air transport. One of the problems is the need for shielding. Shielding requires mass, which in turn means additional weight.

Nuclear reactor plants require a moderator. Among the most successful moderators is water. Water, too, is heavy, creating another weight problem. Water is plentiful at sea. The modern ship makes her own. Weight, a lesser problem at sea, becomes a greater problem on land, and greater yet in the air.

Most of the problems associated with nuclear plants seem to lend themselves to a more ready solution at sea. If nuclear power offers any relative advantage among the several modes of transport, it is clear that the advantage should be awarded to the ship.

In a very real sense, nuclear power at sea does not revolutionize anything. Nuclear propulsion restores to the ship the operating ranges that ships have always had,

218

except for the historically very brief period when power was derived from fossil fuel.

With improved technology it is certain that changes and progress not even known today will bring further increases in capability to land, sea, and air transport. The only gauge of the future is the application and extension of what has been learned in the past.

The past has shown that whatever the technological developments to come, they will find their use in application at sea, and that whatever the power sources that may be devised and applied, they will be used most economically at sea.

Changes resulting from new developments alter the details of individual vehicles and their operation. Technological developments do not change the attributes of the transport systems. The characteristics of land, sea, and air transport systems depend on the functions of the vehicles and the media in which they operate. The fundamentals remain unchanged.

Of vital consideration in any analysis or plans for the future is the one consistent trend observed in men's affairs. Throughout history, all aspects of organized civilization have been increasing in numbers or magnitude. Starting with the people themselves, population, then trade, produce and manufacturing, all are continuously increasing. There is no indication or reason to expect that these trends will not continue.

All these trends create a need for moving things from one place to another, a trend which is not only increasing, but also increasing at a compound rate. As a result, for all forms of transport, there is more to be moved. This increased traffic is met by increases in numbers of vehicles and increases in vehicle size.

▶ *Trucks and Roads*—The increases in sizes are limited by existing clearances and restrictions. An alternative is to increase clearances by replacing structures on limited routes, a big and expensive problem. Increased loadings increase burdens on existing highways. New highways are another big and expensive problem.
▶ *Railroads*—Severely restricted by clearances and loads, railroads are absolutely restricted by track gauge. Alternatives would require rebuilding the entire railway system, roadbed, railway, and rolling stock.
▶ *Aircraft*—Bigger and heavier aircraft require bigger and heavier runways. A new and bigger plane means fewer places it can go, or new facilities, or both.
▶ *Ships*—Ships float; this fact eases the problems and restrictions of size. Additional size means additional capacity; it also means additional weight. In other vehicles, additional weight requires additional support of the static weight of the vehicles and additional power to lift the weight when the vehicle is in motion. The sea is indifferent to the vehicle's weight.

The sea can support a ship as large as man is able to build. The greater weight is still carried by displacement. As for any size, power is not required for lift. Peculiarly, the larger the ship, the less the amount of power required in proportion to size to achieve a given performance.

The practical limitations of ship size are the ability to develop structure. The seaway itself requires no modification. Ships have increased in size enormously in the last few hundred years, but they still use the same ports. Where any work at all is required to accommodate larger ships, it is limited to harbors and approaches. Harbor improvement is relatively simple and inexpensive and capable of further improvement in the future.

Nothing in this discussion has drawn any particular differentiation between military and commercial application of ships at sea. Where the terms seapower or maritime power are properly used, their full meaning embraces both merchant and naval shipping. In the context of transport modes and basic vehicles, there is no need to differentiate. The basic application in both the military and commercial spheres is the same. Transport moves things from one place to another. For the military, the "things" to be moved are weapons, personnel, and logistic support, and the capabilities and limitations of the vehicles operating in their respective media are the same. The relative advantages of ships apply alike to the military and to commercial use, for the ship is still a vehicle, and where weapons are borne and employed in the vehicle, the same rules of speed, economy, and capacity apply.

Other attributes of seaborne movement have particular military advantages. The sea provides 70% of the Earth's surface for maneuvering room to those equipped and able to use it. Because the sea is a naturally interconnected system, no diplomatic footwork or permission is required for movement from any point to any other point.

Countries equipped to do so can carry their influence over 70% of the Earth. And, that is just to the shoreline. The range of influence, of course, can be extended beyond the shoreline. Only a simple exercise in geography and arithmetic is required to plot the range required to achieve a given percentage of coverage—right up to 100% of the Earth's surface.

Of peculiar interest to the military are the physical properties of air and water. Air is quite permissive to transit by all sorts of missiles and weapons. Water is an effective shield. Air is nearly transparent to every known form of detection and observation. The sea is nearly opaque to every known form in the entire spectrum of energy propagation. Recent technological developments are moving in two directions simultaneously, further up in the air space and further down into the depths of the sea. Technological development continually enhances the advantages of operations at sea.

Parallels are easily drawn between military operations and commercial operations. The same sea may be considered as 70% of the Earth for commercial maneuvering room. For those equipped and able to use the sea, it is a highway to the rest of the world, for both the source and the market for materials and goods. To those who cannot use the sea, the commercial world is confined to their own small fragment of the remaining one-third of the world.

As long as men engage in trade and commerce, the greater part of goods and products will be carried by ships at sea. As long as men find it necessary to build and carry weapons, they will be carried and employed in ships at sea.

The sea is the dominant feature of the Earth and ships are its vehicles. In the United States, a nation of global commitments and global commerce, the sea is the dominant factor in our international life.

The preceding discussion was intended to make observations and state facts; then, having tested their veracity, to generalize on their application. A proper generalization is independent of particular circumstances or time. If there is merit in these generalizations, it should be constructive to apply them to:

Circumstances—the U. S. global military and commercial position, and *time*—the latter half of the 20th century.

What is the situation today? By any standard of measure the United States has the greatest global maritime commitments, naval and commercial, in the world today. The Communist nations, led by Russia, are making a determined and dramatic effort at sea, and they are achieving remarkable success in their efforts—with both merchant and naval vessels.

The U. S. Navy, in supporting the national requirements of global policy and commitments, operates a force that is steadily declining in numbers. At this writing, 50 naval ships are scheduled for deactivation as a forced economy measure. Men and equipment are operated at the limits of endurance, not in a short sprint surge effort, but as a continuing level and mode of operation. Major elements of the Fleet face block obsolescence. There are some successful efforts to recognize problems and effect remedies. To the objective observer, however, it is by no means certain that the U. S. Navy will not be eclipsed in number of units, effective age of units, and modernity of weaponry.

While the naval situation is presented with some regularity in both the popular and professional press, less popular concern is evidenced, and less professional notice is taken, of the commercial world at sea—this despite the fact that the vast bulk of the commercial trade in the world, almost the entire dollar volume of international trade, moves, at some point, by water.

Commercial effectiveness requires some degree of control, or at least assurance, of continued use and predictable costs of materials. Similarly, any business will shortly cease to function if a commodity vital to that business is either withdrawn from availability or priced so as to make continued operation economically impossible. In this sense, transportation is a commodity and is no exception to this limitation of use.

The United States is the biggest international trader in the world, importing and exporting the greatest volume of goods of any nation. Yet, this biggest of all the shippers has little or no direct control over the transportation used to move its goods. Variously quoted percentages indicate that less than one-tenth of the nation's trade is now being carried in U. S. ships.

The cost of transportation determines the delivered cost of goods at a destination, and it does not appear rational to pursue deliberately a policy that will enable a competitor to determine the delivered cost of 90% of one's trade.

The unhappy position of American merchant shipping can perhaps best be described by the observation that today, a reader of the PROCEEDINGS, in his middle forties, has witnessed in his adult life the decline of the U. S. merchant marine, from the largest and most modern in the world, to the status of a fifth-rate merchant fleet. He, the reader, may not have noticed, but it happened, and more depressing yet, American shipping falls further behind daily, in numbers of ships and capacity of ships and age of ships.

Consider a ranking of the ten largest merchant fleets, excluding the United States, with position determined by percentage of world gross tonnage (Source: U. S. Maritime Administration, as of 30 June 1969).

Nation	Number of Ships	Gross Tonnage (1,000s)	% of World Fleet
Liberia	1,652	28,686	15.2
United Kingdom	1,810	21,332	11.3
Japan	1,843	20,347	10.7
Norway	1,240	18,562	9.8
U.S.S.R.	1,670	9,630	5.1
Greece	1,059	8,828	4.7
West Germany	915	6,517	3.4
Italy	607	6,314	3.3
France	473	5,489	2.9
Panama	620	5,286	2.8

Now, where would the United States fit in? Figures that are usually quoted to show the good position of the nation are: 2,013 ships of 18,373,000 gross tons, or 9.7% of world shipping. This places the United States in serious contention with Norway for fourth place. Somehow, the purveyor of this particular set of numbers fails to mention that they include 878 ships of 6,307,000 gross tons in the government-owned reserve fleets. Elsewhere, the reader can find, too, that these ships are passing the point of total obsolescence and approaching physical disintegration.

Eliminating the reserve fleets, the figure for the U. S. merchant marine becomes 1,135 ships for 6.4% of the world's fleet. This places the United States somewhere between Russia and Norway. However, 172 of *these* ships are government-owned or charter. Considering only the operating vessels in the merchant service, then, the U. S. merchant service sails 963 ships, 10,774,000 gross tons, or 5.7% of the world's fleet. This places the United States just slightly ahead of Russia.

As dismal as such data may appear, the figures shown are static and refer to 1969. It grows worse every day.* The reader may note the significant gap between Russia and Norway. Among the major shipping nations, these might be termed the upper and lower divisions. All the major fleets in the world are on the increase, and the fastest growing merchant fleet of them all is Russia. The Russians are about to enter the upper division. The United States, by comparison, has the only declining merchant fleet. How could such a calamity occur?

To read the daily newspaper is to observe the complete national lack of comprehension of the significance of ships at sea. This lack of understanding has several facets which ultimately resolve themselves into two factors: first, misinformation—assertions not supported or supportable by facts of analysis; and, second, lack of information—just plain ignorance of details.

A portion of the problem here is superficial over-familiarity with seaborne transportation. It has been around forever, it is old hat, it must be obsolete. If it is not nuclear, electronic or space age, it must be old-fashioned. And what of all the new wonder vehicles, each heralded as the product of a new breakthrough?

Understandably, perhaps, the press treatment of a new wonder vehicle encounters the high risk of slant where it is based on the press release material of the advocates of that particular vehicle. Typically, an article about say, a new surface effect vehicle will extol the virtues and unique capabilities of the vehicle. Little interest is expressed in the comparative capabilities and limitations of other vehicles. By some magic means the new vehicle becomes the answer to all problems everywhere. No attempt is made, for example, to analyze what might be involved when a one-ton payload vehicle would be

asked to move a few hundred million tons of cargo.

Exaggeration? Hardly. Unfortunately, such coverage is not confined to the popular press, but is also found in professional and official publications. All vehicles have their capabilities and limitations which establish their place in the total vehicle spectrum—capacity, speed, and economy compromise. The advocate of capabilities who fails to consider limitations is at best uninformed, and, when so acting in an official capacity, is irresponsible as well.

This lack of information—or acceptance of misinformation—results in the expression of some ideas that seem quite remarkable in the face of pertinent, observable facts. For example: Why, some ask, should we worry about the merchant marine when we have all we need? Such a question ignores the continuing decline of a merchant marine carrying a declining part of our trade.

Why, others wonder, should we bother with conventional ships when the ships of the future—if we are to believe the plethora of artists' renderings—are to be hydrofoil ships the size of transatlantic liners? Such a question betrays an obvious lack of understanding of fundamentals.

But, it is argued, we can pull in our horns and get along without the rest of the world. This attitude ignores the fact that the United States has changed from a "have" country to a "have-not" country, with ever-increasing dependence on importation of raw materials.

We can always rely, the naive among us persist, on cheaper foreign flag charters to move our vital supplies. Yet, even as this is being said, our military cargoes sit idle on the pier because foreign flag crews refuse to load or carry them.

Finally, there are those who say that subsidy is un-American, and besides, we can't afford it. UnAmerican? The very food we eat is part of the most massive subsidy program of them all. The entire Federal appropriation for Maritime Administration construction subsidy, operation subsidy, research and development, field inspection, and operation of MarAd offices, is less than the payment of rental for space to store surplus subsidized grain.

Admittedly, subsidies are no panacea, and government participation is a large and involved topic. Some perspective is required, however, for billions are appropriated for this or that program without the public's batting an eye. The relatively modest appropriation for the Maritime Administration causes great fiscal hue and cry, and as a result, the maritime policy of the United States is no policy at all.

What can be done? By whom?

The maritime posture of the United States is determined by the federal government as a direct matter of policy and federal implementation and indirectly by the national economic and legal climate which is made favorable or unfavorable to maritime affairs. The determinations of the federal government are made by elected and appointed officials whose actions are ultimately responsive to the nation at large.

The majority of people may never even see the sea. Many of those who do may see it only from the shore. Few, except the seafarer, the ship operator, and the professionals, can observe the meaning of ships at sea. It is the responsibility of those who do understand—the naval establishment and marine industry—to share their knowledge effectively.

It is not enough that professionals write to each other in the professional press. Insofar as the national maritime dilemma has its roots in misinformation and lack of information, the solution is to be found in information—truthful, credible, emphatic, and abundant. The writer suggests a massive continuing program of public information—institutional advertising as it were—on a comprehensive scale.

The Navy does have support from organizations such as the Navy League. The Navy has some degree of public information coverage.

But if the Navy presentation to the nationwide public may be limited, the merchant marine's presence is almost nonexistent. The two images—naval and commercial—are really one in the full context of a maritime nation. It is, necessary to reach out through all media—television, motion pictures, publishing, periodicals, education, public, professional, and fraternal groups. Not a one-shot proposition; what is needed is a maritime awareness as a part of the national life.

Propaganda? Fabrication is folly, and fabrication will always be a loser in the long run.

The facts *are* there; solid information is abundant. The United States *is* a maritime nation. The national economy *is* a maritime economy. There *is* a great national heritage of the sea. The U. S. flag ship at sea today *is* vital to every man, woman, and child in the land. it remains for those who know to share these facts. Then the man who may never see a ship, the sea, or even the shore, will nevertheless understand how important the sea and ships are to him. He can be aware and proud of his country at sea. He will know that his way of life, his material possessions, the price of buying and selling goods in the market, his livelihood—all the facets of his economic life—are dependent on the sailing of ships at sea. When he knows these things, he will not be responsive merely to maritime needs, he will demand and get a meaningful, flourishing maritime policy from his government.

These are the fundamentals of our maritime life. National understanding is vital to the survival of our national maritime life.

Following service as an enlisted man in the U. S. Army, Mr. Nichols graduated from the Carnegie Institute of Technology in 1949 and, upon graduation, was commissioned in the U. S. Naval Reserve. He served in the USS *Wiseman* (DE-667) and in the *Samuel N. Moore* (DD-747) from 1950 through 1953. From 1958 until 1969, he was employed by National Steel and Shipbuilding, San Diego, California. He is now employed by Litton Ship Systems, Litton Ship Technology.

U. S. Merchant Marine—
For Commerce and Defense

By Rear Admiral John D. Chase, U. S. Navy

The axiom that seapower is important to all maritime nations is generally accepted. However, the perception that seapower is more important to the United States today than at any time throughout our nation's history is not yet generally understood or accepted. In part, this dependence rests upon the maritime ties that bind the United States to friends and allies around the world. In part it stems from the fact that, when and if the United States wants to exert power or influence, we must do it across the seas. To a considerable degree, it results from the unprecedented and dramatic growth of Soviet sea power in all its aspects, naval, commercial, fishing, and oceanographic research. However, the compelling reason is different from all of these. The United States has become, or is fast becoming, an Island Nation.

Obviously this is not meant in a strictly geographic sense. Rather the term, Island Nation, is here defined as applying to a nation which is absolutely dependent upon maritime ties for the very preservation of its society. Colonial America was an island nation in this sense. The colonists came by sea. They were dependent upon support from across that sea. If the ships did not come, many of the colonists died. Some of the colonies died too. Later with the development of bountiful natural resources, the United States became largely self sufficient.

But, that happy situation is changing and changing fast. England became an island nation about the time of the Napoleonic Wars when she became a permanent net importer of food. Japan became one when she industrialized after the Meije revolution. Today, the Japanese industrial economy could not function without the raw materials and energy resources brought in by sea. The modern, urban Japanese society could not survive without the industrial economy. So, too, the United States is now becoming similarly dependent upon the seas. With about six per cent of the world's population, we use about a third of its energy. Prior to the Arab embargo in 1973–74, oil consumption was estimated to increase by some fifty per cent in a decade with imports rising to about half of this expanded amount. It is not just energy. Sixty-nine of the seventy-one items on the list of critical strategic materials also are imported wholly or in part by sea. These are not all exotic or unusual commodities but include such basics as iron ore and bauxite. We are now an island nation.

The maritime power so vital to an island nation consists of a number of elements. Both a strong and mutually supporting navy and merchant marine must exist, as well as an adequate support base in the way of population, shipbuilding, ports and facilities, financing, and the like.

Seafaring and shipbuilding were early pursuits of Colonial America. It was a seafaring age and the colonists reflected the interest in the sea exhibited by their European antecedents. As the colonies developed and prospered, so did seafaring and shipbuilding. Ships were built and sailed to make a profit. The impetus was purely economic. The necessary materials and skills existed. Every voyage was a venture in the truest sense. While many ended in disaster, many were also the source of fortunes. This condition continued during the early years of the Republic. The sea captains' houses in New England still stand to commemorate the success of these enterprises. Yankee shippers were known for their willingness to "trye all ports" and for their daring in crowding on sail to beat their competitors' time. The clipper ships were the finest expression of this period of American maritime history. Just prior to the Civil War the American merchant marine was second largest in the world. Only the British fleet was larger. American ships sailed on every sea of the globe.

About that time there was a revolutionary change in shipbuilding from wooden to iron ships. The United States was not as well equipped as were European nations to adapt. Coupled with shipping losses during the war, and postwar emphasis on continental development of the West, this change resulted in a drastic reduction in this country's merchant marine. Indeed the decline was so complete that never again has the American merchant marine been among the leaders in the world except when spurred by the clear and immediate demands of war. The 2,318 "merchant" ships built during World War I and the 5,592 during World War II were not built for commerce and profit but rather to meet the military requirement.

The Merchant Marine Act of 1936 and the amending Act of 1970 recognize this dual role of the U. S. merchant marine. The preamble sets forth the purpose of the act as "To further the development and maintenance of an adequate and well-balanced American merchant marine, to promote the commerce of the United States, [and] to aid in the national defense. . . ."

Title I of the Act states that ". . . the United States shall have a merchant marine (a) sufficient to carry its domestic water-borne commerce and a substantial portion of the water-borne export and import foreign commerce of the United States and to provide shipping service essential for maintaining the flow of such domestic and waterborne commerce at all times, (b) capable of serving as a naval and military auxiliary in time of war or national emergency, (c) owned and operated under the United States flag by citizens of the United States insofar as may be practicable, (d) composed of the best equipped, safest, and most suitable type of vessels, constructed in the United States and manned with a trained and efficient citizen personnel, and (e) supplemented by efficient facilities for shipbuilding and ship repair."

Section 8 of the Merchant Marine Act, 1920, is explicit with respect to ports. It states, in part ". . . it shall be the duty of the board [now MarAd], in conjunction with the Secretary of War, with the object of promoting, encouraging, and developing ports and transportation facilities in connection with water commerce . . . to investigate territorial regions and zones tributary to such ports, taking into consideration the economies of transportation by rail, water, and highway and the natural direction of the flow of commerce; to investigate the causes of the congestion of commerce at ports. . . .; to investigate the subject of water terminals, including the necessary docks, warehouses, equipment, apparatus, in connection therewith. . . ."

These policy statements demonstrate a distinct correspondence with the maritime needs of an island nation. They support a merchant marine for purposes of both commerce and defense, U. S. mariners, owners, and operators, adequate port facilities, and a shipbuilding and repair industry in support.

The U. S. Merchant Fleet Today

Now let us examine the American merchant fleet and see how well it is prepared to meet the dual requirements of commerce and defense. It consists of active and inactive ships, oceangoing and Great Lakes fleets, dry cargo ships and tankers. In comparing statistics, it is important to identify the base carefully in order to assure true comparability. Extracting from the Maritime Administration listing, the United States oceangoing merchant marine as of 1 June 1975 is shown in Table 1, which includes all ships of over 1,000 gross tons.

First, the freighters—these are dry cargo, break-bulk ships designed to carry a variety of general cargo, variously packed in boxes, bales, crates, and so on, and secured by dunnage. They are the familiar, conventional ships sometimes with a forest of masts and booms. Cargo space is divided into holds. By current standards the older ships are small and slow. Newer break-bulk ships, built in the early 1960s, run about 15 to 20,000 deadweight tons and steam at about 20 knots. Break-bulk ships, or freighters, may be in either liner (berth) or tramp service. The terms liner, berth, or regular service, often used interchangeably, refer to a service provided by a common carrier operating on a definite, advertised schedule. Non-liner, irregular, or tramp service, on the other hand, refers to operations of ships on an unscheduled basis as cargo offers, usually carrying full cargo lots, generally of a single bulk commodity, with no restricted trading limits as to routes or areas.

Twenty years ago, essentially all dry cargo was carried in break-bulk ships. Ten years ago almost all was so carried. However, today, the picture is changing rapidly with more and more dry cargo moving in "intermodal systems," primarily in containerships, or in bulk carriers.

As the name implies, a containership is specifically designed to carry containers, which are steel boxes, eight feet by eight feet in cross section, and of varying length. Twenty, twenty-four, thirty-five, and forty feet are the principal lengths. The container can be carried on a tractor chassis, on a railroad flat car, or in a barge. On board ship it stacks vertically in a container cell with vertical guides to facilitate insertion. Topside, additional containers are stacked vertically on top of specially strengthened hatch covers. The containerized share of commercial cargo carried in liner service grew from 15 per cent in 1970 to 34 per cent in 1973.

The containership idea originated with the trucking industry. In 1956 Sea Land, owned by Malcolm McLean, who also owned a large trucking firm, loaded fifty-six containers on a specially constructed spar deck on a converted tanker, the *Ideal X*. In April the *Ideal X* sailed from Port Newark, New Jersey, for Houston, Texas. In October of the following year, the *Gateway City,* the first fully containerized vessel, began regular service between New York, Florida, and Texas. The *Gateway City* and her five sisters are 15-knot, 8,400 deadweight-ton ships with a capacity of 226 thirty-five foot containers. The ships, all converted from war-built c-2 freighters, are self-sustaining, which means that they carry gantry cranes which move on guides fore and aft.

The cranes permit the ship to load or unload herself. Normally the containers come from or are placed on trailer chassis dockside.

During the sixties, containerization grew steadily. Break-bulk freighters and tankers were converted into containerships for a number of lines. The majority of these conversions are non-self-sustaining. That is, rather than employing a gantry crane integral to the ship, they rely on specialized container cranes ashore. The absence of a gantry crane results in increased container capacity in a ship, decreased maintenance, and the opportunity to use larger and faster cranes than those installable in the ship.

In addition, a number of freighters were converted into partial containership with facilities to carry both break-bulk and container cargo. These ships are self-sustaining.

Table 1 *United States Oceangoing Merchant Marine June 1, 1975*

	Privately Owned	
	Number Ships	Deadweight Tons
ACTIVE FLEET:		
Freighters	141	1,922,000
Intermodal	138	2,637,000
Combo Pass/Cargo	6	50,000
Tankers	217	7,986,000
Bulk Carriers	15	340,000
Total Active Fleet	517	12,934,000
INACTIVE FLEET:		
Freighters	21	268,000
Intermodal	10	170,000
Combo Pass/Cargo	1	9,000
Tankers	29	933,000
Bulk Carriers	4	203,000
Total Inactive Fleet	65	1,583,000
Total:		
Freighters	162	2,190,000
Intermodal	148	2,807,000
Combo Pass/Cargo	7	59,000
Tankers	246	8,919,000
Bulk Carriers	19	543,000
Total American Flag	582	14,517,000

In addition, the government operates 12 freighters and two tankers of 139,000 deadweight tons, total. The National Defense Reserve Fleet consists of 293 vessels of World War II vintage, of which 72 are scrap candidates. Of the 293, 206 are freighters. The deadweight tonnage of the 293 is nearly 2,900,000 tons.

In the late sixties and in the seventies newly built container ships were delivered to nearly all of the liner companies. The non-self-sustaining Sea Land SL-7 class is the most productive ship in service; 33 knots, 38,800 tons deadweight, with a capacity of 1,096 containers.

The big containerships are the key element in a highly developed, highly integrated, sophisticated intermodal system. The big, fast ships are used as line haul vessels between major ports. From these ports smaller feeder ships fan out to lesser ports. Ashore there has been a requirement for hundreds of thousands of containers, and great numbers of chassis, acres of hardstand for container yards, specialized giant container cranes, electronic equipment, and computers for monitoring and control. Obviously the liner trade is becoming more and more capital intensive. The overall intermodal investment is estimated at something over $7.5 billion.

Partly because of this growth of the intermodal system, the U.S.-flag break-bulk tramp fleet has virtually disappeared, for conventional tramp freighters can no longer compete commercially.

Prior to World War II, the U.S. tramp fleet was a nonscheduled common carrier service. The tramps, after World War II, developed from the sale of surplus ships to speculators. They were quasi-common carriers with tramp characteristics. They became known as tramps probably for want of a better description. Their owners subsisted almost entirely on U.S. government impelled cargo. With the gradual drying up of government cargo, lack of capital, and lack of new construction, it was only a matter of time until the tramp fleet disappeared. The termination of the Vietnam conflict and consequent reduction of government impelled cargo resulted in almost all of the remaining tramp ships being sold foreign or sold for scrap.

The principal advantage of the containership is speed of delivery, not just speed at sea which could be put into any type ship but speed of loading and discharge which really drives the overall delivery time. Containers can be stuffed at source as well as dockside and the simultaneous loading and offloading time for even a big ship like the SL-7 is less than twenty-four hours. In contrast, several days would be consumed in loading and unloading a conventional freighter. Additional advantages accrue to the container shipper from reduction of pilferage and damage losses, and reduction of packaging costs.

Containerships are not the only intermodal carriers. A second variety is the Roll-on Roll-off or RoRo ship. This is a vessel with ramps and large port openings. The primary method of handling cargo is to move it in and out on wheels. The cargoes may be unitized or containerized, or they can be wheeled (tracked) vehicles themselves. The RoRo ship requires few facilities ashore—merely a strong ramp from ship to pier will do—and is compatible with any cargo that can be carried on wheels or caterpillar tracks, whether or not it can be stuffed into a container. Productive space on board is sacrificed to the need to carry chassis. U. S.-flag RoRo service is currently provided to Iran, Puerto Rico, Hawaii, and Alaska, with transpacific service planned for the States Lines ships now building at Bath.

A third variety of intermodal ship is the barge carrier. These ships load, carry, and unload specially designed lighters or barges, each carrying hundreds or thousands of tons of cargo. In the Lighter-Aboard-Ship (LASH) version, five hundred ton barges are lifted out of the water over the stern by an installed special gantry crane. The crane, still carrying the barge, then moves on tracks forward in the ship and lowers the barge into a cell. The barges are stacked vertically, similar to the way boxes are stowed in a container ship. In the Sea Barge (Seabee) version, a huge elevator built into the stern lifts two thousand ton barges to one of several deck levels. Hydraulic transporters then move the barges forward and place them on special jacks. The barges are stowed horizontally on two decks within the ship and on the main deck topside. Barge ships are intended to capitalize on the availability of inland waterway networks in many parts of the world with the opportunity for essentially door-to-door service by water. The barge carriers generally make more ports than do the line haul containerships. Barge carrier schedules feature short stops to offload and load barges. Ideally this operation would not even take place alongside a pier. The barges themselves constitute a feeder system. Additionally, Central Gulf has introduced a specialized feeder barge termed FLASH. The FLASH is not self-propelled but can ballast down, much as an LSD does, to pick up LASH barges; it is towed by a tug. Four have been built, in two sizes, the smaller of which can carry eight barges, and the larger of which can carry 15. A recent example of FLASH use was the discharge of 42 barges of rice from the LASH vessel *Green Island* at Kyuakpyui, Burma. The rice was destined for Chittagong, Bangladesh, a heavily congested harbor. Towed by a local tug, the FLASH then shuttled the barges onward to Chittagong while the *Green Island* continued on her voyage.

The third category in Table 1 comprises combination passenger/cargo ships. Once commonplace, there are only six of these active. There are no pure passenger ships or transports in the active fleet. Point-to-point passenger travel by sea has almost disappeared all over the world. A substantial foreign flag inventory of cruise ships does exist, but for recreation rather than transportation.

Tankers comprise the largest segment of the active U. S. merchant marine. They are the most numerous ships on the high seas. The tanker is defined as a ship designed to carry liquid cargoes in bulk quantities. There are some points that particularly bear on the interrelationship of commerce and defense. Tankers vary tremendously in size. The largest ships, ranging up to almost a half a million tons deadweight, carry crude oil from the producing regions to refineries. They are designated VLCC or ULCC for Very Large Crude Carrier or Ultra Large Crude Carriers. Smaller ships may also carry crude but generally are engaged in the distribution of refined products. Most of the latter are multiproduct ships. Tank cleanliness requirements for refined products are much more stringent than for crude, and jet fuels require specially coated tanks. About half of the tankers belong to oil companies. Because they can better exercise quality control with their own ships, these tankers are used primarily for transportation of products resulting from the company's operations. The remainder are owned by independent operators who charter their ships on a time, voyage, or spot basis.

Tankers can and do carry other liquid cargoes beside POL, including various chemicals and even wine. A specialized type of tanker is the Liquified Natural Gas Carrier or LNG. These are sophisticated and expensive ships designed to carry natural gas liquified under extremely low temperatures. A number are currently under construction in the United States.

One of the peculiarities of tanker operations is that productive voyages tend to be one way only, with a return in ballast. In order to avoid these long, money-losing voyages in ballast, some ships have been designed with dual or even triple capability, i.e., oil/ore or oil/bulk/ore (OBO). Additionally, tankers can and frequently do carry grain in bulk within the ship's cargo tanks.

Bulkers or bulk carriers constitute the final category of the table. These are ships designed to carry dry bulk cargoes, such as wheat, rice, coal, iron ore, and alumina. They can be owned by a company engaged in an industrial operation requiring the cargo they carry. Or, like tankers, they can be chartered from independent operators. Though smaller than tankers, these ships generally run to good size. A small bulker might measure 15,000 deadweight tons, a large one 80,000. The majority of bulk carriers and large tankers, even when owned by American corporations, sail under foreign flags.

One more type of new ship deserves comment. This is the integrated tug barge or notch barge. In this system the tug and barge are designed specifically for each other. The tug fits into the stern of the barge for pushing. She is rigidly restrained so that there is no relative motion between tug and barge. Such a system has the advantage of utilizing one tug for a number of barges with perhaps one barge loading, one discharging, and one in transit. The tug possesses additional advantages over a ship with regard to unit cost and crew size. Some of these barges are very large, up to 50,000 tons deadweight. Current tug-barge combinations are designed for bulk and liquid bulk cargoes. In addition to the new notch barge approach, the employment of conventional barges on the high seas is expanding with more and larger barges coming into service, particularly from the West Coast to Hawaii and to Alaska.

Table 2 summarizes ship construction under contract as of 1 June 1975 (source: Marad).

The concentration on large tankers and LNGs is obvious. In addition, two freighters are undergoing conversion to partial containerships.

To Promote Commerce

This then is our American merchant fleet. Let us see how well it functions to promote the commerce of the United States and to aid in the national defense.

The primary motive underlying operation of the merchant fleet for commercial purposes is, of course, to make a profit. However, circumstances are far different from the early days of our Nation's history when every voyage was a venture. Today seaborne international trade is highly structured and regulated by a variety of laws, by international, governmental and conference agreements, and by administrative regulatory bodies. Almost all nations restrict the carriage of their domestic trade to ships of their own flag. Most also exercise some sort of cargo preference on occasion. In the United States the 1904 Act requires that, except when limited by the unavailability of U. S.-flag ships or the excessive cost of using them, military cargoes be carried in U. S.-flag ships. The so-called 50/50 provision of the 1936 Act requires that at least half of all government sponsored cargoes be carried in privately owned U. S.-flag ships. In some cases there are bilateral agreements between trading partners. A recent example is the U. S.-Soviet agreement on the export of U. S.-grown grain to the Soviet Union. There are also pooling and equal access agreements, basically between steamship lines and a number of South American companies, that have the approval of the U. S. government.

The majority of liner companies throughout the world belong to conferences. There is no supra-national authority with the power to set rates. Accordingly, in order to promote continuity of service and reasonable stability of rates, the liner companies have generally agreed to self-regulation through voluntary associations or conferences. The members of a conference will all charge the same rate. Conferences are particularly strong in the United States, Western Europe, and Japan. Currently there is considerable concern over penetration of Soviet shipping into major trade routes. Often Soviet "companies" do not join the conference concerned with certain trade routes. Rather they will offer substantially lower rates and then, if they see fit, apply for conference membership.

With comparable rates, one would expect a large proportion of American liner trade to be shipped in American ships. This has not been the case. Two reasons are usually cited. One holds that foreign-flag lines are able to provide rebates or incentives to send one's goods in their ships, perhaps in other shipping or other industrial areas. (This argument is nearly always set forth as a general allegation rather than in terms of any specifics.) The other reason is that the record of labor instability in American shipping clearly penalizes efforts to increase the amount of American goods shipped in American bottoms. Responsible maritime labor leaders have realized this situation and have taken action to minimize strikes and promote labor stability. Under the leadership of the Maritime Administration within the

Table 2 *Ships under Contract as of 1 June 1975*

Type	No.	Deadweight Tons per Ship
Intermodal		
RoRo	4	20,000
RoRo	1	14,800
Tankers	1	8,000
	2	25,000
	10	35,000
	3	38,300
	11	89,700
	2	118,300
	2	150,000
	6	160,000
	2	190,000
	2	225,000
	5	265,000
	3	390,000
LNGs	16	63,000 (more than one design)
Ore Carriers	1	31,000
	1	42,000
	3	59,000
	4	62,000
Tug Barge	1	25,000
	1	35,000
	1	40,000
	82	

Department of Commerce, maritime industry and labor are cooperating to promote American-flag shipping through the aegis of the National Maritime Council. However, a more aggressive sales effort than we have yet seen on the part of the individual carriers to capture a greater portion of U. S. trade remains one of the chief means by which the merchant marine can become healthy.

Tramp and bulk operators, liquid and dry, generally operate through the medium of charters. House fleets mainly carry the products of the owner but may be available for charter when their own cargo commitments are slack.

The United States employs subsidies to enable liner shipping firms which meet certain criteria to compete with lower cost foreign-flag ships. The subsidy structure was established by the 1936 act and modified by the 1970 amendment. It consists of a construction differential subsidy and an operating differential subsidy, which are designed to offset higher U. S. building and operating costs. Interestingly, it is the company which receives the subsidy, but it is sailings which measure the extent of the operating subsidy granted.

The performance of the American merchant marine, operating within this framework, can be assessed by examining the statistics of the U. S. trade. Tables 3 and 4, extracted from tables compiled by the Maritime Administration, show the tonnage and dollar value of the commercial cargo moving in United States foreign

After years of idleness in the merchant marine reserve fleet at Mobile, Alabama, the SS Brigham Victory *was activated at the age of 20 for service in the Vietnamese War. Here she is seen being unloaded in DaNang's large, open harbor. Now, at age 31, she is back in reserve, this time in the James River. But whereas once we had thousands of merchant ships in reserve, now we have fewer than 300. Of these, the ancient* Brigham Victory *is one of the best.*

trade and the participation of U. S.-flag ships in that trade in 1964, 1972, and 1973. (With cargo statistics, as with ship statistics, it is important clearly to identify the base when drawing comparisons—i.e., are we comparing total trade or just the liner segment? Are we comparing cargo tonnage or cargo value? Are we including or excluding military cargo? And on and on. It is a slippery area.)

From the tables we can draw a number of conclusions. First, the total U. S. trade has almost doubled in tonnage over the ten year period and has come close to tripling in dollar value, reflecting in part the inflation of the times. Imports have risen more sharply than have exports.

From the figures in the tables simple calculations show that liner volume for all flags in U. S. trade went up by about 2 per cent, for non-liner trade it rose by 75 per cent, and for tanker trade by 146 per cent; the dollar value for liner trade went up by 135 per cent, for non-liner by 325 per cent and for tanker by 230 per cent. Thus, in tons lifted, the liner trade was essentially level while becoming a substantially smaller portion of the total trade. Non-liner volume increased substantially but even so the percentage dropped slightly. The tanker trade increased dramatically as did the percentage of the total (to almost half).

The principal commodities carried are also of interest. Using the figure for 1973 in the liner trade, exports were about twenty per cent greater than imports in tons but about twenty per cent less in dollars. By weight the five leading export and import commodities were:

Liner Trade

Exports	Imports
Pulps and waste paper	Motor vehicles and parts
Animal foodstuffs (feed)	Iron and steel plate
Cotton	Iron and steel bars
Synthetic resins—	& rods
plastics	Alcoholic beverages
Paper and paper board	Coffee

In the non-liner trade, exports were seventy-two per cent greater than imports in tons and sixty-seven per cent greater in dollars.

Non-Liner (Bulk) Trade

Exports	Imports
Coal	Iron ore
Wheat	Non-ferrous ores
Corn	Iron and steel plates
Vegetable oils and seeds	Crude minerals
Crude fertilizer	Inorganic chemicals

Tanker trade—exports were only seven percent of imports in tonnage but twenty-seven percent in value.

Tanker Trade

Exports	Imports
Wheat	Crude petroleum
Petroleum products	Petroleum products
Organic chemicals	Gas products
Inorganic chemicals	Sugar and syrups
Gas products	Organic chemicals

If we look at the U. S. flag carriage only, the picture changes significantly. In the liner segment the tons carried in 1973 by U. S.-flag ships dropped slightly from 1964, and so did the percentage. For the non-liner segment the tons dropped to less than half those they had been nine years earlier, while the percentage plummetted to a meager 1.6 per cent. In the tanker segment the tons carried in U. S.-flag ships more than tripled but, because of the spectacular overall growth, the percentage increase for U. S. flag shipping was modest. In dollar value, the U. S.-flag liner segment more than doubled but the percentage dropped slightly. In the non-liner segment, the value rose slightly but the percentage plummeted. In the tanker segment, the dollar value went up by better than four times but the percentage increase was modest. In tons carried in all categories of U.S.-flag ships, the percentages reach minimums in the latter part of the sixties with upturns now indicated for all except the bulkers. Longer term statistics reinforce this trend. The share of total tons lifted in and out of this country by U.S.-flag ships was 36 per cent in 1950, 4.6 per cent in 1969, and 6.5 per cent in 1974.

The growth of containerized cargo within the liner segment since 1970 is dramatic. In tons the amount more than doubled in just three years and the percentage of total liner trade under all flags has grown from 15 to 34 per cent. This growth is attributed to new container ships coming into service; to new and expanded container facilities ashore; to new market areas for the container trade (once again, at the expense of the conventional freighter), such as South Africa, Eastern Europe, and, to a certain extent, Brazil; and to the containerization of additional commodities. Almost half of the U. S.-flag liner trade went in containers. However, foreign-flag container carriage grew even faster so that whereas in 1970 about 60 per cent of U. S. container trade was under the U. S. flag, in 1973 only about 38 per cent (though of a substantially larger U. S. container trade) was carried under the U. S. flag.

Projections of hardly more than a year ago forecast the disappearance before long of the break-bulk freighter and, most especially, of the American flag break-bulker. Now people are not so sure. Such ships are those most commonly used in carrying trade between this country and ports in most of Africa, South Asia, and Latin America. Unfortunately, port congestion is a severe problem in these areas and the conventional freighter is highly sensitive to such congestion. The use of barge carriers is one way of freeing the ship herself from demurrage imposed by port congestion. As container facilities develop in those ports, one can anticipate that the conventional freighter will disappear from them. However, it does not look as if the shift will take place so fast, or go so far, as many people believed even recently.

At the time of writing, gross 1974 figures were available. They show a slight drop in trade from 1973,

Table 3 *Commercial Cargo Moving in United States Foreign Trade and the Participation of U. S.-Flag Ships in that Trade (Long Tons)*

Year	Total		Liner		Non-Liner*		Tanker	
	Total Tonnage	Percent U. S.	Total Tonnage	Percent U. S.	Total Tonnage	Percent U. S.	Total Tonnage	Percent U. S.
EXPORTS AND IMPORTS								
1964	332,832,000	9.2%	50,319,000	28.1%	161,389,000	6.1%	121,124,000	5.4%
1972	513,566,000	4.6	44,641,000	21.9	242,564,000	1.6	226,361,000	4.5
1973	631,572,000	6.3	51,244,000	25.8	281,910,000	1.6	298,418,000	7.4
EXPORTS								
1964	134,210,000	14.0%	31,904,000	29.9%	86,949,000	7.0%	15,357,000	20.8%
1972	186,103,000	6.0	22,855,000	23.4	146,267,000	2.0	16,981,000	16.8
1973	226,003,000	6.4	28,278,000	27.7	178,249,000	1.7	19,476,000	18.4
IMPORTS								
1964	198,622,000	5.9%	18,415,000	25.2%	74,440,000	5.0%	105,767,000	3.2%
1972	327,463,000	3.9	21,786,000	20.5	96,297,000	.9	209,380,000	3.5
1973	405,569,000	6.3	22,966,000	23.5	103,661,000	1.4	278,942,000	6.7

*Now called "Bulker."

Table 4 *Dollar Value of Commerical Cargo Carried in the United States Foreign Trade and the Participation of U. S. Flag Ships in that Trade*

Year	Total		Liner		Non-Liner*		Tanker	
	Total Value	Percent U. S.	Total Value	Percent U. S.	Total Value	Percent U. S.	Total Value	Percent U. S.
EXPORTS AND IMPORTS								
1964	30,003,000	25.8%	21,296,000	32.8%	5,932,000	8.6%	2,775,000	8.8%
1972	60,529,000	18.4	37,383,000	27.7	17,397,000	2.4	5,749,000	6.2
1973	84,006,000	18.9	49,640,000	29.1	25,216,000	2.5	9,150,000	9.1
EXPORTS								
1964	16,767,000	28.7%	12,016,000	35.1%	3,699,000	11.2%	1,052,000	17.8%
1972	25,592,000	18.7	16,008,000	26.8	8,268,000	3.7	1,316,000	14.7
1973	39,922,000	18.0	22,220,000	29.1	15,773,000	2.9	1,929,000	12.9
IMPORTS								
1964	13,236,000	22.1%	9,280,000	29.8%	2,233,000	4.2%	1,723,000	3.4%
1972	34,937,000	18.1	21,375,000	28.3	9,129,000	1.2	4,433,000	3.6
1973	44,084,000	19.8	27,420,000	29.1	9,443,000	2.4%	7,221,000	8.2

*Now called "Bulker."

but the U. S. share rose a bit, from 6.3 to 6.5 per cent.

Liner shipments were up slightly, as was the U. S. share, from 25.8 to 29.4 per cent.

Non-liner shipments were level with 1973, and so was the U. S. share, at 1.7 per cent.

Tanker total was down slightly from 1973 as a result of Arab oil embargo and the rise in the price of oil. The U. S. share dropped from 7.4 to 7 per cent. Tanker figures include grain shipments in tankers.

These figures indicate a pause in the growth of trade, particularly in the non-liner and tanker segments.

To Aid in the National Defense

Military Sealift

The second purpose of the merchant marine is to aid in the national defense. There are at least five ways in which the merchant marine can so contribute. First of all, in both peace and war, the merchant marine transports most of the material to support military forces. Such material may be destined for support of either U. S. or allied forces and it may be carried in either

U. S. or allied ships. Sealift and airlift are complementary in the provisions of strategic mobility. Airlift provides a small capability but a very fast response. Sealift provides the great bulk of the requirement. In support of the very long war in Vietnam, better than 95 per cent of the goods went by sea. In support of Israel during the very short Yom Kippur war, about 75 per cent went by sea.

Where do we get the ships to do this work? A distinction needs to be made between a large scale NATO type war involving mobilization, and a small contingency fought only with the regular forces. With mobilization, the entire U. S.-flag merchant fleet is subject to requisitioning by the Secretary of Commerce. A considerable number of analyses have been made of the wartime requirements for ships in this situation. Some have involved elaborate computer simulations. They vary in detail depending upon the particulars of the scenario and the analysis. All indicate that the U. S.-flag merchant marine has at best marginal capability to meet military needs and most show an inadequate capability without sizeable reliance upon NATO shipping.

The requirement for numbers in a contingency is smaller than in a NATO war but as we found in Vietnam (400 dry cargo ships), still substantial. In addition, there is a problem of timely response. The ships which might be used come from five sources.

Military Sealift Command. About thirty government owned or government chartered privately owned dry cargo ships of the Military Sealift Command are immediately available to Defense. In the past, rapid and significant expansion of this source has been possible by increasing the number of charters, most of which came from the tramp segment of the merchant fleet. But as we have seen, this segment has now virtually disappeared. Additionally, the coming of sophisticated and integrated intermodal systems makes it difficult for an operator to free his ships for charter purposes. Therefore, the elasticity of this resource is severely limited today.

National Defense Reserve Fleet. The moth-balled fleet of World War II ships once numbered in the thousands. Today, of about 200 dry cargo ships, there are 130 still-useful World War II Victory ships. These ships, even though old, have relatively little mileage on them. Activation procedures have been developed and tested. Nevertheless, the age of the ships will tell, and certainly their value must continue to go down as time goes on. Perhaps they have value for five or six years more. There is a provision in the law which would permit operators to trade in fairly new ships and to trade out on equivalent value of old ships to sell for scrap, but so far little or nothing has come of this. In

the meantime the old ships are being scrapped anyway. It is obviously in the Nation's interest to reconstruct this asset.

Active Merchant Fleet—Sealift Readiness Program. The MSC-controlled fleet is very small. The National Defense Reserve Fleet is much reduced and its usefulness is clearly limited to the next few years. More than ever, therefore, Defense must rely on the active merchant marine in contingency as well as in mobilization situations. The Sealift Readiness Program has been devised to improve the response mechanism. Under this program those berth line operators who desire to carry defense cargo in peacetime must agree to make half of their ships available for call up under certain conditions. The call up is approved jointly by the Secretary of Defense and the Secretary of Commerce. There is a schedule for incremental call up. In a prolonged contingency such as Vietnam turned out to be, the diversion of merchant ships from commercial to defense purposes would weaken the already poor competitive position of the U. S.-flag merchant marine.

Effective U. S. Controlled Fleet. Ships in this fleet are owned by U. S. citizens or corporations but are licensed by and fly the flag of Liberia, Panama, or Honduras. They are sometimes called "flag of convenience" or "runaway fleet" ships depending upon one's point of view. As these names indicate, there is a difference of opinion as to the responsiveness of these ships to United States contingency requirements. However, for the carriage of military equipment and supplies, the question is really moot, since almost all of the EUSC ships are large bulk carriers or tankers.

Foreign Flag. A final source for non-mobilization contingencies is the voluntary charter of foreign-flag ships. As in the case of the EUSC fleet, political drawbacks exist, especially in those instances where the perceived interests of the foreign nations do not coincide with those of the United States.

Modern Demands and Solutions

In addition to the questions of numbers and of timeliness of response, there are other specific requirements for sealift. One of the most critical is the need to lift tracked and wheeled vehicles in large numbers. The trend towards more and more vehicles in all Army divisions, particularly armored and mechanized divisions, is dramatic and this requires more ships than formerly to move a division. This need for more ships, if one can judge from the attrition experienced in the short, intense Yom Kippur war, will be intensified, for tank kills were very high on both sides. Token reinforcements can be flown in by air, but sealift is required to meet the requirements represented by the North Vietnam Easter offensive or the Mid East Yom Kippur war.

The RoRo (Roll on-Roll off) ships are obviously best suited to carry vehicles both for economy of stowage and for facility in loading and discharge. The fact that additional RoRo ships are coming into the commercial inventory is one plus for defense.

The barge carriers have also demonstrated a special capability for handling vehicles, particularly tanks, and, happily, the equipment needed to unload the barges is common in sea and river ports. SeaBee barges have been loaded at military outports on the Gulf Coast. The barges have been taken off the ships at Rotterdam and then have gone up the Rhine for discharge at Mannheim in the heart of Germany. Some LASH barges have similarly carried tanks to Greece and Turkey in the eastern Mediterranean.

Containerships are not suitable for tanks and pose a particular problem for many types of vehicles. Both the vehicles and the container boxes were designed to fit highway criteria. As a result, many vehicles just don't quite fit into the boxes. Flat racks, container frames, and floors without sides have been developed for commercial vehicle handling. Here is an opportunity better to put to use the substantial containership capability with the acquisition by Defense of a considerable number of flat racks. Containerships are well suited for the follow-on resupply phase of a military operation.

A similar specific requirement exists for helicopters, which are best carried below decks, protected from the weather, and in as near to a fly-away condition as possible. During Vietnam the best helo carriers were the Seatrain ships, converted tankers with large open spaces below deck. A few of these ships have been retained in the National Defense Reserve Fleet, but they are very old and tired. In the newer ships, again the Roll on-Roll off and Barge Carrying Ships are best suited. Of note is a Seabee barge delivery to Mannheim where the helos were lifted out of the barge by a large crane and set down adjacent to the wharf. Rotor blades were affixed and the helos flew away. The Army likes to use LASH barges for helo carriage and has tested ways to load and secure helos in such barges. The

During an exercise off the Virginia Coast, the non-self sustaining container ship Warrior *is unloaded with the help of special cranes shipped aboard a lighter and the LST USS* Saginaw. *The object of the exercise was to get containers from the* Warrior *to the beach. The hazards from enemy fire and weather are obvious.*

number of LASH ships in use (20) underscores the need for such tests.

The third specific requirement is for heavy lift for engineer equipment, harbor craft, locomotives, and the like. Two U. S. commercial ships, the *Transcolorado,* and *Transcolumbia,* chartered to the Military Sealift Command, have been fitted with large capacity Stülcken booms. Moreover, if suitable cranes are available ashore, SeaBee or LASH barges can be employed and, with minor modifications, the LASH gantry cranes can accommodate most of the boats in the defense inventory.

Coupled with the need for ships, for timely response, and for the specific requirements posed by vehicle, helicopter, and heavy lift cargo, there is also the need to be able to operate in a difficult shore environment. One of the chief reasons why so many ships were involved in the supply of Vietnam was the inability of the ports to accommodate them. Neither the port unloading fa-cilities nor the inland transportation could handle the loads placed on them and this severely limited the number of ships that could be handled. As a result, hundreds of ships were at anchor off Vietnam's ports or queued in other Southeast Asian ports. In such a situation, barge carriers have an advantage, as do RoRo ships which require merely simple ramp facilities at pierside. In Vietnam we used many World War II LSTs because of their ability to discharge over the beach. Only about a dozen of these useful ships remain, and soon they, too, will be gone. A new beaching ship, able to operate with a smaller crew than the LST, is needed badly. New containerships are non-self-sustaining, and rely entirely on cranes ashore. The installation of such cranes at Cam Ranh Bay played a key role in breaking the Vietnam shipping jam, but it took a long time for the cranes to become operational. Contingencies have a habit of occurring in the less developed parts of the

In the dangerous year 1942 the former merchant tanker Markay, *converted into the escort aircraft carrier* Suwanee, *worked in company with the cruiser* Brooklyn *which had been built from the keel up as a warship. After a period of decline technology has again made it possible for merchant ships and warplanes to be combined into effective fighting elements. As it was in 1942, the problem will be to break high class merchant ships away from pressing logistic demands.*

world and we certainly can't count on having shore container cranes available. Therefore, an urgent need exists to find ways to offload a non-self-sustaining containership without them. (The way this was solved in Vietnam was for the new container ships to carry the goods as far as Cam Ranh Bay. There the small, old self-sustainers, such as the *Raphael Semmes* and *Beauregard,* picked up the containers for delivery to Da Nang, Newport, and Sattahip. Such an arrangement depends, of course, on the continued existence of some self-sustaining container ships.)

Considerable engineering and experimental work has been done involving helicopter discharge, mobile construction cranes on deck, and even a variant of the balloon supported aerial tramway used by lumber operators in the Pacific Northwest. While much has been done with reasonably promising results, much more remains to be done. In airlift, there is a tremendous difference between loading one M-60 tank into a C-5A and carrying out Operation Reforger to strengthen our army in Europe. There is a similar difference between the engineering tests carried out to date and the large scale exercises that need to be carried out in an operational environment. Break-bulk ships have supported military operations for many years and both the military and merchant marine know a lot about their use in such operations. The same is not true for containerships. We need to develop organizational and administrative expertise with these ships, as well as the engineering know-how, and these can come only through operational exercises on a substantial scale.

The Carriage of Strategic Material

In addition to military cargoes, the merchant marine must carry the strategic materials and energy resources which support the civilian economy and defense production of the nation. As in the case of military material such support may be either for U. S. or allied needs and it may be transported in U. S. or allied ships. The import of food to England in World War II was vital.* Today with England as an ally, that would still be true. With Japan as an ally, there is a similar necessity to ensure the continued import of oil. There were minor needs of this nature for our own country in World War II but, today, as we become an island nation, these needs for raw materials and energy resources are as critical for the United States as food for Britain or oil for Japan. Further, in both world wars, the United States functioned as the "arsenal of democracy." The output of the arsenal is essential to the continued fighting capability of an allied force. The output of the arsenal in turn is dependent upon a continued flow of imported raw materials and energy resources. Obviously, transportation alone is not the whole story. We must be able to obtain the materials and POL. We must be able to control the sea to the extent that we can move the cargo across the ocean to the United States with acceptable levels of attrition. We must also have or be able to acquire the ships that actually provide the transport. For these purposes the bulkers, tankers, and

LNGs are as important as the ships in the liner trades. It is in this role that the "Effective U. S. Control" ships would be important.

In considering the wartime carriage of material, the question of attrition is central. From the standpoint of reducing attrition, there is value to a larger number of ships even if for a total given carriage the ships are individually less productive. Commercially, of course, fewer but larger and more productive ships make sense. As we have seen, the trend in most merchant marines is toward bigger and faster ships. The Soviets, however, have the military advantage that most of their merchant tonnage is in a large number of small ships.

With the reduction in number but expansion of productivity characteristic of most countries' shipping, the protection of each ship becomes more important. The increased speed of the ship is some advantage. However, there is a clear need to incorporate defensive features into the ships themselves.

There is some opportunity for this with our own new ships because provision exists for national defense features to be added to ships built with construction subsidy. The features are funded by the Department of Commerce on the basis of Navy recommendations. To date, while important in their own right, these features have not been as significant as they need be or might be. They have included such items as compartmentation, foundations for self-sustaining container cranes, substitution of more rugged materials than would be sufficient for commercial service, and overhead and ramp adjustment to accommodate military vehicles in RoRo ships.* What we need to look at more closely are more imaginative concepts like the modular installation of weapon systems or provisions for operating VSTOL or helicopter aircraft. Additionally, it is important to retrofit some defense features in existing high value ships as well as in new construction.

Direct Support of Military Operations

Thirdly, ships of the merchant marine can be used in direct support of military operations. Such support was important in World War II when merchant ships with only minor modifications helped form the interface between the transpacific supply line and the operating fleet. One of the principal areas for direct support is POL. Commercial tankers fitted with a simple receiver to accept a transfer rig can consolidate cargoes with fleet oilers and can refuel large combatants, which, unlike destroyers, and other ships of modest size, have

*Once refrigerator ships were needed for this service. Now the job is done by refrigerated containers.

*Once gun foundations were a permanent part of the national defense features of subsidized ships, but modern warfare has reduced their importance greatly.

integral transfer rigs of their own. Of course, commercial ships can refuel other ships much more slowly and with less facility than can a fleet oiler. The point is the Navy's need for handy-sized tankers carrying multiple cargoes, mainly jet fuel and marine diesel. (Over the years the definition of "handy-sized" tankers has been rising. Currently it means a ship of 25,000–35,000 tons, about twice what it was when the T-2 tanker was a common sight.) This refueling capability is exercised on an opportune basis by tankers chartered to the Military Sealift Command. The experience and practice proved in good stead during the 1973 Middle Eastern war. In the Mediterranean, the chartered tanker *Spirit of Liberty* provided direct support to the Sixth Fleet. Similarly, in the Indian Ocean, three other "handy-sized" tankers on charter to MSC for routine operations, the *Trojan, Sandy Lake,* and *Exxon Seattle* supported ships of the Seventh Fleet. All these ships were carrying Navy distillate and JP 5, the normal cargo of an MSC tanker.

The utility of break-bulk ships with minor modification (mainly to provide for transfer of cargo at sea) was also demonstrated in World War II. Now with the rapid shift to containerships, it is important to find out and perhaps improve on what containerships can do in this role. Some design work and testing ashore have been accomplished but more remains to be done. Barge ships have a definite potential in direct support. The possibility of augmenting Sixth Fleet resupply in the Mediterranean by LASH barge has been demonstrated, with obvious application to contingencies in undeveloped areas.

The demonstration, or test, consisted of three parts. In the first part, conducted while the Prudential Lines' SS *Lash Italia* was underway from Lisbon to Rota, an unrep was made by helicopter from the *Lash Italia* to an AFS. Naval officers and men temporarily on board the barge carrier could also be moved by helicopter. At Rota the ship dropped off some barges from which cargo was lifted by helicopter to some destroyers in port. Finally the barges were laid alongside the AFS and off-loaded by that ship's cargo-handling gear. Though the test took place at a naval port, it could have occurred in any undeveloped bay or anchorage.

Another example of direct fleet support is the lift of the assault follow-on echelon in an amphibious operation. The assault echelon itself is lifted in the Navy's amphibious ships. The assault follow-on echelon, which should arrive within five days of the landing, consists of a great number of men and many weapons and supplies. The Marines depend on merchant ships to carry all these. Later, normal resupply of the troops ashore will also have to be carried in merchant ships.

The Marines are working to shift the location of much of the logistic support for an amphibious opera-

tion from the beach to ships at sea, for which the barge carrier holds promise of great value. Testing has progressed on the handling of LASH barges in a surf and a LASH barge has been lifted in the well deck of a Navy LSD for use in an amphibious exercise. Possible modification of barges for such support functions as power generation, maintenance facilities, and communications facilities clearly offers exciting prospects.

Auxiliary Combatants

The fourth contribution by the merchant marine to defense needs is service as combatants. The privateer, a privately owned armed ship, was an important factor in the naval history of the Revolution and War of 1812. Many of those ships originally were merchant ships, as were the Q ships and auxiliary cruisers of World War I. Similarly, "jeep" carriers converted from tankers and freighters functioned as combatants in World War II. With the hull size and speeds associated with modern, productive, first line merchant ships, there are all sorts of possible application as auxiliary combatants. If modular installations of defensive weapon systems are developed for the self-protection of high value ships, it takes little extension to pass on to an auxiliary combatant role. The Sea Barge and RoRo ships with their large, relatively clear main decks offer obvious possibilities for helicopter and VSTOL aircraft operation. Indeed, the Sea Barge has been termed a "poor man's LHA." It is of interest that the Soviet Union has contracted to build two of these ships on license in a Finnish yard. The problem in this area does not lie in the possible applicability of modern merchant ships for the auxiliary combatant role but rather in the scarcity of ships. The number available for the carriage of vital military and strategic cargoes is marginal at best, so that it would be very difficult to withdraw highly productive ships for other purposes.

Support of Foreign Policy

The fifth contribution of the merchant marine is to provide peacetime presence in support of foreign policy. Sometimes it is in conjunction with and follows from normal commercial voyages. Historically, the British East India Company was a principal factor in British expansion in India. Certainly the voyages of American merchantmen to China and Japan played a role in the development of our own nineteenth century Far Eastern policy. Today the Soviets actively pursue this course of action. A prime example is their penetration into, and eventual domination of, the East African trade, once almost monopolized by the British. The commercial initiative was followed by political initiatives which, in turn, led to increased Soviet influence, particularly in Somalia. Certainly the current expansion of Soviet shipping in the Pacific has political as well as economic overtones. The effects of the arms sales or grants to many countries all around the world are reinforced when the arms arrive in Soviet ships. The United States has not actively pursued this option in recent years, for much of the U. S. grant aid and most foreign sales go in foreign-flag ships, often in third country ships. In this fashion and others there are opportunities to promote U. S. foreign policy through the medium of the American merchant marine. However, the trend towards larger but fewer ships, with cargoes in containers, lessens the opportunity to "show the flag." The Soviets, with their multitude of small conventional ships able to enter small undeveloped ports, are not so hampered.

Course for the Future

In general, it is fair to say that our merchant marine is at best barely adequate for both commerce and defense. The Merchant Marine Act of 1970 stemmed from recognition of the need to improve the competitive position of the U. S. merchant marine and shipbuilding industries. Obviously more needs to be done. Obviously, too, it can be. One has only to look at the postwar rebirth of Japanese shipbuilding and merchant marine, or examine the U. S. wartime experience, to see what can be done.

First of all, it is essential that we recognize the situation for what it is. An island nation needs a strong merchant marine for both commerce and defense. It is not an either/or situation. We need ships at sea and trained seamen in those ships. We cannot get them for commerce alone. At least we have not been able to do so for over a hundred years. We cannot expect to get them for defense alone since defense budget resources are already severely strained by current programs. Therefore, there must be a cooperative program which will elicit investment of both private and government capital, and which will recognize the operating requirements of both commerce and defense. Further, it is clear that in order to generate private investment there must be an opportunity to make a profit.

Secondly, we need to continue and to do more of what we are already doing. The Merchant Marine Act of 1970 was a valuable stimulus. We need to maintain and accelerate that momentum. It is vital that we make our merchant marine as competitive commercially as we possibly can. This means that we must support expansion of any area that affords commercial opportunity.

We must push technology to cut costs as we did in introducing intermodal systems. Strong support is required for the National Maritime Council and for other efforts to increase the share of American trade shipped in American bottoms. In Defense, we should improve the mechanics of the Sealift Readiness Program to meet the requirement for timely response in contingency situations. We should intensify our efforts to develop modern modular installations for the defense of merchant ships and for the use of containerships in support of the fleet. Most of all, we need to learn more about how to use the ships we actually have in the inventory to support military operations.

Thirdly, we ought to take a hard look at all the interlocking and sometimes contradictory rules and regulations which govern the maritime industry. This includes international and foreign regulations as well as those of our own country.

Finally, we need to consider some more radical approaches, most of which would require legislation. For example:

Should there be a means to support the construction and commercial operation of ships of particular value to defense, such as RoRo ships, barge ships, and small tankers?

Should there be a means to help pay for the construction and commercial operation of ships in support of U. S. foreign policy?

Should there be a means to help pay for the construction and commercial operation of U. S.-flag feeder ships for large intermodal carriers? (Small containerships and FLASH have useful possibilities for defense.)

Should there be a better means to develop and install features in commercial ships that would improve their usefulness for defense? (Provision does exist for national defense features. However, practically speaking, it is difficult to do so with features that clearly penalize commercial operation.)

Should there be a means to upgrade the National Defense Reserve Fleet by incentives powerful enough to impel the acquisition of new ships for that fleet?

Should there be additional means to provide governmental impelled cargo for commercial carriers?

These questions are only examples of those that could be examined. The real point to make is that we need to take positive action to generate a workable, cooperative program that will attract private capital and provide ships for both commerce and defense. Many such ships are required by an Island Nation which the United States has become today.

John D Chase

Influence
of
Geography

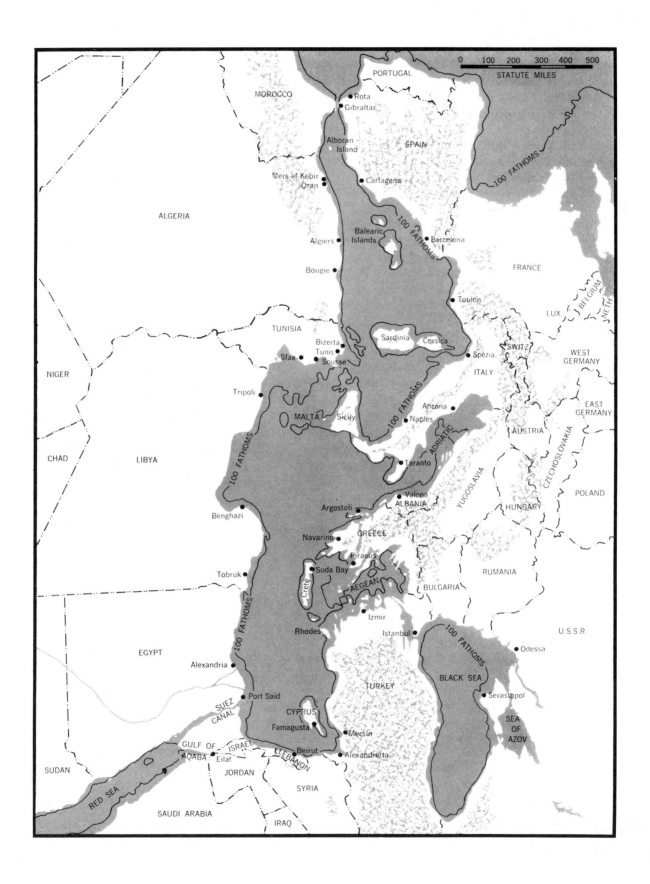

242

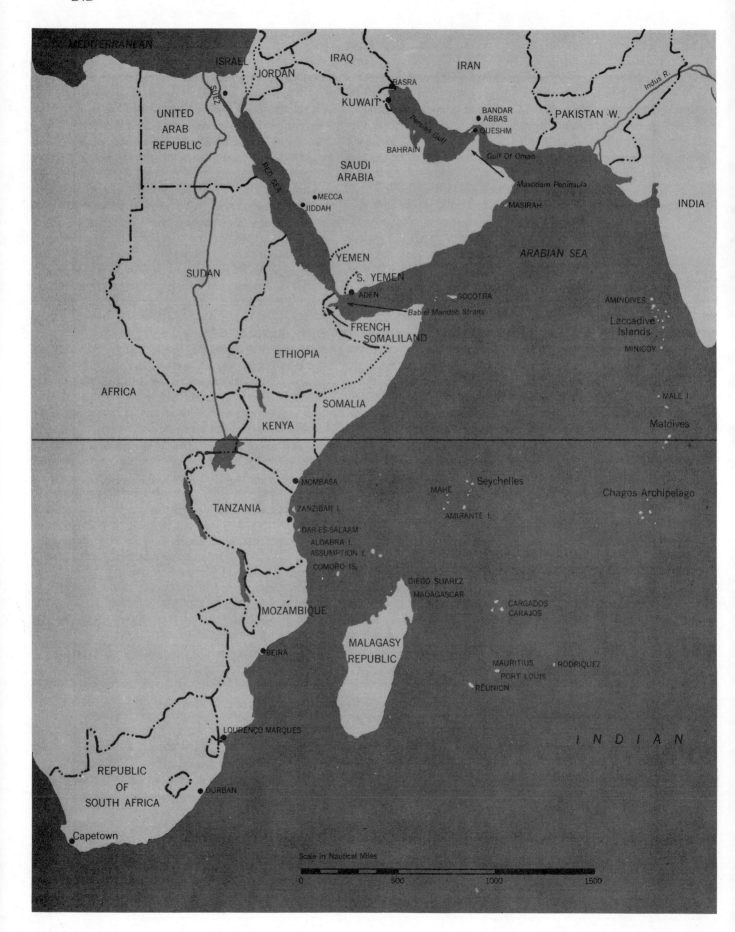

MEDITERRANEAN

ISRAEL
JORDAN
IRAQ
IRAN
Indus R.

SUEZ
KUWAIT
BASRA
BANDAR ABBAS
QUESHM
PAKISTAN W.

UNITED
ARAB
REPUBLIC

SAUDI
ARABIA

Persian Gulf

BAHRAIN
Gulf Of Oman

Masidam Peninsula

INDIA

RED SEA

MECCA
JIDDAH

MASIRAH

ARABIAN SEA

SUDAN

YEMEN

S. YEMEN

SOCOTRA

AMINDIVES

Laccadive
Islands

ADEN
Bab el Mandeb Straits

AFRICA

ETHIOPIA

FRENCH
SOMALILAND

MINICOY

SOMALIA

MALE I.

KENYA

Maldives

MOMBASA

Seychelles

Chagos Archipelago

TANZANIA

ZANZIBAR I.

MAHE

DAR-ES-SALAAM
ALDABRA I.
ASSUMPTION I.
COMORO IS.

AMIRANTE I.

DIEGO SUAREZ
MADAGASCAR

CARGADOS
CARAJOS

MOZAMBIQUE

MALAGASY
REPUBLIC

BEIRA

MAURITIUS
PORT LOUIS
RÉUNION
RODRIQUEZ

LOURENÇO MARQUES

I N D I A N

REPUBLIC
OF
SOUTH AFRICA

DURBAN

Capetown

Scale in Nautical Miles

0   500   1000   1500

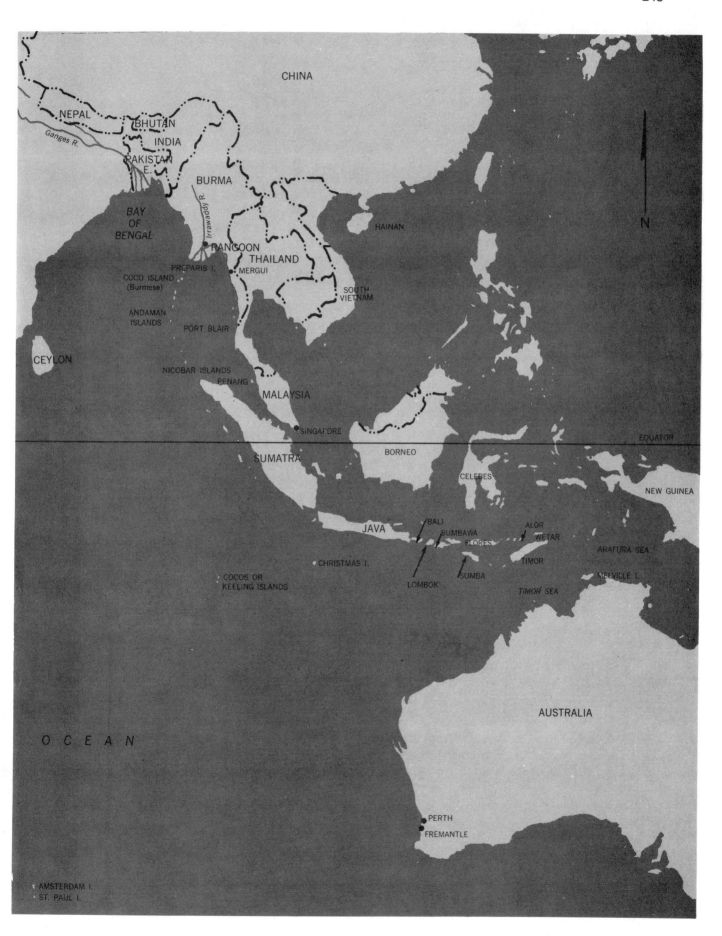

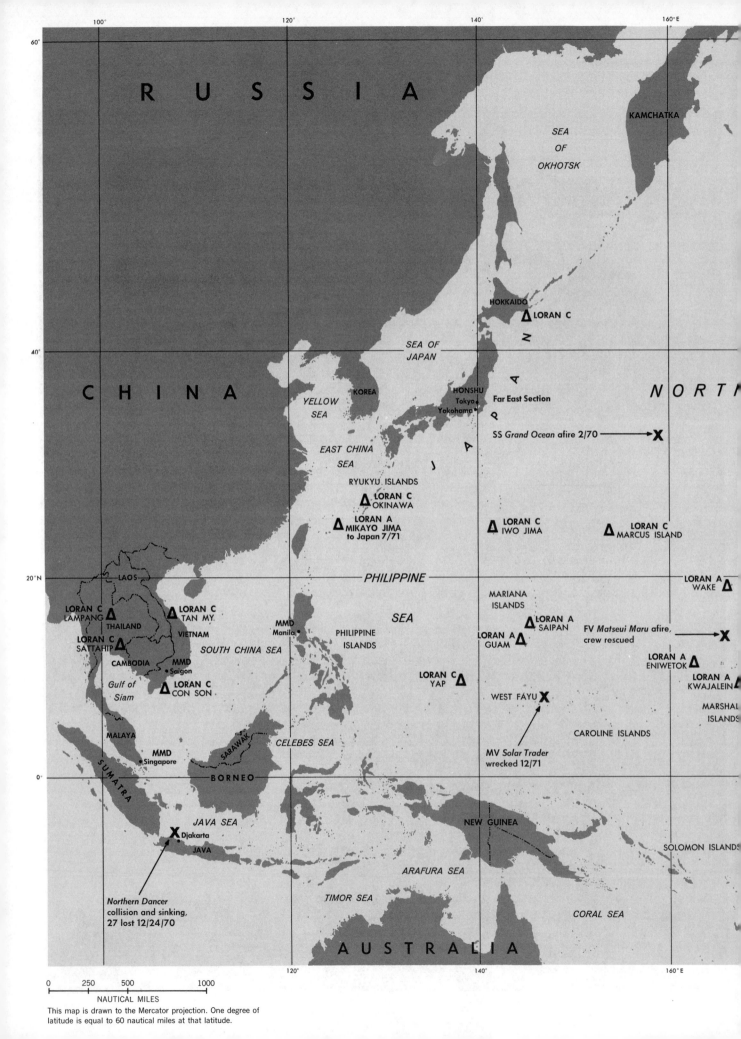

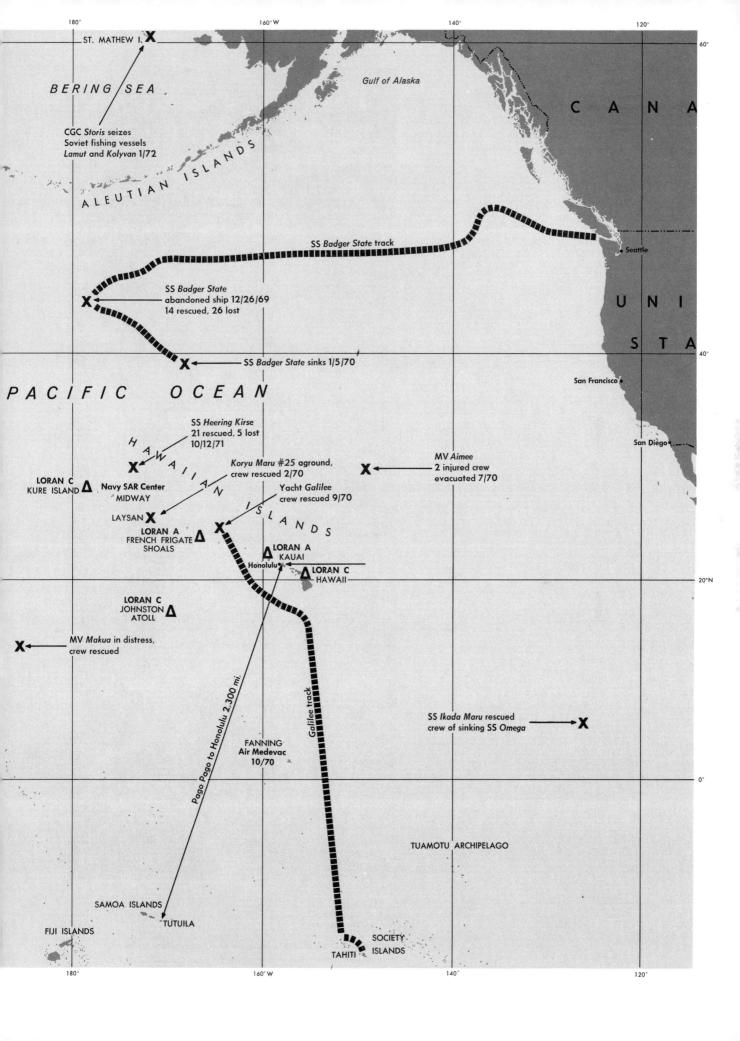

180°   160° W   140°   120°

60°

ST. MATHEW I. **X**

BERING SEA

CGC *Storis* seizes
Soviet fishing vessels
Lamut and *Kolyvan* 1/72

Gulf of Alaska

C A N A

ALEUTIAN ISLANDS

SS *Badger State* track

Seattle

U N I

X   SS *Badger State*
abandoned ship 12/26/69
14 rescued, 26 lost

S T A

40°

X ← SS *Badger State* sinks 1/5/70

San Francisco

PACIFIC   OCEAN

SS *Heering Kirse*
21 rescued, 5 lost
10/12/71

H A W A I I A N

San Diego

X

Koryu Maru #25 aground,
crew rescued 2/70

MV *Aimee*
2 injured crew
evacuated 7/70

X ←

LORAN C
KURE ISLAND △   Navy SAR Center
MIDWAY

Yacht *Galilee*
crew rescued 9/70

I S L A N D S

LAYSAN **X**

X

LORAN A
FRENCH FRIGATE △
SHOALS

△ LORAN A
KAUAI

Honolulu ← △ LORAN C
HAWAII

20°N

LORAN C
JOHNSTON △
ATOLL

X ← MV *Makua* in distress,
crew rescued

Pago Pago to Honolulu 2,300 mi.

Galilee track

SS *Ikada Maru* rescued
crew of sinking SS *Omega* → **X**

FANNING
Air Medevac
10/70

0°

TUAMOTU ARCHIPELAGO

SAMOA ISLANDS

FIJI ISLANDS

TUTUILA

SOCIETY
ISLANDS

TAHITI

180°   160° W   140°   120°

246

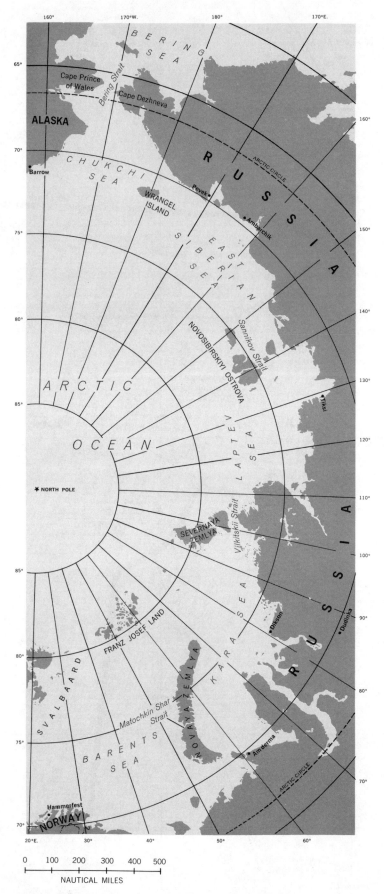

Though secure from attack, compared to its alternatives, the Northern Sea Route, shown here, "can be used for only 130 to 150 days each year and even then the assistance of icebreakers is required."

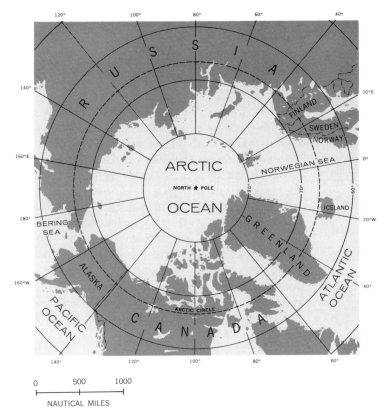

The Arctic Ocean and the surrounding lands. Clearly, "control of the Arctic Ocean is central to the Soviet Union's defense network."

Major Ocean Areas

The major ocean areas in relation to their importance to the maritime interests of the United States are:

a. *Atlantic Ocean.* This is the primary geographical area of maritime interest for the United States. It is an avenue to our allies and trading partners in Europe and is the location of the principal and most probable sea-based threat to this country and its allies.

(1) *Trade Routes and Strategic Points.* Six of the eight major trade routes of the world traverse the Atlantic:

(a) Gulf of Mexico to the East Coast of the United States.

(b) The East Coast of the United States to Northwestern Europe and the Mediterranean.

(c) The Caribbean and Panama Canal to Northwestern Europe and the Mediterranean.

(d) The Persian Gulf to Northwestern Europe and the Mediterranean via the Cape of Good Hope.

(e) South America to Northwestern Europe and the Mediterranean.

(f) Australia and New Zealand to Northwestern Europe and the Mediterranean via the Cape of Good Hope.

Ships transiting these routes converge at focal points as follows:

(a) The Atlantic Coast ports, particularly, New York, Boston, Norfolk and Baltimore.

(b) The Western Approaches to the British Isles and the English Channel.

(c) The Western Approaches to Gibraltar.

(d) The major passages in and out of the Caribbean including the all-important Panama Canal.

(e) The West Bulge of Africa.

(f) The bulge of Brazil.

Virtually all of the strategic raw materials which this country imports are landed at ports on the East and Gulf coasts. These ports process over four-fifths of this country's trade.

(2) *Strategic Imports.* Strategic imports from Latin America and Caribbean nations consist of bauxite, oil, manganese, tungsten and nitrates. Although trade with Africa now represents only about three percent of U.S. world trade, American industry depends on Africa for strategically important cobalt, diamonds, manganese and uranium.

(3) *Access to Markets.* The North Atlantic is the economic seaway which carries ninety percent of the lucrative U.S. trade in manufactured products with Western Europe. The South Atlantic, although of secondary importance, includes the ocean routes for the bulk of raw materials from South America and Africa which help to sustain the U.S. industrial economy. Although the United States perennially enjoys a favorable balance of trade with South America, under the provisions of the Nixon Doctrine the President has pledged his support to promote Latin American trade expansion and generally to improve the lot of the lesser developed countries by improving their access to the expanding markets of the industrialized world.

(4) *Interests and Alliances.* The North Atlantic Treaty Organization (NATO) and the Organization of American States (OAS) are two of our most effective alliances. The large majority of the naval assets of the United States are heavily committed to support the politico-military policies of NATO. A basic feature of the Nixon Doctrine is "Peace Through Partnership," thus it is logical to expect a continued U.S. commitment to NATO with increasing emphasis on the mutual nature of the other members' obligation. In the Western Hemisphere, the United States has strongly endorsed increased cooperation among members of the OAS to enhance peace and stability.

As an expanding population forces the world to rely more heavily upon the sea for food, the Atlantic fishing grounds assume increased importance. The Grand Banks off the coast of Newfoundland is one of the world's largest fishing areas. Here and elsewhere in the Atlantic the fishing interests of the United States are being severely challenged by the Soviet Union. Relatedly, vastly improved technology now permits development of mineral and metallic resources of the seas in areas formerly denied to man. International agreements governing fishing rights and exploitation of ocean resources are needed to permit equitable opportunity for peaceful development.

b. *Pacific Ocean.* The largest of the oceans is of special interest and concern for the United States. It surrounds our newest state and, with the exception of Puerto Rico and the Virgin Islands, all of this country's extra-continental island responsibilities. It is strategically important because of the proximity of the USSR to U.S. territory. Petropavlovsk, a Soviet naval base located on the Pacific-Bering Sea boundary, is less than 500 miles from the Aleutian Islands.

(1) *Trade Routes and Strategic Points.* Four of the eight principal ocean transport lanes traverse the Pacific. Seaborne materials are vital to the very existence of Hawaii, Alaska, Guam, Australia, New Zealand, South Korea, Taiwan and Japan and are economically important throughout the basin. Focal points for sea trade are the points of entry through the Strait of Magellan, the Panama Canal, the Malacca Strait and, of course, the major harbors widely dispersed throughout the area. Pacific Ocean shipping will expand as the population of Hawaii grows, her resources are exploited and three way trade multiplies between Japan, Canada and the U.S., and between these industrial nations and the developing nations of Asia. For example, Japanese imports of U.S. goods are expected to be as high as $20 billion by 1980 and both nations will be deeply involved economically throughout the basin.

(2) *Strategic Imports.* Imports from the Pacific area include: chromite from the Philippines, lead from Australia, manganese from India and Australia, oil from Indonesia, natural rubber from Malaysia and Indonesia, and thorium, tin, titanium, tungsten, zinc and zircon from Australia and Malaysia.

(3) *Access to Markets.* Access is expected to be of increasing importance as the Pacific basin slowly develops stronger economic relationships which may even extend to a Pacific Basin trade area as envisioned by some futurists.

(4) *Interests and Alliances.* Principal U.S. interests are maintaining the integrity of U.S. territory in the Pacific and preserving the ability to utilize the sea for trade, food and development. The United States has military and economic alliances with all free world countries of the Pacific with the exception of Malaysia, Indonesia, the Fiji Islands and those islands associated with France. Despite the planned withdrawal of ground combat troops from Southeast Asia, the Navy is expected to maintain a continuing presence there and throughout the Western Pacific.

As in the Atlantic, the United States depends on the Pacific for a major portion of its seafood. Expansion of Asian trade and the development of the oceans resources are areas of increasing interests.

c. *Mediterranean Sea.* Major U.S. interests are the protection of the southern flank of NATO, the preservation of U.S. economic advantages—particularly with respect to the oil producing countries of the Mid-East, the promotion of peace and stability, the lessening of Soviet influence and the maintenance of access to communication facilities and resources. Of primary concern is the increasing presence of the Soviet Navy.

(1) *Trade Routes and Strategic Points.* The vast majority of seaborne trade passing through the Strait of Gibraltar originates or terminates in countries that border the Mediterranean. These countries import material from and export material to the Americas, the Near East, Northern Europe and Asia. Trade routes in the Mediterranean are the principal lifelines for three of our NATO allies: Italy, Greece and Turkey. In addition to the Strait of Gibraltar, other Mediterranean choke points are the Bosporus/Dardanelles, the Strait of Sicily and the Mediterranean end of the Suez Canal near Port Said. (The Suez Canal choke point is currently not meaningful.)

(2) *Strategic Imports.* Only a very small portion of U.S. strategic imports, including oil, emanate from countries bounding the Mediterranean; however, our NATO and other European and Asian allies are largely dependent on oil from the Middle East which is supplies by tankers transitting the Mediterranean.

(3) *Access to Markets.* Trade with the countries bordering the Mediterranean is estimated to comprise only about five percent of U.S. world trade; however, there is an opportunity for improved trade with the Arab countries if a peaceful settlement of Arab-Israeli problems is achieved.

(4) *Interests and Alliances.* The United States has significant economic investments in the oil-producing countries of the Middle East, particularly in Libya. The Mediterranean is the water boundary of the NATO southern flank and is a major sea line of communications. The Sixth Fleet is proof positive of the continuing interest in and commitment to U.S. allies in the area; accordingly, the preservation of access to the Mediterranean is a vital interest.

The United States is heavily committed to maintaining the integrity of Israel and seeks to prevent Russian domination in the Middle East.

d. *Indian Ocean.* The primary interests of the United States are maintaining stability in the area without domination by either the CPR or the USSR and ensuring continual western access to the oil of the Middle East.

(1) *Trade Routes and Strategic Points.* Trade routes emanate chiefly from the entrances and choke points with no significant trade confined within the ocean basin. Choke points are at the Cape of Good Hope, Bab el Mandeb in the Red Sea, the Strait of Hormung in the Persian Gulf and the Strait of Malacca. If reopened, the Suez Canal will again become a strategic waterway.

(2) *Strategic Imports.* The United States is directly concerned with antimony, chromite and uranium from South and East Africa and beryl and mica from India. However, Middle East oil is of

prime importance to U.S. allies in Europe, Australia and Japan.

(3) *Access to Markets.* U.S. trade in the Indian Ocean area amounts to less than 8% of all U.S. trade; however, because of the underdeveloped nature of most of the countries along the littoral, any foreign trade is important. The emphasis on trade as a means to help the developing nations as expressed in the Nixon Doctrine suggests increased commercial opportunity in the area.

(4) *Interests and Alliances.* SEATO and CENTO tie the U.S. to the area although both alliances are of questionable military strength. Probably more important are the ANZUS Pact and ties with Iran and Ethiopia. Coupled with the British withdrawal of forces, the USSR has expanded its interests and influence in East Africa, the Seychelles, the Arabian Peninsula, Socotra Island and India. The United States has reached agreement with the British for the development of Diego Garcia as a small naval installation. The only other facilities which might be counted on if needed are an Australian naval facility being built south of Perth and the Australian facility at Cocos Island. British and Australian agreements with Malaysia and Singapore might possibly provide an entrée to facilities at Penang and Singapore if required.

In order to fulfill SEATO and CENTO commitments, unrestricted access to and operations within the Indian Ocean are required.

e. *The Arctic Ocean.* Current United States interest in the Arctic centers on the existence of proven mineral and oil deposits. Oil, in particular, exists under the coastal plains north of Alaska's Brooks Range in sufficient quantities to make the United States the world's leading oil producing nation. The problems of oil and mineral recovery in this remote and harsh region are formidable; however, even more challenging is the problem of transporting them to U.S. refineries and processing plants.

(1) *Trade Routes and Strategic Points.* There are presently no Arctic trade routes of significance to the United States or its allies. However, the Soviet Union has developed a viable Northeast Passage across the top of Siberia. Russia's growing capability to keep this route open to Soviet merchant and naval shipping has increased the strategic value of this route. Concomittantly it has permitted Russia's arctic naval skills to be developed to a much higher degree than those of any other nation.

It is in the strategic interest of the United States to develop an arctic maritime capability in support of oil and mineral exploitation in the Alaskan and Canadian Arctic.

(2) *Strategic Imports.* There are at present no strategic imports for the United States either from or via the Arctic Ocean or its coastal areas.

(3) *Access to Markets.* At present the Arctic Ocean plays no geographical role in either providing or denying access to world markets. However, the possibility of a clear and safe Northwest Passage exists and could become a reality in the next decade.

(4) *Interests and Alliances.* It is interesting that of the five littoral states on the Arctic Ocean, four are members of the NATO alliance, the fifth being the Soviet Union. It is therefore important that the United States maintain a capability to project credible naval power into the Arctic in order to preclude an unchallenged Soviet hegemony in the region.

The value of the polar sea for covert operations by nuclear powered submarines has been demonstrated. Surface detection of submerged missile-launching submarines is virtually out of the question. Should the Soviets develop an underwater-launched missile capable of 3,000-mile ranges an attack from the Arctic would be extremely difficult to detect with current warning systems. It is in the interest of the United States to develop a viable ASN capability in the Atlantic.

Priority of Effort

Many of the maritime interests of the United States transcend geographical ocean boundaries; nevertheless, the major ocean areas in order of maritime priority are:

1. The Atlantic, by virtue of the volume of trade with Europe, strategic interdependence with the members of NATO, and the predominant threat to the United States and free-world shipping, is of paramount importance.

2. The Pacific ranks second because of the need to protect the territory of the United States, including the continental United States, from a sea-based attack and to support current commitments requiring a U.S. military presence in the area.

3. The strategic location of the Mediterranean, bordering southern Europe and the Middle East and connecting the Black Sea and the Atlantic Ocean, is the basis for assigning that sea third ranking in priority.

4. The potential power vacuum and the need to deter Soviet expansion results in fourth ranking for the Indian Ocean.

5. The significant economic and strategic potential of the Arctic Ocean belies its relegation to last place in this priority list; however, based on an assessment of current relative importance it is ranked fifth in importance of the major ocean areas.

Where is the Western Navy?
The World Wonders

By Commander Hans Garde, Royal Danish Navy

Prize Essay 1975

During the Cuban Crisis of 1962, it was the Russians' turn to wonder where their Navy was and why Soviet policy could be skewered so swiftly in those warm waters by the cold steel of Western sea power. In a future crisis, the Northeast Atlantic and the frigid waters to the north may prove to be an irresistible temptation for a Soviet maritime response or even for a Soviet demonstration of power which might leave the Western world wondering where, indeed, its own Navy had gone—and why.

On 25 October 1944, Admiral William F. Halsey, Jr., received a message from Admiral Chester W. Nimitz which asked: "Where is, repeat, where is Task Force 34? The world wonders." The last phrase—the end padding—was not part of Nimitz' original message but was not removed before the message was handed to Halsey who, enraged at the time, later conceded that it was "infernally plausible."

Since those days, 30 years ago, when, by its victory at Leyte Gulf, the U. S. Navy again demonstrated the transcendent importance of sea power to maritime nations, the wheel of history has turned many times. Halsey and Nimitz are gone. Apparently abandoned, too, are many of the policies and strategies which had been pursued by Western maritime nations for centuries.

Today, no one has to ask where the Soviet Navy is. But where, for example, are the Western world's navies in the Northeast Atlantic, the North Sea, the Baltic Approaches, and the Norwegian Sea? This area has for centuries been vital to the security of the traditional maritime power, Great Britain. Likewise, it is today of decisive importance for the most modern alliance of maritime states, NATO.

Where once there was a clear dividing line between maritime and continental strategy, today, two traditional maritime powers, England and America, are allied with two traditional continental powers, France and Germany, in defense against the pressure from the nation that occupies the heartland on the Eurasian mainland, the Soviet Union.

Is the Soviet Union pursuing a continental strategy? Years from now, historians analyzing today's world situation may well conclude that the U.S.S.R. had not pursued a continental strategy since the late 1950s or at least since 1962, the year of the Cuban Missile Crisis.

The Soviet Union has made no gains on the continent since the formation of NATO in 1949, and indications of her determination to attempt such continental land acquisitions have become fewer. On the other hand, the Soviet Union has succeeded extremely well, so far, in exerting such pressure on her neighbors, that the maritime powers have forsaken their traditional policy of avoiding continental entanglement.

For more than two centuries, this policy has been one of the most important aspects of England's relationships with continental Europe. It produced the English commitment of an expeditionary force on the continent, to be withdrawn either shortly after restoring the peace, or without serious humiliation before a defeat. The same policy was pursued by the United States after World War I. But, since World War II, the Soviet Union has succeeded in keeping so much pressure on the Central Front in Europe that today, 30 years after the defeat of Nazi-Germany, England finds it necessary to maintain a major part of her army on the continent, not as an expeditionary force, but as the British Army on the Rhine. Likewise, the United States continues to maintain the Seventh Army in Germany, in spite of the heavy domestic pressure for troop reductions. These U. S. forces are of immense importance to the credibility of American support to Europe; but they are expensive, and costs of maintaining the troops in Europe have resulted in reduced budgets for the development of naval forces in the Western World. The Soviet Union, however, has steadily increased her maritime capacity to achieve the now disproportionate balance between the naval forces of East and West in relation to the maritime interests they have to defend. This maritime capacity has given the Soviet Union a new instrument for adopting the maritime powers' traditional elegant strategy of indirect approach. The strategy, so well described by British strategist Liddell Hart, had been pursued by England, for example, in order to avoid continental entanglement, and by the United States in its Pacific drives during World War II.

Since at least the days of Czar Peter the Great, Russia has dreamed of what today has clearly become a Soviet reality. The strategists in the Kremlin seem convinced by Admiral S. G. Gorshkov's arguments, and they apparently understand Mahan better than most continental leaders have in the past. The Russians have also clearly digested Mahan's idea of quantity, and they are willing to pay the price for continued naval power and military preparedness.

Less than 100 years ago, in 1889, the British Parliament based its naval expansion plan on the principle of a navy equal to those of any other two European nations—the "two power standard." Less than 25 years ago, the U. S. Navy not only fulfilled the Naval Act of 1916, authorizing "a navy second to none," but, leading the navies of the Free World, she exercised unchallenged control of the seas. Today, no one in the West is talking of a navy in relation to a "two power standard." In fact, in the *Proceedings* and other forums, the U. S. Navy seems to be asking itself whether it is "a navy second to none."

How did this situation arise? How is it that the country in which Mahan was born has permitted such a development, that the Western World, completely dependent on the sea, has allowed itself to be deprived of the unchallenged control of the sea by the Soviet Union, a country which is almost completely independent of the sea?

The strategy of containment exercised by the United States and the emergence of China as a great world power has closed the ring around the Soviet Union. She, therefore, has only one avenue open for expansion—that of the world's oceans. The Russians have long aspired to sea power, but immediately after World War II they had several major domestic problems. Twenty millions had been killed and 30% of the economy destroyed. It is little wonder that they then proclaimed—and still pretend today—that defense of the homeland is the first and only priority. However, the West has never been convinced by this statement, although the change in the nuclear balance with its related strategies has tended to give the Soviet Union a very good camouflage for her build-up of the Navy. Russia—the country that created the impression in the United States, of a bomber gap and later of a missile gap—is determined to achieve, at the least, a nuclear parity. Similarly, she has with much success initiated and maintained a variety of challenges to the West around her perimeter. These challenges on land have attracted our attention and called for our increased monetary spending, while Russia herself has steadily increased her sea power in such a way that it appears to be an indirect approach to the position of a real maritime power, in possession of the means for projecting her interests on the other side of the oceans and around the globe.

The Soviet naval expansion has taken place while the West has reduced its naval capacity. And had it not been for the SSBNs which again gave life, outside naval circles, to the general public interest in maritime matters, the reductions might have continued to an alarming level. Among political influences which shed light on this situation is, for instance, the 1957 British White Paper, which stated that "the role of naval forces in total war is somewhat uncertain." Yet, the arrival of the age of nuclear parity with its risk of escalation has brought naval forces to the forefront of contemporary strategy. The sea is often described as a neutral environment; it has neither centers of civil population nor of industry—it belongs to no one. Thus, a conflict substantially confined to the sea offers an attractive military option to the Soviet Union.

Consequently, the Soviet Union has been able to establish a naval presence of impressive dimensions around the globe, and maritime problems have again come to public attention. The Soviet build-up in the Mediterranean during the late 1960s and in the Indian Ocean during the early 1970s has especially focused attention on Soviet maritime expansion. In addition, visits and exercises of Soviet warships in Cuban waters and in the Pacific off the U. S. West Coast have drawn the attention of the Western news media. But, outside of professional naval interests, very little attention has been paid to what has happened at the same time in the Northeast Atlantic.

The development in this area is dominated by four characteristics. First, the Northeast Atlantic is the key area to Western vulnerability. The shortest route for exchange of intercontinental missiles between the super powers is an extension of the area, from Greenland in the west, via Iceland, to the Scandinavian countries. Additionally, SSBNs operate in and through this region making it an essential area for the first and principal function of the U. S. Navy, its contribution to strategic deterrence of nuclear war.

Second, the sea is of great importance to all the bordering countries, as recently shown in the fishing disputes between Iceland and Great Britain. Furthermore, the merchant marines of the Nordic countries total more than 14% of the world's fleet, while the Nordic NATO members, together with England, contribute almost a quarter of the world's fleet. These ships provide a most important part of the ships available to the West, and they require protection—in the American term, Sea Control.

Third, the Nordic countries are less influenced by maritime aspects as one proceeds geographically from west to east. In spite of many links, such as common history and culture, this fact has forced the countries into pursuing different security policies. Denmark and Norway, both occupied by the Germans during World War II for purely maritime reasons, are today, together with Iceland, members of NATO. The central country,

Sweden, although dependent on the sea, is not of essential maritime importance, and she has chosen a neutral policy. The easternmost country, Finland, is primarily of importance to the Soviet Union in a continental context. However, these five countries are often regarded as forming a subsystem in the international system. Within this subsystem exists a Nordic balance between East and West, the maintenance of which, for the Western NATO members, is entirely dependent on the ability of their allies, especially the United States, to perform the third mission of the U. S. Navy: Projection of Power ashore.

Fourth, within this area are two of the Soviet Union's four accesses to the open sea, and the major part—more than 60%—of the Soviet Navy is based, maintained, and trained here. The capabilities of the Russian Navy in the area, and the concentration of its amphibious forces are major, perhaps overwhelming, factors in the security of the Nordic countries. A measure of this situation may be the massive and steadily increasing naval presence of the Soviet fleets compared with the presence of the U. S. Navy—its fourth mission area in a period short of war.

The four characteristics of the Northeast Atlantic in relation to the four missions of the U. S. Navy dominate the development in the post-World War II period.

The Soviet Union, using the traditional "salami-tactic," has gradually extended the pattern of naval operations from the fleet base areas of the Baltic and Barents seas to the forward defense zone, established in the Greenland-Iceland-United Kingdom gap, which covers the access routes to and from the remaining Atlantic. This progressive shift to forward deployment has been justified by reference to the traditional Soviet naval doctrine of "Defense of the Homeland" against the Western nuclear threat, posed from sea areas more and more distant from the Soviet Union. On the other hand, Admiral Gorshkov, a member of the Soviet Politburo, has more than once indicated that the role of the Soviet Navy is not limited to "Defense of the Homeland." With naval presence as a measurement, only the word expansion can illustrate current Soviet maritime policies. During the last five years Soviet naval activities in the Atlantic have increased by some 50%.

The largest Soviet exercise to date was the world-wide Exercise *Okean,* in 1970, which at its peak involved 80 naval vessels in the Northeast Atlantic. In comparison, the largest NATO exercise in the same area so far has been Exercise Strong Express, in 1972, which involved only 60 warships.

Since 1969, extensive transfers of surface and submarine units between the two Soviet fleets in the area, and between the fleets and the Mediterranean squadron have taken place, with maneuvers en route. So Soviet warships, including a number of patrolling units, have today established a permanent offshore presence in the Northeast Atlantic between the United States and the Nordic NATO countries, which finally could become located behind the Soviet forward defense zone and beyond that of the United States. In such a situation, the combined Northern and Baltic Soviet Fleet would have fulfilled the important task of creating impressions of Soviet power and thereby reduced the perceived efficacy of U. S. guarantees to Northern Europe. Thus, Admiral Gorshkov's Navy would have obtained, through an indirect approach, what the U. S. continental commitment has denied to the Red Army.

The littoral states in the Northeast Atlantic are all governed in democratic stability; there are no signs of serious internal problems; and conflicting interests between the countries are extremely unlikely to lead to violence. Yet, the fishing dispute between England and Iceland has indicated that a clash of interests can result in temporary cooling of relations; but, much more seriously, this dispute has been connected with the maritime surveillance patrols of aircraft, flying out of Keflavik, and has caused increased anti-NATO opinions in Iceland. Any Icelandic attempt to negotiate an American evacuation from Keflavik would be against the interests of other littoral states and of the United States because the surveillance from Iceland is not only directed against the Soviet deterrent, but it is, in an area where satellite reconnaissance is difficult, of great importance to the credibility of transatlantic reinforcement. Because the defense of Iceland is solely dependent on U. S. assistance, and since the Cod War has been settled, the situation at Keflavik is again normal and the crisis in the area has been relieved by the normal stability without giving outside nations opportunities for interference.

The internal stability in the littoral states area is one of three realities. The second reality is that all the Nordic countries devote their entire defense to anti-invasion missions because of the pressure from the East. Thus, the Nordic countries have been largely content so far to leave the strategic protection of their large maritime trade to Great Britain and the United States. Simultaneously, the littoral states, including the United Kingdom, are unable to maintain a permanent offshore naval presence in the area of more than one or two frigates per country, engaged primarily in fishery protection.

The third reality has grown out of the Soviet struggle for nuclear parity and the related continental confrontation in central Europe. The area is not covered in diplomatic attempts to realize the era of detente through negotiations, for instance, in the Strategic Arms Limitations Talks or on Mutual Force Reduction in Europe. The Northeast Atlantic is an area between the East and the West in which there are no visible or invisible limits on influences between the superpowers.

The extensive offshore oil drilling in the area has added a new defense problem to those of the littoral states. Offshore exploitation of oil resources has until now been concentrated in the northern North Sea, but surveys are being carried out farther north, and drilling north of 62°N off the Norwegian coast is expected to begin this year. The many oil rigs and the pipelines, in being and under construction, are all very vulnerable, and, for the first time, they are placed in areas not clearly controlled by any one power—in contrast to the situation in the Mexican Gulf or in the Caspian Sea. So the Soviet Union and Norway have had exploratory talks on the division of the continental shelf in the Barents Sea, but the Russians are reluctant to negotiate delimitations based on the 1958 Geneva convention on the continental shelf. The Soviets have even been reported to hold the view that the relative power of Norway and the Soviet Union is relevant to a decision on the delimitation of sovereignty on the shelf.

In all countries engaged in offshore oil drilling—Denmark, England and Norway—a major portion of investment and know-how is of American origin, indicating that the United States has two great maritime interests in common with the allies around the Northeast Atlantic—economic and military interests.

The Northeast Atlantic has step-by-step become an area in which the likelihood of a successful Soviet demonstration of power has increased. The Soviet Union has met maritime humiliations in distant waters, for example, during the Cuban crisis in 1962 and as a result of U. S. mining off Haiphong in 1972. In a future crisis, the Northeast Atlantic may well constitute an attractive area for a Soviet maritime response or even for Soviet initiation of a demonstration of power. A demonstration, whether threatened or actual, might take a number of forms, as for instance: deflection of shipping; declared mining of specific areas; or boarding or destruction of oil rigs or ships.

The heavy overload on American defense resources in relation to the global role of the United States has tended to give the Northeast Atlantic a low priority for a deployed U. S. naval presence compared with other areas such as East Asia with the Seventh Fleet or the southern flank of NATO with the Sixth Fleet in the Mediterranean. In the Indian Ocean the United States is taking up the Soviet challenge, after the withdrawal of the Royal Navy. This commitment is taken up by America in spite of the drastic cuts in naval strength, amounting, since 1965, to 25% of the ships, 20% of combat aircraft and 7% of the personnel. In these areas, outside home waters and attracting world attention, the United States is maintaining a naval presence. These preventive deployments, enable the Western World to show a presence in peacetime which is measured in figures, such as the number of surface ships per day, comparable to the effort of the Soviet Navy. Such figures, of course, do not necessarily illustrate factual strength in the area, but they tend to be used—or perhaps manipulated—in each country's interpretation of the credibility of an ally or the intentions of an opponent.

In the Northeast Atlantic, the United States has relied for many years on a minimal naval presence in the form of reactive deployments without any preventive deployments. Thus, the U. S. Navy might be able to respond with surface ships to a crisis in the area only after considerable transit time from the normal operating areas of the Second Fleet.

In the light of the interest the Soviet Union demonstrates in the Northeast Atlantic and considering the background of recent developments in the area, it becomes questionable whether reactive deployments in addition to the permanent but sparse offshore presence of littoral allies is sufficient. Three arguments indicate that preventive deployments of U. S. naval surface ships, although only periodically or in small numbers, would be of relatively great value.

▶ With or without drastic cuts in American continental commitments on the central front in Europe, an increased naval presence along the northern transatlantic route for reinforcements of the northern flank and the central front would add to the credibility of the alliance.

▶ The United States is the only Western country which has concluded an agreement with the Soviet Union to prevent incidents between navies, one of the results of the summit meeting in Moscow in 1972.

▶ The danger that a general war would escalate into a nuclear exchange seems accepted by both sides as too great a risk. Thus, the fear of escalation is most inhibiting for the Soviets, when faced with a U. S. naval presence. Furthermore, this presence would give the American administration greater flexibility for crisis management than would a solely allied naval presence.

The greatest hindrance to such a preventive deployment of surface ships is the number of units available. With a continuous building rate of combatant and amphibious ships, as in the period 1966 to 1971, where more than two Soviet units were built for each American ship, it would soon become impossible for the U. S.

Navy to continue to counter the Soviet naval expansion. In order to avoid a headline in the newspapers like that of this essay, the West needs a strong, deployed navy—founded on a strong U. S. Navy.

Such a navy would give the best possibilities for stability in the world of today where the continental power, the Soviet Union, has been stopped on the continent and, therefore, now pursues the elegant indirect approach of maritime strategy under the existence of nuclear parity and the risk of escalation.

Such a Western navy would continuously be able, in response to any worldwide Soviet attempt of power demonstration, to pose a threat to the Soviet maritime influence in the part of the world's oceans where Soviet naval presence is greatest and most important for the Soviet Union herself—in the Northeast Atlantic. Simultaneously, it would maintain the credibility of NATO.

Such a navy in the Northeast Atlantic, with the four mentioned characteristics, the three realities and the two major U. S. maritime interests, would constitute the best guarantee against a Soviet demonstration in a suitable ocean area close to Soviet bases.

Perhaps we ought to stop thinking of the Russian bear as being brown for, before our eyes, he has become a bear of a different color. His new white coat, like a flag of truce (detente) enthralls us, but it should not make us forget that the polar bear is one of the most completely amphibious (and predacious) of all the mammals and thoroughly acclimated to the frigid waters of the north. The only, but not necessarily lonely, hunter that can cope with him is a strong Western navy.

Commander Garde graduated from the Naval Academy, Copenhagen in 1961 as a Lieutenant. His first assignment on board the corvette HDMS *Flora* was followed by duty in fast patrol boats as Commanding Officer, Division Commander and Senior Division Commander. He served on the staff of the Chief of Defense from 1970-1974. He has lectured at the Naval Academy, Copenhagen on naval warfare, history, and strategy and is now studying staff training at the Royal Navy Staff College, Greenwich, and in Denmark. An avid sailor, Commander Garde has participated in the Bermuda and Transatlantic races. He is a member of the International Institute for Strategic Studies, London.

NATO's Tender Watery Flanks

Where lie the flanks of European NATO and why are they so important?

By JOSEPH PALMER

Commander Joseph Palmer served in the Royal Navy from 1926 to 1962, edited the British Navy Magazine from 1964 to 1970, and is currently editor of Navy International and a much-published writer on maritime defense.

ONCE UPON A TIME, wars were fun, issues simple, excuses superfluous, and the whole field of battle called for little more than a modest acreage with good exits to the rear. At that time flanks were, quite simply, the extremities of the respective armies, easily spotted with the naked eye and of self-evident significance.

Not so in today's East-West line-up. There are, to be sure—for many hundreds of miles across the erstwhile smiling plains and hills of central Europe—the barbed wire, watch-towers, tank-traps, and all the other dreary furniture of politico-military confrontation, a front that even the most obtuse could hardly overlook.

But what about the flanks?

It is not sufficient to point out that, sooner or later, every front line, however emphatically it has been drawn, must end, and that in this case, therefore, the flanks can be found where the front line falls off the continent into the sea.

That is true, of course—up to a point. But it is far from the whole truth. So, before going any further, it might be helpful to put forward a tentative but practical definition of what does constitute a flank in the context of the Cold War in Europe. If, therefore, one can work on the hypothesis that the flanks are "ground or water, not forming part of the front line but associated with its extremities, and of such politico-economic-military interest that one, the other or both contestants wish to operate on it (or in it), dominate or occupy it, or exercise any kind of regime over it," one is halfway to realizing that the matter has spread a long way from those sidelines earlier referred to.

This tentative definition tries to bring out one other important new aspect of flanks: the variety of reasons for their significance. They are not only military redoubts, but also highways to the Great Out Yonder. Possibly most important of all, they are now valuable for themselves. That is, for the resources of harvest (such as fish) and, more important, the oil and other aids to gracious living that can be scooped up from their depths.

Many complications stem from the inconvenient state of affairs that not only are NATO's flanks maritime, for all practical purposes, but also that both sides are maritime powers—a state of affairs that did not exist even a couple of decades ago. Thus the flanks are far from being "ends," but are, instead, "extensions" on, over, or under which the

The attack carrier USS JOHN F. KENNEDY steams through the North Sea during Exercise Strong Express-accompanied by (counter-clockwise): MNLMS AMSTER-DAM (Netherlands); HMS NORFOLK (United Kingdom); MNLMS OVERIJSSEL (Netherlands); and FGNS SHLESWIG-HOLSTEIN (West Germany).(U.S. Navy photo by Lt. R.C. Moen.)

contest can be—indeed, is being—waged just as vigorously as hitherto on land.

The flanks are extensions, but they also have another awkward characteristic: their starting points can usually be discovered around high-water mark, as it were, but where do they end? Like everything else maritime, they cannot be precisely and tidily delineated on a chart and so nailed down like some strategic carpet on which the contestants can be relied on to tread.

The flanks are fluid, which is not to say that they are chaotic. Far from it. Provided that the maritime qualification is borne in mind, there is a great deal to be learned: first, from consideration of the geographical locations, physical natures, natural resources, and politics of the areas; second, from relating those to the desires of the contestants; and, finally, to the various means at each side's disposal for achieving those desires.

View from the Kremlin

As seen by Russia—which, for NATO purposes, is a useful way to look at things once in a while—Western Europe is a many-branched and inconvenient peninsula shutting her off from the open ocean and away from the broad wide world in which she now sees her destiny. If, however, she cannot bulldoze her way through the middle, she clearly must seek a way around the ends: clandestinely

if possible, by pressure if deemed expedient, and by overt force if driven to it—very much in that order.

First, then, one should identify the flanks on which the game will be played, the "areas of interest" defined above.

Four sea areas (with their adjoining land) present themselves:

(1) *Northern.* NATO's near-orthodox left flank, consisting of the north Norwegian Sea, Barents Sea, and Arctic Ocean, together with Finnmark (Norway's northernmost *fylker* or county).

(2) *Baltic.* The shores of that brackish lake are shared by NATO members Denmark and Federal Germany, Pact members Russia, German Democratic Republic, and Poland, neutral Sweden, and all-but-swallowed Finland.

(3) *Black Sea.* Again, shared inland waters—between Turkey-just-in-NATO, Russia and satellites on its northwest shores—but, unlike the Baltic, virtually ice-free.

(4) *Mediterranean.* The whole of that 2,000-mile stretch of water must be thought of as a flank within the present definition, with the added interest that its riparian states include almost every shade of political color: NATO-members (though not contiguous and in some current discord), European neutrals, China-backed Communists, Arabs, Jews—everyone, it might be said, except its one-time rulers, the British.

The Baltic and Black Seas are flanks in that they are

areas of sea adjoining land frontiers and, therefore, liable to be scenes of activities similar to those at the ends of the line, though on a very much smaller scale and of less significance. They should be borne in mind but merit little more than a mention.

The chief geographical significance of the two main flanks is their vast size: that on the north extending virtually to the pole and, in width, as far west as the Denmark Strait; that on the south biting deep into NATO's side all along the Mediterranean. It might even be said that nature has already turned the southern flank. Unlike the north, the water area is limited (though, by the same token, the uncommitted countries of the African littoral could also be seen as flanks in the broadest sense).

Rueful Riches

At first sight the prospect of becoming the richest people in Europe, and without undue exertion, might seem attractive to the Norwegians, but it is possible that Norway's four million will come to rue the day that oil was found in such quantities and so close off their shores. How much oil *is* there in the European Arctic, which, after all, is a pretty large place that offers few comforts to the prospector? The Russians are quoted as claiming that at least half the world's reserves are sitting there—under the ice, it is true, but nevertheless just waiting to be tapped.

Perhaps. At all events, there is reason to expect plenty, and there are quite clear proofs that there *is* a great deal, here and now, in the ice-free Norwegian fields. All of which makes the cold, stormy waters off Nordkap extremely valuable (if waterlogged) real estate, liable to encourage Norway's hefty eastern neighbor—population 60 times that of Norway—to think progressively: first, "reasonable access"; then, through "participation," to ever-increasing influence leading to "irreversible sovereignty."

However, the history of Svalbard (Spitzbergen) since World War I suggests that a Soviet snatch is still some way off. The Svalbard Treaty of 1920, signed by 43 countries, granted sovereignty to Norway and universal rights to all countries to exploit.

Only Russia and Norway took up the latter option (to mine coal) but the interesting point is that Russia's proposal of condominium with Norway was quickly dropped when it met resistance not only from Norway but from the signatories. Egil Ulstein, a Norwegian diplomatist, maintains (in "Nordic Security," Adelphi Paper 81, International Institute for Strategic Studies, London, 1971) that "Historically, Russia has rarely shown aggressive intentions towards its Nordic neighbors."

All the same, the lure is there. However, perhaps to Russians the acquisition of Norwegian oil (they have their own) is not so important as free transit, both military and mercantile.

Transit and Use

In a consideration of the major flanks as transit areas or areas of operations, the politico-military-mercantile problem can be set against a background of geographical fact. First, however, a fundamental question: Why does Russia, being virtually self-sufficient, need to attach any great importance to the ability to use those seas?

The answer is obvious: That, as a world power, she needs

Elements of the U.S. 8th Infantry Division in various stages of crossing the Rhine near Dienheim during 1973 Exercise Laramie Golden Arrow. (U.S. Army photos.) So long as the United States and allies maintain strong ground and air forces along the Central Front, says author Palmer, the result will be a stalemate on land and an inevitably greater focus on NATO's watery flanks.

not only to be able to send her rapidly growing mercantile fleet where and when she wishes, but also sees a similar requirement for her newly acquired instrument of world power, the Red Fleet. What is or tends to be forgotten—whether by accident or design is not always clear—is the newness of the situation. Which, in turn, invites the next questions: What is NATO doing about it? Has the Alliance adjusted its maritime strength and dispositions to take account? Highly important questions, about which more later.

North and South pose similar problems, but conditions are far from the same. The South is very constricted, not only in the Bosporus and Dardanelles, but also within the Aegean and even as far as the Strait of Gibraltar to the west and the Strait of Babel Mandeb near Aden to the south. The degree of constriction varies from a few cables' length to many hundreds of miles in the open Mediterranean— wide enough for most purposes, but decidedly not "open waters" for such purposes as evasive routing, an important factor in running convoys. Likewise, that much easier for one side to dominate.

At first sight, the North looks much freer. It is chilly, but ice-free to the Kola Inlet. The edge of the polar ice is a barrier to all but submarines. But most important are the offshore islands, Iceland in particular.

Iceland holds the key to the extreme northwest of the NATO line and she is, of course, a member of NATO. So all should be well. But is it? In 1940 she was invaded by the Allies and today sees those same allies, some of them, taking away her livelihood by over-fishing what she declares

are her own fishing grounds.

Right or wrong, Iceland does not look kindly on those who in 1940 told her they were saving her from something worse and today make much the same claim. The hard, cold fact is that, irrespective of whether Iceland wants, or will tolerate, NATO, there can be no doubt that NATO needs Iceland.

The main southern front is much more of a political patchwork, and transit along its considerable length or across its eastern end enroute to the Indian Ocean and points east is governed, therefore, by extremely complicated political considerations. The Mediterranean campaigns of World War II showed clearly the interplay between control of the north African littoral and of the seaway itself. Immediately after the war NATO had a firm grip, with bases in the Suez Canal Zone, Libya, and French North Africa—today, all gone. NATO, in its present membership, could not hope to dominate those same southern shores, but it would be highly desirable for the Alliance to have them in friendly hands, which is scarcely the case at the moment.

The northern or European side of the Mediterranean consists of a long and deeply indented coastline all the way from where Turkey meets neutral Syria to the far-off Pillars of Hercules. From east to west it is held (more or less) by: Turkey and Greece (at each other's throat); Albania (Chinese Communist); Yugoslavia (Hands-off Tito Communist); Italy (teetering on the brink of electing herself Communist); France (non-military NATO); and Spain (neutral). As a parade of NATO's military solidarity it leaves something to be desired.

The Wreckage of Ad Hoc

NATO's needs are self-evident: (1) to set its own political house in order; (2) to gain friends in Africa (or at least ensure that their neutrality is benevolent); (3) above all, to strengthen its own position.

The needs are clear; only the means are in question.

Or so it would seem. How otherwise does one explain the absence of Spain, a country implacably anti-Communist and one which, furthermore, has inflicted a resounding defeat on the Communists? No surprise, therefore, that the extreme Left (and often those not so extreme) clutches at every chance to blacken her name or do her an ill service. The wonder lies in the inability—nay, the refusal—of NATO to recognize an ally right under its nose.

Likewise, NATO needs France back where she belongs, as a fully integrated military partner. It is not enough to reassure oneself with the hope that "come the day, France will be there." She will indeed, but what of all those lost opportunities to plan and practice here and now? The full strength of an alliance is not built—or rebuilt—in a day. History is strewn with the wreckage of ad hoc.

The question was earlier posted: What is NATO doing about it? And by "it" is meant the changing situation. (Another vital point to note is that it is "changing," not "changed"; Russian sea power, in all its aspects, including the acquisition of foreign friends, has grown and is still growing. The situation confronting NATO is also still changing, therefore, and nowhere more so than on its maritime flanks.)

A key-word to NATO's strategy in the extreme north is "reinforcement." In the lonely wastes of Finnmark NATO's forces are, to say the least, thin on the ground. Nor do they have any nuclear weapons, tactical or other. That situation arises from Norway's "base and ban" policy, whereby, in deference to the Soviet Union, she (like Denmark) does not allow foreign forces to be permanently stationed on her soil, nor does she allow any of her allies to stockpile nuclear arms on her territory.

Norway has come in for some criticism for her apparent supineness, but, as NATO's Eivind Berdal, Chief of Public Information at AFNORTH, has pointed out (in October

Reefer cargo intended for U.S. forces in Europe is unloaded from USNS BLUE JACKET in Bremerhaven. (Army photo by H. Mueller.) The increased Soviet ability to interdict NATO's sea lines of communications poses a serious new, if not yet fully recognized, threat to allied ground and air forces in Europe.

1975), it is essential to look at the matter in "the whole context of the Nordic situation," with special regard for such factors as:
• Finland's ties with Russia under the 1948 Treaty of Friendship, Co-operation and Mutual Assistance, under which she could be called on ("after consultation," of course) to provide base facilities for Russian forces.
• The consequent NATO build-up that such a move would bring about—highly likely, says Berdal, quoting warnings to that effect made by the Norwegian Government.
• The uncomfortable proximity of NATO forces to the Russian base complex on the ice-free Kola Inlet—uncomfortable for the Russians, that is.

Bad Luck in the Gangway

There are, in short, powerful local factors working for the maintenance of the Scandinavian status quo; at all events, as far as open conflict and attack are concerned. However, it is wise to stress that those factors are, indeed, local. An attack on Norway might merely be part of a wider assault. Egil Ulstein may be confident of Russian benevolence but he also warns that a Soviet attack in the north might be triggered by "events unrelated to the political situation in the area." Which is another way of saying that it would be bad luck for Norway if she found herself standing in the gangway.

NATO's Commander-in-Chief North, General Sir John Sharp, looking at the military side, is in no doubt about the threat, the difficulties, or the urgency. There are, he has pointed out (in an address to the Oslo Samfund in November 1975), "a third of the Soviet submarine strength and a large proportion of their surface ships and aircraft" based on the ice-free Kola Inlet. The Russians must therefore regard the north of Norway as an area from which their sea lines of communication could be threatened, an excellent reason for at least not passing up any chance to gain control.

Even so, Sharp does not envisage "a massive or all-out attack on North Norway"—but he adds the qualification that "the Soviets may be tempted to use their maritime power to outflank the north."

No wonder then that, although Sharp understands the reasons for Norway's attitude, he still sees "base and ban" as making the whole business of reinforcement more urgent and yet "infinitely harder," while making that of a potential aggressor "infinitely easier."

Those difficulties are, of course, compounded by Russia's growing naval power. If left too late, therefore, reinforcements would have to be fought through. Sharp's solution is plain and unequivocal: "Norway's salvation can only lie in the political will to ask for outside help *in time.*" He stresses the phrase "in time," declaring, and rightly so, that it is "the key to their situation."

The Sea Bed and the Law

Exploiting the sea bed many miles offshore is something quite new, and, as ever, the law is taking some time to catch up with the practical needs. Meanwhile, there is little general agreement on who can do what, and where, although, in the case of the North and Norwegian Seas, the interested riparian states have either reached broad agreement or are striving to do so.

The current series of conferences on The Law of the Sea is very much concerned about the problem of oil rigs—although, so far, without any end product at the practical level of the captain of a warship, whose rights and responsibilities vis-a-vis those hostages to good international behavior are currently minimal. One need not venture further into that particular jungle; it is enough to pause outside and observe that the sooner matters are regularized the better.

In the present case there is double urgency, for not only are areas of sea bed valuable in themselves, but structures on them can be seen as threatening legitimate defense interests by their mere presence. It should also be borne in mind that, although the Russians are as willing as any to go where no law says them nay, they have considerable reluctance to be seen as actual breakers of accepted international law.

Much has been made of the Arctic Ocean as a transit area for the Kola-based Russian fleet, but it should also be remembered that a great-circle track between northwest Europe and the Bering Strait represents the shortest route to the Far East by many thousands of miles. Today, it is accessible only to submarines, and then at some hazard. But, as technicians can provide everything but wisdom, the day will no doubt soon arrive when the shortest route also will be the most economic route.

Not yet? Perhaps, but NATO needs to think about it, as the Russians are surely doing so.

Poor Tattered South

That the southern hem of NATO's defensive cloak is currently in tatters is plain for all to see. The damage is, however, almost entirely political and can, therefore, be put right more quickly—given the will.

U.S. Marines race through the surf during NATO Exercise Deep Furrow 73 at Saros Bay, Turkey. (USMC photo by P.D. Martello.) The Soviet sea buildup, combined with current antagonism between Greece and Turkey, has seriously weakened the U.S./NATO position in the Eastern Mediterranean.

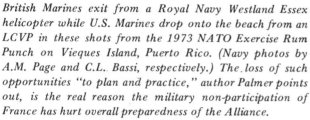

British Marines exit from a Royal Navy Westland Essex helicopter while U.S. Marines drop onto the beach from an LCVP in these shots from the 1973 NATO Exercise Rum Punch on Vieques Island, Puerto Rico. (Navy photos by A.M. Page and C.L. Bassi, respectively.) The loss of such opportunities "to plan and practice," author Palmer points out, is the real reason the military non-participation of France has hurt overall preparedness of the Alliance.

NATO-in-Med is weak and scattered; certainly in indigenous forces. Geography, even more than in the North, dictates a maritime strategy. It is no chance that NATO's Commander-in-Chief, South, is and has always been a sea officer. The then-incumbent, Admiral Means Johnston, USN, hammered home this point in an address to the Royal United Institute for Defense Studies (in London, February 1975): "The seas which wash the shores of our member-nations and preclude their contiguity paradoxically constitute their best unifying element. The dependence of the region on sea lines for such vital defense matters as communications, supply, and reinforcement is immediately obvious. Its susceptibility to isolation, fragmentation, and disarray by the intervention of contravening naval forces should be equally evident."

Johnson also pointed to a further weakness, not readily apparent: what he calls "the technical shortcomings endemic to the region"—a polite way of saying that much of NATO's hinterland is long on donkey-carts, sparse on trucks, and very short on radar sets and those conversant with them.

Nearby industrial backing is, of course, a great advantage to any modern military force. But then the Russians have none at all; so far, they must tote their support along with them. Some comfort here, although not much.

NATO-in-Med *is* militarily weak—save for the mainstay Sixth Fleet (which suffers from the political disadvantage of single-nation command and composition)—and that unhappy state need not continue.

First, there are signs that Greece and Turkey may soon recognize that what pulls them apart is far less important than what should hold them together.

Second, there is what might be termed "reinforcement potential" in the maritime forces of France and Spain,

more than enough to redress the balance in favor of the Alliance: France with her *Force de Dissuasion* of five nuclear-armed submarines, her carrier-borne airpower, and her well balanced and modern fleet; Spain, not quite so powerful, but manifesting a growing awareness of the sea in her rapidly expanding navy (which, incidentally, relies less and less on foreign expertise).

NATO's Crying Need

Two factors have transformed the situation on the flanks of NATO-in-Europe over the last 10-15 years: first, the shift in the balance of sea power; second, increase in offshore exploitation.

Gone forever are the days when NATO's navies could come and go as they pleased, holding the outer ring and dealing promptly with any threat as it arose. (That is by no means to say that Russia is supreme anywhere at sea; merely that she is in a position to dispute control or use.) The possibility of offshore exploitation intensifies the conflict of interest by adding another and important benefit to be drawn from such control or use.

Has NATO adjusted its thinking, its strategy, and, hence, its forces (and their deployment) accordingly?

As always in a maritime situation, the call is for flexibility; for forces that can be both shifted around and play whatever role is required, either in support and supply of the land forces or, less directly, to gain and hold local superiority at sea. The Russian threat today is almost exclusively maritime—the stalemate on the central front makes it inevitable.

It is maritime, but it is still local, for before they can take over the broad ocean the Russians must make sure of those tender, watery flanks, which are theirs just as much as NATO's. To counter the growing threat, NATO must, therefore, have immediately available (although not necessarily deployed) the maritime forces to hold what could be transformed from flanks into the main battle line.

NATO's military commanders are all too well aware of the Alliance's shortcomings, but so far there is no evidence, in the shape of mounting maritime strength, to prove that NATO Governments are likewise alive to a very urgent danger.
∎

262

The South Atlantic:
A New Order Emerging

A Once-Isolated Region
Becomes Increasingly Important

By RICHARD E. BISSELL

Richard E. Bissell is a research associate at the Foreign Policy Research Institute in Philadelphia, and Managing Editor of the Institute's magazine, Orbis, The Journal of World Affairs.

THE emergence of the South Atlantic region as a trouble spot for U.S. policymakers in the last few years is hardly news. The challenges to American interests—military, political, and economic—have been well advertised, with the problem areas ranging alphabetically from Angola to Zaire, and geographically throughout the triangle bordered by Africa, Latin America, and the Antarctic.

The past reputation of the South Atlantic as an isolated outpost, symbolized by the exile of Napoleon to St. Helena, is fast disappearing. Events of the last few years have spurred observers to include the South Atlantic in broader geopolitical calculations. Major changes in the area include the final withdrawal of European colonial power, the growth of Soviet interests and presence, and the emergence of new regional power centers on both sides of the Atlantic.

The emergence of vulnerable new states in southern Africa invites greater involvement not only by the Soviet Union and China, but also by the new "middle powers," such as Brazil and South Africa. New hierarchies of power are evolving in the South Atlantic, and the continuation of

The VLCC (very large crude carrier) BROOKLYN being outfitted with a new smokestack prior to sea trials in 1973. Such supertankers are too big to get through the Suez Canal; those carrying oil from the Persian Gulf to Europe or the U.S. East Coast must go through the South Atlantic, making it now one of the most important of the world's major sea lanes.

past American assumptions about the South Atlantic could be a grave disservice to policy both in the United States and in other nations in the region friendly to U.S. interests.

Trawlers and Supertankers

The present and potential instability of the South Atlantic looms as a major problem. Linking the Pacific and Indian Oceans to the North Atlantic, the region's sea routes carry a major portion of the petroleum needed by the United States and its NATO allies. Nearly all of the oil from the Persian Gulf passes around the Cape of Good Hope into the South Atlantic because supertankers cannot use the Suez Canal. Because they are also too big for the Panama Canal, oil from Alaska may also be shipped around Cape Horn in the supertankers when, as now expected, oil from the North Slope creates a glut of oil on the U.S. West Coast. If so, there could be complications. As if the weather were not already sufficient hazard for the West's oil supply line—so well described in Noel Mostert's *Supership*—the route is now littered with naval vessels of hostile and potentially hostile nations.

Soviet naval power in the South Atlantic (and in the Indian Ocean) is steadily increasing. With more than 30 ships, plus "trawlers," presently stationed in the Indian Ocean, and several transiting the South Atlantic at almost any given time, the Soviet Navy has clearly marked the South Atlantic as its next major focus for development. One can imagine the Kremlin's pleasure over the American decision to withdraw U.S. monitoring ships from the South Atlantic just prior to the Angolan war.

The search for base facilities also is stimulating rivalry in the region, most recently in Angola and now warming up in the rest of southern Africa. The acquisition of base rights by the Soviet Union in Angola, even if relatively "soft" base rights, would enhance Moscow's military position and political leverage in the South Atlantic.

Once bases were established, the Soviet Union would have a growing capability to threaten the blockade of resources vital to Western economies, and thus the potential, in crisis situations, to exert influence on the industrialized economies of the North Atlantic. Such bases would also increase Moscow's capacity for the same kind of "adventurism" already amply demonstrated in Angola. To further complicate matters, the specter of increasing external competition within the region coincides with the discovery of larger oil deposits and other resources along the Atlantic littoral of Africa and off the coasts of Argentina and Brazil.

Economic and Political Changes

Economic trends, too, are changing the strategic rules of the contest in the South Atlantic. Between the industrialized states of the northern hemisphere and the resource-rich "third world" nations there exist increasing prospects for greater rather than less interdependent relationships. As a principal purchaser of Zairian copper, Gabonese iron and manganese, oil from Cabinda and Nigeria, chrome and gold from South Africa, and numerous products of all types from Brazil and Argentina, the United States has an abiding national security interest in retaining a significant influence in the region, either unilaterally or in partnership with regional power centers.

Superpower competition in the South Atlantic is also complicated by other factors:

— the rising potential for nationalistic rivalry between local powers;
— the failure to resolve racial tensions in southern Africa;
— unprecedented diplomatic initiatives by governments in the region reaching out to one another: South Africa to the Latin Americans and a few conservative African states, Brazil to various African states, and Argentina to other middle powers.

The hierarchy of military powers in the South Atlantic is reasonably clear if one excludes the superpowers. The South Africans and Brazilians are today clearly the most powerful (although the Argentines are in the process of negotiating for two aircraft carriers). The South African army of 38,000 and a navy of 32 warships are sufficient to referee the use of force over a large region. On that scale, though, one can imagine the threat posed by the 14,000 Cuban Army regulars in Angola.

One way in which the United States maintains close working relationships with the navies of South America is through the annual "Unitas" naval exercises. Shown here: scenes from Unitas X in 1969. (Navy photos by T. R. Sorenson and J. B. Call.)

The South African sphere, however, extends westward only as far as tacitly approved by the Brazilians, with their 170,000-man army and $2 billion defense budget. The extent of Brazilian influence into the South Atlantic is limited primarily by self-imposed economic constraints, and not by any strategic doctrines infused with a sense of Brazilian "manifest destiny."

The remaining indigenous armed forces in the region, even in a country as important as Argentina, are largely devoted to maintaining domestic order. (Similar missions could ultimately be assigned to South African and Brazilian forces as well, of course, if the present governments lose control.) The inward-looking force alignments are characteristic of the countries bordering the South Atlantic, and illustrate not only the limited reach of the regional states in naval/military terms, but also the relative vacuum of power open to potential external trouble-makers.

Other problems exist which are certain to complicate politics in the South Atlantic of the next decade:

• Possible changes in access to the region, including the routes via the Panama Canal, the Mediterranean, and the Cape of Good Hope.

• The outcome of the U.N. Law of the Sea Conference, affecting the jurisdictions of regional states over areas up to 200 miles wide on both sides of the South Atlantic.

• The simmering dispute between Britain and Argentina over the Falkland Islands (known to the Argentines as the Malvinas)—a dispute, moreover, now exacerbated by excellent oil production hopes.

• Geological soundings in the Antarctic which reveal the presence of oil, gas, and manganese, with no international mechanism to control exploitation of the region.

• The present and prospective bankruptcy of numerous small countries in the region, likely to open them to cheaply-bought influence, up to and including hard basing rights for external military powers.

The Multi-Level Crossroads

The implications for the United States in the South Atlantic thus lie at many levels. From outright military questions to issues of strategic materials and more broadly (if sometimes vaguely) defined national interest, the United States is involved—for better or worse. American policy is at a crossroad, and recent signs (the 1976 Consultation Agreement signed with Brazil, and Secretary of State Kissinger's September shuttle diplomacy in southern Africa), indicate that the United States hopes to maintain,

with the aid of friendly governments, a cooperative, indirect influence within the region. Such an approach has become a topic of debate in the U.S. government, and an object of suspicion on the part of many South Atlantic governments.

The Brazilians, while happy to cooperate with the United States where the interests of the two countries converge, pursue a multi-faceted approach to the South Atlantic region. Political cooperation with the black African states is encouraged by Itamaraty (the Brazilian Foreign Ministry), while economic interchange and military talks are pursued with South Africa by other ministries within the Brazilian bureaucracy.

The Argentines, too, are split. The Argentine Navy reportedly endorses the creation of a regional defense body, or SATO (South Atlantic Treaty Organization). Intense consultation between naval officials of South Africa, Argentina, Brazil, and the United States in the summer of 1976 gave rise to a more activist interpretation of Argentine intentions.

The South African perspective rests largely upon the notion that "beggars can't be choosers." The optimal policy for South Africa probably would involve the exclusion of the superpowers from the region entirely. In that way the South Africans could maintain the peace in their own fashion, as in the past. Since such wishful thinking is fast being invalidated by events, South African Prime Minister John Vorster has more recently called for a coalition of "middle powers," a so-called "sixth world" grouping which would include countries such as Iran, Israel, Brazil, Argentina, and South Africa itself. South Africa's own desire for a South Atlantic Treaty Organization independent of but allied with NATO is no secret, but recent domestic developments in South Africa and neighboring countries may prevent its emergence.

An optimistic view of the future by American planners assumes that the South Atlantic, with its traditional geographic isolation, might remain immune to superpower battles. The Angolan "civil war" put a crack in that theory, however, and subsequent events are likely to shatter it. Whatever the outcome, the emerging challenges of the South Atlantic will not be met by ignoring them. American strategic thinking in the region is undergoing a deserved overhaul.　　　　　　　　　　　　　　　　　　　■

The Soviet aircraft carrier KIEV. (Navy photo by P. D. Adams.) With the building of a more far-ranging blue-water Navy the USSR is now able to project its power ashore from virtually every ocean area of the world; it has already increased its naval presence in the South Atlantic.

The Scrambled Geometry of the New Pacific

West of the Dateline and East of India

By LAWRENCE GRISWOLD

Lawrence Griswold is Contributing Editor of SEA POWER.

UNTIL recently, the power structure of Asia was thought to be a triangle, with the USSR as the hypotenuse. But that shape derived from circumstances which have now changed, twisting the arcs and angles into a new political geometry. The area subtended by the Russian arc has shrunk, while those overshadowed by Communist China and Japan have grown. Since 1972 and the withdrawal from mainland Asia (except South Korea) of the American military presence the long lines of the triangle no longer meet at the south. Southeast Asia remains stickily fluid.

The International Date Line, drawn vertically from Pole to Pole, is not only a temporal borderline between East and West. With some important exceptions, it is also a political battle line where two sharply differing ideologies meet and, in one area, at least, conflict. The state ideologies of the USSR and the People's Republic of China (PRC), for example, may be identical in their socialism, but the present world strategies of the two Communist superpowers appear antipolar. The continental Chinese, a more pragmatic people, confine their immediate aims to Asia while the Kremlin, ridden by doctrinaire Leninism, continues to regard the whole world as its oyster.

Japan—like Britain an island jam-packed with industry and dependent upon foreign sources for raw materials, fuel, and even food—is again becoming an overcrowded nation. But Tokyo shows every evidence of having learned that an expansionist policy demanded by *"lebensraum"* lacks practicality, especially in existing circumstances. Instead of raw manpower, Japan is developing a nation of trained specialists for promotion of an export trade based on quality rather than, as in pre-1941 days, on price.

Still nominally reliant on the United States for protection against external aggression, the Japanese military profile is low, but is supported by a high production capability in every stratum of a broad war potential ranging from nuclear missiles and warships, battle tanks, and aircraft to electronics, optics, and small

arms. With a population of more than 112 million, Japan has great industries, but limited agriculture. The smallest of Asia's Big Three in territory, Japan's industrial potential and available trained manpower—behind its cadres in the Navy, the Air Force, and the Army (which, combined, constitute the Japanese Defense Forces)—are quite sufficient to earn the respect Tokyo requires.

Eastern Ambitions

The Russian Soviet Federal Socialist Republic (RSFSR), centered in Moscow, occupies nearly 80% of the ethnic and political melange comprising the Union of Soviet Socialist Republics and extends from the Baltic Sea to the Bering Strait. But the Russian Slavic type fades into numerous Mongoloid tribes east of the Urals and almost disappears east of the Ob river, only to reappear as an administrative and military elite in Eastern Siberia along the Sea of Japan littoral.

Russia has oceanic ambitions in the East, but the usually ice-burdened Siberian shores of the northern Japan and Okhotsk seas are hardly hospitable for year-round navigation. Even Vladivostok, the southernmost port and naval base of Russia's Maritime Province, is frequently ice-bound during winter months. Farther north, icebreakers are needed most of the year. The growing city of Khabarovsk is the eastern capital. Nikolaevsk, northern terminus of the Trans-Siberian Railway, is used as a submarine and secondary air base.

Other Russian naval-air bases of secondary or less importance—such as Magadan and Gizhiga, opposite the Kamchatka Peninsula—serve merely to underscore Moscow's concern for the integrity of Okhotsk's western coast. The Kamchatka Peninsula itself, a near wasteland of ice-contained fishing villages and sawmills, also has an old naval base and obsolete fortifications at Petropavlovsk, serviced by a small fleet of ice-breakers regularly stationed there.

Petropavlovsk's importance appears to lie in its broad harbor and the fortified hills surrounding it. Its airport is used by naval patrol craft for operations along the western coast of the Bering Sea and around the Chukchi

Peninsula; they also serve in the eastern approaches of the Great Northern Sea Route which runs across the continental roof of the RSFSR from Murmansk, the Kola Inlet, and the White Sea in Western Russia. Petropavlovsk is useful for replenishment of supplies and for minor ship repairs not requiring dockyards. Petropavlovsk's ice-breakers can also, reportedly, be used for minesweeping.

Eastern Siberia encompasses about 2.5 million square miles and, quite possibly, possesses an immense wealth of minerals—much of it below the permafrost. Nevertheless, a major share of Moscow's ninth Five-Year Plan was earmarked for Eastern Siberia's development—possibly the Kremlin's most earnest ambition is to create on its eastern shores a Russian rival to the Pacific Coast ports of the United States. Hampered by nature and by western Europe from easy access to the Atlantic Ocean, it finds itself equally hampered in the East by the interposed geography of a hostile China and an unsubmissive Japan.

Opium Wars and a Long March

Continental China, the hardening core of East Asia and one of the world's oldest civilizations, is now quite likely the most important area power. For the first time, in fact, modern China has managed to secure for itself an authentic place among the world's principal nations. Statistically, the PRC is the largest nation in East Asia with an area of more than 3,700,000 square miles. It is also the most populous country in the world with, in 1974, an estimated 823,000,000 inhabitants.

Rimmed by great deserts and mountain chains to the south and west and cross-hatched by lesser ranges and an assortment of great rivers and lesser waterways, China's huge but largely agrarian population has been provincialized by nature as well as, until recent decades, by poor communications.

Modern Chinese history may have begun with the Opium War of 1839-42, the first European military intrusion, when British forces compelled the Ch'ing (Manchu) Court to permit the sale of Indian-grown opium and, by the seizure of Hong Kong and other coastal ports, opened the way for a general colonizing raid on Chinese territory. After the upheaval of the religious rebellions centered about the T'ai P'ing Revolt (1853-64) displayed the weakness of Manchu rule, the entire country became,

The commerical port area of Saigon during the peak of the Vietnam War. (Military Sealift Command photo.) Enriched by the much improved port facilities and other "infrastructure" elements left behind in the U.S. withdrawal, Vietnam's rulers have concentrated on unification efforts and—so far, at least—eschewed additional adventurism.

The Tokuyama oil refinery plant of the Idemitsu Petrochemical Industries, Ltd., and the Yokosuka thermal power station of the Tokyo Electric Power Co. Japan, fourth in the world in electric power generating capacity and one of the leading petrochemical-producing countries as well, is far behind Russia and Mainland China in territory and population, but her formidable technological and industrial capabilities put her in the first rank of Asia's superpowers.

in effect, a bleeding corpse attacked and dismembered by foreign sharks. By the end of the 19th century and the hysterical outbreak of the Boxer Rebellion, when the Manchu Empress declared war on the world at large, every European and Asian country of genuine importance claimed its own piece of the Chinese coast and exercised a loud voice in Peking as well. China's few railroads were foreign-owned; a Britisher ran the Customs Office and another collected the Salt Tax. Manchu China could claim neither access to the sea nor control over its internal communications.

The fall of the Manchu Dynasty in 1911—the last Ch'ing, Henry Pu-yi, wound up as puppet ruler of Japanese Manchukuo (Manchuria) —led to formation of the Kuomintang under Dr. Sun Yat-sen in Canton. After his death in 1925 the KMT suffered an ideological split which did not, however, become manifest until 1927, when Chiang Kai-shek, commanding the Nationalist Army, temporarily stopped his campaign to expel all foreign intruders and gave vigorous proof of his new anti-Communist credentials by crushing rival war lords, particularly those with strong ties to Moscow. In the Province of Kiangsi, in 1934, Chiang's army dispersed the pro-Communist wing of the KMT—which, with Mao Tse-tung and Chou En-lai among its leaders, re-gathered a few weeks later to commence the storied "Long March" northward. But then the Japanese invasion demanded Chiang's full attention and held it until September 1945.

The Long March ended in the stark and treeless clay caves of Yenan where for over a decade the Red Chinese

army was equipped and trained by Russia and fought, wherever opportunity offered substantial loot or gain, either the Japanese or the Chinese Nationalists. Following the Japanese surrender in Manchuria, the Red Army took the surrendered arms and repulsed the ill-led and poorly disciplined conscripts thrown into battle by Chiang's capital at Nanking. A China still disorganized by the Japanese invasion and long decades of battle, and further torn by printing press inflation, fell easily to the Red Army after Chiang, his government, and a couple of divisions of loyal troops made their way to Taiwan and the shelter of the U.S. Seventh Fleet. The era of the two Chinas had started.

From Stalin to Mao to Chou

Stalin had several times claimed he was an Oriental, and he was often quoted as asserting that the "road to the defeat of western capitalism" lay through China. While he lived, the Sino-Soviet "monolith" flourished. Accordingly, Red China's reputation as an ardent enemy of all things Western may have been well earned between 1950 and 1965. Certainly, Mao did his best until the end of October 1965 to earn Western enmity. But the seriousness of Chinese hostility was undercut by Mao's own follies within China, by the many haphazardly uncoordinated programs of the Great Leap Forward, the wars on dogs, cats, rats, and mice, the backyard "foundries," the treacherous invitation to dissidents to "Let a Hundred Flowers Bloom," and, finally, by the suicidally murderous loosing of armed juvenile Red Guards to uproot the remnants of ancient Chinese traditions—all of which excesses provoked international mirth and pity rather than fear.

But a PRC break with Stalin's successors was suspected as early as 1955 with revelation of the Kao Kang conspiracy to set up an independent state in Manchuria with the intention of ceding it to Russia. Kao, a Deputy

Premier (with Teng Hsiao-p'ing, who acted as prosecutor of Kao), died shortly after his arrest—possibly a suicide, as Teng claimed. Few Chinese were made aware of Kao Kang's defection but it was hard to conceal the PRC rupture with Moscow's military hierarchy, which had until then acted as Red China's own supreme military command.

Less than a year after Stalin's death (in March 1953), Peking ordered formation of an officer corps headed by Chinese marshals and conscription of 450,000 men—out of a military registration potential of approximately 80 million. Fourteen Army corps were to be organized as mobile and garrison troops, the latter to be stationed along the Manchurian and Sinkiang frontiers opposite Eastern Siberia and the Western Sino-Soviet borders.

From 1955 forward the disintegration of the monolith became increasingly evident. Russia stopped work on nuclear plants in northern Inner Mongolia and delayed, then finally stopped, deliveries of military hardware, including W-class submarines and various patrol boats intended for the then-fledgling PRC Navy.

Mao set out on his own strategy of conquest in competition with Moscow. An attempted Jakarta-Peking

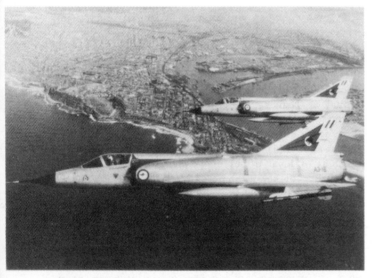

Australian-built Mirage Mach 2 jet fighters fly over the industrial city of Newcastle, north of Sydney, New South Wales. (Australian News and Information Bureau photo.) U.S./Australian relations have improved in recent months, but are yet far removed from the firm and fast friendship of earlier days.

Axis to partition Southeast Asia came to a catastrophic end in October 1965, however, to the vast relief of both Moscow and the West. Shortly thereafter, Mao Tse-tung was elevated as a god-symbol and father-image and day-to-day government control shifted to the more moderate (and more capable) hands of Chou En-lai. Now Chou is dead, Mao may be dying, the future PRC leadership is uncertain, and mutually hostile Chinese and Russian provincial armies glare at each other along an extended border running on the northern side from the Pacific Ocean to Mongolia and on the western side from Mongolia to the Himalayas.

In 1971, by the somewhat elliptical device of dispatching Chinese Ping-Pong teams to western capitals, Chou En-lai let it be known that Peking would be amenable to closer relations with the NATO countries, including the United States. For once, the "conventional wisdom" proved correct: Peking, apprehensive of Moscow's fast growing strength, wanted allies. President Nixon's well-publicized and warm welcome in Peking spoke eloquently of China's desire for and approval of a strong and intelligent U.S. Commander-in-Chief in the White House. The PRC belief that Nixon would restore Washington's waning world power was unfortunately undercut by Watergate and by the continued strangling by a myopic Congress of the U.S. defense budget. Ex-President Nixon was invited back to Peking to reassure the late Chou En-lai's succession, but couldn't. A potential Sino-American alliance, which, if only as a threat, could constitute a valuable strategic bulwark against Muscovite aggression, must now remain in limbo indefinitely.

Four-Sided Triangle

A fourth "side" of the politico-military power triangle west of the International Date Line is comprised of many unsplendored things, chief of which are the various (and shifting) positions and policies of Taiwan, Australia and New Zealand, Korea (North and South), and the nations of Southeast Asia, both insular and continental.

Ironically, perhaps, the most immediately involved of the lesser powers is the government of Taipei. The son of the late Generalissimo who heads the Republic of China (ROC) and the small but sturdy Taiwan/Chinese population he rules now realize the impossibility of conquering the PRC and are also beginning to understand that, one way or another, Taiwan probably must support Peking against Moscow.

There has almost always, it seems, been a triangle in Asia—a triangle, usually, of two sides against the third, although the contest was seldom very well coordinated. There is really little difference now, except that a fourth element may be added when the chips are down and Japan and Taiwan contribute ·their combined strength on the side of a very new and very tough China—or, conversely, should Peking falter because of internal disorder or a disabling nuclear blow, separately pick China's bones.

The ancient enmities of Asia still smolder beneath the thin fabric of post-1950 accommodation, however, and Russia is still Enemy Number One. New China has certainly not forgotten the humiliation and havoc caused by the Japanese attacks and occupation and may yet, if possible, someday present its bill to Tokyo. But for the time the PRC also recognizes Japan as a natural ally against a potentially common aggressor.

As for Japan itself, Tokyo's commercial approach to East Asian conquest seems abundantly more promising than the proven disaster of the military route, and a market of hundreds of millions of Chinese who are friends rather than enemies, and who are no longer compromised by Western politico-industrial domination, is much more attractive.

Moreover, Japan no longer enjoys its pre-WWII

269

freedom of strategic action. In 1940, Tokyo's military planners could debate the options offered by "the North Plan" or "the South Plan." The North Plan envisioned an attack on Russia's Maritime Province, the occupation of Vladivostok and Khabarovsk (as well as areas north of the Amur east of Lake Baikal), and the reoccupation of northern Sakhalin and the Sea of Okhotsk littoral beyond Nikolaevsk as far as southern Kamchatka.

The South Plan, as adopted, was aimed at the military conquest of Southeast Asia and the Philippines and inevitably led to Pearl Harbor and its calamitous consequences. In 1940, the eyes of a disorganized Kremlin were focussed west and the Red Army, demoralized by Stalin's irresponsible purges of its officer corps, was unprepared for war. Today, both of Japan's 1940 alternatives are gone and she must now and possibly forevermore rely principally on her undoubted industrial skills and a sound diplomacy.

Ice-Free Ports and a Manchu Roadblock

From the 16th century through the first half of the 20th, China suffered from Russian intrusion. After the collapse of the Tatar occupation and the slow withdrawal of the Mongol Hordes eastward from the Urals, peasant armies financed by Russian commercial houses followed the oriental retreat to the Heilung (Amur) River south of Lake Baikal. In 1582, acceding to a plea by the Stroganov fur interests, Ivan the Terrible made expansion to the east a semi-permanent policy of the Russian government and backed Cossack and trapper with troops. "Eastward to the Sea" became a tenet of official Russian policy in successive tsarist dynasties, including the Romanov. According to V.A. Yakhontov ("Russia and the Soviet Union in the Far East," George Allen and Unwin; 1932): "Moscow's foreign policy in the XVI century definitely concentrated on two objectives: (1) to monopolize the river route from Europe to Asia ...; and (2) to establish a direct contact with the Western countries having an outlet to the Pacific Ocean." But almost three centuries passed before Russia, having meanwhile colonized Alaska and parts of northern California, seriously schemed against the ice-free ports of China.

Russian progress across undefended Chinese territory ran into occasional roadblocks. In 1652, for example, the freshly installed Manchu rule, not yet having enfeebled itself by luxury, resisted in a war that was interrupted only some 30 years later by the Treaty of Nerzhinsk (forerunner of a long series of subsequently unkept treaties). Several Chinese armies under Manchu leadership won clear victories over Moscow's expeditionary forces. Nevertheless, Russian expansionism increased until, early in the 17th century, the Russian flag flew over future Soviet ports on the Sea of Okhotsk and redirected the conquerors southward along the Ussuri River toward what is now Vladivostok. By 1900, Dairen and Port Arthur on the Gulf of Chihli were also Russian. In 1912 during the turmoil of the republican transformation, pre-Bolshevik Russia deftly provided the foundation of future Soviet political strategy by separating Outer Mongolia from Chinese rule and then adopting it as a Russian protectorate.

Even before that, having reached the Sea of Okhotsk

by a well fortified trail along the Amur (Heilung) River, Russia had turned southward from occupied Sakhalin toward Japan and endeavored by diplomacy to gain a foothold on Hokkaido and, ultimately, on the main islands in the Sea of Japan. That attempt failed, dismally. By the end of the 19th century, recognizing the Japanese naval strength which had led to a significant victory on the Yalu over the British-built but architecturally fanciful Chinese Navy (and to the subsequent loss to Japan of China's Formosa or Taiwan Province), the Romanovs turned their attention to Korea and the Chinese territory south of the Amur. But at that time Russia faced not only Japan but also the entrenched European nations holding dominion in the port cities of the China coast.

That situation, aggravated by rival claims on Peking following the Boxer Rebellion, set the stage for the Russo-Japanese War of 1904 and for the subsequent Treaty of Portsmouth (N.H.), which not only deprived an exhausted and defeated Russia of her own warm water ports on the Gulf of Chihli but also stimulated an almost equally exhausted Japan toward Korea, and inspired Tokyo to conclude a wily but wary de facto alliance with Russia to compel Chinese acceptance of increased spheres of alien influence in Manchuria and Korea. Japan won Korea in that game, but the intervention of World War I and the Russian Revolution left post-1918 Japan free to plan for a Tokyo-dominated Greater East Asia and led to the later, greater war which wrecked Japan and, ironically, made Russia a superpower.

Even today, due to the postwar Russian seizure of the three southern islands of the Kuriles (containing the strategic Kunashiri Strait and the islands of the Habomai Group northeast of Hokkaido), Russo-Japanese relations have not yet been "normalized." Now the ruler of a vastly expanded USSR and adjoining satellites, Moscow holds firm to its Marxist-Leninist doctrine of world

A Soviet-designed P-4 patrol torpedo boat of the type used by North Korea in the 1968 seizure of USS PUEBLO. (U.S. Navy photo.) The Korean Peninsula is now relatively quiescent, but North Korea is still hostile to U.S. interests—and South Korea is the last remaining U.S. naval/military foothold in that part of Asia.

The flag of the Republic of China is raised on the RCS PO YANG during 1972 transfer ceremonies in Long Beach during which the former USS MADDOX was decommissioned and transferred to the ROC Navy. (U.S. Navy photo.) Taiwan remains a dependable ally, but time and the U.S. rapprochement with Communist China have undoubtedly weakened U.S./ROC working relationships.

domination but has thus far been restrained within its larger Eurasian frontiers by a militarily inadequate but nevertheless dangerous NATO alliance to the west and, to the east, by an inchoate and undeclared alliance of western Pacific nations facing Eastern Siberia.

The Awakening Giant

Mainland China, on the other hand, has gained much since 1945: The West has been expelled from the cities of coastal China (except Hong Kong, which lives free more from PRC sufferance than because of British military might); Manchuria south of the Amur has been regained from Japan; even South Korea, although cut off from a hostile North, is friendly; Tibet has been regained from Britain and the Kwangchowwan Peninsula, along with the large island of Hainan, recovered from France; and rapprochement with the West has led to a new international respectability. Finally, since the end of the Vietnam War, the former tributary states of Indochina no longer can be used to nurture a Russian threat from the south.

Industrially, China is beginning to catch up with neighboring Japan and Taiwan. Her rivers are being tamed, her power resources being improved. Communications by sea, air, road, and rail have made notable fissures in China's ancient natural and linguistic barriers. And China's agriculture has now, possibly for the first time in history, become adequate for her population.

Militarily, the new China is new indeed. In nucleonics, China has been improving on designs initially provided by Stalin—Peking now has about 300 nuclear missiles which, although lacking trans-Pacific capability, could easily reach most Russian cities from western China. The Chinese Air Force numbers about 3,800 warplanes—the PRC's aircraft are now designed by Chinese designers and manufactured in Chinese factories, as are Peking's latest naval warships, including submarines and destroyer types, most of which carry surface-to-air missiles and a variety of ASW weapons. The Chinese Army, numerically in excess of 3,200,000 men, is equipped with Chinese-built tanks, artillery, and missiles.

Chinese steel production, according to U.S. News & World Report (8 December 1975), has risen to 26 million tons annually, and petroleum production to 470 million barrels annually. By and large, the weak China of yesterday has taken a healthy lease on life.

Elsewhere; The Final Factor and a Pragmatic Summary

On or north of the equator, other nations west of the Date Line are either militarily impotent, like the Philippines, or determinedly neutral, like Indonesia—where the chaos left behind by Sukarno has not yet been surmounted by his successors in Jakarta. The islands of Micronesia, including the southern Marianas, have little to offer, but can and do serve as naval and air bases for the U.S. Navy and U.S. Air Force.

On the continent, Vietnam, Laos, Cambodia—and even Thailand, Burma, Malaysia, and Singapore—can be categorized as weak neutrals with benevolent sympathies toward nearby Peking. So long as a powerful China endures, they will resist distant Moscow. But probably not a day longer. In Southeast Asia, the Indochinese "revolutionaries" now seem not the ideologues they were once painted, but guerrillas, gangsters, or bandits who wear the appellation "Communist" in order to get weapons and cash. They are, in fact, no one's allies.

The final factor in the complex Pacific equation is the stance of New Zealand and Australia. Until last November, when the English-appointed Governor General deposed Gough Whitlam, the far leftish Prime Minister of Australia's then Labour Government, and appointed Malcom Fraser, a relative conservative, to act in his place, Australia itself seemed headed for left-wing socialism and military as well as economic ruin. And the Labour Government of New Zealand threatened to follow Canberra. Both countries had for some time followed policies hostile to the United States and the West. Last December, however, voters in both countries overturned their Labour Parties and, with them, the anti-western policies and national trends toward socialism (including a closer association with Mrs. Ghandi's India) which had threatened to take the countries out of the Western camp entirely. Today, both countries have resumed a closer and more cordial association with the West and may yet, in time of need, contribute significant naval-air strength to the Western cause.

Like those who govern most European nations, the rulers of Asia's polyglot nations are political pragmatists. They make neither friends nor enemies—and certainly not allies—on sentimental grounds. Like suspicious caravans travelling in the same direction through hostile territory, they occasionally unite in a wary alliance—which lasts so long as the danger lasts. But remove the common danger and the alliance is dead.

That age-old Asian truism has been repeatedly ignored by Washington in the past. If the unintentionally inscrutable present generation of U.S. decisionmakers have finally learned the hard lessons resultant from the American defeat in Vietnam, the "new" Pacific Doctrine of Gerald R. Ford may yet lead to a new dawn for the American position in Asia.

■

By R. M. PAONE

Dr. Rocco M. Paone is a professor of political science specializing in national security affairs at the U.S. Naval Academy, and is co-author of four books in his subject area.

ANY EXAMINATION of strategic implications and considerations of the Indian Ocean peripheral reflects a newly developed interest of the Western powers, the USSR, and the People's Republic of China in that important area of the world. The war in Vietnam, the Six Days War of 1967, the October 1973 War, the question of expanding facilities on the island of Diego Garcia, the fuel crisis, and the reopening of the Suez Canal have all accentuated the interests of major powers in that vast and formerly "forgotten" ocean.

There has been, in fact, such a concentration of

(1) Soviet foreign policy in the Indian Ocean peripheral is political, economic, ideological, and military, and is aimed at gaining political influence for the USSR. The objectives of the USSR are fundamentally political and the other multidirectional aspects of Soviet actions are conduits to that end.

(2) The Soviets have become a major seapower, and now boast a fleet second, if not equal, to the U.S. fleet, a submarine fleet larger than that of the U.S. Navy, and merchant marine and fishing fleets which are the most extensive in the world today. The USSR's maritime research program, moreover, is more ambitious than those of all other major nations combined.

(3) The worldwide exercise Okean conducted by the Soviet Navy in the spring of 1970 and the followup Okean 1975 dramatically illustrate the great improvement in Russian seapower. Participating in each were 200 ships, many of which were missile-equipped surface types and

The Big Three And the Indian Ocean

PRC, USSR Fight for Supremacy While U.S. Seeks 'Reasonable Balance'

attention paid to the policies of the United States and the Soviet Union in the Indian Ocean that many leaders, as well as much of the press and general public, seemingly have concluded that a tremendous and competitive arms race is being structured there by the two powers. But relatively little consideration has been devoted to the aims and activities of the People's Republic of China (PRC), India, and other countries in the area.

The objectives and the nature of the policies of the United States, the USSR, and the PRC in the Indian Ocean Heartland, as well as the interaction of their policies, are of particular interest in today's shrinking world, and are likely to thoroughly test the probability of the old adage that neither the "West" wind nor the "East" wind (China) shall prevail over the East African peripheral.

The Heartland Variables

The character of Soviet activities in the Indian Ocean Heartland is derived from a number of variables:

The Soviet antisubmarine helicopter carrier LENINGRAD underway in the Indian Ocean in June 1974 (U.S. Navy photo). The Soviets now have about 20 ships in the Indian Ocean, according to DoD officials, but the total is closer to 30 or 40 when such non-combatant craft as trawlers and hydrographic research vessels are included.

nuclear-powered submarines, several hundred airplanes, and several amphibious units. Various elements of the force operated simultaneously in the Baltic, Norwegian, Barents, Black, Philippine, Mediterranean, and Japanese Seas, and the Atlantic, Indian, and Pacific Oceans, and all elements were coordinated and directed from Moscow.

(4) Moscow's influence has steadily increased along the rimland of Europe during the past decade. Most of Eastern Europe lies under the control of the hammer and sickle, and now, through her new sea and air power, the USSR has also greatly increased her presence—and, therefore, influence—in the Mediterranean and South Asia regions, two areas among the more strategically important

to Western diplomacy.

(5) There now seems a distinct strategic possibility that the USSR might outflank Europe and hinder the shipment of vital oil supplies to the West. Such a development would have a most serious impact both on the security of the NATO nations of Western Europe and on the global balance of power.

(6) While present Soviet foreign policy is conditioned by U.S. policy and power in the Indian Ocean peripheral, it is also a reaction to Red China's foreign policy. A realization exists in Moscow that Red China purports to become king of the world Communist hill.

Constraints on an Oversimplified Formula

Despite the immense buildup of Soviet naval power during the last six years, however, a number of impediments do exist that could hinder the extension of major USSR naval power in the Indian Ocean. Geographic

oceans and shipping lanes.

If one accepts the oversimplified formula that Size of Navy plus Quality of Navy times Naval Geography equals Naval Power, then the constraint of geography obviously must have a detrimental effect on Soviet naval capability. The previously-held theory that the USSR has a psychological constraint or "land power mentality" which restricts her naval power is no longer applicable. The USSR has not completed construction of her two new aircraft carriers, but she has developed a forward naval capability supported by base and/or landing rights in, among other locales· Hodeida; Socotra; Somalia, lately much in the headlines; Umm Qasr; Mauritius; and South Yemen. All are on the Indian Ocean peripheral. And the Soviet overseas base system is far from being completed. Yet, despite the new Russian awareness of sea power, only two naval officers, Fleet Admirals Sergei Gorshkov and Semen Lobov, were, as of late 1974, among the 41

The U.S. attack carrier HANCOCK and ballistic missile submarine JOHN C. CALHOUN (U.S. Navy photos). Despite occasional deployments of HANCOCK and other surface ships to the Indian Ocean, its principal future value to the United States could be strategic, as a forward base for the Polaris/Poseidon (and, later, Trident) SLBM fleets.

limitations are significant, for example, in measuring power potential and capability. In the case of the Soviet Union, the constraints of geography on the extension of her naval power in the Indian Ocean are particularly significant. Among those constraints:
• The physical vastness of the Soviet land mass itself.
• The physical geography peculiar to Russia which has necessitated fragmentation of the USSR Navy into four fleets and one "squadron."
• The necessity for Soviet ships to pass through narrow straits to reach the open seas.
• The USSR's northern orientation in latitude.
• The distance of Soviet fleets from the major world

senior officers who comprise the Soviet Ministry of Defense and the General Staff of the Armed Forces.

Defending the Homeland

Additional significant variables arise in any analysis of Soviet naval activity in the Indian Ocean. In support of its mission to defend the vast USSR homeland—in the varying contexts of both conventional and mutual deterrence and possible general nuclear war—the Red Navy must, among other things:
(1) Counter the offensive capability of U.S. Polaris and Poseidon submarines;
(2) Neutralize U.S. strike carriers;
(3) Contribute to the USSR's own strategic missile delivery capability;
(4) Assure command of the four fleet areas, particularly the Black, Barents, and Baltic Seas; and
(5) Provide maritime flank support for land operations along the sensitive coastal pivot areas of the world.
Satisfying all those requirements, and others, is a

momentous task. There is little question but that Soviet concepts covering general war provide for seizure of the exits from the Baltic and Black Seas as well as areas in the Eastern Mediterranean, control of the southern portion of the Red Sea area, and amphibious landings along the Norwegian coast. The nature of Soviet naval and political exercises clearly denotes preparations for such tasks, although Soviet landing ships are not designed for far-ranging operations.

The composition of the USSR's fleets and the pattern of their development would indicate that the Soviet Navy purports to simultaneously provide both strategic deterrence and general war capabilities. But there is doubt that it can discharge all of its primary tasks, particularly that of countering U.S. Polaris A3 and Poseidon (and, later, Trident) ballistic missile submarines. Despite her overall naval power, moreover, there also is doubt that the Soviet Union can sustain general naval operations in the Indian Ocean environment and concomitantly defend the Eastern Mediterranean and her four fleet areas.

The Indian Ocean offers geographical advantages for U.S. nuclear-powered submarine operations. The Arabian Sea region, in particular, provides ideal coverage of much of Russia's heartland. Submarines south of India could quickly be deployed to target either the USSR or Red China. The Soviet Navy's ability to counter the strategic nuclear threat which could be effectively posed by the United States from waters 2,000 miles or more from USSR frontiers is therefore highly questionable.

While countering Polaris and Poseidon in the Indian Ocean region constitutes a formidable and perhaps insurmountable challenge, the pattern of Soviet naval operations suggests that any such U.S. threat "will not go unanswered." And it has not.

The Soviets, particularly attuned to control of strategic "choke points" or access routes, are especially conscious of the strategic value of the Suez Canal, the Bab-El-Mandeb region, the Straits of Malacca, and the Somalia Peninsula. They have studied the history of the British and U.S. navies, and have learned their lessons well. As a result, they have sought to gain positions which will allow them to monitor some of the important entrances and exits of the world's third largest ocean—to maintain a

close watch on the movements of the many strategic materials that flow from that area to the free world.

Before 1968, Soviet warships annually spent fewer than 100 ship days in the Indian Ocean. In 1968, the figure for days spent by Soviet ships in the ocean rose to 1,800, and it has increased steadily since—in 1973 it was 8,262.

In 1968, moreover, the Soviet Union had only three ships in the Indian Ocean; it now has between 30 and 40, a total which includes modern missile cruisers and

Men of Naval Mobile Construction Battalion 62 at work on Diego Garcia (U.S. Navy photos by Carnell Coe, Jr.). Navy, Defense Department, and State Department officials view the island as vital to U.S. interests in the Indian Ocean, but additional construction is opposed by many influential members of the House and Senate.

destroyers, nuclear submarines, and such non-combatant craft as fishing trawlers and hydrographic research vessels—which also serve as intelligence gathering bases. The Soviets comprehend clearly that the search for strategic superiority is not only military, but also scientific, technological, and political.

'Sea of the Future'

In five short years, the Soviet Union has established a permanent presence in an ocean now called by many strategists "the sea of the future." There is little doubt that, since the Cuban missile crisis, the Soviet Navy has embarked upon a shift to a forward pattern of deployment, and that the Arab-Israeli conflict in the summer of 1967 opened the door for establishment of a substantial USSR naval presence in the Mediterranean,

274

thus threatening the previous virtually exclusive monopoly of the U.S. Sixth Fleet and other NATO naval forces in that area. Soviet combat ships now regularly visit India, Ceylon, Tanzania, Mozambique, Yemen, and other countries in the Afro-Asian region. And, besides the acquisition of base facilities in Umm Qasr, Iraq, Mauritius, Socotra, Somalia, South Yemen, and Bangladesh, the USSR has supported development by Iraq of anti-submarine forces to help contain the U.S. Navy.

The June 1975 reopening of the Suez Canal clearly should facilitate deployment of Russian Black Sea Fleet vessels to the Indian Ocean. Conceivably, the Soviets could double, triple, or even quadruple their ships on station, and without actually assigning more vessels to the area. The reopening of the Suez route permits a linking of Soviet forces and bases in the Mediterranean with those in the northern areas of the Indian Ocean "to form a strategic compound system going around the Arab peninsula and reaching into the Persian Gulf" (Wolfgang Hopker, "Soviet Global Strategy, A Challenge At Sea," NATO Review, June 1974).

The presence of oil in the region, added to a world energy crisis, has inserted another dimension to the political and strategic implications of the Indian Ocean peripheral. The possibility that the USSR could bar Western access to Arab oil has to be a strong factor giving impetus to current Soviet global strategy. That factor, plus the USSR's achievement in building a chain of bases along the oil shipping lanes of the Persian Gulf area, would seem to reflect a strategy aimed at weakening the power of the West—as well as that of Japan, which imports about 83 percent of its oil from the Kuwait fields.

Waving the Red Flag

Still another variable in considering the nature of Soviet activities in the Indian Ocean relates to the ability of any naval power to "show the flag."

Seapower today is, and traditionally has been, one of the best, effective, and most economical ways to create an overseas presence. It offers complete flexibility and the luxury of a controlled and measured response, and also reflects the fact that great political value can be derived simply from making known the presence of a fleet. The

latter value is not necessarily contingent on the relative strengths of two navies, moreover. In times of peace a navy's political value is strategically relevant, and more. The USSR has demonstrated its appreciation of that fact in extending its political power in the Indian Ocean, and apparently intends to expand use of that same strategy.

Admiral S.G. Gorshkov, the "father" of the modern Soviet Navy, was quoted by the U.S. Naval Institute Proceedings (October 1974) as saying that "the Navy to a greater degree than the other branches of the armed forces, by concentrating in itself the latest achievements of science and technology, has reflected the level of economic and scientific-technical development of a state." During peacetime, he continued, the Navy, because of its "high mobility," can demonstrate the economic and military power of a nation much beyond its borders, and thus may be used by political leaders to demonstrate readiness for decisive actions, to "deter or suppress intentions of political enemies," and "to support friendly states."

In peacetime, visits to foreign shores by the Soviet Navy have been mainly for political purposes. The "imperialist" navies, says Gorshkov, exert political pressures on other states "to support diplomatic moves of one's own country," but the Soviet Navy, in contrast, fulfills the role of "plenipotentiaries" of socialist countries when it visits Indian Ocean ports. Gorshkov admits that recent "show the flag" visits have strengthened the international influences of the Soviet Union, and he states, in effect, that military and political considerations cannot be kept in separate watertight compartments; the increased presence of Soviet naval vessels in the Indian Ocean regions has therefore contributed significantly to the rise of Soviet political influence in the area.

The Scrutable PRC

Besides having an anti-Western motivation, the Soviet naval presence in the Indian Ocean area also reflects an anti-Chinese motivation, aimed principally at creating political barriers in the area for Red China. The PRC cannot yet mount a military strategic capability in those distant waters; it is, however, already engaged in the process of constructing a political presence, and that has caused considerable concern to the USSR.

The Chinese People's Republic, according to Angus M. Fraser, ("Chinese Interests and Activities in the Indian Ocean," an unpublished paper, January 1971), apparently views the Indian Ocean region as a vast political and economic area in which she may "engage in her favorite forms of activity at reasonable cost and with some hope of useful returns," and concomitantly "spoil the efforts of Russia and the United States." The PRC obviously has increased her trade activities in the region. While an Indian Ocean voting bloc in the United Nations does not exist per se, if there were in that body a China-led voting constituency among Indian Ocean nations, previous UN voting records indicate it would include, at least, Afghanistan, Zambia, Chad, Malagasy, Kenya, Indonesia (although official diplomatic relations have not been resumed), Singapore, and even India; all those nations voted with China between 53 and 71 percent of the time in 1973. If the region is extended to include the Philippines and nations of central Africa, then some 43 nations would be included which cast their UN votes with China between 60 and 71 percent of the time during 1973.

There seems little doubt that the PRC has made strong inroads among Indian Ocean nations—and often at the expense of the USSR, incidentally. The USSR and PRC generally, but not always, vote the same way in the United Nations, and most Indian Ocean peripheral states cast their votes, most of the time, with the two Communist superpowers. A review of the 1973 voting patterns of 13 Indian Ocean nations—Afghanistan, Bahrein, Ethiopia, India, Indonesia, Iran, Kenya, Malagasy, Saudi Arabia, Singapore, Sri Lanka, Tanzania, and Zambia—indicates, however, that, when the PRC and USSR do oppose each other in their UN votes, those nations vote with the PRC, and against the USSR, about 75 percent of the time. Russia is, of course, aware of the pattern and probably not too happy about it.

International Conferences and the Tan-Zam Railroad

Corroborating the UN voting pattern has been the PRC-vs.-USSR voting pattern at various international conferences. The records of the Stockholm Conference on the Human Environment (1972), the United Nations Environment Program Conference (Geneva, 1973), the UN Conference on Population Problems (Bucharest, 1974) and the Law of the Sea Conference (Caracas, 1974), demonstrate beyond any doubt that the votes of the developing nations (known to other observers at those conferences as the "solid 77"), including those of Indian Ocean countries, consistently supported the positions of the People's Republic of China over those of the USSR.

The political influence of China among Indian Ocean nations has greatly increased during the last several years, and that development alone has awakened a natural Soviet suspicion of Chinese objectives in the region. Chinese financial and technological support of the Tan-Zam Railroad, creation of a joint Chinese-Tanzanian shipping company, training of the Tanzanian Air Force by China, and the People's Republic assistance program in Kenya, Guinea, Sri Lanka, Zaire, and Mali, among others, have validated and increased the USSR's distrust. As an exporter of warships the PRC has sold six motor gunboats to Sri Lanka, 14 to Tanzania, and over 25 to North Vietnam, mostly of the SHANGHAI class.

The USSR realizes, moreover, that China is on the verge of testing intercontinental ballistic missiles. Because the land mass of China does not provide sufficient range for full testing, there is speculation that the PRC may test the missiles over India and use the Indian Ocean as an impact area. The next step would be construction of

The supertanker NATIONAL DEFENDER. Japan, Western Europe, and, to a lesser extent, the United States, are now dependent on Mideast oil, most of which is carried by such supertankers via various Indian Ocean shipping routes. The strong Soviet naval presence in the Indian Ocean gives the USSR easy interdiction capabilities, however, and has created a serious new problem for U.S. decisionmakers.

tracking stations both in the ocean and along the east African coast. While hard evidence is inconclusive, there have been some intelligence reports that some of the construction under Chinese management in Tanzania is intended for missile testing purposes. Moscow is not unaware of the reports.

The People's Republic also has improved diplomatic relations in the area by completing an exchange of ambassadors with almost all Indian Ocean countries (Indonesia and South Africa are the exceptions), and manning its new embassies with relatively full staffs—including Counselors, Economic Counselors, First, Second, and Third Secretaries, and various non-designated attaches. In several countries the PRC's delegation now exceeds in size those from the USSR and the United States.

Chinese Satellites

In addition, China recently joined the International Satellite Corporation (Intelsat) and has linked up three stations with it. A portable satellite station which carried the 1972 visit of President Nixon to Peking was left behind as a gift; China was obviously pleased with the communications value of the system, and that, it is believed, led to the PRC decision to join Intelsat. The corporation has now completed an Indian Ocean Basin Satellite which serves as a communications systems medium

for such area countries as Bahrein, Kenya, Tanzania, Zambia, Sri Lanka, Iraq, Taiwan, Australia, and Saudi Arabia. The United Arab Emirates and Bangladesh are scheduled to hook up with the satellite in 1975 and 1979, respectively. The PRC's Intelsat membership, once again, admirably complements and reflects Peking's deep-seated interest in the Indian Ocean political arena.

The development of Chinese interest in the Indian Ocean peripheral has added a new dimension to the geopolitical aspects of international politics there, particularly if it is remembered that in such a vast region strategy need not involve control of the sea itself, but only of certain pivotal or key points in or surrounding it. The activities of China, like those of the USSR and the United States, indicate no desire to control the oceanic region. Peking, however, does desire to reap benefits from and assert political leadership in the area. The Chinese offensive, contributing to Soviet distrust of Peking, has created a new conditioning variant in Soviet policy in the Indian Ocean.

U.S. Goal: 'Balanced Stability'

The value of U.S. oil industry capital investments in the Persian Gulf area is almost $4 billion. In addition, Western Europe and Japan, strategically important to U.S. national security, are almost completely dependent upon oil supplies from the Middle East. Under such circumstances, freedom of navigation on the high seas, and particularly in the Indian Ocean, is vital to all members of the world community, including the United States.

Aside from oil, the United States has other huge economic interests in the Indian Ocean—interests which include increasingly substantial trade with India, Pakistan, Saudi Arabia, Iran, the Gulf Sheikdoms, and the African littoral states. The whole region, in fact, is potentially a major market area for U.S. products as well as an important source of raw materials for U.S. industry.

The major objective of U.S. policy in the Indian Ocean is to maintain a balanced stability. That policy requires a strategy aimed at preventing any dominance of the area by either the Soviet Union or the PRC. Within this context the U.S. Navy must maintain a reasonable presence.

Until recently the Navy has had a Mideastern Force comprised of two World War II destroyers and a converted amphibious ship. In view of increasing U.S. interests in the region and the precarious international situation resulting from the October 1973 war, the frequency of U.S. naval deployments to the Indian Ocean has been increased—but is still well within the spirit of "maintaining a reasonable presence." Hence, following the October 1973 war the United States deployed, on a temporary basis, the aircraft carrier HANCOCK (detached from the Seventh Fleet) which was followed by a second carrier, ORISKANY, relieved in turn by the nuclear frigate BAINBRIDGE in early 1974. As of the spring of 1974, the United States had a total of nine naval vessels in the Indian Ocean, and the USSR about 30, including support, auxiliary, and research ships.

A military presence can effectively support diplomacy without necessarily having to be utilized; the U.S. naval presence in the Indian Ocean has a salutary effect by

underscoring the Navy's strategic mobility in support of U.S. diplomatic efforts, as previous sorties into the area by the USS ENTERPRISE have proven.

In early 1974 a significant shift in U.S. strategy occurred when the Department of Defense requested implementation of an agreement signed with the United Kingdom in December 1966 which would make the island of Diego Garcia available for the defense purposes of both governments for a period of 50 years. Funding requests to extend the runways on that island to handle larger transports, to deepen and widen the harbor, and to add fuel storage facilities for ships have been the focus of considerable Congressional debate for the past 18 months.

The United States has no intention to "take over" Diego Garcia, DoD and other witnesses have made clear. The arrangement with the British government permits the United States to have in the island "no less than or more than the kinds of restraints that we have elsewhere, particularly with regard to use of British bases in Great Britain." In the event of unusual developments, moreover, there is "a requirement for consultation" with the British to obtain a "joint decision with regard to the use of the island," State Department official Seymour Weiss has testified. Hoping to quell Congressional fears that a U.S. base in Diego Garcia would invite a heavy Soviet naval counter buildup in the Indian Ocean, Weiss (then Director of the Department's Bureau of Politico-Military Affairs) stressed that the entire Indian Ocean periphery "is an enormously valuable area in terms of oil resources, in terms of communications in connection with these resources which flow to those areas of the world which are critical in maintaining the balance of power ... which has created the relative stability that we enjoy today." He added that "if there were no Soviet naval forces in the area whatsoever ... we would want" to maintain a presence in Diego Garcia. It is very much in the U.S. national interest—as well as in the interest of the region as a

Hungry children in Mali, in western central Africa, anxiously wait in line during U.S. food airlift Operation King Grain in July 1974 (U.S. Air Force photo). Despite such mercy missions, the United States is fast losing influence in Africa, particularly on the Indian Ocean peripheral, to the more ambitious efforts of the USSR and PRC.

whole—for the United States to maintain a stronger presence in the area, Weiss and other witnesses have emphasized.

New-retired Admiral Elmo R. Zumwalt, Jr., then Chief of Naval Operations, supported the State Department's view and added the perceptive point that a rough balance of conventional power has been achieved over the years "with land power superiority conceded to the Soviets in Eurasia and with maritime superiority ... to the free world alliance." Unraveling of that balance, he indicated, would lead to a U.S. inability to prevent more aggressive foreign policy initiatives by the USSR. Weiss said, in corroboration, that, if the U.S. Navy has facilities in Diego Garcia, "the Soviets won't be tempted to interfere with U.S. interests. If it [the U.S. Navy] is not there, the Soviets will be tempted."

Acquisition of U.S. naval and air supply facilities at Diego Garcia, costing an estimated $37 million over a three-year period, would also substantially ease the current strain on supply ships coming from the Philippines and further distances. And the island would provide a base for long-range P-3 Orion patrol planes, thus further reducing the need for ship movements. In addition, while the island's projected runway would not be able to take B-52s, it would support KC-135 tankers. The projected construction also would give the island facilities for a submarine tender and for carrier task force support. There are no plans at present to anchor a submarine tender there, however, nor to make Diego

Garcia a submarine support facility, as Zumwalt and later witnesses have emphasized.

U.S. objectives in the Indian Ocean, it seems clear, are aimed at maintaining a stabilized "balance of power" in the area between U.S. and Soviet naval forces. To do more—strive for "local superiority," for example—might well be counterproductive. But to do less could invite the Soviet Union to initiate overtly aggressive action. It would also indicate to Indian Ocean nations a lack of interest by the United States in the region.

Summary: Three-Way Split

To summarize: Soviet Indian Ocean policy is aimed at gaining influence for the USSR in the region, and also to curtail and reduce the influences of both the United States and Red China. Because most Indian Ocean countries are developing nations, are (at least theoretically) non-aligned in foreign affairs, and have large and rising expectations, the activities of the Soviet Union pose both a potential impediment to the national interests of the United States and a hindrance to achievement of Red China's aims in the region. By the same token, however, the rapid increase and nature of PRC activities in the area present a difficult problem for the USSR, and constitute an additional conditioning dimension in Soviet projections of policy in the Indian Ocean peripheral.

Despite the constraints of geography, tradition, and even detente, the Soviet Union has established a forward naval deployment in the Indian Ocean. The Soviet presence does not necessarily impute a capability of achieving significant far-reaching military objectives, but it does provide strong support for expanding Soviet political influences, particularly in the oil-producing and northwest sections of the peripheral. The Russians do not presently have the capability of mounting a major naval offense in the Indian Ocean. Completion of the two Soviet aircraft carriers now under construction will add to the USSR's forward deployment capability and further support the Soviet diplomatic process already much apparent in such nations as Iraq, India, Sri Lanka, Mozambique, Pakistan, Somalia, South Yemen, and even Iran.

The methodical approach of the People's Republic of China in expanding its influence in the "forgotten ocean" is non-military and appears to be increasingly successful. Even though China does not currently possess strong overseas commercial and naval capabilities, the impact of new PRC diplomatic representation, the pattern of agreement in UN voting by the PRC and Indian Ocean nations, and the leadership of China among the "solid 77" developing nations, including the vast majority of Indian Ocean nations, constitute sufficient cause for Soviet (and U.S.) concern.

Finally, the United States itself, somewhat belatedly realizing, as a nation increasingly dependent on overseas sources of raw materials, the importance to U.S. national interests of the Indian Ocean and its peripheral land area, is now striving to maintain a reasonable balance of naval power in the region, and should certainly be able to do so, provided there is Congressional support for current Administration policy. If there is not, the results could be harmful not only to the United States, but to the Indian Ocean's many developing nations as well. ∎

Soviets at Sea

Soviet Global Strategy:
The Great Challenge to the West at Sea

By Wolfgang Höpker

Translated by Jack Sweetman

© RAND MCNALLY & CO. 75-GP-28

The greatest continental power in the world in surface area has set out to become the greatest sea power as well. Far ahead of Great Britain, once the ruler of the waves, and in intense competition with the United States, the Soviet Union is pressing forward on the high seas with the creation of an oceanic navy. People speak of the greatest challenge to the West since the birth of Soviet imperialism. The ship, not the tank, is the military element to which the Soviets give priority today. The sea, an indestructible highway, is open to all. The Soviet Union has grasped the meaning of command of the sea. Behind the maritime ambitions of the Kremlin leadership is the realization that confrontation in the East-West conflict is shifting ever more strongly from land to sea.

Naval policy is foreign policy. It holds ready a military threat, but has its principal sphere of action in the demonstration of political power. In view of the atomic stalemate of the two superpowers, the Soviet Union cannot want a big war. Its naval buildup is primarily intended to add another means of expansive pressure to

MINISTRY OF DEFENCE

With no direct access to the Indian Ocean, but with an improving capability to replenish its surface fleet, above, the Soviet Union has increased its naval presence in the Indian Ocean tenfold in the past five years.

land-based military power, and not least to win political predominance in Europe.

That may sound declamatory or exaggerated. Yet in a phase of East-West relations called "détente," the Soviet Union most recently demonstrated its strength on the high seas in the last half of April with the naval exercise "Okean 1975." The Red Fleet let it be known that it has the ability to operate far beyond the coastal seas of the Soviet sphere on a global scale. Above all, these farflung fleet movements proved the capability of Soviet commanders to move units from one ocean area to another.

Only hesistantly did the West abandon the traditional military picture, only reluctantly did it begin to recognize in the Soviet advance on the seas a revolutionary change in the world scene. The immense continental empire which covers a sixth of the world's land area has with the construction of an oceanic navy broken the fetters of inland confinement and transformed the claim to be a world power into direct intervention on every continent. For the first time, a navy operating on all the oceans gives Soviet power—dedicated to "world revolution" by V. I. Lenin over half a century ago—the means to direct, worldwide action.

According to Western understanding, armed forces are at their most useful in times of crisis. According to Soviet military doctrine, armed forces are a prominent instrument of policy, even in peace, through presence, pressure, intimidation, and threat. It is exactly in this respect that by the construction of a world-ranging oceanic navy, the Soviets have attained a second option vis-à-vis the Western alliance. In striving to expand their power, they no longer need defeat the enemy on land, and the battle no longer need take place in Central Europe, where in view of the concentration of military forces on both sides of the Iron Curtain, an advance by the Red Army would raise the risk of a third world war.

The NATO alliance can be paralyzed from the sea even without force of arms. In conventional Western thought the security of Europe is still identified with a line, the Iron Curtain, which in case of aggression must be defended, with or without atomic weapons. But why should the Russians attack across the Elbe when a less risky way is open to achieve their aim, the establishment of hegemony over Western Europe? It is high time for the West to redefine its idea of the threat. In view of the danger to the sea-lanes, in view also of the extension of atomic potential to the sea, it has acquired a broader spectrum. It transcends the existing definition of indirect strategy, which sought mainly to incorporate insurgency and guerrilla tactics into the modern military picture.

The continental empire ruled from Moscow, stretching from the Elbe to the Pacific, is economically self-sufficient. It needs no Red Fleet to protect its supply lines. For the West, however, the basic arteries of life run through the sea. What this can mean even in peacetime—but all the more in periods of tension—the Mideast crisis in the fall of 1973 gave a glaring example. The Arabs' attempt to force Israel into isolation and ultimately capitulation through boycotting oil supplies to the Western countries should not be reduced to the "energy crisis" formula and measured solely by its economic consequences. Equally important and in the long run still more critical are its security aspects.

These have opened a new panorama of threats reaching—in previously unparalleled dimensions—far beyond the various Mideastern crises into the East-West conflict. The oil countries could hardly have applied their risky restriction policy so ruthlessly if the great naval power of the Soviet Union had not backed them. Moscow realized that the Arabs had finally succeeded in what, despite all its efforts, the Soviet Union had never achieved: the precipitation of a serious crisis which tested the solidarity of the Western alliance. This can be called an "economic war through proxies." Indirectly through the Arab countries Moscow staged a sort of dress rehearsal of what can be achieved with economic weapons, with control, and—if need be—constriction of the sea lanes to weaken and wear down the Western industrial nations and Japan. In combination with the Soviet Fleet, the Arab oil reserves are conceived as a means of pressure to isolate Western Europe from America, to neutralize and, in the sense of recognizing the hegemony of the Soviet Union, to "Finlandize" it.

Closely linked with this is the intention to take Europe in a pincers on both its "wet flanks." The relaxation of tension in Central Europe, where today Moscow is at pains to attain international legitimization of its annexations through the "Conference for Security and Cooperation," has automatically sharpened Soviet pressure on Europe's northern and southern flanks. In shifting pressure from the relatively stable central sector to Europe's flanks, Moscow sees the most effective method of overcoming the stalemate which developed in Central Europe, in spite of the growing conventional imbalance in favor of the Warsaw Pact.

Militarily checked in Central Europe, the Soviets are reaching around the continent to put primary pressure on its edges. There Moscow believes it has found a field of action for wide-ranging initiatives, which combine military with political and subversive operations to outmaneuver the "Western European bridgehead" on the Eurasian land mass from the sea. All the more regrettable is the general tendency in the West in regard

U. S. NAVY

The eight-year closure of the Suez canal ended for the U. S. Navy with the transit in June 1975 of the USS Little Rock *(CLG-4). The principal strategic advantage of the canal's opening will accrue, not to the United States, but to the Soviet Union.*

to the Vienna talks on troop reduction to look only at Central Europe and to ignore the unprecedented Soviet naval buildup.

The principal concern of the Western alliance today is Europe's elongated southern flank, which stretches from the Atlantic through the Mediterranean to the center of unrest in the Middle East. In a sort of chain reaction, crises have flared up around the Mediterranean basin. Winston Churchill's phrase, "Europe's soft underbelly," has achieved an oppressive reality. With the Mideast crisis, aggravated by the oil situation and the Cyprus conflict which burst into flame in the summer of 1974, the Eastern Mediterranean has become more than ever a storm center of international affairs. The southeastern flank of NATO has lost its reputation as the "pillar" of the Atlantic alliance. Crippled through the Greco-Turkish quarrel, it has become a question mark. With the outbreak of the centuries-old "hereditary antagonism" between the Turks and Greeks, both peoples—for better or worse—lost sight of their dependence upon the alliance against the pressure from the Soviets to the north.

Still another danger sign is Moscow's understanding with Libya. By massive arms shipments, the Soviet Union acquired rights to military bases on the southern shore of the Mediterranean. With the construction of

air bases on the North African coast opposite Italy and Greece, in the very center of the Mediterranean basin, the Soviet Mediterranean squadron would receive the air cover it has lacked until now. The minimum objective of this squadron is the diminution of Western influence, especially American. The maximum objective is hegemony in the Mediterranean—to secure the claim to Soviet superiority. Between its minimum and maximum objectives, Soviet naval activity is designed to outflank Europe from the south by weakening the position of the Western alliance.

A fundamental concept of the Red general staff is the envelopment of Europe on *both* its wet flanks. The critical situation on the southern flank must not obscure the danger on the northern flank. That applies to the Baltic, which with its construction and training potential, is the starting point of the present worldwide Soviet expansion at sea. That applies most of all, however, to the concentration on the Arctic Ocean front, where the Soviets have assembled a mass of naval, air, and land forces which can be characterized as the greatest military complex in the world today. The Baltic and the North Sea, bounded by the Danish Straits, are not just a strategic naval unity in the view of the Soviet Union. The superiority of the Soviet naval forces in the Baltic facilitates operational cooperation with the Norwegian Sea fleet, which forms a sort of pincers around the Scandinavian peninsula. Moscow's flanking concept is in turn inseparably intertwined with strategic land objectives in Central Europe—another sign that the northern, central, and southern sectors of NATO should not be partitioned into individual districts.

The concentration of naval striking forces off Northern Europe aims at a breakout into the open Atlantic, across which run the vital lines of communication of the Western alliance, the arteries binding Western Europe with North America. While the Soviets still pursue limited objectives in the Mediterranean, the north European coastal seas form the basis of their grand strategic offensive, with which they would attempt to cut off Western Europe from its American "hinterland" and thereby automatically cause the European defensive front to collapse. The defensive line Lübeck-Hof-Passau (Lübeck-Trieste) would be overcome from the outside—the sea.

284

War at sea knows no frontlines which opposing forces can change by attack and counterattack. It does not lend itself to Maginot thinking. It can be grasped only in flexible, spatial terms. This fundamental proviso does not exclude a central question: where in the North Atlantic are the West's crucial rallying points to be found? The Barents Sea, extending from the Kolafjord with Murmansk as a nodal point, has already become a *Mare Sovieticum,* removed from Western inspection and control. But the Norwegian Sea also appears to be earmarked to become a sort of Soviet lake in the plans

On "VE" day in 1945, Soviet tanks epitomized the pride and priority of that great continental power; but, 30 years later, two Soviet warships observed the anniversary in Boston and thereby confirmed their country's unmistakable commitment to sea power.

of the Red naval command. From the Red Navy's maneuvers it becomes ever clearer that much of Norway is already *behind* the forward Soviet operational line. The Soviets refer publicly to the calculation that the Western defense would be deployed in the "narrows" between Iceland, Scotland, and central Norway.

The Atlantic stategy takes on a new dimension with the extension of atomic warfare to sea. This exceeds the bounds of classic naval warfare. Nuclear weapon-carrying submarines are not a means of naval warfare, but rather submerged, seagoing missile batteries aimed at land targets. The navy is thus reduced to the role of a trustee. Besides the intercontinental missiles and the far-distant strategic bombers, the U. S. missile submarine fleet is the most effective means of deterrence. An important reason for the current Soviet naval buildup is the intention to paralyze the seagoing atomic potential of the United States in the North Atlantic if at all possible. In the same connection, the Soviet fleet is moving to threaten the NATO coastal areas of both Europe and America through the creation of its own ballistic missile-armed submarine fleet.

The alliance founded a quarter-century ago as a *North* Atlantic union considers only the North Atlantic as its defensive zone. This self-imposed limitation or confinement of NATO to the ocean area north of the Tropic of Cancer has become more and more questionable with the oceanic expansion of the Red Fleet. The vacuum which the South Atlantic exhibits in the picture of the Western alliance represents a growing temptation to the Soviets. The role of Cuba as a Soviet base is connected with the development of Conakry into a naval and air base in West Africa. Thus a control line, patrolled by Soviet aircraft, runs across the narrowest part of the ocean, the "wasp's waist" from Conakry through the Cape Verde Islands into the Caribbean to Cuba. Today the South Atlantic is anything but a "no man's sea." It has gained significance through the rerouting, necessitated by the blocking of the Suez Canal, of the great shipping lanes between Europe and Asia around the Cape of Good Hope. Most important of all was the rerouting of the oil stream, which follows a course from the Persian Gulf—the richest oil region on earth—around the southern tip of Africa to Western Europe. Due to the trend toward supertankers and containerships, the Cape route remains one of the great arteries of world traffic even after the reopening of the Suez Canal.

To be sure, the NATO doctrine that an attack on one alliance partner will be regarded as an attack on all alliance partners can hardly be extended to the South Atlantic. Yet the limitation of Western solidarity to the area of the North Atlantic pact need not mean that NATO naval forces cannot undertake sea control and defensive functions in other areas. Brazil, following the Japanese example, has begun to emerge as a potential new world economic power. By a wide-ranging naval program, she has demonstrated a recognition of her responsibility in the South Atlantic. This in turn relates to the defensive efforts of South Africa. Thanks to her key geostrategic position between the Atlantic and the Indian Oceans, South Africa forms an extremely inconvenient obstacle to the offensive plans of the Soviet fleet. Thus, it would be in the generally understood defensive interests of Western Europe and America to support South Africa through military collaboration.

The reopening of the Suez Canal early in June of this year brings strategic advantages principally to the Soviet Union. For warships of even the largest Soviet cruiser class—indeed even for the soon-to-be-operational Soviet aircraft carriers—the canal is sufficient in its present dimensions. The central issue is Soviet access to the Indian Ocean, which is drastically shortened with the reopening of the canal. The concentration of the Soviet squadron in the Mediterranean remained abortive so long as the connection between the Mediterranean and the Indian Ocean by the direct north-south passage was not assured. The massing of the Soviet Fleet in the Eastern Mediterranean signifies more than a threat to Europe's southern flank; it is applied on a still greater strategic scale.

The Indian Ocean is the only great sea to which the Soviet continental empire has no direct access. Yet despite all the disadvantages of geography, the Soviet Union has increased its naval presence in the Indian Ocean tenfold in the last five years. The thrust of the Soviet leadership toward heightened presence in the Indian Ocean is anti-Western, but also in part anti-Chinese. Here Moscow is moving to contain its great rival China, which shows increasing maritime ambitions, on the sea side as well. Even in the Indian Ocean, Moscow will "show the flag" to increase its influence. Yet stripped of its local psycho-political effects, the general mission of a Soviet fleet in the Indian Ocean emerges as a plan to work in conjunction with the Pacific fleet massed around Vladivostok to alter the strategic situation in South and Southeast Asia as occurred in the Arabian region.

Thereby the Soviet position in the Mediterranean would coalesce with that in the Indian Ocean into a strategic combination which surrounds the Arabian peninsula, extends into the Persian Gulf, and stretches to the coast of India, which is in close military cooperation with Moscow. In regard to the Persian Gulf, the Middle East is now the "Near South" for the Soviet Union. Oil interests mesh with strategy there. The prospect of being able to shut off gulf oil to the West is a major impetus to Soviet global strategy. Consequently, the Red Navy is endeavoring to build a system of bases along the tanker route from the Persian Gulf. This applies to the eastern flank of the African continent as well as to positions on the Red Sea, which like the Eastern Mediterranean ranks as a potential Soviet lake in the planning of the Red general staff.

While the Western countries were inclined to view the navy as a weapon of yesterday, the Soviet Union proceeded to make the fleet a weapon of tomorrow. Behind the smokescreen of the vocabulary of détente, Moscow opened through its naval buildup a whole spectrum of new possibilities of direct—but principally of indirect—strategy to the hegemonial aspirations of Soviet imperialism. From cold war to hot peace—the West has every reason to be on guard against a concept which would replace the *Pax Atlantica* with the *Pax Sovietica*. A maritime epoch has dawned; sea power will be the decisive factor in world power. The Soviet Union is determined to draw the conclusion from that, and with an intensified maritime dynamic to attain not merely equality but superiority.

Dr. Höpker is editor of the weekly Bonn newspaper *Deutsche Zeitung: Christ und Welt* and author of the following books on naval strategy published by Verlag Seewald, Stuttgart: *The Baltic: A Red Lake?, How Red is the Mediterranean?, World Power at Sea: The Soviet Union on the Oceans,* and *Thrust for the Atlantic: The Threat from the North.* Höpker's most recent book is *Storm Center of World Politics: The Indian Ocean in Great Power Rivalry,* published by Verlag Seewald in July 1975. His *Proceedings* article on Soviet naval strategy is an enlarged and updated version of a contribution which appeared in the June 1974 issue of *NATO Review.*

THE SOVIET NAVY'S ROLE

IN FOREIGN POLICY

While the Soviet Navy has been often pictured recently as presenting a new challenge to America's ability to control the oceans of the world in the event of hostilities, Soviet naval forces today are in a much better position to play a more subtle but equally important role in support of Russian foreign policy. By means of eight case studies the author demonstrates the part played by Soviet Navy ships in a variety of situations, revealing how their actions directly parallel and support the Kremlin's political stance abroad.

An article

by

Commander Richard T. Ackley, U.S. Navy (Ret.)

The essential quality of a military navy is obviously its ultimate capacity to engage and fight an enemy. Yet, for the greater portion of its existence, a navy is not engaged in combat. During this time of peace, however, a navy by no means fails to exert an influence upon international affairs. This effectiveness short of war is difficult to characterize but is nevertheless pervasive and may well comprise the most significant benefit a nation derives from its naval investment.

L.W. Martin
The Sea in Modern Strategy

INTRODUCTION

The peacetime role of naval forces in a nation's foreign policy is often obscure and tends to be neglected in foreign policy literature. While the dramatic growth of the Soviet naval fleet has not gone unnoticed, most articles on the subject have stressed the Soviet naval challenge to United States or NATO seapower. The purpose of this essay, however, will be to assess the role played by the Soviet Navy in the overall context of Russian foreign policy. We will look beyond combat capabilities and attempt to associate naval behavior with identifiable Soviet policy goals. Our concern shall center on the time frame from 1950 to 1972, with particular attention being paid to eight Soviet foreign policy thrusts subject to naval influence.

A nation's naval forces can play an impressive role in the furtherance of certain foreign policy objectives, as three centuries of British naval history reveal. In that naval vessels are owned by sovereign states and deployed in response to the will of national political leaders, their operations are directly related to national policy considerations. Further appreciation for the vital role seapower can play in a country's foreign policy is gained from the fact that approximately 90 percent of the world's trade is carried by sea, and about 70 percent of its population lives within 30 miles of the coasts.[1] The linkage between seapower and foreign policy is not new. In the late 1800's Admiral Mahan advocated the doctrine that command of the sea is the dominant form of politics. Mahan emphasized the historical link between diplomacy and naval power. In earlier times, great powers sent gunboats up the rivers of states they were seeking to influence; today the presence of warships offshore and in foreign ports serves as a vehicle of international influence and prestige. In fact, in periods of crisis or tension, the mere appearance of a modern naval force can signal the attitude and degree of interest of its parent power. A naval ship, like an overseas embassy, is an enclave of sovereign territory, serving to symbolize and strengthen the image of the state it represents. The very mobility of warships provides them their unique quality as tools of international diplomacy.

In modern times, particularly since the middle of this century, the U.S.S.R. has capitalized on the diplomatic capabilities of its navy as an adjunct to foreign policy. However, before turning to specific examples of Soviet naval behavior, we shall first identify the Soviet foreign policies concerning us.

By foreign policy we mean a course of action that supports a concept of a state's national goals and purposes. This course of action may be active or passive; and even sometimes may seem inconsistent, as goals and purposes (national interest) may vary with time. Thus, the task of describing a country's foreign policy may be difficult—especially in a closed society such as the Soviet Union. Some Soviet policies are quite explicit; however, others must be derived in a manner that parallels Charles Osgood's image of content analysis. That is, "an attempt to infer the characteristics and intentions of sources from inspection of the messages they produce."[2] On the other hand, the overall trend in Soviet foreign policy since the 1950's is not as difficult to establish as specific policies.

Under Stalin the Soviet Union pursued what might be called a foreign policy of continental dimensions. That is, Stalin's politico-military policy was largely confined in its dimensions to the Eurasian Continent. With the advent of Khrushchev, however, Soviet policy took on a worldwide proportion which was in accord with the new global power status coveted by the U.S.S.R. This global power status increased substantially under Khrushchev's successors—moving more substantially into the "Third World" and into keener rivalry with the United States. Throughout this period Soviet naval development paralleled these expanding foreign policy interests growing in scope from continental to global proportions.[3]

Despite the difficulties inherent in defining clear-cut individual Soviet for-

eign policies, we can identify a set of eight policy trends that have persisted with time—and generally are accepted by specialists in the Soviet field.

First is the policy of strategic nuclear deterrence. Nuclear deterrence is, in fact, an extension of the classical notion of balance of power. It assumes an international harmony of interest at the lowest level—that is, individual and collective survival. This policy is based on the premise that war is a deliberate act, and if each side maintains sufficient nuclear weapons and delivery systems to insure unacceptable damage to the opposing side, nuclear war can be prevented.

Second is a major thesis of communism: expansion and world domination. "For a half-century, Soviet leaders have time and again repeated that Communism's ultimate objective is world domination. But many in the Free World simply refuse to believe that the Soviet leaders mean what they say."[4]

Abundant evidence exists to support expansion and world domination as continuing Soviet policies—both ideological and operational. For example, in a doctrinal context the Communists hold to the theory of historical inevitability, wherein other socio-economic-political systems will succumb to communism. Operationally, coexistence is considered a temporary condition. ". . . that is, coexistence until capitalism becomes weaker, until the Soviet Union becomes stronger, ... After all, if the two systems are to coexist indefinitely, the term coexistence is not necessary."[5]

Third is the Soviet policy of avoiding war with the United States. "It is no exaggeration to state that both the U.S. and the U.S.S.R. have ruled out force in its nuclear form as an instrument of their national policies."[6] Perhaps the one constant feature in Soviet-American relations has been the Soviet motivation to prevent a collision with the United States that might escalate to total war. This policy has been constant, but the motivation for the policy has changed. Herbert S. Dinerstein correctly assessed this position when he wrote:

Earlier Soviet leaders, because they were weaker than their opponents and expected to become stronger, wanted to avoid war as

long as possible. Now that they wanted to avoid nuclear war and since they very much feared that any direct engagement with the United States could lead to such a war, they felt it necessary to avoid any war with the United States indefinitely.[7]

The Soviet policy of avoiding war with the United States may be seen as the antithesis of the basic Communist thesis of expansion and world domination. While in fact, these two policies do contradict in part, it nevertheless can be said with reasonable assurance that the Soviet policy of expansion and world domination has not been dropped but has merely assumed back seat to their fear of risking war with the United States.

Fourth is the Soviet policy of claiming a belt of sovereignty extending 12 miles seaward from Soviet territory. International accord prescribes a 3-mile territorial limit, including the right of innocent passage through territorial straits that connect international bodies of water. The Soviet Union unilaterally enforces or threatens to enforce a 12-mile limit, while disclaiming the right of innocent passage through certain territorial straits connecting international waters.

Fifth is the Soviet policy of opposition to the Montreux Convention. The Kremlin desires to close the Black Sea to warships of all nations, except Black Sea powers. A constant in Russian foreign policy since czarist times, this position has been given considerable emphasis by the Soviet Government. For instance, in March 1945 the Soviet Union terminated its 1925 treaty of friendship with Turkey, applied pressure for a revision of the Montreux Convention, and attempted to gain military control over the straits leading from the Mediterranean Sea to the Black Sea.[8] This initiative was unsuccessful, but nevertheless it served to emphasize Soviet dissatisfaction with the Montreux Convention of 1936—a situation that persists today.

Sixth is the Soviet policy of enhancing the Russian image and influence throughout the world. The most recent manifestation of this Russian design can be seen in the globetrotting expeditions of the Soviet leaders, yet it is a policy of long standing supported by propaganda, cultural exchanges, and international trade fairs. Influence overseas is a traditional byproduct associated with a strong naval presence in support of national policy; and, as such, it has not been overlooked by the Soviets. In 1967 Fleet Admiral Kasatonov declared, "Ships' visits facilitate the development and strengthening of friendly relations between the Soviet people and the peoples of foreign countries, and they strengthen the authority and influence of our homeland in the international arena."[9]

Seventh is the Soviet policy of establishing a sphere of influence in the Arab States. Soviet presence in and support of the Arab States have increased steadily since the 1950's. Most recently the Soviets negotiated a 15-year treaty of friendship and cooperation with Egypt that may insure a Soviet presence for the foreseeable future.

Eighth is the Soviet policy of dispelling American military presence from Europe. Since the end of World War II the U.S.S.R. has worked consistently for the removal of U.S. troops, ships, and aircraft from the European theater. Within this context, persistent Soviet pressure for developing some type of a European security community, has the underlying theme of a secure Europe without the presence of foreign (U.S.) armed forces.

In order to support the above policies, the Soviet Navy required the strength and disposition to create an aura of credibility. This was necessary because at times the Soviets would surely compete with the U.S. Navy, and acting from a position of strength is a self-evident asset.

SOVIET NAVAL STRENGTH

From the standpoint of defending the territory of the Soviet Union, the U.S.S.R. does not require an immense naval establishment. Adm. Sir Nigel Henderson accurately assessed the relative requirement for NATO and Soviet naval strength when he wrote:

> ... the Soviets do not need to rely on the sea for sustaining a military presence in Western Europe to anything like the same

extent as the Alliance (N.A.T.O.). They operate from an enormous land base from which their armies and air force can deploy, and their logistic support uses land lines rather than sea routes. By contrast, N.A.T.O. countries rely, heavily, on the free use of the sea.[10]

Nevertheless, the Soviet Navy has increased steadily in strength and capability. Presently their navy is composed of about 500,000 men, 130 first-line ships, 2,200 small surface vessels, nearly 400 submarines, and a newly formed marine infantry group.[11] While a direct comparison between United States and Soviet naval forces is difficult due to differing ship types and weapon systems employed by each side, (figure 1), the U.S. Navy as of mid-1971 consisted of some 714 ships and 620,000 men.[12] Numbers, however, do not tell the entire story. Warship age, equipment, materiel readiness, and training are other important factors. Everything considered, U.S. naval authorities generally rank the Soviet Navy as a "first-class professional outfit,"[13] with its newness as perhaps, one of its greatest assets (figure 2).

In an overall assessment of Soviet naval power, we must conclude that their navy is competitive with the U.S. Navy in every aspect but aviation. Although absence of aircraft carriers has, in fact, limited the Soviets in their ability to control the sea, their navy has clearly become a significant instrument of diplomacy. In assessing these gains, we shall begin by considering the strategic submarine force in its role of nuclear deterrence. It is the existence of this hidden and potent strategic force which assists the more visible conventional Soviet naval forces in their mission of effectively and directly supporting Soviet diplomacy.

THE SOVIET STRATEGIC SUBMARINE FORCE

The navy contributes its share to the maintenance of a Soviet nuclear deterrent with its missile launching submarines. In demonstrating the rapid growth of Soviet strategic forces, Senator Henry Jackson reported that in the space of 5

years, from 1966 to 1971, the overall strategic balance has moved in favor of the Soviet Union. Jackson revealed that in 1966 the United States had about 600 submarine-launched ballistic missiles and the Soviets had about 100. By mid-1971 the United States had 656 submarine-launched missiles, while the Soviet missile force had grown to almost 400 launchers—and is expected to overtake the United States in 2 or 3 years.[14] In terms of technology and allocation of resources, this is perhaps the most dramatic naval development in recent years.

Nuclear superiority or nuclear parity may heighten a nation's confidence and thus indirectly bolster its willingness to pursue certain foreign policy objectives; however, the diplomatic significance of a large nuclear arsenal is not directly proportional to its destructive capacity. The United States held unquestioned nuclear superiority from the end of World War II through the 1960's, yet it did not extract any vital political concessions from the U.S.S.R.[15] Nuclear superiority or parity does not in itself automatically provide a special claim to success in diplomacy between nuclear powers, but it does enable the nuclear contestants to bargain, influence, and maneuver more effectively with weaker third powers. Accordingly, the Soviet strategic submarine force supports the policy of nuclear deterrence which, at the same time, permits Soviet conventional naval forces to be more impressive and effective in supporting Soviet policy at the lower nonnuclear level.

CONVENTIONAL SOVIET NAVAL FORCES IN FOREIGN POLICY

In assessing the role of Soviet conventional naval forces in foreign policy, we will focus on eight examples that illustrate the navy's role supporting one or more of the foreign policies outlined above.

● **The 12-Mile Limit and the Right of Innocent Passage.** On 21 November 1966, Capt. William K. Earle, USCG (now retired), Commanding Officer of the U.S. Coast Guard icebreaker *Edisto*, proposed to the Commandant of the U.S. Coast Guard that two USCG icebreakers circumnavigate the world via the Arctic basin route with the purpose of collecting new oceanographic and other scientific data. The contemplated voyage would commence at a point north of Spitsbergen on 17 August 1967, proceed easterly across the Eurasian and Canadian Arctic, and terminate 5 weeks later in Baffin Bay on 21 September 1967. The proposed track lay entirely within the high seas, outside territorial waters of the U.S.S.R., and north of the usual Northern Sea Route followed by Russian convoys. The proposed track was north of the Soviet islands of Severnaya Zemlya, but in the event of impassable ice, an alternate passage through the 22-mile wide Boris Vilkitsky Straits was to be followed. (See figure 3.) No Soviet objection to this latter transit was anticipated, in that the proposed route followed the established doctrine of innocent passage, as well as the international concept of the 3-mile limit of full national sovereignty.[16]

The circumnavigation of the Arctic basin was approved for the icebreakers *Edisto* and *Eastwind*. Under constant surveillance by Soviet aircraft, the two icebreakers, with the aid of helicopter reconnaissance flights, failed to find open water or breakable ice north of Severnaya Zemlya and notified the Soviets of their intention to transit the Vilkitsky Straits. On 28 August 1967, in response to the radio message from the ships, the Soviets made it unmistakably clear that the icebreakers would be prevented from sailing the Vilkitsky Straits on the pretext that such a passage would constitute a violation of their frontier.[17] The State Department issued a strong protest, but the icebreakers were ordered to abandon their mission rather than challenge a Soviet warning in an area where the Soviet Union possessed unquestioned sea and air supremacy in the area of possible confrontation. Whether the issue was the 12-mile limit or the right of innocent passage, the threatened use of Soviet seapower was sufficient to cause cancellation of *Edisto's* and *Eastwind's* voyage. Here the threat of confrontation by Soviet seapower supported the policy of a 12-mile limit and disallowed the right of innocent passage through a strait between international bodies of water.[18]

	USSR	USA	UK
Attack Carriers	0	15	3
Anti-submarine Carriers	0	7	0
Helicopter Carriers and Commando Ships	2	8	2
Amphibious Assault Ships	100	150	4
Nuclear-powered Ballistic Missile Submarines	18	41	3
Nuclear-powered Cruise Missile Submarines	25	0	0
Nuclear-powered Attack Submarines	17	40	3
Conventional Ballistic Missile Submarines	35	0	0
Conventional Cruise Missile Submarines	22	0	0
Conventional Attack Submarines	263	62	22
Surface-to-surface Missile Cruisers	8	0	0
Other Missile Cruisers	1	9	0
Conventional Cruisers	11	4	1
Large Missile Destroyers and Frigates	24	60	6
Ocean-going Escorts	176	200	56
Missile Patrol Boats	130	0	0

Figure 1—Active Fleets

Source: Institute of Strategic Studies and *Jane's Fighting Ships.*

Cited in: David Fairhall, *Russian Sea Power* (Boston: Gambit, 1971), p. 250.

Distribution by Age	Number of Ships USA	USSR
0–4 years	108	431
5–9 years	96	486
10–14 years	130	589
15–19 years	39	67
More than 19 years	521	2

Source: Report to the House of Representatives Committee on Armed Services, March 1969.

Distribution by Type	USA Number	USA Average Age	USSR Number	USSR Average Age
Cruisers	14	21	20	12
Conventional Submarines	69	21	300	10
Ballistic Missile Submarines	41	4	15	5
Nuclear Attack Submarines	36	4	20	5
Destroyers	171	22	50	15
Frigates	59	4	30	5
Amphibious Ships	156	19	40	5

Figure 2—Comparative Age of the Russian and American Fleets

Source: Report to the House Committee on Armed Services, March 1969.

Cited in: Fairhall, p. 251.

● **The Black Sea and the Montreux Convention.** As early as 1922 the Soviet Government was opposed to the transit of foreign warships through the Turkish Straits. In fact, the Lausanne Conference of 1922 (forerunner of the Montreux Convention) had as a central theme the opening or closing of the straits to foreign warships, and Moscow's position was that the passage should be closed.[19] In the 1930's Turkey demanded the right to rearm and fortify the straits. The Soviet Union supported Turkey's position because it would place control of the straits in the hands of a friendly power. Hence, the

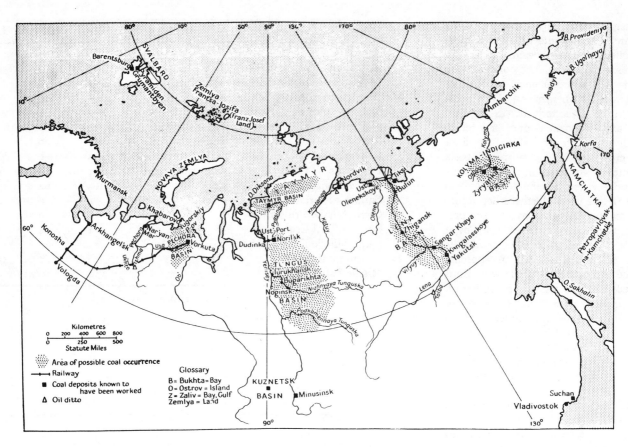

Figure 3.

Source: Terence Armstrong, *The Northern Sea Route* (Cambridge, Eng.: University Press (1952), p. 80.

Montreux Convention was called in June-July 1936 to consider the new straits situation. The Convention fixed limits on the quantity and tonnage of foreign warships passing through the Straits.[20] The only significant restriction levied on the U.S.S.R. was a prohibition against submarines exiting the Black Sea, except to go to another port for repairs.

In August 1946, in an exchange of notes between the Soviet Chargé d'Affaires in Washington and the Acting Secretary of State, the Soviet Government proposed five principles for establishing a new regime for the straits. The first three principles were generally agreed to by the United States and consisted of: open passage of merchant ships of all countries, open passage of warships of Black Sea powers, and a prohibition of passage of warships not belonging to Black Sea powers—except in cases especially provided for. The final two items, to which the United States did not express agreement, were: the straits passage was to be handled by an agency composed of Turkey and other Black Sea powers, and that Turkey and the U.S.S.R. organize the defense of the straits for the prevention of their use by countries hostile to the Black Sea powers.[21] The Soviet proposals were not considered a basis for negotiations and consequently the terms of the Montreux Convention which, incidentally, the United States accepted but did not sign, remain in effect to this day.

The U.S. position is that it has the right to operate warships in the Black Sea in accordance with the terms of the Montreux Convention. Accordingly, it sends two 6th Fleet destroyers into the area every 6 months to show the flag and exercise the U.S. Navy's right to sail anywhere on the high seas.[22] These periodic visits are considered inflammatory by the Soviets who, in turn, dispatch their naval vessels and aircraft to shadow and harass U.S. ships from the time they enter the Black Sea until they depart.[23] The Soviets claim the United States violates the Montreux Convention by sending destroyers equipped with ASROC (antisubmarine rockets) through the straits, as the ASROC caliber exceeds the 203mm. Convention limit. The United States responds that ASROC is not a gun, and the Convention only refers to guns. Nevertheless, the Soviets do not consider the U.S. probes routine sailings. Tass commentator Leonid Velichanskiy said, "... a provocation remains a provocation regardless of the fact that it is repeated twice a year."[24] Along the same vein, A. Sharifov, writing in *Izvestiya*, claimed, "The provocative visit by American ships to the Black Sea is aimed at troubling the clear waters of the good-neighbor relations of the Black Sea countries."[25]

Soviet policy has been constant in its rejection of foreign warships sailing in the Black Sea. The Soviet position is: "The land of the Soviets is a Black Sea power; the waters of the Black Sea are joined with the Mediterranean through the Bosphorous and Dardanelles. The striving of the Soviet Union to protect its vital state interests in the region is completely natural and lawful."[26]

Like the case of the USCG ice-breakers, U.S. warships in the Black Sea are operating in a hostile environment, where the U.S.S.R. maintains the upper hand in sea and airpower. Accordingly, one might reason that the United States, by occasional naval probes into the Black Sea, has made a point *de jure*, while the U.S.S.R., by maintaining effective naval control, has made its point *de facto*.

● **The Soviet Navy in the Korean and Vietnamese Wars.** In assessing the role of the Soviet Navy in foreign policy, we can conveniently discuss the Korean and Vietnamese conflicts simultaneously, as in both events Soviet naval forces avoided scrupulously any direct contact or provocation of U.S. forces. Apparently, the Soviet Union evaluated their interest in both conflicts as peripheral rather than vital. In both conflicts the United States committed ground, air, and naval forces against an invading Communist regime. In both conflicts the Soviet Union backed the Communist regime—but short of committing Soviet Armed Forces. Neither war resulted in severing Soviet-American diplomatic relations nor did it involve military action between the two nuclear powers. Certain tacit rules of warfare were observed including: no nuclear weapons, no Russians, no Chinese territory, no Japanese territory, no bombing of ships at sea or even airfields on the United Nations (and South Vietnamese) sides of the line.[27] Even though both conflicts were costly in terms of lives and supplies, they remained contained geographically. The Soviet Navy has, in effect, avoided any involvement in either conflict, thereby tacitly, but pointedly, supporting the Soviet foreign policy of avoiding war with the United States.

● **The Soviet Navy in the Cuban Missile Crisis.** By 10 a.m., 24 October 1962, warships of the U.S. 2d Fleet were positioned along an arc 500-miles east of Cuba in response to President Kennedy's order to establish a naval quarantine to halt the buildup and force removal of recently discovered Soviet surface-to-surface missiles in Cuba. The

freighters carrying Khrushchev's missiles were only protected by a few Soviet submarines, deadly instruments of war but relatively inflexible and unimpressive for a diplomatic show of force. Admittedly, while the Soviet intent was to install missiles in Cuba surreptitiously—possibly explaining the lack of surface warship escorts—some argue there simply were no surface warships available.[28] In this case, unlike those discussed above, the United States perceived the installation of Soviet medium- and intermediate-range ballistic missiles in Cuba as an immediate threat to the United States itself and consequently was willing to commit the whole of U.S. military power to removing the installations in question. As Herbert Dinerstein points out, the heart of the issue was one of military parity. The installation of the missiles in Cuba would have put the U.S.S.R. within easy reach of achieving parity or superiority in deliverable nuclear weapons systems capable of destroying the United States.[29] The Kremlin, it appears, was attempting to install the missiles surreptitiously because of their strategic weakness vis-a-vis the United States. Thus, when they were caught in the act, the Soviets were willing to take President Kennedy's face-saving way out, rather than become embroiled in a war they could not hope to win. As Admiral Zumwalt points out: "They found that despite their [Soviet] substantial superiority in submarines, they simply did not have the naval capability to oppose with any confidence of success the naval quarantine imposed by us in response to their challenge. Their decision therefore was to withdraw."[30]

The Cuban missile crisis represents a situation for which the Soviet Navy was simply not equipped to support national policy—either diplomatically or militarily. When the Russians were finally faced with a determined U.S. naval quarantine, the Soviet Navy followed the pragmatic policy of Soviet diplomacy since World War II, that of avoiding war with the United States.

● **The Soviet Navy in the Indian Ocean.** Following the 1967 Arab-Israeli war, the Soviet Union intervened in the Yemeni civil war; a first step toward the Indian Ocean. Then, on 16 January

1968, the British announced their military withdrawal east of Suez, to be completed by the end of 1971. A few weeks later a Soviet naval force commenced a historic cruise and goodwill tour of the Indian Ocean and Persian Gulf. The Soviet task force was small, composed of a cruiser, missile destroyer, and an antisubmarine vessel, all of the Soviet Pacific Fleet. The cruise exceeded 4 months in duration and, as the Soviets reported, traveled through two oceans and many seas making friendly visits to India, Somali, Iraq, Pakistan, Iran, Peoples Republic of South Yemen, and Ceylon.[31] Since this initial naval cruise into the Indian Ocean, the Soviets have had as many as 30 ships in the ocean at a time, and rarely fewer than 10.[32]

Why, then, have the Soviets maintained a permanent naval presence in the Indian Ocean? While the initial timing of Russia's naval entry into the Indian Ocean may be explained in terms of sheer opportunism, undoubtedly long-term strategic considerations made the move by the U.S.S.R. inevitable. The Indian Ocean is of strategic interest to the competing superpowers, in part because of its geography—the continents of Africa, Asia, and Australia all touch the Indian Ocean—and in part because of the politics of the riparian states that border it.[33] Because many of the African and Asian Third World states are uncommitted in the East-West struggle, this presents a productive area in which the Soviets might seek to exercise their influence in the hope of bolstering Soviet worldwide prestige and fostering the growth of governments friendly to Moscow. The Soviet Navy, then, has supported and is supporting Russian foreign policy in the Indian Ocean area by enhancing Russia's image and providing a military presence on the scene which might be used in a number of ways to strengthen Moscow's political hand vis-a-vis hostile local governments as well as the United States.

● **Soviet Navy Fleet Exercises.** Fleet exercises are designed primarily for battle training; however, they serve to publicize the capabilities, effectiveness, and war readiness of a navy. In peacetime the reputation of a navy begins with its actual hardware, (ships and

292

equipment), but must ultimately include an assessment of the navy's operational capabilities and materiel readiness. The decade of the 1960's was the period of emergence of the Soviet Navy as an increasingly capable fighting force. This was most apparent in their fleet maneuvers. The increasing complexity of Soviet naval exercises has been well documented in the world's press and certainly has served to enhance the prestige and image of the U.S.S.R. as a real power at sea.

In 1962 a major Soviet naval exercise was conducted in the North Atlantic and Norwegian Sea. It involved four surface warships, about 20 submarines, and a small number of land-based patrol planes. The nature of the exercise was to improve the ability of the Soviet naval forces to protect their homeland.[34]

Just 8 years later, in 1970, however, the Soviets conducted a vastly different exercise named Okean (figure 4). It involved about 150 surface ships, 50 submarines—several of them nuclear-powered—and several hundred aircraft. Included in the surface ship group were two new guided-missile helicopter carriers and new missile-equipped cruisers and destroyers. The exercise was worldwide in scope, ranging through the Baltic, Norwegian, Barents, Black, Philippine, and Mediterranean Seas, the Sea of Japan, the Atlantic, the Pacific, and Indian Oceans. The exercise was several weeks in duration, and in the words of the U.S. Secretary of the Navy John Chafee, "In its global scope, Operation Okean exceeded any previous exercises of any nation in naval history."[35] The Commander-in-Chief of the Soviet Fleet, Adm. Sergei Gorshkov, discussing the maneuvers in Krasnaya Zvesda said,

A century-old dream of our people has become a reality. The flags of Soviet ships now fly in the farthest corners of the seas and oceans. Our navy has become a real power and can successfully protect the state interests of the Soviet Union and of the whole socialist camp.[36]

The Soviet Navy underwent a dramatic change during the decade of the 1960's. They outgrew their traditional role of being the seaward flank of the Red army. Today the Soviet Navy stands as an equal among equals in the Soviet Ministry of Defense.

Soviet naval leaders understand the value of a navy's reputation and have assembled, trained, exercised, and advertised a real force to be reckoned with. Extensive fleet exercises such as Okean have helped raise the status of the Soviet Navy to one of a credible force with a professional reputation—desirable qualities for a first-class navy in battle or in diplomacy. The side effect of a reputation for naval professionalism is a simple transfer of the prestige and capability associated with the navy to a sympathetic attitude toward the Soviet state. In other words, the Soviet state benefits from the favorable impressions created by its navy.

● **The Soviet Navy and Extended Cruises.** In some respects the Soviet Union is emulating the practices of America's Great White Fleet at the turn of the century. They have increasingly conducted distant cruises, shown their new and impressive warships in foreign ports, received widespread press coverage, and, in general, supported a policy of projecting a favorable Soviet image abroad.

The Soviets first claimed an open naval capability in 1962 when the nuclear submarine Leninskiy Komsomol reached the North Pole and later reaffirmed it in 1966, when a detachment of Soviet nuclear-powered submarines, commanded by Rear Adm. A.E. Sorokin, completed their first submerged, and accompanied, around-the-world cruise.[37]

By July 1969 the Soviets made their first naval entry into the Gulf of Mexico. Seven Soviet surface ships and one nuclear-powered submarine penetrated the Gulf of Mexico to a point 300 miles south of the mouth of the Mississippi.[38] Two additional naval visits into the Caribbean took place within 15 months of the first. One observer, James D. Theberge, sees these intrusions into the Caribbean as a challenge to the Monroe Doctrine, strengthening of the image of the Soviet Union as a rising power, and an attempt to undermine the U.S. position in Latin America and the Caribbean while carefully avoiding the risk of direct confrontation with the United States.[39]

In September 1971 the biggest flotilla of Soviet warships ever seen in Hawaiian waters was observed. It consisted of 10 ships; three submarines, a light cruiser, two destroyers, a merchant tanker, submarine tender, and support craft. The voyage originated in Vladivostok, proceeded along the Aleutians and through the Northern Pacific, sailing between the Hawaiian Islands, then returned to Soviet territory. Adm. John S. McCain, Jr., U.S. Commander in Chief Pacific, commenting on this cruise said, "Their visit to our sea frontier is a classic example of the use of sea power to accomplish national objectives. It demonstrated their power, their range and mobility and versatility at sea in a manner that can't be ignored by our nation's defense planners."[40]

Extended deployments by the Soviet Fleet into most all the world's oceans and seas illustrate the increasing Soviet capability and willingness to project their seapower as a worldwide instrument of foreign policy.

● **The Soviet Union in the Middle East and the Mediterranean Sea.** Since the days of Catherine the Great, Russia has viewed the Middle East as an area of considerable interest, but only since the mid-1950's has Moscow been able to make a political impact of significant proportions in the area. After Moshe Dayan's visit to Paris in 1954, France agreed to supply the Israeli Army with tanks, planes, missiles, and radar. The Americans, perhaps in their reluctance to support an enemy of the Baghdad Pact, would only sell arms to Egypt on a cash basis—a condition Egypt could not meet. In any event, the Soviet Union was quick to grasp an opportunity and early in 1955 offered to sell arms to Nasser.[41] The arms agreement, followed by the July 1956 withdrawal of the U.S. offer to finance the Aswan Dam, set the stage for the polarization of the Middle East. It also marked the beginning of an extended and expanding Russian presence in the area. The Soviet position was secured by extending military and economic aid to the Arab States in such quantity and under such favorable terms that virtually all Western influence was eliminated. Equally important, the U.S.S.R. obtained naval base rights on the Mediterranean, thereby fulfilling an objective sought since the days of the czars.[42]

The Soviet Union's increased involvement in the Middle East was reflected at sea, as the bulk of Soviet military and economic aid moved by ship. Perhaps in the Mahanian tradition, the Soviet Navy followed the merchant marine, but whatever the motivation, by the eve of the 1967 Arab-Israeli crisis, the Soviets had 15 to 20 ships operating in the eastern Mediterranean Sea. As the Arab-Israeli situation continued to intensify, the Soviets dispatched an additional 10 naval ships through the Dardanelles. "This action did, however, mark a watershed in the use of Soviet naval power. For the first time, Soviet naval units were used to demonstrate a foreign policy commitment during a crisis."[43] The Soviets claim that their navy was a decisive factor in deterring or "frustrating the adventurous plans" of the Israelis and their "imperialist" backers.[44] In fact, in October 1967, following the sinking of the Israeli destroyer *Eilat* by an Egyptian missile patrol boat, several units of the Soviet Navy entered Egyptian and Syrian ports, quite likely restraining the Israelis from conducting a retaliatory strike.

In addition to providing a visible show of force in support of Soviet Middle East policy, the Soviet naval units provided moral support for the Arab peoples and gained a degree of prestige from world press coverage. Of greater significance, however, was the Soviet naval commitment to the policy of avoiding war with the United States. Despite the Soviet naval (moral) support to the Arab Nations, the Soviets maneuvered carefully to avoid any incident with the U.S. 6th Fleet that might be misinterpreted or escalate out of control.

The buildup of Soviet naval ships in the eastern Mediterranean Sea, in conjunction with the 1967 Arab-Israeli war, proved to be a watershed for Soviet naval policy in the area. Since that time the U.S.S.R. has maintained a permanent naval fleet in the Mediterranean, averaging 35 to 40 ships, including submarines.[45] The existence of a Soviet Mediterranean Fleet has provided new opportunities for the Kremlin to support its foreign policy. Perhaps highest priority has been devoted to the persistent demand for removal of U.S. military presence in Europe.

The Soviet Mediterranean Fleet is allegedly operating in the eastern Mediterranean for the protection of Soviet interests and guarding the approaches to the Black Sea. In turn, the Soviet leadership claims that the U.S. 6th Fleet has no legitimate reason to occupy the Mediterranean. For example, Brezhnev, at the Karlovy Vary meeting in April 1967 said,

There is no justification whatever for the constant presence of the U.S. Fleet in waters washing the shores of Southern Europe. One would like to ask: What are the grounds, 20 years after the end of World War II, for the U.S. Sixth Fleet to cruise the Mediterranean and to use military bases, ports, and supply bases in a number of Mediterranean countries ... The time has come to demand the complete withdrawal of the U.S. Sixth Fleet from the Mediterranean.[46]

The Soviet naval expansion in the

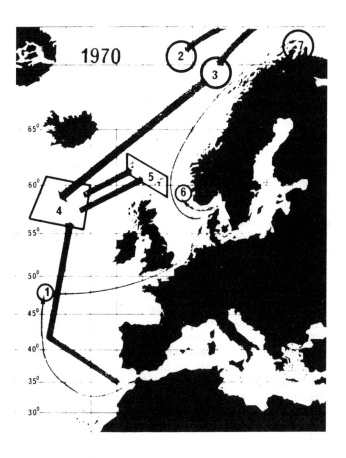

On 14 April the Soviet Ministry of Defence announced a Naval exercise, named "OKEAN", to be conducted in the Atlantic and Pacific Oceans. The exercise started rather badly when a Soviet Nuclear submarine sank in area (1) on 12 April. That same week a Soviet replenishment auxiliary convoy of 9 ships appeared North of North Cape and proceeded to area (2). Some days later two task groups of surface ships from the North Fleet followed, bringing the total deployed strength to 26 ships.

Anti-submarine warfare exercises were conducted in area (3) from 13 to 18 April. On 21 April an exercise with forces from the Mediterranean and the North Fleet battle group was scheduled in area (4). Replenishing of the two major groups took place in area (5).

Two groups of surface vessels moved out of the Baltic and operated in area (6). A landing exercise was held in area (7).

Figure 4—Exercise Okean in NATO Area

Source: NATO Letter, September 1970, p. 10.

294

Mediterranean was noted officially at the December 1967 Brussels meeting of the NATO Council. The Council suggested that the U.S.S.R. might see in the turbulent Middle East an opportunity to expedite the removal of Western influence from the area and establish itself as the dominant power at the strategic meetingplace of the European, Asian, and African Continents.[47] Events since that time have served to confirm the Council's assessment.

As previously noted, the absence of aircraft carriers in the Soviet Fleet places it at a disadvantage in terms of combat capability vis-a-vis the U.S. Fleet. This deficiency has been offset in part, however, by the surface-to-surface missile–systems employed widely throughout the Soviet Navy. Thus, despite their lack of carrier airpower, Soviet Fleet presents the image of a credible threat to the U.S. 6th Fleet, thereby satisfying the military prerequisite for an effective diplomatic offensive in the area.

We can, perhaps, gain an insight into Soviet objectives in the Mediterranean by assessing Soviet criticisms of Western navies operating in the same area. K. Timofeyev, writing in the Soviet Journal, *International Affairs*, defines Western motives as follows:

The imperialist powers keep their navies in what may be called the nerve centres of the world, such as the Mediterranean, which tops the list. The Mediterranean attracts the imperialist powers because of its great strategic importance as a highly suitable area from which to keep threatening the Soviet Union and other socialist countries in Europe. Whoever rules the roost in that area, they contend, can control land, sea and air routes between Europe, Asia and Africa, lord it over the countries of Southern Europe and the Middle East, from which European NATO countries receive up to 75% of its vital oil supply.[48]

Recent developments in Malta appear to be a mirror image of the Soviets following Mr. Timofeyev's thesis. Malta, which controls the narrow seas between Africa and Sicily, was the NATO Mediterranean naval headquarters. At the request of Maltese Premier Dom Min-

toff, NATO agreed to withdraw from the island. Forty-eight hours later the Soviet Ambassador to London, Mikhail Smirnovsky, arrived in Malta for talks.[49] On 28 December 1971, diplomatic sources reported that Malta had concluded a new commercial accord with the Soviet Union and that it appeared to be part of a determined Soviet drive to establish naval facilities on the island for its growing Mediterranean fleet.[50] The following day the British Government announced their decision to withdraw all forces from the island. On 4 January 1972, the U.S. 6th Fleet was barred from using Malta's facilities.[51] While the situation in Malta remains unclear as of this writing, it is apparent that the Soviets are attempting to replace Western influence on that strategic island.

As early as 1968 Soviet naval leaders were convinced that their navy was replacing the U.S. 6th Fleet as the dominant power in the Mediterranean. Fleet Adm. V. Kasatonov, First Deputy of the Main Naval Staff, said in July 1968, "Our surface ships and submarines successfully sail in the Mediterranean Sea, where for a long time the U.S. Sixth Fleet was the undivided master. . . . There is not a sea or ocean where Soviet sailors are not located, nor is there a port they do not know."[52]

The Soviet naval expansion in the Mediterranean has resulted in a corresponding limitation in the freedom of movement for the U.S. Fleet. Arab ports are generally closed to U.S. warships; in fact, nearly all north African states have barred the 6th Fleet from their ports since the June 1967 war. Similarly, anti-American feelings have militated against the U.S. Fleet using many other ports in the area that were previously friendly. Nevertheless, one must now view the eastern portion of the Mediterranean as realistically under Soviet influence.

The Soviet Navy's role in the support of foreign policy is perhaps nowhere more apparent than it is in the Middle East and Mediterranean Sea. It supports Soviet policies of promoting Russia's prestige and influence, avoiding war with the United States, establishing a sphere of influence in the Arab States, and discouraging American naval presence. All of these policies are important,

but Martin Edmons and John Skitt suggest that the principal objective of the Soviet naval presence in the Mediterranean is the creation of the requisite environment for the Communist States as a whole to replace the West as the political, economic, and military mentor of the Middle East countries.[53]

SUMMARY AND TENTATIVE CONCLUSIONS

In a period of two decades, the Soviet Union has developed a modern navy employing the latest ship design, equipment, and weapons systems. Advanced technology has been balanced with rigorous progressive training, both in shipboard and staff functions. The net result is a first-class fleet that competes favorably with the U.S. Navy in every aspect, except carrier-based aviation. The Soviet Fleet presents itself to the world as an effective fighting force, yet this new Soviet Navy has never seen combat. Its primary peacetime function appears to be contributing toward the realization of Soviet foreign policy objectives.

By assessing the role of the Soviet Navy in foreign policy, we may be able to draw some tentative conclusions—tentative because our data are limited in quantity which, in turn, could mislead our qualitative judgments. Nevertheless, the patterns that emerge from our present analysis suggest:

1. The Soviet Navy aggressively supports Soviet policies oriented toward the defense of the homeland in areas peripheral to the Soviet coast, but such support is short of irrevocable combat (e.g., 12-mile limit and in the Black Sea).

2. The Soviet Navy avoids involvement in "limited wars" when U.S. combat forces are participants, thereby avoiding incidents of possible conflict, and lending support to the policy of avoiding war with the United States (e.g., Korean and Vietnamese wars).

3. The navy supports adventuristic Soviet policies, but short of direct hostilities that would lead to war with the United States (e.g., Cuban missile crisis, Arab-Israeli Six-Day war).

4. The Soviet Navy supports the foreign policy of enhancing Soviet international prestige and power by main-

taining an overseas naval presence and by conducting extended cruises and exercises (e.g., naval presence in the Mediterranean Sea and Indian Ocean, fleet exercises, and distant cruises).

It is difficult to determine the relative success of these policies as seen from the Kremlin; yet it appears that the most immediate and far-reaching role of the Soviet Navy has been in the area of ideology and the politics of persuasion. Peoples friendly to the United States are becoming less surprised when they encounter Soviet ships at sea or in port. The technical quality and military smartness of Soviet vessels are viewed as a credit to the Soviet Union. In areas friendly to the Soviet Union, the presence of Soviet warships serves as a moral support the regime in

power and provide an image of support and security for the local people.[54] To uncommitted and nonaligned nations, the presence of Soviet warships may tend to encourage their association with the U.S.S.R.—a friendly, progressive, and industrialized world power.

All in all, it can be seen that the Soviet Navy has been a vehicle for the export of Soviet foreign policy on a grand and worldwide scale. The navy performs diplomatic functions that cannot be duplicated by any other branch of the armed services or by any other civilian agency. The peacetime role of the Soviet Navy is indeed significant and perhaps, in part, explains the motivation of a great land power to construct a modern fleet and carry its ideological battle to sea.

BIOGRAPHIC SUMMARY

Comdr. Richard T. Ackley, U.S. Navy, (Ret.), received his B.A. in history from the University of Southern California, his M.A. in political science from the University of Hawaii, and is a candidate for his Ph.D. degree in international relations at the University of Southern California. He is a graduate of the Naval Intelligence Postgraduate School and the Russian language course at the Defense Language Institute. While on active duty his assignments included command of the submarine *Bream;* Assistant Naval Attache, Moscow, U.S.S.R.; and Commander Submarine Division 31. Professor Ackley has taught at Chapman College in California and is now teaching at the University of Redlands. He is a previous contributor to the *Naval War College Review* and the *Military Review.*

FOOTNOTES

1. Sir Nigel Henderson, "Foreword," *NATO Review,* September 1970, p. 1.

2. Ole Holsti, "East-West Conflict and Sino-Soviet Relations," *Studies in International Conflict and Integration* December 1964, p. 2.

3. Thomas W. Wolfe, *Soviet Power and Europe 1945-1970* (Baltimore: Johns Hopkins Press, 1970), p. 427-28, 442.

4. U.S. Congress, House, Committee on Armed Services, *The Changing Strategic Military Balance, USA vs. USSR,* 90th Cong., 1st sess., July 1967, p. 10.

5. Herbert S. Dinerstein, *Fifty Years of Soviet Foreign Policy* (Baltimore: Johns Hopkins Press, 1968), p. 72.

6. Hans J. Morgenthau, "The Four Paradoxes of Nuclear Strategy," *American Political Science Review,* March 1964, p. 23.

7. Dinerstein, p. 38.

8. Alvin A. Rubinstein, *The Foreign Policy of the Soviet Union* (New York: Random House, 1966), p. 208.

9. James D. Theberge, "The Doorstep Challenge," *Navy,* March 1971, p. 22.

10. Henderson, p. 1.

11. Eugene K. Keefe, et al., *Area Handbook for the Soviet Union* (Washington: U.S. Govt. Print. Off., 1971), p. 569.

12. *Riverside Daily Enterprise,* 29 July 1971, p. D-8.

13. N. Smirnov, "Soviet Ships in the Mediterranean Sea," *Krasnaya Zvezda,* 12 November 1968.

14. Henry M. Jackson, "The Strategic Balance," *Vital Speeches of the Day,* 1 June 1971, p. 483.

15. Wolfe, p. 503.

16. Letter from Commanding Officer, USCG *Edisto* (WAGB-284) to Commandant, U.S. Coast Guard, Ser. 3000, 21 November 1966.

17. "Arctic Trip Frozen Out," *Science News,* 16 September 1967, p. 273.

18. It should be noted that the United States supports the 12-mile limit as the most widely accepted one, but only if a treaty can be negotiated which will achieve widespread international acceptance and will provide for freedom of navigation through and over international straits. The U.S. position is not to recognize territorial seas that exceed 3 miles pending the adoption of a new treaty. "United States Outlines Position on Limit of Territorial Sea," *The Department of State Bulletin,* 16 March 1970, p. 343.

19. Anatole G. Mazour, *Russia, Tsarist and Communist* (New York: Van Nostrand, 1962), p. 645.

20. *Ibid.,* p. 727-28.

21. "Position on Question of the Turkish Straits," *The Department of State Bulletin,* 1 September 1946, p. 421-22.

22. Benjamin Welles, "While Keeping that Flag Flying," *The New York Times,* 15 December 1968, sec. 4, p. 3E.

23. A new edition of the U.S.S.R.'s Diplomatic Handbook carries a demand that the Baltic be made a closed sea to warships of nations not bordering on it. "Scoop and Scuttle," *Sea Power,* December 1971, p. 1.

24. Leonid Velichanskiy, Moscow Tass International Service in English, 1623 GMT, 9 December 1968.

25. A. Sharifov, "Provocateurs at Sea," *Izvestiya,* 8 December 1968.

26. Igor Belyayev, "International Review," *Pravda,* 7 December 1968.

27. Thomas C. Schelling, *Arms and Influence* (New Haven: Yale University Press, 1966), p. 31.

28. David Fairhall, *Russian Sea Power* (Boston: Gambit, 1971), p. 205.

29. Dinerstein, p. 61-62.

30. Admiral Zumwalt's prepared address, as delivered by Vice Admiral Calvert, U.S. Naval Institute Annual Meeting, 18 February 1971.

31. *Krasnaya Zvezda,* 26 July 1968, p. 2.

32. "East-West, Cutting a Chain of Links," *Time,* 4 January 1971, p. 41.

33. Alvin J. Cottrell, "Indian Ocean of Tomorrow," *Navy,* March 1971, p. 11.

34. Zumwalt.

35. *Ibid.*

36. *Krasnaya Zvezda,* 16 April 1970, p. 1.

37. D.E. Sokha, "The Submarine Force, Yesterday and Today," *Morskoi Sbornik,* September 1971, p. 29.

38. *Riverside Press Enterprise,* 21 February 1971, p. A-5.

39. Theberge, p. 22-23.

40. James Basset, "Naval Power—Russ Challenge Circles Globe," *Los Angeles Times,* 5 December 1971, p. B-6.

41. Andre Fontaine, *History of the Cold War* (New York: Random House, 1969), p. 161-62.

42. Keefe, p. 505.

43. David R. Cox, "Sea Power and Soviet Foreign Policy," *United States Naval Institute Proceedings,* June 1969, p. 42.

44. Smirnov.

45. Horacio Rivero, "The Soviet Union, NATO and the Mediterranean," *NATO Review,* September 1970, p. 15.

46. Brezhnev, cited in Claire Sterling, "The Soviet Fleet in the Mediterranean," *The Reporter,* 14 December 1967, p. 16.

47. Wolfe, p. 336-37.

48. K. Timofeyev, "The Role of Navies in Imperialist Policy," *International Affairs,* Moscow, November 1969, p. 43.

49. *Riverside Daily Enterprise,* 16 August 1971, p. A-5.

50. *Redlands Daily Facts,* 28 December 1971, p. 1.

51. *Redlands Daily Facts,* 4 January 1972, p. 2.

52. V. Kasatonov, "Ocean Watch of the Motherland," *Krasnaya Zvezda,* 28 July 1968, p. 1.

53. Martin Edmons and John Skitt, "Current Soviet Maritime Strategy and NATO," *International Affairs,* v. XLV, p. 39.

54. Georgetown University, The Center for Strategic and International Studies, *Soviet Sea Power,* Special Report Series No. 10 (Washington: 1969), p. 26.

The Gorshkov articles represent a "window" into the planning offices of the Soviet Navy. Admiral Gorshkov speaks from a background of vast experience and from a position of authority. He presents a clear message that the Soviet Navy is no mere transitory phenomenon on the world's maritime stage.

THE MEANING AND SIGNIFICANCE
OF THE GORSHKOV ARTICLES

A research paper prepared for the

Naval War College Strategy Study

by

Commander Clyde A. Smith, U.S. Navy

Introduction. The Gorshkov series represents 11 articles which appeared in *Morskoy Sbornik,* the Soviet *Naval Digest,* from 1972 into 1973.[1] The entire series was entitled "Navies in War and Peace" and consisted of 50,000 words of sustained, forceful prose. The author of the work is Adm. Sergey Georgievich Gorshkov[2] who, since 1956, has been the Commander in Chief of the Soviet Navy and who has reputedly enjoyed the trust and confidence of both Khrushchev and Brezhnev. He is the architect of the modern Soviet Navy and is, by this accomplishment alone, the most distinguished naval officer that Russia, the great landpower, has yet produced. Without a doubt the Gorshkov articles are by far the most significant and comprehensive pronouncement on seapower ever to come out of Russia. Because of their breadth, because of their authorship, because of their publication in the professional naval journal of the Soviet Navy, and because they have occurred at a time when historic shifts in the

distribution of naval and world power are in progress, these papers merit a most careful consideration.

The general title of the series and the subtitles listed below suggest the general content and comprehensive nature of the writings.

● [Navies in War and Peace] No subtitle (Ed.)
● Russia's Difficult Road to the Sea
● Into the Oceans on Behalf of Science
● The First World War
● The Soviet Navy
● The Building of the Navy (1928-1941)
● The Second World War
● The Soviet Navy in the Great Patriotic War
● The Basic Missions Executed by Navies in the Course of the Second World War
● Navies as a Weapon of the Aggressive Policy of the Imperialistic States in Peacetime
● Some Problems in Mastering the World Ocean

Gorshkov's announced purpose for publishing the series was to "foster the development in our officers of a unity of views on the role of navies under various historical conditions" and "to determine the trends and regularities in the role and place of navies in war, and also their peacetime use as an instrument of state policy."[3] It is an official interpretation of Russian naval history, and while it is by no means objective history, it serves admirably as a vehicle for Gorshkov's ideas. In his description of history and historical lessons, it becomes obvious that he intends to present modern analogies and that he wishes these to be abundantly clear. Throughout this book-length naval history, Gorshkov constantly reiterates the vital necessity for having large modern naval forces, both for use in war and in peace. Benefits deriving from such a navy have been great, penalties for not having such a navy severe. The tone of the articles is assertive, at times polemical; and while it is apparent that Gorshkov is under pressure from budget constraints, the army, and possibly SALT negotiators, he seems self-assured with the situation. He justifies a larger, more balanced navy by advancing, seemingly, every conceivable argument, including the protection of state interests and the requirements for a modern version of gunboat diplomacy. The articles provide a powerful rationale for expanded Soviet seapower that is often Mahanian in the force of its appeal and in its urgency.

Nevertheless, a search for the real reason *why* the series was written ultimately resolves into the question: "Is it announcement, or is it advocacy?" Is Gorshkov *announcing* that a new, long-term naval program to construct a larger, even more modern navy has already been approved? Is he then acting as the spokesman for this decision, providing explanation and rationale to support it? Or is he *advocating* a large and modern navy in an ongoing defense debate in which substantial criticism of such a fleet exists? Is he then rebutting critics, arguing for a favorable, yet to be made decision on the size and role of the future Soviet Navy? The contention of this commentary is that Gorshkov is announcing a decision already taken. At the same time, he is using the series as a forum to rebut critics and the various arguments they have advanced. On basic questions he seems to be making authoritative pronouncements. Not only does he announce continued expansion of Soviet naval power, but he announces the continued growth of Soviet seapower in other areas—merchant marine, fishing fleet, oceanography, and even ocean mining and ocean exploitation in general. Accepting this "announcement" interpretation, the Gorshkov series is a significant forewarning of the future magnitude of the total Soviet maritime effort and of the challenge it represents to Western seapower.

An acknowledged Soviet custom calls for the most authoritative person available to treat comprehensively any important subject on which an official position has not been established previously. Ideally, this authority should be a professional man in a high official position. Admiral Gorshkov—a member of the Central Committee of the Communist Party, a Deputy Minister of Defense, and the Commander in Chief of the Soviet Navy—is admirably suited to deal with naval strategy. Therefore, while some of Gorshkov's conclusions are questionable and a bit contrived, they do reflect the Soviet Navy's official view of the lessons of history on seapower.

It is unlikely that Gorshkov established this official interpretation of history solely to justify larger appropriations for the navy or solely to preserve allocations at present levels, although these elements are present in the series. His routes for appropriations are through either the Politburo, the Central Committee of the Communist Party of the Soviet Union, the General Staff, the Ministry of Defense, or the Council of Ministers or a combination of these. An appeal for appropriations through the pages of *Morskoy Sbornik* would not only be futile under the Soviet system, but unthinkable as well. Publication of the series seems to reflect a Soviet command desire to acquaint as many Soviet officers as possible with the official interpretation as the reasoning behind current and forthcoming naval developments.

The main idea, the constantly recurring theme in the Gorshkov series, is that the Soviet Union requires a large, modern, and powerful navy commensurate with her global interests, both in war and in peace. He provides what purports to be a historical review of Soviet naval power, reinterpreting history as necessary to support his view. This historical review contains numerous and intended modern-day analogies, each supporting his view that a large and modern navy is an essential power ingredient of the Soviet state. Once he has established the general requirement that such a navy is needed in war and peace, he then discusses Soviet naval requirements and the uses of naval power in war and peace in present and past contexts. Lesser themes recur sporadically throughout the series. But before examining this central idea, as well as the diffuse lesser themes, it is necessary to look first at the strategies and general compositions of the Soviet and United States Navies. The Gorshkov series, to be understood, must be interpreted in the framework of the differences in philosophy and historical development of the world's two most powerful navies.

Differing Strategies. Soviet naval strategy is defensive and deterrent.[4] It is a strategy of sea denial rather than sea control. It is a strategy reactive to our Navy, designed to prevent us from accomplishing our mission. Their navy has traditionally been subordinated by landpower thinking Soviet generals.[5] This army-dominated thinking has traditionally assigned the Soviet Navy to an inferior, defensive role in direct or indirect support of the Soviet Army. Consistent with this thinking and with a defensive strategy, their major mission in war is to destroy or repulse our Navy should it attempt to approach the Soviet Union.[6] They have not included in their navy sea-control and projection capabilities such as aircraft carriers or any significant amphibious capabilities. Their capital ship, itself a sea-denial weapon, is the nuclear submarine, which they have constructed in quantity. Many of their ships and submarines are equipped with surface-to-surface missiles designed to destroy U.S. ships and deny them the use of the seas. In wartime the Soviets envision operating their ships within the range of land-based air cover, a condition that further commits them to a defensive posture. Nor do they have, even if air cover were available, either the overseas base structure or the at-sea distant-water support capabilities to permit sustained blue-water naval operations in wartime.

Soviet geographical constraints, of which Gorshkov reflects an acute awareness, have further oriented their navy to the strategic defensive. To protect their maritime frontiers, they have been forced—because of peculiarities of their geography—to fragment their navy into four fleets in peripheral seas. The Soviet Northern Fleet is stationed in the Barents Sea, while the other two European fleets are situated in the Baltic and Black Seas. They also maintain a permanent "squadron"[7] in the Mediterranean with the ships for this force drawn primarily from the Black Sea and Northern Fleets. Their fourth fleet—stationed over 5,000 miles away from their other fleets—is the Pacific Fleet located in the Sea of Japan. This geographic separation has forced each fleet to be organized largely as an independent fleet since their geographic locations negate close mutual support.

Each separate fleet must also pass through interdictable straits to reach the open sea. The Northern Fleet must pass through the Greenland-Iceland-United Kingdom Gap, the Baltic Fleet through the Danish Straits, the Black Sea Fleet through the Turkish Straits, the Mediterranean "Squadron" through the Sicilian Straits and Gibraltar, and the Pacific Fleet through straits leading from the Sea of Japan. These fleets are distant from the major world maritime routes which they must interdict if they are to deny an enemy use of the sea. Finally, the extreme northerly orientation of their country ensures hostile climatic conditions for their Northern, Baltic, and Pacific Fleets, with attendant problems of severe weather, closed harbors, ice, et cetera for significant parts of the year. In sum, a consistent landpower mentality and physical handicaps of geography have further inclined the Soviets toward a defensive, sea-denial strategy as opposed to an offensive, sea-control strategy.

U.S. naval strategy, by contrast, is an offensive, sea-control strategy. It is a strategy which seeks to gain and maintain control of the seas, to ensure their use by friendly forces, and to deny their use to an enemy. Central to this strategy are aircraft carriers, which ensure the availability of organic fleet air cover in seizing control of the seas and protecting naval formations and amphibious operations. Not confined to operations under the narrow umbrella of land-based air, the U.S. Navy has global sea-control capabilities. Consistent with this strategy, it has developed efficient amphibious projection capabilities which provide the capability to project power across oceans and onto hostile shores. It also possesses well-developed at-sea support capabilities and forward bases to permit sustained distant-water operations and, in response to the huge Soviet submarine force, has developed considerable antisubmarine warfare capabilities—maintaining a sizable lead over the Soviets in this area.

Nor does U.S. naval power suffer from serious geographic handicaps. Granted, the U.S. Navy is divided into two fleets, but this fleet fragmentation problem is in no way as severe as the Soviets'. U.S. naval bases front on the open ocean, and the major world maritime routes are at our ocean doorstep. While a landpower mentality and geographical constraints on naval power seem almost to have predestined the Russians to a defensive sea-denial strategy, the U.S. maritime mentality and relative lack of geographical constraints on naval power seem almost to have predisposed an offensive, sea-control strategy.[8]

The "Big-Navy" Theme. Gorshkov maintains that great national power and a powerful navy are indispensable concomitants. To be a great power, a state must also be a maritime power; and when maritime power declines, great-power status diminishes also. "All of the modern great powers are maritime states."[9] Further:

> Naval might has been one of the factors which has enabled certain states to advance into the ranks of the great powers. Moreover, history shows that states which do not have naval forces at their disposal have not been able to hold the status of a great power for a long time.[10]

And again: It is evident . . . that every time ruling circles in Russia failed to properly emphasize development of the Fleet and its maintenance at a level necessitated by modern-day demands, the country either lost battles in wars or its peacetime policy failed to achieve designated objectives.[11] In the 16th century Spain neglected to maintain an adequate navy and, as a result, lost her overseas possessions "and was gradually transformed from a great power into a third-rate state."[12] In the 17th century, Holland lost her great-power status and colonies because her navy was not sufficiently strong; she "became a second-rate colonial power."[13] Conversely, in the 18th century, England became the leading capitalist country through her naval power, and in the early 19th century Napoleonic Wars, "the course of the war at sea and the gaining of domination by the English Fleet had a great effect on the further policy of the belligerents."[14] Therefore, to be and remain a great power, a country must also be a great maritime power; and

Russia "has been and remains a great seapower."[15]

Gorshkov—in support of the big-navy theme of the series—cites historical precedents and arguments to assert the existence of a longstanding navalist tradition for Russia.[16] He states that the more enlightened czars, Lenin, and even the Communist Party itself, since 1917, have followed a strong navy policy. The people too are seen as having a historic affinity for the sea. Peter the Great, in Gorshkov's second article, is thus shown as seeing the requirements to build both an army "and a powerful Navy with all urgency."[17] Presumably, if the need for a powerful navy was evident to Peter the Great, it should be clear to present-day Soviet officials. In article five he alludes to "Leninist theses," associating them with the growing importance "of our building an oceanic fleet,"[18] to show that Lenin too was a strong navalist. Invoking the authority and prestige of Lenin on the side of naval expansionism, no matter how speciously done, establishes a powerful precedent. In this same article he further associates the party with these same Leninist theses "which comprise the basis of the military policy of the Party."[19] This last touch seems to place any opponents of continued expansion in opposition to the party. Throughout Russian history, "the qualities of a sea-going people" have been "inherent in Russians since ancient times."[20] It has been a "slanderous assertion that the Russians are not a sea-going nation but rather a dry-land nation, that the sea is alien to them, and that they are not gifted at seafaring."[21]

Running through the Gorshkov series is the proposition that the naval expansion program should occur as rapidly as the Soviet economy and shipbuilding capacity will permit. He states this idea in the first article, saying that: "Every social-economic system has built up armed forces, including navies, commensurate with its economic and technical capabilities."[22] Also in the first article, he cites the British example, which he would obviously like the Soviet Union to follow: "Supported by a powerful economy which provided England the supremacy of the strongest fleet in the world . . ., it took over the leading position among the capitalist countries and held it for almost two centuries."[23] To support his ideas with naval activity during the Lenin and Stalin eras, Gorshkov must largely engage in generalities while lauding whatever navy achievements he can. However, he can state that in 1938 the U.S.S.R. attained the world's largest submarine force, indicating that this was but part of an approved larger construction program—interrupted by the war—for a "large sea and oceanic fleet" in which "major surface ships were . . . to be its nucleus."[24] Pursuing this claimed precedent on into the present, Gorshkov states in his last article: "The need to build a powerful ocean-going Navy . . . was backed up and is being backed up by the vast capabilities of the military economic potential of the Soviet state and by the achievements of our science and technology."[25]

Gorshkov then seems to conclude this proposition with the forthright assertion that the Soviet economy can well support such a large and sustained naval construction program:

> In speaking of the military-economic potential of our country, it should be noted that it possesses vast, practically inexhaustible energy, raw material, and fuel resources. This high, stable rate of growth of the economic power of the USSR, observed throughout its entire history, confirms the stability, planned nature, and harmoniousness of the Soviet state.[26]

Gorshkov, in this proposition for an all-out naval expansion program, seems to be advocating more than announcing. If he is in fact announcing here too, then surely he must realize—as must the Soviet leadership—that the United States is likely to respond with an expanded naval construction program of its own. Therefore, it seems likely that, while continued and diversified Soviet naval expansion may be forthcoming, it will not be so dramatic as Gorshkov would like.

Gorshkov also sees the solution to Russia's traditional fleet fragmentation problem as residing in a larger, more powerful navy. In the third article he recounts historic Russian problems of inadequate or nonexistent naval strength in the Baltic, the Black Sea,

and the Far East. Speaking of czarist times, for which the obvious modern-day analogy exists: "The considerable difficulties for Russian seapower stemmed from its geographical position, which required having an independent fleet capable of ensuring the performance of the missions confronting it in each of the far-flung naval theaters."[27] He goes into particular detail with Russia's great naval disaster at Tsushima in 1905. In this recounting he is implicitly arguing for stronger fleets to handle any potential enemies in these areas, since time-distance and other factors prevent one fleet from effectively reinforcing another in wartime.

He criticizes czarist governments because they constructed a fleet "basically from considerations of prestige, and not the true interests of the state."[28] They did not, Gorshkov asserts, take into account operational conditions and ignored "requirements, unique to Russia, stemming from her geographical location."[29] For "Russia needed a separate fleet on each sea, which was usually weaker than the fleets of potential opponents in the given theater."[30] Further, "One of the most important characteristics of utilization of the Russian Fleet was the need for intertheater maneuvers, governed by the absence of the necessary quantity of naval forces in individual theaters."[31] Thus, Gorshkov's resolution of his navy's fleet fragmentation problem is classically simple: provide each of the four fleets with sufficient naval power to independently handle any potential opponents!

As further big-navy justification, Gorshkov depicts a powerful navy as a force to assist in the historic Russian drive for open ocean access through the interdictable straits. Gorshkov's solution to this problem is a wartime breakout strategy. He portrays czarist naval history as consisting of a sustained struggle to gain free access through seizure of the straits. Having lost her window on the Baltic and her Black Sea outlet prior to Peter the Great, "Russia was not resigned to being cut off from the seas and continually waged a struggle for outlets to them."[32] As he devotes attention to czarist efforts to obtain the use of the Turkish Straits, it becomes apparent that Gorshkov intends a

modern analogy and that he does not rule out the possibility of seizing them in a limited war scenario. In articles two and three, he seems to argue for a strengthened Soviet Mediterranean Squadron that could control the Eastern Mediterranean against 6th Fleet and NATO naval forces while the Soviet Army seized the Straits. In article three, he says: " . . . historically it has turned out that when a threat arises of an enemy encroachment on the territory of Russia from the southwest, the Russian Fleet has been moved into the Mediterranean Sea where it has successfully executed great strategic missions in defending the country's borders from aggression."[33]

While Gorshkov presents a scenario only for the Turkish Straits, it is easy to project a similar breakout strategy for the Greenland-Iceland-United Kingdom Gap or the Danish Straits as well. It also seems clear in article four of the series that Gorshkov views the lack of open ocean access for his fleets vis-a-vis NATO and the United States to be analogous to the strategic German dilemma with her fleet, bottled up in the Baltic, vis-a-vis the British in World Wars I and II. Breakout is Gorshkov's recommended solution, which will require in part a big navy both to effect and to make the effort worthwhile.

Gorshkov describes unique peacetime uses of a navy to support the global interests of a powerful state as a further rationale for a large navy. He couches this rationale in both general and specific terms. As a general proposition, it is a "special feature" of a Navy that it "can be used in peacetime for purposes of demonstrating the economic and military might of states beyond their borders."[34] And "over a period of many centuries it has been the solitary form of armed forces capable of protecting the interests of a country overseas."[35] It will therefore be "useful to examine questions related to this specific feature of naval forces as a . . . part of the military organization of a state."[36] It is, Gorshkov asserts, quoting Engels, "the political force at sea" which has "a most important significance as a political weapon of the great powers."[37] He notes that "the fleets of the Western states have represented not only a part of the armed forces, which were employed in war in the naval theaters, but also a weapon of state policy in peacetime. . . . "[38] Western nations with numerical and fire-power superiority have in the past "striven to employ . . . naval forces as an important political instrument to create definite prestige in the international arena and in mutual relations with other states."[39] While this is his general thesis, he also cites two specific roles for navy use in peacetime as being gunboat diplomacy (although he does not call it this by name) and as being a negotiating lever.

In gunboat diplomacy applications, "Maritime states with great economic capabilities have," says Gorshkov, "widely used their naval forces in peacetime to put pressure on their enemies, as a type of military demonstration, as threats of interrupting sea communications, and as a hindrance to ocean commerce."[40] He notes in his 10th article that the sudden appearance of naval forces in an area has sometimes "permitted the achievement of political goals without resorting to military operations by only threatening to initiate them."[41] He then goes on to define further his conception of gunboat diplomacy:

> Consequently the role of a Navy is not limited to the execution of important missions in armed combat. While representing a formidable force in war, it has always been a political weapon of the imperialist states and an important support for diplomacy in peacetime owing to its inherent qualities which permit it to a greater degree than other branches of the armed forces to exert pressure on potential enemies without the direct employment of weaponry.[42]

While most of his examples of gunboat diplomacy are drawn from alleged actions and policies of Western navies, he leaves no doubt that he thinks that it should be a policy of the Soviet Navy as well. In the second article, Gorshkov provides historical examples of successful Russian gunboat diplomacy. In one example, in 1769 a Baltic Fleet squadron was sent to the Mediterranean "to support the making of important political moves by Russia by threatening

Turkey from the sea. . . . "[43] In his final article, Gorshkov leaves no doubt in his belief in the efficacy and desirability of using gunboat diplomacy in select situations, when he asserts:

> . . . it is the Navy which is this kind of force, capable in peacetime of visibly demonstrating to the peoples of friendly and hostile countries not only the power of military equipment and the perfection of the naval ships, embodying the technical and economic might of the state, but its readiness to use this force in defense of state interests of our nation or for the security of the Socialist countries.[44]

Having a large navy, Gorshkov indicates, permits a state to negotiate from a position of strength and protects it from unnecessary concessions to other strong maritime powers. In article three he illustrates this concept from Russia's unfortunate experiences of the Crimean War:

> The significance of the Navy in this war was also determined by the extent to which its presence in a given theater could be used by the diplomats of the belligerent sides to support their positions at the peace talks. Russia, almost totally deprived of her fleet in the Black Sea, was unable to oppose the fleets of the enemy states with her own naval power, and therefore had to accede to the provisions of the Paris peace treaty. Great Britain and France, having consolidated their position at sea, acquired new possibilities for exerting pressure on Russia with the threat of attacks against her from the southwest, consolidating their control over the Turkish Straits zone, and increased their influence in the Near and Middle East.[45]

Earlier, in his first article, Gorshkov also indicated that a strong navy was valuable in any type of negotiations:

> Many examples from history attest to the fact that . . . all problems of foreign policy were always solved on the basis of taking into account the military might of the "negotiating" sides, and that the potential might of one state or

another, built up in accordance with its economic capabilities and political orientation, permitted it to conduct a policy advantageous to itself to the detriment of other states not possessing a corresponding military power.[46]

While unspoken, the importance of negotiating from a position of strength with a large and powerful navy in any arms limitations talks is obvious, as Gorshkov undoubtedly intended it to be.

The Navy, the Army, and the Budget. Gorshkov clearly reflects that he is under budget constraints. He is either competing with the army for an increase in present resources or is attempting to forestall arguments for diminishing the navy budget or both. Although he and the navy are subordinate to Marshal Grechko (and other marshals in the Ministry of Defense), he nevertheless competes fiercely for resources and is often, directly or indirectly, sharply critical of the army and of their land-power mentality in the process. He constantly stresses the navy's unique capabilities and favorably compares it with the army at every opportunity. Thus, in the first article:

> The hallmark of naval forces is their high degree of maneuverability, and ability to concentrate secretly and to form powerful groupings which are of surprise to the enemy. At the same time naval forces are more stable against the effects of nuclear weaponry than land forces. All of this has catapulted the navies into the front ranks of the diverse modern means of armed combat.[47]

He also implies that the navy either now is, or should be, ascendant in the budget: "In some stages of the history of states ground forces have played the main role, and in others, the Navy."[48] In discussing the Seven Years' War (1756-1763), he states that events then required restoration of the fleet and "an increase in its role within the system of armed forces."[49] A contemporary analogy seems intended here—that the navy now merits a larger budget share. He further states, polemically:

> The opponents of Russian sea-power have widely used (and are

widely using) falsification of its military history. In particular they assert that all of Russia's victories have been gained only by the Army and that it can be powerful only by strengthening the Army at the expense of the Navy.[50]

He frequently cites the uneven historical development of the Russian Navy. He is obviously attempting to avert a recurrence. Historically, he says: " . . . the . . . Fleet developed rather unevenly. Surges in the naval might of Russia gave way to declines. And each time a reduction in its seapower evoked new difficulties on the historical path of the state and led to serious consequences.[51]

While he blames czarist officials, landpower enthusiasts, and Western imperialists and their propaganda for many of the Russian Navy's historic travails, it is apparent that he holds equally guilty the living and that he seeks, or seeks to retain, present resources. The answer may be, in accord with the announcement postulation, that he is rebutting critics who desire to cut back on his approved program. This supposition then explains his pointed quotation of Lenin in the fifth article: "Like a red thread the idea runs through all of Lenin's directives, letters, and orders concerning the need for firmness and purposefulness in carrying out intended plans, and of the falseness of any kind of wavering and indecisiveness at the crucial moments of the struggle."[52]

Gorshkov forthrightly defends Soviet Navy deployments to the Mediterranean. Presumably, the permanent presence of the Soviet Mediterranean Squadron and its attendant high costs have been under attack. He justifies its cost-effectiveness in terms of the defense[53] it provides the Soviet Union against attack by 6th Fleet aircraft carriers and missile-equipped submarines:

Today, when the capabilities of the imperialist aggressors to attack the Soviet Union directly from the Mediterranean Sea have increased extraordinarily, this region has assumed especially important significance in the defense of our Homeland. The constant presence there of the U.S. Sixth Fleet with aircraft carriers and missile-carrying submarines has as its basic mission a surprise attack against the Soviet Union and the countries of the Socialist community. The U.S. Navy command openly states that the missiles of the nuclear-powered submarines and the carrier aircraft from the Mediterranean Sea are aimed at objectives in the USSR and the states of Eastern Europe and are in a constant state of readiness to deliver nuclear strikes against them.

It is natural that in response to the direct threat the Soviet Union is forced to undertake defensive measures and implement its indisputable and legal right to have warships in the Mediterranean Sea. They are there not to threaten peace-loving peoples, and not to implement any sort of expansionist desires, which are alien to the very nature of our Socialist state, but in order to nip aggression in the very bud, if the imperialists attempt to undertake it from this region.[54]

Gorshkov's arguments for the necessity for the operations of the Mediterranean Squadron are among the most direct and vigorous in his series. By implication he also defends distant-water deployments and their costs in general to the Indian Ocean, the Hump of Africa area near Guinea, and the Caribbean. Gorshkov obviously believes that his navy should operate beyond home waters and that the associated costs are well worth it. He seems in effect to be announcing that Soviet naval deployments out of home waters will continue.

Weapons, Weapon Systems, and Projection. On weapons and weapon systems, Gorshkov at the very outset of his series remarked on the difficulty of making meaningful modern-day comparisons of warships and navies:

The qualitative transformations which have taken place in naval forces have also changed the approach to evaluating the relative might of navies and their combat groupings: we have had to cease comparing the number of warships of one type or another and their total displacement (or the number of guns in a salvo or the weight of this salvo), and turn to a more complex, but also more correct appraisal of the striking and defensive power of ships, based on a mathematical analysis of their capabilities and qualitative characteristics.[55]

This problem is particularly acute in the case of the Soviet and American Navies because the navies are differently configured in response to different strategies and missions in war and peace. He is also aware this difficulty has important ramifications in assessing relative levels of Soviet and United States naval strength[56] and in naval arms limitation talks. In part, Gorshkov makes use of this difficulty as another reason for approaching any naval arms limitation talks (which he clearly opposes) between the Soviet Union and the United States with caution. In Gorshkov's opinion, the Soviet Union should engage in such talks when it has a big and powerful navy in being, well in excess of current capabilities.

While he has in the past been identified with antidétente[57] (he is a hardliner), Gorshkov bases his present opposition on the alleged ineffectiveness of such talks in curbing naval arms races, on the fact that they only affect navies and not armies and air forces as well, and on the supposed advantages they confer on imperialist powers. He is obviously concerned with the effects that any naval arms limitations talks might have on the size of his navy, as well as on the large construction program which may have been approved and which he may, in part, be announcing in his series. Again, he presents his arguments circuitously, using historical examples which have modern analogies:

Recognizing the essential role of navies in war and in peace, the imperialist powers repeatedly attempted in the period after the First World War to regulate the growth of naval arms in special conferences (it is interesting that other forms of armed forces were not subjected to this). However, as is well known, all of these attempts did not lead to a reduction of the navies of the powers, and from the mid-1930's a new unrestrained and in no way regulated naval arms race began.[58] In the early articles of his series, Gorshkov made the point that negotiations should proceed from strength, that one should, by implication, consider engaging in naval arms talks only if one already has a large and powerful navy to provide a negotiating edge. But such talks are, in Gorshkov's view, only the "war of the diplomats for supremacy at sea."[59]

While he maintains that such talks do not contain naval arms races anyway, he also pointedly notes that armies seem exempt from similar talks. The conferences of the 1922-1935 period:

. . . fulfilled only a delaying function in the naval construction of the largest states and then only up to the mid-1930's (thereafter the naval arms race proceeded without any sort of limitations). It is interesting that no such attempts were undertaken until our day with respect to the other branches of the armed forces. Even today, when the arms limitation talks have become a reality and ways of solving this problem have been defined, arms control is still only being extended to strategic missiles, including those belonging to the navies.[60]

Imperialist powers invariably initiate naval arms talks to seek allies or to delimit the naval power of a competitor, Gorshkov alleges. He claims that the London naval arms limitation talks only showed that "the imperialist powers were aligning themselves not for . . . limiting naval armaments, but to wage the forthcoming war and to seek allies. . . ."[61] Further:

The failure of the 1936 London Conference . . . served as a signal for an unlimited arms race by the imperialist powers. Just the very fact of repeated attempts to regulate naval armaments by international agreements, especially after the First World War, attests to the important significance the major imperialist powers attached to naval forces.[62]

Gorshkov provides no meaningful clues concerning what the Soviet Union will or will not do about constructing aircraft carriers. He simply does not discuss it, and we are left only to speculate. It is, in any event, the major area in which the Soviet Navy remains clearly inferior to the U.S. Navy. Regardless of what the Soviets may do, it is not a shortcoming that they can readily correct. Even under a parity principle achieved through naval arms talks, the costs of constructing a fleet of carriers would be enormous. Our lead in operating carriers is great, both in technology and in experience. Soviet carriers would suffer from the geographic handicap of no direct access to the open ocean. They also lack overseas bases for forward support and distant-water, at-sea replenishment capabilities. Gorshkov does not discuss these matters but neither does he withdraw his previous criticisms of carrier usefulness in nuclear war. Likewise, Gorshkov fails to mention the new Kiev class of small carriers which intelligence has now confirmed the Soviets are constructing in the Black Sea.[63] In his final article he defends the unique construction paths his navy has taken, saying that these have met their needs "to the maximum degree" without copying Western construction, presumably including carriers:

The utilization of the achievements of science and industry together with the introduction of scientific methods in determining the more valuable mix of weapons and equipment characteristics, taking into account economic factors, has made it possible for naval development to approximate the Navy's vital needs to the maximum degree, without copying naval construction in the Western countries and following our own national path which best corresponds to the specific tasks facing the Navy and the conditions for carrying them out.[64]

The nuclear-powered missile submarine remains, in the Gorshkov perspective, the capital ship of the Soviet Navy. This is the result of the confluence of developments in nuclear weapons, ballistic and cruise missiles, nuclear propulsion, and electronics.[65] Nuclear weaponry has been "the decisive factor"[66] that has permitted the navy's submarine forces to become a part of the country's strategic nuclear forces. These strategic forces employ ballistic missiles for use against "strategic targets of the enemy deep in his territory from different directions," while tactical nuclear submarines employ cruise missiles for "the delivery of powerful and accurate attacks from great distances against the enemy's major surface ships."[67]

Nuclear power plants have transformed submarines into "genuine undersea warships, incorporating . . . such basic earmarks of sea power as maneuverability, hitting power, and concealment."[68] Equipping "submarines with nuclear power plants has made possible a sharp increase in the speed and range of their underwater navigation. And this is understandable, since the power-to-weight ratio of submarines with a nuclear-power plant considerably surpasses that of diesel submarines."[69] Electronics decisively permits "depicting the situation"[70]—presumably through radar and other displays of tactical information from assisting air platforms. Thus, "a course has been charted in our country," Gorshkov states, "toward the construction of an oceangoing Navy whose base consists of nuclear-powered submarines of various types."[71]

The Gorshkov articles may imply a withholding strategy[72] for Soviet ballistic missile submarines in a nuclear exchange, while other wartime missions may be interdiction of Western sea lines of communications and antisubmarine warfare. He stresses the desirability of employing surface and submarine forces in concert, which also constitutes an argument for a large, balanced navy. If the withholding strategy is correctly inferred from the Gorshkov series, it probably derives from the greater survivability of ballistic missile submarines, compared to land-launch facilities. Even after a general nuclear exchange that would leave Soviet land-launch capabilities destroyed, submarine-launch capabilities would remain to ensure destruction of any strategic targets left in the United States.

A wartime mission of interdicting Western sea routes emerges from Gorshkov's discussion of German submarine operations in both World Wars and from the known capabilities of his huge submarine force. Specifically, he says that "it is clear that submarines in World War

II were, and even more so under modern conditions are, the main means of combatting the enemy's shipping.''[73] Concerning antisubmarine warfare, he notes that in World War II submarines ''operated successfully against enemy submarines.''[74] In his final article, he states that ''Submarines are also becoming valuable anti-submarine combatants capable of detecting and destroying the enemy's missile-carrying submarines.''[75]

That Gorshkov is sharply critical of the Germans for not using surface and aviation forces to support their submarines implies that he would not make the same mistake. Despite the successes of Hitler's armies in Europe, England remained unconquered and the attempted submarine blockade on Britain failed. Gorshkov feels this was because: ''... despite the exceptional threat to submarines on the part of anti-submarine forces, the German naval command did not conduct a single operation or other specially organized combined action aimed at the destruction of these forces.''[76] While German submarines inflicted great losses, they failed.

One of the important reasons for this was that the submarines did not have the support of other forces and above all of aviation, which could have carried out reconnaissance for the submarines and destroyed anti-submarine forces, as well as operated against the enemy's economy by hitting his ports and targets in the shipbuilding industry, not to mention his ships at sea. These reasons considerably reduced the effectiveness of German submarine employment in cutting off the enemy's shipping in the Atlantic.[77]

In sum, says Gorshkov: ''... a modern fleet, designed to conduct combat operations against a strong enemy, cannot be simply a submarine fleet. The underestimation of the need to support submarine operations with aviation and surface ships cost the German command dearly in the last two world wars.''[78]

Gorshkov has relatively little to say about other areas of naval power in which the United States enjoys a substantial lead and advantage—antisubmarine warfare (ASW), amphibious projection and intervention, at-sea and dis-

tant-water replenishment, and forward bases. As with carriers, the Soviet Union cannot overtake the U.S. lead in any of these areas without large costs and without years of concentrated effort. Gorshkov denigrates, for example, the efficacy or potential of ASW as a realistic counter of Polaris. He seems to accept that a large and expensive effort to attempt to counter Polaris through at-sea detection and prosecution is both unrealistic and cost-ineffective. The reality of the relative invulnerability of Polaris has become more manifest with the expanded missile ranges of U.S. missile submarines which provide even greater expanses of ocean in which to roam and hide. As noted above, he recognizes the value of another submarine as an ASW platform, but no large or costly effort to expand the ASW capabilities of submarine platforms seems evident.

No increases in amphibious forces to a level of strategic significance seem apparent. Accordingly, Soviet naval infantry (marines) will probably remain peripherally tasked in areas such as the Baltic, Black Sea, and the Scandinavian Peninsula. This suggests that no strategic intervention capability such as the United States possesses seems forthcoming, except for the possibilities of naval gunboat diplomacy. Again, costs appear to be a major factor. The allocation of resources in designing and constructing the wide range of amphibious ships and craft required, in expanding and training the Soviet marines, and in providing means to protect and support them at sea and in the amphibious objective area would be enormous. Such costs appear prohibitive in view of other, competing, and more urgent Soviet naval requirements.

While the papers reveal no apparent major program to improve at-sea and distant-water replenishment capabilities, some progress can be expected over a period of years, and their new *Chilikin* class oiler is a step in this direction. They also do not possess multicommodity ships which permit replenishing of an entire formation, task group, or force with fuel, food, ordnance, and supplies in one operation, using alongside and helicopter replenishment techniques. Soviet underway replenishment problems in distant waters

are compounded by vast distance from home bases. Placing nuclear power in surface ships would partially solve the problem the Soviets would have in supporting distant operations in wartime, but there is no indication that this is planned for surface ships, and Gorshkov states that only submarines will be so powered.

In his final article, Gorshkov stresses ''balanced forces'' and new requirements for forces and for the means to support them. He speaks of long oceanic cruises and the long stay of ships in the ocean. He notes the importance of improved habitability standards which permit sustaining a high combat capability [79] for extended at-sea periods. Extended employments to the Mediterranean—and presumably elsewhere—thus appear likely to continue. Gorshkov seems well aware of his at-sea and distant-water support problems, their magnitude, and the need to overcome them. Despite these problems and the large costs involved, a major effort will probably continue to keep substantial Soviet naval units in distant deployments.

Finally, Gorshkov is acutely aware that he does not have a system of forward bases for his navy. In his third article, he complains that: ''Many islands discovered by Russian seafarers in the Pacific were not added to Russian possessions, although as their first discoverer she was fully entitled to this right.''[80] The tone in his articles concerning forward bases is pessimistic: the inference is that he either does not expect to get them or at this point in time he cannot count on them. He obviously recognizes this as a critical deficiency which the United States does not have—what with the base facilities available to the United States in NATO countries, the Mediterranean, the Caribbean, at Pearl Harbor, in Japan, in Taiwan, at Subic Bay, in Australia, et cetera. Absence of forward bases and lack of an at-sea replenishment capability are problems which mutually compound each other. In summary, it is in these additional areas of naval power in which the United States has a decided advantage—ASW, amphibious projection and intervention, at-sea and distant-water replenishment, and forward bases—that the Soviet Navy will likely remain in arrears, perhaps substantially, for at least a number of years.

Components of Soviet Seapower. Gorshkov, in his final article, makes a bow, elegant but brief, to the other "necessary components" of the Soviet Union's "constantly strengthening... seapower."[81] These three components are oceanographic research, the merchant marine, and the fishing fleet. He further indicates that the Soviets' sea and ocean industry will be increased to exploit ocean resources. His navy directly controls some of the oceanographic research effort and exerts influence on the course of many of its other activities. The Soviet oceanographic effort, much of it in response to navy requirements, will also expand: "We are presently conducting a large volume of research on the hydrosphere. Yet the World Ocean still remains the least studied section of the globe, and the scale of work on trying to understand it must and will be expanded in the future."[82]

Gorshkov describes the value and the comprehensiveness of the Soviet oceanographic effort:

In order to exploit the World Ocean and to utilize its resources, it is essential to have detailed and comprehensive knowledge of the hydrosphere of the Earth, to understand the processes occurring in it, and its effect on the land and the atmosphere, and on the formation of weather. Knowledge ensuring navigational safety in the oceans and seas and flights over them is also needed. Moreover, reliable information on the various resources existing in the hydrosphere and on possible methods of exploiting them is necessary. Special expeditionary research oceanographic ships, scientific organizations, equipment, and, of course, the appropriate personnel are required to understand the seas and oceans. All of this is one component of the seapower of a country.[83]

The Soviet merchant marine is also growing. The shipbuilding and ship repair industry he mentions are of course important to his navy. One reason for having a large navy is, ostensibly, to be able to protect the interests of the merchant marine, as well as those of the distant-water fishing fleet and the oceanographic research effort. Nevertheless, he disposes of the Soviet merchant marine in two paragraphs:

An important integral part of seapower is the equipment and personnel which make possible the practical utilization of the oceans and seas as transport routes connecting continents, countries, and peoples. For this, it is essential to have a merchant marine, a network of ports and services supporting its operation, and a developed shipbuilding and ship repair industry.

In 1972 the Soviet Merchant Marine, which is growing at a rapid rate, was sixth among the merchant fleets of the world. A majority of its ships have been built in recent years and are among the more technically advanced ships.[84]

While what Gorshkov says here is true, the Soviet merchant marine has not yet commercially adopted, to any substantial degree, such advanced methods of sea cargo transportation as containerization, LASH (lighter aboard ship) type ships, and roll-on, roll-off ships. Yet the Soviet merchant marine is huge, is growing rapidly, and is a significant component of Soviet seapower.

As a final component of seapower Gorshkov discusses the Soviet fishing fleet which appears regularly off the New England and Newfoundland coasts with large modern ships: "The next component of seapower is the ships, technical equipment, and the personnel needed for the practical exploitation and utilization of the resources of the World Ocean, that is, the fishing fleet. Today our country has the strongest fishing fleet in the world at its disposal."[85] Elsewhere in his final article, he speaks in glowing terms, as a true resources of food which the Soviet fishing fleet, as a part of the world fishing fleet, is exploiting:

The reserves of animal protein, i.e., fish, sea animals, plankton, etc., in the World Ocean (if measures are taken to restock them) make it possible to consider it to be one of the most important sources for solving the food problem for the growing population of the world. Today the catching of fish and other "gifts of the sea" is carried out only in a small section of the ocean surface, consisting of about 10% of it. The annual world catch of fish equals some 60 million tons, but in the near future it may reach 100 million tons or more.[86]

In his discussion of the fishing fleet, he indicates that the Soviets' "sea and ocean industry" will expand:

The sea and ocean industry will also be developed in the future, will exploit new areas, and will expand the assortment of products of the sea being captured. The broadest prospects are opening up in the creation of equipment for extracting mineral resources from the water, from the sea bottom, and from beneath it.[87]

In his final article, Gorshkov includes an eloquent discussion on the resources of the ocean waters, the deep seabed, and the Continental Shelf. He refers to the tides, currents, temperature gradients of the water, et cetera as "truly inexhaustible energy resources" and notes that seawater contains all the elements, that manganese nodules rich in metallic content cover considerable parts of the deep seabed, and that vast reserves of oil and gas lie within the ocean floor.[88] He speaks, somewhat inaccurately, of the truly inexhaustible wealth of the World Ocean which, presumably, the expanding sea and ocean industry will exploit: "The reserves of metals, minerals, fuels (oil, gas, and coal), various chemical raw materials, nuclear material, power and food reserves, locked in the seabed, are so vast that there is no comparison whatsoever with the known reserves existing on land."[89]

This "industry" probably refers to ocean mining and offshore drilling ventures. Magnesium, salt, and other minerals and substances may be extracted from seawater; manganese nodules may be scooped up from the deep ocean seabed in the Pacific for their manganese, cobalt, copper, and nickel content; and oil and gas wells may be drilled in offshore locations on the Continental

Shelf. U.S. firms are now exploiting the oceans, their seabeds, and the Continental Shelf for such minerals and fossil fuels. That the Soviets will follow suit in such endeavors to exploit ocean wealth is hardly surprising.

While Gorshkov argues for the continued growth of Soviet seapower on virtually all fronts—navy, oceanographic research, merchant marine, resource exploitation—it is quite clear that in his mind the navy is the preeminent component. "However, we must consider the most important component of the seapower of the state to be the Navy, whose mission is to protect state interests of the seas and oceans and to defend the country from possible attacks from the direction of the seas and oceans."[90] A few paragraphs later, he says yet again that the Soviet Navy is expanding into a new, oceangoing navy: "The Communist Party and the Soviet government fully appreciated both the threat to our country which is arising from the oceans, and the need to deter the aggressive aspirations of the enemy through the construction of a new, ocean-going Navy. And this need is being answered."[91]

In his closing work, Gorshkov expresses considerable concern over those law of the sea matters which have significant impact on Soviet naval power. His positions on these are in many cases identical with those of the U.S. Government. Littoral states, he notes, have increasingly begun to divide up the World Ocean because of the possibilities for exploitation of its resources. His implicit concern is that such actions will curtail naval power through restricting the areas in which a navy operates. He criticizes, in particular, the highly alarming symptom of some states to expand the limits of their territorial seas out to 200 miles, a practice he views as extreme and nothing other than an attempt to seize great expanses of the ocean.[92]

Expansions of the territorial seas are having a definite and deleterious effect on the status of the high seas and freedom of navigation. Yet experience has shown the viability of the 12-mile limit which the Soviets claim as their territorial waters for the breadth of the territorial sea. While he avoids the Soviet positions on the Arctic seas

peripheral to Russia and on the Sea of Okhotsk (over which, in both cases, the Soviets exercise considerable control), he is concerned that other areas, such as the Mediterranean, may be divided up among littoral nations through expansion of the territorial seas. Such action could virtually prohibit the operations of the Soviet Mediterranean Squadron, although Gorshkov does not openly express this fear.[93]

He is concerned with the problem of the innocent passage of combatants and auxiliaries and of aircraft overflights through international straits. Obviously, should some or all of the more than 110 straits being used for international shipping turn out to be closed territorial seas of littoral states, then this too will restrict Soviet naval power. He criticizes, as have Western writers, the vagueness of the 1958 Geneva Convention on the Continental Shelf in defining the limits of the shelf over which littoral states have jurisdiction. The vagueness of the definition has helped precipitate controversies over division of the seabed adjacent to the coasts of littoral states. He also urges the complete demilitarization of the seabed, ostensibly in conjunction with ending the arms race.[94] Adoption of this standard Soviet line would of course outlaw any devices on the seabed for submarine detection, which—in view of the huge Soviet submarine force and the alleged existence of such devices in Western hands—would redound to Soviet naval advantage.

Gorshkov seems preoccupied with the potential effects on Soviet naval power of any dividing up of the seabed. In the vigor of his condemnation of this danger to expanding Soviet seapower, he not only defends international maritime law, but even criticizes developing countries in Africa, Asia, and Latin America for opting for such practices:

Today the serious threat of a further division of the World Ocean exists. Therefore, it is not by chance that many countries and a great number of international organizations, beginning with the UN and ending with dozens of different types of intragovernmental and nongovernmental organizations and organs, are engaged with questions of the legal regime and with the develop-

ment of new norms regulating the use of the World Ocean. The most characteristic feature in their work in the current stage is the fact that several Afro-Asian and Latin American developing countries are insisting on a review of all existing norms regulating the use of the World Ocean, based on the fact that they are not participating in the exploitation. In particular, they assert that current international maritime law is outmoded and does not reflect changes which have occurred in the world since 1958. Representatives of these countries put their position on the plane of a struggle between the poor and the rich, the backward and the industrially developed countries. . . .[95]

Gorshkov is painfully aware of the potentially profound effects that law of the sea matters may have on the naval power resident in world navies. Freedom to use the seas is essential for the application of naval power. The degree that that freedom is diminished through dividing up of the World Ocean among littoral states—through the extension seaward of territorial seas, through the nationalizing of previously international straits, through closed sea regimes imposed by countries littoral—is the degree that naval powers will lose their ability to effectively employ their forces.

Conclusions. The major and overriding conclusion to this commentary is that the Gorshkov articles are essentially announcement, particularly in their broad outlines. Accepting this proposition, Gorshkov has told us a great deal, and it appears possible that the content of his articles allows one to make some reasoned judgments on the course of Soviet seapower in general and of Soviet naval power in particular.

The most positive element in the Gorshkov announcements is that Soviet seapower—of which the navy is the key component—will, in general, continue to expand on virtually every front. Gorshkov clearly said that the Soviet merchant marine, the Soviet oceanographic effort, and the Soviet ocean exploitation effort will all expand. He did not elaborate on the fishing fleet, merely noting that it was already the world's strongest fleet. Soviet seapower will therefore present an increasingly larger challenge in the aggregate to traditional Western seapower superiority.

The Soviet Navy seems destined in particular to grow into a larger, more modern, more balanced navy. While submarines will remain at least for several years as the Soviet Navy's capital ship, their navy is likely to see increased numbers and variety of modern, but conventionally powered, surface ships. The future role of aircraft carriers in the Soviet Navy remains unclear and will probably remain so at least until the new *Kiev* class carriers now being built in Russia begin operations. (This writer believes that the Soviets have not yet made a commitment to build a fleet of carriers but wish to analyze the *Kiev's* performance before making the costly, long-term, and strategic decision to proceed with additional construction.) Soviet at-sea and distant-water replenishment and support capabilities seem

likely to improve, perhaps substantially, in coming years; but no major increase in Soviet amphibious projection capabilities or in antisubmarine warfare seems forthcoming. The Soviets continue to need, and lack, a system of forward bases to support deployments beyond home waters; this deficiency will probably continue for some time.

The Soviet Navy will thus continue to lag behind its U.S. competitor in several key areas, but particularly in the at-sea air cover in the open ocean which at present only fleet carriers can provide. At the same time, the huge Soviet submarine force will continue to pose both a strategic nuclear threat against the continental United States and a strategic interdiction threat against its sea lines of communication. The Soviets will continue to work under the strategic hardships of unfavorable geography which both fragments and encloses their naval power. From the vantage point of this writer, the Gorsh-

kov papers confirm that Soviet Naval Strategy will generally remain defensive and deterrent for the next several years and perhaps for a decade or more.

BIOGRAPHIC SUMMARY

Comdr. Clyde Smith, U.S. Navy, holds undergraduate degrees from both Oklahoma State University and the University of Maryland, a master's degree from Oklahoma State University, and is a graduate of the Russian Language School. As an intelligence officer he has served in West Berlin, on the staffs of Commander 7th Fleet and Commander Cruiser-Destroyer Group 8, and has had three separate tours in Vietnam— Naval Intelligence Adviser in the Naval Advisory Group (1964-65), Staff Intelligence Officer to Commander River Assault Flotilla 1 (1966-67), and Chief of Operational Intelligence to Commander Naval Forces Vietnam (1970-71). Commander Smith is currently a student in the College of Naval Warfare.

NOTES

1. Each of the 11 articles of the Gorshkov series will be published, on a one-per-month basis, in the January through November issues of the 1974 *United States Naval Institute Proceedings*.

2. For biographical information on Admiral Gorshkov, see Edward L. Crowley, et al., eds., *Prominent Personalities in the USSR* (Metuchen, N.J.: Scarecrow Press, 1968), p. 194.

3. *Morskoy Sbornik* (Hereinafter *MS*), No. 2, 1972, pp. 20, 23.

4. For a more comprehensive discussion of these aspects of Soviet naval strategy, see Robert W. Herrick, *Soviet Naval Strategy* (Annapolis: United States Naval Institute, 1968), pp. 143-57.

5. For example, in Marshal V.D. Sokolovsky, ed., *Military Strategy* (Moscow: Soviet Ministry of Defense, 1968), all of the authors and reviewers of the official Soviet view of military strategy were army marshals, generals, or colonels.

6. In such efforts the Soviets have stressed anticarrier operations. See John T. Funkhouser, "Soviet Carrier Strategy," *United States Naval Institute Proceedings*, December 1973, pp. 27-37, for a good discussion of this aspect of Soviet naval strategy.

7. While it is common in U.S. Navy circles to refer to this Soviet Mediterranean force as a "fleet, the Soviets themselves call it a "squadron" (*ehskadra*).

8. For further discussion of the influences of geography on Soviet and United States naval strategies and on fleet composition, see the exchange of letters between Senator Proxmire and Admiral Zumwalt, in May and June 1972, as appearing in the U.S. *Congressional Record*, vol. 118, No. 94, pp. S9179-95. Herinafter, the "Zumwalt-Proxmire Exchange."

9. *MS*, No. 2, 1972, p. 24.

10. *Ibid.*, p. 23.

11. *MS*, No. 4, 1972, p. 23.

12. *MS*, No. 2, 1972, p. 25.

13. *Ibid.*

14. *Ibid.*, p. 29.

15. *MS*, No. 3, 1972, p. 20.

16. For further discussion of Gorshkov's "big-navy" theme, see Herrick, "The Gorshkov Interpretation of Russian Naval History," as contained in Michael K. MccGwire, ed., *Soviet Naval Developments: Capability and Context* (Halifax: Centre for Foreign Policy Studies, 1972), pp. 275-89; and Robert W. Herrick, "Soviet Navy Commander-in-Chief Advocates Construction of a Much Larger Navy," Working Paper, Center for Naval Analyses, Arlington, Va., 9 May 1973.

17. *MS*, No. 3, 1972, p. 22.

18. *MS*, No. 6, 1972, p. 14.

19. *Ibid.*

20. *MS*, No. 3, 1972, p. 22.

21. *Ibid.*, p. 20.
22. *MS*, No. 2, 1972, p. 24.
23. *Ibid.*, p. 27.
24. *MS*, No. 8, 1972, p. 18.
25. *MS*, No. 2, 1973, p. 19.
26. *Ibid.*
27. *MS*, No. 3, 1972, p. 22.
28. *MS*, No. 4, 1972, p. 22.
29. *Ibid.*
30. *Ibid.*, p. 23.
31. *Ibid.*, p. 23.
32. *MS*, No. 3, 1972, p. 24.
33. *Ibid.*, p. 31.
34. *MS*, No. 2, 1972, p. 23.
35. *Ibid.*
36. *Ibid.*
37. *MS*, No. 5, 1972, p. 24.
38. *MS*, No. 2, 1972, p. 29.
39. *MS*, No. 5, 1972, p. 22.
40. *MS*, No. 2, 1972, p. 29.
41. *MS*, No. 12, 1972, p. 16.
42. *Ibid.*
43. *MS*, No. 3, 1972, p. 27.
44. *MS*, No. 2, 1973, p. 21.
45. *MS*, No. 4, 1972, pp. 13-14.
46. *MS*, No. 2, 1972, p. 21.
47. *Ibid.*, p. 20.
48. *Ibid.*, pp. 21-22.
49. *MS*, No. 3, 1972, p. 26.
50. *Ibid.*, pp. 20-21.
51. *Ibid.*, p. 21.
52. *MS*, No. 6, 1972, p. 14.
53. As if in illustration of this concept, Gorshkov, in the name of the Soviet Union, deployed over 90 ships into the Mediterranean during the recent Arab-Israeli crisis. This was the highest number of Soviet Navy ships ever deployed to the Mediterranean at one time and is over twice the size of the normal Soviet Mediterranean Squadron.
54. *MS*, No. 3, 1972, pp. 32-33.
55. *MS*, No. 2, 1972, p. 20.
56. Both Admiral Gorshkov and Admiral Zumwalt are in essential agreement on this. As Admiral Zumwalt stated in the Zumwalt-Proxmire Exchange:
   . . . a direct comparison of the two fleets, unless heavily footnoted, cannot mean very much. With very few exceptions, U.S. ships are not designed to fight Soviet ships of similar classes. Therefore it is of little value to contrast . . . characteristics. . . . What is important is how well the platform, or the fleet, can carry out its assigned tasks.
57. Michael K. MccGwire, "The Gorshkov Series—'Navies in War and Peace'—a Summary Report," Working Paper, Center for Naval Analyses, Arlington, Va., 8 May 1973, p. 2.
58. *MS*, No. 5, 1972, p. 24.
59. *MS*, No. 8, 1972, p. 14.
60. *MS*, No. 12, 1972, p. 18.
61. *MS*, No. 8, 1972, p. 24.
62. *MS*, No. 9, 1972, pp. 14-15.
63. Two *Kiev* class carriers are currently under construction there.
64. *MS*, No. 2, 1973, p. 19.
65. *Ibid.*
66. *Ibid.*
67. *Ibid.*
68. *Ibid.*, p. 20.
69. *Ibid.*
70. *Ibid.*, p. 19.
71. *MS*, No. 2, 1973, p. 20.
72. For a full exposition of this possible withholding strategy, see James M. McConnell, "Admiral Gorshkov on the Soviet Navy in War and Peace," Working Paper, Center for Naval Analyses, Arlington, Va., 1 October 1973, pp. 1-21.
73. *MS*, No. 11, 1972, p. 27.
74. *Ibid.*, p. 25.
75. *MS*, No. 2, 1973, p. 20.
76. *MS*, No. 11, 1972, p. 25.
77. *Ibid.*, p. 28.
78. *MS*, No. 2, 1973, p. 20.
79. *Ibid.*, pp. 21-22.
80. *MS*, No. 4, 1972, p. 11.
81. *MS*, No. 2, 1973, p. 18.

82. *Ibid.*
83. *Ibid.*
84. *Ibid.*
85. *Ibid.*
86. *Ibid.,* p. 14.
87. *Ibid.,* p. 18.
88. *Ibid.*
89. *Ibid.,* pp. 13-14.
90. *Ibid.,* p. 18.
91. *Ibid.,* p. 19.
92. *Ibid.*
93. *Ibid.,* p. 16.
94. *Ibid.,* p. 18.
95. *Ibid.,* p. 15.

―――――――――― ψ ―――

Superiority in naval power will henceforth consist in keeping up a proper naval establishment in discipline. The first naval nation to fall will be the one that is first caught napping.

Sir Charles Napier, 1786-1860

CONSTRAINTS OF NAVAL GEOGRAPHY
ON SOVIET NAVAL POWER

The element of geography poses clear limitations on both the development and employment of naval powers by the Soviet Union. Failure on the part of naval planners to recognize and exploit this strategic advantage would be a disservice to the defense budget, the national economy, and the United States citizenry.

An article prepared

by

Commander Clyde A. Smith, U.S. Navy

Introduction. This commentary focuses on the psychological and physical constraints, arising from geography,[1] which diminish Soviet naval power in the naval power equation. Naval power is inseparably linked to national geography, and while an oversimplification, the essential naval power equation is nevertheless:

(Size of Navy + Quality of Navy)
X Naval Geography = Naval Power.

In this case study of the Soviet Navy, it is apparent that naval geography largely drives naval strategy which, in turn, drives force structure.

Admittedly, this paper has a tendency toward geographic determinism. It proceeds in three steps: by identifying the psychological and physical constraints which flow from Russia's unfavorable naval geography; by discussing the significance of these constraints on Soviet naval strategy, defense economics, and decisionmaking and fleet and forward base structure; and by positing objectives that should be pursued in *our* defense economics and

decisionmaking in view of these constraints and their influences.

Assumptions. Two assumptions underlie this paper. First, when it speaks of "war" or "wartime," it refers either to nonnuclear war or to a nuclear war confined to the sea. In an all-out exchange between the American and Soviet nuclear arsenals, what might transpire at sea between the two navies would be academic since both civilizations would already have perished on the land. Second, it assumes that a satisfactory means can be worked out to qualitatively compare the ships, submarines, and planes of the Soviet and United States Navies, that differ both in missions and in configurations. Undoubtedly such means can be determined via systems analysis, although both Admirals Gorshkov and Zumwalt have noted its difficulty.[2]

Constraints of Geography and Geographic Determinism. Constraints of psychology and physical geography have, throughout history, imposed

severe restrictions on Soviet naval power, constraints which present the United States with strategic and tactical advantages that the Soviets cannot overcome. We need but to understand this and to resolve, with our larger and more efficient industrial base, to maintain and exploit these advantages. While Western observers often note the existence of some or all of the major geographic constraints, they do not consider their historic and long-term ramifications. As long as the total ship, submarine, and plane capabilities of the two navies, appropriate to their missions, remain approximately in balance, the burdens imposed by geography will continue to diminish the effectiveness of the Soviet Navy. The Russian bear has learned to swim, but he nevertheless remains a prisoner of his physical geography.

The Psychological Constraint: Land Power Mentality. By history, tradition, and necessity, Russia has long been a landpower with a landpower's mentality. This psychological constraint, flowing from Russian physical geography, suffuses and dominates Soviet decisionmaking throughout her Defense Establishment. Historically she has lived with vulnerable frontiers, and her fears and ambitions have therefore been directed inward, upon the land, rather than seaward. This historical preoccupation with the land has focused major attention on Russian armies, and her seapower has suffered accordingly. The historic Soviet fear of eventual invasion from Europe remains, and she now has the added concern of an unfriendly China upon her Asiatic border.

Maintenance of huge armies is costly and diverts resources away from the sea. At the same time, army domination of military policy councils[3] assures that the Soviet Navy will not receive the fullest share of attention and consideration in competition for budget, resources, and industrial capacity. The accomplishments of the incumbent Soviet Navy Commander in Chief, Admiral Gorshkov,[4] and whatever other naval enthusiasts are in alliance with him in Russia, therefore loom even larger. While this landpower mentality is a major psychological constraint on Soviet naval power, it has not—in view of the vast resources and centralized direction which Russia possesses— precluded her from becoming a great naval power as well. Nor does it preclude her from making further great advances in growth of her naval power, a growth which Admiral Gorshkov seemingly announced in his series of articles in *Morskoy Sbornik*.

The Five Geographic Constraints. There are five major geographic constraints on Soviet naval power. These are:

• the vastness of the Soviet Union
• the geographic fragmentation of the Soviet Navy into four fleets and one "squadron"
• the existence of narrow straits through which her fleets must pass to reach the open oceans
• the northerly orientation, in latitude, of the Soviet Union
• the distance of her fleets from major world oceans and shipping lanes.

These five geographic constraints, in conjunction with the all-encompassing psychological constraint, profoundly affect Soviet naval power. They significantly influence Soviet naval strategy and defense decisions, Soviet perceptions of the utility of the world's oceans, and Soviet views on material requirements to operate successfully upon them.

As Germany learned in both World Wars, a naval fleet and the national geography from which it must project its naval power are two parts of an inseparable system. Like the Germans, the Soviets can have a great navy, but not necessarily be a great naval power. Deficiency in the "Naval Geography" term in the naval power equation translates into severe constraints on national naval power. In essence, the Soviet Navy's geographic dilemma vis-a-vis the U.S. Navy is analogous, on a grander scale, to that of the German Navy vis-a-vis the British Navy during both World Wars.

Constraint One: The Vastness of the Soviet Union. The Soviet Union's size is a major liability to her naval power, but a major asset to her landpower. Her hugeness dilutes and separates her naval power, but, at the same time, ensures her a wealth in natural resources and a capacity for the defense in depth appropriate to a landpower. Nearly three times as large as the United States, Russia's east-west extent is more than the distance from New York City to Honolulu, and her north-south extent is twice the distance from Maine to Miami. Her great size ensures that her naval power, operating as it must only on the periphery of her landmass, will be physically divorced from political and economic centers of power. In the extreme example, Vladivostok, the headquarters of the Pacific Fleet, is well over 5,000 miles from Moscow. With her navy situated in peripheral seas, with her severe climate, and without a maritime tradition, the ascendancy of the landpower mentality and its historic subordination of the navy to the army in Russia seems predestined.

Transportation between distant regions of Russia is at best underdeveloped, at worst nonexistent. For example, no highway spans Siberia, and the only railway across this huge area is the Trans-Siberian. In short, the Soviet Union lacks a modern road, highway, rail, and air transport system. This factor, together with size and climate, dictates that any exchange of spare parts, personnel, and even publications will be difficult, time-consuming, and expensive. The vastness of the Soviet Union thus effectively prohibits an integrated and efficient supply system for her Naval Establishment, as well as limiting naval coordination and reinforcement in wartime by means of her vast maritime perimeter.

Constraint Two: Fleet Fragmentation. Physical geography has dictated the division of the Soviet Navy into four fleets—Northern, Baltic, Black Sea, and Pacific. The "Mediterranean Squadron,"[5] drawn from units of the Black Sea and Northern Fleets primarily, is maintained in the Mediterranean and compares in size to the U.S. 6th Fleet. Each of the four fleets has a commander in chief, and each comprises seagoing units, naval infantry,[6] naval air forces, support bases, dockyards, and associated facilities. Land-based naval forces include coast defense units—artillery and air defense—together with operational troops, such as naval infantry and engineer units. This division of the Soviet Navy into four fleets, concomitant with the distances involved and with the lack of free access of each fleet with the others, ensures that the fleets cannot provide timely mutual support or reinforcement in wartime.

Each fleet is configured to function independently, which presents severe command and control problems, and each has specialized functions. Since the Soviet Navy has no aircraft carriers[7] and since it is extremely risky to operate warships at sea without air cover in a hostile environment, the Soviet Navy's effective operational range in time of war is restricted to the range of land-based air. This, in turn, not only prevents global operations in wartime, but constricts the Soviet Navy to operating its surface ships (under existing technology) near home waters where land-based air can protect them with continuous air cover.

Geography also divides the U.S. Navy, forcing us to maintain both Atlantic and Pacific Fleets. Passage from one fleet to another must either be by way of the Panama Canal or around

Cape Horn. The Panama Canal is, of course, vulnerable to bombs, mines, and sabotage, not to mention Panamanian nationalism, and the locks are also not large enough to accommodate most of our carriers. Even so, while we ourselves do have a fleet fragmentation problem, it simply is not nearly so severe as that of the Soviets.

The Northern Sea Route (NOSE-RO). Some alternatives, none satisfactory, are available to the Soviets in attempting to alleviate this problem of fleet fragmentation. These alternatives are the Northern Sea Route (NOSERO) and the Soviet canal system. The Soviet NOSERO runs from Murmansk on the Barents Sea across the top of Russia to Providéniya on the Bering Sea (or conversely), with Vladivostok usually the ultimate destination. This route is strategic and in the Soviet view internal. They control the icebreakers on the route, provide charts and weather services, conduct ice reconnaissance, and exercise jurisdiction over passage of key straits. The route also services various small ports along Russia's northern periphery.

The route is open to surface transit only a few months each year, and icebreaker assistance is required. The route passes through numerous interdictable straits, and both convoys and icebreakers are vulnerable to submarine or air attack. The Germans effectively operated submarines in the Kara Sea in World War II. The entire NOSERO would now pose far fewer operational problems for modern nuclear submarines than it did for the World War II German diesel submarines. If the Soviet icebreakers should be lost, so too is the route itself.

Soviet Canals. Nor does the extensive Soviet canal system present relief. There does exist a significant canal system in European Russia which provides a means for interchange of small naval vessels, equipment, and supplies between the Baltic and Northern Sea Fleets. The Baltic Fleet-Northern Fleet interchange is via the White Sea-Baltic Sea Canal and the Baltic Fleet-Black Sea Fleet interchange is via a series of canals and rivers. The White Sea-Baltic Sea Canal's capacity is limited, and it cannot take either the larger Soviet ships or submarines. It is susceptible to aerial mining in wartime, and its locks and canal walls are vulnerable to bombing. (German Stuka dive bombers put the canal out of operation in June 1941 in the first month of the invasion of Russia.) Limited capacity and vulnerability to mining and bombing similarly curtail the usefulness of other Soviet European canals in wartime.

Icing is also a serious problem because Soviet canals and rivers freeze for a considerable period each year. The Northern Dvina River, which empties into the White Sea, is frozen for 188 days each year, while the lower Dnieper, emptying into the Black Sea, is frozen for 80 days. Freezing periods for other canals and rivers in European Russia lie somewhere between these figures. Thus, Soviet canals, while useful, do not significantly alleviate fleet fragmentation problems.

Constraint Three: Interdictable Fleet Egress Routes. Each of the four fleets, as well as the Mediterranean Squadron, must transit interdictable straits to reach the open sea. The Northern Fleet, with headquarters at Murmansk in the Kola Inlet, is the most powerful of the four Soviet fleets. It contains most of the Soviet Navy's "blue water" forces, including the majority of its long-range attack and missile submarines. Geography, again, demonstrates why. Of the three fleets positioned around the periphery of European Russia—where most of its industrial resources are located—the Northern Fleet has the relatively freest access to the open ocean. Submarines of this fleet would in war be the cutting edge that would attempt to sever the lifeline between America and Europe. By the very nature of this Soviet submarine threat, we have been forced to achieve a significantly higher level of antisubmarine warfare (ASW) expertise than the Soviets.[8]

Nevertheless, while relatively better off than either the Baltic or Black Sea Fleets, the Northern Fleet still must run the gauntlet around Norway and down through the Greenland-Iceland-United Kingdom Gap before reaching the strategic North Atlantic. To return to home waters, the gauntlet has to be run in reverse. Not only is the gap interdictable by friendly submarines, air, and surface forces, but Norway, the United Kingdom, and Iceland are NATO partners, while Greenland is under NATO control. Attrition of the Northern Fleet attempting to reach the North Atlantic or to return to home waters would be severe. The U.S. Navy does not suffer a comparable handicap to reach the North Atlantic.

The Baltic and Black Sea Fleets and the Mediterranean Squadron labor under even more severe geographic constraints. Narrow and minable or otherwise interdictable straits confine these fleets to their home waters and deny them open access to the ocean. The Danish Straits lock up the Baltic, while the Turkish Straits lock up the Black Sea Fleet. Even if the Baltic Fleet could escape the problem of the Danish Straits, severe attrition could take place in any crossing or recrossing of the North Sea. Like the German Navy in both World Wars, the Soviet Baltic Fleet could find itself imprisoned in the Baltic Sea. Likewise, even if the Turkish Straits problem were somehow solved for the Black Sea Fleet, it would have to transit the length of the narrow, interdictable Mediterranean and force passage through Gibraltar. Like the Baltic Fleet, the Black Sea Fleet is confronted with either wartime confinement to home waters or to destruction.

Nor is the much vaunted Mediterranean Squadron better off. Not only is the Mediterranean narrow, with NATO countries arrayed along its northern border, but the Strait of Gibraltar, under British control, locks up the sea itself. The opening of the Suez Canal to Soviet use does not change the situation appreciably since the canal is minable and ships in transit are vulnerable to air attack. These geographic constraints, together with United States and NATO naval and airpower, ensure that in time of war the Baltic and Black Sea Fleets along with the Soviet Mediterranean Squadron would either be confined to home waters or perhaps—in the case of the Mediterranean Squadron—destroyed in its geographic cage.

The Soviet dilemma is not much better in the Pacific. The Soviet Pacific Fleet is largely penned up in the Sea of

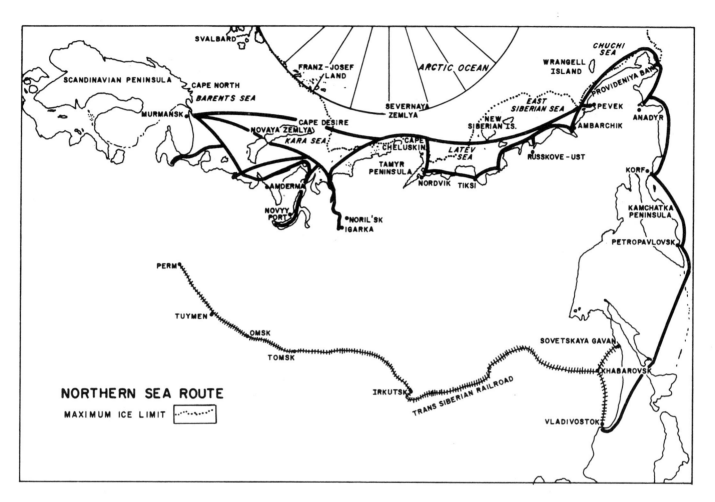

NORTHERN SEA ROUTE

MAXIMUM ICE LIMIT

Japan. Access is again via interdictable straits—La Pérouse between Hokkaido and Sakhalin, Tsugaru between Hokkaido and Honshu, and Korea and Tsushima between Kyushu and Korea.

Similarly, the Kuril Island chain encloses the Sea of Okhotsk, with the interstices between the islands interdictable. In the Pacific only Petropavlovsk on the Kamchatka Peninsula used mainly by submarines, fronts on the open ocean. Presumably, Petropavlovsk—like Murmansk and the Kola Inlet in the Northern Fleet—would be an early target for airstrikes, mining, submarine interdiction, and blockade.

Constraint Four: Climate. The freezing periods for Soviet canals and rivers noted above illustrate the fourth geographic constraint on Soviet seapower: climate. Nearly all of the Soviet Union lies north of the latitude of Portland, Me. Of their major naval bases in the Pacific, Baltic, and Barents, only Murmansk is ice-free the year around—

warmed by the terminus of the Gulf Stream looping around Norway. The Black Sea, however, is a warm-water basin, and Black Sea ports are open to navigation throughout the year. Arctic ice encroaches upon northern Russia, and it closes the NOSERO except for a few months each year. As a consequence of the pervasive cold climate and icing, the Soviets lead the world in cold weather operational capabilities. At the same time, cold and ice severely limit their naval operations in home waters as they must divert considerable resources in combat of these conditions.

Mahan saw the factors of numerous deep harbors, navigable rivers providing internal access to the country, length of coastline, and climate. As pertinent to seapower taken without the limitation of climate, the Soviet Union would be particularly well endowed. For example, several of her great rivers in Siberia are considerably longer than any navigable stream in Central or Western Europe. However, they flow into the Arctic, are

too far north, and are frozen and unnavigable for much of the year. She has enormous expanses of coastline, but again much of this fronts uselessly on the Arctic, distant from world trade routes.

Climate also influences Soviet ship design and characteristics. Since major battles contesting control of the sea-lanes will likely be fought in warmer climates, Soviet ship designers must come up with ships capable of operating in the semitropics and tropics to accomplish their missions. Their ships must also be able to operate in cold home waters, and their shipbuilding technology must allow for this in hull strengths and design, insulation of piping and equipment, operation and design of equipment and propulsion, and the selection of lubricants and fuels. Climate thus further constrains Soviet naval power.

Constraint Five: Distance From World Oceans. This northerly orientation of the Soviet Union also produces

314

the fifth constraint: distance of Soviet naval power from major world oceans and shipping lanes. Only the Northern Fleet—which has the relatively freest access to the open ocean—need be considered. As previously noted, the Baltic and Black Sea Fleets and, to a lesser extent, the Pacific Fleet, are contained within semi-enclosed seas, as is the Mediterranean Squadron. The Northern Fleet's submarines, which constitute the greatest threat to Western maritime routes, are at least 2,500 miles distant from the major America-Europe reinforcement and resupply sea routes. Not only do their submarines have to run the gauntlet past Norway and through the Greenland-Iceland-United Kingdom Gap, but they must expend considerable "dead time" in transit to and from patrol station.

Transit time to and from operating areas is dead time. We do not live with the same handicap. The Atlantic and other major ocean routes in the Northern Hemisphere Temperate Zone are at our ocean doorstep. Further, with organic air cover in our carriers, with the availability of land-based air, and with our better ASW, we can hope to protect our merchant marine[9] on the major ocean routes. The Soviets, lacking organic naval air cover, cannot provide the same protection. In time of war, they must either keep their merchant marine (and their large distant-water fishing fleet) in port or sacrifice them needlessly at sea.

Soviet Naval Strategy: Predilection for Defense, Deterrence, and Reaction. Soviet naval strategy, decisively influenced through history by geography, is essentially defensive, deterrent, and reactive in its relationship with the U.S. Navy.[10] Subordinate to army doctrine and needs, lacking maritime traditions and a trading seafaring people, and confronted by severe geographical constraints, it would seem natural that their employment strategy for naval forces would be essentially defensive. Only in recent times have they created a credible strategic deterrent force of nuclear ballistic missile submarines.

Their naval strategy, flowing from their geography, has traditionally been a strategy of *denial*,[11] of *preventing* hostile fleets from accomplishing such mis-

sions as sea control and the projection of power ashore. Their naval strategy is today aimed not at asserting their use of the sea, but in denying its use to us. While geography has dictated this strategy, it has also influenced the character of the Soviet Navy. In design and capability their ships, submarines, and aircraft are—appropriate to their mission—reactive to our Navy. To combat our carriers and surface ships, they have emphasized maximum firepower, largely through missiles, in ship and submarine design. Their submarines, ships, and naval aircraft are well equipped with tactical missiles designed to destroy surface targets. A variety of the features evident in these missile systems clearly indicates that our Navy is the projected target.

Aircraft Carriers. Stalin initially, and Khrushchev later, postponed building the aircraft carriers needed for organic fleet air cover. This was a momentous strategic decision in the great-power rivalry between the Soviet Union and the United States, inasmuch as it relegated the Soviet Navy to a position of long-term "blue water" inferiority vis-a-vis the U.S. Navy in terms of distant sea control and projection of power onto the land.

Although Western intelligence has confirmed that the Soviets are building two medium-sized aircraft carriers in the Black Sea on which vertical- or short-takeoff-and-landing (VTOL/STOL) aircraft will be embarked, our lead in aircraft carriers is immense, both in the short and long terms. Launch and recovery operations and the proper maintenance of aircraft at sea are no simple matters. Our Navy has had over 50 years of experience in operating carriers, and our level of operational efficiency cannot be attained in the short term. The VTOL/STOL aircraft to be embarked on the Soviet aircraft carrier will of necessity be of short range, will be restricted to small ordnance and fuel loads, and will therefore be mission-limited.

Projection Capabilities. The essentially defensive strategy growing from the geographic constraints has also forestalled the Soviet development of capabilities to project power from sea to

shore. Again, since they have no carriers, they cannot provide air cover to fleets operating distantly from their shores in wartime. They have not developed a long-range capability of any significance for an at-sea replenishment, for assertive sea control, for amphibious assault ships, nor have they developed technologies and expertise required to project power ashore. Neither do they possess substantial and well trained forces in amphibious operations. The U.S. Marines have no real counterpart in the Soviet Union since Soviet naval infantry is neither so large, well trained, nor experienced as our Marines in amphibious operations. Even given a scenario of Soviet success in a war at sea, they would still lack the amphibious assault capability and the required air cover over the amphibious objective area to invade the Western Hemisphere from the sea.

Underway Replenishment (UNREP). The Soviet Navy lacks ships and experience in open-ocean and distant-shore replenishment-at-sea operations, although they may be closing this gap. Their ships now routinely operate in the Mediterranean, the Indian Ocean, the "Hump of Africa" area near Guinea, and, to a lesser degree, in the Caribbean. They are also building some modern replenishment ships, such as the *Chilikin* class which permit the more efficient alongside refueling at sea,[12] as opposed to the standard Soviet bow-stern refueling method. They have yet to construct multicommodity replenishment ships which can provide simultaneous replenishment at sea of fuel, food, ordnance, and other supplies and material, using alongside and vertical UNREP methods.

Forward Bases. The Soviets do not possess a forward base structure, at least not one which could support any significant overseas force deployment. Our forward base structure is again a concomitant of the long-term endurance and effectiveness of our seapower. In part a residue of the imperialistic era, it is one that has nevertheless bequeathed us a system of forward bases in modern times. Since geographic constraints and their ramifications have dictated a historically weak Soviet Navy, the Russians heretofore have not had the means and needs to acquire and retain forward bases to support distant-water deployments of naval forces, a circumstance which Gorshkov in his series lamented.

However, it appears that as Soviet naval power continues to develop, there is an inclination to acquire a forward base structure. Their naval forces have been expelled from Yugoslavia, Albania, China, Indonesia, and Egypt since World War II, yet they have acquired footholds in Cuba, Guinea, Syria, and Somalia. They may, in time, regain naval base rights in Egypt and obtain base privileges in Algeria or even Malta. In the Pacific and Indian Oceans, they could eventually obtain base rights in India, Singapore, and Yemen or on the Island of Socotra or even in North Vietnam. But until such further expansion into an overseas base system occurs, the U.S. Navy retains a significant edge in forward deployment and support capabilities.

Antisubmarine Warfare (ASW). While the U.S. Navy surpasses the Soviets in ASW, the fact may not be as significant as it first appears. Nevertheless, it is an area in which the Soviets cannot overtake us in the short term, regardless of the level of resources applied. They have no effective means for detecting and destroying, for example, our strategic missile submarines nor do they seem to entertain any hope that such means may be forthcoming via technological breakthrough. Their ASW inferiority is a circumstance which the Soviets both understand and acknowledge, as the statements of the recent Gorshkov series of articles attest.

At the same time, our *need* for a better ASW capability than the Soviets is critical. While the carrier platform is crucial to our strategy, the submarine—which in its attack and mining roles is an interdiction and sea-denial weapon—is essential to theirs. [In the type of war postulated in this paper, they must interrupt our river of merchantmen which will pour materiel into Europe.] The Germans had this same requirement for victory, failed to achieve it, and lost both World Wars. Their submarine force must also prevent us from exercising our capabilities for assertive sea control and for the projection of power ashore.

Their submarine force is large, with a backbone of modern, nuclear boats which, aggregatively, have significant antiship missile, torpedo, and mine capabilities. If we cannot contain and defeat this submarine force, then our strategy is for naught. In addition to carriers, ASW is an area in which we must maintain both a clear and sufficient advantage over the Soviets.

In particular, the Soviet submarine force may be able, despite our best efforts, to prevent our rapid reinforcement of NATO in a nonnuclear war in Europe. For example, assuming a predeployment scenario for their submarine force in response to rising tensions or prior plans, their submarines could have a dominant advantage over our convoy defenses during the first weeks of war. Their minelaying capabilities, if exercised, would pose further problems. Even a small number of their nuclear submarines might be able to destroy a significant proportion of our oil and modern dry cargo ships. The magnitude of such potential losses is dramatized in consideration that a single supertanker can now carry as much oil as some entire convoys of World War II. While Soviet submarines would have to return to port and suffer consequent attrition en route, and while using our advantages in naval geography and ASW we would hope to eventually prevail over their submarines, high initial losses to Soviet submarines could prevent the rapid reinforcement on which our NATO defense strategy depends. [13]

Conclusions. This commentary has two conclusions. First, the major objective of our naval defense strategy must be to ensure that we maintain at least parity with the Soviets—within the combined parameters of the "Size of Navy" and "Quality of Navy" in the naval power equation. Again, we cannot simply count numbers of ships alone, but must, as Gorshkov indicated, turn to some form of systems analysis to weigh the relative capabilities of navies. If we maintain—in numbers and quality of ships, submarines, and planes appropriate to our missions—parity within the naval power equation, then Soviet psychological and geographic constraints will ensure that our superiority in naval power remains secure. This realization has been insufficiently articulated and understood within the U.S. Navy and at higher levels of government. The naval power equation may yield the naval budgetary key to the heretofore unanswerable question: "How much is enough?" As responsible military managers and naval officers, the ramifications to our Navy of the naval power equation merit careful consideration.

Second, we should attempt to engage in naval arms limitation talks with the Soviets. We should continue this attempt as long as we can negotiate from superior strength within the naval power equation and as long as we perceive what is essential in the strategies and force structures of the two navies. It is then to our advantage, as in chess, to "trade down." Casting out naval strength in equal proportions—predicated upon the combined "Size of Navy" and "Quality of Navy" of the Soviet and United States naval power equations—*increases* our relative margin of superiority in naval power. To possess such superiority but to be unwilling to engage in such talks disserves our defense budget, national economy, and the American people. Such a policy ignores enormous opportunity costs—

BIOGRAPHIC SUMMARY

Comdr. Clyde Smith, U.S. Navy, holds undergraduate degrees from both Oklahoma State University and the University of Maryland, a master's degree from Oklahoma State University, and is a graduate of the Armed Forces Staff College and the Russian Language School. As an intelligence officer he has served in West Berlin, on the staffs of Commander 7th Fleet and Commander Cruiser-Destroyer Group 8, and has had three separate tours in Vietnam—Naval Intelligence Adviser in the Naval Advisory Group (1964-65), Staff Intelligence Officer to Commander River Assault Flotilla I (1966-67), and Chief of Operational Intelligence to Commander Naval Forces Vietnam (1970-71). Commander Smith is a recent graduate of the College of Naval Warfare and is completing a second master's degree at the University of Rhode Island in marine affairs.

---

the alternative uses to which those unnecessarily expended resources could have been productively put.

Admiral Gorshkov clearly believes that naval arms limitations talks are not to his navy's advantage. While inferen-tial, this may be a further indication that such talks could redound to our national benefit. In view of the tradi-tional Soviet landpower mentality, it seems conceivable that Soviet leaders might accept such talks over the objec-tions of Gorshkov. Army-navy inter-service rivalries in the Soviet Union are severe, and a United States proposal for such talks might greatly appeal to the army-dominated Soviet Military Estab-lishment.

NOTES

1. My principal concern in this paper is with physical geography and with ways in which the Soviets have responded to that physical environment. To a geographer certain causal relationships which I have postulated between this physical geography and Soviet perceptions on the utility of the World Ocean may seem overly simplified, although I felt simplification necessary in order to keep this commentary within reasonable confines.

2. Admiral Gorshkov, in the lead article in his series "Navies in War and Peace" (*Morshkoy Sbornik*, No. 2, 1972), p. 20, states:

The qualitative transformations which have taken place in naval forces have also changed the approach to evaluating the relative might of navies and their combat groupings: we have had to cease comparing the number of warships of one type or another and their total displacement (or the number of guns in a salvo or the weight of this salvo), and turn to a more complex, but also more correct appraisal of the striking and defensive power of ships, based on a mathematical analysis of their capabilities and qualitative characteristics.

Admiral Zumwalt has stated in the U.S. *Congressional Record*, vol. CXVIII, No. 94, p. S9187:

... a direct comparison of the two fleets, unless heavily footnoted, cannot mean very much. Nor is a direct comparison of platforms very useful. With very few exceptions, U.S. ships are not designed to fight Soviet ships of similar classes. Therefore, it is of little value to contrast ... characteristics. ... What is important is how well the platform, or the fleet, can carry out its assigned tasks.

3. For example, in Marshal V.D. Sokolovsky's (ed.) *Military Strategy* (Moscow: Soviet Ministry of Defense, 1968) all of the authors and reviewers of this official Soviet view of military strategy were marshals, generals, or colonels. The Soviet Navy was apparently not permitted any substantial contribution to this Soviet statement of strategy. While the 1968 edition of *Military Strategy* was the third edition of this work, this same circumstance appertained in the first two editions also.

4. Admiral Gorshkov has been Commander in Chief of the Soviet Navy since 1956, is the father of the modern Soviet Navy, and is, by this achievement alone, the greatest naval officer Russia has yet produced. In 1972 and early 1973, he published in the Soviet Naval Digest (*Morskoy Sbornik*), a series of 11 articles containing about 50,000 words. While individual articles had individual titles, the series itself was entitled "Navies in War and Peace" and is the most comprehensive and authoritative pronouncement on seapower ever to come out of the Soviet Union. This series is being published and examined piecemeal throughout 1974 by the *United States Naval Institute Proceedings*.

My article, entitled "The Meaning and Significance of the Gorshkov Articles," presents an analysis of this series as a whole in the March-April 1974 issue of the *Naval War College Review*, pp. 18-37.

5. The Soviets call this force a "squadron" (eskadra), while it is U.S. Navy policy to refer to it as a "fleet" in official writings. This force has in fact assumed the proportions of a fleet in size and composition. It draws its ships from the Black Sea and Northern Fleets primarily, to which they return after completing their "Med cruise."

6. "Naval infantry (morskaya pehota) are Soviet marines.

7. The Soviets are, however, now building at least two aircraft carriers in the Black Sea of the *Kuril* class. These are small carriers and will not have the capabilities of our modern attack carriers.

8. As early as 1968, as Robert Herrick noted in *Soviet Naval Strategy* (Annapolis: United States Naval Institute, 1968), p. 111, the Soviet Union believed that the United States had a system of long-range underwater sound detection for making initial detection and tracking of submarines. The Soviets have no long-range or sophisticated capability against our strategic missile submarines or modern nuclear attack boats. Even Gorshkov, in his series in *Morskoy Sbornik* admits this, albeit indirectly. The U.S. Navy possesses a clear edge in active and passive sonar technology and in general ASW expertise over the Soviets.

9. As quoted by David Fairhall, *Russian Sea Power* (Boston: Gambit Inc., 1971), pp. 46-7, Robert McNamara described in 1969 our general war at sea strategy and the way in which we would try to preserve our merchant marine:

... our war at sea strategy is based essentially on the rapid emplacement of ASW forces, comprised of submarines and land and sea based ASW aircraft, between the enemy submarines and their potential targets. Recent studies have reaffirmed the potential effectiveness of this concept and the probability that in an all-out war at sea we would be able to destroy a very large proportion of the Soviet submarine force in a matter of a few months while losing only a relatively small part of the free world merchant fleet.

10. Herrick, pp. 143-57. When Herrick's book first appeared, statements therein similar to this caused consternation in U.S. Navy circles. For if this were true (and it was and is), it affected U.S. Navy budget requirements, our conceptions of what a proper strategy to counter the Soviet Navy should be, and our force structure to implement this strategy. We have an honest but inaccurate bias to see the Soviet Navy through our eyes instead of theirs. We tend to view their navy as one, like ours, designed to exercise assertive sea control in "blue water" areas or near foreign shores and to project power ashore. However, the structure of the Soviet Navy, their lack of organic at sea air cover, and the constraints which naval geography imposes on them do not reflect this philosophy.

11. Admiral Zumwalt has candidly noted this in the U.S. *Congressional Record*, vol. CXVIII, No. 94, p. S9187: "The Soviet Navy . . . as a Navy in support of a nation whose vital interests are those of a landpower, is designed largely to prevent the U.S. Navy from carrying out its missions."

12. The alongside method which the U.S. Navy uses is more efficient primarily because it is faster, which limits the period of vulnerability of the replenishment formation to submarines or air attack. The alongside method also requires special refueling rigs and expertise.

13. For a perceptive analysis of this problem, see Frank B. Case, "Time to Secure the Seas," *United States Naval Institute Proceedings*, August 1973, pp. 25-31.

Power is an elusive quantity, incapable of being quantified in purely numerical terms. Rather, it is a derivative of the perceptions of power. For this reason, trends relating to the waxing or waning of strength and determination and how they are perceived by oneself, friends, and enemies are crucially important. Professor Ra'anan takes issue with the minimalists who view the increase of Soviet naval power as motivated primarily by Soviet defensive considerations. Instead, he argues strongly that the Soviet Union, recognizing the limitations nuclear weapons have imposed upon direct conflict with the West, now seeks unilateral gains in the Third World by the use of surrogates. The Cuban involvement in Angola is only the most recent example.

THE SOVIET VIEW
OF NAVIES IN PEACETIME

based on a lecture

by

Professor Uri Ra'anan

It may be helpful to start by attempting to place this topic within its proper parameters: that is, to focus upon the issue of perceptions, as viewed by theoreticians and policymakers alike within the Soviet Union and, hopefully, if one can educate Western analysts, outside the U.S.S.R. as well. The reason for this emphasis is that the concept of perceptions relates to the crux of the great "game" of international competition and conflict.

I had the honor, some 4½ years ago, to be asked by the Senate Subcommittee on National Security and International Operations (of the Committee on Government Operations) to prepare an evaluation of the power balance between the United States and the Soviet Union. That particular task raised in my mind some conceptual and methodological questions, in response to which I developed a theory or, if you prefer, an equation. Although published by the Senate some 4 years ago, my conclusions appear to have been "rediscovered" recently.

My main point was that the leadership of the Soviet Union, as evidenced by the extensive defense and political literature printed in that country, has identified power, quite correctly, as a derivative of *perceptions* of power. This means that there are no "concrete," objective factors that, without further refinement and qualification, can be equated, as such, with "power"—i.e., no purely numerical, quantifiable elements. Rather, the power of an "actor" on the international scene (usually a state) —that is to say, its ability to influence others and also its own evaluation of what it may be capable of doing to influence others—is a function both of its perception and of its adversary's perception of what either is able and willing to do. That perception may or may not be related directly to the objective, numerical power factors that can be measured and quantified.

Who are the "customers" to whom a perception of power has to be conveyed in order to achieve the degree of influence required by any regime? They include several segments of that regime's own population: the leadership itself— the elite (whether it be the decision-making bureaucracy or the broader elite within which the decisionmakers operate), and the masses who participate in the political process actively or passively, depending on the nature of the society. All of these elements have to be convinced of the power of their own state in order that the regime may be able to perform with credibility during an encounter in the arena of international conflict. Similarly, on the adversary's side, the decisionmakers themselves, the broader elite, and the masses all have to be persuaded that their state really is not capable of standing up to the image of strength that, hopefully with success, the other regime has attempted to project. Finally, but by no means unimportantly, other recipients of this impression of power should be one's own allies, as well as the clients of the adversary, in addition to the usually large number of so-called third parties—

neutrals and "unaligned," i.e., those who can be tempted with the mirage of a "bandwagon" on which it is worth jumping while there still is time.

It is necessary to dazzle all of these "customers" with a certain perception of strength if one is to attain credibility in confrontation situations. Absolute strength in purely objective terms is not very effective unless one can success-fully project—to those in one's own ranks, as well as to the other side—the image of being strong. For example, if really I am weak, but I believe that I am strong, and the other side feels that I am strong, why, then, I *am* powerful! My intrinsic weakness becomes irrelevant, until and unless it is put to the test of actual warfare.

An example of this proposition may be found in the history of Mussolini's Italy during the 1920's and 1930's. The whole world was impressed by the strength and daring projected by this new Fascıst state. The term "the eight million bayonets of Italy" was propa-gated throughout the international arena as a major factor to be borne in mind. This general perception of might successfully propelled Mussolini's state into the upper echelons of European powers—until he made the fatal mistake of actually resorting to his military forces and putting them to the test in invading Ethiopia! Then observers began to realize that, while Mussolini might possess eight million bayonets, he cer-tainly did not have an operational army of eight million soldiers! Until then, Italy had been a major power to be reckoned with on the European and, indeed, on the global scene.

Now, what are the elements that constitute the power equation? What is it that creates the perception of power? First and foremost, there are what may be called the "available" physical in-puts: strategic forces, general purpose forces, and the geographic propinquity of a state to the primary arenas of confrontation. Rightly or wrongly, the will and determination of a country to employ the means at its disposal in the pursuit of its perceived interests tends to be measured in proportion to the propinquity of that state to the arena where the main conflict is taking place. There is no question but that, quite apart from other aspects, which re-dounded to the advantage of the United States, it was the fact that Cuba is 90 miles away from Miami, whereas the Soviet Union is remote, which made a major difference to the outcome of the Cuban missile crisis. It was perceived correctly that the U.S.S.R. was unlikely to place the same degree of national effort and determination as the United States behind a move in this relatively faraway area.

The second element in the equation consists of so-called potential physical inputs: e.g., mobilizable manpower, technological and economic potential. These factors are not immediately available to be brought to bear upon a conflict in any specific area, but they are mobilizable and they must be borne in mind if there is any likelihood of a protracted conflict.

However, both of these fairly con-crete and quantifiable elements perhaps are less important than the third, which is of a subjective, less tangible nature. I refer to it as the psychological input. This element is made up of several ingredients that are difficult to measure. However, its essence is the will and determination of a regime as *demon-strated*, i.e., not expressed in words, but shown in action; it may be defined as the will and determination of a leader-ship visibly to apply its available and its potential physical inputs in the pursuit of a given political goal. There are many elements that comprise the psycho-logical input: a "forward" (or offensive) societal posture and a willingness to pay a relatively high price for "victory," i.e., for prevailing in a confrontation, per-haps are the most significant.

These three elements in the power equation cumulatively make up an aggregate that may be equated generally with the perception of power—but not quite, because this aggregate is projected upon a screen (the minds, the views, of all the parties concerned) through a lens or a prism, so to speak. That lens is constituted of certain, so-called dy-namic factors.

What are they? One such factor is the willingness of one party in an adversary relationship to seize and maintain the political and military initiative, to take and keep taking the first steps. Such willingness is of tremendous importance in a thermonuclear age, because it places the ball squarely in the adversary's court. What is *he* going to do about this development? Is he going to react at all? And, if he reacts, to what type of means is he willing to resort? This question frequently produces agonizing dilem-mas. In this context, the Cuban missile crisis is highly relevant. The Soviet Union took the first step. It held the initiative. It left the agonizing decisions, for a protracted period, in the court of the United States. (Of course, subse-quently, America, with the imposition of the blockade, wrested the initiative from the Soviet Union.) From Lenin's day onward, this particular penchant for seizing and maintaining the initiative has been a hallmark of Soviet policymakers.

A second dynamic factor that helps to magnify or to diminish the image or perception of power is the visible fixity of purpose with which a regime pursues its aims. It is not sufficient to display will, to resort to the various physical means at one's disposal, in the pursuit of a political aim, and to seize the initiative. An equally important factor is one's staying power: the ability, once embarked upon a course of action, to see it through to the bitter end and not to flinch, regardless of apparently dis-couraging cost-benefit analyses.

The final dynamic factor relates to the important concept of "trend." In evaluating a power image, it is not enough to snap a "still photo" and to say, "This is where we are at the moment, and this is where the adversary is right now." Much more important is the question, "Where was I yesterday in comparison to where I am today? And where was the adversary yesterday in comparison to where he is today?"

All of you know this factor ex-tremely well from the arena of sports. When the score in a baseball game or in a hockey game is 3-3, it can have quite different connotations. It could mean a tie between two roughly equal teams, but it may mean something entirely different. A team has momentum if it was 3 to 1 behind, 2 minutes ago, and now has tied the score at 3-3. It is moving forward and its hopes and ex-pectations are rising. The team that has lost the lead is declining and, probably, demoralized. Therefore, 3-3 as a "still photo" does not present the correct picture of what is going on. What one has to take into consideration is: Where were both of these teams during the previous stage? Which is waxing, and which is waning in power? In other words, the human mind tends to project forward into the immediate future (or point C) the trends that have been established by connecting point A, the immediate past, with point B, the present. In our context too, it is not the "still photo" but the "movie," the cinematographic approach, which is of great significance.

It is only when one takes all of these elements into consideration, the three primary ingredients, or inputs—available physical power, potential physical power, and psychological inputs, plus the dynamic factors that I have mentioned—initiative, fixity of purpose, or staying power, and "trend," that one arrives at the final picture which is projected onto the screen or onto the retina, or the mind, of one's *own* people, one's *own* allies, the adversary, the adversary's clients, and, last of all, third parties.

This is a very complex, a very difficult, but a very *real* way of translating the realities of politics, of policymaking and of decisionmaking, into some kind of definite order—a product that determines how the various parties will line up. It helps to decide whether there is confidence on one's own side and lack of confidence or even despair on the other side, and whether there is a bandwagon effect which causes previously uncommitted parties to say to themselves: "I have now discovered to whom the future belongs, and I am going to jump on the bandwagon at the earliest possible moment, before it's too late—before everyone else has already jumped on and I am one of the last to do so, with all the penalties that accompany such poor timing."

A look at Soviet defense and politico-strategic literature will demonstrate that all of these concepts very clearly are present in the minds of Soviet analysts and decisionmakers. Although this literature no doubt owes a great deal to Lenin and to Leninist semantics, the concepts I have described are, of course, much older in origin than Lenin or communism or the Communist Party. These elements may be found in all of classical literature that relates to

power, from the period of the Renaissance and of Machiavelli onward, through Clausewitz, to the recent past.

This is a picture that we disregard at our own peril and at the expense of our own clarity of mind and our lucidity in approaching the decisionmaking process.

It is *because* of these factors that I tend to have reservations about the interpretations of several friends and colleagues concerning the precise meaning of the political concepts that have been advanced by Gorshkov and others, including Kasatonov and, more recently, even Grechko himself.

In analyzing the political objectives and attainments of the "peacetime uses" of power, and particularly of naval power as described in Soviet publications, there is a tendency here, in Britain, and in Canada, to support what I would call the "minimalist" school of interpretation. Many fine and very knowledgeable Western scholars may be mistaken in saying that the Soviet escalation of terminology (to be discussed anon) which has taken place in tandem with the expanding deployment of Soviet naval power during the last decade is merely, if you like, an afterthought. In their view, the main motivation for the buildup of Soviet naval power essentially has been reactive or defensive; they feel that it was done primarily for purposes of protecting the Soviet Union itself, but that the development of technology carried it to areas further and further away from the immediate coastal waters of the U.S.S.R. They add that, in order to justify and to support the significant proportion of resources devoted to this task, the naval advocates, and particularly Gorshkov himself, tried to explain to the party leadership that there were byproducts to this buildup of immediate political and psychological utility. Consequently, massive naval expansion could be defended on other than purely military and technological grounds and, so these Western analysts hypothesize, probably there was a "debate" in which Gorshkov was on the defensive and within the parameters of which he had to justify (and perhaps even to plead for) a special allocation of resources and that this political argument proved to be very useful to him.

I do not mean to infer that there is nothing whatsoever to this particular version of history. There are some aspects of this view, which are founded fairly accurately, I believe, on content analysis of the kind of "debates" that apparently took place in the Soviet Union some years ago. However, I believe that the Soviet escalation of terminology and, of course, of deployment is to be viewed in a far more offensive and far less minimalistic context than is recognized by those of my colleagues who have argued otherwise.

How, precisely, does the escalation of terminology manifest itself? The original slogan accompanying Soviet naval development was "Defense of the Motherland,"—a predominantly defensive concept. However, this phrase started changing a long time ago, with the first incursion of the Soviet Navy into areas outside the waters immediately adjacent to the Soviet Union (the Black Sea, the Baltic shore) to far-off stations, particularly the eastern Mediterranean, eventually reaching the Indian Ocean among other areas. The slogan was altered then from "Defense of the Motherland" to "Defense of State Interests."

Many Western analysts have attempted to define what was meant by "Defense of State Interests." The minimalistic school has tended to believe that it was not much more than a description of the heavy maritime development that was and still is taking place: the vast expansion of the Soviet merchant fleet, particularly trawlers. This development has occurred under conditions of increasing pressure on resources, causing the Soviet leadership to try and supplement land resources with those taken from the sea. Therefore, said the Western minimalists, "Defense of State Interests" meant no more but that the Soviet Navy had acquired a second mission, in addition to "Defense of the Motherland," i.e., simply the protection of the new Soviet maritime development.

If the Soviet naval slogan really had remained this way, one might have been inclined to say, "Well, maybe there's something to it." However, it escalated very quickly beyond "Defense of State Interests" as early as 1967, long before the famous Gorshkov series was published. The new phrasing read "The Strengthening of the Prestige and Authority" of the Soviet Union. (Even more overt langauage has been used, such as:

> to vividly demonstrate the economic and military power of a country beyond its border . . . to show readiness for decisive actions, to deter or suppress the intentions of potential enemies, as well as to support friendly states. . . . to surprise probable enemies with the perfection of the equipment being exhibited, to affect their morale, to intimidate them right up to the outbreak of war, and to suggest to them in advance the hopelessness of fighting. . . . [this] in many cases has permitted the achievement of political goals without resorting to military operations by only threatening to initiate them. *Morskoy Sbornik*, No. 12, 1972, "Navies in War and Peace," Adm. S.G. Gorshkov.)

The utilization of these particular words, both in the context of speeches and slogans used on Red Navy Day each July and in the Gorshkov series itself, obviously implies much more than the earlier phraseology. It refers—as I see it, at any rate—to the whole concept of projecting power and the perception of power, into the no-man's land between the United States and the U.S.S.R., primarily, of course, what we call the "Third World," and particularly the areas upon which the Soviet Union clearly has focused most: the Middle East, the Red Sea, the approaches to the Indian Ocean.

In the context in which the new slogan has been used and in view of the somewhat envious words with which Admiral Gorshkov has described the behavior patterns of non-Soviet navies—"imperialist navies" in the past and present—*very evidently* it implies Soviet willingness to maintain a "presence," to take risks, and to present a credible picture of preparedness to clash with Western interests. At the least, it may intimate that Moscow might take steps to isolate areas in which Soviet clients, heavily armed and trained by the U.S.S.R. itself, could win at least limited military victories

against friends and allies of the United States. It also implies that the Soviet Navy, by its very presence, could deter any U.S. counterintervention, or undertake a "picket-fence" operation, interposing itself.

In practice, the Soviet Navy actually has gone one step further. Starting as early as 1970-1971, and continuing through 1973, Soviet naval practice reached its visible apex with the Cuban expedition to Angola. The Soviet Navy stood by as a deterrent shield while Moscow's Communist allies and friends were employed in an ancillary way to aid Russia's overseas client states win local victories, with the United States discouraged from taking counteraction. Soviet literature charmingly calls all of this "preventing the export of counter-revolution."

Incidentally, in almost all of these cases, the Communist allies and friends used as surrogates of the Soviet Union were not members of the Warsaw Pact, but rather North Vietnamese, North Koreans, and Cubans.

This is what, I believe, Gorshkov and others have in mind when they speak of "The Strengthening of the Influence and Authority" of the U.S.S.R. That is to say, within the parameters of a global thermonuclear stalemate which prohibits major advances by either side in the Northern Hemisphere (the Central NATO sector and, perhaps, the Pacific area around Japan), the Soviet Union can score *unilateral gains* in the Southern Hemisphere, i.e., generally the area from the Mediterranean on southward. In view both of the domestic constraints that impinge upon the possibility of U.S. action and the visible Soviet naval "presence" that intensifies the reluctance of Congress and portions of the bureaucracy to become engaged within that area, the Soviet Union can give its overseas clients surrogate victories, through the good offices of Cubans, North Koreans, and North Vietnamese. The Soviet Union can turn to the United States and say baldfacedly, "Well, look, the Warsaw Pact is not involved—or, at least, only logistically. Therefore, if you react and intervene, you will force us to resort to our strategic power against you!"

Here, one might argue, "Well, this is all very good; however, is the Soviet

Navy really in a position operationally to implement such a task?" I would say that, at this stage, the question is hypothetical, because the Soviet Navy's posture of interposition, to shield clients which are scoring unilateral gains against potential U.S. counterintervention, is based on the assumption that this stance itself will be sufficient to deter the United States from becoming involved. Therefore, operational conclusions will not be required. Consequently, the operational capabilities of the Soviet Navy, in its current state, are less relevant than the visibility of the Soviet presence and its implications in terms of power perceptions, vis-a-vis the West and vis-a-vis the Third World countries that are concerned.

The question now arises whether the picture I have painted correctly reflects the views only of a small group within the Soviet leadership, that perhaps temporarily holds the upper hand, or whether these are, in fact, the concepts that have been followed, certainly since the overthrow of Khrushchev, by what may be called the mainline of the leadership itself?

Here one can only speculate, but my own instinctive reaction is one of aversion to the whole idea of "hawks and doves," or "hardliners and softliners" in the Kremlin. My studies, which have been devoted largely to the question of factional struggles and "debates" within the Soviet leadership, do not bear out the concept of the existence of permanent "hardliners" or "softliners." Soviet decisionmaking elites, and factions within these elites, are not permanently wedded to ongoing issues. Issues serve as tactical devices whereby one faction attacks another and tries to weaken it, to deprive it of support, and hopefully, to replace it. Having done so, the victorious faction is under *no obligation whatever* to stick to the slogan or to the issue which it used as a battle flag during the period of struggle. Once one side has won, it can throw away its own banners and—so to speak—pick up the fallen banner of the enemy. This has happened time and again in Soviet history. Stalin fought Trotsky over the question of the quick industrialization of the Soviet Union. Stalin objected. Trotsky lost. He was exiled. Almost immediately Stalin adopted the first 5-year plan, which really had been the Trotsky platform in the period of the struggle. Again, as between Malenkov and Khrushchev, Malenkov was the supporter of consumer goods against heavy industry. Khrushchev fought Malenkov tooth and nail, and finally defeated and humiliated him. No sooner had this occurred, than Khrushchev adopted the Malenkov platform!

It is very misleading, therefore, to view Soviet leaders in terms of permanent allegiances to permanent issues. It is true that, lower down, in what I would call the middle-level or technical echelons, there are specific job interests which carry with them certain commitments, particularly in regard to the allocation of resources. However, the whole point about the decisionmaking elite, the top leadership, is that it is *not* made up of technical experts, but rather prides itself on consisting of generalists; therefore, it feels that it is "above the limitations" of job-vested interests. Or, as the old Chinese slogan has it: Red, rather than Expert! At that upper level of the top 20 or 25 leaders who really make the decisions, there is an extraordinary "flexibility" or, of you like, lack of consistency or lack of principle, where issues are concerned!

I see no sign whatever, therefore, that one can speak of Soviet "hardliners" and "softliners." On the contrary, if anything, the faction that has been described, mostly by Western commentators and columnists, as being the "Stalinist hardliners"—persons like Suslov, Ponomarev, and others—is cautious and conservative, being the group within the Soviet leadership whose primary task is fostering the relationship between the Soviet Communist Party and Communist Parties abroad. This so-called "dogmatist, hardline" faction is precisely the group that is *least* interested in military adventures abroad. Its outlook, as was the case with Stalin himself, is essentially cautious and patient. That is to say, like the Vatican, it sees itself as operating *sub specie aeternitatis*—under the view of eternity: "We have lots of time. What's your hurry? Why take risks? Why not rather build up the local Communist Parties to the point where they will eventually take over power without the need for

adventures and the grave dangers attending them?"

Thus, if anything, these so-called "Stalinist hardliners" are less likely to support provocative deployment than are the so-called "moderates" or, as I would call them, the Khrushchevian group—Khrushchev's successors—and particularly Brezhnev himself (who is deeply wedded, as was Khrushchev himself, to trying to prove a point: namely, that it is possible to score unilateral gains, even in a thermonuclear age).

If there is a theme to which Soviet defense literature comes back again and again, it is precisely that the limitations of the thermonuclear era are not such as to bring the dialectic itself to an end (meaning that these limitations do not require terminating international conflict between main adversaries). That conflict merely has to be fought out in slightly different ways and in slightly different arenas; in other words, preferably in the Third World rather than in Europe, and, if possible, by paramilitary means, including Soviet logistical aid and the utilization of Communist friends, like the Cubans, the North Vietnamese, and the North Koreans, rather than by direct and overt use of Soviet troops. It should be pointed out, however, that the Soviet Union by no means has eschewed even the utilization of Soviet personnel itself. Two examples will suffice. In 1970, the Soviet Union sent into Egypt combat personnel, during the "War of Attrition," in the form both of MiG-21's piloted by Soviet flyers and Soviet crews for the anti-air missile system. In fact, these Soviet pilots engaged in combat with the Israelis over the Suez Canal, and five of the Soviet-flown MiG's were shot down. Again, in 1973, although it has never been publicized, Soviet operational personnel *did* participate on the Syrian front, at least in small numbers, and some were killed.

However, certainly there are other and better means available to Moscow than directly involving Soviet personnel. One of these is the utilization of surrogate forces, which has worked extremely well so far, sometimes the same elements being employed successively in different areas. Thus, a Cuban armored unit that was dispatched to Angola had previously been present in Syria, at least since the end of October 1973. Some

Cubans still are in Syria. Surrogate forces, therefore, have been used in the Middle East as well as in Africa.

Consequently, I believe that it's a basic mistake to look upon the decisionmaking process in the Soviet Union as a struggle between alleged supporters of "détente," like Mr. Brezhnev, and some unnamed military "hawks" who supposedly are trying to push the number one leader in a different direction.

I have seen no evidence whatever—and I have gone through the literature fairly extensively—of the existence of any major forces in the Soviet leadership that question the implementation by Mr. Brezhnev of what has become known as the "détente policy." Why should they? The Soviet Union has done extremely well as a result of this line. There is no sign that anyone seriously is challenging this policy. Certainly no one in Moscow is questioning the semi-adventurous, paramilitary byproduct of "détente" that I have mentioned, with the possible exception of the so-called "die-hard Stalinists," who feel a little uneasy. *They* would much rather see the Italian Communist Party being invited to share power in a general atmosphere of good-will, and avoid awakening and alerting the sleeping tiger of public opinion in Western societies to the possible dangers of what the Soviet Union is doing now.

Finally, let me say that before, during, and since the 25th Party Congress, I have not seen any real sign that the leadership of the party has abandoned its aversion to "Bonapartism," that is to say, its aversion to allowing military personnel to make major political decisions. It is true that Grechko has been allowed membership in the hallowed ranks of the Politburo. It may surprise you to learn, however, that that body is only theoretically a decisionmaking organ. Reportedly, it meets in plenary session no more than once a week. Very rarely can it boast of full attendance. There are several members and candidate members who stay in the provinces and hardly ever come to the Moscow meeting at all. The only really meaningful sessions it has are in subcommittees, where three, four, or, at the most, five of the directly affected leaders participate (although, sometimes, they bring in, prior to reaching their decisions, so-called star witnesses—i.e., experts, both from the armed services and the so-called Institutes—who present information and suggestions, usually concerning non-Communist governments, and then are thanked for their testimony and sent outside). At that point, three or four generalists will make final, although rather broadly phrased, decisions. To the best of my knowledge, Mr. Grechko rarely, if at all, is to be found among the inner group that makes these decisions. His entry into the Politburo, I believe, may mean no more than, if you like, a further watchdog function by the Party over the military, rather than the other way around. Nor is it at all certain that he would be succeeded in the Politburo by another military professional. The military services are firmly controlled by the Main Political Administration and also by the Administrative Organs departments of the Secretariat, which make very sure that they have the last say over personnel and appointments—questions that matter more than "mere" issues, as I have explained already. In this way the party leadership can keep out officers who may develop worrisome signs of independence. Thus, the concept of a so-called military-industrial complex in the Soviet Union, to my mind, remains unproven. It is a Western hypothesis, based on Western terminology, with very little to bear it out in Soviet documentation. My plea to you is *not* to view the U.S.S.R. as a mere "mirror image" of currently fashionable perceptions of our own society.

ψ

BIOGRAPHIC SUMMARY

Professor Uri Ra'anan is Professor of International Politics and Chairman of the International Security Studies Program at the Fletcher School of Law and Diplomacy. He is a member of the editorial board of *Orbis*. Concurrently he is an affiliate of the Center for International Studies at MIT and an associate of the Russian Research Center at Harvard. He has previously taught political science and government at MIT, at Columbia, and at City University, New York. He was educated at Oxford University, and he is the author of works on Soviet foreign policy, on Soviet military aid to the Third World, on Soviet policy in the Middle East, on the diplomatic history of the Middle East, on Chinese factional struggles, and on the politics of the *coup d'etat*.

Recent discussions of the roles and missions of the Soviet Navy have been marked by wide differences of opinion. Briefly, one of the two main schools of thought maintains that the Soviet Navy has been built as a reaction to Western naval dominance and as a reaction to the deployment of strategic weapons in submarines. The other school of thought ascribes the more traditional Mahanian concepts to the Soviet Navy. Lieutenant Commander Hynes avoids the extremes of both schools in his discussion of the capabilities and possible missions of the Kiev, *the new Soviet "ASW cruiser," which has a capability of embarking fixed wing V/STOL aircraft as well as helicopters. The political tasks* Kiev *could perform may well prove to be more important than her operational capabilities.*

THE ROLE OF THE KIEV

IN SOVIET NAVAL OPERATIONS

by

Lieutenant Commander William R. Hynes, U.S. Navy

The report in 1971 of a Soviet "aircraft carrier" under construction at Nikolayev was not totally unexpected, despite Soviet rhetoric condemning Western carriers as highly vulnerable, expensive platforms. Stalin recognized the value of aircraft carriers and apparently had approved construction of an unspecified number, although none were built. Khrushchev had been instrumental in the development of the naval air arm and the submarine force, and it was clear to the Soviets that carriers had been important to the Allies during World War II in gaining control of the sea.

The development of *Kiev* must be considered within the overall context of how the Soviets see the Western naval threat facing them. Such an approach may imply a defensive role for *Kiev*, but in the final analysis, the primary mission of the Soviet Navy is to protect the homeland from attack from the oceans. Following an extensive debate in the early 1960's, the fleet has been forward deployed as a means to counter the West's seaborne strategic weapon delivery capability. According to Michael MccGwire, the Soviet naval objective in wartime would be to limit the damage caused by sea-launched strikes and, as a deterrent measure, to deny the West the option of withholding SSBN's from the initial exchange. Specifically, maritime defense zones have been extended into the potential operating areas of the SSBN, and through active peacetime presence the Soviets seek to establish a deterrent force that could, in wartime, deny use of the strategic sea areas to the West, particularly the United States.[1]

The increasing capability of U.S. submarine-launched strategic missile systems undoubtedly caused the Soviets to reevaluate their strategic defensive posture. The Polaris A-1 system deployed in 1960 was limited in range to approximately 1,200 miles. The A-3 system that became operational in 1964 more than doubled the threat range, and the development of the Poseidon system with its MIRV warheads added a new dimension to the problem. Clearly, if the Soviets were to be able to counter this threat they needed to develop ASW platforms capable of operating at great distances from the Soviet homeland. The Soviet Navy's text for higher naval schools states that the "principal task confronting the Soviet Navy is that of combating these forces."[2]

Admiral Gorshkov has emphasized the importance of building task-specific ships, i.e., ships designed to accomplish a particular mission. Some countries, Gorshkov says, have tried to economize by building a single class of surface ship that can do everything, but have not been successful.[3] However, in December 1974 Gorshkov apparently took a different stand when he stated that

. . . the sharp increase in naval offensive and defensive capabilities is being achieved not only and not so much by an increase in the number of ships and other weapon platforms as by expanding the range of missions which each platform is able to prosecute through its more advanced weaponry. In other words, clearly it is not the quantity but the quality of the weapons platforms, i.e., the total power of the potential combat capabilities concentrated on them, which is becoming the final criterion of the scope of operations.[4]

As platform capabilities increase, there can be a corresponding increase in assigned tasks. Although there is no reference to aircraft carriers implicit in Gorshkov's remarks, his views provide a vantage point from which to observe *Kiev* and her capabilities.

Kiev's Design Characteristics. The Soviets probably decided as early as 1963 or 1964 to develop "ASW cruisers" capable of carrying large numbers of helicopters. The development of the V/STOL aircraft, especially Freehand, suggests that they may have been included in their early plans for shipborne aviation. The subsequent testing of V/STOL aircraft aboard *Moskva* offers conclusive evidence of their long-range plans.

Moskva and *Leningrad* apparently served as operational test beds for the evaluation of airborne ASW systems and tactics. When the *Moskva* program was terminated, the Soviets obviously had a follow-on ship in the planning stage; that ship was *Kiev*, the first of the *Kuril* class. The final details were probably held in abeyance pending the test and evaluation of the *Moskva* units and the development of a suitable V/STOL aircraft.[5] The Soviets have experimented with a number of V/STOL aircraft types. In addition to the Freehand, variants of the Fishbed and Flagon series and the Faithless have all demonstrated a vertical lift capability.

Kiev, at 35-40,000 tons, is the largest warship ever built in the Soviet Union. Like her predecessor *Moskva*, she is classified by the Soviets as an ASW cruiser. The greatest similarities between these two ships appear to be in the weapons and electronics systems. Both carry the SA-N-3 (Goblet) for air defense, a surface-to-underwater missile launcher, ASW rocket launchers, and 57mm guns. Additionally, *Kiev* will carry the SA-N-4 missile system for point defense.[6] The principal elec-

tronics appear to be the same. Both ships carry the Top Sail and Head Light radars.[7]

Forward, both ships give the appearance of cruiser hulls; but the similarities end there. *Kiev's* displacement is approximately twice that of *Moskva*. She has a 550-600 foot angled flight deck that extends almost two-thirds of her overall length (925 feet). *Moskva's* flight deck is only 295 feet long and is located aft of her superstructure. While both ships can easily accommodate the Hormone ASW helicopter, only *Kiev* is designed to permit operation of a significant number of V/STOL aircraft.[8]

Because of the absence of catapults and arresting gear on *Kiev*, her fixed wing aircraft operations would necessarily be limited to V/STOL type aircraft. These aircraft could be used for a variety of missions, including reconnaissance, strike, or air defense. In the absence of superior U.S. aircraft carriers, Soviet V/STOL aircraft could be employed in a limited sea control role and conceivably could conduct air strikes against shore installations or troop concentrations. However, unless and until the Soviets have achieved a major breakthrough in design technology, the payload and performance limitations inherent in V/STOL aircraft would severely limit their mission capabilities.

The evidence indicates that a follow-on to the Freehand has been developed. Since 1967, trials of what is apparently an improved version of the Freehand have been conducted at Ramenskoye airfield near Moscow. This aircraft is the same type as the one tested aboard *Moskva*.[9]

Kiev's Most Likely Missions. In "Navies in War and Peace," Admiral Gorshkov describes the primary missions of the Soviet Navy.[10]

Under today's conditions the basic mission of navies of the great powers in a world-wide nuclear war is their participation in the attacks of the country's strategic nuclear forces, the blunting of the nuclear attacks by the enemy navy from the direction of the oceans, and participation in the operations conducted by

ground forces in the continental theaters of military operations. In this instance, navies will perform a large number of complex and major missions.

Important missions in protecting the interests of the Soviet state and the countries of the Socialist community confront the Navy in peacetime too.

The primary wartime missions of the Soviet fleet, then, may be characterized as:[11]

• strategic offense—nuclear powered submarines armed with ballistic missiles;
• strategic defense—denial of the use of the sea to Western SSBN's and attack carriers;
• support of ground operations—securing the flanks of the Warsaw Pact nations against invasion from the sea (control of local seas), interdiction of enemy sea lines of communication, i.e., the disruption of enemy supply lines as a means of indirect support of the land battle, and projection of power ashore through amphibious operations.

In peacetime, the primary role of the Soviet Navy is strategic deterrence. This mission is carried out by Soviet SSBN's on patrol within striking distance of the United States and by the presence of the Soviet Fleet in strategically important areas such as the Mediterranean and the Norwegian Seas.

The protection of Soviet interests overseas is becoming an increasingly important mission. Does the Soviet Union plan to develop a capability for worldwide support of so-called wars of national liberation? The Gorshkov series, while it expresses a clear appreciation for the importance of naval power as an instrument of foreign policy, gives no clear indication as to what Soviet intentions might be with regard to a global capability.[12] Nevertheless, the Soviet naval presence off the coast of Guinea (since 1970) and more recently during the Angolan civil war provide examples of Soviet intentions toward Africa.

In the context of Admiral Gorshkov's mission statement outlined in "Navies in War and Peace" and proceeding from the premise that Soviet naval strategy is largely reactive to the strategic threat posed by the West, it is possible to postulate a number of possible missions for *Kiev*.

● **Antisubmarine Warfare**

With the deployment of U.S. SSBN's commencing in 1960, the Soviets decided to concentrate on the development of ASW ships as well as submarines. The value of sea-based ASW helicopters was recognized at that time, and with the development of the *Moskva*, the Soviets had their first "helicopter cruiser." *Moskva* and *Leningrad* were ostensibly developed as test platforms for *Kiev*. But *Kiev* is a radical departure primarily because of her size and angled flight deck. According to Adm. Thomas H. Moorer, USN (Ret.), she can carry 25 V/STOL or 36 helicopters, with a mixture of the two considered most likely.[13] *Moskva*, however, is limited to the operation of about 18 Hormone helicopters and has only a very limited V/STOL capability.

Kiev is almost certainly a follow-on to the *Moskva* class. Her capability to deploy with organic fixed-wing aircraft indicates that the Soviets are preparing to counter the long-range Poseidon C-3 and Trident missile systems with a surface ASW platform that can operate at great distances from the U.S.S.R. and, if necessary, beyond the range of shore-based air cover. Gorshkov has emphasized the fact that the range of American SLBM's more than doubled between 1964 and 1974, and he has indicated a keen awareness of the Trident threat which, he says, will again double the threat range and expand the front of operations accordingly.[14]

Another aspect of strategic ASW operations concerns the use of *Kiev* in a pro-SSBN role, i.e., to protect Soviet SSBN's from attack by Western ASW forces, principally submarines. A 1971 *Morskoi Sbornik* article by Capt. First Rank D.P. Sokha stated that the primary mission of U.S. nuclear attack submarines was "combatting other submarines and protecting their own guided missile submarines."[15] The following year Capt. First Rank N. Aleshkin wrote that Western SSN's were intended "to track and destroy nuclear powered guided missile submarines and attack submarines."[16]

Senior Soviet spokesmen evidently have not publicly addressed the broad question of the total U.S. ASW mission during wartime, although writings at the "technical level" have indicated general awareness of U.S. efforts in the field of ASW. From these sources we know that the Soviets at least recognize that the U.S. ASW capability can be targeted against their SSBN's.[17]

In his final chapter of "Navies in War and Peace," Admiral Gorshkov emphasized the importance of supporting submarine operations with surface ships and aircraft. He stated that:

> . . . a modern navy, whose mission is to conduct combat operations against a strong enemy, cannot be only an undersea navy. The underestimation of the need to support submarine operations with aircraft and surface ships cost the German high command dearly in the last two wars. . . . one of the reasons for the failure of the "unlimited submarine war" prosecuted by the Germans was the absence of such support for the submarines, which forced them to operate without the support of other forces.[18]

Given the importance that the Soviets assign to their SSBN's as a deterrent force, it seems reasonable to assume that SSBN protection is a major consideration in the development of the *Kuril* class carrier, particularly in view of the historical Soviet concern with defensive missions for their navy. Bradford Dismukes argues that the SSBN is the greatest high-value unit in the Soviet Navy and that its importance is likely to increase as long as mutually assured destruction remains the basic theme of United States-Soviet strategic arms negotiations.[19]

● **Sea Control**

The Soviet view of sea control differs from that of the United States.[20] While sea control is essential to the maintenance of U.S. overseas alliances, geography and politics have removed this necessity from the U.S.S.R.. Nevertheless, the Soviets do have economic/political interests in overseas nations and are expanding the scope of their naval operations considerably. From a strategic point of view, the Soviets, in wartime, would attempt to deny the West the use of sea areas that could be used to project power ashore. This, of course, means that the Soviets would concentrate their efforts against Western attack carriers and SSBN's. They would also attempt to exercise control of their sea frontiers to protect the flanks of the army. In this regard, the Soviet concept of sea control would be similar to that of the United States: the Soviets would attempt to gain and maintain control of local seas such as the Baltic, the Barents, and the Sea of Japan by asserting their own use of the seas and by attempting to deny use to the enemy.

The most likely utilization of *Kiev* in a sea control role would be to provide protective air cover for Soviet surface combatants operating beyond the range of shore-based naval aircraft. The Soviets recognize that they are not assured of the use of overseas bases in periods of tension or in time of war. The loss of their submarine base in Albania in 1961 and their airbase rights in Egypt in 1972 cannot be ignored by their planners, and they have only to look at the U.S. experience in the Mediterranean and the Atlantic for further evidence of the unreliability of foreign bases. Admiral Sergeev, the Chief of Naval Staff, has commented that his greatest problem in the forward deployment of the Soviet fleet was "bases."[21] This requirement for bases is founded on the need for logistics and repair facilities and the need for air cover to protect surface units.

The Soviets' concern over the threat of air attack at sea is evidenced by the wide variety of air defense systems built into their ships. The deployment of standoff air-to-surface missile systems such as Harpoon and Condor will further complicate their air defense problem. Although *Kiev*, with a complement of approximately 25 V/STOL aircraft, would be no match against a large deck U.S. CV, she could provide a measure of protection for Soviet surface forces operating in a relatively low threat environment. Development of a shipborne aircraft air defense capability could provide the Soviets with an alternative to overseas bases.

● **Projection of Power Ashore**

In a general war against NATO the Soviets would probably use their amphibious forces to protect the seaward flanks of their army. The control of vital chokepoints, such as the Danish and Turkish Straits, would be important. The Soviet naval infantry is small (15,000 men) but, when viewed in conjunction with their airborne assault capability, the Soviet projection forces pose a formidable threat to NATO.

The Soviets have given no indication that they consider their projection capability inadequate or that they consider airborne assault from the sea necessary to support the land battle. Their intentions toward development of an over-the-beach airborne assault capability in the Third World are less clear. Soviet amphibious units have deployed regularly to the Mediterranean and, to a lesser extent, the Indian Ocean. Although the Soviets have used their navy to create an image as the protector of client states overseas, there has been a noticeable lack of deployed forces that could support these countries with an over-the-beach assault by troops launched from an amphibious carrier.[22]

According to one observer, the Soviets have apparently opted for a different strategy, especially in those countries where they have strong politico-economic interests. In these countries the Soviets apparently plan to develop a strong foothold in peacetime so that, in the event of hostilities, a beachhead will already have been established. In a situation such as this, the Navy would attempt to control the sea frontier of a Third World country, perhaps in much the same way it would defend the shores of the U.S.S.R.[23] This strategy, however, would require a strong Soviet position in the host country, and its success would depend upon the reactions of the West. Should the United States decide to intervene, the Soviets would require forward-based logistics support and shore-based air cover to counter the carrier threat.

The operations conducted by *Moskva* and *Leningrad* have given no indications that the Soviets plan to utilize their helicopter carriers in an amphibious assault role. The Hormone is primarily an ASW helicopter and although it could be used to carry troops, this seems unlikely because of its relatively small capacity. The larger Soviet troop carrying helicopter (Hip) and assault

helicopter (Hind) could be deployed aboard *Kiev;* but due to their size and the restrictions imposed by the inboard location of *Kiev's* aircraft elevators, these helicopters could not be moved below the flight deck.

The possibility remains, however, that *Kuril* class carriers with V/STOL aircraft embarked could be employed in a strike role. Admiral Gorshkov has indicated that advances in weapons technology have permitted an expansion in the range of missions which each ship is able to perform.[24]

● **Peacetime Presence**

In his 1972/1973 series "Navies in War and Peace," Admiral Gorshkov points to the

> special features of the Navy as a military factor which can be used also in peacetime for purposes of demonstrating the economic and military power of states beyond their borders . . . it has been the solitary branch of armed forces capable of protecting the interests of a country beyond its borders . . . .[25]

Gorshkov has indicated that a navy, more than any other branch of the armed forces, is an indicator of the level of development of a country's economy. He quotes Engels as saying that, "A modern warship is not merely a product of major industry, but at the same time is a sample of it . . . ."[26] Further, Gorshkov has shown a keen awareness of the role of navies in show of force operations. He has written that

> . . . the capability of navies to suddenly appear close to the shores of different countries and immediately proceed to carry out their assigned missions has been used for ages by various aggressive states as an important weapon of diplomacy and policy in peacetime, which in many cases has permitted the achievement of political gains without resorting to military operations by merely threatening to initiate them.[27]

With the forward deployment of the Soviet Navy there has been a marked increase in foreign port calls. Gorshkov has indicated that from 1971 to 1974 some 1,000 Soviet combatants and

auxiliaries visited ports in 60 countries in Europe, Asia, Africa, and Latin America. He stated that these visits have made it possible for the people of many countries to see with their own eyes the "creativity of the ideas of Communism" and to gain an appreciation for the level of development of the U.S.S.R.[28]

McccGwire has divided the peacetime role of the Soviet Navy into three tasks: securing state interests, increasing prestige and influence, and countering "imperialist aggression."[29] MccGwire defines securing of state interests as the building up, consolidating, and preserving the infrastructure on which war related missions depend. This includes actions such as the overthrow of a client state and the acquisition of base rights. Thus the berthing of Soviet units in Port Said and Alexandria in July 1967 not only provided a deterrent against Israeli strikes but, more importantly from the Soviet view, insured Soviet access to Egyptian port facilities.

Increasing prestige and influence implies the use of naval power as an instrument of foreign policy. Showing the flag, port clearing operations in Bangladesh, and intervention in the Iraq-Kuwait border disputes are examples.

Countering "imperialist aggression" entails the use of Soviet naval forces to contest the West's use of the sea for projection of military power. Two illustrative examples are the counter-presence of Soviet naval forces in the eastern Mediterranean during the Arab-Israeli wars of 1967 and 1973 and the Jordanian crisis of 1970.

There are several political tasks that *Kiev* can perform in furtherance of the Soviet "presence" mission. The deployment of embarked fixed wing aircraft will demonstrate the power of the U.S.S.R. for purposes of prestige and influence; it will increase the Soviet capability to influence potential adversaries with Soviet power, intimidate them, lower their morale, and help to secure political objectives without actually fighting.[30] Deployment of a number of *Kuril* class ships will add to the loss of American naval credibility, especially in those ocean areas where U.S. capabilities are already marginal, such as the Norwegian Sea, the Northwest Pacific, and the Indian Ocean. And,

328

perhaps most important, *Kiev* will help the U.S.S.R. in its quest to deny the United States unimpeded use of the oceans for the projection of naval power, particularly the projection of strategic nuclear power. In this role *Kiev* and her sister ships are probably viewed by the Soviets as important elements of strategic deterrence.

Conclusions. Although a variety of missions for *Kiev* are possible because of the capability to embark fixed wing V/STOL aircraft as well as helicopters, the strategic defense role during wartime appears to be of the utmost importance to the Soviets. In peacetime, the political effect *Kiev* could produce relative to Western nations and Third World countries remains an important consideration.

Although *Kiev* has the capability to deploy both fixed wing and helicopter aircraft, her size would tend to argue against her effectiveness in a multimission combat role. The fact that she is a hybrid design—part cruiser and part carrier—will limit both aircraft operating and maintenance spaces. Further, the inboard location of her aircraft elevators will further reduce space and will restrict aircraft operations somewhat unless the elevators are in the up position. While the deployment of large numbers of both V/STOL aircraft and helicopters would require diverse logistic and technical support, the effect of a multimission combat role would be a reduction in primary mission effectiveness. Therefore, in a general war the aircraft mix would more than likely be tailored to accomplish a strategic ASW mission, either in countering enemy SSBN's or in support of Soviet SSBN's. A number of V/STOL aircraft could be embarked to oppose enemy surface ASW platforms and patrol aircraft, thereby providing an additional measure of protection for Soviet SSBN's and self-protection in hostile forward areas where shore-based air cover is not available. However, in all probability ASW operations would primarily be directed against the Poseidon SLBM threat and the eventual deployment of Trident in the 1980's.

During "show of force operations," *Kiev* could be deployed as an effective instrument of Soviet foreign policy, particularly in support of Moscow's political and economic interests in the Third World. The appearance of *Kiev* off the coast of a client state would undoubtedly have more influence than a destroyer or cruiser with little or no capability to provide direct support to friendly forces ashore.

The best evidence, of course, is lacking. We will undoubtedly learn much more about the *Kuril* class when *Kiev* enters the Mediterranean for the first time and provides Western observers an opportunity to witness her operations first hand. Until that time, the best indications are to be found in Soviet writings.

BIOGRAPHIC SUMMARY

A graduate of the University of Miami, Lt. Comdr. William R. Hynes is a graduate of the Defense Intelligence School. He has served on the staff of Commander, Carrier Division 2, and at Headquarters, U.S. European Command. He is a 1976 graduate of the College of Naval Command and Staff, Naval War College. Currently he is assigned to the staff of Commander in Chief, U.S. Pacific Fleet.

NOTES

1. Michael K. MccGwire, "The Evolution of Soviet Naval Policy, 1960-74," Michael K. MccGwire, et al., eds., *Soviet Naval Policy, Objectives and Constraints* (New York: Praeger, 1975), pp. 531-532.

2. Norman Polmar, "The Soviet Aircraft Carrier," *United States Naval Institute Proceedings*, May 1974, pp. 153-154; Sergei Gorshkov, "The Development of the Art of Naval Warfare," *United States Naval Institute Proceedings*, June 1975, p. 57.

3. Peter Vigor, "Admiral S.G. Gorshkov's Views on Seapower," *RUSI, Journal of the Royal United Services Institute for Defense Studies*, March 1974, p. 59.

4. Gorshkov, p. 56.

5. MccGwire, p. 514.

6. John E. Moore, ed., *Jane's Fighting Ships, 1975-1976* (New York: Franklin Watts, 1975), pp. 551-552.

7. Polmar, p. 159.

8. *Jane's Fighting Ships, 1975-1976*, pp. 551-552.

9. *Ibid.*

10. Sergei Gorshkov, "Navies in War and Peace," *United States Naval Institute Proceedings*, November 1974, p. 63.

11. See Vice Adm. Stansfield Turner's commentary on the final chapter of "Navies in War and Peace," *United States Naval Institute Proceedings*, November 1974, p. 68.

12. *Ibid.*

13. John W.R. Taylor, *Jane's All the World's Aircraft, 1975-1976* (New York: Franklin Watts, 1975), p. 523.

14. Gorshkov, "Development of the Art of Naval Warfare," p. 56.

15. D.P. Sokha, quoted in Bradford Dismukes, "The Soviet Naval General Purpose Forces: Roles and Missions in Wartime," Michael K. MccGwire, et al., eds., *Soviet Naval Policy, Objectives and Constraints* (New York: Praeger, 1975), p. 576.

The Soviet Merchant Fleet

By Commander Richard T. Ackley, U. S. Navy (Retired)

All of the four kinds of merchant ships the Soviet Union needs to make a major impact on world trade—the really fast cargo liner, the containership, the huge bulk carrier, and the supertanker—are only just beginning to appear on the world's oceans. Newest of the supertankers is the 150,000-ton Krym, forerunner of a 370,000-ton class that will vie for international oil trade, but not with Soviet oil.

The Soviet Union has more territory than any nation in the world. It is essentially independent of sea lines of communications other than for supplying some nearly inaccessible areas in the Arctic and Pacific Far East. Strategically, the U.S.S.R. is almost self-sufficient in energy and raw materials; yet it has one of the world's largest and fastest growing merchant marines. In fact, the Soviet merchant fleet is capable of carrying more than half of all Soviet foreign trade, of delivering military and economic aid to client nations, of earning currency from foreign nations by hauling their commerce, while at the same time satisfying domestic needs for coastal transport. It seems, then, that the U.S.S.R. is employing its merchant marine less from necessity than for political-economic advantage. That is, the Soviet merchant marine serves as a positive contributor to the overall economy by its favorable impact on the balance of payments; by being an important employer, taxpayer, and customer of the U.S.S.R.'s products; and, additionally by hauling foreign products for profit.

Within the context of maritime power and foreign policy, the Soviet merchant fleet's four essential roles might be defined as follows:

▶ To reduce the Soviet Union's dependence on Western shipping to carry its trade and aid, including routine arms supplies

▶ To ensure that large quantities of arms and equipment can be supplied to client nations at short notice if required

▶ To provide the lift for follow-up forces in the event of overseas intervention

▶ To serve (through the presence of its ships and their companies in distant parts of the world) as an influence-building instrument of policy

Ranking of world merchant fleets is subject to statistical manipulation and varied definitions. Accordingly, one should at least be aware of the common frames of reference used by specialists and the data bases often employed in statistical analyses.

Most common, perhaps, is the numerical reporting and ranking of all merchant ships registered by a given state. Side-by-side ranking may appear in terms of gross registered tonnage or deadweight tonnage, neither of which necessarily coincides with numerical ranking.[1] Additionally, in certain reporting, it is common practice to list only ships of 1,000 or more gross registered tons. Unfortunately, combinations of the above are sometimes intermingled, producing data that can be just as confusing as informative. For instance, a recent comparison of Soviet and American merchant fleets revealed:

> "Overall, the Soviet merchant fleet of 1500 vessels of approximately 1000 gross registered tons is the world's fifth largest merchant marine fleet in number of ships and ninth in total tonnage. In contrast, the U. S. fleet of 971 ships ranks ninth in total number, but the tonnage capability of these ships is the seventh largest in the world since U. S. ships normally are larger than the Soviets'."[2]

One is unsure if the 1,500 Soviet merchant vessels considered are over or about 1,000 gross registered tons and if the remaining comparisons are expressed in gross, deadweight, or net tonnage. As an example of how tonnage nomenclatures differ, four tonnage figures typical of modern freighter of 10,000 tons deadweight carrying capacity might be:

Net registered tonnage	4,000
Gross registered tonnage	6,000
Deadweight tonnage (dwt.)	10,000
Displacement tonnage (loaded)	13,350

Table 1 shows a 20-year growth pattern of the total Soviet merchant fleet in comparison with that of the U. S. and of the world fleet. Soviet fleet expansion in both quantity and deadweight tonnage is indeed spectacular, particularly when one notes that Soviet totals have grown from 483 to 2,140, an increase of about 443%. Equally unsettling to American observers is the fact that U. S. totals have decreased in the same period from 3,440 to 1,550, a decrease of about 66%.

Table 1 *Growth of U. S. and U.S.S.R. Merchant Fleets (Millions of dwt.)*

	1953		1963		1973	
	Ships	*dwt.*	*Ships*	*dwt.*	*Ships*	*dwt.*
World	14,019	114,946	17,861	185,843	21,009	399,552
U. S.	3,440	36,961	2,733	31,106	1,150	17,949
USSR	483	1,937	1,002	5,922	2,140	15,413

Source: *The World Almanac, 1954, 1964, & 1974,* (New York: Newspaper Enterprise Association, 1953, 1963, & 1973.

Table 2 *Soviet & American Merchant Fleets as a Percentage of World Shipping and Deadweight Tonnage, 1953–73*

	1953 % of world		1963 % of world		1973 % of world	
	Ships	*dwt.*	*Ships*	*dwt.*	*Ships*	*dwt.*
U. S.	24.5	32.2	15.3	16.7	5.8	4.5
USSR	3.5	1.7	5.6	3.2	10.2	3.9

Additionally, the average age of the Soviet merchant fleet is less than ten years, while the average age of the U. S. fleet is about 20.

In a worldwide context, however, Soviet merchant shipping statistics are not nearly so impressive as when directly compared with those of the United States. The Soviet fleet represents about 10.2% of the world's merchant ships and only 3.9% of the worldwide deadweight tonnage (Table 2). In other words, the Soviet "share of the pie" may not be so menacing as some Western shippers might want us to think, if in fact one granted their assumption that numbers are all-important.

Indeed, growth rate, up-to-dateness, and fleet mix (balance) may be every bit as important as numbers and tonnage when assessing the effectiveness and capability of the Soviet merchant marine. Moreover, another significant factor is that the entire Soviet fleet is owned and operated by one organization—the Soviet government. Therefore, a major concern is how the Soviet merchant fleet is employed for political, economic, and military support purposes, rather than just its static proportion of the world shipping tonnage. The merchant marine, after all, is an instrument of national policy in the real world, not merely another form of transportation.

Granting the U.S.S.R. an "up-check" in numerical and dwt. growth rate does not, in fact, imply that the fleet is economically rational or indeed competitive with major world shippers. In point of fact, the Soviet Union does not now have a well balanced fleet in terms of either ship composition or modernity (state of the art equipment). It still has few bulk carriers and is just starting to operate containerships. Supertankers and lighters aboard ships are planned but not in service. The Soviets have large numbers of small vessels but relatively few modern, cost-effective, specialized vessels. In part, the lack of extensive modern automated handling facilities in Soviet ports impairs up-to-dateness in Soviet shipping, as does the backwardness of port facilities in many of the U.S.S.R.'s client nations. Nevertheless, Soviet planners are aware of their shortcomings and are

making concerted efforts to shape their maritime fleet into an effective tool of foreign policy in addition to being an economic success on the world scene. This is in contrast to operating the fleet as an essential vital lifeline of commerce, which is often the case in other countries.

Robert E. Athay identifies two principal theses advanced in the literature of Soviet merchant marine development:

▸ The U.S.S.R. has expanded its merchant fleet largely for political and military reasons with little or no regard for economic costs involved.
▸ This development poses a serious threat to the political and economic interests of the Free World.[3]

Close scrutiny of the Soviet record, however, fails to support either of these theses. In fact, it appears more likely that the Soviets expanded their fleet largely for economic reasons, and that the Soviet fleet as it exists today is not a serious threat to Western shipping interests.[4] A brief review of the Soviet merchant marine buildup may make this clear.

During the period of stabilization following the Russian Revolution, the Soviets possessed about 200,000 dwt. of merchant shipping. Yet, by the beginning of World War II, the Soviet merchant fleet had increased to about 1.5 million dwt. Despite severe losses during the war, the Soviet commercial fleet was bolstered by 84 American Lend-Lease ships, and after the war the U.S.S.R. received German and Italian vessels as war reparations. The final postwar result was a Soviet merchant fleet that exceeded its previous all-time high of the century, namely 507 ships totaling an estimated 2.7 million dwt.

It was in the early 1950s that Soviet merchant ship construction began in earnest. After Joseph Stalin's death in 1953, the *Sverdlov*-class cruiser program was terminated, and the building ways were available for merchant hulls. Additionally, the U.S.S.R. built four new shipyards, three of which were used for only merchant and fishing ship construction.[5] In fact, it has been estimated that 144 ships were added to the Soviet

One of the vessels built during the recently concluded ninth five-year period (1971–1975) is the Soviet Union's first oil and ore-carrying tanker, a multipurpose sea-river-sea vessel which can transport 1,800 tons of dry cargo or 2,700 tons of oil without costly reloading operations.

NOVOSTI FROM SOVFOTO

inventory between 1950 and 1954. This expansion was only in part tied to First Secretary Nikita Khruschchev's policy of economic penetration of the less developed countries. The real impetus was to broaden trade relations with non-Communist nations for economic gain.

A political decision to increase Soviet trade and aid, then, served to stimulate the acquisition of more Soviet-flag shipping. Thus, by 1957, the Soviet Union had doubled its prewar commercial tonnage. The most dramatic shipbuilding developments, however, did not occur until after 1957. In part, this was because of the increase in Soviet foreign trade and aid that exceeded the available supply of Soviet-flag merchant vessels. In other words, the Russians had to charter Western shipping to meet their seaborne freight commitments, and this cost the Soviets valuable foreign exchange.

Additional demands on Soviet-flag shipping arose after the break with China in 1960. Goods that formerly went overland to China were then available to less developed countries and had to travel long distances by sea. Also, in the wake of the Cuban Missile Crisis of 1962, Soviet vessels had to accommodate most of that country's foreign trade. In fact, a boycott organized by Western oil companies against non-Soviet tankers carrying Soviet oil to Cuba aggravated the situation. These realities led to an unprecedented growth in the Soviet merchant marine from 1961 to 1966.[6] In point of fact, in 1961 the U.S.S.R. had to charter foreign ships to carry 19.3 million tons of cargo, 31% of its total seaborne foreign trade. It has been estimated that the costs involved exceeded $100 million—certainly a motivating factor for merchant fleet expansion! Indeed, S. Mikhailov, writing in *Voprosy Ekonomiki,* stated:

> "The creation of our own merchant fleet made it possible to guarantee the U.S.S.R.'s independence from the world charter market and to begin the transportation on Soviet ships of cargo and passengers of other countries."[7]

The point remains, however, while that conceding economic gain as the major motivating factor behind the Soviet drive for merchant marine ascendency, political opportunities were not overlooked, and they were often exploited with vigor.

Several years ago, then Soviet Maritime Minister Viktor Bakayev stated that his fleet would continue to expand at the rate of approximately one million tons annually until 1980, when 23 million dwt. of shipping would be in service.[8] Subsequently, planning figures for the 1971–1975 five-year plan supported Bakayev's assertions by directing a 40% increase in tonnage—only slightly less than Bakayev's total of 23 million tons.[9] The 1980 Soviet projection now appears overoptimistic when one notes that since 1965 the Russian merchant fleet has, in fact, grown at an average rate of 600,000 tons per year, rather than the projected one million (Table 3).

The inevitable conclusion, however, remains that the Soviet merchant fleet seems destined to exceed the U. S.-flag fleet in both quantity and tonnage by the end of 1980, but it will gain only slightly in relation to worldwide totals. Furthermore, as David Fairhall has noted, the ship types the Russians must deploy to make a major impact on world trade—the really fast cargo liner, the containership, the supertanker, and the huge bulk carrier—are only just beginning to appear on the world's oceans and just beginning to affect shipping statistics.[10] Nonetheless, as Soviet foreign trade has grown, the U.S.S.R. has made significant strides in reducing chartered tonnage, and now carries more than 50% of its trade in Soviet bottoms (Table 4). This increased carrying capacity permits additional flexibility in the pursuit of attractive political-economic (as well as military) support activities.

If, in fact, the Soviet merchant fleet's reason for being is in support of the four roles suggested at the beginning of this paper, then each role should be examined in order to assist us in arriving at some reasonable assessment of the fleet's capabilities—present and projected.

▶ *Reducing the Soviet Union's Dependence on Western Shipping:* In this role, the term "dependence" can be considered in both an economic and political aspect. Politically, the Russians would consider it desirable to haul all their cargo—as well as a significant percentage of other nations' cargo—in Soviet bottoms. And economically, if the former is not possible, it is second best to turn a profit in convertible currency through earnings from available shipping assets. In other words, a corollary to reducing dependence on Western shipping is to earn convertible currency to help offset the cost of necessary foreign charters, and if possible, to pay for it all and even show a profit. These two facets of the Soviet maritime problem are recognized and being aggressively dealt with by the U.S.S.R.

A paradox of Soviet maritime transport is that

Russian foreign trade turnover, numbers of merchant ships, and fleet deadweight tonnage are all on the increase. Since 1960, as noted in Table 4, the dilemma is improving inasmuch as Soviet dependence on Western shipping has decreased. Nevertheless, the U.S.S.R. still depends on Western carriers to haul somewhat less than half of its foreign trade. (Table 5 shows the annual increase [ruble value] of Soviet foreign trade turnover from 1971–74, while Table 3 shows the increase in merchant fleet size.)

An indication of the Soviet desire to reduce dependence on Western shipping while increasing foreign trade turnover is apparent from Soviet literature. For example, official Soviet statistics reveal that in 1970 Soviet ships engaged in foreign trade visited 995 ports in 105 countries, making 23,700 individual port calls. The target goals set for the ninth five-year plan, ending in 1975, called for Soviet ships to visit more than 1,000 ports in various countries and carry 70% more cargo for foreign freight owners than was shipped during the preceding five-year plan. In the past, the Soviets add, their foreign trade shipments grew largely through the

Table 3 *Soviet Fleet Expansion**

Year	Inventory as of December 1972		Net Increase in tonnage		Deliveries during year (million of deadweight tons)
	Number	Million of deadweight tons	Millions of deadweight tons	Percent	
1959	590	3.3	0.3	10	0.4
1960	650	3.9	.6	18	.6
1961	680	4.2	.3	8	.4
1962	740	4.8	.6	14	.7
1963	820	5.7	.9	19	.9
1964	900	6.9	1.2	21	1.3
1965	990	8.0	1.1	16	1.2
1966	1,070	8.9	.9	11	1.0
1967	1,150	9.7	.8	9	.8
1968	1,230	10.4	.7	7	.8
1969	1,320	11.2	.8	8	.8
1970	1,400	11.9	.7	6	.8
1971	1,470	12.4	.5	4	.5
1972	1,500	12.7	.3	2	.5
1973	1,550	13.5	.8	6	1.0

* In the 13 years between 1946 and 1959 (the beginning of a new 5-year plan), the Soviets succeeded in restoring its parts and repair facilities and continued to expand its shipbuilding program in the U.S.S.R. and the Comecon nations.

Source: *Soviet Ocean Activities: A Preliminary Survey*, p. 18.

Table 4 *Percentage of Foreign Trade Carried in U. S. and U.S.S.R. vessels*
   (*in thousands of short tons*)

Year	U. S. Trade	% in U. S. Ships	USSR Trade	% in USSR Ships
1950	159,389	39.3	33,700	72.0
1960	322,717	12.3	75,900	41.0
1967	444,233	6.5	141,400	52.0
1969	487,906	4.9	148,700	over 50.0
1970	538,933	5.6	161,900	56.0
1971	517,000	5.6	170,900	—
1972	581,000	5.0	178,000	—

development of new long-distance routes. Now the routes and distances are the same, but shipping volume in 1975 was expected to show an increase of 37.4% in tonnage and 42% in freight turnover in comparison with 1970.[11] This is based on a new trend of long-term agreements with countries of Western Europe and Asia. It is not surprising that with this anticipated increase in foreign trade, the ninth five-year plan called for an additional 550 merchant ships totaling 5.3 million dwt. by 1975.

Soviet trade with the United States for instance, totaled 2.4 million rubles in 1972–74, or 380% more than in the preceding three-year period. The Russians purchase U. S. machine equipment deemed necessary to carry out the broad program of development in many branches of their economy. However, this trade results in an unfavorable balance for the Soviet side.[12] In order to offset such an imbalance, the U.S.S.R. increased its overall foreign trade turnover in 1974 by 8.3 million rubles as compared to 1973. Exports reached 20.8 rubles, and imports were 18.8 million rubles. As a result, the U.S.S.R. had an overall favorable trade balance of some 2 million rubles.[13] Profits, then, are made principally in cross-trade, and to a lesser extent in winter charters. That is, non-Soviet cargos are being hauled for foreign countries and more and more ships are being let out on charter (voyage or time) to other countries during the months when the northern and far eastern Soviet ports are frozen over.

In terms of profitability, one might note, the Soviet merchant fleet has a commercial advantage derived from centralized management of a large-scale operation without middlemen. And profit is, indeed, important in the Russian maritime industry. Since January 1968, the Soviet merchant fleet is supposed to fund all new investments from earned profits. Certainly the need for foreign exchange is an additional inducement to earning profits, but one's fleet must consist of a cost-effective

combination of modern specialized vessels in order to compete successfully for cross-trade with Western shippers. Of course, specialized vessels permit more efficient handling of Soviet cargo too, and it is in the area of supertanker and containership development that the Soviets are currently concentrating.

Tankers and Supertankers: The U.S.S.R. is becoming increasingly involved in the international oil trade, but not with Soviet oil. A few years back, Timofei Guzhenko, the Soviet merchant marine minister, said the Soviet Union hopes to reduce the dependence of smaller countries, particularly those in the oil trade, "on the shipping concerns of the imperialist powers."[14] Thus, it follows that the Russians plan to build a record number of tankers during the next five years. The Soviet Union wants to provide friendly producing and consuming nations, such as Algeria and India, with enough tankers to eliminate their dependence on capitalist shipping monopolies. It has been suggested that the Soviets plan to make their tankers available to these countries on very attractive charter terms.[15]

The current Soviet production tanker is the 150,000-ton *Krym* series. However, Deputy Minister of the U.S.S.R. Shipbuilding Industry Yevgeniy Nikolayevich Shaposhnikov reported that design work is underway for the construction of a 370,000-ton displacement supertanker to be manned by a crew of 35. He reports she will have a length of 344 meters (1,129 feet) and sides higher than a ten-story building. Furthermore, this tanker will be able to call at more oil ports than the non-Soviet 500,000-ton supertankers. A fleet of such tankers has political-economic implications for the Western world, and also should provide subsidy to the Soviet state.

Containerships: Perhaps of all new types of speciality ships, the containership has made the greatest impact on international trade. In fact, containerization has been introduced into conferences of which the Soviet steamship lines are members, thus forcing the issue of Soviet containership construction.

The first Soviet containership, *Svetlogorsk,* was built in Vyborg in 1971 and can carry only 218 containers. There are now only some 55 full, partial, and feeded container-type ships registered under the Soviet flag, with a total carrying capability of about 10,000–11,000 containers.[16] This represents a low percentage of world containerized seaborne commerce. For example, the largest Soviet container-carrying ship is about 12,000 dwt. and has a capacity of 368 20-foot containers. Other merchant fleets have about 100 ships ranging up to 40,000 dwt. and with a carrying capacity from 1,000 to 2,300 standard 20-foot containers.[17]

Yet, by 1976, the Soviet merchant fleet will be augmented by some 70 ships totaling about 894,000 dwt., with a collective capacity of more than 33,000 standard containers.[18] Additionally, the U.S.S.R. has sufficient containerships on order or under construction to make their presence felt within the next five years. It appears that containerization will be the Soviets' ploy to reduce their dependence on Western shipping, while increasing their seaborne cross-trade for profit. Some have estimated that the U.S.S.R. should theoretically be in a position to carry all the country's seaborne foreign trade by 1980; however, such a judgment seems rather premature.

▶ *Supplying Large Quantities of Arms and Equipment to Client States on Short Notice:* One of the most important factors in the Soviet merchant ship buildup has been its growing capability for long-range sealift that can sustain Soviet proxy forces over extended periods. In recent times, the Soviet merchant service has been able to supply friendly governments with war materials while enjoying immunity from retaliation. For example, in support of North Vietnam, about 100 Soviet merchant ships—many built in the West—were in regular use on the Haiphong run. Earlier the *Poltava*-class cargo ship became famous as a carrier of missiles to Cuba.[19] Furthermore, it was the Soviet merchant fleet, not naval

From such ports as Riga on the Baltic, the Soviet merchant fleet has demonstrated its ability to deliver large quantities of materials by sea, as well as an ability to deliver smaller quantities of war materials on short notice to client nations. But its capability of withstanding military opposition remains untested.

At Kherson, one of the 11 seamanship schools in the Soviet Union, some of the 2,000-man student body undergoes instruction in navigation while others study marine, electrical, and radio engineering in preparation for careers in the Soviet merchant marine.

squadrons, that made the initial inroads into the Middle East. Soviet merchant ships carried materials for the Aswan Dam to Egypt, brought back cotton on the return voyage, and carried Soviet equipment to rearm the Arab nations for their several wars with Israel. It was, in fact, after the 1967 Arab-Israeli War that the U.S.S.R. demonstrated a real proficiency for adjusting its shipping from programmed commercial schedules to a total resupply operation of military equipment. Notably, the Soviets exhibited for the first time a sealift capability adequate to support their ambitious political objectives in the Mediterranean basin.

Another objective of Soviet capability to deliver military equipment overseas took place in Angola. A United Press International dispatch of 23 July 1975 reported that Portuguese refugees from the war-torn capital of Angola in West Africa said Soviet ships waited in the harbor to unload military supplies for leftist liberation troops and young boys ran through the streets carrying Russian-made guns. One refugee said "The Soviets have four ships in the harbor and unloaded armored cars and weapons for the Popular Movement; the people protested about it and they stopped, but the ships are still in the harbor."[20]

The Soviets have demonstrated an ability to deliver large quantities of materials by sea, as well as an ability to deliver smaller quantities of war materials on short notice to client or would-be client nations. This capability, however, has been unopposed militarily. Successful delivery of war materials in the face of armed opposition would indeed depend upon the nature of the opposition, geographic location, and other factors too numerous to consider here.

▶ *Providing the Lift For Follow-up Forces in the Event of Overseas Intervention:* The West has long known that shipping plays a dominant role in supplying military ground operations overseas. In fact, without secure maritime transport, no substantial overseas military operations could be conducted at all. For instance, in the Vietnam War, two out of every three men and 98% of this nation's cargo were shipped by sea.[21] Accordingly, one must be alert to the reality that the Soviet Union is acquiring adequate merchant shipping and operational experience supporting military operations to be able to undertake distant limited war operations herself some-

day. In this context, agreements between the U.S.S.R. and a number of less developed countries in Africa and Asia (such as Mauritius, Yemen, and Socotra) may make it possible for civilian Soviet logistic support ships to refuel and resupply for subsequent delivery to Russian sea- or land-based forces deployed overseas.

Merchant ship support available for the Soviet Navy increased substantially between 1961 and 1964 due to an increase in the number of oilers, repair ships, transports, and supply ships. The U.S.S.R. now has some 370 cargo ships and 112 tankers which are believed to be equipped and suitable for long-range military sealift. All are less than 20 years old, capable of speed in excess of 14 knots, and have the needed heavy-lift booms and hatch size for such use. As a comparison, the United States operates 239 similar ships and 162 tankers which could be employed for comparable military requirements.[22]

Evidence exists to demonstrate the Soviet merchant marine's ability to support deployed naval squadrons for prolonged periods. For instance, the Soviet warship probes into the Caribbean Sea and cruises off the Hawaiian Islands are proof positive that the merchant service can provide necessary logistic support to deployed naval formations. From this, it might be inferred that similar support to intervention forces is possible. Yet, a limiting factor to Soviet military engagement in an overseas area is control of the air. Until the U.S.S.R. acquires attack aircraft carriers or sufficient airfields to provide air superiority, overseas projection of Soviet military force in the face of sophisticated opposition is not a feasible option.

▶ *Serving As An Influence-Building Instrument of Policy:* Although the opportunity to spread a favorable image is inherent in worldwide maritime operations, the less developed countries seem to provide especially fertile grounds for the U.S.S.R.

As previously noted, while the total number of Soviet merchant vessels has increased considerably, the rise in total deadweight tonnage has been rather modest—a condition contrary to contemporary shipbuilding efficiency. However, in the politics of persuasion, small ships with specialized self-unloading equipment are particularly suitable for trade with small countries—that is, the less developed countries with their less developed ports. Although economic gain from trade with less developed countries is modest, it appears that establishing a foothold in the economy and political structure of these countries is a motivating force for Soviet actions. By extending aid to such countries in Africa, Asia, and South America—and by establishing trade relations with them—the Soviets are able to decrease the economic dependence of these countries upon the West, thereby at least making the political alternative of neutralism more acceptable.

In assessing the significance of the numerous foreign port calls made by Soviet merchant ships, it is important to note that some form of Russian trade organization and Soviet consular representation is provided for each visit. In other words, Soviet commercial and consular expansion ashore parallels increased Soviet merchant marine activity overseas. Even in areas where Soviet atheism is rejected, such as the Arab states, clean, modern, and smart Soviet ships can be forceful advertisements in themselves. Especially in developing countries, modern ships tend to reinforce the Soviet claims to

scientific and technological supremacy and to enhance the appeal of the Soviet model as the route to rapid national development.

Besides trade, the Soviet merchant marine has a sizable stake in military aid and technical assistance programs in the less developed countries. Transportation of technicians to and from the U.S.S.R. and these countries is, for the most part, accomplished in Soviet-flag ships. Additionally, the aid and trade cargos and supplies are transported in Soviet-flag shipping. Indeed, it is the Soviet merchant marine that has provided the wherewithal for large-scale programs between the U.S.S.R. and the developing nations.

In the developed nations, the Soviet merchant marine is increasing its volume of trade and consequently its presence in Western European, North American, and Pacific Basin ports. Of special interest, however, is a new subtlety in peddling influence while earning convertible currency: the Soviet passenger fleet as an international carrier. The passenger liners of the Western world, it seems, have succumbed to the jet aircraft. Liners are no longer competitive. Yet, in this age of jet travel, the Soviet Union builds passenger ships.

In the late 1940s, the U.S.S.R. had only a few old passenger vessels; today, it has passenger service on about 150 regular routes totaling more than 120,000 miles.[23] According to Edmund E. Davis, president of American Maritime Management, Inc., Morposflot, the Soviet agency which has jurisdiction over the domestic and foreign passenger ship traffic, will probably become the largest passenger ship company in the world—if it is not already! Today the U.S.S.R. has more than 70 modern passenger ships and several medium sized new ships, each with a capacity of carrying 700–800 persons on 16 international lines connecting the U.S.S.R. with 22 countries.[24]

It was not until the mid-1960s that a major effort was undertaken to capture a share of the international cruise market. The *Ivan Franko*-class ships spearheaded this effort. The *Franko*-class are modern ships that carry about 700 passengers in fully air-conditioned accommodations and at a speed of about 20 knots. Beginning in 1966, Soviet passenger ships were chartered to Western European operators for cruises from the U.S.S.R. and Western European ports to the Mediterranean and Caribbean areas, and in June 1973 the new 700-passenger, 21,000-ton sister ship of the *Pushkin*, the *Mikhail Lermontov*, set sail on her maiden voyage in the New York to Leningrad trade.[25]

The Soviets have purchased West Germany's seven-year-old *Hamburg* (renamed *Maxim Gorky*) and Britain's Cunard liners *Franconia* and *Carmania*. Now they reportedly are eyeing the *France*. The Soviets can make money on the same ships that drive capitalist owners

Table 5   *U.S.S.R. Foreign Trade Turnover in 1971–1974*
(billion rubles, in prevailing prices for each year)

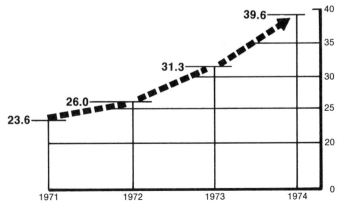

Source: *Ekonomicheskaya gazeta,* April 1975, p. 21.

toward bankruptcy because the state controls sailors' wages and pays them in nonconvertible rubles. For the most part, they do not have to import fuel at inflated costs, and can obtain a sizable percentage of food and other materials at home at constant prices.[26] In pushing this advantage, the Russians set a 1975 goal of carrying more than 50 million passengers, 20 million of which were to be tourists. Meeting this goal would mean a five-fold increase over 1970.[27]

At least three reasons become apparent for Soviet entry into international passenger trade: the accumulation of hard currency from Western tourists, a favorable flow of gold from chartering ships to the West, and a fringe benefit not lost on the Soviets—gaining national prestige and influence. Despite the fact that "influence" is difficult, if not impossible, to measure, the Soviets seem bent on continuous expansion of their merchant marine and increased contacts with the outside world that might be advantageous.

Alarmist rhetoric concerning a Soviet maritime threat, other than in perhaps passenger traffic, is simply not borne out by the facts.[28] Despite the unprecedented growth of Soviet maritime forces, they are a small percent of world totals and will remain as such for years

to come. This is not to suggest that Soviet shipping will not continue to grow in both numbers and deadweight tonnage. In 1972, for example, 958 merchant ships of 41,931 dwt. were delivered worldwide. Of these, the Soviet Union received 76 ships amounting to 570,000 dwt. or 7.9% of the ships and 1.4% of the total dwt. (Table 6). This is hardly destabilizing on a worldwide basis when one notes no other Communist country was the recipient of any of the 958 merchant ship deliveries.

It appears that an economic imperative, now as in the past, drives Soviet maritime activity. The Russians have said that approximately 65% of their foreign exchange earnings from shipping services are in hard currency, and that this is higher than for other types of export. So to maintain this momentum, Soviet emphasis is now on advanced specialized vessels rather than small- and medium-sized freighters. This is because, in comparison with major mercantile fleets of the world, the Russian merchant fleet is not yet well balanced in terms of ship composition. It has very few bulk carriers, is just starting to operate containerships, and still only planning to build lighters aboard ships (LASH) and "near-super-tankers." A fleet of specialized ships, then, will reduce significantly Soviet dependence on Western charters and render the Soviet commercial fleet more competitive in

Table 6 *Shipbuilding—Leading Nations, Merchant Ship Deliveries—1972*
(*Oceangoing ships—Deadweight tons in thousands*)

For whom built	Number of ships	Deadweight tons	Rank	Where built	Number of ships	Deadweight tons
Liberia	138	11,140	1	Japan	417	22,756
Japan	198	9,406	2	Sweden	38	3,695
United Kingdom	132	5,213	3	Spain	63	1,913
Norway	77	4,062	4	United Kingdom	61	1,849
Greece	72	2,577	5	Germany (West)	85	1,764
Sweden	28	1,264	6	Denmark	17	1,677
Italy	13	1,249	7	Italy	25	1,669
Spain	27	1,207	8	France	23	1,620
Panama	18	1,097	9	Norway	58	1,401
Denmark	29	1,087	10	Netherlands	41	1,254
France	22	1,067	11	Yugoslavia	17	1,088
Germany (West)	89	1,034	12	Poland	45	653
United States[1]	15	658	13	United States	13	602
U.S.S.R.	76	570	14	U.S.S.R.	42	364
Brazil	24	300	15	Germany (East)	31	314

[1]1973 deliveries—34 ships at 883,600 gross tons. Source: Department of Defense.

dollar-earning cross-trade with Western maritime nations.

Chances are that in the face of insufficient sealift capacity, and with the current emphasis on specialized vessels, the Soviets will continue to add to their merchant fleet in order to bring it closer into balance with competing Western nations. Furthermore, it is likely the U.S.S.R. will not retire its older merchant ships but instead will operate them until they are no longer cost-effective. (This judgment has some precedent in the Soviet retention of many old warships—notably *Sverdlov* cruisers from the 1950s.) The first Soviet ships of the postwar years, however, are now nearing 20 years old. So if, in fact, they are to be retained, the average age of the Soviet merchant fleet will increase progressively over the next decade.

In substance, then, what the Soviets are doing is increasing the capability of their fleet to satisfy their requirements for expanded trade and aid, to earn hard currency, to reduce dependence on Western shippers, to maintain a capability to supply client nations with arms and equipment, to be capable of supporting Soviet interventionary forces overseas if required, and all the while to gain any prestige and influence available as a low-cost bonus.

Professor Ackley, a retired commander, received his B.A. in history from the University of Southern California, his M.A. in political science from the University of Hawaii, and his Ph.D in international relations from the University of Southern California. He is a graduate of the Naval Intelligence Postgraduate School and the Russian language course at the Defense Language Institute. While on active duty his assignments included command of the submarine *Bream* (SS-243) and Submarine Division 31. He also served as Assistant Naval Attache in Moscow and as Command Center Director, Submarine Force Pacific Fleet. Dr. Ackley has taught international relations and defense strategy at U.S.C. and the University of Redlands, and he is the author of many articles in the field of international security and defense strategy. Professor Ackley is a consultant for Lulejian & Associates, Inc., and Associate Dean of Academic Administration and Assistant Professor of Political Science at the California State College, San Bernardino. His article "The Fishing Fleet in Soviet National Strategy" appeared in the July 1975 *Proceedings*.

[1] Gross registered tonnage is the content of a merchant ship's closed-in spaces; one registered ton equals 100 cubic feet. This figure is used principally for assessing port dues and canal tolls. Deadweight tonnage is an expression of the number of tons (2,240 pounds) of cargo, stores, and bunker fuel that a vessel can transport, e.g., the difference between a ship's displacement light and her displacement loaded. Net registered tonnage is a vessel's gross tonnage minus deductions of space devoted to crew accommodations, propulsion plant, fuel, and other spaces necessary for operating the vessel. It is a measure of earning capacity but is seldom used in statistical comparisons.

[2] General George S. Brown, USAF, *United States Military Posture for FY-1976,* edited by Norman Polmar and Richard Ackley (San Bernardino: California State College, 1975), p. 94.

[3] Robert E. Athay, "Perspectives on Soviet Merchant Shipping Policy," in *Soviet Naval Developments: Context and Capability,* edited by Michael MccGwire (Halifax, Nova Scotia: Dalhousie University, 1973), p. 83.

[4] *Ibid.*

[5] Norman Polmar, *Soviet Naval Power: Challenge for the 1970s,* (New York: Crane, Russak and Co., Inc., 1974), p. 91. For an analysis of the Soviet fishing fleet, see Richard T. Ackley, "The Fishing Fleet and Soviet Strategy," *U. S. Naval Institute Proceedings,* July 1975, pp. 30–38.

[6] Nicholas G. Shadrin, "The Soviet Merchant Marine, A Late Developing Economic Growth Sector," *Soviet Economic Prospects for the Seventies,* United States Congress. Joint Economic Committee, 93rd Cong. (Washington: U. S. Government Printing Office, 27 June 1973), p. 720.

[7] S. Mikhailov, "The Development of the USSR's Maritime Economy," *Voprosy Ekonomiki,* No. 7, July 1972; *The Current Digest of the Soviet Press,* 1 November 1972, p. 4.

[8] Viktor Bakayev, cited in Commander Tyrone G. Martin, USN, book review of *Soviet Merchant Ships, 1945–68, U. S. Naval Institute Proceedings,* March 1970, p. 104.

[9] *Krasnaya Zvezda,* 7 April 1971, p. 4.

[10] David Fairhall, *Russian Sea Power,* (Boston: Gambit, Inc., 1971), p. 263.

[11] M. Bruskin and P. Pustovoit, "High Goals of the Merchant Marine," *Vodny Transport,* 30 November 1971; *The Current Digest of the Soviet Press,* Vol. XXIV, No. 1, 2 February 1972, pp. 3–4.

[12] *The Current Digest of the Soviet Press (CDSP),* Vol. XXVII, No. 14, 30 April 1975, pp. 3–4.

[13] *Ibid.* p. 4.

[14] *The Sun* (Baltimore), 21 June 1973.

[15] U. S. Senate, Committee on Commerce and the National Ocean Policy Study, *Soviet Ocean Activities: A Preliminary Survey,* (Washington: U. S. Government Printing office, 30 April 1975), pp. 19–20.

[16] Irwin M. Heine, "Russia's Containerships: Today and Tomorrow," *Sea Power,* June 1974, p. 15.

[17] *Ibid.,* p. 16.

[18] *Ibid.,* p. 17.

[19] Anthony C. Sutton, "The Soviet Merchant Marine," *U. S. Naval Institute Proceedings,* January 1970, p. 42.

[20] "Angola's Leftists Get Soviet Help," *Sun Telegram* (San Bernardino, Calif.) 23 July 1975, p. A-5.

[21] L. W. Martin, *The Sea in Modern Strategy,* (New York: Praeger, Inc. 1967), p. 55.

[22] Brown, *op. cit.,* p. 94.

[23] U. S. Congress, House of Representatives, Committee on Armed Services, *The Changing Strategic Naval Balance, USSR vs. USA,* 90th Congress 2d session, December 1968, p. 28.

[24] Shadrin, *op. cit.,* p. 737.

[25] U. S. Department of Commerce, Maritime Administration, Irwin M. Heine and Muriel W. Coe, *The Soviet Merchant Marine,* (Washington: U. S. Government Printing Office, 1967), pp. 10–11; U. S. Congress, House of Representatives, *The Soviets and the Seas,* Report No. 1809, 89th Cong., 2d sess., 1966, p. 19; "The Good Ship 'Lermontov' is on Her Way to New York," *The Sun* (San Bernardino), 1 June 1973, p. C-10.

[26] Ralph Hubley, "Russians Making Big Splash on Cruise Scene This Season," *Christian Science Monitor News Service,* October 13, 1974.

[27] M. Bruskin and P. Pustovoit, p. 3.

[28] For an analysis of the Soviet maritime threat in terms of Major General A. N. Lagovskiy's "Weak Link" strategy, see Richard T. Ackley, "The Weak Link in U. S. National Strategy," *Sea Power,* August 1974.

Uses and Laws
of the Sea

Towards a Rational Use of the Oceans

By R. H. Charlier and M. Vigneaux

The needs of man are growing incessantly. This results from the demographic growth, roughly 2% yearly, or 10,000 additional humans per hour. Within 50 years, at this rate, there will be at least twice as many people on earth. Another cause lies in the improvement of living standards: more sophisticated food, more comfort, more energy, to name a few. Man will be forced to turn to the sea, perhaps because there is no other solution. The ocean is a repository of most of the raw materials man needs, and perhaps technologists will find in the water domain nuclear energy, living space, and food. Yet, although exploitation of the ocean has barely begun, the spectrum of marine pollution is becoming steadily more real. We must aim not toward a wild rush, but toward a well planned move.

Human and animal needs for fresh water have already become a major concern; further demands are made by agriculture, industry, tourism, and recreation. Within 20 years, the need for fresh water and food will have been doubled. Man cannot afford to ravage the ocean as he did the earth: he must adapt his fishing techniques, his harvesting methods, so that the ecosystem is not endangered. Similarly, the true challenge of the present decade is, for the marine "mining" engineer, to develop exploitation methods and techniques which will not constitute a danger to the marine environment.

An important question raised in official and private quarters alike is "Which catalyst could bring together maritime powers towards a rational management, and an international management, of marine technology in order to extract the hoped for benefits of the oceans?" A first step in the right direction might well be the preparation of an atlas of economic oceanography, illustrating the resources of the ocean, showing pollution sources, and picturing the circulation models of ocean waters. Such an atlas would contribute to protection of the oceanic environment from man's continuous depredations. The Soviets, for example, are ready to start a 200-vessel campaign to draw the map of the economic wealth available in the 7 billion square kilometers which constitute their national territorial waters.

Edward Wenck wrote, some time ago, that marine technology should be considered on a worldwide basis and not be limited to the development of exploitation means of ocean organic and mineral products. This global image encompasses wastes disposal, maritime trade, maintenance of peace, scientific research, natural conservation. To this already lengthy list one should add tourism, recreation, climate control, and production of energy. Such an economic atlas is by no means an idealist's dream: today technologists can determine the geographic distribution of minerals located at depths exceeding 300 meters by using a nuclear probe containing man-made Californium-252 followed by area scanning with a detector. Minerals, indeed, absorb Californium-252, then emit gamma rays. Gold, silver, copper, and manganese were thus detected, and the proponents of this method claim that quantities as minute as 20 grams per ton could thus be located.

Nuclear probe detection of minerals has been the object of a research grant from the U. S. Atomic Energy Commission for tests in Sequin Bay, Washington. This nuclear probe could be instrumental in drawing a map of the ocean bottom using geophysical methods and will facilitate the evaluation of mineral deposits, in various stations, in a matter of minutes.

Obviously, the viewpoints of the technologist and of the champion of conservation are at antipodes. Yet, should we not ask: "Is such opposition permanent?" Is there really no path which may lead to a rational exploitation of the Earth without running the risk of irremediable damage to environment and humanity? The promise that the oceans hold is considerable and its resources might well be inexhaustible, providing we use the sea carefully and wisely. Using the oceans will certainly be a major objective of this century's end.

France is one of 19 nations which have put upwards of 500 scientific vessels into service, each searching for a share of the knowledge—and wealth—of the oceans' depths. The oceanographic vessel Jean Charlot, *above, is seen taking on board a self-contained laboratory.*

Exploitation of the oceans. Attracted by the probable wealth held by the oceans, several countries have set up scientific, technical, and industrial organizations to first explore, then exploit the marine resources. Nineteen nations have put more than 500 scientific vessels into service, each searching for a share of the wealth. Computer studies concluded that an investment in exploitation of ocean resources will return in 20 years more than three times the same sum placed at 10% yearly interest. These studies considered the ocean as a source of food, an area of fishing, of aquaculture, mariculture, ostreiculture, conchyculture; yet, the success of such exploitation is challenged by looming pollution. The studies also considered the ocean as a source of raw materials, and foresaw exploration, recon-naissance, pre-exploitation planning, and extraction of petroleum, gas, and ores.

The gigantic thermo-dynamic engine constituted by the ocean-atmosphere complex is a primordial study theme: ocean action upon meteorological conditions. The theme "ocean, source of recreation and health" has gained a considerable momentum as humanity becomes steadily more concentrated in asphalted urban zones where green spots and sky glimpses are increasingly rare. Still another theme, of current interest, is to find ways of transforming products extracted from the ocean into consumer goods, and to ensure their marketing. Oceanography is important to the consumer because of its "products", and to the producers because of its technical needs. "Oceanography is one of the most promising markets of the current decade," stated J. Jamison Moore. "It offers a potential that has unleashed the imagination and the enthusiasm of industrial planners."

If, on the one hand, opportunities have been pictured as an exceptional cornucopia, we cannot afford to lose sight of the need to acquire first a thorough understanding of the environment. Today, a sluggish market supports only a limited effort, except in petroleum and gas exploitation. A sober assessment of priorities is imperative; expansion of existing markets must be kept apart from the creation of new industries; the ocean must be considered as a milieu subject to technological and ecological limitations; finally, reaping of the ocean's resources will be a function of an honest profit for the investor and of the trends in national and international economies.

In 1968, coastal locations accounted for 84% of all marine exploitation activities, 14% were off-shore endeavors, and only 2% of the operations were deep water projects. The trend is rapidly changing and agreements signed in Geneva, in 1958, which granted sovereign rights to riparian nations, up to a depth of 200 meters, are well outdated since the ocean is readily exploitable beyond the 200-meter depth limit. With the new and increased demands of an exploding population, the economy of the ocean is a matter for immediate attention.

Water. One of the first resources of the ocean is water itself, whether it is used to extract salts, construct electrical power plants, or to quench the thirst of man and parched lands.

The shortage of fresh water poses a pressing problem: water levels are dropping on the continent; occasionally wells are invaded by brackish waters; artesian wells run dry; deeper and deeper drilled wells are needed. Kings County, outside New York City, woke up one morning to find its wells put out of use by seepage of the Long Island Sound waters—this was a half a century ago. Today, New York City and the surrounding communities import their drinking water from the Catskill Mountains, hundreds of kilometers away. Tapping the ocean for fresh water, an unthinkable luxury not so long ago, is now a necessity. Engineers have examined the possibility of towing icebergs from Antarctica to Australia and to the west coast of the United States. An iceberg with dimensions of 1,000 by 1,000 by 250 meters represents 250 million cubic meters and could be towed in 300 days near the Atocoma desert in Chile. It would lose 86% of its water mass but would still represent 35 million cubic meters of fresh water worth 2.7 million dollars. The trip would have cost 1.3 million dollars and thus, theoretically, the operation would be profitable.

Today, there are numerous desalting plants throughout the world providing fresh water for man, cattle, and irrigation purposes. Salt removal is done through a variety of processes such as distillation, the membrane process, congealing, solar distillation, chemical processes, physical and electrical methods, and the flash distillation process used in the San Diego, California, plant. This was the first plant in the United States to use the multiple flash process and is one of the world's largest. The U. S. Office of Saline Water disclosed, in

1968, that no less than 627 plants were then in use, being built, or on order, with a production capacity of 800,000 cubic meters per day. In many cases the energy needed to run the plants is provided by petroleum or gas, an ideal energy source in the Middle East. Kuwait has the lead in fresh water production with 100,000 cubic meters per day and is building two more plants which together will provide an additional 130,500 cubic meters of fresh water daily.

The major problem, of course, is the cost of the produced fresh water. Since fuel is no problem in Kuwait, water can be produced at a cost of 12 cents per cubic meter; otherwise, it would cost about 30 cents.

The price can probably be cut by planning larger plants, treating at least 100,000 cubic meters per day, and establishing agricultural-industrial complexes which will recuperate the waste products. If plans to build nuclear powered plants go through, then giant desalting factories will further reduce production costs by furnishing between 300,000 and 500,000 cubic meters per day.

Therapeutic uses. Is salt water beneficial to health? Agreement was reached long ago on the favorable effects of marine heliotherapy and of the curative properties of the combination air-sea-sun. However, there is also a marine thermal medicine, called thalassotherapy, which has achieved appreciable results in the treatment of several illnesses, among them rheumatism, healing of bone fractures, and rhinitis. Drugs from the sea constitute a segment of the pharmacopoeia. A symposium was organized, in 1970, dealing exclusively with the ocean as a source of useful drugs. Many old medical treatments are based upon the use of marine plants. Thalassotherapy stations are not of recent vintage; there are several such cure centers in France (Roscoff, Biarritz, Quiberon), in Germany, and elsewhere (e.g., Ostend, Belgium).

Under given conditions, sea water can be administered to patients orally, or by intravenous injections. Hot and cold baths, often accompanied by high pressure water streams, have been successfully used to combat obesity, nevritis and polynevritis, lumbago, cellulitis, and nasal conditions. Thousands of children were saved in pre-World War I days by sea water injections in specialized clinics at Paris, Brest, Reims, and Nancy, in France. Nasal absorption of sea water has proven beneficial in curing sinusitis. Yet, the medical use of sea water faded away after the end of World War I. Just as an interest is developing in the Western world for the use of needles in medicine, Chinese acupuncture, there is now a renewal of interest in thalassotherapy.

346

Energy. If there is a "water crisis", there is also an "energy crisis." Perhaps, with the help of the ocean, black-outs of the type experienced in New York and London can be avoided. Fossil energy production needed per-person in 1800 was 300 calories; by 1970, the requirements had reached 22,300 calories. The world is facing an electrical energy crisis, stated recently Nobel Prize winner Glenn T. Seaborg, former Chairman of the U. S. Atomic Energy Commission. Seaborg felt that the additional source of production should be the atom. Conservationists contend that the atom is a source of thermal pollution whose effects are not known. Another alternative is perhaps the harnessing

of the energies of the oceans, energy which is dissipated by tides, waves, and currents.

The Ancient Greeks had already attempted to take advantage of the Euripus tides, a channel separating Euboea and Boeotia. Near Chalcis, water mills put the energy of currents to use, while near Agostoli, on the isle of Cephalonia, energy to run mills was obtained from the tides. Tide mills were in use in England and Wales as early as the year 1000; even in the United States, in New England, and on Long Island, tide-powered mills were numerous. A major treatise on the subject of using the force of the tides was published in France in the late 18th century by Bernard Forest

ELECTRICITÉ DE FRANCE

Of all the world's nations, only two—the Soviet Union and France—have built tidal power plants. In this photograph, taken during the construction of the first French plant on the Rance River, near St. Malo, the massive central portion of the enclosure dam (being built inside a ring of cofferdams) dwarfs the French workmen.

de Bélidor. But plans on a larger scale were placed on the drawing boards after World War I. Possibilities of using the tides to produce energy have been examined in England, Wales, France, Australia, Argentina, the United States, and elsewhere. Under President Franklin Roosevelt, work was actually started on a tidal power plant near Passamaquoddy, Maine, in 1935, but it halted when Congress failed to appropriate funds. Under President John Kennedy, a similar plan was revived and approved, but Congress failed again to appropriate funds.

Tidal energy is derived from the force inherent in the earth's rotation. Only France and the U.S.S.R. have actually built tidal power plants: the first in the estuary of the Rance River, near St. Malo on the coast of Brittany, and the others on Kisgalobskaia Bay near the White Sea.

The price tag of such plants has been the main deterrent to their construction; it was the motivating factor in deciding not to construct the Severn River plant in Great Britain; and, yet, it is freely admitted today that, had the Severn plant been built, when first considered in 1933 or next in 1945, the operation would have paid off handsomely within 10 years. In Australia, the possibilities defy the imagination and a plant built on the Kimberley coast in western Australia would provide over 300,000 kw, or about 50 times the present production of electricity of Australia. A negative decision was taken because energy cannot be stored and there is not yet a sufficient market in Southeast Asia to use that much power. Meanwhile, the French plant has proved to be a boost to the development of Brittany and a worthwhile addition to the French national grid at peak demand times.

There are other sources of energy provided by the ocean besides that of the tides. Among these are thermal and electromagnetic energy, waves, and marine currents. Electromagnetic energy seems rather limited when compared to the total energy available. Thermal energy results from temperature differences between two water supplies of unlimited discharge. Warm surface waters, in equatorial regions and in the tropics, and deep cold waters flowing from the polar regions come into contact in these areas. An experimental plant was built in Abidjan, Republic of Ivory Coast, but was abandoned after a short period of time. Such plants, whose most favored locations are upwelling zones, near coasts, in tropical areas exposed to winds of constant direction, nevertheless hold great promise since the production of electricity can be coupled with fresh water production, air conditioning, and extraction of sodium chloride, sodium sulfate, chlorine, and hydrochloric acid. Recently, the physicist Barjot discussed the possibility of building thalassothermal plants in polar areas where the difference of temperature between the ocean water and the overlying air layers reaches some 50°C. Neither the tidal power plants nor the ocean thermal plants interferes with the environment.

No efforts have been made to harness the energy of marine currents, though the possibility was examined. In the last few years there has been a revival of interest for the harnessing of wave energy. A Boston firm has proposed a model plant; other projects have been under consideration in Chicago, on the west coast, in Biarritz, and in Japan. A Columbia University team has conducted a project to use thermal energy in the Virgin Islands and has coupled the plant with a high productivity mariculture effort. While production was very successful, using the warm waters, ecologists object strenuously, warning of environmental destruction, multiplication of algae, invasion of starfish, and possible ruin of the coral reefs.

Biological resources. Putting water itself and the production of energy aside, ocean resources can be classified into three categories: biological, chemical, and geological resources. The notion of resource can of course be extended to include the ocean bottom and its edges, offering sites for cables, pipelines, gasoducts, harbors and resorts, and the water itself as the geographical locale of maritime routes. During the last Oceanographic Congress held in Moscow in 1966, some oceanographers insisted on the inexhaustible quality of ocean bio-resources, insisting even that the then-current catch of 60 to 80 million tons of animal products, could be increased to 200 millions. Yet, it appears that the productivity of the Atlantic and Pacific oceans has reached its peak. Perhaps there is a possibility of increasing the catch in the Indian Ocean. But, if the ocean is not the panacea that alone can solve the hunger problem in the world, it can resolve, in part, the protein deficiency of some diets and certainly can provide more than the present 1% which it now contributes to worldwide nutrition. To increase ocean products consumption, education concerning religious tabus and diet are necessary.

The use of the biological resources of the ocean is a function of its productivity capacity, of its accessibility (because refrigeration is far from widespread), and of the cultural heritage. The plant life of the sea surpasses that of the land, indeed, but the algae are the principal constituent. It is thus probably toward the source of proteins rather than toward the vegetal matter that our attention should be turned. Infant deaths are due, in major percentages, to the lack of proteins in their diets, even though 3.5 to 7 kilograms of proteins per year would suffice. An investment of about $3.00 per year would provide a sufficient quantity of proteins per child, in the shape of food protein concentrate (FPC). A bit less than half the total catch of American fishermen is used to make fodder for cattle and developing countries can their sea food products in order to sell them as pet food in foreign countries— an incredible waste as far as human consumption is concerned since one ton of fish represents 115 kilograms of protein.

Aquaculture and Aquafarming. Aquaculture is the husbandry of marine species in closed basins and maricul-

348

ture is the same activity in open waters. With improved technology, both offer important new horizons, and the Japanese are leading the way. Three years ago, anchovies were successfully raised in basins at La Jolla, California; more recently, the Fisheries Ministry of the Republic of the Ivory Coast put special basins into use for the production of shrimps (*Penaeus ducrarum*), near Abidjan, and over 500,000 shrimps are being fattened in special lagoons. In the Morbihan region of France, similar efforts with prawns have been successful, and the production of lobsters and crayfish is expanding; aquaculture has been improved in Brittany and Aquitaine. Commercial production of shrimps in Japan has increased by 10% the supply which could not meet the demand. Encouraging results have been obtained with ambulatory basins for tuna, but in this instance efforts will be slowed down until an international agreement is reached guaranteeing to the producer the harvest of his "crop."

A major consideration in aquaculture and aquafarming is that the species which are being grown find in their new environment sufficient food and reproduction conditions which are favorable, while not becoming

CNEXO

In an aquaculture laboratory, at the Oceanographic Center in Brittany, French scientists and technicians conduct studies in the husbandry of such marine species as prawns, lobsters, and crayfish.

competitive with the indigenous species and not perturbing the alimentary equilibrium upon which they depend. Encouraging results were registered, near Angleton in Texas, where shrimps were raised in closed-off basins and fed a commercially produced diet. Near Manchester, in the State of Washington, Coho and Chinook salmon were raised in Puget Sound, starting from free males' sperm. Under the Sea Grant program, high sea mariculture experiments are conducted off the coast of Hawaii.

Since man has practically abandoned hunting in most regions of the world as a source of nutrition, in favor of animal husbandry, and gathering in favor of agriculture, would it not be possible to consider a similar trend in the ocean environment? Plankton yields 4,000 tons of vegetal matter for each 2.5 square kilometers, while such a surface yields only 600 tons on land. Naturally, since algae are the main plant life, the danger of pollution must be kept in mind and rivers and seas must be stocked, acclimating species if necessary, in order to avoid over-fertilization which may lead to eutrophication.

Denmark's Zealanders have produced commercially oysters and mussels for centuries. Today they place the young on rafters putting them out of reach of their carnivorous enemies and increasing fourfold their rate of growth by placing the mussel banks in the path of faster currents. Phytoplankton production can be intensified through a strictly supervised control, by mixing waters and even, perhaps, by using the heated waters poured out by nuclear plants. Nevertheless, the pollution factor remains staggering; without it, oyster production in the United States would easily reach 800 million tons. Two years ago, 90% of the oysters died in the Arcachon Bay, a major production center on the Atlantic Coast of France. The disappearance of shrimps and eels from the Belgian North Sea Coast, and the decline in the herring population, are definitely a consequence of the ecosystem's disruption.

According to Soviet scientists, the spawn of the sea urchin has wonderful healing properties and they believe that it can compete with ginseng, occasionally called "root of life." Each gram of the spawn contains as much as 35 milligrams of fat and 20 milligrams of protein, as well as an abundance of useful microorganisms. The waters washing Kunashir and Shikotan islands, in the Kuriles, are the only place in the world, it is believed, where sea urchins are available on a commercial scale. They are caught at a depth of 80 to 110 meters by special dredges installed on fishing vessels. The spawn is extracted from the sea urchins, canned at the Yuzhno-Kurilsk fish processing plant, and sent to medical institutions both within the U.S.S.R. and abroad. Aquaculture and aquafarming are not a new activity in the U.S.S.R.; they have even recently put into service a fish incubator; at the fish hatchery near Volgograd, white salmon are artificially bred. The male and female fish are kept in special pools of cold water for eight months. The spawn is incubated and the fry kept in covered pools with circulating cold water and then placed in special ponds. When the fry are large and strong enough, they are released into the Volga River and the Caspian Sea. The complete cycle takes a year. Nevertheless, the results are impaired by the pollution plaguing river and sea, and by existing hydroelectric dams.

Six years ago, Professor Shelbourne reported raising 300,000 plaice in Ardere Loch (Scotland). He had created in the loch conditions close to those of the ocean and showed that the death of the fry, under natural conditions, is almost exclusively caused by the voracity of marine flesh eaters. Marine husbandry could thus be a remedy to this situation.

Fish husbandry could even, it appears, help man combat pollution. In the last five years Asiatic Amurs have been raised in Arkansas and their incredible voracity has cleaned up several of the state's rivers.

Hunting. Environment and conservation conscious groups have been successful in putting some countries out of the whaling business and prohibiting the import of products of cetacean origin by the United States. Fur coats are suffering from a wave of reprobation. Seal and sea lion hunting are in great popular disfavor. Some voices even object to the training of porpoises for military aims. Efforts are made to avoid the killing of dolphins caught in the tuna fish nets. The hunting of sea mammals appears to be declining, since only Australia, Japan, and the U.S.S.R. continue large scale operations. Instead, the cooperation of some of these mammals is sought to help man retrieve objects lost at sea and to study sound transmission in the oceanic milieu.

Fishing. Fishing remains, even in these days of high technology, an enterprise based on nets, hooks, human labor, and a good deal of luck, yet the use of biomarine resources is still a sociological, cultural, and political matter. Areas which are rich in fish products are jealously protected by the riparian states. Peru strives to increase its anchovies catch from one-half to ten billion tons; the Soviet Union has pressed into service factory ships which accompany the fishermen's craft. Iceland has extended its territorial limits to keep other nations from exhausting the waters surrounding the island. The United States, once the second most important fishing nation, has dropped to sixth place, behind Peru, Japan, China, the U.S.S.R., and Norway. The fishing industry

of the Soviet Union has made amazing progress in the last years. If whaling is declining, its flotillas of over 100 fishing vessels are exceedingly efficient; it has built new fishing harbors, new factory ships, new spotting units, new harbor-to-fleet commuting vessels, and has provided developing nations with ultra-modern trawlers. The Soviets consider fishing as a very important source of hard currency and, for that reason, they reduced the production of salted, smoked and dried fish, increasing sales of fresh, frozen, and canned products. So far, however, they have not signed conservation agreements.

Soviet techniques have made considerable progress: in the Caspian Sea, fishermen use spotlights to find the fish, then use suction pumps to bring them aboard, while the sonar is used in locating currents, upwellings, schools, and in checking weather conditions. One submersible is used exclusively for fisheries research. Both Japan and France have improved their technological equipment; France has put to sea large vessels for tuna fishing; these vessels carry a helicopter whose task it is to spot schools of fish and to direct the fishing operations.

There is no doubt that the biological resources of the ocean constitute a precious contribution to the feeding of a world in which hunger is an endemic condition for large segments of humanity; it is equally true that more nations should turn to the sea in their efforts to solve the problem, but it is of paramount importance that no nation overlook the threat of overfishing which would rob the ocean of its regenerative capability. A primordial step is to acquire a better knowledge of the capital which the wealth of the seas represents, so that only a reasonable interest be collected.

Raw materials. Marine resources, we pointed out, are either chemical, geological or biological. Geological resources can be either authigenic, detrital, or organic. They are very numerous although specialists are not sure whether they are, under present conditions, profitably exploitable.

Phosphorite contains usually 30% of economically worthwhile material (P_2O_5) and is generally found where other materials brought from land are not accumulated. Exploitable areas include the Pacific coasts of both California and northwest Mexico, Peru, the northwest and the south of Africa, and probably the northwest of Australia as well. The Indian geological survey claims to have found deposits near the Andaman islands. The composition of phosphorite is sand, gravel, calcareous organic remains, and fossil phosphorite. Appreciated as fertilizer, phosphorite is mined, on land, in coastal North Africa and in Florida. One ton is worth $13, and costs more than a ton of marine phosphorite at $6.

It is already more than a hundred years since the *Challenger* reported the presence on the ocean bottom of nodules containing manganese; in 1968, an easily exploitable deposit was located under the waters of Lake Michigan, spreading over 500 square kilometers and at depths varying from 30 to 60 meters. The yield was assessed at 40,000 to 60,000 tons per-square-kilometer. These nodules are actually made up of several metals and nonmetals. A partial list, in order of decreasing importance, includes manganese, iron, aluminum; nickel, copper, and cobalt. The American concern Teneco announced in 1969 its plans to gather these nodules; the operation was actually to be carried out by its subsidiary, Deep Sea Ventures, which had gathered 40 tons of nodules off the Florida and Carolina coasts. In 1970, an area covering 390 square kilometers, in waters of medium depth, was located near Hawaii; heaviest concentrations were found near the north coast of Lihue and south of Kapaa. A French expedition picked nodules off Tuamotu (Tahiti) from depths varying between 1,000 and 1,600 meters: most samples were small but one specimen weighed 128 kilograms. A year ago, a team of oceanographers from Columbia University (New York) made a map of the manganese nodule sites which might well prove to be a valuable sheet of the economic atlas of the ocean we spoke about at the beginning of this paper.

Ferrous-manganetic concretions have been sited in the Sea of Japan and chromite could be exploited along the Sakhalin coast. According to John Mero, the Pacific Ocean alone has reserves of 10^{12} tons of manganese and a single gathering operation could provide up to 50% of the world's production of cobalt. P. L. Bezrukov of the U.S.S.R. Academy of Sciences Oceanology Institute describes as follows the 1969 to 1970 *Vitiaz* campaign: "Nodules of manganese are found at depths of 4 to 6 kilometers at rather large distance from continental masses in regions of accidented relief and slow sedimentation. The sediments are red clays and diatomeceous or radiolarae oozes. At lesser depths, 1 to 2 kilometers, nodules rest upon igneous or carbonaceous rocks and upon the ocean bottom. The highest density is 50 to 75 kg/m^2 in the central Pacific where phosphatic rocks are abundant on the slopes of submarine mountain chains which stretch westwards from Hawaii." These observations conform to the photographic reconnaissance made by American scientists. If the Soviets are right, then reserves of over 100 billion tons of cobalt, manganese, and nickel rest on the bottom of the Pacific Ocean. If all this data is correct, then less than 1% of ocean bottom reserves would suffice to satisfy current needs in manganese, nickel, copper

and cobalt for 50 years. According to Brooks, the price of manganese production could drop by 45%, that of nickel by 7%, and that of cobalt by 30%. His views are challenged by Sorensen and Mead who see only reductions of 3% and 4% for manganese and nickel, respectively, but still 27% for cobalt.

According to D. S. Cronan of the University of Ottawa, manganese at depths exceeding 3,300 meters is mostly todokorite, while at lesser depths it is manganese dioxide. Todokorite concentrates nickel and copper which replace the bivalent dioxide which concentrates, instead, cobalt and lead; todokorite is more common in an oxidation milieu.

Though some scientists doubt the development of a large ocean mining industry, ocean mining is already a reality. Sands and gravels are extracted from the ocean. Some, containing organic remains, have been used as building stone: San Marcos Castle, in St. Augustine, is built from coquina. Sands and gravels are used for artificial beach building, land fill, cement production and in the making of prestressed concrete. They are inexpensive and easily transported.

Ocean Cay is an artificial island built in the Bahamas Archipelago using dredged material. Aragonite is sucked up and treated on this island; production reached two million tons during 1971 and reserves are estimated at 575 million tons. Near Muiden, in The Netherlands, sand is dredged from a depth of 75 meters under the surface of the former Zuiderzee. Off the British Isles, more than 50 dredges exploit sand and gravel deposits. Recently, high quality calcareous sands have been located near the Laccadive Islands. These mining operations might prove dangerous if carried out too close to the coasts as the Lebanese and the Israelis found out: beaches can be ruined. Yet, the need for marine sands and gravels will increase: some countries fail to find sufficient quantities on land and the French foresee that within a decade the Channel will be tapped for the materials needed by Paris, Normandy, and the north of France.

Some sands contain gold; gravels contain diamonds and often where gold is found, there is also platinum. Shell Oil is prospecting off Alaska. Goodnews Bay has provided, since 1935, close to 90% of the platinum needed by the United States. Extraction is presently carried out on Australian and South African beaches; here diamonds have been mined from the sea since 1962, all along the coast from the Orange River mouth to Deay Point. Kimberlite is transported by the river and deposited along the littoral by marine action. The yield is not negligible: in 1964, one company extracted 16,118 carats from a single marine deposit. In Alaska, Inlet Oil exploits petroleum deposits, but also discovered gold deposits in the channel off Bluff and continues its search in Goodnews Bay for gold, platinum, mercury, and chrome, and in the southeast for gold, silver, copper, zinc and uranium. Beyond the Burdekin River (Queensland), Australians found gold deposits whose worth is estimated at $100 million.

Off the southeast coast of Greenland, Danish enterprises are prospecting for chromite, rutile, and platinum. Near southeast Alaska, 1,000 tons of barite are mined per day. Heavy minerals have concentrated on the continental platform at depths averaging 200 to 300 meters and ilmenite and rutile are currently mined off the Australian coasts where 95% of the world's reserves of rutile are located (east coast). Yearly, 450,000 tons of ilmenite are mined off the Australian west coast. Both ilmenite and rutile are often associated with zirconium and with thorium-containing monazite. Zircon and monazite are extracted simultaneously with titanium in Florida, Ceylon, and Australia. Though deposits of monazite have been located off India and Alaska, Australia remains the leader with 30% of the world's production. Near Liepaja, in the Baltic Sea, uranium has been mined since 1972; the Soviets are looking for deposits of titanium, ilmenite, and rutile in the same area. Already, magnetite and titanium placers have been detected in the sands of the northwest coast of the Black Sea; similar deposits were found near Batumi and in the Sea of Azow. These placers also contain chromite—already mined off the Oregon coast—magnetite, cassiterite, and aragonite. Magnetite was exploited, until very recently, by the Finns, and the Japanese still extract 40,000 tons per year south of Kyushu Island.

Construction is under way in the Maritime Territory district of the U.S.S.R. of a metallurgical complex which will process manganese, cobalt, nickel, and copper-containing materials of marine origin. Among others, the plants will treat magnetite- and titomagnetite-rich placers mined from the Baltic and Black seas. Other such deposits have been located in the Sea of Azow and near the Kurile Islands. Still among the Soviet plans are recovery of tin from the Laptev Sea and the east Siberian coasts, and of amethyst along the southern littoral of the White Sea. Cassiterite, a tin ore, has been mined from the ocean for some time: in the State of Selangor (Malaysia) tin is mined from 50 meter depths. The 65th anniversary of tin mining near Tongkah (Thailand) was celebrated in 1972. Five years ago, new deposits of cassiterite were spotted in the Andaman Sea near Takuapa, and exploitation started in 1968. In Indonesia, eluvions and alluvions containing tin ore are dredged from the ocean bottom, close to the isles of Singkep, Banka, and Billiton. In 1971, an American concern tested a hydraulic mining system which proved functional at depths down to 1,000 meters. The largest tin ore dredge was built recently by the Japanese: they scrape the ocean bottom then suck up the material made up of sands and muds. Once aboard the ship, the ore is automatically separated from the bulk of the material which is then returned to the ocean. Japanese experiments are under way with a continuous belt dredge which could perhaps work at depths of up to 4,000 meters.

The Soviets reported large tin reserves in the Vankina Guba (Yakutia), near Selyakhskaya, stretching from Cape Svyatoi Nos, to the Strait of Dmitri Laptev, south of Bolshoi Lyakhov Island, and in the harbors of Khuntazeyev and Siahu, and also in the Japan Sea. They claim to be ready to extract diamonds, platinum, and especially gold near Kalyma (Lena River), Nakhodka (Okhotsk Sea) and along the northern and southern coasts of the Kamchatka Peninsula. Specially equipped ore processing ships are being built. They will also serve for prospecting and be equipped with a probe with a radio-isotope sensor which, when put to sea, will reveal on a shipboard indicator the presence of lead, gold, and manganese through gamma ray absorption.

In the Atlantic Ocean, off the coast of Cornwall, in St. Ives Bay, recovery of tin-containing sands has started and important deposits have been located off Brest, on the coast of Brittany. In closing this impressive, yet far from complete, survey, let us mention copper and zinc mining operations in Maine, potash in Great Britain, and barite in Alaska. Here, natural forces have not barred operations even though tides reach seven meters, winds reach speeds of 170 km/hour and temperatures fall below −15°C.

Muds. As a result of erosion, and from alluvial accumulations, muds are deposited at the sea bottom at lesser depths than on the continental platform. They can be divided into two types: calcareous muds and red muds. The first type originates from shell deposits and can be used in the production of whitewash, as fertilizer, or for its content of calcium, potassium or barite. Such muds cover about 35% of the ocean bottom at depths ranging from 700 to 6,000 meters with layers whose thickness is estimated at 400 meters on the average. This calcareous cover would thus spread over 128 million square kilometers and accumulate at the rate of one billion tons per year, or eight times the quantity yielded by contemporary land operations.

The red muds are agillaceous and constitute a source of aluminum, iron, copper, nickel, cobalt, and vanadium. According to some oceanographers, they cover one-half of the floor of the Pacific Ocean and one-fourth of the Atlantic Ocean bottom at an average depth of 3,000 meters.

Dissolved substances. Since time immemorial, man has extracted from sea water common salt or sodium chloride; it still represents some 30% of the world production today. Its use is both domestic and industrial. Bromine and magnesium compounds are simultaneously extracted: 70% of the total production of bromine and 60% of the magnesium used are of marine origin. Dow, Kaiser, and Merck extract magnesium in Texas, and Dow alone provides, from marine origin, 75% of the U. S. needs in bromine. Near Los Angeles, iodine is extracted from the petroleum fields' brackish solutions.

A few years ago, hot brines were discovered in the Red Sea. The estimated value of the mineral materials contained in these brines is estimated at more than 1.5 million dollars. Layers, occurring at depths of more than 2,100 meters, are sometimes 200 meters thick and contain, besides precious metals, zinc, lead, copper, and cobalt. Joseph Lassiter, of the Massachusetts Institute of Technology, wrote that in the Atlantic Deep II of the Red Sea, there are reserves, in the upper 11 meters layer, worth $2.3 billion. Such wealth is tempting but, so far, no extraction method has been devised. The Hughes Tool Company and Deep Sea Ventures are conducting research to develop an appropriate system.

Sea water composition is well known and analyses have put in evidence quantities of dissolved copper, cobalt, zinc, gold, uranium, and deuterium. Concentrations, however, are small, yet, these elements could perhaps be recovered as a side operation of desalinisation plants.

Indirect exploitation. Some activities are not *sensu stricto* ocean mining, but they are closely linked with the ocean domain, albeit because of the technological problems involved or the location of the zones of extraction. The Japanese extract coal in mines which stretch under the sea. African concerns such as De Beers, in the Republic of South Africa, gather diamonds off the coast of the Southwest Africa Territory. It is only in the last 25 years that petroleum companies have been drilling through the ocean floor, first at modest depths, then at ever increasing depths, to reach the petroleum reserves stored under the ocean. Progress in petroleum extraction in the ocean has raised questions of international law which have not yet been answered.

Even before the Christian era, mines were under exploitation by Greeks beneath the sea at Laurium. Since then, coal, limestone, iron ore, tin, copper, and nickel have been extracted near the British Isles, Ireland, the Atlantic coast of France; near Greece, Turkey and Spain in the Mediterranean; Finland in the Baltic Sea; Japan and China in Asia; and on the American west coast off Alaska, Canada, the United States, and Chile.

Among the organic geological resources are shells, petroleum, and natural gas. We mentioned shells earlier; as for gas and petroleum, they are being depleted at a faster rate than extraction progresses. Not so long ago, wells dug at depths of 25 meters were considered quite an achievement; today depths of 250 meters are not unusual and current prospecting is considering deposits more than 400 meters under the water surface. Petroleum demand doubles approximately every ten years, a situation which has triggered worldwide prospecting. Some salt domes come close to the ocean surface and through dissolving of the halite, bacteria can bring about sulfate reduction and transform non-soluble matter into sulfur. Contemporary sulfur production, from the sea, accounts for more than 10% of the total sulfur production in the United States, or about 60,000 tons in 1965.

Coal, like gas and petroleum, is not extracted from the ocean but rather from under the ocean; such coal mines are operated in China, Japan, Turkey, Great Britain, Nova Scotia and Newfoundland, and in Chile. Some two million tons were extracted in 1965. While petroleum and gas production is progressing at an accelerating pace in the North Sea, important reserves of methane have been discovered and are also being tapped. A listing of indirect exploitation of the ocean should include such products as corals, used to manufacture jewelry (Bahamas), amber (Baltic), and limestones, used for building and cement manufacture.

Hydrocarbons, however, remain the most abundant mineral resource extracted from the oceans today. New sites are continuously discovered throughout the world. One of the richest fields underlies the North Sea. Some finds are spectacular because of their reserves, others because of the technological difficulties in tapping them. In 1972, one find was sited 135 miles off Aberdeen (Scotland) with an estimated daily production of 4,000 barrels of petroleum and 60,000 cubic meters of natural gas. The North Sea "Brent concession" is about 100 miles north of the Shetland Islands, at 91°N. latitude, at a depth of 150 meters, in an area where winds reach speeds of 160 km/hour and waves are frequently 30 meters high! The Soviets have found considerable gas and petroleum reserves east of the Crimean Peninsula in the Black Sea, along the Romanian Dobrudja littoral and on the submarine plateau stretching from Varna (Bulgaria) to the Bosporus. Monthly petroleum industry periodicals list new sites, new areas under exploration, new concessions being granted. But this flurry of economic exploitation of the oceans is not without dangers. Petroleum companies and shipping companies are severely taken to task by environment-conscious groups. Collisions of giant tankers, wells out of control, bursting of a layer, or fires on

C. G. DORIS

drilling platforms, all contribute to disasters known as the black tide, with its ensuing pollution of water and air, destruction of aquatic life, and spoiling of ocean beaches. Though cases brought to court are dealt with severely, unbridled commercial efforts continue; the frenzy is such that there are not sufficient drills to satisfy the demand, especially those for great depths. In 1971, one company brought a giant drill back from Australia to the North Sea at a cost of two million dollars, and found the investment profitable.

As of 1969, one fifth of the world's petroleum production was of submarine origin and close to 400 million tons of gas and oil had already been extracted from the ocean milieu. It is foreseen that by 1980, or 1985, wells will be drilled at depths of 2,000 meters. Considering that, in 1965, 15% of the world production of liquid hydrocarbons came from the ocean, in addition to 6% of the gaseous hydrocarbons, the increase is about 5% per year. It is foreseen that by 1980, 30% will come from the ocean, and by 1990 more than two billion tons will be extracted, which represented

Such ultra-modern oil storage facilities as this one in the North Sea, coupled with successful experiments that have been conducted with pre-stressed concrete tanks on the bottom of the Red Sea, are dramatic examples of the petroleum companies' continuing efforts to minimize the environmental and financial costs of oil spills.

the total world production of liquid hydrocarbons in 1971. Within 20 years, the number of drilling platforms grew from none to 360. Yet, some believe that these quantities will not satisfy the demand.

From a technological viewpoint, oil drilling operations still follow the traditional pattern involving a derrick and a drilling platform, some of which are sufficiently large to accommodate a heliport. Humble Oil is pursuing research to refine a remote flow control system; diving bells would be used to periodically inspect installations, while the oil itself would be stored in pre-stressed concrete tanks resting upon the ocean bottom. Experiments with such storage facilities were quite satisfactory when conducted in the Red Sea.

The demand for oil, estimated at 8,000 million tons by 1980, and the need to spread the geographical sites of operations so as not to be at the mercy of political crises, are sufficient motivation to drill at ever greater depths even though the cost of installations doubles each time depth increases by 600 meters. Since 1970, 75 countries have engaged in geological and geophysical exploration along their coastlines and 42 have drilled in the sea.

The ocean as real estate. Oceanic bottoms represent a very important piece of real estate today. For more than a hundred years telephone and telegraph cables have rested on its floor; the last such cable linked Japan and Hawaii in 1964. More numerous, and covering shorter distances, are the pipelines and gaslines. Underwater tourism, once a science fiction dream, was a highly popular attraction during a world exhibit in Geneva, when Piccard used his mesoscaphe to take tourists on an underwater ride in Lake Geneva. In Florida and the Virgin Islands, the U. S. National Park Service created, several years ago, the two first underwater national parks, providing scuba divers with an opportunity to observe, along marked paths, aquatic flora and fauna in an undisturbed environment; popular response was such that a third such park was inaugurated in Hawaii in 1970.

The futuristic views of Athelstan Spilhaus, former dean of the Institute of Technology at the University of Minnesota, were taken tongue in cheek a decade ago. Even though underwater cities and resorts have not left the drawing boards, the Japanese, surrounded by an incredibly polluted environment, plan to build housing complexes beneath the waters of the Sea of Japan; if construction has been delayed, it is not because of technological handicaps, but rather because authorities want to ascertain that fishing, and the coastal environment, will not suffer ill effects from such a project.

Since the end of World War I, tourism has become accessible to the popular masses and has given rise to an ever expanding industry; in some countries the tourism industry represents the major part of the national income. Water tourism attracts thousands of men, women, and children, and ocean shore recreation is perhaps the leader in this type of activity, including fishing, nautical sports, swimming, and just plain beach relaxation. Unfortunately, total anarchy has characterized the development of shore resorts. Beach erosion, dune bulldozing, lack of sanitary facilities, damages caused by the tourists themselves, and commercial de-

velopments, have wrought havoc with coastal areas, brought about the virtual disappearance of entire stretches of beach, led to the toppling of valuable properties and buildings. Unless we have given up hope of salvaging the tourist resources constituted by the ocean, drastic measures must be taken immediately. The United States has already passed strict legislation to protect the shore areas, but only a few other Western countries have managed to timidly "protect" a few natural sites.

The ocean offers travel lanes in depth and in surface, unhampered so far, and its shores provide choice locations for the establishment of harbors. The intensity of today's traffic on some routes and towards specific ports and the ever increasing tonnage of ships have caused traffic jams, incidents, and multiply accidents which often result in the spilling of dangerous, dirtying, and noxious substances. It is high time that some order be brought to the maritime lanes, to safety, to environmental protection and that laws be updated.

Who owns the ocean? Several proposals dealing with the ownership of the ocean, beyond territorial waters, as well as with the extent of territorial waters, have been placed before the United Nations organization. Private firms are hesitant to invest large sums required by prospecting and exploiting of ocean areas, as long as ocean ownership is not clearly defined. They can hardly be blamed, since several have been hit hard in their pocketbook by sudden nationalizations which, in several instances, were outright confiscation. And yet, some companies have announced definite plans for the coming years to start mining in the Pacific Ocean as deep as 5,000 and 6,000 meters. Japanese commercial enterprises are backed by the government and an increase of 15% was decided in 1972 over the preceding year's budget for mineral exploitation of the ocean. But Japan is by no means alone in its expanding interest in the ocean; the efforts of the Soviets have been widely publicized and the United States has been in the forefront of oceanographic activities for some time. It was inevitable that legal problems would arise from positions which are unavoidably divergent. There is virtually no marine law jurisprudence; there is no clear definition of the boundary separating two states at sea. The only international agreement with some relevance to present conditions is more than ten years old and, since then, technological progress has outdistanced the legal wisdom. At that time, the continental plateau was defined as the bottom of the sea and the sub-bottom layers of the adjacent marine regions, located outside the national territory, up to a depth of 200 meters, or beyond that limit if "the depth of the overlying waters permitted the exploitation of the natural resources of said regions." This satisfied the signatories of the convention because no techniques existed then which would permit penetration at greater depths. It left virtually without any "marine" territory countries bordering areas where the continental plateau is non-existent. An example is Peru which is asking, in compensation, territorial limits of 300 km, and patrols its "territory" in consequence, often capturing foreign vessels and demanding heavy fines. U. S. fishing vessels often fall victim of this practice and the U. S. Government, which refuses to recognize the Peruvian limits, bails them out. However, some countries, which have neither the manpower nor the financial means of enforcing respect of their territorial limits, could quite well entrust this task to third parties and thereby upset political situations. Finally, must we ignore the objections of land-locked countries which, perhaps rightfully, feel that the ocean belongs to all of humanity and demand their share of the wealth of the "last frontier on earth?"

Discussion about international law for the economic uses of the sea started when the U. N. delegation from Malta suggested that the ocean should not be up for grabs but should instead be shared by all of mankind. Vociferous objections were instantly raised against all proposals in this direction, especially from the firms who have been tapping the mineral sources of the sea, oil and gas.

Today it is obvious that legislation regarding the sea is no longer adequate. When the agreements were reached in Geneva in 1958 nobody realized that nations would ever want to exploit the sea at a greater depth than 200–300 meters. But today it seems quite possible that by the year 1980 the oceans could be exploited to depths of 4,000 meters. However, legislation means restriction. The idea of an international sea bed regime means limiting national jurisdiction and the question is where to set the limits and over what.

In this respect there are several problems to be solved; for instance, the problem of the continental shelf, which has not yet been defined; territorial sea and zone, fishing banks, innocent passage, international regulation and regime, exploitation and conservation of resources, and measures against pollution. Furthermore, since World War II, the fishing fleets of the world have been renewed and changed radically and catches increased rapidly. There is reason to believe that fishing might start to decline in the near future. Oil and gas now represent 90% of all the mineral wealth extracted from the sea, but today we see signs of exploitation of other minerals as well.

There is widespread belief that an international regime is necessary in order to avoid clashes over the riches of the sea but the world's nations have quite different views of the form of such a regime. Some want to give the authority in this matter to the United Nations or to the International Court in the Hague, but experience has taught that these institutions have no means of enforcing their decisions and thus must have the consent of all parties involved in order to achieve agreement.

There seems to be common agreement that an international regime of the sea must encourage peaceful economic exploitation of the sea and that it must ensure maximum benefits, not only for coastal states, but for the entire international community. Such a regime must furthermore be flexible enough to be adapted easily to new technology. The Geneva agreement in 1958 was very flexible, at that time, but signatories did not expect that it would shortly be possible to exploit resources at great depths.

Committees, preparing the conference of the United Nations on the Law of the Sea (1973), discussed topics such as freedom of passage through straits, coastal states' preferences as regards fisheries, international regime versus national jurisdiction, conservation, and scientific research, and so on.

Various types of proposals concerning international machinery were put forward. The four main types are:

▶ International machinery for information exchange and preparation of studies.
▶ International machinery with intermediate powers.
▶ International machinery for licensing and registration.
▶ International machinery with comprehensive powers.

Many nations made proposals: the United States, Malta, Tanzania, Latin American countries, France, Britain, the Soviet Union, Canada, a group of land-locked and shelf-locked nations, and others. And, naturally, numerous theses are put forward. Among these, one position insists on the rights of first occupancy, which would grant ownership to the first discoverer, going as far back as the 15th century when new lands were annexed by European nations. This would unavoidably lead to armed conflict and guarantee possession to the most powerful nations. The world ocean would soon be divided among these and become a private lake. Another thesis is based upon the logical continuity of the coast and the continental slope; hence, the national territory would continue underneath the sea, as long as the sea bottom would be, without fracture or break, the extension of the coast. Still another position recommends the subdivision of the entire ocean bottom, beyond the continental plateau, among all countries. One point that remained unsettled in this last plan was whether all shares would be equal, or which rules would determine the various shares. A final proposal would apply the high seas rule to the ocean bottom, and thus all countries would own, jointly, the ocean bottom while no nation would acquire an individual property title over a given area.

With joint ownership, new problems arise: exploitation would then be done either by the community of nations or else the community would grant concessions for which research permits and exploitation permits would be granted in exchange for the payment of license fees. Were the community itself to attempt exploitation, the ultimate outcome would lead to a colonization of the oceans by the superpowers, since they alone possess a sufficiently advanced technology. On the other hand, a system of licensing with payment of fees, would theoretically benefit the entire community, with each country getting a share of the fees even though the work would be done by highly developed countries.

The American proposal would substitute for a regime of *laissez faire,* of which the United States was at one time the determined supporter, a supranational collaboration which would not hamper freedom of navigation on the high seas and beyond reasonable territorial limits. This proposal recognizes the overall interests of all humanity, the need to protect the environment, and the obligation to fairly apportion the benefits reaped from the ocean. This plan can be summarized as follows: first, beyond 200 meters depth, resources extracted from the ocean would be used partly for scientific research and partly for improvement of the economic conditions in the underdeveloped countries. Respect of the convention and administration of a common fund would be ensured by an international authority, which would have the necessary instrumentalities to impose rules enforcement, e.g., control services, courts, parliamentary assemblies, political councils and technical commissions.

The administrative domain of this authority would encompass all supra- and extraterritorial waters when they have been defined. This international authority would also grant exploration and exploitation licenses, pass anti-pollution regulations, and, in general, be the watchdog over the aquatic environment.

Although national sovereignty would affect areas of less than 200 meters depth, national sovereignty would nevertheless be somewhat reduced. The coastal state would have exploitation rights in its national area but, nevertheless, would have to pay the international authorities some fee, based on the product harvested. This fee could be as high as two-thirds of the sum collected at the time the license was granted. The proposal provides special consideration for islands and coastal states very dependent on fisheries.

This clause places riparian states under control of the international body and makes it impossible for them to extend their territory into the international area. The greed and indifference of coastal states would thus be constrained. Such nations would be prohibited from transforming their "maritime territory" into pollution factories. The main opposition to the American proposal is the Tanzanian proposal, which is favored by many developing countries. Tanzania wants each state to set its own limitation of territorial waters with resources outside the national jurisdiction distributed according to a rule which states roughly "to each country according to its needs." Members of the U.N. shall provide money on a basis proportional to contributions to the United Nations, which means that the United States and Europe would bear the burden. Then, income would be used for administration, exploration and exploitation expenses. The remainder, if any, would be distributed to the states that belong to the U.N. in inverse proportion to what they contribute to support the U.N. Thus, when there was an income, it would be used at first to pay back the sums paid to this international body and the remainder shared by all, with the poorest nations getting the largest share.

The Soviet proposal favors creation of an international authority to administer the sea bed resources. This authority would be governed by a small executive committee and controlled by an assembly of the signatory states.

This executive committee would be empowered to enforce adherence to the terms of the treaty, control industrial activities, assess reserves, distribution, and localization of resources, deliver licenses, and determine disposition of benefits. On the other hand, this international authority would not have jurisdiction over the sea bed nor the immediately underlying layers, nor would it have exploration and exploitation rights.

These two restrictive clauses do not appear in the Tanzanian proposal, which would authorize the international authority to own mining equipment, establish research and oceanographic institutes, and provide experts and technological assistance to developing countries which would become active in ocean exploration and exploitation. The international authority would be empowered to set prices and to decide the quantity of products that may be offered for sale, thereby protecting the smaller nation's economy.

The Latin American group has come up with a proposal similar to Tanzania's. It does not foresee an international machinery nor the right for such as authority to grant licenses; nor does it vest in anyone de facto or de jure ownership of the sea bed. The general trend is to put territorial limits at 20 km, with the right of innocent passage for any vessel, and economic jurisdiction at 300 km.

A proposal which has gathered strong support calls

for the creation of international machinery with comprehensive powers. This receives the widest consideration from the U.N. General Secretariat, and appears in proposals from the United States, France, and Great Britain. Yet the two most powerful countries—the United States and the U.S.S.R.—seemingly agree to support an extensive international regime for the oceans, with modest claims of national jurisdiction. The American proposal has reaped much criticism from large international consortiums which claim that it would stymie scientific research and exploration, and would foster exploitation conflicts. While this argument is not without merit, private concerns managed to find, and exploit, mineral resources on land, notwithstanding legislation that was quite restrictive; as a matter of fact, exploitation was so anarchic that reserves are often exhausted and the countryside is left with scars; the land is polluted. Perhaps a slower paced exploitation might be wholesome and benefit future generations.

Unfortunately, progress is very slow and probably no treaty will be signed before 1980. The workload is heavy since so many international conventions must be re-examined. Some examples are: territorial sea, contiguous zones, high seas, continental platform, fisheries, and conservation of high seas' biological resources. It is difficult to be optimistic when one realizes that of the 127 states that are members of the United Nations organization, barely 28 have ratified the 1958 Geneva Convention.

The ocean, ideal dumping ground. About ten years ago, the ocean was praised not only for the promise it held to solve some of humanity's problems, but also because it provided an ideal dumping ground for both human wastes and, for radioactive wastes. Since then, concrete containers containing nerve gas, ypresite, and others with radioactive wastes have been thrown into the ocean; so have street-cars, cars, untreated sewage and used water. The list is far from comprehensive. Yet, *in fine,* air pollution, land pollution and water pollution are all ocean pollution; the ocean is endangered ecologically, chemically, physically. We cannot allow further deterioration of the ocean. Furthermore, the ocean does not destroy matter as rapidly as was once thought. The recent experiments conducted on food retrieved from the submersible *Alvin* refloated after one year at the bottom shows that conservation in the ocean is quite surprising. The sea has favored the biological balance by absorbing refuse and diluting the substances which could have been destructive. Through the action of the marine flora and fauna, of absorption, digestion, transformation and concentration phenomena, regeneration of the vital environment fa-

vorable to life upon our planet takes place, but the noxious elements cannot be allowed to exceed the regenerative capacity of nature. Until this century, nature's capacity has never been challenged, but now it is endangered. The challenge has taken on new dimensions because, in addition to the large quantities of wastes brought to the ocean by rivers or directly thrown in it at the coast, and to chemical refuse and nuclear wastes poured into the ocean, we are faced with petroleum wastes and the cleansing of ships at sea. Soviet researchers found hydrocarbon derivates at depths of 100 meters in the Baltic Sea and a natural reserve near the Hange peninsula would be certainly destroyed if a planned refinery were to be constructed in the area. As far as ecologists are concerned, either we prevent exploration and drilling for marine-derived hydrocarbons, or we will founder and die in a polluted quagmire.

The exploitation of the ocean for the benefit of all humanity must be conducted as part of an overall plan that provides the clean-up of the marine environment, the fight against further pollution, the improvement of existing conditions, and the protection of the environment. Whether we consider chemical, biological, or geological resources, ocean exploitation should not be allowed to take place amidst juridical anarchy, moral irresponsibility or at the expense of future generations. Richard Cowen once compared the man who lives from what the earth provides as living off his capital, while the man who lives from the exploitation of the oceans is like a man living off his dividends. The capital-ocean must be well cared for.

Professor Vigneaux studied at the Universities of Lille, Bordeaux, and Paris, and was awarded the degrees of Doctor of Sciences and of Pharmacist. He is Vice President of the University of Bordeaux I and member of the Scientific and Technical Committee of the Centre National pour l'Exploitation des Océans. He is Director of both the Natural History Museum of Bordeaux and the Geological Institute of the Aquitaine Basin. President of the Organizing Committee of the International Congress on the Exploitation of the Oceans of Bordeaux, Professor Vigneaux manages the Department of Geology and Oceanography of the University of Bordeaux.

Professor Charlier was born in Belgium and studied in various European universities and in America, and has earned three doctoral degrees. Now a U.S. citizen, he is a professor of oceanography at the University of Bordeaux I, he holds the chair of regional geography at the Vrije Universiteit Brussels, and is professor of oceanography at Northeastern Illinois University (Chicago). In his words, "he commutes." He has authored articles in various American and European periodicals and has written a book on oceanography to be published by McGraw-Hill.

Who Owns the Oceans?

By Commander Richard C. Knott, U. S. Navy

The Law of the Sea Conference, scheduled for 1973, must come to grips with such thorny international problems as those typified by the seizure, below, of a U. S. fishing boat in 1971 for "illegally" fishing within Ecuador's 200-mile territorial sea.

The winds of change which have so altered human concepts and attitudes in recent years are now blowing across the oceans of the world. Nations have begun to look at the sea with new interest, and some have even decided that it is entirely proper and in keeping with their sovereign rights to claim huge portions of it for themselves. Principles governing the use of the sea once considered sacrosanct are being challenged or ignored with increasing frequency, and the law of the sea is in danger of disintegration. Moved to action by this alarming trend, the international community is now preparing for a world conference to begin in late 1973, which would attempt to resolve major problems through multilateral agreement. But it is far from certain that such an ambitious undertaking can be successful. The issues are politically complex, the obstacles to accommodation are formidable, and the stakes are enormous. Yet the alternative to multilateral agreement is maritime anarchy, a development which can only work to the detriment of all.

The law of the sea has evolved from both custom and treaty. It is a collection of rules which, over the years, has attempted to accommodate various international interests to create order in the marine environment. The law of the sea is unique in that it is one area of international jurisprudence which has enjoyed almost universal acceptance with minimal change for over three centuries. Its most basic tenet is the principle expounded by Hugo Grotius who, in 1604 declared "that no part of the sea may be regarded as pertaining to the domain of any given nation;" ergo the sea is open to use by all.

There can be little doubt that Grotius' arguments were tailored to suit the interests of Dutch commerce and the Dutch East India Company in particular. It is not surprising therefore that his thesis drew fire from certain major maritime powers who saw their commanding positions threatened.

The concept of the free seas survived, nevertheless, and eventually gained widespread acceptance. Regardless of his motivation, Grotius' reasoning was sound and ideally suited to the requirements of the times as subsequent history has proven. European leaders were beginning to see, albeit in terms of national aggrandizement, that the economic and political growth of Western civilization increasingly would depend upon the use of the sea for trade, exploration, warfare, and communication of ideas. Moreover, it was plain that there was more than enough ocean for everyone who possessed the assets and was willing to compete. Considering the vastness of ocean space and man's feeble ability to control and exploit the sea, it must have seemed presumptuous for any one country to claim large sections for its exclusive use. Grotius had wisely perceived that the sea was not susceptible of possession or occupation and that assertions of ownership would be difficult to defend with either logic or force.

A state, however, is thought to possess the inherent right to defend itself and to provide for the safety of its citizens. Consequently, it became generally accepted that a coastal state must be afforded the right to exercise sovereignty over a narrow band of the sea adjacent to its coast for reasons of national security. By the 1800s, it was widely conceded that three miles, based on cannon-shot range, was a reasonable limitation to the breadth of the territorial sea.* This idea prevailed without serious challenge until the early 1900s when Imperial Russia claimed a 12-mile exclusive fisheries zone. The Soviets in their turn declared that this was in reality a territorial sea, thus producing a significant crack in the international consensus. This crack was to widen further as a result of underlying forces born of technology, population growth, and political change.

It was World War II which provided the catalyst for major adjustment. Great navies and merchant fleets busying themselves in the business of global conflict ranged the seas revising old concepts of security and strategy. A tremendous acceleration in the development of ocean technology took place and new devices came into existence which not only affected the techniques of warfare but also had important implications for the exploitation of ocean resources. In 1945, President Harry S. Truman, recognizing the importance of these technological developments as they could be applied to undersea deposits of petroleum and minerals, declared that the natural resources of the continental shelf were henceforth to be considered as "appertaining to the United States, subject to its jurisdiction and control." But while great care was taken to differentiate between the continental shelf and the water column over it, many countries chose to overlook this important distinction and took the position that the U. S. action established a precedent for unilateral claims over all or any part of the marine environment.

Perhaps the most significant consequence of the war was the political change it wrought. Power balances shifted and colonial empires disintegrated. Former colonies grasped the opportunities presented. But emerging nations soon found that independence was hollow without economic viability. Large, industrially-developed countries still controlled the wealth of the world and the normal give and take of international economic competition seemed certain to widen rather than narrow the development gap. Developing coun-

*See G. G. Carlisle, "Three-Mile Limit—Obsolete Concept?" U. S. Naval Institute *Proceedings*, February 1967, pp. 24–33.

tries found themselves faced with an accelerating population growth rate and a decreasing capability to satisfy rising expectations and even basic needs. To many, the sea seemed to offer a way out of their dilemma. The possibility of finding rich oil and mineral deposits or of establishing lucrative fisheries off their coasts had great appeal. This idea set in motion a new undercurrent of change and a new threat to freedom of the sea as well.

In 1952, three developing Latin American countries, Chile, Ecuador, and Peru took a bold step. These countries, it should be noted, have virtually no continental shelf and therefore no economically exploitable mineral resources off their coasts. For them, the potential yield from the sea was viewed in terms of fish. Drawing an analogy to the U. S. continental shelf claim of 1945, these countries, in the Declaration of Santiago, claimed sovereignty and jurisdiction over an area extending seaward from their coasts not less than 200 nautical miles.

The analogy to the Truman Declaration was invalid. The United States had gone to great lengths to point out that its claim applied only to resources of the continental shelf, which is in fact a submerged extension of the continental plateau. The U. S. claim did not apply to the water column above the continental shelf nor did it in any way interfere with the traditional concept of freedom of the seas. In contrast, Chile, Ecuador, and Peru had claimed sovereignty over the entire marine environment adjacent to their coasts to a minimum of 200 miles, implying the right to extend jurisdiction still further if circumstances warranted. But to these countries such action was only logical and just. In their view, the United States had set an important precedent which established the right of a state to extend its jurisdiction over the adjacent marine environment as dictated by national interests. U. S. interests, they said, happened to be in the seabed; their interests were in fish.

By this time the need for an international conference had become widely apparent. The International Law Commission had already begun to move in this direction and, by 1958, the nations of the world assembled at Geneva. Four conventions were produced, but none of these resolved the root problem of the breadth of the territorial sea. In 1960, a further attempt to reach agreement on this critical issue also resulted in failure.

Since then, there has been a marked tendency, mostly on the part of developing countries, toward unilateral claims to areas of the high seas varying in size and the nature of the claimed jurisdiction. Some have actually extended their jurisdiction while others have only indicated a desire to do so. Many of those in the latter category are merely waiting to see what the Law of

the Sea Conference brings before acting unilaterally. In the meantime, coastal geography is already beginning to resemble an ill-conceived patchwork quilt with each country designing claims to meet its own peculiar requirements.

In May of 1970, the President of the United States made a policy statement on the problem. "The stark fact," he said, "is that the Law of the Sea is inadequate to meet the needs of modern technology and the concerns of the international community." "If it is not modernized multilaterally, unilateral action and international conflict are inevitable." In December of that same year, the U.N. General Assembly resolved to convene a comprehensive Law of the Sea Conference in 1973.

A preparatory committee has met four times in preparation for this Conference. Its mission is to seek out areas of basic agreement, to define the issues and to prepare draft treaty articles for consideration by the Conference. The General Assembly, however, recognized that even basic agreement may not be attainable, and made provisions for the Conference to be postponed if necessary. Initial efforts of the preparatory committee seemed to confirm the fears of the pessimists, but by the end of the fourth session sufficient progress had been made for the General Assembly to schedule the conference to begin in late 1973.

It is generally conceded that six basic issues are involved; the breadth of the territorial sea, passage through straits, fisheries, the seabed, marine pollution, and scientific research. All of these are interrelated to some degree. The United States has submitted to the preparatory committee of the Law of the Sea Conference a draft seabed treaty and three draft articles dealing with the territorial sea, passage through and over straits, and fisheries. These were an initial attempt to define U. S. interests and to accommodate them with those of the international community.

The United States as a major maritime power is particularly concerned with the issue of navigation. This concern, of course, involves international trade and seaborne communication in general. Most nations recognize that freedom of navigation in this context serves the interests of all. But, for the United States and other major maritime powers, freedom of navigation also means freedom of mobility for military forces as may be necessary to meet the requirements of self-defense. In addition, freedom of the high seas is important to those countries which depend upon the major powers for their survival and in an even larger context it is a major factor affecting the maintenance of political stability throughout the world.

It is clear that the navigation interests of the United

States would best be served by international agreement on the narrowest possible territorial sea. Three miles is still adhered to by 31 coastal states, but the trend toward extension is unmistakable. Reluctantly, the United States has come to accept the proposition that 12 miles is probably the minimum which would be acceptable to a majority of nations. Even the Soviet Union, whose navigation interests are somewhat similar to our own, would be reluctant to agree to a territorial sea of less than 12 miles. Consequently, in a draft Article, the United States proposed that each state, at its discretion, shall have the right to claim a territorial sea of up to 12 nautical miles. Indications are that there is considerable support for a 12-mile territorial sea, and if this issue could be taken separately, it is probable that agreement among a majority of states could quickly be reached.

Nevertheless, the United States has unequivocally stated that its willingness to accept 12 miles is contingent upon agreement on the right of free transit and overflight through and over international straits as set forth in its second draft Article. The issue is a critical one for maritime nations. If the territorial limit is increased to 12 miles, over 100 straits now navigable as high seas would become the territorial seas of the riparian states. Included in these are Gibraltar, Malacca, and others of considerable strategic importance. The United States has taken the position that the right to transit such straits "should be regarded in law for what it is in fact: an inherent and inseparable adjunct of the freedoms of navigation and overflight on the high seas themselves."

Spain, Malaysia, Indonesia, and others see it quite differently. They believe that they have an indisputable right to assert sovereignty over the straits in question and point to problems of pollution and traffic safety as well as dangers to their national security as justification for their position. Maritime nations, they argue, have no real cause for alarm because users would be protected by their right of innocent passage.

In fact, the right of innocent passage would not solve the problem for the United States and other maritime nations, because the strait state is ultimately the judge of what is innocent and what is not. There are some who have suggested that the passage of a warship, because of the nature of the vessel, cannot be innocent. Others are of the opinion that a vessel's registration, destination, or cargo are valid criteria for the determination of innocence. Unquestionably, aircraft and submerged submarines would not enjoy the right of innocent passage if the terms of the territorial sea convention of 1958 were applied. Clearly, the mobility of U. S. forces cannot be subjected to the whims of straits states. Yet it is equally clear that such

states have legitimate concerns which must be addressed. Recognizing this, the United States has indicated that it seeks only a limited right of free passage; "merely one of transiting the straits, not of conducting any other activities." Moreover, under the U. S. proposal, vessels which abuse this right would subject themselves to appropriate action by the strait state.

The limits of the territorial sea and freedom of passage through and over international straits as expressed in the U. S. drafts are basic, interrelated elements of U. S. policy. The Chairman of the U. S. Delegation emphasized the importance of these issues when he stated that the United States "would be unable to conceive of a successful Law of the Sea Conference that did not accommodate the objectives of these articles." This should not be surprising since the United States has always relied on its location athwart the two great oceans of the world for its security and its ability to project its influence as a world power. Americans discovered early that the oceans not only provided them with in-depth protection but also with the means of making common cause with others who have similar interests, no matter how distant they may be. On the other hand, those who would threaten these interests are effectively deterred because they know that the military, industrial, and economic might of the United States can be quickly employed anywhere in the world. This geographic advantage, coupled with sea and air power, provides the United States with the capability to move men and equipment on and over the sea for great distances at a moment's notice as well as the ability to furnish continuous logistic support for sustained military operations of any kind or size. It should be expected then that the U. S. position on all law of the sea issues will be influenced to some degree by the imperative of such considerations.

The issues of fisheries and seabed exploitation, are of major importance to most coastal states. For the United States, the fisheries problem is complicated by domestic pressure generated by coastal fishing interests to declare a 200-mile exclusive fisheries zone from which foreign fishing vessels can be excluded. Such action, however, would cause serious damage to U. S. distant-water-fishing interests, particularly the tuna fleets, and would be viewed as tacit recognition of the right of other countries to make their own claims as they saw fit. These countries would certainly object to any U. S. attempt to dictate limitations on these claims and even if broad multilateral agreement could be reached which limited countries to control over living resources only, the door would be open to "creeping jurisdiction," that is, the tendency for a country to expand one form of control to encompass another.

The dilemma facing the United States is one which

demands protection for both coastal and distant water fishermen while not compromising navigation and security interests of maritime nations. An attempt was made to do just that in the U. S. fisheries proposal. Basically, the United States envisions a species approach wherein the coastal state might exercise control over its coastal species as far out as they may range, while highly migratory oceanic stocks, such as tuna, would be managed by international organizations. While this concept goes a long way to accommodate both major segments of the U. S. fishing industry and hopefully many developing coastal states as well, its most important feature from a military point of view, lies in the fact that it does not rely on geographic boundaries which might offer a temptation to extend sovereignty over other ocean uses such as navigation.

A somewhat different problem exists with regard to the seabed. Here, the U. S. proposal provides for exclusive coastal state jurisdiction over resources out to the 200-meter isobath which coincides roughly with the average seaward edge of the continental shelf. Beyond that would be a trusteeship zone in which the coastal state would exercise considerable authority, but which would be subject to a degree of international control. Still seaward of this and encompassing the entire deep ocean floor would be a zone completely under international jurisdiction. It is important to note here that beyond the territorial sea, jurisdiction over these zones would apply only to the seabed and not to the water column above. Further, the international implications which would attach to both the trusteeship and international areas would serve as an effective deterrent to creeping jurisdiction. Thus, freedom of navigation would be given maximum possible protection.

The remaining major issues involve marine pollution and freedom of scientific research. The latter poses less serious threats to vital U. S. navigation interests but is understandably a matter of considerable concern to the scientific community. The issue of marine pollution, on the other hand, is fraught with potential navigation-related difficulties. While so-called Third World countries seem primarily interested in ocean resources, some may see growing concern over marine pollution as a vehicle by which they may be able to exercise a degree of control over the strategic mobility of larger powers. Consequently, they might be tempted to take advantage of world concern to harass or deny passage of warships on the high seas off their coasts under the guise of pollution control.

The United States has gone far in attempting to accommodate legitimate interests of developing coastal states. Still, a wide gulf seems to exist in many cases between these states and the maritime countries which give considerable weight to traditional freedom of the seas. Significantly, this latter category includes not only the United States but also other influential powers, such as the United Kingdom, Japan, and the Soviet Union. All are industrially developed and have sizeable investments in distant water fisheries. All have a strong interest in the maritime aspects of commerce and defense. Several other countries, mostly European, tend to identify strongly with the interests of this group.

Others who have reason to associate themselves with narrow limits are the landlocked and shelf-locked group. (The term shelf-locked refers to those countries the breadth of whose shelf or the length of whose coast, is limited by the proximity of other jurisdictions).

UPI PHOTO

The Icelandic Coast Guard gunboat Aegir, *rear, circles the British trawler* Wyre Victory *off Reykjavik, Iceland, on 12 September 1972. Iceland escalated the "Cod War" by cutting the trawl lines of the* Wyre Victory *and another British fishing boat which were said to be operating inside Iceland's new 50-mile fishing limit.*

These countries stand to lose from the proliferation of extended coastal state claims made by geographically advantaged nations. It is not surprising, then, that they tend to see such unilateral claims as gobbling up the "common heritage of mankind" from which, in their view, all should reap the benefits of exploitation. These benefits, they feel, could be derived through international control of ocean resources and equitable sharing of the profits among the members of the world community. Since most exploitable resources of the sea, both living and non-living are generally found above the continental shelf or margin or within two or three hundred miles of land, landlocked and shelf-locked countries can be expected to oppose extended jurisdiction by coastal states which would claim these resources for themselves. Thus, whether a landlocked state is developed, such as Austria, or developing, such as Bolivia, it would be likely to support narrow limits of national jurisdiction. For this reason, the landlocked and shelf-locked states share the maritime powers' concerns, but for different reasons.

At the other end of the spectrum is a growing number of coastal states in the developing stage which strongly advocate extended national jurisdiction in various forms. Some have already claimed sovereignty over the ocean out to 200 miles and beyond, off their coasts. Others have claimed a more limited jurisdiction, such as exclusive rights to resources. In general, however, these countries believe that each coastal state has the right, and indeed the duty, to extend its jurisdiction into the high seas to whatever extent it deems necessary in pursuance of its economic needs. Many see the development of coastal fisheries as the answer to their more immediate problems, since fishing does not require the technology or tremendous capital needed for offshore mining or petroleum exploitation. Other developing countries hope to persuade foreign companies with capital, equipment, and know-how to explore and exploit the seabed for a share of the profits. Still others have no capability at all to harvest certain ocean resources, but plan to claim jurisdiction over them and permit others to exploit them in return for large license fees. They consider annexation of ocean space to be a legitimate means to compensate for the uneven distribution of the world's wealth. This view, of course, ignores the inequities of geography—e.g., Chile has over 1,000 miles of coastline while Bolivia has none.

As a generalized matter, then, the lines of confrontation are clear. On one hand are the maritime powers, the distant-water-fishing, landlocked and shelf-locked countries. On the other, a large group of developing coastal and straits states which tend to gravitate together. What chance, then, does the Law of the Sea Conference have of success?

In order for agreement to be reached at the Law of the Sea Conference, a two-thirds majority of the U.N. members present and voting may be required. Obviously, one-third of the members plus one can constitute a "blocking third." This becomes critically important when one considers that there are those states, particularly the Latin American hard-core proponents of extended jurisdiction, which may feel that a successful conference is not in their interests. Certainly, if success is to be achieved in 1973, it will require some compromise of their position. The delaying tactics employed by some countries at both the March and the July/August 1972 session of the preparatory committee tends to confirm the suspicion that there are those who may be bent on hamstringing the deliberations as much as possible. Even though it now appears that preparations for the Conference will be completed in time, developing coastal states which see time as working to their benefit are certainly capable of mustering a blocking third if they wish to carry their demands to that extreme.

There are also dangers from the other end of the spectrum. Let us suppose that a large number of states favored conferring total jurisdiction over coastal resources upon the coastal states—even as far out as 200 miles. Important distant-water-fishing nations would, no doubt, strongly oppose such a solution. They might, in concert with landlocked and shelf-locked countries, be moved to form a "blocking third" of their own.

Still another possibility is that two-thirds of the members or more might agree on a solution which is satisfactory to most, but which seriously impairs the vital interests of a few. These few might refuse to be bound by the convention and, if they happen to be major maritime powers, the usefulness of the agreement would be questionable as there is always a qualitative as well as a quantitative aspect to multilateral agreements.

Placing states into neat categories is, of course, an over-simplification of a very complex problem. Some states are schizophrenic over their interests. As previously mentioned, the United States itself is both a coastal and a distant-water-fishing nation and must walk a fine line when dealing with this question. Still others have not clearly identified their interests or projected them very far into the future. These countries tend to drag their feet on the theory that it is better to do nothing than to make a serious mistake.

Some states will act on the basis of considerations which have very little to do with law of the sea. For example, the prospects of deep-sea mining may cause concern for countries which rely to varying degree on the export of certain minerals for their economic well-being. Chile relies heavily on copper and Canada is the world's largest exporter of nickel. The mining of manganese nodules in the deep-ocean basins is becoming technically feasible and may within a few years bring large quantities of these minerals to the international market place at greatly reduced prices. Middle East countries, on the other hand, may be concerned over the exploitation of offshore oil deposits by countries which were previously dependent upon them for this resource. Kuwait reflected this concern by offering a resolution which would halt much exploitation of the seabed until an international treaty could be agreed upon.

There are still other examples of how unrelated matters can affect deliberations on the law of the sea. The People's Republic of China, attending the preparatory committee session in March 1972 for the first time, registered strong support for the proponents of extended jurisdiction. While this may be partly owing to China's interest in oil deposits on the floor of the East China Sea, such conduct indicates that China is even more interested in establishing a credible position of leadership within the Third World.

No one can predict the outcome of the Conference at this point. But it seems reasonable to assume that failure to arrive at a satisfactory agreement will almost certainly be followed by a deluge of extreme claims. Those who have waited to see what the Law of the Sea Conference would bring will feel compelled to make up for lost time. States will undoubtedly compete with one another in this respect and those which have already extended their jurisdiction may decide that they must extend it still further, beyond any conceivable needs as a matter of status or in reaction to the claims of neighboring states. Under such conditions the possibilities for area or regional conflicts would increase. Some states might even exploit the confusion to further

unrelated objectives. If the situation deteriorated sufficiently, maritime nations, their economic and security interests threatened, would be hard pressed to avoid being drawn into the fray.

The prospects of achieving satisfactory agreement on the major law of the sea issues are not particularly encouraging. Yet, the situation is far from hopeless. The conflicts are reconcilable but any compromise, to be viable, must give recognition to the basic interests of all without threatening the vital interests of any. The United States as a world leader has proposed solutions which attempt to strike a balance between its own national interests and those of the international community. The proposals are by no means perfect but they constitute a beginning, a framework for further progress. But others will have to contribute reasonable solutions of their own if a proper blend is to be achieved. Success will depend, to a great extent, on whether the participants sincerely desire to reach agreement or are only interested in presenting a facade of good faith. Whatever the case, all must surely be aware that this may be the last opportunity to achieve a stable regime for the oceans and ensure continued orderly use of the sea.

Commander Knott graduated from the University of Maryland in 1957. Completing flight training in 1958, he served with Patrol Squadron Forty-Five until 1961, and was Assistant Professor of Naval Science at Villanova University until 1964. Upon receiving an M.A. in Political Science from Villanova, he served with Patrol Squadron Sixteen until 1967, when he was assigned to the Military Armistice Commission in Korea as Chief, Plans & Policy for the U.N. component. During this tour, he was a member of the team which negotiated with the North Koreans for release of the crew of the USS *Pueblo*. From 1968 to 1971, Commander Knott served with the Politico Military Policy Division of OpNav as an Asian specialist. He is currently assigned to the State Department preparing for the upcoming Law of the Sea Conference.

By MERLE MACBAIN

Merle Macbain, a frequent writer on maritime subjects, is a retired Navy commander and former public affairs officer on the staff of the Oceanographer of the Navy.

WHILE the United States is celebrating its 200th year as a constitutional democracy, delegations from virtually every nation on earth are gathering this month in New York for another try at writing a constitution for the two thirds of the earth still outside the realm of law.

Times have changed since the days when all of the oceans beyond cannon shot range could happily belong to everybody in the special sense that they could not belong to anyone exclusively. Opinions on what the consequences will be if the third session of The Third United Nations Conference on the Law of the Sea (LOSC) accomplishes no more than the first two range from "nothing" to "chaos" to "war." If the latter predictions seem extreme, reflect that a bloody war and nearly a decade of turmoil followed the closing by Egypt in 1967

of a single strait, the Strait of Tiran, to Israeli shipping.

Admiral James L. Holloway III, who as Chief of Naval Operations has thought more about such matters than most of his fellow Americans, assessed the consequences as follows in a recent statement before the Senate Armed Services Committee: "Our studies by the Joint Chiefs of Staff in recent years have pointed to the potential for ever increasing confrontations, chaos, challenges, and conflict in the oceans, unless a new, comprehensive Law of the Sea Treaty is concluded."

The Geneva Four

In the simpler days before World War II the law of the sea consisted of old usage fairly well understood and observed by all. Piracy was punishable by death, international straits were open to all comers, and a three-mile "territorial sea" was legally a part of the adjoining coastal state—but open to "innocent passage."

But those old rules of "customary law" took no account of new modes of passage, such as those made by submerged submarines, and aircraft on "overflights." The

LOS '76:
Constitution or Chaos
for the World's Oceans?

changing situation still was not too serious until some states made claims, largely to protect fishing rights, to territorial seas of 12 miles or greater, and other states refused to recognize such claims.

The evolving course of events led to the First Law of the Sea Conference in Geneva in 1958, from which emerged four Geneva Conventions: the Convention on the Territorial Sea and the Contiguous Zone; the Convention on the High Seas; the Convention on the Continental Shelf; and the Convention on Fishing and Conservation of Living Resources of the High Seas.

Neither at the First Geneva Conference nor at a second one in 1960 were the nations represented able to agree on the breadth of the territorial sea, the extent of fisheries jurisdiction, or the outer limits of a coastal state's exclusive rights to continental shelf resources. The Contiguous Zone Convention provided an extra nine-mile strip in which the coastal state controlled fish and mineral rights and could police smuggling, immigration, and health regulations—but beyond that still narrow strip there lay the high seas, where all could sail, fly, fish, and pollute without restriction.

"Creeping jurisdiction" soon turned many contiguous zones into territorial seas. In some South American countries, where the tuna run far offshore, 200-mile contiguous or economic zones were decreed which in turn and by unilateral edict became "territorial seas."

Blue-Eyed Powers and a Detente Ally

The tangle of conflicting claims, uncertainty over the outer limits of the oil-bearing continental shelf, and the demonstrated ability of the United States and other technologically developed nations to mine the deep oceans for metal-rich manganese nodules made another LOS conference a matter of some urgency. Phase One of that conference was held in Caracas in 1974 and demonstrated principally that such conferences are no longer a "gentlemen's" gathering of blue-eyed big powers. The one agreement reached was to reconvene in Geneva from March to May of last year.

Some two thousand delegates from 141 countries were represented at Geneva, making it the largest international conference ever held. From the first the sessions were dominated by two contending viewpoints.

The great industrial and maritime nations, powered by the United States and its sometimes detente ally, the Soviet Union, favored the traditional freedom of the seas with strictly limited jurisdiction for coastal states in the economic zone, now thought of by one and all in terms of 200 miles.

The underdeveloped (or, rather, developing) countries were led by a monolithic bloc dubbed the "Group of 77." Among other advantages, such as an automatic majority vote, the bloc had the best slogans. To the cry that sounded in the corridors of Caracas, "The seas are the common heritage of mankind" (which Secretary of State Henry Kissinger has aptly described as merely a statement of the problem) were added "One Nation, one

The extent to which coastal states can enforce anti-pollution laws is but one of many thorny issues dividing the developed and non-developed nations at the LOS Conference. Shown here: oil pollution cleanup equipment near the U.S. Naval Station, Newport, R.I. (Navy photo by Duane E. Marsh.)

New York Meeting may be Last Chance for a World Law of the Sea Treaty

Oil rig and oil slick off the coast of Santa Barbara, Calif. Offshore oil is the most evident of the non-living resources in the new coastal economic zones, "now thought of by one and all in terms of 200 miles."

vote" and a more revolutionary concept sloganeered as "A new international economic order." The latter lofty utterance translates roughly into "share the wealth."

For efficiency the awesome agenda was divided among separate working committees. The First Committee was concerned with setting up an international regime to deal with exploitation of seabed resources beyond the limits of national jurisdiction. The Second Committee had responsibility for establishing the tacitly agreed on 12-mile territorial sea and 200-mile economic zone and the many related problems, particularly passage through straits. The Third Committee was given the deceptively simple task of assessing responsibility for protection of the marine environment and making rules for the conduct of scientific research within restricted economic zones. None of the committees reached any formal agreements.

Informal Advance

What did come out of the conference was an Informal Single Negotiating Text for a treaty designed primarily to serve as an agenda for the New York meeting. Although in its entirety it pleases no one, that text represents the only solid advance since the Conventions of 1958. Agreement, if any, to be reached in New York will be based on the issues in the text.

Ambassador John R. Stevenson, Chief of the U.S. Delegation at Geneva, and Bernard H. Oxman, U.S. representative in Committee II, summarized in the October 1975 issue of *The American Journal of International Law* what they personally regard as the ten elements of the negotiating text which offer the best basis for agreement in New York.

Those issues, paraphrased for brevity, are:

(1.) A 12-mile territorial sea, subject to the right of innocent passage.

(2.) Unimpeded passage through international straits for all vessels and aircraft.

(3.) A 200-mile economic zone in which the coastal state exercises sovereign rights over both living and non-living resources and over exploitation of the seabed of the continental margin where it extends beyond 200 miles, but is subject to a contribution of international payments for mineral production on the margin beyond 200 miles, with all states retaining their traditional freedoms of navigation, overflight, and communications in the area.

(4.) Coastal state control of all drilling and economic installations in the economic zone.

(5.) Modernization of the regime of the high seas to allow for far-traveling tuna and shrimp fleets and for state-of-origin interest in anadromous species of fish such as salmon; also: new rules for control of unauthorized offshore broadcasting and suppression of illicit traffic in narcotics.

(6.) A new regime for unimpeded passage through sea lanes and on air routes that traverse archipelagoes.

(7.) International rules for marine pollution control, with limited coastal state enforcement rights against vessel-source pollution.

(8.) Provisions for international cooperation in marine scientific research and transfer of marine technology.

U.S. Navyman views Suez Canal activity from the deck of the amphibious assault ship BOXER in 1966 photo, and the Japanese merchant ship TOYOTA MARU transits the Pedro Miguel Locks of the Panama Canal. (U.S. Navy photos.) The long Suez closure and the anti-American posture of the present Panamanian government dramatically illustrate the vital importance of those canals and other of the world's narrow straits and "chokepoints" to the U.S. economy as well as to the ability of the U.S. Navy to carry out its assigned missions.

(9.) Machinery to deal with the exploitation of seabed resources beyond the outer limits of national jurisdiction.

(10.) A system for binding third-party settlement of disputes which cannot be resolved by negotiation.

No Details, No Definition

Although U.S. delegates are reluctant to discuss specific details, there is reason to believe that substantial agreement was reached in Committee II on the first six items. If so, it would represent significant progress, since the articles pertaining to the economic zone, where most of the known offshore oil and gas fields and commercial fisheries are found, affect more interests of more states than any of the other articles.

One important matter not agreed on was a definition of the high seas. If the various national economic zones and continental shelves are not included in the "new" high seas area, as the Group of 77 would have it, the area

Reconnaissance of a Soviet "Z" class ballistic missile submarine by a U.S. Navy Orion P-3 patrol aircraft near the Rock of Gibraltar illustrates one LOS issue on which the U.S. and USSR are firmly agreed: that the present "freedom of the seas" in and through international straits must be preserved for naval/military ships and aircraft as well as for merchant ships and civil aircraft. (Navy photo by Walter J. Dumbek.)

in which the traditional freedom of the seas could survive would be reduced by 40 percent, a matter not taken lightly by the maritime powers.

The real crunch, however, came in Committee I, where the only thing agreed on was the need for a legal regime for the deep seabed. At stake is the rich treasure trove of manganese nodules (nuggets of copper, nickel, and cobalt) carpeting great areas of the seabed at depths of 12,000 feet or more. The big problem, not yet solved, is to reconcile the views of those favoring a system of direct exploitation (by a new international authority—that "new international economic order") with the views of those desiring guaranteed access to specified mining areas, with security of tenure, for their nationals.

The view of the developing nations, as reflected in the text, is that the one-nation, one-vote Assembly should be the supreme policy-making organ for a new seabed authority—an economic czar for the oceans. American miners, who have hundreds of millions of dollars invested in preliminary development work, and investment bankers, who would have to furnish the much larger sums required for mining the deep sea on a commercial scale, are unanimous in their conviction that risk capital could not be raised on such terms.

Science Si, Pollution No

The fairly recent pot-of-gold aura over deep sea mining has dimmed with a realization of the problems involved.

However, expectations are still a factor and emotional ideology plays a strong role in the Committee I divisions and has doubtless been encouraged by land-based miners of the metals present in the nodules. The Group of 77 countries want an Authority with real power over the developed nations in what they see as the world's last unexploited area of natural resources. Since it is not an immediate pocketbook issue for them, moreover, they can afford to be adamant. Such authorities as Leigh S. Ratiner, ocean mining administrator for the Department of the Interior, doubts that they will retreat from their one-country, one-vote position.

The division in Committee III seems more surprising since, by definition, pollution is bad and science is good.

Although some developing countries take the interesting view that the rich got rich by polluting the environment and it's now their turn, the principal point at issue is whether coastal states can have control over vessel-source pollution in the economic zone. By extension, however, such control would enable them to dictate design features of ships entering a zone and could therefore impinge on rights of innocent passage; e.g., they could deny passage to oil tankers per se.

The more serious Committee III differences arose out of the opposition of developing nations to foreign-flag scientific research near their shores. Progress here appears to run up against paranoia. The developing nations charge that, where such research is not a cover for espionage, it will be used to uncover and exploit new sources of wealth for the benefit of others. The U.S. position is that permission for research is a high seas right that may not be denied in an economic zone. A U.S. counter-proposal, rejected outright, stipulated that adjoining coastal states would be invited to participate and to share in the findings. There may be some chance for agreement in a USSR-led socialist-bloc proposal that coastal state consent be required for research related to resources, with other scientific research subject only to "reasonable" treaty obligations.

Arbitration a Must

The last major item in contention, an arrangement for binding third-party settlement of disputes, would apply to all parties and to all substantive elements of an LOS treaty. The United States will insist on such an arbitration provision as part of any overall treaty package. The essential issue involved in compulsory settlement of disputes is the need for a guarantee of both coastal state and international rights in the economic zone. It would not be difficult to surmise that those who already favor excluding the economic zone from the high seas foresee that without compulsory dispute settlement the zone could easily evolve into a territorial sea.

Such are some of the more difficult problems which face the New York negotiators—plus the fact that the Group of 77 is now the Group of 105, so designated by outgoing U.S. Ambassador to the United Nations Daniel Patrick Moynihan, who has had occasion to count them. Their leaders are tough and smart; a number of them were educated at Harvard and Oxford. The United Nations is their true forum and the oceans their chosen battleground. They want international indexing, tech-

Marine life on the bottom of McMurdo Sound, Antarctica, and near Andros Island, the Bahamas. (Navy photos by W.R. Curtsinger and F. McCraw.) The food potential of the oceans is still enormous, but international agreement on conservation of numerous species is mandatory if current stocks are not to be depleted.

Oceans and Atmosphere (NACOA) shifted position in its 1975 report to the President and Congress and now strongly favors unilateral U.S. action establishing a wider economic zone—both to encourage deep sea mining (to reduce dependence on foreign mineral sources) and to provide preferential rights to U.S. fishermen in a 200-mile resources conservation zone.

Coastal mineral resources, principally oil and natural gas, are already protected under the earlier Continental Shelf Convention.

There seems to be relatively little to agrue about concerning "the navigation issue"; merchant ships would undoubtedly continue to sail unimpeded through international straits since the economies of all nations are dependent upon such traffic.

As for navigational rights for naval/military ships and aircraft, it can be assumed that NATO and Warsaw Pact countries have too much at stake in the free mobility of their defense fleets and aircraft to tolerate interference with transit through international straits or impediments to navigation on the high seas.

Nothing Good Preferred to Something Bad

There are numerous other factors to bolster the argument, frequently heard of late, that no treaty at all is better than any treaty that can conceivably come out of the New York conference.

On the other hand, most knowledgeable U.S. leaders—diplomatic, political, and military—appear to believe that prospects both for peaceful settlement of disputes and for orderly exploitation of the earth's last frontier are worth the investment of time, patience, and reasonable concessions that a treaty worthy of world consensus would require—always provided that essential U.S. rights on the high seas are preserved.

Even if more good will is shown this time around than was evident in Geneva and Caracas, however, the eight-week session in New York still seems too short to permit resolution of all still existing differences. And there will not be time enough for final action in the short session contemplated for August, which must end with the opening of the fall meeting of the United Nations in September.

Two more LOS failures will, however, probably result in strong unilateral legislation being passed by the U.S. Congress regulating the field of deep sea mining as well as strengthening U.S. claims to a broader economic zone. Such legislation, if signed into law (or passed over the President's veto), would undoubtedly be followed by both cooperative and retaliatory action by other nations. The resulting chaos of claims and counter-claims, accompanied by threats, and possibly by force, could, however, result in a new and probably final U.N. effort at LOS agreement early in 1977.

If that effort is also unsuccessful, the dream of a world constitution for the seas will, in the view of one senior State Department official, either go away for good or just drag on to no avail.

In any case, there are few, if any, on either side of the dispute who believe that a bad treaty would be better than none at all.   ∎

nology transfer, and "a place in the world," and their stance, so far, on matters of substance is "Don't give an inch."

The most important factor favoring success in New York is the consciousness even among the underdeveloped nations that: (1) 1976 may well be the last chance for an LOS treaty; and (2) they are the ones with the most to lose.

Congress Acts, President Waits

The alternative to failure, for the United States and other developed nations, is a combination of unilateral and cooperative actions. A significant step toward establishing a broader U.S. economic zone was made with Senate passage of the Magnuson Fisheries Management and Conservation Act (S.961); a similar bill (H.R. 200) was passed earlier in the House. Both bills establish a 200-mile U.S. fisheries zone. President Ford has indicated he will sign a conference bill into law, providing it incorporates a Senate provision delaying its effective date until 1 July 1977. The intentional delay would allow time to see what happens at the eight-week LOS session starting this month as well as another short session scheduled, if needed, to begin sometime in August.

Senator Lee Metcalf (D-Mont.), whose Subcommittee on Minerals, Materials, and Fuels has held exhaustive hearings on deep sea mining, is sponsoring legislation designed to set up a licensing system for deep sea miners and provide them indemnification against any loss of tenure in their claims due to later establishment of an international authority. Representative John Murphy (D-N.Y.), Chairman of the House Subcommittee on Oceanography, is sponsoring similar legislation. Sponsors of both bills favor a cooperative arrangement with other nations possessing deep sea technological capabilities (Japan, West Germany and France, so far) which would provide mutual protection for each other's claims.

The prestigious National Advisory Committee on

The rights and responsibilities of both maritime and coastal states must be weighed and considered in any convention of the law of the sea. In addition, changing conditions brought about by technology, environmental concerns, and political factors complicate even further the prolonged negotiations now in progress. Nevertheless, the historic concept of freedom of the high seas holds the greatest promise for the most equitable balancing of rights, interests, responsibilities, and duties of all nations concerned.

THE POSSIBLE EFFECTS ON MARITIME OPERATIONS

OF ANY FUTURE CONVENTION

OF THE LAW OF THE SEA

by

Admiral Sir Edward Ashmore G.C.B., D.S.C., A.D.C., Royal Navy

Chief of Naval Staff and First Sea Lord

When the Chief of Naval Operations kindly invited me to initiate our discussions on this important subject, I had hoped that the recent session of the conference at New York would have got a little further. That progress was made, I am in no doubt. I am also in no doubt that it is very important that at their August 1976 session in New York enough progress is made to enable governments to agree to the broad terms of a new convention which could be finalized in 1977.

But because of this rate of progress, it does mean that we can discuss the crucial issues the conference has before it in an unrestricted way and not feel bound by any positions our own governments might otherwise by now have adopted. Indeed, I must stress from the outset that my views are those of a professional naval officer, not of a

maritime lawyer nor of an official negotiating for his national interests in the matter. But it is inevitable that I will have frequently to refer to the arguments that are still taking place in the conference for it is these that will colour the backcloth against which any future maritime operation will take place.

Such operations in such a context are of, course, a peaceful exercise of maritime power. I do not address the question of belligerence.

My theme in this discussion of how a new convention might affect future maritime operations is that the cornerstone of any future convention must be the maintenance of the often challenged but long established freedoms of the seas. I hope to show you that both maritime and coastal states stand to gain by the maintenance of this concept.

Freedom of the seas, of course, implies not only a freedom of action but a responsibility to respect the rights of others. I acknowledge from the start, and I will go over the ground in more detail later on, that we are living in a changing world and that there is a very reasonable case to be put which calls for more careful definition of the rights of states on, in, and under the oceans of the world. States have every right to look to their security and economic interests: and the better understanding that is reached on these issues, the less chance there is of friction and tension. A new convention will depend entirely on a sound balance of all interests being struck. The United Kingdom has both maritime and coastal state interests. We firmly believe in the maintenance of the balance of strategic deterrence and depend extensively for our livelihood on unfettered contacts with our trading partners—we have the third largest mercantile marine in the world (after Liberia and Japan). At the same time, our geographical position as an island state, separated from our European neighbours by the busiest straits of the world, on a continental shelf rich in hydrocarbons and fish, gives us significant coastal state interests. A balanced convention is therefore as vital to my country as to any.

We have only reached this view after many years as a maritime nation and in common with most of us here could not claim to have been consistent in our views over the last 2,000 years. Let me say something since nothing is new under the sun, least of all the ocean, about those 2,000 years and the sum of human experience they convey to us.

In the earliest days the sea was believed not only to hold inexhaustible stocks of fish, which were free for anyone to take, but to extend over such vast distances that the waters themselves could not similarly be taken. What could not be taken was free for common use by all men. To the Romans who enshrined this principle in the Justinian Code, such a view was probably more a luxury that the undisputed masters of the Mediterranean could well afford, since it was unlikely that anyone would challenge it, rather than an act of liberal statesmanship.

Nevertheless, after the collapse of the Roman Empire there was no major change to this principle until the crusades brought a Europe emerging from the Dark Ages into contact with the Mediterranean. This stimulus to commerce allowed Mediterranean practice, Roman in origin, to spread to the Atlantic seaboard, and the rolls of Oleron gained immediate success and wide recognition among the nations of North West Europe. But although these codes talked of freedom, this freedom began to become discretionary. As Mediterranean trade revived in the 13th and 14th centuries, the conflicting claims of the trading nations on the waters around their coasts became the dominant issues.

The Venetians began to charge a fee for entering the Adriatic, and Venice's chief rival, Genoa, claimed similar jurisdiction over the Ligurian Sea. In northwest Europe, countries made similar claims: The Danes, Swedes, and Poles claimed various parts of the Baltic and the English, with what some of you may feel was characteristic expansiveness, the channel, the North Sea, and the whole of the Western Atlantic. Slowly the sea from being free from any jurisdiction became, like the land, subject to the authority of those who had the power to enforce that authority. But the two great naval powers of the day were Spain and Portugal and, using the Pope as a maritime arbitrator which had the wholly desirable effect of giving their claims the authority of God, they began to apportion the oceans of the world between them so that both countries' interests in their newly discovered possessions in the Americas, East and West Indies, Africa, and India were protected. Their dominance culminated in the Treaty of Tordesillas which, in effect, divided the globe in half; a feature which even the Pope had sought to avoid.

With the growth of English naval power in the middle of the 16th century, her ships began to challenge the monopoly of Spanish trade with the Indies. The first Queen Elizabeth sought to justify the activities of men like Sir Francis Drake by an appeal to the principle of the freedom of the seas—the first time this concept had been expressed for four or more centuries. Her Majesty refused to concede that Spain "had any right to debar British subjects from trade or from freely sailing that vast ocean, seeing that the use of the sea and air is common to all: neither can any title to the ocean belong to any people."

While England was having difficulties with Spain, Holland, which was also increasing in power, was having the same difficulties with Portugal. The Portuguese cited the Papal Bull of 1493 in support of their trade monopoly; to counter their arguments Grotius wrote his famous treatise on the law of the sea. He stated quite categorically that "Since the sea is just as unsusceptible of physical appropriation as the air, it cannot be attached to the possession of any nation."

By this time, however, the British had forgotten their late Queen's stand and her successor, King James I, commissioned John Selden to write a refutation of Grotius supporting the concept of a closed sea; a principle which was duly followed so long as the British felt that their interests were best served by protecting their trade against foreign competition. However, during the 18th century there was a slow and gradual change in British policy. The old order whereby strong maritime powers waged war to protect their trade was changed by the Industrial Revolution in England. There was for a time thereafter no foreign competition, and so British interests were now best served by completely free and unrestricted trade. Thus, by the early 19th century Britain was once again an unequivocal supporter of the freedom of the seas.

It seems clear that the policy of the superior maritime power, and not for the first time, carried the day. When one power has been predominant, freedom of the seas has been its policy. It would be an oversimplification to say that when dominance of the sea was in doubt nations pursued a policy of closed seas which went unchallenged until one power again became predominant, but it is nevertheless not far from the truth.

Later on I will attempt to show how the maintenance of the freedom of the seas has developed from being principally in the interests of major maritime powers to the situation today when it safeguards the interests of the international community.

As trade increased, piracy became a growing nuisance on an international scale. Initially countries were content to rid the seas of pirates harassing their own trade while being quite content to let them do their worst among their rivals. Nevertheless, the consciences of some enlightened men and the timing of history ensured that piracy and the slave trade were suppressed in an era when the principle of the freedom of seas was being upheld under the umbrella of Pax Britannica. It could not have been effected in the absence of the freedom of the seas, and the dividend this then gave is enjoyed by all nations.

Another example of benefit from the freedom of the seas is to be found in the contribution to the surveying and charting which has been done for over 200 years by the hydrographic fleets of our various countries. Their freedom of navigation and their cooperation results in world chart series for all the mariners of every nation. There is no ship which does not benefit from the ability to sail and work on the seas of the world with hydrographic data which has resulted from this very freedom of access. Long may it continue.

That having been said, we all know that the law of the sea is not merely an affirmation of unfettered freedom. The freedom of the high seas became a regulated freedom through agreements by flag states that their ships should follow certain rules about safety, avoidance of collisions, interference with submarine cables, and similar matters of general concern. It is important to recognize, however, that ships were to be regulated only by their own flag states.

In more modern times came the recognition that the coastal state had an interest, and indeed a claim, on the belt of water immediately surrounding its own coastline. This claim was ultimately recognized in the concept of the territorial sea. The development which balanced this concession to absolute freedom at sea was the establishment of the right of innocent passage through the territorial sea. Coastal states accepted the erosion of full sovereignty implicit in the acknowledgement that a foreign ship could not be prevented arbitrarily from passing through the territorial sea so long as she was doing no harm.

This harmonious compromise was further developed by the 1958 Geneva Conventions on the law of the sea. What started as an attempt to codify all past practice, in fact, went further and resulted in recognition of the increasing attention being given to the exploitation of the resources of the sea and the seabed, and whilst high seas freedoms were to a large extent preserved, these conventions for the first time addressed the rights to exploit the resources of continental shelves and the conservation of the living resources of the high seas.

The 1958 Geneva Conventions have, I believe, served the international community well. The listing of the freedoms of the high seas was useful, as were the provisions concerning nationality for all ships, piracy, and slave trading. So also were the definition of innocence of passage in the territorial seas as being not prejudicial to the peace, good order,

and security of the coastal state; the definition of the rights of hot pursuit; and the safeguarding of the right of passage through straits. There were also many other valuable provisions relating to navigation and resource exploitation. But there were major omissions too, the most far reaching being the failure of the 1958 conference to agree on a maximum breadth for the territorial sea and the failure to set objective limits to coastal state rights in respect of fisheries and the continental shelf. The large increase since 1958 in the number of merchant ships sailing under flags of convenience has also called into question whether dependence on flag state regulation is sufficient to safeguard coastal state interest.

The main pressure for a new law of the sea convention has, however, been generated by the increase of man's knowledge associated with a desire to exploit the resources of the sea and the seabed. "The common heritage of man should be used for the benefit of mankind as a whole" is a popular cry. If we are to use the seas and the resources in and under the sea for the benefit of the international community in an orderly fashion, we must aim to reexamine and strengthen existing law to fit today's circumstances and fill in the gaps in the 1958 conventions that I have already mentioned.

There are, of course, a number of ways of doing this, and it is precisely because of this fact that negotiations in the conference directed toward reaching a consensus have been prolonged and difficult. A position somewhere between the somewhat imprecise but possibly, maritime oriented regime that came from the 1958 conventions and those states who have been calling for extensive coastal state sovereignty and jurisdiction must be found.

We must not be discouraged by the length of negotiations on this complex subject. Each member state of the United Nations surely has to attend to its own immediate needs before acting as a member of the international community to safeguard the broader world interest.

With good reason coastal states are concerned with sovereign rights, and the obvious proof of the growing concern for this is to be found in the large

increase in the number of states now claiming a wider territorial sea. The numbers have increased markedly since 1958. Some states believe that an extension of sovereignty over the sea is an essential safeguard to their security. There is much public discussion of security, both in the defense or military sense and also in the civil or police sense. Many newly emergent and emerging states think of increased sovereignty as an essential precursor of economic well-being. Many states also, and my own is no exception, look to the wealth of the natural resources of the continental shelf to contribute substantially to economic well-being and are showing a real concern about conservation of fish stocks and an understandable feeling that they should have prime responsibility for assuring the future of a resource they claim for their own country. However we must remember the other side of the coin.

This is that to extend the frontiers of sovereignty is at the same time to increase the burden of national security and certainly not to make it easier. If we are to develop new laws, we must ensure that either the coastal state or the international community has the ability to enforce them. Laws that cannot be upheld fall into disrepute and are certain sources of international friction. While I well understand the importance of the work being done in the present conference on the settlement of disputes, I am sure we would rather that its aim should be a consensus likely to minimize the occurrence of disputes. Moreover, it is axiomatic that the greater area of the continental shelf or greater volume of water that the coastal state can lay claim to, the less the resources freely available to others.

One of us here represents a land-locked state, and there are others amongst us whose countries say that they are geographically disadvantaged. Any view that the seas are free requires that the rights of every member of the international community be considered in drawing up the balance between the interests of the coastal state and the community as a whole. There is no shortage of public discussion on this either.

Coastal states have a third interest

which is gaining in importance as the worldwide lobby for the protection of the environment grows. None of us here would quarrel with the need to take every reasonable precaution to minimize the risk caused by collisions and groundings or by poor construction of ships. Pollution control, too, is listed high in the requirements of all these days. It is an important matter which the convention must address.

I mentioned earlier that flag states had come to accept the need for certain rules to guide the conduct of shipping. An amalgam of these rules on safety, the avoidance of collision and pollution control add up in many minds not merely to the maintenance of good order but to the need for traffic regulations as the means of assuring it. Sealanes and traffic separation schemes do, of course, have a valuable part to play. The United Kingdom and France believe that they have already been instrumental in improving traffic conditions in the Dover Strait, and they look forward to the observance of these schemes becoming mandatory. I would welcome also the establishment of similar schemes in other busy shipping areas around the world. Latterly the International Maritime Consultative Organization (IMCO) has taken the lead in initiating international conventions in this broad field of good order at sea. However, IMCO neither lays down nor enforces law. Governments use the IMCO machinery to conclude agreements, and it is their responsibility to give these agreements the force of law. Should we not agree to urge our governments to place their trust in IMCO and make proposals to it? Furthermore, should we not also agree that we should urge our governments to ratify conventions agreed through IMCO and to enforce rigorously the ensuring legislation?

The international community currently accepts that outside the territorial sea it remains the flag state's responsibility to enforce regulations on their own shipowners and masters. To overcome the laxity of some flag states and in particular to regulate those ships that sail under a flag of convenience, it may be necessary to introduce a different enforcement regime. Consideration should be given to what seems a very sensible idea that a form of port state jurisdiction may well provide a better balance between the interests of the coastal state and those of the international community, the theory here being that a coastal state whose regulations have been flouted and who does not have confidence that the flag state will take appropriate action will appeal to the state into whose port the offending ship next calls to prosecute that ship.

Let me now summarize the coastal state's interests as I have outlined them to you. They amount, I suggest, to "a requirement to extend their sovereignty and jurisdiction into the sea area and on to the continental shelf, adjacent to their shores so as to ensure their state's security, militarily, economically and ecologically."

I have previously laid emphasis on the meeting of these justifiable aims while preserving the natural maritime rights of the international community as a whole. Furthermore, in examining the history of those rights, we saw how we arrived at the basic doctrine of high seas freedoms on the back of maritime power. In the remainder of my talk I would like to show that these freedoms developed in the last 150 years now safeguard the rights of the international community.

The high seas freedoms stipulated in the 1958 convention were the freedom of navigation and overflight, the freedom to fish, the freedom to lay submarine cables and pipelines, and other generally recognized and customary international freedoms.

I would like to dwell for a while on what to us, as mariners, must be the most important aspect, "freedom of navigation and overflight."

We are not in this convention addressing the historic rights of warships in time of war. Nevertheless, in spite of the fact that I have barely mentioned any military matters so far, I still see a very clear role for the military in the wake of a new convention. We are all here because our countries deem it necessary to maintain navies for reasons of national security. Warships have traditionally been involved with maintaining the freedom of navigation of merchant ships, and we would claim that the deployment of our navy in support of trade has been a stabilizing factor in increasing world prosperity.

In the past the number of ships engaged in trade that plied the seas was miniscule compared with the number today. Under the umbrella of high seas freedom and as the economies of the countries of the world partly under imperial influences expanded during the 19th century, trade began to flow in all directions. This expansion has accelerated as the colonial empires have waned and the colonies and protectorates have become independent countries. With the growth of international companies and the complex economic relations that exist today, the very foundation of our society depends for its future on economic efficiency. To carry cargo by sea is and will remain in the foreseeable future the most cost effective manner of trading. We see examples everyday of the world's dependence on energy supplies, and the battle against poverty and starvation can only begin to be tackled with any hope of success if trade across the sea is allowed to proceed about its lawful occasions, unhampered and unmolested.

Economic stability is intrinsically bound up with the balance of power and in this imperfect world in which we live the balance of strategic deterrence is of the utmost importance. We surely must accept the fact that navies have a part to play in maintaining that balance of power and that they must operate and train in the areas in which they need to exert their power. These areas coincide with the world sea routes which, in many cases, pass through what we expect to become economic zones. Efforts in the past to declare zones of peace have much to commend them, but they will never be zones of peace for all the fine words that are spoken unless we can be confident that no one will cheat. Let us not delude ourselves, we cannot be certain of that today. No doubt we all look forward to the day when world tensions are eased and that the opportunity occurs for the major alliances to scale down the effort deployed to maintain this strategic balance, but we must deal with things as they are and not as we would wish them to be. Meanwhile we should, I think, take advantage of the phenomenon that we are in the presence today of an expanding maritime power, which is far from achieving that position of maritime dominance that I have historically associated with allegiance to the freedom of the seas and which seems to be content, for reasons which are not yet clear, to support a doctrine of maritime freedom.

I have now outlined to you why I see a requirement for the coast states' needs to be put in perspective with the requirements to safeguard the rights of the international community.

Let us then assume that we achieve an acceptable balance of interest in an internationally agreed convention. The need will then arise for coastal states to evolve internationally acceptable methods of enforcing the laws which they will be entitled and indeed have a duty to enact.

Varying historical and constitutional factors will influence the way different countries tackle the task. It would be wrong to assume that there is a single correct way and if others do not do things in the way we do, either they or we are in error. I would like to explain to you how we in the United Kingdom see ourselves undertaking this. We could have established some kind of force on the lines of the U.S. Coast Guard and this may be an attractive model for many countries to follow. We have, however, decided to meet our expected increased responsibilities by the development and improvement of the existing pattern involving continuing cooperation between the civil authorities concerned and our Armed Forces rather than by some radical change. The Royal Navy has for many years provided ships for fishery protection duties, and though the extent of this task will increase, it will hopefully be carried out in an atmosphere of international accord.

As regards fixed offshore installations, these are of course subject to the normal external threat posed by another power and in this respect we see the services defending them within the framework of their normal function to defend the realm. But today we face an increasing threat from terrorists. Many people advance the theory that an oil platform, like an aircraft, is an attractive target for hijackers wishing to gain

publicity. Around our shores, in the stormy waters of the North Sea and off the Coast of the Shetlands, to hijack an oil rig to make a political point such as demanding the release of political prisoners would be very difficult and require considerable skill and resources. There are many targets associated with the oil and gas industries ashore which it would be much more easy to tackle.

Nevertheless, there is a threat, and in our view that is best met by mounting deterrent patrols by ships and aircraft. Sophisticated ships are not needed for this. The important thing is to deploy ships with good seakeeping qualities and good communications. If the ships and aircraft can be seen and heard they deter, and if any incident occurs they have the ability to get to the scene quickly and observe and report. This is also a priceless asset in the event of an accident. A new convention will, we assume, confirm the existing entitlement of the coastal state to establish safety zones around installations on its continental shelf and even enhance their status. In the light of this we envisage a requirement to operate a force of about eight ships backed up by fixed wing surveillance aircraft and shorebased helicopters to undertake concurrently fishery protection and deterrent patrols in the area of offshore installations. We have chosen a 200-foot lightly armed ship of about 1,300 tons to fulfill these tasks. In the poor weather conditions around our coasts we have decided that an all-weather capability is more important than high speed, and thus the fast patrol boat, an attractive option for many countries, is not a realistic one for the United Kingdom.

We also envisage these ships being useful in reporting incidences of pollution and for assistance in maintaining good order in traffic separation schemes. Here our aim is to advise shipping on the state of traffic so that it can more easily follow the traffic separation scheme. We have not found it either practical or desirable to attempt to positively control the traffic, believing that no sea captain would take kindly to being controlled from shore and that an attempt to do so would be likely to lead to more radio assisted collisions than it avoided.

In all these tasks we see our forces being used to safeguard our coastal states' rights and at the same time to ensure that the rights of the international community will be served as well—they will be there to monitor and report. The legal action that ensues from any incident they observe will be taken up by the civil authorities.

Maybe in due course an international force should be set up to carry out these tasks. Perhaps regional arrangements can be expanded. We already have in the Northeastern Atlantic a fisheries convention whereby some 14 countries (both East and West) agree to the monitoring of each other's fleets by fishery protection ships flying an international fishery protection flag.

But before that kind of situation can become commonplace we must achieve an agreed and acceptable convention. Inevitably there will have to be compromises. Some may not be to the liking of the coastal states who may feel that their sovereignty, their ability to exploit their resources, is weakened. Some may not wholly suit the maritime powers who will find rights and privileges long

BIOGRAPHIC SUMMARY

Admiral Sir Edward Ashmore G.C.B., D.S.C., A.D.C., joined the Royal Navy in 1933. Serving on the China Station before World War II, he saw action in the Norwegian Campaign and he took part in the convoys to the Soviet Union and to Malta. He qualified as a Russian interpreter in 1946 and served as Assistant Naval Attache to Moscow. Subsequently he commanded H.M.S. *Alert*, H.M.S. *Mercury* and H.M.S. *Blackpool*. Following duty with the Ministry of Defence, with the rank of commodore, he was appointed Flag Officer Second-in-Command, Far East Fleet in 1967. He was Vice Chief of the Naval Staff in the Ministry of Defence before becoming Commander in Chief Fleet, which carried with it the NATO posts of CINCHAN and CINC-EASTLANT. In March 1974 he relieved Admiral of the Fleet Sir Michael Pollock as First Sea Lord and Chief of Naval Staff and as First and Principal Naval Aide-de-Camp to the Queen.

taken for granted will become conditional. And in the balance it will be the coastal states who will have the major increase in the responsibility for safeguarding all our rights in their waters. Those of us who know how very seriously the progress of mankind can be hampered by failure to resolve issues such as those the convention has to address can only wish the negotiators well. I do not think I would be guilty of heresy if I said that it would be nice to

think that the convention would put all us naval men out of a job, that there would be no need for armed forces at sea. But, as things stand today, there can be little prospect of this, and only by maximizing the flexibility of maritime forces can the burden they impose on national economies be reduced.

Against this background of a future where the rights and responsibilities of maritime and coastal states will need some degree of enforcement and a

future where power politics may make the movement of naval forces a sad but necessary condition of preserving peace and good order, may I suggest that we could usefully discuss the following points amongst ourselves: the rights and duties of warships under a new convention; the enforcement of the laws at sea; and the need to continue to operate and train in key areas to maintain the balance of deterrence.

———— ψ ————